KENTUCKIANS
IN
OHIO
AND
INDIANA

KENTUCKIANS
IN
OHIO
AND
INDIANA

BY STUART SEELY SPRAGUE

Professor of History
Morehead State University

CLEARFIELD

Reprinted for
Clearfield Company, Inc. by
Genealogical Publishing Co., Inc.
Baltimore, Maryland
2001

Copyright ©1986 by
Genealogical Publishing Co., Inc.
Baltimore, Maryland
All Rights Reserved
Library of Congress Catalogue Card Number 85-81212
International Standard Book Number 0-8063-1142-8
Made in the United States of America

FOREWORD

Kentuckians in Ohio and Indiana is intended to be of use primarily to genealogists seeking ancestors from Indiana or Ohio of Kentucky descent. However, it will also prove useful to those seeking ancestors of Kentuckians who never left the Commonwealth. The trick is to work through siblings who did.

Kentucky was a classic breeder state, sending her children to newly opened areas where it was believed their prospects would be brighter. So pronounced was this propensity to move that in the *antebellum* period nearly one-third of all native-born Kentuckians were living out of state. With families being large by modern standards, there could have been few families unaffected by this emigration. Doubtless many of those who moved were of the proverbial rolling-stone variety and put down shallow roots in Ohio, Indiana, Illinois, or Missouri, and finally ended their days farther west.

The information abstracted for this book comes from approximately 200 rare county histories and county atlases published between 1876 and 1916. The atlases often list patrons by name, birthplace, and year, and give the year they migrated to the county. Thus, post-Civil War migrants as well as early settlers are listed. In county histories the biographical information usually includes the date and county and state of birth of the biographee. In many cases similar information appears for the parents.

Arranged in tabular form under county of origin (if the county is unknown, the individual is listed separately), the entries include some or all of the following information: the name of the Kentucky migrant, his birthdate, the names of his/her parents and their dates and places of birth (if known), and the date of migration. The division by Kentucky county is useful for several reasons. For the genealogist it provides a small bundle of other surnames, many of which may already be familiar since settlers often migrated in multi-family groups. For local Kentucky libraries and historical societies the information as to sources, visible at a glance, will indicate which county histories might be valuable to them.

Source citations with specific page references are included. Women are listed both by maiden and married name when known. The following symbols are used throughout the work:

( ) maiden name
[ ] married name
**   born in same county as biographee
/   divides information pertaining to the father from that of the mother
--   no information
c   circa, as in c1821 (about 1821)

STUART SEELY SPRAGUE
Center for Historical Studies
Clearfield, Kentucky

AERI   Lewis Cass Aldrich
           History of Erie County, Ohio with Illustrations
           and Biographical Sketches of Some of Its Promi-
           nent Men and Pioneers.
           Syracuse, New York: D. Mason & Company, 1889.

ALUW   An Illustrated and Historical Atlas of Lucas and a
           Part of Wood Counties, Ohio. Maps ... of Town-
           ships and Plates made by S.W. and P.A. Durant,
           R.P. Hickley, D.P. Kayner, J.N. Wheeler, George
           Rossiter, Civil Engineers.

AMWA   Martin R. Andrews
           History of Marietta and Washington County, Ohio,
           and Representative Citizens, Edited and Compiled
           by Martin R. Andrews, M.A., Douglas Putnam Pro-
           fessor of History and Political Science, Mariet-
           ta College.
           Chicago: Biographical Publishing Company, 1902.

ARIC   Alfred Tredone Andreas
           Atlas Map of Richland County, Ohio. Compiled,
           Drawn and Published from Personal Examinations
           and Surveys.
           Chicago: A.T. Andreas, 1873.

ATRU   Atlas and Directory of Trumbull County, Ohio, Includ-
           ing a Directory of Freeholders and Official Reg-
           ister of the County with Illustrations Compiled
           from Recent Surveys, Official Records and Per-
           sonal Examinations.
           Cleveland, Ohio: American Atlas Company, 1899.

BCLA   A Biographical Record of Clark County, Ohio, Illus-
           trated.
           New York and Chicago: S.J. Clark Publishing
           Company, 1902.

BHCL   Albert J. Brown
           History of Clinton County, Ohio, Its People, In-
           dustries and Institutions, with Biographical
           Sketches of Representative Citizens and Geneal-
           ogical Records of Many of the Old Families. Il-
           lustrated.
           Indianapolis: B.F. Bowen & Company, Inc., 1915.

BNEO   Biographical History of Northeastern Ohio, Embracing
           the Counties of Ashtabula, Trumbull and Mahoning,
           Containing Portraits of All the Presidents of
           the United States, with a Biography of Each, To-
           gether with Portraits of Joshua R. Giddings, Ben-
           jamin F. Wade, and a Large Number of the Early
           Settlers and Representative Families of To-day.
           Chicago: The Lewis Publishing Company, 1893.

CBNW Commemorative, Biographical Record of Northwestern
Ohio Including the Counties of Defiance, Henry, Williams, and Fulton, Containing Biographical Sketches of Prominent and Representative
Citizens, and of Many of the Early Settled Families. Illustrated.
Chicago: J.H. Beers & Company, 1899.

CCHA A Centennial Biographical History of Champaign County, Ohio, Illustrated.
New York and Chicago: The Lewis Publishing Co., 1902.

CCRA A Centennial Biographical History of Crawford County,
Ohio. Illustrated.
Chicago: The Lewis Publishing Company, 1902.

CHAN A Centennial Biographical History of Hancock County,
Ohio. Illustrated.
New York and Chicago: The Lewis Publishing Co., 1902.

CHCA Commemorative, Biographical Record of the Counties of
Harrison and Carroll, Ohio Containing Biographical Sketches of Prominent and Representative Citizens, and of Many Early Settled Families. Illustrated.
Chicago: J.H. Beers & Company, 1891.

CINC Cincinnati Past and Present: Or Its Industrial History As Exhibited in the Life-Labors of Its Leading Men, by M. Joblin & Company. Photographical-
ly Illustrated by James Landy.
Cincinnati: Elm Street Printing Company, 1872.

CSOT Commemorative, Biographical Record of the Counties of
Sandusky and Ottawa, Ohio Containing Biographical
Sketches of Prominent and Representative Citizens,
and of Many of the Settled Families, Illustrated.
Chicago: J.H. Beers & Company, 1896.

CUVC Cuvier Press Club
Cincinnati: The Queen City: Newspaper Reference
Book.
Cincinnati: The Cuvier Press Club, 1914.

CWHO Commemorative, Biographical Record of the Counties of
Wayne and Holmes, Ohio Containing Biographical
Sketches of Prominent and Representative Citizens,
and Many of the Early Settled Families, Illustrated.
Chicago, Illinois: J.H. Beers, 1889.

CWOO Commemorative, Historical and Biographical Record of Wood
County, Ohio; Its Past and Present, Early Settlement
and Development; Aboriginal History; Pioneer History;
Political Organization; Agricultural, Manufacturing,
Commercial Interests, Including Oil and Gas; History
of the County, Townships, Towns and Villages; Relig-
ious, Educational, Social, Political and Military
History, Including Roster by Townships; Statistical
and Miscellaneous Matter; Biographies and Portraits
of Early Settlers and Representative Citizens, etc.
Illustrated.
Chicago: J.H. Beers & Company, 1897.

DHGR   R.S. Dills
          History of Greene County, Together with Histor-
          ic Notes on the Northwest, and the State of Ohio.
          Gleaned from Early Authors, Old Maps and Manu-
          scripts, Private and Official Correspondence,
          and All Other Authentic Sources. Illustrated.
          Dayton, Ohio: Odell & Mayer Publishers, 1881.

DSJE   Joseph B. Doyle
          Twentieth Century History of Steubenville and
          Jefferson County, Ohio and Representative Ci-
          tizens.
          Chicago: Richmond-Arnold Publishing Co., 1910.

ESCI   Nelson W. Evans
          A History of Scioto County, Ohio, Together
          With a Pioneer Record of Southern Ohio.
          Portsmouth, Ohio: Nelson W. Evans, 1903.

FHCI   Henry A. Ford and Kate B. Ford
          History of Cincinnati, Ohio, with Illustrations
          and Biographical Sketches.
          Cleveland, Ohio: L.A. Williams & Co., 1881.

GCCI   Charles Theodore Greve
          Centennial History of Cincinnati and Representa-
          tive Citizens.
          Chicago: Biographical Publishing Company, 1904.

GCIN   Rev, Charles Frederic Goss
          Cincinnati: The Queen City. 4 volumes.
          Chicago and Cincinnati: S.J. Clarke Pub. Co., 1912.

GFPE   A.A. Graham (compiler)
          History of Fairmont and Perry Counties, Ohio.
          Their Past and Present, Containing a Comprehen-
          sive History of Fairfield and Perry Counties;
          Their Townships, Cities, Villages, Towns, Schools,
          Churches, Societies, Industries, Statistics, etc.
          A History of Their Soldiers in the Late War; Por-
          traits of Early Settlers and Prominent Men; Mis-
          cellaneous Matters, Maps of the Counties; Biogra-
          phies and Histories of Pioneer Families, Etc., Etc.;
          Illustrated.
          Chicago: W.H. Beers & Company, 1883.

GVWE   Thaddeus S. Gilliland
          History of Van Wert County, Ohio and Representa-
          tive Citizens Edited and Compiled by Thaddeus S.
          Gilliland, Van Wert, Ohio.
          Chicago: Richmond and Arnold, 1906.

GWIL   Weston Arthur Goodspeed
          County of Williams, Ohio, Historical and Biographi-
          cal, With an Outline Sketch of the Northwest Terri-
          tory of the State, and Miscellaneous Matters by
          Weston A. Goodspeed [and] Charles Blanchard.
          Chicago: F.A. Battey & Company, 1882.

HALL   History of Allen County, Ohio. Containing a History
of the County, Its Townships, Towns, Villages,
Schools, Churches, Industries, Etc.; Portraits
of Early Settlers and Prominent Men; Biographies;
History of the Northwest Territory; History of
Ohio; Statistical and Miscellaneous Matters, etc.,
etc.
Chicago: Warner, Beers & Company, 1885.

HBRO   History of Brown County, Ohio, Containing a History
of the County; Its Townships, Towns, Churches,
Schools, etc.; General and Local Statistics;
Portraits of Early Settlers and Prominent Men;
History of the Northwest Territory; History of
Ohio; Map of Brown County; Constitution of the
United States, Miscellaneous Matters, Etc., Etc.
Chicago: W.H. Beers & Company, 1883.

HBUT   A History and Biographical Cyclopedia of Butler Coun-
ty, Ohio with Illustrations and Sketches of Its
Representative Men and Pioneers.
Cincinnati: Western Biographical Pub. Co., 1882.

HCHA   The History of Champaign County, Ohio, Containing a
History of the County, Its Cities, Towns, etc.;
General and Local Statistics; Portraits of Early
Settlers and Prominent Men; History of the North-
west Territory; History of Ohio; Map of Champaign
County; Constitution of the United States, Miscel-
laneous Matters, etc., etc.
Chicago: W.H. Beers & Company, 1881.

HCIN   History of Cincinnati and Hamilton County, Ohio;
Their Past and Present, Including Early Settle-
ment and Development; Antiquarian Researches;
Their Aboriginal History; Pioneer History; Pol-
itical Organization; Agricultural, Mining and
Manufacturing Interests; A History of the City,
Villages and Townships; Religious, Educational,
Social, Military and Political History; Statis-
tics; Biographies and Portraits of Pioneer and
Representative Citizens, Etc.
Cincinnati: S.B. Nelson & Company, 1896.

HCLA   The History of Clark County, Ohio, Containing a His-
tory of the County; Its Cities, Towns, etc.;
General and Local Statistics; Portraits of Early
Settlers and Prominent Men; History of the North-
west Territory; History of Ohio; Map of Clark
County; Constitution of the United States, Miscel-
laneous Matters, etc., etc. Illustrated.
Chicago: W.H. Beers & Company, 1881.

HCLE   History of Clermont County, Ohio with Illustrations
and Biographical Sketches of Its Prominent Men
and Pioneers.
Philadelphia: Louis H. Everts, 1880.

HCLI   History of Clinton County, Ohio Containing a His-
        tory of the County; Its Townships, Cities,
        Towns, Schools, Churches, Etc.; General and
        Local Statistics; Portraits of Early Settlers
        and Prominent Men; History of the Northwest
        Territory; History of Ohio; Map of Clinton
        County; Constitution of the United States,
        Miscellaneous Matters, etc., etc.
        Chicago: W.H. Beers & Company, 1882.

HCOL   History of Columbiana County, Ohio and Representa-
        tive Citizens Edited and Compiled by William
        B. McCord of Salem, Ohio.
        Chicago: Biographical Publishing Co., 1905.

HCOS   N.N. Hill, Jr.
        History of Coshocton County; Its Townships,
        Its Townships, Towns, Villages, Schools, Chur-
        ches, Societies, Industries, Statistics, etc.;
        A History of Its Soldiers in the Late War;
        Portraits of Its Early Settlers and Prominent
        Men; Views of Its Finest Buildings and Various
        Historic and Interesting Localities; Miscellan-
        eous Matter; Map of the County; Biographies and
        and Histories of Pioneer Families, etc., etc.
        Newark, Ohio: A.A. Graham & Company, 1881.

HDAR   The History of Darke County, Ohio, Containing A His-
        tory of the County, Its Cities, Towns, etc.;
        General and Local Statistics; Portraits of Early
        Settlers and Prominent Men; History of the North-
        west Territory; History of Ohio; Map of Darke;
        Constitution of the United States, Miscellaneous
        Matters, etc. etc.
        Chicago: W.H. Beers & Company, 1880.

HDAY   History of Dayton, Ohio. With Portraits and Bio-
        graphical Sketches of Some of the Pioneer and
        Prominent Citizens.
        Dayton: United Lutheran Publishing House, 1889.

HDEL   History of Delaware County and Ohio. Containing a
        Brief History of the State of Ohio, From Its
        Earliest Settlement to the Present Time. Em-
        bracing Its Topography, Geological, Physical
        and Climactic Features; Its Agricultural,
        Stock-Growing, Railroad Interests, etc.; a
        History of Delaware County, Giving an Account
        of Its Aborignal Inhabitants, Early Settlement
        by Whites, Pioneer Incidents, Its Growth, Its
        Improvements, Organization of the County, Its
        Judicial and Political History, Its Business
        and Industries, Churches, Schools, etc.; Bio-
        graphical Sketches, Portraits of Some of the
        Early Settlers and Prominent Men, etc., etc.
        Chicago: O.L. Baskin & Company, 1880.

HFPI   History of Franklin and Pickaway Counties, Ohio,
        with Illustrations and Biographical Sketches
        of the Prominent Men and Pioneers.
        Cleveland: Williams Brothers, 1880.

HHAN   History of Hancock County, Ohio. Containing a History of the County, Its Townships, Towns, Villages, Schools, Churches, Industries, etc.;
Portraits of Early Settlers and Prominent Men;
Biographies, History of the Northwest Territory; History of Ohio; Statistical and Miscellaneous Matters, etc., etc.
Chicago: Warner, Beers & Company, 1886.

HHAR   The History of Hardin County, Ohio Containing a His-
tory of the County, Its Townships, Towns,
Churches, Schools, etc., General and Local Sta-
tistics; Military Record, Portraits of Early
Settlers and Prominent Men; History of the
Northwest Territory; History of Ohio; Miscel-
laneous Matters, etc., etc.
Chicago: Warner, Beers & Company, 1883.

HHOC   History of Hocking Valley, Ohio, Together With
Sketches of Its Cities, Villages and Townships,
Educational, Religious, Civil, Military, and
Political History, Portraits of Prominent Per-
sons, and Biographies of Representative Citizens.
Chicago: Inter-state Publishing Company, 1883.

HKNO   N.N. Hill, Jr.
History of Knox County, Ohio. Its Past and Pre-
sent Containing a Condensed, Comprehensive His-
tory of Ohio, Including an Outline History of the
Northwest; A Complete History of Knox County;
Its Townships, City, Towns, Villages, Schools,
Churches, Societies, Industries, Statistics, etc.;
A Record of Its Soldiers in the Late War; Por-
traits of Its Early Settlers and Prominent Men;
Views of Its Finest Buildings; Miscellaneous Mat-
ter; Map of the County; Biographies and Histories
of Pioneer Families, Etc. Compiled by N.N. Hill,
Jr. Illustrated.
Mt. Vernon, Ohio: A.A. Graham & Company, 1881.

HLIC   N.N. Hill, Jr.
History of Licking County, Ohio. Its Past and
Present Containing a Condensed, Comprehensive
History of Ohio, Including an Outline History
of the Northwest; A Complete History of Licking
County; Its Townships, Cities, Towns, Villages,
Schools, Churches, Societies, Industries, Statis-
tics, etc.; a History of Its Soldiers in the Late
War, Portraits of Its Early Settlers and Prominent
Men; a Chapter on Noted Pioneers; Views of Its Fi-
nest Buildings and Various Historic and Interest-
ing Localities--such as the "Old Fort," etc.; Mis-
cellaneous Matters; Map of the County; Biographies
and Histories of Pioneer Families. Illustrated.
Newark, Ohio: A.A. Graham and Company, Pubs., 1881.

HLOG History of Logan County and Ohio. Containing a
History of the State of Ohio, From Its Earl-
iest Settlement to the Present Time, Embra-
cing Its Topographical, Geological, Physical
and Climactic Features; Its Agricultural,
Stock-growing, Railroad Interests, etc.; a
History of Logan County, Giving an Account
of Its Aboriginal Inhabitants, Early Settle-
ments by Whites, Pioneer Incidents, Its
Improvements, Organization of the County,
Its Judicial and Political History, Its
Business and Industries, Churches, Schools,
etc.; Biographical Sketches; Portraits of
Some of the Early Settlers and Prominent
Men, etc.
Chicago: O.L.Baskins& Company, 1880.

HMAD The History of Madison County, Ohio; Containing
a History of the County; Its Townships,
Towns, Churches, Schools, etc.; General and
Local Statistics; Portraits of Early Settlers
and Prominent Men; History of the Northwest
Territory; History of Ohio; Miscellaneous
Matters, Etc., Etc.
Chicago: W.H. Beers & Company, 1883.

HMAR The History of Marion County, Ohio, Containing a
History of the County; Its Townships, Towns,
Churches, Schools, etc.; General and Local
Statistics; Military History; Portraits of
Early Settlers and Prominent Men; History of
the Northwest Territory; History of Ohio;
Miscellaneous Matters, etc., etc.
Chicago: Leggett, Conaway & Company, 1883.

HMED History of Medina County and Ohio. Containing a
History of the State of Ohio, From Its Earl-
iest Settlement to the Present Time, Embra-
cing Its Topographical, Geological, Physical
and Climactic Features; Its Agricultural,
Stock-growing, Railroad Interests, etc.; a
History of Medina County, Giving an Account
of Its Aboriginal Inhabitants, Early Settle-
ments by Whites, Pioneer Incidents, Its
Improvements, Organization of the County,
Its Judicial and Political History, Its
Business and Industries, Churches, Schools,
etc.; Biographical Sketches; Portraits of
Some of the Early Settlers and Prominent
Men, etc., etc.
Chicago: Baskin & Battey, 1881.

HMIA The History of Miami County, Ohio, Containing a
History of the County; Its Cities, Towns,
etc.; General and Local Statistics; Portraits
of Early Settlers and Prominent Men, History
of the Northwest Territory; History of Ohio;
Map of Miami County; Constitution of the United
States, Miscellaneous Matters, etc., etc.
Chicago: W.H. Beers & Company, 1880.

HMMV   John C. Hover, etals.
Memoirs of the Miami Valley (Volume III con-
tains biographies. References are keyed to
this volume).
Chicago: Robert O. Law Company, 1920.

HMON   The History of Montgomery County, Ohio, Containing
a History of the County; Its Townships, Cities,
Towns, Schools, Churches, etc.; General and Lo-
cal Statistics; Portraits of Early Settlers and
Prominent Men; History of the Northwest Terri-
tory; History of Ohio; Map of Montgomery County;
Constitution of the United States, Miscellaneous
Matters, etc. etc.
Chicago: W.H. Beers & Company, 1882.

HMOR   History of Morrow County and Ohio. Containing a
Brief History of the State of Ohio From Its
Earliest Settlement to the Present Time, Em-
bracing Its Topographical, Geological, Physical
and Climactic Features; Its Agricultural, Stock-
growing, Railroad Interests, etc.; A History of
Morrow County, Giving an Account of Its Aborigin-
al Inhabitants, Early Settlement by the Whites,
Pioneer Incidents, Its Growth, Its Improvements,
Organization of the County, Its Judicial and Po-
litical History, Its Business and Industries,
Churches, Schools, etc.; Biographical Sketches,
Portraits of Some of the Early Settlers and
Prominent Men, etc., etc.
Chicago: O.L. Baskin & Company, 1880.

HPRE   History of Preble County, Ohio, with Illustrations
and Biographical Sketches.
Cleveland: H.Z. Williams & bro., 1881.

HRHI   History of Ross and Highland Counties, Ohio with
Illustrations and Biographical Sketches.
Cleveland: Williams Brothers, 1880.

HSEN   History of Seneca County, Ohio. Containing a History of the County, Its Townships, Towns, Villages, Schools, Churches, Industries, Etc.;
Portraits of Early Settlers and Prominent Men;
Biographies; History of the Northwest Territory; History of Ohio; Statistical and Miscellaneous Matters, etc., etc. Illustrated.
Chicago: Warner, Beers & Company, 1886.

HTMA   History of Trumbull and Mahoning Counties; with
Illustrations and Biographical Sketches.
Cleveland: H.Z. Williams & bro., 1882.

HTUS   The History of Tuscarawas County, Ohio. Contain-
ing a History of the County; Its Townships;
Towns, Churches, Schools, etc.; General and
Local Statistics, Military Record; Portraits
of Early Settlers and Prominent Men; History
of the Northwest Territory; History of Ohio;
Miscellaneous Matters, Etc., Etc.
Chicago: Warner, Beers & Company, 1884.

HUNI   The History of Union County, Ohio, Containing a
History of the County; Its Townships, Towns,
Churches, Schools, Etc.; General and Local
Statistics; Military Record; Portraits of
Early Settlers and Prominent Men; History of
the Northwest Territory; History of Ohio; Mis-
cellaneous Matters, Etc., Etc.
Chicago: W.H. Beers & Company, 1883.

HUPP   History of the Upper Ohio Valley. With Historical
Account of Columbiana County, Ohio, A State-
ment of the Resources, Industrial Growth and
Commercial Advantages: Family History and
Biography.
Madison, Wisconsin: Grant & Fuller, 1891.

HVWM   History of Van Wert and Mercer Counties, Ohio.
With Illustrations and Biographical Sketches
of Some of Its Prominent Men & Pioneers.
Wapakoneta, Ohio: R. Sutton & Company, 1882.

HWAR   The History of Warren County, Ohio, Containing a
History of the County; Its Townships, Towns,
Churches, Schools, etc; General and Local
Statistics; Portraits of Early Settlers and
Prominent Men; History of the Northwest Terri-
tory; History of Ohio; Map of Warren County;
Constitution of the United States, Miscellan-
eous Matters, Etc., Etc.
Chicago: W.H. Beers & Company, 1882.

HWOA   C.W. Williamson
History of Western Ohio and Auglaize County
with Illustrations and Biographical Sketches
of Pioneers and Prominent Public Men.
Columbus: W.M. Linn & Sons, 1905.

HWYA   The History of Wyandot County, Ohio, Containing a
History of the County; Its Townships, Towns,
Churches, Schools, etc.; General and Local Sta-
tistics; Military Record; Portraits of Early
Settlers and Prominent Men; History of the
Northwest Territory; History of Ohio; Miscel-
laneous Matters, Etc., Etc.
Chicago: Leggett, Conaway & Company, 1884.

KHIG   Reverend J.W. Klise
The County of Highland: A History of Highland
County, Ohio, From the Earliest Days, With Special
Chapters on the Bench and Bar, Medical Profession,
Educational Development, Industry and Agriculture;
and Biographical Sketches by Rev. J.W. Klise, A.E.
Hough, editor.
Madison, Wisconsin: Northwestern Hist'l Assoc., 1902

KHLO   General Robert P. Kennedy
The Historical Review of Logan County, Ohio. To-
gether with Biographical Sketches of Many of the
Leading and Prominent Citizens and Illustrious
Dead. Illustrated.
Chicago: The S.J. Clarke Publishing Company, 1903.

LAKS   Samuel A. Lane
           Fifty Years and Over of Akron and Summit County.
           Akron: Beacon Job Department, 1892.

LCCI   John W. Leonard
           The Centennial Review of Cincinnati: 100 Years.
           Cincinnati: J.M. Elster & Company, Pubs., 1888.

LGCI   Lewis Alexander Leonard
           Greater Cincinnati and Its People: A History.
           New York: Lewis Historical Publishing Company,
           4 vols., 1927.

MALL   Charles Christian Miller
           History of Allen County, Ohio and Representative
           Citizens; Edited and Compiled by Charles C. Miller
           Ph.D., Assisted by Dr. Samuel A Baxter, Lima, O.
           Chicago: Richmond & Arnold, 1906.

MAPA   Oliver Morrow
           Historical Atlas of Paulding County, Ohio Con-
           taining Maps of Paulding County Townships,
           Town and Village by O. Morrow & F.W. Bashore.
           Also Maps of the United States and State of
           Ohio, Together with a Statement of Settlement,
           Growth and Prosperity of the County. Includ-
           ing a Personal and Family History.
           Madison, Wisconsin: Western Pub. Co., 1892.

MBUT   Memorial Record of Butler County, Ohio, Containing
           Biographical Sketches of Representative Citi-
           zens of the County Together with Biographies
           and Portraits of All the Presidents of the
           United States.
           Chicago: Record Publishing Company, 1894.

MCHA   Judge Evan P. Middleton
           History of Champaign County, Ohio. Its People,
           Industries and Institutions, Representative Ci-
           tizens and Genealogical Records of Many Old
           Families. Illustrated.
           Indianapolis: B.F. Bowen & Co., 2 vols., 1917.

MDUM   Memorial Record of the Counties of Delaware, Union
           and Morrow, Ohio. Illustrated.
           Chicago: The Lewis Publishing Company, 1895.

MLIC   Memorial Record of Licking County, Ohio, Containing
           Biographical Sketches of Representative Citizens
           of the County, Together with Biographies and
           Portraits of all the Presidents of the United
           States.
           Chicago: Record Publishing Company, 1894.

PALS   Portrait and Biographical Record of Auglaize, Logan
           and Shelby Counties, Ohio. Containing Biographi-
           cal Sketches of Prominent and Representative
           Citizens Together with Biographies and Portraits
           of All the Presidents of the United States.
           Chicago: Chapman brothers, 1892.

PAVW   A Portrait and Biographical Record of Allen and Van
                  Wert Counties, Ohio Containing Biographical
                  Sketches of Many Prominent and Representative
                  Citizens ... Together with Biographies and
                  Portraits of All the Presidents of the United
                  States.
                  Logansport,IN: A.W. Bowen & Company, 1896.

PFPM   Portrait and Biographical Record of Fayette, Picka-
                  way and Madison Counties, Ohio. Containing
                  Biographical Sketches of Prominent and Repre-
                  sentative Citizens, Together with Biographies
                  and Portraits of All the Presidents of the
                  United States.
                  Chicago: Chapman Brothers, 1892.

PGCL   Portrait and Biographical Album of Greene and Clark
                  Counties, Ohio, Containing Full Page Portraits
                  and Biographical Sketches of Prominent and
                  Representative Citizens of the County Together
                  With Portraits and Biographies of All the Presi-
                  dents of the United States.
                  Chicago: Chapman Brothers, 1890.

PMHA   Portrait and Biographical Record of Marion and Hardin
                  Counties, Ohio, Containing Portraits and Biographi-
                  cal Sketches of Prominent and Representative
                  Citizens of the Counties, Together with Biographies
                  and Portraits of all the Presidents of the United
                  States.
                  Chicago: Chapman Publishing Company, 1895.

PMNO   Progressive Men of Northern Ohio.
                  Cleveland: Plaindealer Publishing Company, 1906.

PPFA   Rufus Putnam
                  Pioneer Record, and Reminiscences of the Early
                  Settler of Fayette County, Ohio.
                  Cincinnati: Applegate, Pounsford & Co., 1872.

PPSU   A Portrait and Biographical Record of Portage and
                  Summit Counties, Ohio, Containing Biographical
                  Sketches of Many Prominent and Representative
                  Citizens, Together with Portraits and Biogra-
                  phies of the Presidents of the United States.
                  Logansport, Indiana: A.W. Bowen & Co., 1898.

PSCI   Portrait and Biographical Record of the Scioto Valley,
                  Ohio.
                  Chicago: The Lewis Publishing Company, 1891.

RCIQ   George Mortimer Roe, editor
                  Cincinnati: The Queen City of the West: Her
                  Principal Men and Institutions, Biographical
                  Sketches and Portraits of Leading Citizens.
                  Published by the Cincinnati Times-Star Company.
                  Cincinnati: C.J. Krehbici & Company, 1895.

SHME   S.S. Scranton
                  History of Mercer County, Ohio and Representative
                  Citizens.
                  Chicago: Biographical Publishing Co. 2 vols., 1907.

VPIC   Aaron R. Van Cleaf
           History of Pickaway County, Ohio and Representa-
           tive Citizens Edited and Compiled by Hon. Aaron
           R. Van Cleaf.
           Chicago: Biographical Publishing Co., 1906.

WCBR   Byron Williams
           History of Clermont and Brown Counties, Ohio,
           From the Earliest Historical Times Down to
           the Present. In Two Volumes.
           Milford, Ohio: Hobart Publishing Co., 1913.

WHAN   Eugene B. Willard, etals., editors
           A Standard History of the Hanging Rock Region
           of Ohio. An Authentic Narrative of the Past,
           With an Extended Survey of the Industrial and
           Commercial Development.
           Chicago: Lewis Publishing Co., 2 vols., 1916.

Numerous additional volumes were examined which included no
Kentuckians. They are listed by short title and date below:

Aldrich, History Henry and Fulton (1888).
Andrews, Washington County (1877).
Atlas of Lorain County (1896).
Atlas of Medina County (1897).
Beardsley, History of Hancock County (1881).
Biographical Record Fairchild County (1902).
Caldwell, History Belmont and Jefferson (1880).
Centennial History Hancock County (1903).
Commemorative Record Northwestern Ohio (1899).
Commemorative Record Huron and Lorain (1894).
County of Miami (1894).
County of Richland.
Douglas, Lawyers of Wayne (1900).
Everhart, History of Muskingum (1882).
First Atlas Tuscarawas County (1908).
Gould, Atlas Crawford County (1873).
Graham, History Richland County (1880).
Hill, Ashland County (1880).
History Ashtabula County (1878).
History Columbiana County (1879).
History Noble County (1887).
History Portage County (1885).
History Sandusky County (1882).
History Washington County (1881).
History Crawford County (1881).
History Geauga and Lake Counties (1878).
History Lorain County (1879).
Hunt, Historical Collections Coshocton Co. (1876).
Johnson, History Cuyahoga County (1879).
Martin, History Franklin County (1858).
Mead, Twentieth Century Sandusky County (1909).
Moodie's Atlas Delaware County (1908).
Mowry, Atlas Union County (1877).
Murray, Atlas Morgan County (1902).
Nollings, Pioneer History Medina County (1861).
Norton, History Knox County (1862).
Perrin, History of Stark County (1881).
Perrin, History Summit County (1881).
Portrait Stark County (1892).   Shinn, Co. of Williams(1905).
Portrait City of Toledo (1895).   Williams, Jackson Co. (1900).
Portrait Portage and Summit (1898).

A D A I R   C O U N T Y   (N O N E)

A L L E N   C O U N T Y

BIRTHDATE	NAME OF BIOGRAPHEE	PARENTS/BIRTHPLACE/BIRTHDATE		SOURCE/PAGE	DATE
28 Jan 1822	Warren Ledbetter	Thomas & Dorothea(Linkhart)	Va/Va	PGCL 235	1828

A N D E R S O N   C O U N T Y   (N O N E)

B A L L A R D   C O U N T Y

BIRTHDATE	NAME OF BIOGRAPHEE	PARENTS/BIRTHPLACE/BIRTHDATE	SOURCE/PAGE	DATE
07 Feb 1844	Dr. J.L. Wylie	Thomas & Sarah(Cook)	HBRO B90	1844

B A R R E N   C O U N T Y   (N O N E)

B A T H   C O U N T Y

BIRTHDATE	NAME OF BIOGRAPHEE	PARENTS/BIRTHPLACE/BIRTHDATE		SOURCE/PAGE	DATE
18 Jun 1830	George W. Anderson	William & ---(Graham)	Va/x	ESCI 887	----
00 000 1845	Maj.Samuel Bigstaff	Dr. O.S. & Fenton(Bean)	x/Ky	GCIN B366	----
00 000 1822	James M. Campbell	Alexander & Elizabeth(Davis)	Tn/Tn	HBRO B152	----
00 000 1807	Thomas Cartmill	William	Va1779/x	HMAD 992	1812
23 Oct 1808	Thomas Cartmill	William & Isabel(Ferguson)	Va1779/x	PFPM 649	1825

BIRTHDATE	NAME OF BIOGRAPHEE	PARENTS/BIRTHPLACE/BIRTHDATE	SOURCE/PAGE	DATE
12 Nov 1847	William E. George	Robert & Drusilia(Raborn) **14/**18	WHAN 698	----
11 Oct 1831	Dr.Cornelius Honaker	Charles W. & Sarah(England) Va/x	ESCI 1010	----
00 000 0000	Presley Said		HDEL 735	----
25 Dec 1822	Eliza J.Shoat[Bryant]Augusta & Sarah	Md/Va DHGR 480	1841
28 Nov 1851	J.D. Sorrell	Elisha & Eliza(McCullough)	WCBR B320	1863
20 Feb 1807	Samuel A.Williams	Capt.Wm. & Harriet(Forrest) Eng./Eng.	WHAN 825	----

B E L L   C O U N T Y   (N O N E)

B O O N E   C O U N T Y

BIRTHDATE	NAME OF BIOGRAPHEE	PARENTS/BIRTHPLACE/BIRTHDATE	SOURCE/PAGE	DATE
07 Jul 1867	Claude Ashbrook	Benjamin & Elizabeth(Tucker) 38/44	GCIN D97	----
00 000 0000	J.W.R. Bradford	William R. & Anna(Wrightman)	HMMV C367	----
00 000 1806	Benjamin F.Brashear		HCIN 575	----
25 Nov 1836	Dr. James H.Buckner	Henry M. & Etheline E(Conn)	GCCI B669	----
06 Apr 1853	David L. Carpenter	Caleb	GCIN C919	----
03 Apr 1880	Dr.Carleton G.Crisler R.H.		GCIN C520	----
01 Jun 1874	Thomas T. Fenton	Capt. H.B. & Eliza(Sebree) In/x	GCIN D41	----
01 Jun 1874	Thomas T. Fenton		HMMV C259	----
02 Jul 1841	Frank M. Foster	James A. & Prudence(Knight) Tn/Pa	CCRA 225	----
00 Jul 1843	Reuben F. Freeman		HRHI 84	----
25 Aug 1855	Thomas S. Harlow	Michael & May	GCIN C258	----
23 Jul 1873	Charles J. Iredell	James W. & Virginia(Rust)	CUVC 169	----
23 Jun 1873	Charles J. Iredell	James W. & Virginia Pa41/**43	GCIN C258	----
00 000 0000	Edith E. Lancaster	William W. & Martha A(Tanner) **/**	HMMV C242	----
25 Aug 1863	Capt.Jacob LindenburnPhilip & Martha(Eckstein) Ger/x	GCIN D857	----

BIRTHDATE	NAME OF BIOGRAPHEE	PARENTS/BIRTHPLACE/BIRTHDATE		SOURCE/PAGE		DATE
22 Mar 1846	A.B. McIntosh	William R. & Ann C.	Oh/Pa	DHCK	510	---
05 Aug 1879	Dr.Gordon F. McKim	William F. & Florence		CUVC	123	---
28 Apr 1839	Wenden O'Neal	George & Sarah(Sleet)	Ky/Ky	HCIN	577	---
30 Aug 1833	Capt.James D. Parker	Richard & Sallie(Hogan)		RCIQ	283	---
00 000 0000	Judge George Perkins	John H & ---(Stansifer)	**/**	RCIQ	307	---
00 000 0000	Benjamin M. Platt	Jacob		CINC	199	---
00 000 0000	John H. Platt	Jacob		CINC	199	---
03 Sep 1841	Maj.Kentuck B.Platt	Gen.A.Sanders & Hanna Ann	Oh21/**23	KHLO	477	---
22 Feb 1843	R.J. Platt	Gen. A.S. & Anna(McCoy)	Oh/Ky	HLOG	677	---
00 000 0000	Harry M. Piper	George	Ger/x	HCIN	1033	---
00 000 0000	Dr. L. Southgate	Bernard & Eleanor(Fleming)	Va21/x	GCIN	C824	---

B O U R B O N   C O U N T Y

BIRTHDATE	NAME OF BIOGRAPHEE	PARENTS/BIRTHPLACE/BIRTHDATE		SOURCE/PAGE		DATE
13 Aug 1855	George Alexander	Charlton & Kitty		CUVC	151	---
00 000 1845	Brent Arnold			FHCI	495	---
00 000 1847	Brent Arnold		**/Mercer	GCIN	B224	---
00 000 0000	Brent Arnold	J.U. & Lucy J.		RCIQ	43	---
18 Dec 1806	Mathias W. Baker	William & Mary D(Winans)	Ky81/Ky85	DHGR	721	1828
28 May 1812	William G. Baker	William & Mary(Wynans)	Va/Pa	PGCL	425	---
17 May 1805	Robert Bickham			HLOG	798	---
08 Jan 1810	Joseph C. Brand	Thomas & Fannie(Carter)	Md/Md	CCHA	628	1830
15 Mar 1802	George E. Bunnell	Jonas & Sallie(Tomlin)	NJ/x	HWAR	894	---
03 Nov 1815	IsaiahD. Counts	Elijah & Margaret(Wiley)	Va87/x	HMIA	480	1819
29 Jul 1794	Thomas Corwin	Mathias		HWAR	372	1798
29 Jul 1794	Gov. Thomas Corwin	Mathias		PPSU	141	1798
13 Sep 1794	John Creath	William & Margaret		HMAD	1085	---
29 Mar 1785	Sarah [Daniel]			HCHA	778	---
00 000 0000	Robert Davidson			HDAR	744	---
00 Oct 1806	James Fry			HBRO	562	1812
06 Feb 1824	J.L. Galloway	Samuel & Elizabeth(Kirkpatrick)**94/x		HCIN	954	---

BIRTHDATE	NAME OF BIOGRAPHEE	PARENTS/BIRTHPLACE/BIRTHDATE	SOURCE/PAGE	DATE
00 000 1784	Rachel Green[Johnson]	George	HHAR 1046	1811
23 Nov 1785	Aaron Greer		HDAR 759	----
00 000 1789	John J. Hawkins	Col.Samuel & Christian(Worthington) Va/x	HPRE 146	1806
00 000 1784	Joseph Hawkins	Col.Sam'l&Christian(Worthington) Va62/x	HPRE 146	1806
07 Aug 1829	Jonathan D. Hearne	Cannon & Sallie(Owen)	GCCI B507	----
25 May 1801	D.C. Hitt		HCHA 655	c1803
00 000 1789	Sarah Hutson		HMAD 1022	----
00 000 0000	Thomas Johnson		PAVW A338	1830
01 Nov 1803	Elam Kenney	David & Martha Ky/Ky	HCLA 859	1807
00 000 1791	James Kilgore	John & Lydia Ky/Ky	HMAD 1022	----
15 Sep 1849	Agnes McKee[Scott]		HBUT 559	----
16 Jul 1805	William McKee	John & Elizabeth(McClintock)	HBUT 558	1844
00 000 1852	Thomas Miller		HKNO 743	1866
00 000 1805	Elizabeth Moore		PFPM 720	----
00 000 0000	William Moore		BHCL 320	c1806
00 000 0000	William Parker		HMAR 854	----
00 000 0000	Mary Patton		PFPM 827	----
12 Apr 1793	John Purviance	David & Mary(Ireland)	HPRE 256	----
00 000 1783	John Railsback		HPRE 178	1806
00 000 0000	Absalom Reed		BHCL 294	1803
00 000 0000	Samuel Reed		BHCL 294	1803
17 Feb 1804	Margaret Sanders		HMAR 556	----
22 Feb 1858	John Seggerson	Patrick & Margaret(Cahill) Ire20/24	BCLA 627	1875
00 000 0000	John L. Shuff	Isaac & Elizabeth(Cleveland) Va/x	LGCI D399	----
10 Dec 1811	Louise Stipp[McClintock]		HBUT 558	1844
00 000 0000	Nancy Van Kirk[Mark]		PGCL 203	----
26 Aug 1829	Barton W. Wasson	Joseph & Sarah(Hearne) Pa95/Md	GCIN C125	----
00 000 1829	Barton W. Wasson	Joseph & Sarah(Hearne)	RCIQ 101	----
02 Jan 1841	William H. Willette	Carlton & Nancy(Coons) Md/Pa	HCIN 972	----

BIRTHDATE	NAME OF BIOGRAPHEE	PARENTS/BIRTHPLACE/BIRTHDATE	SOURCE/PAGE	DATE
13 Jun 1859	Dr. William Burgess	George R. & Martha M(Spurlock) Va14/x	CHCA	645	1882
05 Aug 1858	Michael Corkery	Andy & Mary(Farbery) Ky/Ky	WHAN	1266	----
00 000 0000	Katherine Falter[Winter]	Joseph & Rosa(Bahn) Ger20/Ger23?	WHAN	798	----
00 000 0000	Dr. James W. Fitch	George & Mary(Martin) **40/**42	WHAN	861	----
12 Oct 1865	James W. Fitch	George & Mary(Martin)	ESCI	564	----
24 Feb 1860	Oscar E. Kinkead	William & Susan E(Haskill) Ky/Oh42	WHAN	738	----
28 Oct 1871	William L.Schweickart	Frederick & Louisa(Fridley)Ger33/Oh38	WHAN	1266	c.1896
17 Jun 1873	John B. Winspear	Wheelock & Ellen(Rowe) NY/Eng	WCBR	B464	----
00 000 1862	Mary E. Witting[Frecka]		WHAN	760	1872

BIRTHDATE	NAME OF BIOGRAPHEE	PARENTS/BIRTHPLACE/BIRTHDATE	SOURCE/PAGE	DATE
31 May 1898	Benjamin P. Pink	Abraham J. & Bertha(Gold)Russia/Russia	LGCI	D739	----
19 Jun 1796	Dr. William Thompson	Rev. William J & Lucretia(Webster)	HCLE	145	----
00 000 1796	Dr. William Thompson		WCBR	B53	1808

BIRTHDATE	NAME OF BIOGRAPHEE	PARENTS/BIRTHPLACE/BIRTHDATE	SOURCE/PAGE	DATE
20 Jan 1821	James F. Chalfant	Thomas & America(Coburn)	HCIN	1014	----
29 Oct 1820	Mitchell Evans	Abraham & Esther(Turner) Md/Md	ESCI	971	----
29 Oct 1820	Mitchell Evans	Abraham & Esther(Turner) Md/Md	WHAN	959	1832
00 000 0000	Charles S. Furber	John N & Martha M(Smith) NH13/Ma26	LGCI	D361	----
02 Feb 1878	Pearl C. Harber	John N & Ida J(Poe)	WCBR	B153	1881

BIRTHDATE	NAME OF BIOGRAPHEE	PARENTS/BIRTHPLACE/BIRTHDATE		SOURCE/PAGE	DATE
00 Jan 1840	William T. Hicks	Samuel J & Melinda I		HBRO B226	1880
00 000 1820	George O. McMillen	---- & Martha		BCIA 602	----
20 Mar 1817	Augustus M. McNight	Alexander & Sarah(Lemon)	x/Pa	HDAR 747	1830
31 Mar 1824	Henry T. Ogden	Henry & Lucy C(Metcalfe)	Md/Va	HCIN 827	----
07 May 1813	William W. Perkins	William		HCLE 280+	----
01 May 1815	Andrew Poe	David & Elizabeth(Richey)		PMHA 147	1815
23 Dec 1805	Adam Powell	Joseph & Elizabeth(Dillman)	Pa/Pa	HBRO B189	----
16 Nov 1828	Benjamin F. Power	Robert & Nancy(Meyers)	Va/Ky	HCIN 515	----
27 Feb 1837	Robert D. Rice	Michael & Lutitia(Ham)		HBRO 190	----
11 Nov 1812	Dr.Samuel J.Spees	George & Mary(Wright)	Pa88/Pa89	PSCI 108	----
11 Feb 1819	Gen. Durbin Ward	--- & Rebecca(Patterson)		FHCI 427	----
11 Feb 1819	Durbin Ward			HWAR 787	----
09 Sep 1884	William A. Williams	Anderson & Lucy(Boyd)	**46/Ky	WCBR B55	----
00 000 1811	James Young			HBRO 599	----
00 000 1802	William Young	William		HBRO B127	1828

B R E A T H I T T   C O U N T Y   (N O N E)

B R E C K I N R I D G E   C O U N T Y

BIRTHDATE	NAME OF BIOGRAPHEE	PARENTS/BIRTHPLACE/BIRTHDATE		SOURCE/PAGE	DATE
01 Sep 1835	James McNeil	David G & Harriet(Lay)	Pa96/Va08	HDAR 756	1844
00 000c1812	David Poe			HHAR 700	----

B U L L I T T   C O U N T Y

BIRTHDATE	NAME OF BIOGRAPHEE	PARENTS/BIRTHPLACE/BIRTHDATE		SOURCE/PAGE		DATE
26 Sep 1859	Charles Freyhof	James & Eva	Ger/Ger	MCHA	B229	----
00 000 1795	Phillip Lewellen			HPRE	300	----

B U T L E R   C O U N T Y

BIRTHDATE	NAME OF BIOGRAPHEE	PARENTS/BIRTHPLACE/BIRTHDATE	SOURCE/PAGE		DATE
02 Nov 1800	Rachel Mann(Stone)		HCLI	910	----

C A L D W E L L   C O U N T Y   (N O N E)

C A L L O W A Y   C O U N T Y   (N O N E)

C A M P B E L L   C O U N T Y

BIRTHDATE	NAME OF BIOGRAPHEE	PARENTS/BIRTHPLACE/BIRTHDATE		SOURCE/PAGE		DATE
11 Feb 1880	Fred W. Brehmer	Frederick & Catherine(Summers)		LGCI	C306	----
00 000 1812	William H. Bushman	Henry & Sophia(DeMoss)	1766/x	WCBR	B378	----
21 Dec 1868	John V. Campbell	John S. & May(Valentine)	Va/x	GCIN	B285	----
05 Oct 1891	Dr. Ralph G. Carothers	Dr. Robert & Clara(Cole)		LGCI	D587	----
00 000 1884	J.D. Cloud			HMMW	C367	----
26 Apr 1866	Dr. Henry J. Cook	Simon A. & Sybia(Doerr)	Ger/Ger	GCIN	D704	----
24 Sep 1864	Charles W. Crawford	James R. & Martha(Ward)		CJVC	147	----
29 Jul 1871	Otto Creutz	Christopher & Julia(Cohn) Sweden/x		GCIN	C589	----
10 May 1868	Gilbert I. Cullen	James & Sarah E(Gallup) Scotland/NY		HCIN	710	----

-23-

CAMPBELL COUNTY (CONT.)

BIRTHDATE	NAME OF BIOGRAPHEE	PARENTS/BIRTHPLACE/BIRTHDATE	SOURCE/PAGE	DATE
17 Apr 1855	Frank Cummings	Samuel & Eliza	HWAR 942	----
25 Oct 1867	William J. Davidson	W.A. & Sarah J(Schofield) Scott/Ky	GCCI B384	----
25 Oct 1867	William J. Davidson	W.A. & Sarah J(Schofield) Scott/Ky	HCIN 621	----
28 Mar 1864	J. Hazard Davis	John H. & Melissa(Coppin)	CUVC 163	----
00 000 1849	Dr. William DeCourcy		FHCI 478	----
19 Jul 1876	William T. Denis	Harry & Cecelia	CUVC 141	----
00 000 1863	William H. Donaldson	William M.	GCIN D465	----
19 Apr 1868	William H. Dyer	William H. & Virginia P(Hawthorne)Eng/*	LGCI C259	----
06 Jan 1800	John Ewing	John & Margaret Pa/Pa	DHGR 492	1801
17 Apr 1894	Dr. Victor W. Fischbach	Dr. Frederick & Emma(Fischer)Oh/Oh	LGCI C248	----
00 000 0000	J.W. Frelinger		HMMV C380	----
24 Feb 1859	Dr. Frederick C.Gunkel	Dr. Henry C. & Katherine(Weber)	HCIN 695	----
06 Jun 1826	Richard H. Hayman	Isaiah T. & Elizabeth(Tarvin)	ESCI 156	----
27 Mar 1859	George Hobson	James & Elizabeth	RCIQ 287	----
00 000 1860	Simon Hubig	Simon & Catherine(Gruber) Fr/Fr	GCIN D414	1860
04 Oct 1852	John D.Inderrieden	Henry & Elizabeth(Wehmoff) Ger/Ger	PALS 140	1860
00 000 1851	George B. Jennings		GCIN D774	----
00 000 0000	C.J. Jones, Jr.	Charles J. & Mary(Holland)	HCIN 779	----
18 Feb 1892	Samuel E. Kaiper	Charles H. & Nellie C(Wilson)Kenton/**	LGCI D511	----
00 000 0000	Joseph Knecht		HMMV C514	----
04 Apr 1797	Andrew Lewis	Andrew & Martha(Montgomery)	HBUT 445	1804
15 Aug 1822	H.D. Lombard	Jesse & Olive(Carlton)	HMAD 973	1827
00 000 1883	William P. McCone	James & Irene(Nelson)	GCIN D383	----
00 000 0000	William J. McMurrays	Robert & Mary(Hurst) Eng/Eng	PALS 303	1860
12 Aug 1877	Chris Milus	Jacob & Louisa	CUVC 129	----
09 Aug 1879	P. Lincoln Mitchell	Richard H & Mary(Lincoln)	GCIN D645	----
00 000 1879	Col.P.Lincoln Mitchell	Robert H& Mary(Lincoln)	HMMV C361	----
28 Jul 1876	Capt.W.Emerson Mooar	Capt.Luke M. & Cornelia(Moore) 42/x	GCIN D183	----
20 Mar 1865	William L. Ortblieb	Constance & Catherine(Smith)	HCIN 779	----
07 Jul 1870	Emery C. Pyle	Lemuel T. & Liza(Willison)	GCIN C335	----
11 Mar 1889	Dr. Louis H. Schriver	Walter A. & Mary P(Betz) **60/**	LGCI D418	----

BIRTHDATE	NAME OF BIOGRAPHEE	PARENTS/BIRTHPLACE/BIRTHDATE		SOURCE/PAGE	DATE
17 Apr 1859	William D. Smith	Daniel & Caroline(Wagner)	Ky/Ger	PMHA 464	----
03 Feb 1840	Walter J. Todd	Charles W. & Catherine	Ky/Ky	HDAR 531	1861
03 Sep 1850	William P. Walker	William P. & Eliza L(Stewart)	Ky/Ky	HCIN 794	----
12 Jan 1881	Harry C. Winston	L.C. & Elizabeth		HMMW C53	----
15 Nov 1872	Charles H. Zuber			RCIQ 402	----

C A R L I S L E   C O U N T Y   (N O N E)

C A R R O L L   C O U N T Y

BIRTHDATE	NAME OF BIOGRAPHEE	PARENTS/BIRTHPLACE/BIRTHDATE		SOURCE/PAGE	DATE
00 000 0000	John W. Clifton	William & Lavina	Ky/Ky	DHGR 485	----
00 000 0000	Angelina Linn[Blair]	Joseph & Sophia(Johnson)		MBUT 181	c1844

C A R T E R   C O U N T Y

BIRTHDATE	NAME OF BIOGRAPHEE	PARENTS/BIRTHPLACE/BIRTHDATE	SOURCE/PAGE	DATE
21 May 1865	John W. Evans	John & Mahala(Ward)	ESCI 972	----
01 Jul 1847	William E. Evans	David & Frances(Evans)	HHOC 456	----

C A S E Y   C O U N T Y   (N O N E)

C H R I S T I A N   C O U N T Y

BIRTHDATE	NAME OF BIOGRAPHEE	PARENTS/BIRTHPLACE/BIRTHDATE	SOURCE/PAGE	DATE
03 Jun 1808	Dr. Thomas V. Morrow Thomas		GCCI B733	----

CHRISTIAN COUNTY (CONT.)

BIRTHDATE	NAME OF BIOGRAPHEE	PARENTS/BIRTHPLACE/BIRTHDATE	SOURCE/PAGE	DATE
07 Apr 1817	J.C. Smith	William W. & Elizabeth(Chrisman)Va/Va	HMAD 1164	c1840

CLARK COUNTY

BIRTHDATE	NAME OF BIOGRAPHEE	PARENTS/BIRTHPLACE/BIRTHDATE		SOURCE/PAGE	DATE
15 Nov 1829	Reason R. Baxter	Sill & Mary		NBUT 446	1877
08 Feb 1798	James Black	Alexander & Janet(Crocket) Va65/Va		CCHA 527	1809
08 Feb 1798	James L. Black	Capt.Alexander & Janet(Crockett)Va/Va		MCHA B371	1809
08 Nov 1808	Robert Crockett	Robert & Patsy(Cartmill)		HLOG 595	1812
09 Dec 1785	John Dewitte			PPFA 19	1796
23 Apr 1856	Thomas M. Greene	Col.William & Mary E(Smith)	Ky/Ky	GCIN C63	---
12 Jan 1812	Eleanor Huls[Harris]			HCLI 995	---
00 000 0000	Robert Neil			HMAD 913	1811
22 Sep 1844	Charles W. Parido	William & Mary H.		GFPE 341	---
00 000 1822	Benjamin F. Ragland	Henry		WCBR B322	1828

C L A Y   C O U N T Y   (N O N E)

C L I N T O N   C O U N T Y   (N O N E)

C R I T T E N D E N   C O U N T Y   (N O N E)

C U M B E R L A N D   C O U N T Y   (N O N E)

F A Y E T T E   C O U N T Y

BIRTHDATE	NAME OF BIOGRAPHEE	PARENTS/BIRTHPLACE/BIRTHDATE		SOURCE/PAGE	DATE
01 Jun 1814	Hon.Charles Anderson	Col. Richard C.	Va/x	HMON A486	----
00 000 0000	Ann Bain[McConnel]			HWYA 874	----
00 000 1793	George Balintine			HWAR 793	----
21 Aug 1895	Dr.Ernest N.Beatty	James P. & Mary E(Nutter)		LGCI C305	----
00 000 0000	John Brooks			HBRO B180	----
00 000 1799	John Clinton	Isaac & Elizabeth(Harcourt)	Ire/Ire	---- ----	1807
00 000 1808	Jeptha Davis			HCIN 707	----
00 000 1839	W.D. Grierson	John & Ann(Greenhow)	Scot01/Eng04	HBRO B164	----
29 Apr 1807	John Hoagland	Levi & Lucy(Mallory)		HBUT 652	1818
00 000 0000	Frederick Hutchinson	John & Catherine(Snyder)	**/Va	HWAR 750	----
00 000 1800	Robert January	James		PGCL 626	----
00 000 0000	Lydia Johnston	Walter		HCHA 777	1803
00 000 1802	Harriet Kemper	Caleb		HMIA 580	c1810
00 000 0000	Martha J. McClure	John & Jane	Va/Ky	MLIC 359	----
00 000 0000	James Mark			PGCL 203	----
00 000 0000	Thomas S. Noble	Thomas H. & Rosamond(Johnson)		GCCI B543	----

FAYETTE COUNTY (CONT.)

BIRTHDATE	NAME OF BIOGRAPHEE	PARENTS/BIRTHPLACE/BIRTHDATE	SOURCE/PAGE	DATE
00 000 0000	Orene Parker		CUVC 143	----
07 Mar 1793	Catherine Patterson		HMON A378	----
27 May 1801	Jefferson Patterson		HMON A378	----
27 May 1799	Robert L. Patterson		HMON A378	----
22 Oct 1847	Elder J.H.P. Payne Jacob		GFPE 502	1867
00 000 0000	Elizabeth Perry Bechtle Captain		PGCL 493	----
00 Mar 1792	John C. Short	Peyton & Mary(Symmes)	FHCI 416	----
00 000 0000	Thomas Spencer		WHAN 1348	----
01 Apr 1791	Dr. John Steele	Robert & Agnes(Coulter)	HDAY 522	----
01 Apr 1791	Dr. John Steele	Robert & Agnes(Coulter)	HMON B243	----
20 Nov 1833	J.B. Tennell	Joseph Ky96/x	HDAR 595	----
00 000 0000	Nancy Tompkins[Gordon]		MCHA B60	----
07 Mar 1790	Jacob Walterfield		HCLE 352+	----
00 000 1797	Dr. James Webb		HRHI 215	----
18 Jul 1802	Charles W. White	Charles Vac59/x	CCRA 828	1810
00 000 1817	William Wilkinson		ARIC 18	----
00 000 0000	John Winters		HBRO B90	----
03 Jul 1831	Col.Chas.W.Woolley	Hon.A.H. & Sallie(Howard)	GCCI B654	1855

FLEMING COUNTY

BIRTHDATE	NAME OF BIOGRAPHEE	PARENTS/BIRTHPLACE/BIRTHDATE	SOURCE/PAGE	DATE
03 Dec 1833	Johnson P. Ansley	George & Dilly(Johnson)	KHLO 727	1835
04 Feb 1803	William D. Baird	William & Dorothy(Camerer) Md62/Md60	HCLA 954	1808
00 000 1826	Robert P. Bennington	Thomas & Mary(Rains)	HBRO B53	----
20 Sep 1818	William Bennington	Thomas & Mary(Rains)	HBRO B53	----
00 000 1815	George Bishop		GCIN B460	----
04 Nov 1812	Richard M. Bishop	Henry Va/Va	CINC 143	----
04 Mar 1812	Hon.Richard M. Bishop		GCIN B50	----

FLOYD COUNTY

BIRTHDATE	NAME OF BIOGRAPHEE	PARENTS	BIRTHPLACE	SOURCE	PAGE	DATE
04 Nov 1812	Gov.Richard M.Bishop			PPSU	157	----
00 000 0000	Mahala Q. Browning[Renner]			BHCL	687	----
15 Jun 1834	Mahala Q. Browning	Basil & Mary(Bright)	Md90/x	HCLe	501	----
22 Apr 1811	Balden C. Carpenter	Simeon & Sally(Fee)	Va/Va	PFPM	589	----
00 000 0000	Baldwin C.Carpenter			HFPI	338	1837
03 Apr 1811	Solomon G. Clements	Gustavus A. & Mary(Gregg)		HALL	577	1850
26 Mar 1837	J.T. Cunningham	Reuben & Sarah(McClelland)	Ky/Ky	HHAR	996	----
01 Dec 1805	J.J. Dinsmore			HMIA	632	----
06 Mar 1803	George Dynes		Ky/x	HWAR	737	1807
12 Jul 1809	Thomas F. Eckert	Leonad & Susan	Pa/x	CINC	139	----
23 Jan 1823	David B. Glasscock	Asa & Mary(Penquie)	Va/Pa	HWAR	740	----
14 May 1817	Allen Hendrixson	Enoch & Nancy(Fryman)	Sweden/Ky	HBRO	B203	----
00 000 0000	Jacob Hess			CCHA	171	----
09 Apr 1828	Evan McD. Jackson	Thomas & Nancy	Va84/**10	PMHA	503	----
17 Apr 1813	Henry G. Johnson	Jacob & Rachel(Green)		HHAR	1045	----
00 000 0000	John Johnson			HLOG	635	----
29 Jul 1811	Peter Johnson	Jacob & Rachel(Green)		HHAR	913	1816
14 Feb 1791	John Judy			HCLA	959	1800
17 Nov 1840	Gordon F. Lauman	George M.	Pa05/x	ESCI	1041	----
17 Nov 1840	Hon. Gordon F.Lauman	George M. & Anna J(Shanklin)	Pa/Ky	WHAN	1147	----
15 May 1809	James Mills	Thomas & Jane(Dale)	Va85/Va	HCLA	1052	1812
24 Jun 1798	Samuel Pearce	John & Mary(Taylor)	Ca/x	HMAD	917	----
00 000 1835	Dr. Robert T. Prine	Henry		WCBR	B482	----
28 May 1803	James Rawling	Thomas & Mary(Tribbe)	Va/Ky	CCHA	580	c1823
06 Dec 1868	Harry F. Taylor	George H. & Eliza(Thornton)	**/40	GCIN	D455	----
02 Oct 1799	Isaac Tharp	Jacob		HCHA	899	1811
00 000 0000	Lucy Wells[Bishop]			GCCI	B461	----

BIRTHDATE	NAME OF BIOGRAPHEE	PARENTS/BIRTHPLACE/BIRTHDATE	SOURCE/PAGE	DATE
13 Sep 1816	Spencer Spears	Spencer & Tabitha(Chaffin)	HBRO B85	1817

FRANKLIN COUNTY

BIRTHDATE	NAME OF BIOGRAPHEE	PARENTS/BIRTHPLACE/BIRTHDATE	SOURCE/PAGE	DATE
22 Jul 1866	James H. Butler	Edward & Jane(Hollywood) Ire/Ire	GCIN D322	---
24 Jan 1864	R.H. Butler	Edward & Jane(Hollywood) Ire/Ire	GCIN D322	---
21 Jan 1865	James H. Cleveland	Francis L. & Laura(Harlan)	GCCI B336	---
21 Jan 1865	James H. Cleveland	Francis L. & Laura(Harlan)	RCIQ 298	---
21 Jan 1865	James H. Cleveland	Francis L. & Laura(Harlan)	GCIN D765	---
14 Oct 1815	Joseph D. Collins	Thomas & Mary A(Bowan) Va/Va	HBUT 647	1839
15 Sep 1897	George E. Kearns	Martin J. & Josephine(Salendar) Ky/**	LGCI D705	---
07 May 1808	Elder J. Neal	Benjamin & Mary(Sellers) Ky77/Va76	HPBE 280+	1811
00 000c1821	Caroline Payne		HBUT 436	---
00 000 1800	Reuben R. Springer	Charles & Catherine(Runyan) WV/NJ	HCIN 511	---

F U L T O N   C O U N T Y   (N O N E)

G A L L A T I N   C O U N T Y

BIRTHDATE	NAME OF BIOGRAPHEE	PARENTS/BIRTHPLACE/BIRTHDATE	SOURCE/PAGE	DATE
09 Sep 1846	John R. Hance	Richard & Margaret J(Knox)Bourbon24/ky MALL	381	---

G A R R A R D   C O U N T Y

BIRTHDATE	NAME OF BIOGRAPHEE	PARENTS/BIRTHPLACE/BIRTHDATE	SOURCE/PAGE	DATE
01 Jan 1791	David Lamme	Nathan & Nancy(Ralston) Va/Pa	DHGR 614	1796

BIRTHDATE	NAME OF BIOGRAPHEE	PARENTS/BIRTHPLACE/BIRTHDATE		SOURCE/PAGE	DATE
20 Feb 1847	James A. Collins	James W. & Cordelia(Carlisle)		GCIN D412	---
22 Oct 1884	Richard T. Dickerson	William W.		HMMV C28	---
00 000 0000	Henrietta Stroud[West]Edward		Pa/x	BHCL 672	---

G R A V E S   C O U N T Y   (N O N E)

G R A Y S O N   C O U N T Y   (N O N E)

G R E E N   C O U N T Y

BIRTHDATE	NAME OF BIOGRAPHEE	PARENTS/BIRTHPLACE/BIRTHDATE	SOURCE/PAGE	DATE
27 May 1827	Jerry Sheeler	Jacob & Elizabeth(Canon)	GFPE 542	---
18 Feb 1810	Thomas Upton		HVWM 403	---
00 000 0000	William D. Wilson	Valentine	PFPM 684	---

G R E E N U P   C O U N T Y

BIRTHDATE	NAME OF BIOGRAPHEE	PARENTS/BIRTHPLACE/BIRTHDATE		SOURCE/PAGE	DATE
15 Feb 1822	Stout Barklow	Benjamin		ESCI 896	---
16 Jan 1830	William Biggs,Jr.			ESCI 905	---
12 Sep 1839	Robert Clutts	Archibald A. & Mary(Gantz)	Oh/x	ESCI 933	---
22 Jan 1847	William H. Crawford	John	Ire/x	HHOC 942	---
12 May 1868	William C. Culkins	John & Elizabeth J	27/Va38	GCIN D60	---
12 May 1868	William C. Culkins	John & Elizabeth J(McStead)		LGCI D416	---

G R E E N U P   C O U N T Y   (C O N T.)

BIRTHDATE	NAME OF BIOGRAPHEE	PARENTS/BIRTHPLACE/BIRTHDATE		SOURCE/PAGE		DATE
01 Jan 1852	Eugene M. Funk	Thornton A & Anary(Gray)		ESCI	986	---
13 Dec 1839	Joshua M. Gammon	Joshua L. & Harriet(Stewart)		ESCI	987	---
08 Oct 1871	Thomas C. Lantz	Henry & Lovina(Bennett)		ESCI	1040	---
25 Jun 1859	John M. Lawson	Jacob & Elizabeth(Rawling)		ESCI	1291	---
17 Dec 1850	Col.Henry A. Marting	Henry & Mary E(Knaper)	Ger/Ger	ESCI	1066	---
15 Apr 1846	John W. Myers	John A. & Isabella(White)	Pa/Pa	GVWE	665	1865
29 Oct 1848	Charles L. Raison	Charles L & Amanda K(Corum)	Ky/Ky	HCIN	596	---
00 000 1836	Michael Scherer			WHAN	1217	---
16 Mar 1838	Abraham G. Sellards	Andrew J. & Mary G(Hartley)		ESCI	574	---
28 Jan 1869	Dr. Martyn Taylor	Dr. Martyn & Lydia J(Draper)	NY/x	SHME	429	---
13 Nov 1857	Armour K. Veasey	Joseph W. & Elizabeth(Campbell)	Pa/Pa	WHAN	934	---
13 Nov 1857	A. King Veazey	Joseph W. & Elizabeth(Campbell)		ESCI	1169	---
09 Nov 1815	Emiline White[Wood]	David		ESCI	876	---
23 Sep 1876	William M. Willis	Edward & Helen(Coron?)	**54/**58	WHAN	1260	---

H A N C O C K   C O U N T Y

BIRTHDATE	NAME OF BIOGRAPHEE	PARENTS/BIRTHPLACE/BIRTHDATE		SOURCE/PAGE		DATE
28 Jan 1839	George Peach	John & Fannie(Taylor)	Engl2/Eng	HCOI	555	---
00 000 1839	George Peach	John & Fannie(Taylor)	Engl2/Eng	HUPP	350	---

H A R D I N   C O U N T Y

BIRTHDATE	NAME OF BIOGRAPHEE	PARENTS/BIRTHPLACE/BIRTHDATE	SOURCE/PAGE		DATE
24 Oct 1843	John A. Murlin		HVWM	403	---
26 Dec 1832	Susanna Murlin		HVWM	384	1833
06 Sep 1821	P. C. Parker	Daniel & Sally	HMED	697	---

BIRTHDATE	NAME OF BIOGRAPHEE	PARENTS/BIRTHPLACE/BIRTHDATE		SOURCE/PAGE		DATE
12 Jan 1866	Dr. Jacob G. Smith	Albertus & Mary E(Gardner)	Oh/**	PFPM	497	1870
12 Jan 1866	Dr. Jacob G. Smith			VPIC	309	---
00 000 1800	Edward Upton	Edward		SHME	703	1834
17 May 1824	John Upton	Edward & Ann(Murlin)	OhOO/x	SHME	704	---

H A R L A N   C O U N T Y   (N O N E)

H A R R I S O N   C O U N T Y

BIRTHDATE	NAME OF BIOGRAPHEE	PARENTS/BIRTHPLACE/BIRTHDATE		SOURCE/PAGE		DATE
09 May 1865	William B. Adams	Robert S. & Mary A(Batson)	23/28	WCBR	B200	---
03 Mar 1814	Hamilton Anderson			KHIG	229	---
00 Dec 1804	Stephen Barnes			HCIN	955	1808
25 Feb 1799	Robert Braden	Samuel & Jane(Newell)	Ire/x	KHLO	432	---
27 Oct 1877	Dr. A.R. Conner	Alpheus & Susan A(Reed)		CUVC	135	---
15 Sep 1798	Andrew Coulter	John	Ire/x	PALS	207	---
22 Apr 1792	Polly Hall[Dugan]	John		PGCL	757	1808
00 000 1822	Richard Hall	Richard	Ky/x	HCLI	1099	---
00 000 1817	M. G. Harter	Jacob & Elizabeth(Smizer)		HMIA	---	1821
00 000 0000	Benjamin Hinkson	Thomas		BHCL	135	---
00 000 0000	Judge Benj. Hinkson	Judge Thomas		HCLI	394	1806
00 000 0000	Ruth Ketherwood	Charles	Ire/x	PALS	207	---
00 000 0000	Samuel McCluer			HALL	608	---
17 Nov 1793	Samuel McClure			PAVW	AL392	c1815
02 Feb 1798	Hon.Joseph McCutchen			HWYA	1053	1827
10 Mar 1781	William McDonald	William		HLOG	676	---
00 000 0000	John Makemson			KHLO	495	1806
00 000 0000	Margaret Newell			PALS	369	1816
06 May 1795	James C. Page	Jonathan & Hannah(Jones)	NC66/73	PGCL	213	---
23 Mar 1844	Hon.Hiram D. Peck		x/Va	GCCI	B332	---
23 Mar 1844	Hon.Hiram D. Peck			GCIN	D638	---
23 Mar 1844	Hon.Hiram D. Peck	John W. & Jane(Veach)	NY/Ky	HCIN	577	---

HARRISON COUNTY (CONT.)

BIRTHDATE	NAME OF BIOGRAPHEE	PARENTS/BIRTHPLACE/BIRTHDATE		SOURCE/PAGE	DATE
00 000 0000	Dr. Edith Smith	N. Frank & Alice(Lair)		GCIN C902	----
00 000 1845	Rev. Jesse H. Smith	Simpson & Sallie	Va/Ky	DHGR 525	----
00 000 1795	David Smizer	Philip & Mary		WCBR B630	1795
00 000 1791	Charles Waits			WCBR B290	----
31 May 1812	Andrew Whitely	John & Christiana(Hall)	NC/Ky	HCLA 942	----
04 Oct 1805	Dr. Allen Woods	Allen		HCLE 145	1806

H A R T C O U N T Y (N O N E)

H E N D E R S O N C O U N T Y

BIRTHDATE	NAME OF BIOGRAPHEE	PARENTS/BIRTHPLACE/BIRTHDATE		SOURCE/PAGE	DATE
21 Aug 1848	Dr. Charles M. Humston	Dr.		AMWA 1429	----
30 Nov 1835	Andrew Motz	Joseph & Magdalene(Weaver)	Ger/Ger	HCIN 928	----
10 Feb 1875	Stewart D. Ruggles	Caleb F. & Henrietta(Dixon)		ESCI 580	----

H E N R Y C O U N T Y

BIRTHDATE	NAME OF BIOGRAPHEE	PARENTS/BIRTHPLACE/BIRTHDATE		SOURCE/PAGE	DATE
06 Mar 1852	William B. Bryant	William F. & Frances(Russel)		HCIN 1031	----
21 Oct 1796	James Loudon		Pa/Pa	HBRO 355	----
27 Aug 1832	William T. Moore	John & Dorcas(Masterson)	Va/Va	CINC 228	----

H I C K M A N C O U N T Y (N O N E)

H O P K I N S   C O U N T Y

BIRTHDATE	NAME OF BIOGRAPHEE	PARENTS/BIRTHPLACE/BIRTHDATE	SOURCE/PAGE	DATE
10 Mar 1880	Dr. E.R. Earle	Dr. Benjamin P. & Mary(Roberts) Ky/Ky	MCHA B152	----
06 Feb 1877	Polk Laffoon	Polk & Hattie(Parker) **/x	LGCI C41	----

J A C K S O N   C O U N T Y

BIRTHDATE	NAME OF BIOGRAPHEE	PARENTS/BIRTHPLACE/BIRTHDATE	SOURCE/PAGE	DATE
00 000 1862	L.F. Parks		GCIN D492	----

J E F F E R S O N   C O U N T Y

BIRTHDATE	NAME OF BIOGRAPHEE	PARENTS/BIRTHPLACE/BIRTHDATE	SOURCE/PAGE	DATE
01 Jun 1814	Gov. Chas. Anderson	Richard C.	PPSU 152	----
09 Mar 1836	Charles Barnes	Alfred & Florence(Todd) Eng/Eng	LGCI C168	----
09 Mar 1808	Rev. F.G. Black		HMIA 727	----
21 Jan 1868	Charles Boldt	Charles & Margaret(Schwenck)**36/Ger	GCIN L652	----
00 000 1829	Edmond C. Boyce	Charles F.	GCCI B364	1831
00 000 1842	Louis C. Brankamp		GCIN D101	----
07 Feb 1859	Leon J. Brumleve	Ger/x	LGCI D711	----
14 May 1865	Dr. Asher Buxbaum	Morris C. & Sarah Ger39/La42	HCIN 728	----
07 Jan 1850	John S. Crowell	S.B	HCLA 812	----
14 Jun 1828	John H. Eaton	William G. & Elizabeth(Bridgewater)KyKyHLOG 621		----
25 Apr 1858	Phillip C. Fosdick	William & Louise	RCIQ 115	----
20 Apr 1855	George F. Klotter	George F. & Magdalene Ger/x	GCIN D72	----
00 000 0000	W.G. Layer	Gottlieb & Louise(Engelhart)	GCIN C768	----
01 Dec 1835	Capt.Tim.D.McGillicuddy		LAKS 432	----
29 Jan 1873	Edwin L. Neilson	James D.	HMMV C252	----

-35-

JEFFERSON COUNTY (CONT.)

BIRTHDATE	NAME OF BIOGRAPHEE	PARENTS/BIRTHPLACE/BIRTHDATE	SOURCE/PAGE	DATE
24 Aug 1840	Lloyd Phillips	Abraham & Nancy(Lewis)	MAPA 82	---
00 000 1852	Francis H. Prenat	Francis X. & Mary J(Johnson)	HBRO B145	1866
16 May 1885	Francis L. Scott	Thomas P. Ky/x	GCIN D651	---
00 000 1853	Mrs.Clara C.Shambs		ARIC 14	---
17 Jul 1875	H. George Sickles	Simon & Ida(Rice)	CUVC 153	---
00 000 1832	Col.Wm. H. Vodrey	Jabez Eng/x	HUPP B366	---
27 Dec 1819	Sarah Walter[Woodruff]		CHAN 284	1827
00 000 1847	Robert H. West		FHCI 449	---
17 Jan 1847	Robert H. West	John A. & Margaret(Knowles) Pa97/x	HCIN 901	---
17 Jan 1847	Robert H. West	Captain John A.	GCIN C959	---
08 Mar 1855	Rev.Pacific Winterhead	George & Mary(Engel) Ger/Ger	HMMV C75	---

JESSAMINE COUNTY

BIRTHDATE	NAME OF BIOGRAPHEE	PARENTS/BIRTHDATE/BIRTHPLACE	SOURCE/PAGE	DATE
30 May 1805	John Darland		HDAR 691	1810
00 000 0000	Michael Funk		KHLO 508	---
00 000 1825	Catherine Oyler[Nye]		HMON B433	---
25 Sep 1801	William Scott	Hugh & Mary(Moffatt) NC/x	HMIA 616	1808

JOHNSON COUNTY

BIRTHDATE	NAME OF BIOGRAPHEE	PARENTS/BIRTHDATE/BIRTHPLACE	SOURCE/PAGE	DATE
00 000 1800	Abram Brewer		HWAR 968	---

KENTON COUNTY

BIRTHDATE	NAME OF BIOGRAPHEE	PARENTS/BIRTHPLACE/BIRTHDATE	SOURCE/PAGE	DATE
10 Aug 1852	A.J. Anderson	Thomas B. & Bathsheba Scot/Va	GCIN C432	----
00 000 0000	Priscilla Atkins	John & Alice(Atkinson)	HMAR 1004	----
00 00c 1820	Elizabeth Belt[Sprague]		GCIN C358	----
25 Jul 1880	Henry Bentley		HMW C517	1890
27 Oct 1848	C.F. Brent		HKNO 609	1850
01 Aug 1868	Charles G. Brooks	Lee H. & Laura(Tone)	GCIN C898	----
03 Dec 1886	W.A.R. Bruehl, Jr.		GCIN D130	----
21 Feb 1871	John R. Bullock	William R & Mary T(Clayton)	CUVC 163	----
00 000 1858	William R. Buselman	Henry & Mary(McCarthy) Ger/La	WCBR B788	----
22 Nov 1851	Braxton W. Campbell	A. Morgan & Susan(Love)	CUVC 169	----
22 Nov 1851	Braxton W. Campbell	Morgan	GCIN C265	----
22 Nov 1851	Braxton W. Campbell	Morgan & Sally	LGCI C242	1869
20 Sep 1841	Dr. John L. Cleveland	Washington & Hannah(Allen)	GCCI B363	----
14 Aug 1887	William M. Coffin	William M. & Leonora(Moore) In33/In51	LGCI D363	----
11 Nov 1884	Rev.James J. Conroy	Charles & Catherine(O'Rourke)Campb/**	HMW C237	----
00 000 1867	Louis G. Dittoe	George M.	GCIN C404	----
04 Nov 1881	Dr. William McDoughty	Charles L. & Ann(Parvin) Oh/x	GCIN C937	----
03 Feb 1844	Alexander G. Drury	Rev. Asa & Elizabeth W(Getchell)Ma02/x	----	----
25 Jul 1878	Benjamin F.Dulweber	John & Anna(Lineman)	GCIN D784	----
00 000 0000	Wade H. Ellis	S.A.C. & Katherine(Blackburn) Ky/x	GCIN B216	----
28 Feb 1858	Richard P. Ernst	William & Sarah A(Butler)	GCIN B254	----
28 Feb 1858	Sen.Richard P.Ernst	William & Sarah(Butler)	LGCI C144	----
28 Feb 1858	Richard P. Ernst	William & Sarah(Butler) x/Fayette	RCIQ 330	----
20 Jan 1855	Charles C. Glidden	Daniel A. & Ellen(Robinson)	ESCI 991	----
00 000 1844	Robert Gray	John & Jane Ire98/Ire02	DHGR 565	----
00 000 1851	Walter E. Gray	Francis	MALL 618	----
14 Jun 1879	Ransom C. Hall	Ransom A & Mary C(Rivarde) **/Fr	LGCI D474	----
23 Aug 1847	John H. Havlin	Joseph & Margerrette(Creighton)	RCIQ 230	----
21 Aug 1856	Dr.Harmon H. Hays	Samuel K. & Elizabeth(Smith)	HMW C119	----
18 Mar 1853	Rev. Raphael Hesse	Anthony Ger/x	MBUT 320	----
18 Mar 1853	Rev. Raphael Hesse	Anthony	MLIC 320	----

-37-

BIRTHDATE	NAME OF BIOGRAPHEE	PARENTS/BIRTHPLACE/BIRTHDATE	SOURCE/PAGE	DATE
10 Oct 1848	John W. Hill	Edmund & Amanda	RCIQ 343	----
20 Mar 1856	Edwin J. Howard	James G. & Della(Peck) Ky/x	HCIN 604	----
00 000 1849	Richard B. Jones	William & Mary(Calvert)	HBRO B70	----
22 Feb 1867	Henry C. Kasson	Henry & Frances	HMMV C399	----
26 Nov 1851	George A. Keen	Archibald & Rebecca(Kirkpatrick)Ky/**	WCBR B441	----
23 Oct 1869	Dr. Edwin J. Kehoe	Timothy & Elizabeth(McHenry) Ire/Ire	GCIN D63	----
08 Feb 1876	Thomas G. Kennedy	John M. & Florence G Pa40/x	GCIN D420	----
06 Jun 1867	E.G. Kinkead	Joseph D. & Edna A(Manser)	CUVC 163	----
16 Nov 1886	Dr. Elmer A. Klein	Charles E. & Katheryn(Peters)	LGCI D526	----
10 Dec 1855	Simon Labold	Henry & Fannie(Rosenfeld) x/Ger	ESCI 1035	----
12 Apr 1889	Dr. Charles W.Larkins	George W. & Susan(Blennerhassitt)	HMMV C159	----
27 Jul 1855	Eugene Lewis	Alexander H. & Sarah(Marion)	RCIQ 289	----
15 Aug 1822	Harry D. Lombard	Jesse & Olive(Carleton) Vt93/Vt	PFPM 368	1828
00 000 1867	James A. McEntee	Patrick & Maria(McKean) Ire/Ire	GCIN D73	----
00 000 1852	Alexander McGregor	Alexander & Rachel(Willoughby)Scot/Eng	BCIA 116	----
16 Jun 1881	William Macke	Bernard & Margaret(Weber) **/**	CUVC 169	----
18 Jul 1874	Harry B. Mackoy	William H. & Margaret C(Brent)**39/x	GCIN D278	----
18 Jul 1874	Harry B. Mackoy	Wm. H. & Margaret C(Brent) **/Bourbon	LGCI C220	----
00 000 0000	W.H. Mackoy	John & Elizabeth(Hardin) Ky/Va	HCIN 577	----
02 Sep 1872	R.S. Magee		HMMV C475	----
06 Oct 1872	Cliff E. Martin	Absalom Oh/x	HMMV C274	----
05 May 1875	John B. Morris	Benjamin W & Sarah(Funk) Oh/**	GCIN D193	----
18 Jun 1851	James H. Morrison		ESCI 1080	----
27 Apr 1864	William D. Nixon	John S. & Mary(Clemens) In22/**	LGCI D394	----
21 Jun 1856	Edward J. Nolan	James & Ellen(Daniels)	RCIQ 250	----
12 Dec 1861	Frank H. Perkins	John H. & Maria(Stinsifer) 08/14	GCIN C256	----
00 000 0000	R.H. Ransom		HMMV C476	----
11 Feb 1856	George J. Renner	George J. & Saraphina(Appleman)Ger/Ger	BNEO 541	----
28 Jun 1891	Burton E.Robinson	Albert & Annie(Stevenson)	LGCI D673	----
09 Apr 1857	Enoch J. Salt	Enoch & Elizabeth(Davis) Eng/Eng	ESCI 1122	----

25 Oct 1877	A. Clifford Shinkle	Bradford & Ann J(Hemingray)		CUVC	159	----
25 Oct 1877	Amos C. Shinkle			GCIN	D50	----
21 Nov 1870	Hon. William W. Smith	William W.		GCCI	B349	----
13 Aug 1874	Jackson W. Sparrow	William & Mary E(Wolcott)Eng45/NY48		GCIN	C483	----
13 Aug 1874	Jackson W. Sparrow	William & Mary E(Wolcott)Eng45/NY48		LGCI	D661	----
08 Oct 1872	Dennis J. Sweeney	John & Julia	Ire/Ire	MCHA	B64	----
21 Jun 1861	Dr. August R.Walker	Rudolph & Margaret(Nieman)Ger/Ger		HCIN	694	----
28 Nov 1867	Charles A.J. Walker	Rudolph & Margaret(Neiman)Ger/Ger		LGCI	D524	----
22 Aug 1856	Orville J. Wiggins	O.B. & Rachel(Adams)		RCIQ	97	----

K N O T T   C O U N T Y   (N O N E)

K N O X   C O U N T Y   (N O N E)

L A R U E   C O U N T Y   (N O N E)

L A U R E L   C O U N T Y   (N O N E)

L A W R E N C E   C O U N T Y

BIRTHDATE	NAME OF BIOGRAPHEE	PARENTS/BIRTHDATE/BIRTHPLACE		SOURCE/PAGE		DATE
10 Oct 1858	Alexander G. Chafins	Kenas M. & Margaret(Goans)	**35/**	HCOL	551	----
00 000 0000	William Tipton	Wiley C. & Nancy(Vance)	NC35/NC40	WHAN	1001	----

L E E   C O U N T Y   (N O N E)

L E S L I E   C O U N T Y   (N O N E)

L E T C H E R   C O U N T Y   (N O N E)

L E W I S   C O U N T Y

BIRTHDATE	NAME OF BIOGRAPHEE	PARENTS/BIRTHPLACE/BIRTHDATE		SOURCE/PAGE		DATE
00 000 0000	Capt. John Barrett			GCCI	B441	---
00 000 1834	C. W. Boyd	James & Mary(Gibson)	Oh/Va	HBRO	B54	1849
00 000 1834	Capt.Charles W.Boyd			WCBR	B487	---
00 000 0000	S. G. Boyd	James & Margaret(Gibson)	Ky/Ky	GCIN	C684	---
20 Jul 1811	Hannah M. Brewer[Johnson]	John & Rachel(Dunavon)	Md/Md	PGCL	348	---
11 Oct 1862	Jackson Cropper	Wheatley & Elizabeth(Frame)	Md/Oh	ESCI	942	---
22 Aug 1827	Capt. D.H. Henderson	James & Elizabeth(Truesdale)	**01/**00	HUNI	E406	---
00 000 1865	Joel D. Hendrickson	Daniel & Elizabeth(Rummans)		ESCI	568	---
14 Oct 1839	James S. Pollit	Alexander & Eleanor		ESCI	297	---
31 Oct 1858	Robert H. Putnam	Thomas D. & Hannah		HMMV	C467	---
19 Feb 1854	James T. Shepherd	John & Mary A(Smith)		DSJE	---	---
04 Jan 1846	Francis A. Swearingen	John & Mary(Loveland)	**21/Oh	WHAN	905	1850
02 Oct 1810	Andrew H. Thompson			MDUM	120	---
24 Apr 1827	George W. Thompson	Mathew & Sarah(Bassett)	Pa/Pa	PSCI	278	---
00 000 0000	Denton Tolle	Stephen	Va/Md	PSCI	82	---

L I N C O L N   C O U N T Y

BIRTHDATE	NAME OF BIOGRAPHEE	PARENTS/BIRTHPLACE/BIRTHDATE	SOURCE/PAGE	DATE

14 Dec 1793 Solomon Fitzpatrick   HCIN 670 ----
26 Aug 1812 Zerilda Vanhook[Fitzpatrick]   HCIN 670 ----

L I V I N G S T O N C O U N T Y (N O N E)

L O G A N C O U N T Y

BIRTHDATE	NAME OF BIOGRAPHEE	PARENTS/BIRTHPLACE/BIRTHDATE	SOURCE/PAGE		DATE
00 000 1845	Major Samuel R. Crumbaugh		GCCI	B383	----
00 000 0000	Harriet Rial[Bailey]		HHAR	918	1854

L Y O N C O U N T Y (N O N E)

Mc C R A C K E N C O U N T Y (N O N E)

Mc C R E A R Y C O U N T Y (N O N E)

Mc L E A N C O U N T Y (N O N E)

M A D I S O N C O U N T Y

BIRTHDATE	NAME OF BIOGRAPHEE	PARENTS/BIRTHPLACE/BIRTHDATE	SOURCE/PAGE		DATE
08 Mar 1786	Silas Dooley	Moses & Mary(Boyd)	HPRE	176	----
05 Jun 1861	Talton Embry	Talton	GCIN	C271	----
25 Sep 1790	Charles Johnston		PALS	476	1800

M A R I O N   C O U N T Y

BIRTHDATE	NAME OF BIOGRAPHEE	PARENTS/BIRTHPLACE/BIRTHDATE	SOURCE/PAGE	DATE
00 000 0000	Lucius S. Howard		MCHA B160	----

M A S O N   C O U N T Y

BIRTHDATE	NAME OF BIOGRAPHEE	PARENTS/BIRTHPLACE/BIRTHDATE	SOURCE/PAGE	DATE
10 Feb 1797	Sylvanus Allen	Jeremiah	HMIA 471	1805
05 Jul 1834	Benjamin F.Applegate	Vincent & Ann(Lemon) Ky/Md	HBRO B294	---
00 Jun 1816	Daniel W. Applegate	Benjamin & Rebecca(Wall)	HBRO B245	---
00 000 1795	Vincent Applegate		HBRO 559	1836
20 Jan 1800	Wesley Arrowsmith	Ezekiel & Elizabeth(Kenton)Md71/Va78	---	---
08 Jan 1854	William A. Bennett	George W. & Matilda(Nichols) Vt/**	HCIN 833	---
08 Jan 1854	William A. Bennett	George W. & Matilda(Nichols) Vt19/**	GCIN C566	---
12 Oct 1845	Benjamin D. Best	Abner & Louisa(Reynolds)	RCIQ 181	---
00 Aug 1841	William C. Blades	William & Amanda(Gates) Ky/Ky	HCIN 857	---
00 000 0000	Charles C. Boyd	Samuel & Susan A(Calvert)	LGCI C149	---
00 000 1799	Nancy Brookover[Case] A.		HBRO B152	---
00 000 1807	Rachel Campbell[Martin]		HBRO B75	---

Date	Name	Parents	Origin	Code	No.	Year
15 Sep 1793	John F. Chenoweth	Elijah & Rachel(Foster)	Pa/Va	HMAD	863	---
08 May 1837	Alexander Cole	Thomas & Mary(Wallingford)	Pa/**	ESCI	934	---
04 Aug 1820	James B. Collins		Ma/x	HWAR	1030	---
18 Oct 1818	John R. Crosby		x/Md	HBRO	B10	---
27 Apr 1887	Dr. W.C. Crowell	Joseph & Elizabeth(Jackson)	**/**	WCBR	B817	---
10 Apr 1778	James S. Daniels			MALL	221	---
00 000 1775	Rhoda [Daniels]			MALL	221	---
00 000 1799	John Davidson			WCBR	B817	---
00 000 1790	William Dixon	William & Grizzy A(Bell)	Ire/x	HBRO	B60	1799
00 000 1795	Anthony Barley	William		HCLI	1048	---
08 Mar 1844	John R. Foster	Joshua & Eliza(Frizell)		ESCI	981	1852
18 Aug 1836	Otho D. Foster	Joshua F. & Alice(Fiusant)		ESCI	982	1851
00 000 1844	R.C. Fristo	Thompson		HCLI	1097	---
11 Jan 1825	Joseph Fulton	Joseph & Elizabeth(Bennett)		HBRO	B160	---
20 Jul 1813	Titus B. Fulton	Joseph & Elizabeth(Bennett)	Md81/Md	HBRO	B160	1831
00 000 1824	William Fulton	Joseph		HBRO	B160	---
03 Apr 1829	Elijah Garrison	James & Mary(Sullivan)	Va/Va	HBRO	B162	1841
23 Dec 1845	William P. Gault			LCGI	135	---
13 Jan 1809	Benjamin Ginn	Benjamin & Lucy(Triplett)	Va/Va	HLOG	710	---
18 Sep 1782	William Givens			ESCI	70	---
18 Sep 1782	Judge Wm. Givens	--- & Mary(Mitchell)		WHAN	892	---
27 Sep 1800	Azel Glover			ESCI	723	1820
00 000 1854	William H. Grundy	Rev.R. & E.S(Kemper)	Oh/Oh	HDAY	537	---
00 000 1854	William H. Grundy	Rev.R.C. & E.S(Kemper)		HMON	B211	---
05 Aug 1801	Rev. William Haller	John & Sarah(Arrowsmith)		HCHA	B521	1812
05 Aug 1801	Rev. William Haller			MCHA	A1103	1812
21 Dec 1860	Charles Hanauer	Andrew & Mary A.M.		CUVC	133	---
00 Nov 1793	John Hatfield			HMON	B265	---
30 Jun 1792	David F. Heaton			HPRE	66	---
00 000 1810	James Helm	Samuel H. & Phoebe	Ky/Ky	HBRO	B167	1820
00 000 1797	Samuel Hill[Thompson]			WCBR	B53	---
28 Jan 1814	Jacob Howser	Jacob & Sarah(Loveless)	Md/Ger	PMHA	372	1822
08 Mar 1819	Joseph R. Johnson	James & Clemency(Donovan)	Va/Va	BCLA	257	1826
10 Jul 1808	William D. Johnson			PGCL	348	1828

BIRTHDATE	NAME OF BIOGRAPHEE	PARENTS/BIRTHPLACE/BIRTHDATE	SOURCE/PAGE	DATE
00 000 0000	Elizabeth Logan Claypool]		HHAR 839	---
17 Nov 1823	James M. McMichael	William & Agnes(Kerr) Ire/Pa	HBRO B30	1839
00 000 1848	Louisiana Mannen[Broadwell]		WCBR B102	---
00 000 1803	Thomas Mefford		HBRO 603	1825
00 000 0000	Samuel Naylor	James Ma/x	PSCI 381	---
00 000 1850	Dr. William N.Nelson		FHCI 479	---
12 Mar 1851	J.C. Newcomb	James & Nancy(Mannen) Fleming00/**	HBRO B79	1861
00 000 1871	Dr.Charles D.Pearce	Charles	GCIN C77	---
25 Oct 1820	Daniel Perrine	Joseph & Susan(Downing)	HWAR 771	---
23 Feb 1806	William C. Perrine	Joseph & Susan(Downing) NJ/Pa	HWAR 771	---
00 000 1801	Lovell Pickerell	Samuel	HBRO B80	1805
10 Apr 1813	Grandison Pinckard	William & Elizabeth(Duff) Va/Va	HBRO B36	---
05 Oct 1845	J.W. Pinckard	G.	HBRO B112	1861
17 Dec 1808	Alfred Purcell		HBRO B292	1820
21 Nov 1815	Henry Putnam	Zecharia	MCHA B544	1816
00 000 0000	Robert H. Putnam		GCIN C545	---
21 Jan 1840	Capt. Wm. J.Rannells	Samuel & Rachel(Hughes) Pa91/SC06	HHOC 1259	1841
00 00c 1790	Josiah Rhoten		KHIG 447	---
00 000 1801	Elizabeth Scott[Caven]		HMIA 478	---
00 00c 1798	Mary T. Simpson		HTMA B177	---
14 Sep 1841	William D. Spaulding	Daniel & Matilda(Campbell) Can./Va	HCIN 858	---
04 Jun 1796	Mary Stansell[Carmony]	Henry	HMON B398	1820
04 Apr 1845	R.J. Stevens	Samuel Ky/x	HBRO B41	---
00 000 1797	Griffin Taylor	John & Sarah(Mackinnon)	GCIN C760	---
07 Dec 1814	Andrew J. Thorpe	John & Mary(Hall) Ky/NJ	HWAR 885	1820
19 Jan 1796	Wilson Vance	Joseph C. & Sarah(Wilson) Va/Va	HHAN 538	1800
09 Jun 1801	Mary Wallace	Thomas & Catherine Ire/Pa	HBRO B86	1815
25 Oct 1773	Abraham Watson	Michael	PSCI 383	1804
07 May 1793	Gen. John Webb	John & Richard(Davis) Va/Pa	HMIA 540	1797
01 Jan 1815	Maj. A.J. Whipps	Col. Wm. & Cecil(Finch) x/Ky	HCIN 525	---

08 Feb 1824	Col.Carr D.White	John D. & Margaret R(Baker)	Va/Va	HBRO	B47	1824
00 000 1845	T.J. White	Peyton & Virginia(Owens)	Ky/Ky	HBRO	B90	----
01 Sep 1826	Henry Worthington	Thomas T & Arah(Whipps)	Md/Md	HCIN	521	----
00 000 0000	Linda Wright[Halenshade]			CINC	349	----

M E A D E   C O U N T Y   (N O N E)

M E N I F E E   C O U N T Y   (N O N E)

M E R C E R   C O U N T Y

BIRTHDATE	NAME OF BIOGRAPHEE	PARENTS/BIRTHPLACE/BIRTHDATE		SOURCE/PAGE	DATE
26 May 1780	John A. McDowell	Samuel & Ann(Irvin)		HMAD	393	----
26 May 1780	John A. McDowell	Samuel & Ann(Irvin)		HMAR	358	c1815
03 Mar 1806	Lyne Starling	William & Mazy(McDowell)		HFPI	69	1830
27 Sep 1812	James H.Thompson	John B. & Nancy P(Robards)	Va/Va	PSCI	202	----
00 000 0000	Andrew Wilson			MCHA	B148	1807
11 Sep 1806	Thomas C. Wilson	James & Anna(Cleland)	Va/Md	PGCL	491	----

M E T C A L F E   C O U N T Y   (N O N E)

M O N R O E   C O U N T Y   (N O N E)

M O N T G O M E R Y   C O U N T Y

BIRTHDATE	NAME OF BIOGRAPHEE	PARENTS/BIRTHPLACE/BIRTHDATE	SOURCE/PAGE	DATE
30 Jul 1809	Bennett Barrow		WCBR B315	----
19 Oct 1800	William Biggs	Andrew & Judith(Robertson)	ESCI 1257	----
19 Jan 1810	Benjamin E. Cave	Benjamin & Mary(Mounts) Va/Ky	HHOC 1113	1815
00 00c 1756	Rev.Simon Cochran		MALL 713	----
00 000 1862	Isaac N. Crain	Richard M. & Elizabeth(Ketron)Va33/Va29 WCBR 751		----
30 Dec 1804	Joseph Dean	Daniel & Jenny(Steele) Ire/x	PGCL 128	1812
00 000 0000	George Elliston	Joseph L. & Ida(Givens)	LGCI D563	----
00 000 1840	Clara French	Charles & Alice	HBUT 446	----
00 000 1800	James H. Hodge	Andrew & Isabell(McTeer)	CGHA 567	1808
00 000 1800	James H. Hodge	Andrew	HCHA 907	1808
11 Dec 1796	Samuel E. Hodge	Andrew & Isabel(Mateer) Va/Ky	PGCL 436	1806
01 Jan 1848	John Jones	David E. & Elizabeth(Edwards)	ESCI 1016	----
00 000 0000	Harriet Smith[Albro]		GCCI B743	1831
28 Jul 1846	Edwin S. Wallace	Dr. Joseph H.	HCLA 938	1855

M O R G A N   C O U N T Y   (N O N E)

M U H L E N B U R G   C O U N T Y   (N O N E)

N E L S O N   C O U N T Y   (N O N E)

N I C H O L A S   C O U N T Y

BIRTHDATE	NAME OF BIOGRAPHEE	PARENTS/BIRTHPLACE/BIRTHDATE	SOURCE/PAGE	DATE
01 Mar 1805	William Baker	Jacob & Barbara	HCLI 1134	----

15 Aug 1823	O.P. Fite	John W. & Millie(Cotterill)	Pa/Ky	HBRO	B184	---
00 Jan 1833	Melville M. Gaunce	Martin		PGCL	511	---
09 May 1797	George Mann	Jacob & Catherine(McDaniel)	Va/Va	HCLI	1145	---

O H I O   C O U N T Y   (N O N E)

O L D H A M   C O U N T Y

BIRTHDATE	NAME OF BIOGRAPHEE	PARENTS/BIRTHPLACE/BIRTHDATE	SOURCE/PAGE	DATE
00 000 1846	John B. Washburn	Ira D. & Mary(McKnight)	RCIQ 258	---

O W E N   C O U N T Y

BIRTHDATE	NAME OF BIOGRAPHEE	PARENTS/BIRTHPLACE/BIRTHDATE	SOURCE/PAGE	DATE
15 Apr 1860	D. Howard Gayle	James & Sarah C(Green) **/**	GCIN C346	---

O W S L E Y   C O U N T Y   (N O N E)

P E N D L E T O N   C O U N T Y

BIRTHDATE	NAME OF BIOGRAPHEE	PARENTS/BIRTHPLACE/BIRTHDATE	SOURCE/PAGE	DATE
00 000 1878	George W. Berger	Hugh & Margaret(Chalfant)	GCIN C564	---
00 000 1849	William A. Bradford	George P. & Aurelia M(Bennett)Eng/NY13	GCIN C624	---
13 Jul 1845	Fred A. Goulding		HCLI 1071	---
00 000 1880	Hall Hagemeyer	C.C. & Mary E(Hall) Ger49/x	GCIN D844	---

PENDLETON COUNTY (CONT.)

BIRTHDATE	NAME OF BIOGRAPHEE	PARENTS/BIRTHPLACE/BIRTHDATE		SOURCE/PAGE		DATE
23 Oct 1865	Andrew J. Halfhill	John & Elizabeth(Kellum)	Oh29/x	GCIN	C696	----
15 Aug 1835	William M. Rogers	Jacob & Mary A(Truston)	NJ08/x	HMON	B303	----

PERRY COUNTY (NONE)

PIKE COUNTY (NONE)

POWELL COUNTY (NONE)

PULASKI COUNTY

BIRTHDATE	NAME OF BIOGRAPHEE	PARENTS/BIRTHPLACE/BIRTHDATE	SOURCE/PAGE		DATE
00 000 1812	David Carnahan	Aaron & Alvira(Mitchell)	BHCL	469	1831
23 Oct 1812	David Carnahan	Aaron & Elvira	HCLI	1070	1813

ROBERTSON COUNTY

BIRTHDATE	NAME OF BIOGRAPHEE	PARENTS/BIRTHPLACE/BIRTHDATE	SOURCE/PAGE		DATE
06 Dec 1869	W.C. Deming	Judge O.S.	ATRU	172	----

ROCKCASTLE COUNTY (NONE)

S C O T T   C O U N T Y

BIRTHDATE	NAME OF BIOGRAPHEE	PARENTS/BIRTHPLACE/BIRTHDATE		SOURCE/PAGE	DATE
13 Aug 1835	David Davidson	John & Margaret	Oh/Oh	DHGR 488	----
00 000 1839	John W. Fitzgerald	John M. & Mary S(Smallwood)		HMON B312	----
00 000 0000	Elizabeth J.Flournoy[Stevenson]	Rev.David J&Elizab(Cunningham		MCHA B448	**Ky
00 000 1802	Sarah Ireland[Wilson]			BHCL 484	----
18 Jul 1854	Tom L. Johnson			PMNO 12	----
03 Mar 1861	Dr.Benj.F. Lyle	Dr. John & Mary(Phillips)	Oh/34/Oh37	HCIN 688	----
03 Jan 1790	Nancy Mann[Waddle]			HCLA 1075	1798
27 Nov 1845	Allen Robinson	Alfred		HHOC 1295	----
26 Jun 1820	Joab Rudulph			CWOO 518	----
00 000 0000	Bolton Smith	Oliver & Ann(Bolton)	Pa/x	MBUT 137	----
00 000 0000	John Smith	Oliver & Ann(Bolton)	Pa/x	MBUT 137	----
14 Jul 1794	John T. Tullis	Aaron		HMIA 717	1804
00 00c 1824	Dr. James H. Williamson			HBUT 436	----
22 Sep 1800	Nelly Wilson			BHCL 88+	----

S H E L B Y   C O U N T Y

BIRTHDATE	NAME OF BIOGRAPHEE	PARENTS/BIRTHPLACE/BIRTHDATE		SOURCE/PAGE	DATE
14 Jul 1809	Elias Carman	James & Comfort(Clinton)	Ger/Fr	HALL 817	----
14 Jul 1809	Elias Carman	James & Comfort(Clinton)	Va82/Va	PAVW AL222	c1811
24 Sep 1799	John Easton	Redwood & Polly(McMichael)	RI/Va	HLOG 749	----

BIRTHDATE	NAME OF BIOGRAPHEE	PARENTS/BIRTHPLACE/BIRTHDATE		SOURCE/PAGE	DATE
00 000 1804	Patience Easton			HLCG 755	---
07 Oct 1814	Francis Johnston	Arthur & Frances	Ire/Ire	HCLA 1044	1829
00 000 0000	Solomon Jones			HMIA 487	---
10 Aug 1813	Joseph Moxley			MAPA 81	---

S I M P S O N   C O U N T Y

BIRTHDATE	NAME OF BIOGRAPHEE	PARENTS/BIRTHPLACE/BIRTHDATE	SOURCE/PAGE	DATE
00 000 1843	James Pattan		HVMW 439	---

S P E N C E R   C O U N T Y   (N O N E)

T A Y L O R   C O U N T Y   (N O N E)

T O D D   C O U N T Y   (N O N E)

T R I G G   C O U N T Y   (N O N E)

T R I M B L E   C O U N T Y   (N O N E)

WARREN COUNTY

BIRTHDATE	NAME OF BIOGRAPHEE	PARENTS/BIRTHPLACE/BIRTHDATE	SOURCE/PAGE	DATE
08 Aug 1872	Louis B. Sawyer	Nathan L.R. & Ella M	GCCI B351	----
08 Aug 1872	Louis B. Sawyer		GCIN D293	----

WASHINGTON COUNTY

BIRTHDATE	NAME OF BIOGRAPHEE	PARENTS/BIRTHPLACE/BIRTHDATE		SOURCE/PAGE	DATE
21 Sep 1867	Walter J. Bagby	William & Mahala I(Bruce)	Ky41/x	ESCI 894	----
12 Apr 1848	Henry D. Graham	Ancil & Sarah(Urton)	Ky/Ky	HCIN 985	----
25 Dec 1791	Ezekial S. Woods			HLIC 810	1818

WAYNE COUNTY

BIRTHDATE	NAME OF BIOGRAPHEE	PARENTS/BIRTHPLACE/BIRTHDATE		SOURCE/PAGE	DATE
06 May 1838	Green B. Buster	Garrett & Sophia(Hudson)	**04/**09	HCLI 1138	----

WEBSTER COUNTY (NONE)

WHITLEY COUNTY (NONE)

W O O D F O R D   C O U N T Y

BIRTHDATE	NAME OF BIOGRAPHEE	PARENTS/BIRTHPLACE/BIRTHDATE		SOURCE/PAGE	DATE
00 000 1775	Nancy DeCoursey[Cooper]			HPRE 164	1816
00 000 0000	James W. Faulkner	James W. & Martha	**/x	HBRO B276	----
00 000 1832	Laura G. Graves[Wasson]	R.C. & Lucy(Mitchell)		GGIN C126	----
17 Feb 1798	James D. Moffett	George		HMIA 609	----
00 000 0000	Martha A. Sallee[O'Neall]	Joseph & Susan(Downing)	Ky/Ky	HWAR 767	----
00 000 1837	Dr. Jefferson B. Scearce			HRHI 218	----

C O U N T Y   N O T   G I V E N

BIRTHDATE	NAME OF BIOGRAPHEE	PARENTS/BIRTHPLACE/BIRTHDATE		SOURCE/PAGE	DATE
00 000 0000	Lamyan Adams			HALL 561	----
00 000 0000	Jeremiah Allen			HBRO 604	1817
06 Mar 1818	William Allen	E. & Nancy(Young)	Va/Va	HMAD 1107	----
23 May 1808	Steven Anderson	Thomas & Rebecca	Va/Va	HMAD 1030	1808
04 Aug 1814	Charles Ansley	William & Mary	Md/Md	HHAR 931	1835
00 000 0000	John Arnold			SHME 531	----
00 000 0000	Rachel [Arnold]			SHME 531	----
00 000 0000	Adrian Aten			HDAR 472	----
00 000 0000	Henry Atley			BHCL 801	----
00 000 0000	Sarah [Atley]			BHCL 801	----
00 000 0000	William D. Baird			PGCL 533	----
00 000 0000	John W. Baker	William		PGCL 922	----
00 000 1799	William Baker			HCLI 799	c1809
00 000 0000	Elizabeth Banta[Hatfield]			HWAR 744	1800

Date	Name	Parents/Notes	Origin	Code	No.	Year
00 000 0000	Joseph Barnes			HBRO	B178	---
00 000 0000	James Barr			HCHA	877	---
00 000 0000	Herman A. Bayless	Herman G. & Mary A(Strong)Kenton/Brack.		GCIN	D253	---
00 00c 1799	Joel Beard			CHAN	407	---
00 000 0000	John Beard			CHAN	407	---
00 00c 1803	William Beard	James & Margaret(Blue)	Pa78/81	MBUT	390	---
00 000 0000	John Bigger			DHGR	645	---
00 000 0000	Thomas Bigger	John & Mary	Ire/Pa	DHGR	590	1806
00 000 0000	Edward Biggs			HMW	C366	---
08 Feb 1798	James Black	Alexander & Jane(Crocket)	Va/Va	HCHA	806	1809
00 000 0000	Sarah Black[McIlvain]Alexander			CCHA	446	1809
00 000 0000	Ezekiel Boggs	Aaron	Oh/x	HMIA	727	---
00 000 1838	Eliza Bonwell[Pulse]			KHIG	440	---
00 000 1797	Robert Braden			PALS	395	1815
00 000 0000	Major Joseph C.Brand Thomas		Md/x	MCHA	B820	1830
00 000 1808	Isaac P. Brandon			HMIA	804	c1815
00 000 0000	Susan [Bremer]			HTUS	899	---
17 Jan 1800	Abraham Brewer			HDAR	479	---
00 000 0000	Nancy[Brittingham]		Ky/x	HBRO	B150	1808
00 000 0000	Benjamin F. Brown	James & Martha(Summers)	Va/Va	HMIA	578	1805
00 000 0000	D.D. Brown			HBRO	B180	1800
00 000 0000	Harlin S. Brown			CWOO	709	---
00 000 1795	James Brown			BHCL	418	---
23 Oct 1794	John Brown			HMIA	579	---
22 Dec 1806	Mary Brown[Walker]	Asa & Anna	Me/Ky	HCLI	1023	c1812
00 000 1793	Mary A. Brown			HBRO	559	---
00 000 1786	Vincent Brown			HBRO	559	1801
02 Dec 1822	William Brunson	John & Elizabeth(Ellis)		HLOG	733	---
00 000 0000	Henry Buchanan			ESCI	664	---
00 000 0000	Thomas Cahall			HBRO	B7	---
00 000 0000	Sarah Cainbell[Daniels]			CCHA	657	1813
00 000 0000	Vincent Calvin			HBRO	665	1807
00 000 0000	Jane Campbell	William		PFPM	146	---
00 000 1803	Folly Campbell			HLOG	815	---
00 000 0000	Folly Campbell			PMHA	234	---

COUNTY NOT GIVEN (CONT.)

BIRTHDATE	NAME OF BIOGRAPHEE	PARENTS/BIRTHPLACE/BIRTHDATE		SOURCE/PAGE	DATE
00 000 0000	David Cantrill			HCLI 983	---
00 000 0000	David Carpenter			HBRO B214	---
00 000 0000	Margaret [Carpenter]			HBRO B214	---
00 000 1798	William Carroll			HCLI 850	c1805
00 000 0000	William Cast	Ezekiel & Mary		HCLI 1138	---
00 000 1792	John F. Chenoweth			PFPM 147	1804
00 000 0000	Jacob Claypool			HHAR 839	---
14 Jan 1792	James H. Coleman			HWOA 720	---
00 000 0000	Allsey Collett[Boring]	John	Pa/x	BHCL 773	1793
00 000 0000	Elsie Collett[Boring]			BHCL 590	---
06 Dec 1811	Dr. John Colliver			HMAD 442	1841
19 Jan 1841	Jefferson T. Colliver	John & Matilda(Robinson)		HMAD 442	---
13 Sep 1798	L. W. Colvin	Henry & Catherine(Williams)		HMIA 479	1820
00 000 0000	Mary A. Colvin[Brown]			CWOO 709	---
00 000 0000	Sarah Colvin[Deck]	James & Martha		KHIG 279	---
00 000 0000	William Colvin	Henry		BHCL 615	---
00 000 0000	Abraham Compton	Jacob	NJ/x	MBUT 415	---
29 Feb 1796	Abraham Compton	Jacob	NJ/x	MLIC 415	---
00 000 0000	Jonathan Conry			DHGR 790	---
00 000 0000	Mathias Corwin	Joseph	Pa/x	HDAR 728	---
00 000 0000	Jacob Counts	Jacob	Md/x	HMIA 544	1816
00 000 0000	Hannah Cowgill[Swann]			HUPP A266	---
00 000 0000	Lewis F. Crain	Lewis	Ky/x	CCHA 422	---
00 000 1805	Thomas Cramer	John & Margaret(Hoover)		DHGR 646	c1807
00 000 0000	Thomas Crawford			HDEL 621	---
00 000 0000	Jabez Cretcher	John & Sarah(Oldfield)		HLOG 819	---
00 000 0000	Jabez Cretcher	John & Sarah(Oldfield)		KHLO 519	---
00 000 0000	Robert Crockett			KHLO 497	---
01 Jan 1866	Edward H. Cronenger			HMMW C502	---
00 000 0000	Benjamin Cummins			HHAN 829	1831

Date	Name	Parents/Spouse	Origin	Code	No.	Year
00 000 0000	Thomas Daniels			CCHA	657	1813
00 000 1804	Benjamin Davis	Elijah T. & Elizabeth(Vance)		HCHA	475	----
00 000 0000	I. Davis	Issachar		HBRO	B10	----
00 000 0000	William Dawson			GWIL	660	1830
00 000 0000	Charlotte [Decker]			HHAR	978	1818
00 000 0000	I.G. Decker			HHAR	978	1817
10 Sep 1801	Maia R. Dickey	Rev. William		HCHA	805	----
00 000 0000	William Dill			HWAR	735	1798
00 000 0000	Samuel Dills			HCHA	832	----
22 Apr 1801	Wesley Diltz	Joseph & Mary(Jarrard)	NJ/x	----	B216	1804
00 000 1801	John Donley			HBRO	B216	----
27 Nov 1809	Thomas Doty			CWHO	693	----
00 000 0000	Catherine Dudley[Monahan]	John & Catherine(Sparrow)	Md/Md	PGCL	474	----
00 000 0000	Mary Dugan[Young]			HBRO	B92	1832
00 000 0000	Gideon Dunham			HBRO	B12	----
26 Oct 1800	Mary Dunlap[Powell]	Rev. James & Emily(Johnson)	Va73/Va77	CCHA	514	----
00 000 0000	Isaac Dunn			HDAR	708	----
00 000 0000	May Dutterrow[Kelley]			PGCL	37	----
10 Jan 1798	Daniel Earley			HCLI	1047	1799
00 000 1820	D.W. Early	D.W. & Elizabeth(Lynn)	Va/Pa	HBRO	B155	1836
00 Aug 1818	Eliza[Eleyet]			HCHA	779	----
00 000 0000	Michael Ellsberry			HBRO	B13	1805
00 000 1800	John B. Evans			HBRO	B15	1801
00 000 0000	William Evans	Hugh	Wales/x	PSCI	319	1808
27 Oct 1789	William Ewing			HMON	B360	1797
25 Mar 1832	Rachel A. Farrow	Orson D. & Elizabeth(Brewer)	Mason/Mason	PGCL	198	----
09 Oct 1799	Jesse Fenton	Jeremiah		HBRO	B277	----
00 000 1782	B. Fisher			HPRE	246	----
00 000 0000	Lavina Fitch[Colwell]			CCHA	17	c1806
00 000 0000	John Fletcher			HHAR	979	----
00 000 0000	David Floro			CSOT	886	----
00 000 0000	George Fogle			HMOR	706	1832
00 000 1807	Mordecai S. Ford			HDAR	730	----
00 000 0000	Elizabeth Frame[Counts]			HMIA	544	1816

-55-

COUNTY NOT GIVEN (CONT.)

BIRTHDATE	NAME OF BIOGRAPHEE	PARENTS/BIRTHPLACE/BIRTHDATE		SOURCE/PAGE		DATE
00 000 0000	Fred Friesner			PAVW	VW190	---
00 000 0000	Nancy Frizell[Hance]			HMIA	485	1815
17 Oct 1806	James Fry	Jacob & Elizabeth	Va/Va	HBRO	B217	1812
00 000 0000	Jeptha D. Garrard			GCIN	D606	---
00 000 0000	Gershom Gard	Job	NJ/x	HCLA	1001	---
02 Dec 1801	William Gilliam	Richard & Martha(Hodge)	Va/Va	HMON	B320	---
00 000 0000	Elizabeth Giltner[Licklider]			HMIA	606	1813
00 000 1817	John R. Glasscock	Gregory & Elizabeth(White)	Va/Va	HBRO	B163	1807
00 000 0000	John Graham	James & Mary		HHAN	371	---
00 000 0000	John Graham			HMAD	881	---
00 000 1807	James S. Gray	Mathew & Nancy	Pa/Pa	HBRO	B163	1821
00 000 0000	John Hall			HBUT	447	1806
00 000 1792	John Hamilton			MCHA	A1091	1814
19 Feb 1820	Justus Hamilton	Hon. Justin & Eliza(Rhodes)	NY/x	SHME	648	1822
22 Sep 1791	Benjamin Hance	William	Eng/x	HMIA	524	1810
00 000 0000	Joseph Hance		Eng/x	HMIA	565	c1812
00 000 1809	David M. Harlan			HMON	B285	---
00 000 0000	Perkins Harper	Cynthia		AERI	576	1857
00 000 0000	Sanford Harper	Cynthia		AERI	576	1857
00 000 0000	William Harper	Cynthia		AERI	576	1857
00 Nov 1809	Robert Harris	Joseph & Sarah J.		HBUT	572	1810
19 Feb 1819	Bennett J. Harter	Jacob & Elizabeth	Va/Ky	HMIA	566	c1820
00 000 0000	Emily Harter[Shidaker]			HMIA	573	---
00 000 1799	Andrew Hemphill			HHAR	701	1800
24 Mar 1799	Andrew Hemphill			HHAR	982	1---
00 000 0000	Capt. D.H. Henderson			MDUM	439	---
00 000 0000	Sarah Hendricks[Lemen]			HCHA	818	---
00 000 1796	John C. Henry			HBRO	604	1818
12 Jun 1819	George L. Heslar	William & Catherine(Waits)	Ger/Pa	HBRO	B296	1829
22 Feb 1852	Thomas Hetzler	David & Mary A(Thornell)		HBUT	651	---

Date	Name	Parents/Spouse	Origin	Code	No.	Year
00 000 1801	John W. Hitt	Rev. Samuel		CCHA	715	----
00 000 0000	Sarah M. Hodge[Baird]			PGCL	533	----
00 000 0000	Barbary Hoey			HHOC	1126	----
00 000 0000	John Hoffman			PFPM	237	----
00 000 0000	Susan Hoffman			PFPM	237	----
00 000 0000	Caroline Holden[Downs]			HSEN	848	----
12 Jun 1791	Dr. A.V. Hopkins			HCLE	145	----
00 000 0000	David Houston			HWYA	606	----
00 000 0000	John M. Houston			PFPM	440	----
28 Jan 1814	Jacob Howser	Jacob & Sarah(Loveless)		HMAR	732	----
10 Aug 1806	Capt. Manasas Huber			HLOG	730	----
30 Mar 1806	Cornelius Hufford	Christopher	Va/x	CSOT	493	c1815
00 000 0000	Capt. David Hughes	Jesse		PGCL	826	1803
00 000 0000	Benjamin Hull			HCHA	907	----
01 May 1802	John Hurd	Thomas & Dorcus(Morrison)	Pa/Md	HCHA	836	----
00 000 0000	Jane Irwin[Wright]	Thomas	Pa/x	HLOG	833	----
00 000 1803	Israel Johns			HWOA	797	1828
00 000 0000	Henry G. Johnson			HHAR	939	----
00 000 0000	James Johnson			DHGR	662	1815
00 000 0000	Jesse Johnson			HCHA	838	----
00 000 0000	Rebecca Johnson[Michael]		Ky/Ky	HCLA	1006	----
00 000 0000	Ruth Jones[Thornhill]			BHCL	469	----
00 000 0000	Sarah Jones[Whitmore]			HMIA	541	----
28 Mar 1828	William H. Jones	Samuel & Mary		HVWM	480	----
00 000 0000	Jesse Judy			HUNI	E391	----
00 000 1792	Jacob Juvinall			HWYA	609	----
00 000 0000	Anna Kavanaugh[Covington]			HLOG	817	----
00 000 0000	G. M. Kearns			HMMV	C458	----
00 000 0000	Mark Kenton	William & Susan(Markley)	Va/Md	CCHA	590	1802
00 Jun 1807	Sarah Kline			BHCL	88+	----
00 000 0000	Asa M. Lake	Asa & Cloe	Ky/Ky	HHAN	398	----
00 000 0000	Lydia Lake[Wolford]	Asa & Cloe	Ky/Ky	HHAN	398	----
00 000 0000	Martha Lake[Rose]	Asa & Cloe	Ky/Ky	HHAN	398	----
00 00c 1795	David Lamme			HMON	B268	----

C O U N T Y   N O T   G I V E N   (C O N T.)

BIRTHDATE	NAME OF BIOGRAPHEE	PARENTS/BIRTHPLACE/BIRTHDATE	SOURCE/PAGE	DATE
00 00c 1782	Samuel Lamme		DHGR 613	----
00 000 0000	Dr. Zachariah M. Lansdowne		HDAR 507	----
00 000 1792	Charles Larsh		HPRE 167	----
00 000 0000	John Latimore		HHAR 607	----
00 000 0000	Mary Lewis[Rutledge]		HHAR 1025	----
22 Nov 1875	Benjamin J. Lindeman Joseph & Mary		GVWE 652	----
00 000 0000	Margaret Lindsey[Makemson]		KHLO 495	----
00 000 0000	Benjamin Logan Samuel & Phoebe(Richards)		HCHA 665	----
00 000 0000	Elijah Logan Samuel		CCHA 420	1812
00 000 0000	Elijah R.Logan Samuel & Phoebe(Richards)		HCHA 665	----
29 Feb 1824	David R. Lombard Jesse & Olive		HMAD 1067	----
00 000 0000	Mary Long[Adams]		NALL 858	1833
00 000 0000	Mary Long[Adams]		HCHA 306	----
23 Feb 1801	Robert Long John & Isabella(Thompson)	Pa/Pa	HHAN 675	1826
08 Aug 1798	Stephen Long		HDAR 610	----
00 000 1807	William Long		HMIA 778	----
00 000 0000	Joseph Longfellow	Me/x	HCIN 646	----
00 000 0000	Charles Loudon		HBRO B27	----
00 000 1800	Mary McCane[Richardson]		HLOG 781	----
00 000 1789	William McCartney		CSOT 357	c1810
00 000 0000	William McCartney		AERI 600	c1815
00 000 0000	John McClary		HMIA 741	c1812
00 000 0000	Daniel McConkey Archibald		HGLA 977	----
00 000 0000	James B. McCoy Joseph & Charlotte	Ky/x	PSCI 249	c1798
00 Jan 1796	Nancy McCoy		PALS 476	----
00 000 1795	Elizabeth McClellan[Line]		HBUT 483	----
17 Apr 1818	Robert McClellan Joseph & Jane	Pa/Pa	HSEN 995	1822
00 000 0000	Elizabeth McClure[Ellsberry]		HBRO B13	----
00 000 0000	Rev. S.W. McCracken		HBUT 544	----
02 Sep 1808	James McCrosky		HCHA 782	1812

Date	Name	Parents / Notes	Code	No.	Year
00 000 0000	Stephen McDougal		HLIC	722	---
00 000 0000	Polly M. McDuffie[Taylor]		PFPM	532	1805
00 000 1798	Margaret [McGinnis]		HHAR	984	1811
00 Jan 1788	William McGee		HLOG	654	1811
00 00c 1799	Moses McIlvain	Samuel	CCHA	445	1808
00 Jul 1804	William McKee	John & Elizabeth(McClintock) NX78/Pa	HCIN	682	---
00 000 0000	W.H. McKoy	John & Elizabeth(Hardia) Greenup/x	GCCI	B402	---
00 Jul 1817	Ingels McLeod		HDEL	851	1831
00 000 0000	John McMaken	John	HMIA	607	---
00 000 0000	John McMaken		HMIA	742	---
00 000 0000	George McManis		BHCL	308	1807
00 000 0000	William McNelly		ESCI	1062	---
00 000 0000	Jane W. McPherson[Cowan]		HWAR	733	---
00 000 0000	William McRoberts	Ire/x	CCHA	583	---
00 000 0000	John Mahan		HHAR	568	---
00 000 0000	Nancy Makeinson[Huber]Thomas		HLOG	730	---
00 000 0000	Margaret Mann[Bobbitt]		PSCI	9	---
00 000 1789	Hugh Marshall		HPRE	258	1813
00 000 0000	Jane Marshall		DHGR	505	c1800
00 000 0000	Jesse Marshall		DHGR	505	c1800
00 000 1790	Elizabeth Martin[Lamme]		DHGR	613	---
00 000 0000	Henry Martin		HBRO	B75	---
11 Jul 1811	Henry Massie	General Nathaniel	PSCI	107	---
00 000 0000	Mary Meyers[Hite]		DHGR	839	---
00 000 0000	Susan Middleton[Thompson]		MCHA	B866	---
14 Aug 1799	Elizabeth Miller[Rumbarger]		HMON	B348	---
23 Dec 1811	Milton M. Miller	Robert & Elizabeth(Hanson) Va/Md	HCLA	993	1812
00 000 0000	Samuel Miller		BHCL	281	1804
00 000 0000	William Miller		HWYA	919	1833
00 000 1807	Abner C. Mills		KHIG	406	c1830
00 000 0000	Abner C. Mills		HCLI	888	1840
00 000 0000	Lucy Minter		HDEL	756	1804
00 000 1796	Lewis Mitchell	Elijah & Hugh	HPRE	258	1813
00 000 0000	Vincit Mitchell		HPRE	78	c1800

BIRTHDATE	NAME OF BIOGRAPHEE	PARENTS/BIRTHPLACE/BIRTHDATE		SOURCE/PAGE		DATE
00 000 0000	Christiana Moore[Coon]			MALL	780	----
00 000 0000	M. Moore			HCLI	891	----
24 Nov 1807	David Morris	Joseph & Levina(Drake)		HMAD	1068	1812
00 000 0000	David Morris	Joseph & Levina(Drake)		PFPM	475	1814
00 000 0000	Jane [Morton]			HCLI	1009	c1820
00 000 0000	Joab Morton			HCLI	1009	c1820
00 000 0000	John Morton			HCLI	1107	c1813
00 000 1795	Providence Mounts	William & Catherine		HWAR	953	1796
21 Jul 1859	John T. Myers	Abram & Elizabeth	Ky/Ky	BHCL	864	----
00 000 0000	Richard Neal[Ginn]			DHGR	600	1814
00 000 1800	Michael Neff			HDAR	684	----
00 000 0000	Michael Neff	Michael & Leonard	Va/x	HMON	B386	1815
00 000 0000	Samuel Nicholson			HMIA	745	1815
00 000 0000	Charlotte Nolan[Newcomb]			HMON	A272	----
00 000 0000	Martha North			DHGR	515	1825
00 000 1805	George Northcutt			HMIA	703	----
00 000 0000	Runyan Northcutt	Shadrick & Ruth(Taylor)		MCHA	B80	c1810
31 May 1787	Aaron Nutt	Aaron & Michael(Archer)	NJ58/56	HMON	A363	----
24 Sep 1790	Abigail Nutt	Aaron & Michael(Archer)	NJ58/56	HMON	A363	----
24 Oct 1792	Ann Nutt	Aaron & Michael(Archer)	NJ58/56	HMON	A363	----
02 Feb 1795	Bethesda Nutt	Aaron & Michael(Archer)	NJ58/56	HMON	A363	----
05 Feb 1780	Levi Nutt	Aaron & Michael(Archer)	NJ58/56	HMON	A363	----
28 Apr 1783	Mary Nutt	Aaron & Michael(Archer)	NJ58/56	HMON	A363	----
22 Aug 1797	Moriah Nutt	Aaron & Michael(Archer)	NJ58/56	HMON	A363	----
07 Jul 1781	Sarah Nutt	Aaron & Michael(Archer)	NJ58/56	HMON	A363	----
00 000 0000	Diana Oard[Teegardin]			HHAR	888	----
00 000 0000	Adam Orewiler			CBNW	460	1820
00 000 1787	David Osborn	David	Va/x	PFPM	564	----
00 000 1801	George Parks	Samuel & Charity		HPRE	163	1811
00 000 0000	Sarah Patton[Ferguson]			KHIG	301	----

Date	Name	Parents	Origin	Code	No.	Year
07 Aug 1793	Samuel Paxton	Thomas & Martha		HCLE	487	---
00 000 0000	Dennis Penny			HMIA	787	---
00 000 0000	Lewis Penny			HBRO	B189	---
00 000 0000	Peter Penny			HBRO	B188	---
00 000 0000	Middleton Perfect			MDUM	409	---
00 000 1797	William Perfect			HDEL	691	---
00 000 0000	Aaron Perkins			HBRO	B189	---
28 Mar 1844	Columbus Phillips	P.T. & Susan(Kendrick)	Va/Ky	HBRO	B36	1844
14 Mar 1799	Jesse C. Phillips	Elijah & Hanna(Corwin)	Pa/Pa	HCHA	910	1799
22 Jan 1831	Marion Phillips	John & Anna(Ross)		HBRO	B299	1844
18 Nov 1804	William F. Pickerill	Samuel & Mary		HBRO	B303	1810
00 000 1808	W.D. Piper	Alexander		HLOG	838	1818
00 000 0000	Jeremiah Plummer			HVWN	470	---
11 May 1800	Andrew Porter			HHAR	392	---
11 May 1800	Andrew Porter			HHAR	580	---
11 May 1800	Andrew Porter			PMHA	246	---
00 000 0000	Andrew Porter			PMHA	452	1833
00 000 1790	--- Pottenger			HPRE	165	---
02 Mar 1791	Abram Powell			MCHA	B336	---
00 000 0000	Roxoline Powell[Logan] Samuel			CCHA	420	1806
00 000 0000	Timothy Powell			MCHA	B584	---
25 Jan 1841	Thomas Preston	Thomas & Mary(Owens)	Ky/x	HMAD	924	1858
02 Mar 1844	William F. Price	William		KHIG	437	---
00 000 0000	Agnes Priest[Flinn]			HMIA	563	---
00 000 0000	William Prince			PGCL	396	---
00 000 1807	William Prince			HCHA	725	---
00 000 0000	Mary Prine[Rhoten]			KHIG	447	---
00 000 0000	John Prior			CSOT	245	1813
00 000 0000	Elizabeth Purdum[Rees]			HBRO	B37	---
00 000 0000	Martha Rafferty[Johnson]		Ky/x	CCHA	494	---
00 000 1806	Isaac C. Railsback	John & Hannah(Conger)		HPRE	178	1806
00 000 0000	James Rawlings			PGCL	573	1823
00 000 0000	Absalom Reed			BHCL	323	1810
00 000 0000	Cyrus Reed			BHCL	323	1810

BIRTHDATE	NAME OF BIOGRAPHEE	PARENTS/BIRTHPLACE/BIRTHDATE	SOURCE/PAGE	DATE
00 000 0000	Margaret Reed[Arthur]Isaac		HBRO B294	----
00 000 0000	Abel Rees		HBRO B37	----
00 000 1800	John Rhea		HPRE 165	----
00 000 0000	Henry Ritter		HCHA 459	----
00 000 0000	Jane Robb[Cook]	Robert & Susan(Gray) Pa/Pa	HLOG 744	----
00 Aug 1827	Miranda Roberts[Bloom]		BHCL 694	----
00 000 0000	Aaron Robuck		HCLI 1111	----
00 000 1806	Katherine Rogers[Brown]		WHAN 789	----
05 Aug 1879	Wilson H. Rucker		LGCI D481	----
00 000 1785	Robert Runyon		HPRE 178	1810
00 000 0000	Richard Sales		HHAR 1025	1804
22 Jul 1798	James Sallee	Abraham & Lucy(Nelson) Fr/Fr	HBRO B114	----
00 000 0000	Mary Sanders[Turner]		DHGR 813	----
00 000 0000	Edward Sapp		WCBR B39	----
00 000 0000	Elizabeth[Schnurrenberger]		BNEO 664	----
00 000 0000	Jane Scott		HMIA 327	----
00 000 1801	Robert Scott	John	HBRO B175	1816
00 000 0000	Henry Shafer		HLOG 811	----
00 000 0000	David Shaw		KHLO 420	----
00 000 1835	John T. Shaw		HPRE 320	1840
00 000 0000	Louisa Shawman[Clayton]		CHAN 393	----
00 000 0000	John Shepherd	Abraham & Mary	HCHA 896	----
00 000 0000	Joseph Shepherd		HBRO B38	----
00 000 0000	William Shields	William	HBRO B39	1815
00 000 1873	John Shipp		ARIC 14	----
00 000 0000	Mahala Shockey[Kiplinger]		HCLA 1003	----
00 000 0000	John Slade		HCLE 247	----
00 000 0000	Charles S. Smith		FHCI 503	----
10 May 1901	Forrest W. Smith	Samuel H. & Ina(Wardill) Ky/Ky	LGCI D483	----
00 000 1795	Isabelle Smith[Mounts]		HWAR 953	----

Date	Name	Father/Parents	Origin	Code	No.	Year
00 000 0000	Margaret Sparks[Perrill]			DHGR	843	
00 000 1784	Francis Spencer			HDAR	593	
00 00c 1768	Ezekiel Spurgeon			HCLI	1112	1808
00 00c 1777	Martha J[Spurgeon]			HCLI	1112	1808
00 000 0000	Sarah Starling[Sullivant]			HFPI	580	
20 Nov 1796	Charles W. Stevenson			HHAR	816	
00 000 0000	Rachel M. Stevenson[Dills]			HCHA	832	
00 000 0000	Lot Stratton			HBRO	B256	1810
00 000 1811	Louise Stipps[McKee]			HCIN	682	
00 000 1777	John Strom			HCOS	800	
00 000 1818	W.W. Sutton	Jonathan	Ky/x	PALS	210	
00 000 1859	William S. Swan			ALVW	31	
00 000 0000	Jacob Swank			HDAR	646	
00 000 0000	Josiah G. Talbott		Md/x	HCHA	826	
00 000 1798	James Tatman	Samuel & Mary	Md/Md	HBRO	B118	
00 000 1798	Sarah Taylor			HLIC	224	
00 000 1791	James Templin	John	Eng/x	PSCI	243	1801
00 000 0000	Susan B Thompson[Massie]	John B.		PSCI	107	
00 000 0000	Mary Thomson[Irwin]			HHAR	846	
00 000 0000	Barnett Thornhill			BHCL	469	
00 000 0000	Elizabeth Todd[Spyker]			HALL	820	
16 Jun 1818	Harrison Tolle	Joseph		KHIG	495	
00 000 0000	Elizabeth Turner[Jacobs]			HALL	820	
00 000 1794	Jacob Ulrey	Jacob & Hannah(West)	Md68/x	HCLE	382	
20 May 1788	Sarah Vance[Pringle]			HCLA	1073	
00 000 0000	Henry Vandament			HBRO	B257	
00 000 0000	Amelia Van Pelt[Brothers]	Cyrus N. & Mildred(Hope)	Oh/Ky	NCHA	257	
00 00c 1814	William Vaughn			KHLO	798	
00 000 1802	William Walker	Robert & Nancy	Pa/Va	HCLI	1023	
00 000 0000	Harry D. Wall			HMW	C406	
00 000 1814	William Wallace			HLOG	815	
00 000 0000	William Wallace	Isaac		PMHA	234	
00 000 0000	James Waters			HBRO	B211	
18 Jun 1810	Cooper K. Watson			HSEN	302	c1812

BIRTHDATE	NAME OF BIOGRAPHEE	PARENTS/BIRTHPLACE/BIRTHDATE	SOURCE/PAGE	DATE
00 000 0000	Samuel Watt		HALL 616	1812
07 Nov 1835	Dr.Benjamin F. Welch	Thomas B. & Druzilla(Drummond) Va/Ky	----	---
11 Jun 1803	Thomas White	Stephen & Mary(Bigger) Ire68/Ire60	DHGR 660	1806
17 Oct 1790	Margaret Wiley		HMIA 524	---
00 000 0000	Dr. Benjamin C.Willes	Samuel W. & Anna(Coleman) Ky/x	GCIN 0456	---
00 000 0000	Elizabeth[Wilkerson]		BHCL 199	1805
00 000 0000	Elizabeth Wilkerson[Vandervoort]	James & Sarah(Moore) Va58/Va	BHCL 1018	---
00 000 1787	James Wilkerson		HCLI 1175	---
00 000 0000	John Wilkerson		BHCL 199	---
00 000 0000	Charles Wilkinson		HPRE 190	1810
00 000 0000	Joseph Williams		HHAR 987	---
00 000 0000	Melatiah [Williams]		HHAR 946	---
00 000 0000	Micaiah Williams		HHAR 946	---
02 Jul 1801	Andrew P. Wilson		HDAR 716	1805
05 Jun 1801	Dr. Daniel Wilson		HMAD 450	---
00 000 0000	Isaac Wilson		BHCL 308	1802
00 000 0000	Isaac Wilson	Jacob Ire/Ger	HMAD 1119	---
00 000 1812	Robert M. Wilson		HPRE 228	1831
23 May 1803	William B. Winters		HVWM 457	1812
00 000 0000	Nicholas Wood		HBRO B196	---
00 000 0000	Phebe [Wood]		HBRO B196	---
00 000 0000	Sarah Wood[Meharry]	Nicholas		---
00 000 0000	George Woodward			---
00 000 1805	John W. Yocom	Solomon	MCHA B891	1820
00 000 0000	Alexander Young		HUNI E261	---
28 Dec 1796	John Young	Thomas	HWOA 789	1819
00 000 1832	Robert L. Young		HBRO B92	1832

E N D   O F   O H I O

ADEA   Atlas of Dearborn County, Indiana, From Actual Sur-
              veys by D.J. Lake and B.N. Griffing.
              Philadelphia: Lake, Griffing & Stevenson, 1875.

AGIP   An Atlas of Gibson and Pike Counties, Indiana, From
              Actual Surveys Under the Direction of B.N. Grif-
              fing.
              Philadelphia: D.J. Lake & Company, 1881.

AGRE   An Atlas of Greene County, Indiana, From Actual Sur-
              veys Under the Direction of B.N. Griffing.
              Philadelphia: D.J. Lake & Company, 1879.

AHAR   An Atlas of Harrison County, Indiana, From Actual
              Surveys Under the Direction of B.N. Griffing.
              Philadelphia: D.J. Lake & Company, 1882.

AJEN   An Atlas of Jennings County, Indiana, From Actual
              Surveys by J.M. Lathrop and J.H. Summers.
              Chicago: D.J. Lake & Company, 1884.

AKNO   An Historical Atlas of Knox County, Indiana, From
              Actual Surveys Under the Direction of B.N.
              Griffing.
              Philadelphia: D.J. Lake & Company, 1888.

ALAG   An Illustrated Atlas of LaGrange County, Indiana.
              Map Work of Townships and Plats Made by S.W.
              and P.A. Durant, R.P. Hinkley, D.A. Kayner,
              Civil Engineers.
              Chicago: Andreas & Baskin, 1874.

ARIP   An Atlas of Ripley County, Indiana, From Actual
              Surveys Under the Direction of B.N. Griffing.
              Philadelphia: D.J. Lake & Company, 1883.

ASPE   An Illustrated Historical Atlas of Spencer County,
              Indiana, From Actual Surveys Under the Direct-
              ion of B.N. Griffing.
              Philadelphia: D.J. Lake & Company, 1879.

ASOH   An Atlas of Switzerland and Ohio Counties, Indiana,
              From Actual Surveys Under the Direction of
              B.N. Griffing.
              Philadelphia: D.J. Lake & Company, 1888.

AVAN   Griffing's Atlas of Vanderburgh County, Indiana,
From Actual Surveys Under the Direction of
B.N. Griffing.
Philadelphia: D.J. Láke & Company, 1880.

AWAR   An Illustrated Historical Atlas of Warrick Coun-
ty, Indiana, From Actual Surveys Under the
Direction of B.N. Griffing.
Philadelphia: D.J. Lake & Company, 1880.

AWAS   An Atlas of Washington County, Indiana, From Act-
ual Surveys Under the Direction of B.N.
Griffing.
Philadelphia: D.J. Lake & Company, 1878.

BART   History of Bartholomew County, Indiana.
Chicago: Brant and Fuller, 1888.

BAWE   Biographical and Historical Record of Adams and
Wells Counties, Indiana. Containing Por-
traits of All the Presidents of the United
States from Washington to Cleveland, With
Accompanying Biographies of Each; A Condensed
History of the State of Indiana; Portraits
and Biographies of Some of the Prominent
Men in the State; Engravings of Prominent
Citizens in Adams and Wells Counties, With
Personal Histories of Many of the Leading
Families, and a Concise History of the
Counties; Their Cities and Villages.
Chicago: The Lewis Publishing Company, 1887.

BGAS   Rebecca A. Shepherd, etals. (eds)
A Biographical Directory of the Indiana
General Assembly, 1816-1899.
Indianapolis: Indiana Historical Bureau,
1980.

BELA   Rev. Timothy Horton Ball
Encyclopedia of Genealogy and Biography of
Lake County, Indiana, With a Compendium of
Its History 1834-1904, A Record of Achieve-
ment of Its People in the Making of a Com-
monwealth and the Founding of a Nation.
Chicago: The Lewis Publishing Company, 1904.

BEGR   Jack Baber
The Early History of Greene County, Indiana,
as Taken from the Official Records and Compiled from Authentic Recollections; by Pioneer Settlers ... from 1813 to 1875 ...
Worthington: N.B. Milleson, 1875.

BHCL   Lewis C. Baird
Baird's History of Clark County, Indiana,
Illustrated.
Indianapolis: B.F. Bowen & Company, 1909.

BHOT   Charles Blanchard (ed.)
             Counties of Howard and Tipton, Indiana. His-
             torical and Biographical. Illustrated.
             Chicago: F.A. Battey & Company, 1883.

BHV I   Henry C. Bradsby
             History of Vigo County, Indiana with Biographi-
             cal Selections. Illustrated.
             Chicago: S.B. Nelson & Co., Publishers, 1891.

BJAB   Biographical and Historical Record of Jay and Black-
             ford Counties, Indiana, Containing Portraits
             of All the Presidents of the United States from
             Washington to Cleveland, with Accompanying Bio-
             graphy of Each; a Condensed History of the
             State of Indiana; Portraits and Biographies of
             Some of the Prominent Men.
             Chicago: The Lewis Publishing Company, 1887.

BJAY   Biographical Memoirs of Jay County, Indiana, To
             Which is Appended a Comprehensive Compend-
             ium of National Biography--Memoirs of Eminent
             Men and Women in the United States.
             Chicago: B.F. Bowen & Company, 1901.

BJOH   David Demaree Banta
             A Historical Sketch of Johnson County, Indiana.
             Chicago: J.H. Beers, 1881.

BKOS   Biographical and Historical Record of Kosciusko
             County, Indiana, Containing Portraits of All
             the Presidents from Washington to Cleveland,
             with a Biography of Each, a Condensed History
             of the State of Indiana; Portraits and Biog-
             raphies of Some of the Prominent Men of the
             State, Engravings of Pioneer Citizens ...
             Chicago: The Lewis Publishing Company, 1887.

BMMB   Charles Blanchard (ed.)
             Counties of Morgan, Monroe and Brown, Indiana,
             Historical and Biographical.
             Chicago: F.A. Battey & Company, 1884.

BMON   Hiram Williams Beckwith
             History of Montgomery County, Together with
             with Historic Notes on the Wabash Valley Glean-
             ed from Early Authors, Old Maps and Manuscripts,
             Private and Official Correspondence and Other
             Authentic, Though for the Most Part, Out-of-the-
             Way Sources with Map and Illustrations.
             Chicago: H.H. Hill & N. Iddings, Pubs., 1881.

BPUT   Biographical and Historical Record of Putnam County,
             Indiana, Containing Portraits of All the Presi-
             dents of the United States from Washington to
             Cleveland, With Accompanying Biographies of Each;

a Condensed History of the State of Indiana;
Portraits and Biographies of Some of the Prominent Men of the State; Engravings of Prominent
Citizens, With Personal Histories of Many of
the Leading Families, and a Concise History of
the County and Its Cities and Villages.
Chicago: The Lewis Publishing Company, 1887.

BSCC Biographical and Historical Souvenir for the Counties
of Clark, Crawford, Harrison, Floyd, Jefferson,
Jennings, Scott, and Washington, Indiana, Illustrated. Compiled and Published by John M. Gresham & Company.
Chicago: Chicago Printing Company, 1889.

BTWJ Biographical History of Tippecanoe, White, Jasper,
Newton, Benton, and Pulaski Counties, Indiana,
Illustrated.
Chicago: The Lewis Publishing Company, 1899.

BVAN Biographical Cyclopedia of Vanderburgh County, In-
diana, Embracing Biographies of Many of the
Prominent Men and Families of the County.
Evansville: Keller Printing and Publishing
Company, 1897.

BVER Biographical and Historical Record of Vermillion
County, Indiana, Containing Portraits of All
the Presidents of the United States from
Washington to Cleveland ... Histories of
Many of the Leading Families and a Concise
History of the County and Its Cities and
Villages.
Chicago: The Lewis Publishing Company, 1888.

BVPA Hiram Williams Beckwith
History of Vigo and Parke Counties, Together
With Historic Notes on the Wabash Valley,
Gleaned from Early Authors, Old Maps and
Manuscripts, Private and Official Corres-
pondence and Other Authentic, Though for the
Most Part, Out-of-the-way Sources with Map
and Illustrations.
Chicago: H.H. Hill and N. Iddings, 1880.

BWAB Biographical Memoirs of Wabash County, Indiana,
Together with ... a Comprehensive Compendium
of National Biography--Memoirs of Eminent
Men and Women in the United States Whose
Deeds of Valor or Works of Merit Have Made
Their Names Imperishable ...
Chicago: B.F. Bowen & Company, 1901.

BWEL   Biographical Memoirs of Wells County, Indiana, Embracing a Comprehensive Compendium of Local Biographies--Memoirs of Representative Men and Women of the County Whose Works of Merit Have Made Their Names Imperishable and Special Articles Prepared by Hon. Hugh Smith, Hon. Joseph Dailey, George E. Fulton M.D. and Thomas Stugils D.D.S. Illustrated. Logansport: B.F. Bowan, 1903.

CLOW   Charles Blanchard (ed.) Counties of Clay and Owen, Indiana. Historical and Biographical. Illustrated. Chicago: F.A. Battey & Company, 1884.

CSHE   Edward H. Chadwick Chadwick's History of Shelby County, Indiana. Indianapolis: B.F. Bowen, 1909.

DGIN   Jacob Piatt Dunn Greater Indianapolis: The History, The Industries, The Institutions, and the People of a City of Homes. Chicago: The Lewis Publishing Company, 1910.

DIND   Jacob Piatt Dunn Indiana and Indianans. A History of Aboriginal and Territorial Indiana and the Century of Statehood. Chicago and New York: American Historical Society, 1919.

DTCE   Anthony Deahl A Twentieth Century History and Biographical Record of Elkhart County, Indiana. Illustrated. Chicago and New York: The Lewis Publishing Company, 1905.

EBOO   Early Life and Times in Boone County, Indiana, Giving an Account of the Early Settlement of Each Locality, Church Histories, County and Township Officers ... Down to 1886. Histories of Some of the Pioneer Families of the County, Biographical Sketches of Some of the Prominent Men and Women. Lebanon: Harden & Spahr, 1887.

EIND   A Biographical History of Eminent and Self-made Men of the State of Indiana with Many Portraits--Illustrations on Steel Engravings Expressly Made for This Work. Cincinnati: Western Biographical Publishing Company, 1880.

FDAV   A.O. Fulkerson (ed.)
        History of Daviess County, Indiana; Its
        People, Industries and Institutions with
        Biographical Sketches of Representative
        Citizens and Genealogical Records of Many
        of the Old Families ... Illustrated.
        Indianapolis: B.F. Bowen, 1915.

FHSM   J.L. Forkner
        Historical Sketches and Reminiscences of
        Madison County, Indiana. A Detailed His-
        tory of the Early Events of the Pioneer
        Settlement of the County, and Many Hap-
        penings of Recent Years, as Well as a
        Complete History of Each Township, to
        Which Is Added Numerous Incidents of a
        Pleasant Nature ...
        Anderson: Press of Wilson, Humphreys, 1897.

FMAD   Same as FHSM.

FMWA   Henry Clay Fox
        Memoirs of Wayne County and the City of
        Richmond, Indiana. From the Earliest
        Historical Times Down to the Present In-
        cluding a Genealogical and Biographical
        Record of Representative Families in
        Wayne County.
        Madison, WI: Western Historical Associ-
        ation, 1912.

FWAR   Will Fortune
        Warrick and Its Prominent People. A His-
        tory of Warrick, County, Indiana, From the
        Time of Its Organization and Settlement,
        with Biographical Sketches of Some of Its
        Prominent People of the Past and Present.
        Evansville: The Courier Company, 1881.

GBRD   A Genealogical and Biographical Record of De-
        catur County, Indiana; Compendium of Na-
        tional Biography.
        Chicago: The Lewis Publishing Co., 1900.

GCEV   Frank M. Gilbert
        History of the City of Evansville and Van-
        derburgh County, Indiana.
        Chicago: The Pioneer Publishing Co., 1910.

GIBS   History of Gibson County, Indiana with Illustra-
        tions Descriptive of Its Scenery and Biog-
        graphical Sketches of Some of Its Prominent
        Men and Pioneers.
        Edwardsville: James T. Tartt & Co., 1884.

GIND   Dewitt C. Goodrich
            An Illustrated History of the State of In-
            diana; Being a Full and Authentic Civil
            and Political History of the State From
            Its First Exploration Down to 1875 Includ-
            ing an Account of the Commercial, Agri-
            cultural and Educational Growth of Indi-
            ana with Historical and Descriptive Sketches
            of the Cities, Towns and Villages Embracing
            Interesting Narratives of Pioneer Life, To-
            gether with Biographical Sketches and Por-
            traits of the Prominent Men of the Past and
            Present ... History of Each County Separate-
            ly.
            Indianapolis: Richard S. Peale & Company,
            Publishers, 1875.

GPLA   Weston A. Goodspeed and Charles Blanchard
            Counties of Porter and Lake, Indiana. His-
            torical and Biographical. Illustrated.
            Chicago: F.A. Battey & Company, 1882.

HALL   History of Allen County, Indiana, with Illustra-
            tions and Biographical Sketches of Some of
            Its Prominent Men and Pioneers to Which is
            Appended Maps of Its Several Townships and
            Villages.
            Chicago: Kingman Brothers, 1880.

HCAR   History of Carroll County, Indiana, with Illus-
            strations and Biographical Sketches of Some
            of Its Prominent Men and Pioneers to Which
            Is Appended Maps of Its Several Townships.
            Chicago: Kingman Brothers, 1882.

HCLI   History of Clinton County, Indiana, Together
            with Sketches of Its Cities, Villages and
            Towns, Educational, Religious, Civil, Mil-
            itary and Political History; Portraits of
            Prominent Persons and Biographies of Repre-
            sentative Citizens. Also a Condensed His-
            tory of Indiana Embodying Accounts of Pre-
            historic Races, Indian Wars, a Brief Review
            of Its Civil and Political History. Illus-
            trated.
            Chicago: Inter-state Publishing Co., 1886.

HDEK   History of DeKalb County, Indiana, Together with
            Sketches of Its Cities, Villages and Towns,
            Educational, Religious, Civil, Military and
            Political History, Portraits of Prominent
            Persons, and Biographies of Representative
            Citizens. Also a Condensed History of In-
            diana Embodying Accounts of Prehistoric
            Races, Aborigines, Winnebago and Black Hawk
            Wars, and a Brief Review of Its Civil and
            Political History. Illustrated.
            Chicago: Inter-state Publishing Co., 1885.

HDOH   History of Dearborn and Ohio Counties, Indiana
        From Their Earliest Settlement Containing
        a History of the Counties, Townships,
        Towns, Villages, Schools and Churches;
        Reminiscences, Extracts, Etc.; Local Sta-
        tistics; Portraits of Early Settlers and
        Prominent Men Containing Biographies;
        Preliminary Chapter on the History of the
        North West Territory, the State of Indi-
        ana and the Indians.
        Chicago: F.E. Weakley & Company, 1885.

HELK   History of Elkhart County, Indiana; Together
        with Sketches of Its Cities, Villages,
        and Townships, Educational, Religious,
        Civil, Military and Political History;
        Portraits of Prominent Persons and Biog-
        raphies of Representative Citizens. His-
        tory of Indiana Embracing Accounts of
        Pre-Historic Races, Aborigines, French
        and English Conquests, and a General Re-
        view of Its Civil, Political and Military
        History. Illustrated.
        Chicago: Charles C. Chapman & Co., 1881.

HENR   George Hazzard
        Hazzard's History of Henry County, Indi-
        ana 1822-1906. Military Edition.
        New Castle: George Hazzard, 1906.

HGSU   History of Greene and Sullivan Counties, Indi-
        ana.
        Chicago: Goodspeed Publishing Co., 1884.

HHAN   John H. Binford
        History of Hancock County, Indiana, From
        Its Earliest Settlement by the "Pale Face"
        in 1818, Down to 1882 ...
        Greenfield: King & Binford, 1882.

HHEN   History of Henry County, Indiana; Together with
        Sketches of Its Cities, Villages and Towns,
        Educational, Religious, Civil, Military and
        Political History; Portraits of Prominent
        Persons and Biographies of Representative
        Citizens. Also a Condensed History of In-
        diana Embodying Accounts of Pre-Historic
        Races, Aborigines, Winnebago and Black Hawk
        Wars, and a Brief Review of Its Civil and
        Political History.
        Chicago: Inter-state Publishing Co., 1884.

HHHE   John V. Hadley
        History of Hendricks County, Indiana. Her
        People, Industries, and Institutions with
        Biographical Sketches of Representative
        Citizens and Genealogical Records of Many
        of the Old Families. Illustrated.
        Indianapolis: B.F. Bowen & Company, 1914.

HJOH   History of Johnson County, Indiana. From the Earli-
est Time to the Present, with Biographical
Sketches, Notes, etc., Together with a Short
History of the Northwest, the Indiana Terri-
tory, and the State of Indiana ...
Chicago: Brant & Fuller, 1888.

HKDA   History of Knox and Daviess Counties, Indiana, From
the Earliest Times to the Present; with Biog-
graphical Statistics, Reminiscences, Notes,
etc., Together with an Extended History of
the Colonial Days of Vincennes and Its Progress Down to the Present Time ...
Chicago: Goodspeed Publication Co., 1886.

HLOW   History of Lawrence, Orange and Washington Counties, Indiana [reprinted from 1884 edition].
Paoli: Stout's Print Shop, 1965.

HMIA   History of Miami County, Indiana. From the Earliest
Time to the Present, With Biographical Sketches,
Notes, etc., Together with an Extended History
of the Northwest, the Indiana Territory, and
the State of Indiana.
Chicago: Brant & Fuller, 1887.

HPDB   History of Pike and Dubois Counties, Indiana. From
the Earliest Time to the Present, with Biographical Sketches, Reminiscences, Notes, etc., Together with an Extended History of the Northwest,
the Indiana Territory and the State of Indiana.
Illustrated.
Chicago: Goodspeed Brothers, 1885.

HPOS   History of Posey County, Indiana. From the Earliest
Time to the Present, With Biographical Sketches,
Notes, etc., Together with an Extended History
of the Northwest, the Indiana Territory, and
the State of Indiana. Illustrated.
Chicago: Goodspeed Publishing Company, 1886.

HSHE   History of Shelby County, Indiana, From the Earliest
Time to the Present, With Biographical Sketches,
Notes, etc., Together with an Extended History
of the Northwest, the Indiana Territory, and
the State of Indiana. Illustrated.
Chicago: Brant & Fuller, 1887.

HSTJ   History of St. Joseph County, Indiana; Together
with Sketches of Its Cities, Villages and
Townships; Educational, Religious, Civil,
Military and Political History; Portraits of
Prominent Persons and Biographies of Represent-
ative Citizens. History of Indiana Embracing
Accounts of the Prehistoric Races, Aborigines,
French, English and American Conquests ...
Chicago: Charles C. Chapman Co., 1880.

HSTU   History of Steuben County, Indiana, Together with
           Sketches of its Cities, Villages and Townships,
           Educational, Religious, Civil, Military and
           Political History; Portraits of Prominent Peo-
           ple and Biographies of Representative Citizens;
           Also a Condensed History of Indiana Embracing
           Accounts of Pre-historic Races, also Winnebago
           and Black Hawk Wars, and a Brief Review of Its
           Civil and Political History.
           Chicago: Inter-state Publishing Co., 1885.

HVAN   History of Vandenburgh County, Indiana, From the
           Earliest Times to the Present, With Biographi-
           cal Sketches, Reminiscences, etc. Illustrated.
           Madison, WI: Brant & Fuller, 1889.

HWAY   History of Wayne County, Indiana; Together with
           Sketches of Its Cities, Villages and Townships,
           Educational, Religious, Civil, Military and Po-
           litical History; Portraits of Prominent Persons
           and Biographies of Representative Citizens Il-
           lustrated.
           Chicago: Inter-state Publishing Co., 1884.

HWBJ   Counties of Warren, Benton, Jasper and Newton, Indi-
           ana. Historical and Biographical. Illustrated.
           Chicago: F.A. Battey & Company, 1883.

HWSP   History of Warrick, Spencer and Perry Counties, Indi-
           ana. From the Earliest Times to the Present,
           Together with Interesting Biographical Sketches,
           Reminiscences, Notes, Etc. Illustrated.
           Chicago: Goodspeed Brothers & Co. Pubs., 1885.

JACK   History of Jackson County, Indiana. 1886.

KTCD   G.W.H. Kemper
           A Twentieth Century History of Delaware County,
           Indiana. Illustrated.
           Chicago: The Lewis Publishing Company, 1908.

LHDP   William P. Leonard
           History and Directory of Posey County. Also
           Biographical Sketches of Prominent Citizens of
           the County ...
           Evansville: A.C. Isaacs, 1882.

LLDM   Living Leaders; an Encyclopedia of Biography. Spec-
           ial Edition for Daviess and Martin Counties,
           Indiana.
           n.pl.: American Publishing Company, 1897.

MHMA   Daniel McDonald
           History of Marshall County, Indiana, 1836-1880.
           Carefully Written and Compiled From Official
           and Other Reliable Sources ... To Which Is Added

Maps of Its Several Townships.
Chicago: Kingman Brothers, 1881.

MONT History of Montgomery County, Indiana, With Personal Sketches of Representative Citizens.
Indianapolis: A.W. Bowen & Company, 19--.

MPRO Men of Progress. Indiana. A Select List of Biographical Sketches and Portraits of Leaders in Business, Professional and Official Life, Together with Brief Notes ... Will Cumback and J.B. Maynard, editors.
Indianapolis: The Indiana Sentinel Co., 1899.

MSTE Harvey W. Morley
The 1955 History of Steuben County, Indiana; An Historical, Pictorial, Complete County Atlas and Biographical County Album.
Angola: 1956.

NSPC John H.B. Nowland
Sketches of Prominent Citizens of 1876, with a Few of Its Pioneers of the City and County Who Have Passed Away: A Sequel to Early Reminiscences of Indianapolis 1820-1876.
Indianapolis: Tilford and Carlon, Printers, 1877.

OPMM Thomas Gains Onstot
Pioneers of Menard and Mason Counties; Made Up of Personal Reminiscences of Early Life in Menard County, Which We Gathered in a Salem Life from 1830 to 1840, and Petersburg Life From 1840 to 1850; Including Personal Reminiscences of Abraham Lincoln and Peter Cartright.
Peoria: J.W. Franks & Sons, Printers, 1902.

PBES Pictorial and Biographical Memoirs of Elkhart and St. Joseph Counties, Indiana; Together With Biographies of Many Prominent Men of Northern Indiana and of the Whole State, Both Living and Dead.
Chicago: Goodspeed Brothers, Pubs., 1893.

RAJR Martha C. Lynch
Reminiscences of Adams, Jay, and Randolph Counties.
Fort Wayne: Lipes, Nelson & Singmaster, 1897?

RCAR James Hervey Stewart
Recollections of the Early Settlement of Carroll County, Indiana.
Cincinnati: Hitchcock and Walden, 1872.

RUSH   History of Rush County, Indiana. From the Earliest
            Time to the Present, with Biographical Sketches,
            Notes, Etc., with a Short History of the North-
            west, the Indiana Territory, and the State of
            Indiana.
            Chicago: Brant & Fuller, 1888.

SGIB   Gilbert R. Stormont
            History of Gibson County, Indiana, Her People,
            Industries and Institutions.
            Indianapolis: B.F. Bowen & Company, 1914.

SHMI   John H. Stephens
            History of Miami County, Indiana.
            Peru: John H. Stephens, 1896.

SIND   B.R. Sulgrove
            History of Indianapolis and Marion County,
            Indiana. Illustrated.
            Philadelphia: L.H. Everts, 1884.

SCWA   Warder W. Stevens
            Centennial History of Washington County, Indi-
            ana. Its People, Citizens and Genealogical
            Records of Many of the Old Families.
            Indianapolis: B.F. Bowen, 1916.

TCMA   Daniel McDonald
            A Twentieth Century History of Marshall County,
            Indiana.
            Chicago: The Lewis Publishing Company, 1908.

TRAN   E. Tucker
            History of Randolph County, Indiana, with Ill-
            ustrations and Biographical Sketches of Some
            of the Prominent Men and Pioneers to Which Are
            Appended Maps of Its Several Townships.
            Chicago: A.L. Kingman, 1882.

VUMR   Valley of the Upper Maumee River with Historical Ac-
            count of Allen County and the City of Fort
            Wayne, Indiana. The Story of Its Progress from
            Savagery to Civilization. Illustrated.
            Madison, WI: Brant & Fuller, 1889.

WFUF   Biographical and Genealogical History of Fayette,
            Union and Franklin Counties, Indiana. Illustrated.
            Chicago: Lewis Publishing Company, 1899.

WHSU   Thomas J. Wolfe (ed.)
            A History of Sullivan County, Indiana. Closing
            of the First Century's History of the County ...
            N.Y./Chicago: The Lewis Publishing Co., 1909.

A D A I R   C O U N T Y

BIRTHDATE	NAME OF BIOGRAPHEE	PARENTS/BIRTHPLACE/BIRTHDATE		SOURCE/PAGE		DATE
09 Apr 1823	Alexander Breeding	David & Mary(Hendrickson)		HJOH	401	1828
11 Feb 1821	Elza Breeding	David & Mary M(Hendrickson)	Ky/Ky	BART	793	1828
00 000 1830	Henry C. Daugherty	Stephen & Jane(Smith)	Va/Ky	HPOS	621	1834
00 000 0000	J.M. Daugherty			AGIP	12	---
00 000 0000	Mary A. Daugherty[Montgomery]			GIBS	242	1834
02 Mar 1843	Simon Grider	William & Mary(Bailey)	Ky/x	SCWA	1091	---
27 Nov 1837	J.W. Hood	Bonaparte		HJOH	422	1852
00 000 0000	F.M. Judd			AWAR	58	1851
21 May 1863	Dr.LafayetteF.Page	Robert & Mary(Irving)	Va/Va	DGIN	1034	---
00 000 0000	E.F. Roe			AGIP	17	1871
00 000 0000	Martha Shaw[Vermillion]			BPUT	386	---
00 000 0000	John M. Smith			GIBS	240	1823
00 000 0000	John M. Smith			GIBS	240	1836
11 Nov 1827	James H. Tilman	Morris A. & Mary(Brown)	Va/NC	HWSP	229	1828
00 000 1816	Juda Wheeler[Williams]			HJOH	501	---

A L L E N   C O U N T Y

BIRTHDATE	NAME OF BIOGRAPHEE	PARENTS/BIRTHPLACE/BIRTHDATE	SOURCE/PAGE		DATE
27 Sep 1815	Thomas V. Mitchell	Richard	RUSH	440	1836
10 Dec 1806	William Pruitt	Moses & Phoebe(Williams)	HVAN	674	---

A N D E R S O N   C O U N T Y

BIRTHDATE	NAME OF BIOGRAPHEE	PARENTS/BIRTHPLACE/BIRTHDATE	SOURCE/PAGE		DATE
00 000 1834	George Corbin		ASUL	49	1852

BIRTHDATE	NAME OF BIOGRAPHEE	PARENTS/BIRTHPLACE/BIRTHDATE	SOURCE/PAGE	DATE
00 000 1839	J.T. Corbin		ASUL 49	1852
00 000 1841	Sarah F[Corbin]		ASUL 39	1852
02 May 1822	Calvin A. Elliott		NSPC 336	---
22 May 1825	Lewis T. Hancock	Stephen F. & Martha(Lacey)	BMMB 329	1826
25 Jun 1833	Pleasant Huffman	Henry & Barsheba(Craig) Ky/Ky	HJOH 617	---
00 000 1810	Isham Kelley		FWAR 148	1820
00 000 0000	Parady Payne	Thomas B. & Mary(Coffman)	BHCL 916	---
00 000 1834	J.R. Robertson		ASUL 132	1864
31 Jan 1828	Gabriel Robinson	Gabriel & Mary(Rice)	BMMB 290	---
00 000 0000	Rev. John Stott		AJEN 47	1816
31 Dec 1842	Minerva Walts	Woodford & Lacy(Steele)	WHSU B272	c1855
30 Dec 1835	Margaret Wheat[Tilson]	Richard A. & Lucy(Jordan) Va/Ky	HJOH 836	---
30 Dec 1835	Margaret Wheat[Vorles]	Richard A. & Lucy(Jordan) Va/Ky	HJOH 836	---
26 Dec 1813	John Woods	Joseph & Keziah(Bell) Ire/Pa	CLOW 415	---

B A L L A R D   C O U N T Y

BIRTHDATE	NAME OF BIOGRAPHEE	PARENTS/BIRTHPLACE/BIRTHDATE	SOURCE/PAGE	DATE
27 Sep 1872	John W. Bowen	James A. & Charity(Davidson) Oh/Tn	WHSU B336	1878

B A R R E N   C O U N T Y

BIRTHDATE	NAME OF BIOGRAPHEE	PARENTS/BIRTHPLACE/BIRTHDATE	SOURCE/PAGE	DATE
25 Sep 1809	Pleasant Allee	William & Susan	BPUT 779	1830
01 Jun 1817	William M.Allee	William & Susan Va/Va	BPUT 447	---
09 Apr 1842	Charles A. Allen	William & Elizabeth	BPUT 445	---
17 Nov 1839	John Branstetter	John & Catherine(Amyx) Va/Va	BJAB 389	---
17 Nov 1839	John Branstetter		BGAS 36	---
00 000 0000	Fannie Carlton		ASPE 66	1863
00 000 0000	J.A. Coleman		AGIP 17	1838

BIRTHDATE	NAME OF BIOGRAPHEE	PARENTS/BIRTHPLACE/BIRTHDATE		SOURCE/PAGE		DATE
18 Nov 1815	Thomas Drake	Greenberry & Nancy(Lane)	Va/Va	CLOW	399	---
00 000 0000	Dr. B.F. Forbis			AHAR	45	1877
05 Jun 1807	Benjamin T. Goodman			BGAS	146	---
00 000 0000	J.J. Hardy			AGRE	53	1868
06 Jul 1791	Joshua Harlan			HWAY	B408	---
24 Sep 1825	William Hert			HGSU	372	1829
25 Aug 1812	James B. Hicks	John & Eleanor		HLOW	862	---
00 000 0000	L.F. Hoffman			AGIP	9	1861
22 Feb 1825	Livingston Isbell			BVPA	469	---
00 000 0000	Susan Johnson[White]			SHGI	654	---
24 Apr 1830	William H. Jones	Thompson & Margaret(Gilliland)	**/**	HSWP	817	---
27 Sep 1840	Edward A. Junken	Harvey & Betsey(McHatteon)	In/In	RUSH	508	1845
04 Feb 1823	Joseph Lee			BPUT	346	1816
00 000 0000	George McKay	Alexander	Scot/x	BSCC	B247	---
00 000 0000	Mary McManus[Glover]			HLOW	253	---
01 Jun 1838	Joseph A. McMurtry	Samuel B & Louisa(Perkins)	**/**	BPUT	340	1859
11 Dec 1806	Simon S. Monk			BGAS	277	---
00 000 0000	O.D. Oldham			AGIP	9	1851
25 Jun 1845	Beverly T. Pace	Joseph W. & Harriet L(Whitlow)	Ky/Ky	HLOW	871	---
11 Feb 1804	Curtis Parks	Samuel & Charity(Runyan)	NJ/NJ	HWAY	B296	---
06 May 1831	John T. Scott			EIND	H44	1846
00 000 0000	Clement N. Shields	Patrick	Va/x	BSCC	B112	---
00 000 0000	Mary Stewart[Shields]			BSCC	B112	---
08 Mar 1842	George P. Stone	Stanford & Margaret(Smith)	Me/Me	HGSU	355	1867

B A T H   C O U N T Y

BIRTHDATE	NAME OF BIOGRAPHEE	PARENTS/BIRTHPLACE/BIRTHDATE		SOURCES/PAGE		DATE
18 Nov 1818	Samuel W. Austin	John B. & Nancy(Vanhook)	Va96/x	MONT	890	--
27 Jul 1817	John R. Baird	Archibald & Elizabeth	Va/Va	BPUT	516	--
14 Nov 1823	Capt.William Bough	Frederick & Rebecca(Sexson)		HGSU	382	1827
00 000 0000	Van S. Brandon			ASOH	46	1854
29 May 1831	Francis M. Busby			EBOO	243	--
00 000 0000	Harriet Campbell	Williamson & Nancy(Choshow)		HCLI	677	--
20 Feb 1824	Scythia Carpenter[Goodpaster]	Michael & Sallie(Jones)		BMMB	353	1844
00 000 0000	William Clow	John		DIND	2103	--
10 Aug 1819	Arthur D.Doggett	Henry & Nancy(Smith)	Va/Va	BHOT	T304	--
00 000 0000	James J. Duckworth			MONT	1079	--
24 Feb 1823	John A. English	John & Joenna(Kincaid)		RUSH	840	1832
03 Jun 1821	Samuel P. Evins	Thomas & Anna(Martin)	Ky/Ky	CLOW	945	c1824
00 000 1829	J.I. Farley			BVPA	259	1831
00 000 0000	Solomon P. Garner			HHHE	638	--
30 May 1810	Jonathan Gill			BMON	467	1837
24 Nov 1822	Anthony J. Goodpaster	Michael & Margaret(Carpenter)		BMMB	353	1844
00 000 1811	Nancy Griffith			HHHE	344	--
10 Jan 1828	B.F. Hart	John & Hester(Adams)		CLOW	892	1841
13 Sep 1807	Harvey G. Hazelrigg			BGAS	174	--
13 Sep 1807	Harvey G. Hazelrigg	Joshua & Frances(Wright)		EIND	116	--
01 Apr 1839	James T.J.Hazelrigg			HHEN	489	1859
02 Sep 1852	Frederick Heiner	Samuel & Rossalinda		EIND	G88	--
04 Feb 1806	John H. Hendrix	Moses M. & Frances(Honey)	74/82	BPUT	495	--
08 Sep 1806	Eldridge Hopkins	William & Sarah(Smathers)	**/**	BART	830	1826
16 Dec 1817	Seyth Ingraham[Gill]			BMON	467	1837
15 Oct 1835	William W. Leach	Meredith & Eliza(Allison)	Ky/Ky	HHHE	629	1836
24 Jun 1829	Catherine Lowe[Shanklin]			BMON	189	--
00 000 0000	Deborah Lyons[Garner]			HHHE	638	--
15 Dec 1829	David F. McClure			BMON	256	--
15 Dec 1829	David F. McClure			MONT	1275	--
14 Dec 1845	Gov.Claude Matthews	Thomas A. & Eliza(Fletcher)		PBES	17	--
14 Dec 1845	Claude Matthews	Thomas A.		MPRO	470	--
14 Dec 1845	Claude Matthews			BGAS	265	--
14 Dec 1845	Claude Matthews	Thomas A. & Eliza A(Fletcher)	Ky/Ky	BVER	489	--

BATH COUNTY (CONT.)

BIRTHDATE	NAME OF BIOGRAPHEE	PARENTS/BIRTHPLACE/BIRTHDATE		SOURCE/PAGE	DATE
08 Oct 1828	John T. Morgan	William C. & Lorilda(Turman)		CLOW 495	1834
10 Mar 1834	Thomas M. Powell	John & Elizabeth L(Patrick)	Ky/Ky	BMON 551	1840
22 Mar 1809	Sarah Richart[Jackson]			HSHE 593	1825
19 Feb 1813	Henry Robertson	John H. & Anna(Burton)		HWBJ 385	1835
15 Jul 1803	Philip Sicks			EBOO 369	---
00 000 0000	Alexander B. Tolin			BFUT 508	1829
19 Jul 1841	Drury B. Vice	Martin & Jahazy(Barber)	Ky/Va	BHOT T329	1862
06 Jan 1855	Benjamin F. Whaley	Benjamin & Jane(Bush)		CSHE 431	---
00 000 0000	Keziah Williams[Patrick]			BMmB 311	---
06 Oct 1840	L.R. Young			BVPA 188	1848

BELL COUNTY

BIRTHDATE	NAME OF BIOGRAPHEE	PARENTS/BIRTHPLACE/BIRTHDATE		SOURCE/PAGE	DATE
00 000 1824	James H. Ray	Joel & Malinda J(Brown)	**/**	SCWA 990	---

BOONE COUNTY

BIRTHDATE	NAME OF BIOGRAPHEE	PARENTS/BIRTHPLACE/BIRTHDATE		SOURCE/PAGE	DATE
28 Sep 1827	Mason W. Anderson	Henry & Mildred(Cornelius)	x/Ky	HDOH 613	---
00 000 0000	O.P. Burns			ASOH 45	1859
00 000 1837	Samuel Canby			NSPC 323	1837
07 Jun 1813	Newton Canfield			HDOH 658	---
00 000 1838	Charles Carpenter	Asahel & Ann F(Bates)		HDOH 1198	---
00 000 1860	Capt.William F.Cisco	Francis & Elizabeth(Hedges)		BHCL 537	---

00 000 1821	Simeon Clore		BMON	354	----
00 000 0000	Joseph Connell		ARIP	49	1818
00 000 1823	William A.Connely		BGAS	75	1826
00 000 0000	J.J. Craven		ARIP	51	1828
00 000 1828	Joel Deer		BWON	350	1847
00 000 0000	William Dobbins	Israel & Frances(Deer)	AGRE	53	----
00 000 1802	John Doyle		BGAS	105	----
28 Sep 1805	John P. Dunn	Isaac & Frances(Piatt) NJ1785/x	BGAS	109	----
27 Feb 1855	R.E. Graves	Rev.R.K. & Sarah E(Mothershead)**/Owen	HVAN	410	----
15 Mar 1826	Rev. R.K. Graves	Absalom Va91/x	HVAN	410	1864
00 000 0000	J. Greene		ADEA	50	1864
00 000 0000	W.H. Greene		ADEA	50	----
00 000 1810	Owen Griffith	Abel & Jennie(Windsor) Va/Va	HHEN	696	----
00 000 0000	Robert Hamilton		ARIP	51	1842
28 Dec 1815	Edmund D. Herod		BGAS	180	----
00 000 0000	Nancy Hoffman[House]		HSHE	715	----
00 000 0000	George W. Horton		ARIP	51	1871
00 000 0000	Masten House		HSHE	715	----
21 May 1858	Robert Johnson	Andrew & Mary(McClure) Ky/Ky	GBRD	409	----
00 000 1798	Sarah Jones[Ryker]		BSCC	B264	----
00 000 0000	John H. Kelly		ADEA	72	1863
06 May 1866	Clarence L. Kirk	John W. & Augusta(Calvert)	DIND	1350	----
11 Mar 1847	Rev. Eusebius Kirtley		HDOH	1238	1880
24 Oct 1844	William P. Knight	John & Amanda(Winans) Ky/x	HPDB	400	----
00 000 0000	William P. Knight		AGIP	17	1869
07 Nov 1812	George W. Lane		HDOH	807	1814
07 Nov 1812	George W. Lane	Amos & Mary	BGAS	228	----
01 Feb 1810	John B. Lantz	Mary & Polly(Arnold) Va/Bourbon	HSHE	740	1834
00 000 0000	C.W.H. McClure		AGIP	16	1854
00 00c 1811	William W. McCoy		BGAS	248	----
24 Dec 1844	Hon.Gustavus Menzies	Dr.Samuel G. & Sally(Winston) Ky10/x	HPOS	508	----
00 000 1815	Alfred Mitchell	Benjamin & C. Garnett Va62/73	BMON	353	1831
07 Apr 1830	John C. Noble	George T. & Louisa(Canby}	HJOH	803	1834
10 Aug 1828	Noah E. Noble	George T. & Louisa(Canby)	HJOH	805	1835

BIRTHDATE	NAME OF BIOGRAPHEE	PARENTS/BIRTHPLACE/BIRTHDATE		SOURCE/PAGE	DATE
13 Jul 1831	Rev.Samuel C.Noble	George T. & Louisa(Canby)	Ky/Va	HJOH 804	1833
12 Feb 1827	Dr. Thomas B.Noble	George T. & Louisa(Canby)		HJOH 805	1835
00 000 0000	J. Patterson			ASOH 46	1854
00 000 1849	James N. Perkins	James & Mildred(Calvert)	**/**	HDOH 870	---
00 000 0000	J. Plow			ASOH 46	1835
00 000 1820	Micajah Powell			HSHE 524	1831
21 Jul 1824	Lucinda Powers[Lindsay]			HDOH 814	---
00 000 0000	J.T. Ratcliff			ARIP 49	1876
00 000 1820	Alfred Records	Alexander & Elizabeth(Aldridge)	De/De	HPOS 654	---
00 000 1798	Elias Rogers	William & Sally(Strickler)		HCLI 819	---
14 Sep 1819	Nathan Ross	William O. & Elizabeth(Wilson)	Ct/**	EIND K41	---
14 Sep 1819	Nathan O. Ross	William O.	Ct/x	TBAB 718	---
00 000 1826	William Rowen	Francis & Lydia(Brunner)		HDOH 1261	1826
09 Oct 1814	Mary Scott[Gipson]			EBOO 288	---
07 Nov 1830	John G. Shryock	Valentine J. & Mary(George)		HWSP 177	---
00 000 0000	David E. Stevenson			ARIP 49	1821
08 May 1820	John Stump	George & Martha(Talbot)		BMON 199	1821
03 Sep 1839	George L. Summers	Moses & Jenetta(Ross)	**/**	BPUT 492	---
00 000 0000	Andrew Tanner			ADEA 66	1873
00 000 0000	J.L. Tanner			ARIP 49	1878
00 000 0000	A.R. Voshell			ADEA 72	1858
04 Mar 1803	James Walker			BGAS 404	---
11 Jan 1816	John S. Watts			BGAS 410	1816
00 000 0000	Sarah B. Watts[Vawter]			BSCC B297	---
00 000 0000	Hon.Delano E. Williamson	Robert & Lydia(Madchen)		BPUT 343	---
19 Aug 1822	Delano E. Williamson	Robert & Lydia(Madden)		BGAS 419	---
19 Aug 1822	Delano E. Williamson	Robert & Lydia(Madden)		TBAB 698	---
19 Aug 1822	Delano E. Williamson	Robert & Lydia(Madden)		EIND E47	---
19 Aug 1822	Delano E. Williamson	Robert & Lydia(Madden)		MPRO 229	---
00 000 0000	James D. Willis			ADEA 66	1847

BIRTHDATE	NAME OF BIOGRAPHEE	PARENTS/BIRTHPLACE/BIRTHDATE	SOURCE/PAGE	DATE
07 Jan 1810	James Aikman	John & Mary(Barr)	HKDA 743	----
22 Nov 1813	Joel R.M. Allen	Joseph & Hannah(Levy) Md/Pa	BPUT 406	----
10 Jan 1811	William Allen		BGAS 5	----
10 Jul 1814	John F. Allison	Md/Md	BEGR 89	----
10 Jul 1814	John F. Allison	John B.	BGAS 6	----
00 000 0000	H. Alsman		WHSU B409	1830
30 Sep 1803	J.J. Amos	Nicholas & Ann(Jones) Md/Md	RUSH 425	1823
30 Jun 1816	William Amos	Elijah & Rebecca(Neal) Md/x	HSHE 738	1828
25 Mar 1799	Jacob Anthony		BGAS 7	----
25 Mar 1799	Jacob Anthony		BSCC B66	1820
00 000 1802	Elisha Bailey		HKDA 309	----
07 Jul 1811	Milton Ballenger		HCLI 681	----
12 Oct 1835	Martha A. Barnes	Aaron & Ann **/**	RUSH 372	1837
24 Jul 1809	Ambrose Barnett		HJOH 743	----
10 Oct 1820	William H. Barnett	Thomas & Sarah(Jackson) **98/**96	HJOH 589	----
10 Oct 1820	William H. Barnett		BGAS 15	----
00 000 1792	Robert Barr		HKDA 412	----
00 000 0000	James A. Barton		RUSH 351	----
05 Aug 1847	Nancy Beatty	John & Sarah(Patterson) **/Fayette	HJOH 798	----
17 Sep 1799	James F. Beckett		BGAS 20	----
00 000 1817	William Beckett	Samuel & Mary(Thornley) Va89/Ky	HKDA 809	----
00 000 1809	Elijah Bell		BGAS 21	----
00 000 0000	William H. Benfiel	Samuel & Elizabeth	BVER 465	1826
00 000 0000	Isaac Bennett		SHGI 788	----
12 Aug 1803	Richard Biddle	Richard & Ann(Clark) De/Md	BPUT 437	1831
00 000 1791	Nancy Boyd[Robbins]		HSHE 532	----
14 Nov 1812	Joseph F. Brandon	Joseph	KTCD 1060	----
05 Dec 1824	Barker Brown		BGAS 39	----
05 Dec 1824	Hon.Barker Brown	John & Polly(Seabright) Mason96/**00	RUSH 353	1825
00 000 0000	John G. Brown		NSPC 222	1828

BIRTHDATE	NAME OF BIOGRAPHEE	PARENTS/BIRTHPLACE/BIRTHDATE		SOURCE/PAGE		DATE
00 Apr 1812	Harriet [Broyles]			KTCD	767	--
18 Sep 1824	Alexander J. Bryan	Alexander & Elizabeth	Va/Md	BPUT	460	1834
04 Mar 1801	Lucinda Buris[McGinnis]			BPUT	517	1831
00 000 0000	William H. Bryan			BGAS	43	--
22 Feb 1806	John H. Callaway	Micajah & Frankie(Hawkins)		HLOW	856	1810
15 Mar 1809	Noble Callaway	Micajah & Frankie(Hawkins)		HLOW	856	1810
00 000 1819	Letitia McDole Carr			BHOT	T332	1841
00 000 0000	Cheaney & Bros.			AVAN	64	1870
20 Jan 1819	James H. Clay	Littleberry & Arabella(McCoun)		HHHE	714	1840
20 Jan 1819	James H. Clay	Littleberry & Arabella(McCoun)		HHHE	254	1840
06 Feb 1815	Gilbert Clutter	John & Mary(Gilchner)		HWSP	141	1823
04 Jun 1816	Albert H. Coffman	Abraham & Susan	Va/Ky	BPUT	480	1821
23 Mar 1795	Joseph Cowan			BGAS	81	--
17 Mar 1837	Benjamin F. Cummins			BGAS	88	--
06 Oct 1827	Joseph Custer	Conrad & Leanna	Va/Va	RUSH	856	1827
20 Nov 1814	Dillard C. Donnohue			BGAS	103	--
12 Jan 1790	John Dunn			BGAS	109	--
28 Sep 1805	John P. Dunn	Isaac & Frances(Piatt)	NJ85/x	BGAS	109	--
22 Oct 1813	Hosier J. Durbin			BGAS	110	--
00 000 1813	Greenup Eaton			HHHE	764	--
05 Oct 1810	James C. Ferguson	Clemons & Sarah(Cochran)	Ire/x	EIND	G39	--
00 000 1808	George Field			HLOW	293	--
22 Oct 1810	Harrison Field	Joseph & Jemima(Wright) Va/Woodford		HLOW	292	--
00 000 1812	William Frame	William & Margaretta(Jerette)	Va/Va	GPLA	382	1822
14 May 1814	Willis Francis	William & Sarah(Hardesty)	Va/**	HSHE	745	--
14 Nov 1813	Alexander Gorham	Alexander & Sarah(Tyler)	Va/Va	BPUT	364	1829
17 Sep 1825	William J. Gray	John & Margaret(Dick)		RUSH	773	1833
16 Sep 1828	Henry Hall	Daniel & Milly(Yelton)	Va/Ky	RUSH	775	1828
01 Jul 1827	Moses F. Ham	Michael & Elizabeth(Mathers)	Va/x	HLOW	643	--
17 May 1797	S.R. Hamilton	James & Hannah(Ramsey)	In/Pa70	BVPA	428	1816

Date	Name		Parents/Spouse	Origin	Code	No.	Year
24 Dec 1812	Polly Harper[Wasson]				HSHE	737	1833
00 000 0000	Frances Harris[Patterson]				HJOH	647	---
25 Sep 1889	John J. Hawkins				RAJR	174	---
00 00c 1784	Joseph C. Hawkins				BGAS	172	---
31 Mar 1801	William Herod				BGAS	181	---
31 Mar 1801	William Herod	William			TBAB	355	1824
29 Jun 1817	Sarah Highland[Shrout]				CSHE	693	---
22 Jul 1810	James M. Holmes	Alexander & Sarah		NC/Va	RUSH	544	1835
00 000 0000	M.M. Hon				AHAR	46	---
00 000 1815	Hiram A. Hopkins	Ezekiel & Polly(Benson)			SHGI	548	1818
01 Jan 1800	John M. Hudelson				BGAS	195	---
01 Jan 1800	Hon.John M. Hudelson	John M. & Catherine(Irvin)		Pa/Pa	RUSH	380	1828
20 Apr 1810	William H. Hudelson	David & Sally(Donnell)			HLOW	589	---
21 Sep 1808	David S. Huffstetter				BGAS	196	---
21 Sep 1808	David S. Huffstetter	George & Catherine(Sears)		Md79/NC79	HLOW	609	---
28 Jun 1807	S.I.H. Ireland	Andrew & Elizabeth			HSTJ	819	---
07 Mar 1807	Carter T. Jackson				BGAS	203	---
07 Mar 1807	Carter T. Jackson	James & Martha(Chambers)		NC/NC	BHOT	T438	1812
22 Mar 1809	Newton J. Jackson				BGAS	---	---
00 May 1796	Sarah Jackson[Barnett] William				HJOH	589	---
28 May 1798	Thomas Jackson	Thomas & Nancy			BPUT	370	1821
00 000 1809	John M. Jameson				BGAS	204	---
00 000 1792	Hannah Johnson[Barr]				HKDA	412	---
05 Dec 1832	Prof.Benj.F.Kennedy	Thomas & Mary(Kimbro)		Ky/x	HJOH	707	1836
10 Jul 1829	Peter S. Kennedy				BGAS	218	---
10 Jul 1829	Peter S. Kennedy	Joseph			DIND	1305	---
10 Jul 1829	Peter S. Kennedy	Joseph & Elizabeth(Sharrer)		83/x	TBAB	783	1832
18 Nov 1821	James Kiser	Joseph & Rebecca		Ky/Ky	RUSH	871	---
15 Jan 1820	William Knox	John & Margaret(Hammer)		Ky97/Tn99	BJAB	840	1832
19 Mar 1805	Henry Liter	Henry & Katie(Boyers)		Pa/x	BMON	351	---
00 000 0000	Narcie Lockwood[Ritter] Benjamin & Rebecca(Smith)				DGIN	776	---
22 Jan 1796	Andrew Lydick				BMON	351	---
08 Feb 1813	Fleming McCray	Samuel & Rebecca(Hedges)		Pa/Md	BPUT	388	1840
27 Mar 1818	William McCray	Samuel & Rebecca			BPUT	358	1837

B O U R B O N   C O U N T Y   (C O N T.)

BIRTHDATE	NAME OF BIOGRAPHEE	PARENTS/BIRTHPLACE/BIRTHDATE	SOURCE/PAGE	DATE
04 May 1803	David McDonald		BGAS 250	---
04 Mar 1801	Reuben McGinnis	John & Mary(Houston) Scotland58/Va	BPUT 517	---
21 Apr 1818	Oliver McLoed	George & Katie(Miller) Va/Ky	BMON 356	---
00 000 0000	John Maple		RUSH 872	1829
00 000 1797	Sophia Marsh[Wood]		BHOT T332	---
23 Aug 1819	Thomas N. Mathers	James & Jane(Ardrey)	HLOW 629	1840
00 000 0000	Hannah Mauzy[Browne]		TRAN 306	---
00 000 0000	Hannah Mauzy[Browne]		TBAB 513	---
00 000 0000	William Mauzy		RUSH 782	---
00 000 0000	Lucinda Mawzy[Pattison]		SIND 157	---
30 Jan 1803	John Maxwell		WHSU A66	1806
03 Nov 1808	Thomas Maze		RUSH 873	---
30 Oct 1824	William A. Montgomery	Zachariah & Rebecca(Donovan) Va/Md	CLOW 896	1834
09 Aug 1804	Austin W. Morris		BGAS 282	---
13 Mar 1820	William Morris	Morris & Mary(Cummings)	RUSH 785	1834
00 000 0000	Leander Morrison	Andrew Scotland/x	BJAY 828	---
00 000 0000	Leander Morrison	Andrew Scotland/x	BJAY 899	---
08 Feb 1794	William Morrow	William Scotland/x	BHCL 656	---
29 Mar 1834	Charles W. Neal	Nathaniel & Sallie(Sandusky)	HHHE 606	---
00 000 0000	Tavner Neal	Charles W. & Emma S(Bradley) **/**	HHHE 188	---
00 000 1782	John Nesbit		SIND 634	1829
24 Dec 1807	Isaac J. Nicolson		CLOW 469	---
22 Mar 1826	James H. Paris	Stephen & Sarah(Peoples) Ky/Ky	HGLI 578	---
20 Mar 1813	James O. Parks		BGAS 306	---
20 Mar 1813	Hon.James O. Parks		MHMA 131	---
20 Mar 1813	James O. Parks	James & Elizabeth(Hughes) Md/Va	EIND M49	---
00 000 0000	Rev.John H. Payton		BJAB 318	---
00 00c 1801	George Piercy, Jr.		BGAS 314	---
00 000 0000	Malinda Pierson[Smith]		BMMB 348	---
00 000 0000	Rev. Henry R. Pritchard		DGIN 694	---

Date	Name	Parents	Origin	Code	No.	Year
08 Apr 1796	Lewis W. Purviance			BGAS	320	----
26 Jan 1835	Levi R. Retherford	David & Elizebeth(Hall)	Ky03/Ky13	RUSH	743	1836
00 000 0000	C.L. Roberts			AVAN	72	1867
08 Oct 1814	William N. Roseberry			BGAS	338	----
25 Aug 1800	Joseph B. Ross	Samuel & Margaret B(Walton)	Eng/Eng	BPUT	506	----
23 Jul 1815	Dr. J.P. Russell			BMON	356	1845
00 000 0000	James Sandusky			HHHE	581	1864
20 Jun 1808	James C. Scott	John & Jane		HWAY	B511	1813
00 000 0000	Daniel Sears	Jaob & Mary(Hffstutter)	NC/Pa	BVER	456	1830
04 Jun 1889	Nancy Sellers			RAJR	174	----
22 Nov 1833	James M. Sharp	George & Julia(Darnall)		BPUT	387	1854
12 Oct 1823	A.W. Shrout			CSHE	692	----
09 Sep 1837	Michael M. Simms	Craven & Amanda(Smith)	Ky/Ky	RUSH	750	1849
13 Nov 1840	Alfred Smalley	Jackson & Elizabeth(Combs)		MONT	1191	1848
05 Oct 1817	John P. Smith	Peter & Margaret(Smelser)	Md/Ger	HWAY	B233	----
19 Nov 1815	George W. Snoddy			BGAS	365	----
05 Dec 1823	Charles Soper			HHHE	216	1853
04 Sep 1825	Moses Standley	Moses & Jane(Minery)	Va/Pa	HCAR	347	1827
12 Dec 1826	Harvey Steele	Samuel & Polly(Donovan)	NC/Ky	CLOW	900	----
04 Sep 1804	Courtney Talbot	Nicholas & Aria(Kennedy)		BMON	232	----
18 Oct 1845	Priscilla Thomas[Balleger]			HCLI	681	----
20 Apr 1803	William Thomas			BGAS	388	1826
20 Apr 1804	Hon.William Thomas	Daniel & Sarah(Amos)	Del/**	RUSH	364	1822
00 000 0000	John Todd			FDAV	689	----
00 000 0000	Ann E.Townsend[Weir]			BSCC	B117	----
00 000 0000	Sarah J. Traylor			AGIP	16	1830
00 000 0000	B.F. Trester			ADEA	44	1849
27 Mar 1806	Capt.Martin Trester	William & Elizabeth(Hesler)	Pa61/Pa64	HDOH	950	1815
00 000 0000	Anderson Turpin	Robinson & Rachel(Powell)	**05/**07	HHHE	189	1834
00 000 0000	Annie Turpin[Neal]	Anderson & Eveline(Reupert)	**/x	HHHE	189	----
07 Apr 1805	Robinson Turpin	Jacob & Martha	Md85/x	HHHE	189	1834
18 May 1821	Stephen B. Van Cleave			BPUT	421	----
01 Jan 1802	Martin Van Hook			BMON	208	----
10 Feb 1809	Anna R. Waler[Hendrix]			BPUT	495	----

BOURBON COUNTY (CONT.)

BIRTHDATE	NAME OF BIOGRAPHEE	PARENTS/BIRTHPLACE/BIRTHDATE	SOURCE/PAGE	DATE
01 Oct 1849	William I. Warner	Josiah & Mary E(Riker) Ky/Ky	CLOW 441	1851
01 Jan 1807	Fleming Wasson		HWAY B803	----
05 Dec 1810	John J. Wasson		HSHE 737	1833
12 Oct 1828	Joseph Wasson	Samuel & Susanah(McLeod)	BMON 422	1835
00 000 0000	Elizabeth Wilson[Reed]		HLOW 612	1832
05 May 1819	James Wilson	William & Devora(Custer)	RUSH 446	1832
00 000 1790	George Wood		BHOT T332	----
00 000 1803	Adam Zener		BVER 258	1812
03 Feb 1803	Adam Zerner		BVER 476	----

BOYD COUNTY (NONE)

BOYLE COUNTY

BIRTHDATE	NAME OF BIOGRAPHEE	PARENTS/BIRTHPLACE/BIRTHDATE	SOURCE/PAGE	DATE
00 000 1797	William Bilbo	Archibald & Mary Ky69/Ky77	BVPA 460	1829
00 000 0000	James E. Bottom		AGIP 17	1861
26 May 1822	Rev. John Brazelton	-- & Elizabeth(League)	EIND C3	c1826
09 Jun 1815	James B. Brumfield		BGAS 43	----
00 000 0000	J.N. Brumfield		AGIP 17	1863
22 Jan 1835	Stephen G. Burton		BGAS 48	----
12 Oct 1814	Isabel D. Caldwell[Durham]	John & Mary(Knox)	BMON 472	----
03 Sep 1823	J.W. Carver	Sterling & Jane(Durham)	BPUT 462	----
10 Dec 1829	Martin Conder	Peter & Lucinda(Hack) Ger/Va.	HPDB 390	1863
05 Feb 1829	Dr. William H.Craig	William H. & Sarah J(Handley)Rockc/NJ	HDOH 679	----
11 Oct 1817	Rev. John B. DeMott	Daniel & Mary(Brewer) **88/***93	BVPA 249	1831

Date	Name	Parents / Notes	Birth	Code	No.	Year
09 Aug 1809	Samuel C. Dunn			BGAS	110	---
25 Dec 1781	Williamson Dunn			BGAS	110	---
20 Nov 1820	J.Y. Durham			BMON	358	---
00 000 0000	Jacob Durham			BMON	349	---
06 May 1808	Jesse Durham			BMON	472	---
09 Mar 1788	Jesse B. Durham			BGAS	110	---
00 000 0000	John Durham	John	Va/x	HHHE	792	1835
26 Oct 1844	Dr. John L. Durham	Jesse Y. & Martha(Tarkington)**20/Tn20		WHSU	B251	1850
26 Oct 1844	Dr. John L. Durham	Jesse Y. & Martha(Tarkington)		HGSU	799	---
00 000 0000	Mary M. Fields[Durham]			HHHE	792	1835
04 Jun 1829	Jacob H. Fleece			BGAS	128	---
04 Jun 1829	Capt.Jacob H. Fleece	Charles & Mary(Harlan)		HHHE	209	1836
00 000 0000	John Fleece	Charles & Mary(Harlan)		HHHE	277	1836
00 000 0000	Susan Fleece[Clay]	Charles		HHHE	254	---
19 Nov 1784	William Hite			BGAS	185	---
00 000 0000	G. Hollon			AGIP	16	1850
24 Oct 1784	Judge Jesse L. Holman			HDOH	152	---
24 Oct 1784	Judge Jesse L. Holmon			EIND	D34	---
12 Mar 1810	Jesse M'Callister			BMON	542	1829
14 Aug 1840	John W. Minor	John & Polly(Owens)	90/Ky90	HWIA	650	1854
00 000 0000	N. Morton			AGIP	16	1857
00 000 0000	Lt.Col. Frank Neff			WHSU	A69	---
00 000 1830	Willis G. Neff			BGAS	289	---
00 000 1830	Willis G. Neff			BPUT	453	---
00 000 0000	Willis G. Neff	John & Elizabeth(Kenton)	Va/Ky	WHSU	B294	---
05 Jan 1815	Albert G. Prewett	Joseph & Jane(Little)	Ky/Ky	HJOH	810	1838
05 Feb 1801	William Protsman			HDOH	1258	1814
00 000 0000	Mary Pruett[Wilkinson]			HPOS	636	1812
21 Apr 1796	Joseph Rawlins	Charles & Aristica(Gregory)		HLOW	267	1812
00 000 1800	John Rheuby			BVER	415	---
00 000 0000	Gen.James M.Schackelford			EIND	A50	---
00 000 1834	Robert Spears	John & Martha		HHHE	487	1835
00 000 0000	E.H. Vager			AGIP	17	1861
00 000 1820	Alvin T. Whight			BGAS	413	1836

BIRTHDATE	NAME OF BIOGRAPHEE	PARENTS/BIRTHPLACE/BIRTHDATE	SOURCE/PAGE	DATE
08 Jun 1811	Henry Boyd	James & Phebe(Webster) Va51/78	HDOH 1195	1819
00 00c 1822	Fielding Clark		SIND 632	c1822
01 Aug 1795	Henry Devore	Jerry & Nancy(Mann) NJ/NJ	CLOW 951	---
00 000 0000	Mary Dickson		MHWA 47	1836
31 Oct 1839	E.C. Elliottt		BHOT T275	1865
19 Aug 1826	Jesse P. Elliott	John & Rachel(Pigman) Va00/05	WFUF 749	1833
06 Apr 1824	Benjamin Frazee	William & Catherine(King) Ky00/Ky01	RUSH 430	1829
00 000 1795	Moses Ferree		RUSH 357	---
00 000 1801	Covey Gallaway		BAWE 551	---
00 000 1824	James Giles		SIND 545	---
00 000 0000	J. Hardy		HWSP 462	1830
00 000 1798	Nathan Harlan		DGIN 1139	---
28 Apr 1823	Samuel Lamberson	Thoughgood Md97/x	WFUF 1066	---
17 Oct 1828	George W. Leak	William & Elizabeth(Kitch)	HHHE 736	1836
20 Oct 1841	James M. Leak	Louis & Elizabeth Ky08/Ky	HHHE 707	---
00 000 0000	Jesse L. McMahan		FMWA B187	---
00 000 1817	Dr. Isaac Miranda	Jonathan Spain/x	HHSJ 967	---
31 Oct 1842	Wilford W. Moore	John & Dulcina(McGinnis) Ky15/1n21	HCLI 690	---
06 Aug 1848	Dr. Thomas B. Morris	John P. & Mary Ann(McClennahan) Ky/Ky	BWEL 567	---
00 000 0000	Thomas Norman		AVAN 64	1867
08 Feb 1805	Edward Norris	Norris J. Md/x	HSHE 520	---
12 Jun 1832	William R. Norris	Edward & Catherine(Brightwell)**05/**	HSHE 520	---
06 Oct 1846	James W. Ogden	John & Frances(Threlkeld)	EIND B26	---
00 000 1822	A.F. Patterson	Anderson	KTCD 550	---
15 May 1840	William A. Pigman	George W. & Caroline A.	HCAR 261	---
26 Mar 1853	Evan L. Patterson		BGAS 308	---
00 000 0000	John C. Shaw		ARIP 50	1842
03 Feb 1815	Seymour Smith	Aquila & Polly(Seymour) Md/Va	HM1A 553	---
00 000 1805	Andrew Stewart		CSHE 653	1808

BIRTHDATE	NAME OF BIOGRAPHEE	PARENTS/BIRTHPLACE/BIRTHDATE		SOURCE/PAGE	DATE
30 Sep 1808	Fletcher Tevis			BGAS	387	----
00 000 1816	Thomas Tevis			RUSH	490	1836
00 000 1809	George W. Thatcher			HCLI	593	----
26 May 1819	Jesse Thatcher	Joseph & Mary(Keithler)	NJ/Ky	BHOT	T328	1821
06 Nov 1837	George H. Thompson			BGAS	389	1840
11 Feb 1832	Isaac D. Tull	Joseph & Hester A(Pilchard)	Md/Md	HSHE	627	1834
00 000 1828	William S. Turvey	William M. & America(Cupp)		HWBJ	389	----
00 Nov 1842	Mary A.Whalen[Bond]			HCLI	668	----
26 Dec 1806	Robert Woods	Jeremiah & Margaret		EIND	F106	----
26 Dec 1806	Robert Woods	Jeremiah & Margaret		HHEN	906	1810

B R E A T H I T T   C O U N T Y

BIRTHDATE	NAME OF BIOGRAPHEE	PARENTS/BIRTHPLACE/BIRTHDATE	SOURCE/PAGE	DATE
06 Sep 1832	Daniel N. Davidson	Silas & Elizabeth(Stamper)	HHHE 300	----

B R E C K I N R I D G E   C O U N T Y

BIRTHDATE	NAME OF BIOGRAPHEE	PARENTS/BIRTHPLACE/BIRTHDATE		SOURCE/PAGE	DATE
07 Feb 1812	Andrew Ackarman	Andrew & Maria(Reinhart)	Ger/Ger	HWSP	776	----
10 Aug 1825	William F. Bandy	William & Elizabeth(Jordan)	Va/Va	BHVI	665	1830
02 Jun 1842	John Barger	George & Susan(Sherman)	Pa/Pa	HWSP	778	----
27 Apr 1825	Cyrus W. Blackwell			HLOW	632	----
00 000 0000	Joseph Brashear			HWSP	779	----
22 Oct 1813	Rev.Allen Brooner	Peter & Nancy(Rusher)		HWSP	557	----
05 Apr 1815	Alfred Bruner	Adam & Nancy(Arnes)		HLOW	625	----
00 000 0000	Cassandra Biddle[Mitchell]			HWSP	818	----
31 Aug 1827	Martin V. Burnett	Green B. & Nancy(Gibson)		HWSP	755	----
00 000 0000	Mary Cart[Groves]			HWSP	785	----

BIRTHDATE	NAME OF BIOGRAPHEE	PARENTS/BIRTHPLACE/BIRTHDATE	SOURCE/PAGE	DATE
22 Aug 1824	Charles Cox	John & Lucy(Sexton) Va/Va	HWSP 497	--
06 Apr 1848	Scott Cunningham	Joel D. & Jane(Barr) Ky/Ky	HWSP 815	--
00 000 0000	J.M. Dailey		ASPE 67	1862
00 000 0000	Dr. T.G. Dailey		AWAR 57	1863
00 000 0000	T.G. Dailey		FWAR 175	1856
00 000 0000	W.W. Dailey		FWAR 175	1860
08 Mar 1842	Dr. James M. Dailey	John H. & Elizabeth(Glasscock)	HWSP 447	--
29 May 1824	Dr. Thomas G. Dailey	John H. & Elizabeth(Glasscock) Ky/Ky	HWSP 142	--
22 Jul 1825	Dr. John W. Compton	Jeremiah D. & Nancy(Ball) Va01/Va04	HVAN 239	--
22 Jan 1810	Arnold A. Elder		BGAS 115	--
12 Jan 1819	Henry Frank	John & Phebe(Miller) Ky/Ky	HWSP 450	1831
00 000 0000	L. Gasaway		AGIP 12	--
23 Jun 1814	James Hardin		BGAS 166	--
21 Dec 1832	John T. Harlan	John & Mary(Farmer)	HWSP 817	--
00 000 0000	Gabriel Harrison		HWSP 519	--
01 Apr 1829	Jefferson Hawkins	Silas & Polly(Kephart) Va/Pa.	HWSP 787	1851
15 Aug 1822	John H. Haynes		BGAS 174	--
02 Feb 1850	Dr. Samuel B. Howard	Huston & Elizabeth(Herron) Pa09/x	SCWA 1037	--
00 000 0000	Henry Huff		HWSP 788	--
14 Feb 1812	Wilson Huff		BGAS 196	--
00 000 0000	Wilson Huff		ASPE 66	1815
14 Feb 1812	Hon.Wilson Huff		HWSP 572	1815
00 000 0000	Mahala[Jenkins]		BSCC B20	--
00 000 0000	J.W. Kelly		ASPE 67	1860
17 Feb 1828	Dr.Isaac L. Milner	Patrick D. & Mary Ann(Wilkerson)	HWSP 474	--
00 000 0000	Solomon Mitchell		HWSP 818	--
00 000 0000	Elizabeth Nix[Harrison]		HWSP 519	--
00 000 0000	William O. O'Bannon		DIND 2283	--
01 Jan 1810	Nicholas Peckinpaugh John	Pa/x	BSCC B59	--
00 000 0000	Nicholas Peckinpaugh		BGAS 310	--
00 000 0000	Peter Peckinpaugh		BSCC B58	1818

BIRTHDATE	NAME OF BIOGRAPHEE	PARENTS/BIRTHPLACE/BIRTHDATE		SOURCE	PAGE	DATE
00 000 1818	William D. Piety	Thomas & Mary(Duncan)	Pa/x	HKDA	438	1814
06 May 1814	Horace E. Raff	Charles & Edie(Mallory)	NY/NY	HWSP	793	---
00 000 0000	L.A. Riely			AHAR	45	1874
00 00c 1800	Thomas Ryan			BGAS	342	---
00 000 1810	Nelson Siner	Benjamin	Va/x	WHSU	B103	---
00 000 0000	Ellen Spencer[Mills]			GIBS	234	1883
09 Nov 1837	Rev.Hugh Stackhouse	William & Jane(McNab)	Eng/NC	BMMB	239	1841
00 000 0000	Sanford Stackhouse			MONT	977	1828
00 000 1796	Frederick Stucky			HPDB	408	1814
00 000 0000	A. Thompson			AGIP	17	1826
00 000 0000	Sarah Wagoner[Weatherholt]			HWSP	797	---
16 Jul 1813	John Walls			BGAS	407	1820
00 000 0000	F.H. Wealthy			AKNO	60	1839
00 000 0000	Jacob Weatherholt			HWSP	797	---
00 000 0000	William Weatherholt			HWSP	797	---
00 000 0000	James Wheeler			HWSP	799	---
27 May 1812	Hugh T. Williams			BGAS	417	---
27 May 1812	Dr. Hugh T. Williams Rev. Otho			HDOH	174	---
27 May 1812	Dr. Hugh T. Williams Rev. Otho			EIND	D74	---
00 000 0000	Nancy Young[Morris]			HSHE	708	---

B U L L I T T   C O U N T Y

BIRTHDATE	NAME OF BIOGRAPHEE	PARENTS/BIRTHPLACE/BIRTHDATE		SOURCE	PAGE	DATE
00 000 1780	Asa Allison			BSCC	B123	---
00 000 0000	Melvina A[Broadstreet]			BPUT	462	---
09 Sep 1808	John Fuquay			HWSP	188	1817
08 Dec 1819	Gentry Giles	John & Elizabeth(Gentry)	NC/Va	HWSP	531	---
15 Jul 1789	Benjamin Irwin			BGAS	202	---
10 Jun 1820	Dennis B. Kitchen			BGAS	224	---
11 Jul 1823	Abraham Lasher			HWSP	809	---
06 Jul 1847	William H. McKay			BSCC	B100	---

BULLITT COUNTY (CONT.)

BIRTHDATE	NAME OF BIOGRAPHEE	PARENTS/BIRTHPLACE/BIRTHDATE		SOURCE/PAGE		DATE
02 Aug 1868	John Magruder	Levi & Mary(Straney)		BHCL	838	---
00 000 1780	Rebecca Mason[Allison]			BSCC	B123	---
16 Jun 1848	Lizzie F. Polk[Wilson]	William & Sarah(Shoptaugh)	Nels/Nels	HJOH	832	---
26 May 1792	Ezekiel Riley			AGAS	331	---
00 000 0000	A.H. Shaptaw			AGRE	54	1833
11 Oct 1822	Ellison Slegar	David & Margaret(Stafford)	Pa/Pa	EMMB	319	---
13 Sep 1824	Rev.Jacob Smock	David & Dorcas(Cole)	**/**	BHVI	933	1825
22 Dec 1816	Bluford Steele			BVPA	439	1842
09 Oct 1820	Elizabeth Williams[Allen]			WHSU	B80	---

BUTLER COUNTY

BIRTHDATE	NAME OF BIOGRAPHEE	PARENTS/BIRTHPLACE/BIRTHDATE		SOURCE/PAGE		DATE
00 000 1839	Benjamin Bridwell			ASUL	35	1856
09 Jul 1822	Capt. F.P. Carson	Thomas E. & Jane B(Carson)	Va/Va	HVAN	435	---
00 000 0000	R.N. Hubbard			GIBS	237	1862
07 May 1838	Robert A. Jenkins	Thomas & Martha(Webster)	Oh/Oh	SHGI	702	---
00 000 1822	L.W. Marymee			ASUL	102	---
16 Sep 1811	Joshua Strode	William & M(Osborne)	x/Ky	HWSP	540	1814
21 Jan 1782	William Stalling	Samuel & Sarah		BSCC	B187	---

CALDWELL COUNTY

BIRTHDATE	NAME OF BIOGRAPHEE	PARENTS/BIRTHPLACE/BIRTHDATE		SOURCE/PAGE		DATE
00 000 1806	John A. Bailey			HPOS	544	---
00 000 1807	Elizabeth Nichols[Rice] Noah		Va/x	HVAN	161	---

| 00 000 0000 | H.E. Read | | AVAN | 72 | 1839 |
| 09 Feb 1823 | Hiram E. Read | DeGranton & Eliza May(Hunter)But/Logan | HVAN | 159 | ---- |

C A L L O W A Y   C O U N T Y

BIRTHDATE	NAME OF BIOGRAPHEE	PARENTS/BIRTHPLACE/BIRTHDATE	SOURCE/PAGE		DATE
00 000 0000	Hiram H. Stice		GIBS	233	----

C A M P B E L L   C O U N T Y

BIRTHDATE	NAME OF BIOGRAPHEE	PARENTS/BIRTHPLACE/BIRTHDATE	SOURCE/PAGE		DATE
10 May 1810	Elisha M. Arnold	John & Mary Va/Va	HSHE	684	1835
16 Feb 1836	Rev.T.Warn Beagle		EIND	D3	----
00 000 0000	A. Benedict		ASOH	46	1865
00 000 1828	Americus Benedict	Jeremiah & Elizabeth(Herbert)	ADOH	1191	1865
00 000 0000	Dr. J.L. Benedict		ASOH	46	1865
00 000 0000	Mary G. Burrer[Dannettall]		HVAN	199	1850
22 May 1854	George Erdel	George & Catherine(Barnhart) Ger/Ger	HCLI	831	----
00 000 0000	Dr. D.S. Fisher		AHAR	47	1854
10 Apr 1830	John P. Hearn	Isaac & Nancy A(Mason) Md07/Va08	BJAB	349	1839
25 May 1819	William J. Herbert	Charles & Elizabeth	BVER	397	1831
15 Jun 1815	James Hopkins		BGAS	189	----
29 Oct 1817	William M. Janes	Samuel & Elizabeth(McCollum)Va96/Ky98	TRAN	412	----
03 Apr 1824	Robert T. Kercheval		BGAS	219	----
03 Apr 1824	Hon. Robert T. Kercheval		HWSP	467	----
31 Dec 1847	Samuel E. Kercheval		BGAS	219	----
31 Dec 1847	Samuel E. Kercheval	Robert T. & Maria A. Ky/Va	EIND	B20	----
26 Oct 1854	Thomas B. Laycock	William H. & Minerva B(Dawson)Oh29/**	DGIN	1117	1862
00 000 1826	Dr. Benjamin McFarland		SIND	587	----
06 Jun 1825	Esther Moore[Chamberlain] Alexander & Rhoda(Miner)		HDOH	660	----

C A M P B E L L   C O U N T Y   (C O N T.)

BIRTHDATE	NAME OF BIOGRAPHEE	PARENTS/BIRTHPLACE/BIRTHDATE	SOURCE/PAGE	DATE
19 Dec 1815	Alexander L. Patterson		BGAS 308	----
23 Feb 1871	Richard J. Pfingstag	Switzerland/x	MSTE 590	----
20 Sep 1820	Stacy L. Reeves	Stacy & Sarah(Lawrence) NJ78/Va84	BPUT 438	----
16 Jun 1833	Stacy Reeves	John & Elizabeth(Dicks) Ky/Ky	BPUT 519	1833
21 Apr 1828	William F. Reiley		BGAS 326	----
20 Jun 1853	George W. Shaw	Coleman & Mary E(Riley) **18/29	HKDA 389	----
20 Jun 1853	George W. Shaw		TBAB 630	1879
29 Jan 1817	John N. Shaw		BGAS 351	----
00 000 0000	Adam Smith		AKNO 64	----
00 000 0000	William C. Stubbs		FWAR 178	1844
18 Oct 1820	Napoleon B. Taylor	Robert	SIND 214C	----
18 Oct 1820	Napoleon B. Taylor	Robert A. & Mary(Vyze) Mason/Va	TBAB 317	1826
02 Mar 1854	William J. Tebleman	Henry & Catherine Ger/x	HWSP 525	----
14 Oct 1811	Dr. James V. Wayman	Moses	HWAY B605	1829
00 000 1812	Frank S. White	Convard & Sarah(Spillman)	GBRD 329	----
00 000 1820	Absalom Yeager	Joel & Anne(McDonald)	GIBS 176	1826
00 000 0000	William Young		AGIP 17	1872

C A R R O L L   C O U N T Y

BIRTHDATE	NAME OF BIOGRAPHEE	PARENTS/BIRTHPLACE/BIRTHDATE	SOURCE/PAGE	DATE
00 000 0000	James T. Arnold		ARIP 49	1833
00 000 0000	Luther Bailey		ARIP 49	1849
00 000 0000	James Brown		ASOH 46	1846
00 000 0000	Andrew Cockerell		HHHE 517	----
11 Jul 1805	William T.S. Cornett		BGAS 79	----
00 000 0000	T.H. Farris		ASOH 45	1879
24 Jan 1824	D.A. Fish	John B. & Elizabeth(Wilson) Ky/Ky	BHOT T338	----

BIRTHDATE	NAME OF BIOGRAPHEE	PARENTS/BIRTHPLACE/BIRTHDATE	SOURCE/PAGE	DATE
27 Dec 1856	Dr.Ernest E.Gegelbach	Christian & Sophia(Martin) Ger/Ger	HWSP	565	----
09 May 1830	John G. Haines		HWSP	459	1847
00 000 0000	Willis Haines		ASPE	67	1847
07 Mar 1828	Willis Haines	Garrett & Nancy(Chadwell) Ky/Va	HWSP	458	----
00 000 1872	Henry W.Harrison	R.F. & Kate F(Gibson)	BHCL	577	----
00 000 1804	Matilda May[Miller]		BART	726	----
00 000 1825	Joseph H. Netherland	Christian P. & Sarah(McIntyre)Va91/Ire	HDOH	1253	----
18 Nov 1837	William L. Owen	William & Frances(Driskel) Ky/Ky	BHOT	T320	1855
13 Aug 1839	Richard Sarels	Richard & Julia(Everston)	HPOS	524	----
17 Jun 1851	Dr. John F. Thompson	Thomas F. & Macy C(Carpenter)	HHEN	538	----
02 Sep 1827	John M. Wallace		BART	759	----
03 Sep 1852	Dr. Thomas E,Warring	Dr. John M. & Tabitha M(Hopkins)Ky/Ky	BWMB	771	----
20 Jun 1853	George C. Wyatt	James S. & Mary(Campbell) Ky/Ky	RUSH	765	1861

C A R T E R   C O U N T Y   (N O N E)

C A S E Y   C O U N T Y

BIRTHDATE	NAME OF BIOGRAPHEE	PARENTS/BIRTHPLACE/BIRTHDATE	SOURCE/PAGE	DATE
21 Oct 1823	William Jarvis	Reason & Betsey(Heath) Md/Md	MONT	1062	----
29 Jan 1826	Aaron Overstreet	James & Susan	HHHE	659	----
10 Feb 1849	Rev.Z.T. Sweeney	Rev.G.E. & T(Campbell)	EIND	E43	1857
10 Feb 1849	Rev.Z.T. Sweeney	Rev.G.E. & T(Campbell)	BART	753	----
03 Mar 1827	Dandridge Tucker	Lee & Miranda(Durham) Va03/Va05	HHHE	656	----

C H R I S T I A N   C O U N T Y

BIRTHDATE	NAME OF BIOGRAPHEE	PARENTS/BIRTHPLACE/BIRTHDATE	SOURCE/PAGE	DATE
06 Sep 1836	Dr. Charles P.Bacon	Charles A. & Susan(Roulette) Va/Va	BVAN	65	----
06 Sep 1836	Dr. Charles P.Bacon	Charles A. & Susan(Rowlette) Va/Va	HVAN	259	----

C H R I S T I A N C O U N T Y (C O N T.)

BIRTHDATE	NAME OF BIOGRAPHEE	PARENTS/BIRTHPLACE/BIRTHDATE	SOURCE/PAGE	DATE
00 000 0000	Mildred A[Grubs]		HJOH 486	----
00 000 1840	Maj.James B. Harrison	J.J. & Sarah A(White) Va/Va	HVAN 412	----
00 000 1833	Thomas S. Harrison		HVAN 412	----
00 000 0000	Capt. C.C. Harrison John		SHGI 597	----
22 Feb 1823	Dr.Thornton A.Johnson John		MPRO 96	----
22 Feb 1823	Dr.Thornton A.Johnson	Lawson W. & Mary A.W(Stubblefield)Va/Va	IGIN 896	----
24 Jan 1782	Dann Lynn		BGAS 243	----
00 000 0000	Mahala Young[Clark] Caleb	Pa/x	SHGI 669	----

C L A R K C O U N T Y

BIRTHDATE	NAME OF BIOGRAPHEE	PARENTS/BIRTHPLACE/BIRTHDATE	SOURCE/PAGE	DATE
22 Apr 1815	Cyrus McCracken Allen Thomas		HKDA 306	----
22 Apr 1817	Cyrus McCracken Allen		BGAS 4	----
28 Oct 1826	William A. Allen	James & Sarah(Gilkey) Va/Va	BPUT 439	1847
02 Mar 1809	David S. Danaldson		BVPA 185	1833
22 Aug 1802	Walter C. Danaldson		BGAS 91	----
22 Aug 1802	Judge Walter Danaldson John & Ellen		BVPA 185	1834
25 Oct 1821	Capt.Jeremiah Dean	James & Mary(Campbell)	--- ---	----
00 000 0000	Ailsey Flynn[Ragland]		HHHE 227	----
17 Jul 1819	Thomas Francis	Jesse & Catherine(Lowman) Va/Md	HSHE 745	----
00 000 1839	Phillip Fritz		ASUL 65	1872
08 Mar 1814	Lysander H. Gillaspy Martin & Lydia(McGuire)		CLOW 952	1827
04 Oct 1811	Hulbert L. Hamilton James & Hannah(Ramsey)	Ky/Ky	BPUT 497	----
00 000 1809	Thomas Irwin		HWBJ 545	c1832
00 000 0000	Valentine Lingenfelter		BPUT 367	----
18 Dec 1823	James H. McConnell		BGAS 247	----
00 000 1821	John W. McCoun		HHHE 695	1826
21 Sep 1814	William E. McLeland Robert & Esther(Benefiel)Mont91/Mont		BSCC B248	----

BIRTHDATE	NAME OF BIOGRAPHEE	PARENTS/BIRTHPLACE/BIRTHDATE		SOURCE/PAGE		DATE
19 May 1846	Charles E. Massie	A.W. & Salestine(Ford)	Ky/Ky	BART	886	---
00 000 1816	Lucy Miller[Ramsey]	Michael & Mary	Va/Va	HHHE	740	---
25 Feb 1821	C.W. Mobley	Walter G. & Elizabeth(Burton)Md86/Fay		HLOW	870	---
17 Feb 1799	Preston Morgan	William & Rachel(Farmster)		CLOW	468	---
00 000 0000	Horatio Owen			HHHE	794	1833
00 000 1825	Berry Parris	James & Anna(May)	Pa/Va	HWBJ	534	---
22 May 1818	Capt.James D. Parvin			BVAN	72	1840
00 000 0000	Dudley Ragland			HHHE	227	---
21 Jun 1821	Alexander Ramsey	Andrew & Jennie(Browning)		HHHE	740	---
25 Dec 1827	James A. Rea	William & Leanna(Rice)	Oh/Ky	BVPA	237	1828
23 Feb 1819	Dillard Ricketts			BGAS	330	---
00 000 0000	Hon. Dillard Ricketts			NSPC	437	---
00 000 0000	Margaret Sears[Owen]			HHHE	794	1833
00 000 1818	Sebith Sears[Applebay]			HHHE	528	---
06 Sep 1820	Dr.Hubbard M.Smith	Willis R. & Elizabeth(Taylor)	Ky/x	HKDA	392	---
06 Sep 1820	Dr.Hubbard M.Smith	Willis R. & Elizabeth W(Taylor)		EIND	B32	---
11 May 1830	John W. Smith	Daniel & Eliza A. Montgomery/**		CLOW	899	---
11 May 1830	John W. Smith	Daniel & Eliza A(Gardner)Mont01/**06		EIND	E41	---
15 Sep 1825	L.D. Stone	William & Nancy(Oliver)	**/**	BMON	359	1830
06 Mar 1827	Leroy D. Stone	William & Nancy(Oliver)	Ky/Ky	HLOW	632	---
23 Oct 1820	Mary Strange	John & Harriet(Eubanks)		BMON	415	---
00 000 1800	Samuel G. Taggat	James	Ire/x	BSCC	B40	---
12 Jun 1805	Williamson Terrell			BGAS	386	---
00 000 1847	Catherine White[Spry]			BELA	449	1879
18 Jul 1816	C.T. Williams			HWAY	B252	1830

CLAY COUNTY

BIRTHDATE	NAME OF BIOGRAPHEE	PARENTS/BIRTHPLACE/BIRTHDATE		SOURCE/PAGE		DATE
00 000 0000	Frances Asher[Walters]			BWMB	324	---
00 000 0000	Isaac Gipson	William & Nancy		EBOO	287	1829
28 Oct 1826	Samuel E. Sevier	James & Susanna(Warren)	77/79	HGSU	813	1871
00 000 0000	Richard Walters			BWMB	324	---

CLINTON COUNTY

BIRTHDATE	NAME OF BIOGRAPHEE	PARENTS/BIRTHPLACE/BIRTHDATE	SOURCE/PAGE	DATE
00 000 0000	W.W. Shy		AGIP 17	1865
03 Nov 1799	William Stoops		BGAS 374	1830
00 000 0000	John F. Yates		AKNO 64	1875

CRITTENDEN COUNTY

BIRTHDATE	NAME OF BIOGRAPHEE	PARENTS/BIRTHPLAVE/BIRTHDATE		SOURCE/PAGE	DATE
14 Jun 1826	John W. Cofield	Robert & Amanda(Wallingford)	NC/Ky	HDOH 667	1835

CUMBERLAND COUNTY

BIRTHDATE	NAME OF BIOGRAPHEE	PARENTS/BIRTHPLACE/BIRTHDATE		SOURCE/PAGE	DATE
00 000 0000	T.S. Adams			FWAR 174	1817
22 Jun 1813	Thomas S. Adams	Joseph & Nancy(Barton)	Va/Va	HWSP 133	1817
00 Jul 1840	Daniel A. Bohanan			BGAS 30	---
00 000 0000	J.O. Carter			AGIP 16	1852
29 Sep 1842	George Cromeans	John & Jemimiah(Dobbs)	**/**	HWSP 141	---
00 000 0000	John Eskew			GIBS 238	1848
26 Apr 1808	John T. Gwinn			BGAS 158	---
00 000 1810	Jacob B. Lough	Thomas & Nancy(Bishong)		BVPA 465	---
00 000 0000	Kate[Massie]			FWAR 177	1868
00 000 0000	J.W. Pace			AWAR 57	1841
00 000 0000	Isabell[Patton]			ASUL 120	1865
01 Jan 1807	Joel Ray			BGAS 323	---
04 May 1833	Thomas J. Rowland	Wade & Winnie(Murphy)		HVAN 591	---
00 000 0000	Joseph H. Stone			FWAR 178	1848
00 000 0000	Joseph H. Stone			AWAR 57	1848

BIRTHDATE	NAME OF BIOGRAPHEE	PARENTS/BIRTHPLACE/BIRTHDATE	SOURCE/PAGE		DATE
08 Aug 1826	Dr. J.R. Tilman		FWAR	167	----
00 000 0000	J.R. Tilman		AWAR	58	1849
10 Dec 1843	James C. Tweedy	Thompson & Sarah A(Zimmerman)	HWSP	181	1852
24 Feb 1855	Judge Jordan G. Winfrey	Ky/Ky	BVAN	29	----

D A V I E S S   C O U N T Y

BIRTHDATE	NAME OF BIOGRAPHEE	PARENTS/BIRTHPLACE/BIRTHDATE	SOURCE/PAGE		DATE
00 000 0000	W.H. Beecher		AVAN	69	1865
00 000 0000	Rachel Bristow[Roby]	Benjamin P. & Sallie(Crawford)	SHGI	642	----
15 Oct 1877	Dr. Gustavus Brown	Christopher D. & Anna(Crow) Ky/Ky	DGIN	788	1830
00 000 0000	James Brown		ASPE	65	----
29 Jul 1855	Eugene Bryan	Gabriel & Susan M(Hayden) Ky/Ky	HPOS	481	----
00 000 0000	Dr. James H. Bryant		ASPE	66	1833
19 Dec 1824	James H. Bryant		BGAS	43	----
19 Dec 1824	Dr. James H. Bryant	Louis & Mary T(Morris)	HWSP	551	----
00 000 0000	F.M. Coomes		ASPE	65	1865
08 Aug 1850	Francis Dickson	Francis & Maria S(Bliss) Ire/Mal9	HJOH	787	----
00 000 0000	James H. Douthitt		AWAR	58	1879
08 Dec 1832	James H. Douthitt		HWSP	214	----
06 Feb 1842	A.J. Fulkerson		CLOW	426	1864
00 000 0000	E.E. Gabbert		ASPE	65	----
11 Oct 1816	Levi Hale	Levi & Catherine(Tucker) Va/Va	HWSP	532	1819
00 000 0000	James Hatfield		ASPE	67	1865
01 Feb 1843	James Hatfield	Elijah & Emiline(Morgan) Ky/Ky	HWSP	545	----
00 000 0000	V.W. Husk		AWAR	58	1860
00 000 0000	W.J. Husk		AWAR	58	1864
25 May 1821	Hon. Calvin Jones	James & Rebecca(Kirk) NC/NC	HWSP	466	1827
25 May 1821	Calvin Jones		BGAS	210	----
00 000 0000	Rose Knott[Davis]		HWSP	447	----
00 000 0000	Thomas Lang		ASPE	67	1837
25 Jan 1852	P.S. Lashbrooke	Grayson & Emily(Fearman) Ky/Ky	HWSP	471	----

DAVIESS COUNTY (CONT.)

BIRTHDATE	NAME OF BIOGRAPHEE	PARENTS/BIRTHPLACE/BIRTHDATE		SOURCE/PAGE		DATE
05 Mar 1811	Joseph McCool	William & Margaret(Baker)	SC/SC	HWSP	471	----
00 000 0000	Green McFarland			AVAN	64	1864
09 Apr 1831	William T. May	William & Maria	Ky/Ky	HWSP	505	----
18 Dec 1820	Gabriel Medcalf	George & Elizabeth(Winkler)	Pa/NC	HWSP	561	----
00 000 0000	Dr. A.F. Metcalf			ASPE	65	1828
00 000 0000	J.W. Moffet			ASPE	67	1844
00 000 0000	John Roby	Robert	Va/x	SHGI	642	----
25 Dec 1814	Dr. James J. Taylor	Manuel & Rebecca(Lee)	NJ/Ky	HWSP	832	1826
00 000 0000	A.D. Troutman			AVAN	72	1863
10 Jul 1887	Elmer S. White	Willis G. & Rebecca J(Dearinger)	**/x	GGEV	B360	----
17 May 1845	Isaac T. Wilkinson	John G. & Eliza(Bishop)	Nelson/Nelson	HWSP	222	----
00 000 0000	Robert Wood			ASPE	65	1820

EDMONSON COUNTY

BIRTHDATE	NAME OF BIOGRAPHEE	PARENTS/BIRTHPLACE/BIRTHDATE		SOURCE/PAGE		DATE
00 000 0000	W. Carlisle			AKNO	60	1826
00 000 0000	A.C. Clifford			AGIP	9	----
24 Jul 1875	Mayor James M. Gossom	W.G. & Mary Emma(Jordan)	Warren/Barr	DIND	2167	1898
00 000 0000	E.C. Stice[Bourland]			GIBS	233	1883
00 Nov 1814	James Wilton			HVAN	261	----

ELLIOTT COUNTY (NONE)

ESTILL COUNTY

BIRTHDATE	NAME OF BIOGRAPHEE	PARENTS/BIRTHPLACE/BIRTHDATE	SOURCE/PAGE	DATE
00 000 0000	John C. Adams	James & Eleanor	HHHE 364	----
00 000 0000	Rev.Greenup Kelly		SIND 581	----
00 000 0000	Sarah E. Park[Adams]		HHHE 364	----
17 Jan 1867	John L. Portland	Leonard & Martha(Portwood) Ky/Ky	HHHE 840	----
27 Nov 1830	Enoch Spry	John & Vina(Kimbrell) NC/x	HWBJ 807	----
00 000 1835	John D. Williams	William & Margaret(Bradley)	HHHE 333	----

F A Y E T T E   C O U N T Y

BIRTHDATE	NAME OF BIOGRAPHEE	PARENTS/BIRTHPLACE/BIRTHDATE	SOURCE/PAGE	DATE
27 Mar 1808	Samuel L. Anderson	James & Mary(Logan) Pa/Pa	RUSH 539	----
00 000 0000	Wilson Anderson		SHGI 470	----
25 Mar 1799	Jacob Anthony		BGAS 7	----
08 Apr 1782	Eunice Atherton[Lee] Aaron		WFUF 940	----
10 Jul 1799	Willis G. Atherton		BGAS 9	----
00 000 1828	James A. Baird		BHCL 877	----
00 000 0000	Jesse Baker	Andrew & Martha(Griggs)	HHHE 615	----
30 Sep 1830	Eliza A. Beatty[Patterson] John & Sarah(Patterson)		HJOH 647	----
00 000 0000	Osee Bell[Ward]		DGIN 1098	----
08 Nov 1819	James E. Blythe		BGAS 29	----
00 000 0000	Louisa Bridgewater[Wallace]		HLOW 615	----
00 000 0000	William Bridgewater		HLOW 615	----
17 Sep 1817	John H. Buchanan	Smith & Mary(Minton) Va/Va	HLOW 617	----
23 Mar 1799	Lewis Burk		BGAS 46	----
00 000 0000	Catherine Carrico[Trimble]		WHSU B387	1800
00 000 1794	William Casey		BGAS 58	----
16 Aug 1816	Uriah Chandler	Daniel Scc88/x	PBES 630	----
01 Apr 1824	John J. Childers	Lindsey & Catherine(Lydic)	BMON 274	----
00 000 1821	John H. Clay		DGIN 1137	1841
25 Mar 1816	A.W. Clifford		HPDB 688	c1838
00 000 0000	Mary[Cooke]		HPDB 450	----

F A Y E T T E   C O U N T Y   (C O N T.)

BIRTHDATE	NAME OF BIOGRAPHEE	PARENTS/BIRTHPLACE/BIRTHDATE	SOURCE/PAGE	DATE
11 Feb 1828	William Cordrey	John & Malinda(Johnson) Md/Ky	BSCC B218	----
25 Jun 1820	James J. Curtis		BGAS 89	----
23 Mar 1817	Cranston T. Dodd	Thomas & Elizabeth(Myers) Scott/x	HLOW 347	----
00 000 0000	Betsey J Duke[Todd]		HJOH 827	----
00 000 0000	Dr. E.D. Ehrman		ASPE 67	1876
08 Nov 1853	Edward D. Ehrman	Christian & Sophia(Withers) Ger/x	HWSP 448	----
25 Dec 1812	Jefferson Farr	James & Catherine(Kurry)	BMMB 364	----
29 Jun 1807	Sally A. Fisher[Lydick]		BMON 351	----
09 Aug 1809	Sophia Fisher[Galey] Samuel		BMON 347	----
08 Mar 1842	Maggie R. Fowler[Johnson] William A. & Jane(Riley) **04/Ky		HCLI 812	----
00 000 0000	Barry Gentry		BMMB 302	----
00 000 0000	Abraham B. Giltner		BMON 357	----
00 00c 1790	Daniel Harrah		BGAS 168	----
00 000 0000	John P. Henderson		HJOH 798	----
00 000 0000	Alexander Hudelson		SHGI 1031	1813
20 May 1818	Fabius Hull		BGAS 197	----
18 Sep 1825	William D. Hutchins		BGAS 200	----
07 Jun 1842	Edward T. Johnson		BGAS 206	----
07 Jun 1842	Edward T. Johnson		NSPC 422	----
01 Mar 1819	Nelson R. Keyes		TBAB 641	----
00 000 0000	Judge Nelson R.Keyes John L. & Mary A(Coons) NY17/Ky14		BART 711	----
20 Jan 1815	Col.William C. Kise		EBOO 315	1821
00 000 0000	Benjamin Leavell	Robert Va/x	FMWA B562	1811
00 000 0000	Nancy Liter[Giltner]		BMON 357	----
16 Oct 1796	Judge T.A. Long	Benjamin & Margaret A.	BHOT H401	1826
00 000 0000	Elizabeth J. Ludlow[Gentry]		BMMB 302	----
00 000 0000	Sarah Lyons[Voris]		HJOH 826	----
19 Aug 1832	William F. McCorkill Bryson		BHOT T283	1837
00 000 1798	James McIlvain		SIND 631	----
17 May 1813	James H. McIntosh	David & Jane(McAuley) Scotland/x	HWBJ 173	1830

Date	Name	Parents	Notes	Code	No.	Year
00 000 0000	Samuel McKee	James & Esther		HKDA	370	----
30 Mar 1811	James W. McKinney			HGSU	775	1811
18 Sep 1803	Thomas R.McKinney			HGSU	755	1815
00 000 1800	Rebecca McKittrick[Lindley]			HVAN	457	----
08 Aug 1827	Robert L. McOut	Thomas & Janette(Lockerbie)		SIND	160	1830
08 Aug 1827	Robert L. McOust			NSFC	198	1830
29 Apr 1799	Douglas Maguire			NSFC	100	1823
00 000 0000	John G. Marshall			BGAS	262	----
00 000 1799	Margaret Maze[Titus]			HSHE	793	----
16 Oct 1818	Thomas S. Metcalf			EBOO	331	----
00 00c 1808	Nathan Miles			WHSU	A69	----
00 000 0000	James Miller			KTCD	833	----
00 000 0000	Ann Monroe[Anderson]			SHGI	470	----
00 000 0000	Dr. John Moore	Rev. James & Betsey(Todd)		HJOH	828	----
22 Jul 1800	Nathaniel Moore			BGAS	280	----
07 Dec 1820	Clement H. Nutter	Hewitt & Susan(Talbot)	**85/**87	BMMB	200	1823
29 Aug 1817	John Nutter	Hewitt & Susan(Talbot)	**85/**87	BMMB	199	1823
00 000 1793	Agnes H. Oliver[Wishard]			HJOH	834	----
00 000 0000	Eliza Patterson[Kelly] Robert			HJOH	797	1811
24 Apr 1801	Thomas Patterson	Robert & James(Henderson)		HJOH	647	1847
00 000 0000	Thomas J. Patterson			MHMA	47	1842
26 Jun 1825	Melinda Pinkston[Minter]			WHSU	B236	----
00 000 0000	Laura G. Prentiss[Van Trees]	Thomas G. & L.G(Porter) Vt/Vt		FDAV	365	----
00 000 0000	William T. Ramsey			MONT	815	----
30 Apr 1818	Isaac A. Rice			BGAS	328	----
00 00c 1795	John Robbins			WHSU	B258	----
00 000 0000	Annie Roberts[Rousk]			HCLI	763	1837
31 Jul 1859	Louis Saunders	Charles & Zelphy(Duncan)	21/x	BHCL	559	----
09 Aug 1814	Thomas Scantlin	James & Elizabeth(Young)	Ky/Ky	HVAN	180	1814
22 Oct 1810	Robert H. Scrogin	Joseph & Martha(Campbell)	Ky/Pa	BWmB	362	----
13 Oct 1806	Franey Sears[Bush]			SCWA	907	----
02 Aug 1808	Thomas H. Sharpe	Ebenezer & Eliza(Lake)		DGIN	1082	1826
02 Aug 1808	Thomas H. Sharpe	Ebenezer & Eliza(Lake)		SIND	220	1826

FAYETTE COUNTY (CONT.)

BIRTHDATE	NAME OF BIOGRAPHEE	PARENTS/BIRTHPLACE/BIRTHDATE	SOURCE/PAGE	DATE
00 000 0000	George Sumption		HSTJ	945	----
06 Sep 1841	Capt.Henry H.Talbot	Courtney & Elizabeth(Harp)	DIND	1310	----
06 Sep 1841	Capt.Henry H.Talbot	Courtney & Elizabeth(Harp)	MONT	1124	----
29 Oct 1819	James Talley	John & Catherine(Grady)	BART	780	1844
00 000 1827	Caleb B. Tarlton		BGAS	383	1834
22 Nov 1811	Robert Tegarden	Bazil & Nancy(Todd)	HLOW	613	1813
00 000 0000	John Thompson		BHVI	958	----
03 Mar 1803	Lewis G. Thompson		BGAS	390	----
07 Aug 1800	James Thornburg		EBOO	378	----
26 Jul 1791	Levi L. Todd		BGAS	393	----
04 Jan 1827	Robert N.Todd		BGAS	394	----
04 Jan 1827	Robert N.Todd	Levi L. & --(Ashby)	SIND	283	----
26 Nov 1797	Thomas J.Todd		BGAS	394	----
00 000 0000	Thomas J.Todd		HJOH	827	----
03 Feb 1796	Joseph Trimble		WHSU	B387	----
00 000 0000	Abraham B. Voris		HJOH	826	----
22 Jan 1827	Sampson Walters	Frank	WHSU	B94	1837
00 000 0000	James Ward		DGIN	1098	----
08 Oct 1793	Howard Watts		BGAS	409	----
07 Jul 1794	Johnson Watts		BGAS	410	----
07 Jul 1794	Col.Johnson Watts	Judge John & Fannie(Sebree)	HDOH	967	----
09 Apr 1808	Zachariah Webb		HJOH	672	----
00 000 1800	Rebecca Welch[Scott]		BSCC	B271	----
20 Apr 1824	Harriet Wilson[Lydick]	John	BMON	352	----
00 000 0000	Rachel Worland		HSHE	743	----

FLEMING COUNTY

BIRTHDATE	NAME OF BIOGRAPHEE	PARENTS/BIRTHPLACE/BIRTHDATE	SOURCE/PAGE	DATE

Date	Name	Parents	Origin	Code	No.	Year
00 000 0000	William Alexander			RUSH	496	---
19 Jan 1812	Ambrose W. Armstrong			BGAS	8	---
19 Jan 1812	Ambrose W. Armstrong	Henry & Elizabeth(Fisher)		BWON	417	1829
00 000 1834	S.W. Asbury			ASUL	21	1844
05 Aug 1840	Dr. W.H.H. Asbury	W.D. & Elizabeth(Bowman)	Ky/Ky	HGSU	428	1849
14 May 1828	James A.B. Baird	William & Ary A(Rose)		HCLI	616	1835
22 Feb 1819	Abner Bebout	Peter & Elijah		RUSH	706	1826
20 Oct 1803	James Beck	J.		HELK	924	---
05 May 1825	Catherine Bridges[Dicks]	Hon. Moses T.		BPUT	518	---
05 Jun 1812	Dillon Bridges			BGAS	37	---
00 000 0000	Sarah Bright[Quinn]			HHHE	728	c1820
08 Jul 1833	John T. Burns			BGAS	47	---
00 000 0000	Peter O. Carpenter			HSHE	758	---
00 000 1818	William Carr			BWAB	671	1823
18 Jun 1818	William Carr			BWAB	697	---
20 Feb 1814	Daniel T.Carter	Henry & Mary(Green)	Va76/Va91	RUSH	372	1841
19 May 1811	Jesse Chambers	Stacy & Margaret(Starkey)		EBOO	361	---
15 Oct 1818	Mary Collins	William & Elizabeth(Berkner)	Ky/Ky	RUSH	514	1825
19 Nov 1827	Samuel Conaway	John & Phebe(Plank)	Lewis/**	RUSH	503	1836
30 Apr 1823	Clarington G. Cross	John & Mary(Johnson)	Tn/Va	HKDA	862	---
00 000 1805	Ell Davis			MPRO	254	1819
03 Jun 1831	Samuel H. Davis	Robert & Elizabeth(Henry)	**99/**05	RUSH	354	---
09 Jul 1813	Samuel Davis			BGAS	95	---
06 Feb 1832	Robert S. Dorsey	John & Nancy(Spiers)	83/94	DGIN	1195	---
01 Jan 1832	Louisa S. Duley[Whicker]			HHHE	466	---
28 Jun 1815	William Duncan	Martin & Mary(Henry)	Pa77/Pa91	RUSH	355	1824
01 Jan 1799	Jacob D. Early	Joseph & Catherine(Drennen)	Va10/x	EIND	H11	---
12 Jul 1827	Samuel S. Early	Jacob D. & Mary(Stockwell)		EIND	H13	---
00 00c 1793	William Eaton			WHSU	A51	---
00 Aug 1806	Delana R. Eckels			BGAS	112	---
09 Sep 1843	William W. Ewings	James & Harriet(Bishop)		BWON	471	1852
07 Dec 1821	Andrew Faris	John & Sarah(Truitt)	Va/De	HWBJ	573	1826
29 Jun 1813	Ell Faris	John		HWBJ	573	---
23 Feb 1805	James P. Foley			BGAS	130	---

BIRTHDATE	NAME OF BIOGRAPHEE	PARENTS/BIRTHPLACE/BIRTHDATE		SOURCE/PAGE		DATE
04 Apr 1817	James H. Foxworthy	Samuel & Mary Ann(Calvert)	Va/x	RUSH	378	1846
22 Jul 1815	John Gilkinson	Robert A. & Annie(Hunt)		HGSU	725	1816
00 000 1815	John Gilkison			WHSU	A53	1816
20 Jan 1824	Judge David S. Gooding Asa & Matilda			TBAB	507	1827
20 Jan 1824	Judge David S. Gooding Asa & Matilda			HHAN	450	1826
20 Jan 1824	David S. Gooding	Asa & Matilda(Hunt)	Ky/x	MPRO	522	1827
20 Jan 1824	David S. Gooding			BGAS	146	----
20 Jan 1824	David S. Gooding	Asa		GIND	680	1827
12 Jan 1814	Willis A. Gorman			BGAS	148	----
00 000 0000	Sarah Goslin[Moore]			BHVI	869	----
11 Mar 1819	Orville S. Hamilton			BGAS	162	----
00 000 1816	S.B. Harrah			BEGR	93	1825
14 Jan 1816	Samuel B. Harrah	Robert & Elizabeth(Baldwin)	Va/Md	HGSU	360	1825
00 000 1811	James Havens	Rev. James & Hester(Jarvis)		RUSH	706	1822
18 May 1821	Joseph Heaton		Pa/Pa.	RUSH	433	1822
00 0c 1829	Adam Hester			MONT	1095	----
00 000 0000	Abram Hillis			BPUT	348	----
00 000 0000	J.C. Hinton			AKNO	61	1869
04 Feb 1817	Malinda R. Hunt[Garrett] Rev. Bazell & Mary	Tn90/Ky91	BGAS	199	----
00 000 1808	Miles Hunt	Basil		TRAN	480	---+
10 Sep 1808	Miles Hunt			TRAN	400	1811
10 Sep 1808	Miles Hunt			TRAN	478	1824
00 000 1813	Lewis S. Hunter			HHHE	771	----
13 Feb 1826	Dr. John J. Inlow	Abraham & Sophia(Bell)		RUSH	843	----
05 Jun 1825	Perry C. Johnson	Arthur	Pa/x	HLOW	635	----
04 Mar 1847	Martin Jones	John F. & Lucinda(Myers)		CSHE	432	----
04 Mar 1847	Martin Jones	John F. & Lucinda(Myers)		HSHE	619	1850
03 Jun 1843	Thomas A. Jones	Thomas D. & Jane(Kirk)	Va/Pa	RUSH	846	1863
00 000 0000	John J. Kelly			MHMA	47	----
02 Jul 1840	Elizabeth Jane King[Williams] Enoch W. & Lucy(Campbell) 12/15HHHE			333	----

Birth Date	Name	Parents	Origin	Origin 2	Code	No.	Year
00 000 0000	George B. Leavitt				AGRE	53	---
20 Oct 1804	James McClary	John & Margaret	Va/x		BPUT	382	1833
00 000 0000	Abraham McCorkle				SIND	600	1824
29 May 1792	Isaac Mahan				BGAS	258	---
07 Feb 1824	Col. John R. Mahan	Isaac & Margaret(Knight)		Md/Md	BPUT	418	1826
18 Jan 1800	Joseph G. Marshall	Rev. Robert & Elizabeth(Glass)			EIND	D47	1828
16 Sep 1831	James W. Meredith	William R. & Harriet(Davis)			HCLI	572	---
00 000 1819	James Mershon			Md/Md	BVPA	210	1836
17 Apr 1834	Dr. Abraham Miller	John & Eleanor(Beckett)		Pa/Va	HJOH	801	1834
00 000 1801	John Miller	William			SIND	604	---
07 Dec 1791	Lewis D. Mills				BMON	452	1827
04 Jun 1815	William R. Montgomery	John & Polly(Donovan)	Va/Mason		CLOW	928	---
00 Oc 1818	William Moore				BHVL	869	---
00 000 0000	I.N. Morrison				AGRE	53	---
00 000 1795	James Morrison				HCLI	881	---
01 Oct 1829	Sally Ann Morrison[McClary] Joseph				BPUT	382	---
00 000 1846	Sarilda Myers[Camp]				FDAV	557	---
15 Mar 1830	James Neiles	James & Sarah			EBOO	344	---
00 000 0000	Jane Z. Parker[Smith]				DIND	1754	---
00 000 1837	D.H. Patton	Andrew D. & Nancy(Cowan)			HWBJ	547	---
00 000 0000	Elizabeth Peck[Hillis]				BPUT	348	1825
00 Jul 1832	Alexander D. Pollitt	Nehemiah & Jane(Hoffer)	Md/Va		HSHE	643	1834
24 Nov 1825	Dr. A.M. Porter	Seth W. & Cynthia(Davis)	Md91/x		HWBJ	178	---
29 May 1821	Albert G. Porter	Seth W. & Cynthia(Davis)			EIND	136	---
04 Aug 1806	James Prather,Sr.	Basil & Mary(George)	Va85/NC84		BMMB	202	1817
09 Feb 1820	James E. Quinn	John			BPUT	358	---
00 Oc 1820	John Quinn				HHHE	728	---
12 Jul 1825	William C. Randall	Richard S. & Sarah(Havens)	Va/Ky		CLOW	948	1826
30 Apr 1808	Andrew W. Reeves				BGAS	325	---
22 Oct 1827	Sarah Reeves[Long]				DGIN	739	---
22 Nov 1812	John Ricketts	Edward & Sarah(Story)	**/**		HCLI	862	1830
21 Mar 1820	William Ricketts	Edward & Sarah(Storey)	Pa91/Ky89		RUSH	361	1831
18 Aug 1797	Thomas Robison				HJOH	496	---
08 Apr 1797	Jonathan H. Rose				BGAS	338	---

FLEMING COUNTY (CONT.)

BIRTHDATE	NAME OF BIOGRAPHEE	PARENTS/BIRTHPLACE/BIRTHDATE	SOURCE/PAGE	DATE
17 Mar 1820	Johnson H. Ross		NSPC 323	----
00 000 1819	Wesley Sanders	John & Jane	WFUF 1023	1827
00 000 1806	Henry Secrest		BGAS 348	----
11 Apr 1804	James Secrest		BGAS 348	----
00 000 1811	James Seybold		BVPA 435	1822
12 May 1812	Samuel Shockley		BGAS 354	----
00 000 0000	Fountain P. Smith		DIND 1754	----
00 000 1834	Lucinda Smith[Talbott] Robert & Elizabeth(Cohorn)		BPUT 479	1834
23 Apr 1819	William A. Sommervill Joseph & Elizabeth(Lee) Ire92/**92		RUSH 363	----
00 000 0000	Elizabeth Stephens[Crowe]		SHGI 446	----
16 Sep 1818	John M. Stockwell		BGAS 374	1838
00 000 1818	G.W. Story	Va/Pa	ASUL 145	1832
00 000 1826	James Story	Lewis & Annie(McGhee) Va/Pa	HGSU 379	1832
16 Aug 1831	Austin Sweet	Benjamin & Harriet(Mills) Ky98/Va	BMMB 208	----
23 Jul 1825	Jonathan Talmage		BWAB 672	1845
23 Jul 1825	Honathan Talmadege	Jesse & Mary(Beabout)	BWAB 453	----
05 Mar 1789	Stephen Tatman		WFUF 535	----
00 000 0000	David Terhune		AGRE 54	----
24 Mar 1818	David Terhune		HGSU 380	1844
00 000 0000	Thomas P. Terhune		AGRE 54	----
13 Dec 1834	Dr.Charles E.Triplett Charles & Clarissa(Duckings)		HWBJ 794	----
18 Jan 1818	James H. Turner	Joel & Anna(DeBell) Ky/Ky	BHVI 972	----
00 May 1801	Jeremiah Vanlaningham		SIND 544	----
00 000 1839	Martha J. Vanlandigham[Hunt]		TRAN 400	1852
18 Dec 1812	L.T. Vanscholack		MHMA 103	----
00 000 0000	Ann M. Van Zandt[Hester] **/x		MONT 1095	c1829
00 000 0000	Dr. William O. Walker William M.		BPUT 496	----
02 Dec 1840	Luther F. Warder Hiram K. & Mary(Wallingford) Ky/Ky		EIND C40	----
00 000 0000	Julia A. Watson[Carpenter]		HSHE 738	----
08 Oct 1793	Dr. Howard Watts		EIND D74	----

BIRTHDATE	NAME OF BIOGRAPHEE	PARENTS	BIRTHPLACE/BIRTHDATE		SOURCE	PAGE	DATE
13 Dec 1822	James E. Welch	Noble & Lydia A(Secrest)			BMON	420	1825
25 Oct 1816	Alfred P. White	Nelson & Elizabeth(Perry)	Ky/Md		RUSH	445	1825
18 May 1846	Thomas T. White	Hazel & Martha(Rigdon)	Ky/Ky		BWAB	278	1848
05 Apr 1825	James Wilson	Samuel & Polly(Natchet)	Ky/Ky		HSHE	664	1827
03 Nov 1815	John H. Wilson	Thomas & Jane(Hughes) Pa75/Fayette89			BPUT	468	----
29 Aug 1803	Capt.Robert C.Wishard	William & Elizabeth(Furlow)	Ire/Pa		HJOH	835	1823

F L O Y D   C O U N T Y   (N O N E)

F R A N K L I N   C O U N T Y

BIRTHDATE	NAME OF BIOGRAPHEE	PARENTS/BIRTHPLACE/BIRTHDATE		SOURCE/PAGE		DATE
01 Jul 1836	E.G. Bondurant	Thomas L. & Elizabeth(Woodfill) Va/Ky		HKDA	751	----
07 Jul 1795	Henry Bradley	Thomas & Philadelphia(Ficklin)		NPRO	577	----
29 Mar 1819	James L. Bradley	Henry & --(Ficklin) **95/**99		NSPC	135	1821
29 Mar 1819	James L. Bradley	Henry & Mary(Jenkins)		NPRO	578	1821
15 Feb 1794	Eli P. Farmer			BGAS	123	----
00 000 1824	Elizabeth Faught[Bailey]			HKDA	309	----
00 000 0000	James Forsee			NSPC	443	----
00 000 1803	Joseph Gray	Thomas		WHSU	B249	1818
00 000 0000	Margaret A. Gresham[Wood]	Christian	Ger/x	DGIN	818	----
15 Mar 1836	M.L. Jett	John W. & Virginia(Hancock)	Va/Ky	CLOW	432	----
15 May 1814	James M. Leathers			EWMB	228	----
17 Feb 1837	Maurice J. Lee	Morris & Cecilia Jane(Runey)	Ire/Ire	EIND	H30	----
17 Feb 1837	Maurice J. Lee	Maurice & Cecilia(Runey)		MONT	1207	----
17 Feb 1837	Maurice J. Lee	Morris & Cecilia Jane(Runey)	Ire/Ire	BMON	284	----
00 000 0000	James H. Lemmon			BHCL	556	c1850
00 000 1837	Nancy Long[Pool]			WHSU	B350	1852
12 Oct 1813	John H.B. Newland			NSPC	565	----
00 000 1807	Matthias T. Nowland			NSPC	51	----
16 Jun 1811	John J. Peyton			BGAS	313	----

F R A N K L I N   C O U N T Y   (C O N T.)

BIRTHDATE	NAME OF BIOGRAPHEE	PARENTS/BIRTHPLACE/BIRTHDATE		SOURCE/PAGE		DATE
01 Jul 1814	Wesley Pottorf	George & Nancy(Phillips)	Pa/Tn	BART	838	1815
00 000 0000	Alexander W.Russell	James		NSPC	29	1821
00 000 1799	James A. Stewart	James & Anna(Abel)		HDOH	1271	1799
00 000 1811	Rev. John Stott	William T.	Ky88/x	HJOH	659	---
00 000 1802	David W. Stucker			EIND	B35	1810
00 000 1802	Rev. David W. Stucker		NC73/x	HLOW	601	---
00 000 0000	J.F. Taylor			AGIP	16	1859
10 Dec 1800	Lytle Wiley	William		HPOS	658	---
07 Feb 1822	Vincent E. Williams	Parker & Mary(Farmer)	NC/Ky	CLOW	943	1828
06 Jun 1820	Robert Woods	John & Elizabeth	Va/x	BVPA	266	---
02 Sep 1835	Simeon T. Yancey			BGAS	432	---

F U L T O N   C O U N T Y   (N O N E)

G A L L A T I N   C O U N T Y

BIRTHDATE	NAME OF BIOGRAPHEE	PARENTS/BIRTHPLACE/BIRTHDATE		SOURCE/PAGE		DATE
00 000 1843	Robert T.F. Abbett			HDOH	1185	1866
00 000 1845	James H. Beard	John & Emily J(Morris)	Pa/x	BHCL	505	---
00 000 0000	J.H. Beard			ASOH	46	1874
00 000 1848	Thompson Blunt			ASPE	65	---
00 000 0000	William Boggs			ASOH	45	1877
00 000 0000	Samuel Brenton			BGAS	36	---
22 Nov 1810	Hon. Samuel Brenton	Robert & Sarah		HALL	98+	---
22 Nov 1810	Charles Bruce			HDOH	643	---
20 Mar 1798	James H. Burnes			ARIP	50	1838
00 000 0000	Louisa E. Clem[Smith]	Isaac & Nancy(Shepherd)		HJOH	819	---

Date	Name	Parents/Spouse	Origin	Code	No.	Year
00 000 0000	Thomas J. Comboe			ASPE	66	1831
26 Apr 1824	Joel Copher	Joel & Sarah(Foley)		BHOT	T301	---
24 Mar 1829	Benjamin F. Deer	Simeon & Mary E(Close)		HWBJ	373	---
00 000 0000	J.R. Dickson			AGIP	17	1843
21 Oct 1847	Eugene A. Ely	Dr. John E. & Elizabeth(Hatfield)Oh/Ky		HPDB	392	1864
00 000 0000	T.R. Furnish			ASOH	45	1881
00 000 0000	G.W. Griffin			ASOH	46	1880
29 Dec 1840	William H. Hardesty	Richard & Amelia(Rudd)		HWSP	461	---
00 000 0000	J.A. Hearick			ASOH	46	---
00 000 0000	Kate Hobbs[Harris]	Emory		HDOH	744	---
22 Sep 1847	Alexander Hutchinson	John & Lydia Ann(Fuller)	Ct/Ky	HPOS	500	c1850
12 Jun 1835	William W. Ireland	James B. & Sallie(Lancaster) Scott97/x		BVAN	137	1819
29 Mar 1816	Wade H. Jack			HDOH	1230	1874
00 000 0000	Dr. J.M.W. Langsdale			ASOH	46	---
00 000 1847	Dr. J.M.W. Langsdale	John & Wealtha(Dill)	**/Md	HDOH	1240	---
00 000 0000	Leander Lindsey			ADEA	72	1855
23 Dec 1843	Leander Lindsay	Charles & Minerva(Williams) In07/Scott		HDOH	813	---
23 Feb 1814	Isaiah McCoy	William & Nancy(Waple) Vac62/x		GBRO	228	1819
17 Jul 1830	George W. Marsh	William & Abi(North)		HWSP	472	---
27 Apr 1858	Ida N. Moore[Wheatcraft]	John & Josephine(Krutz)		HJOH	828	---
09 Oct 1863	Archie C. Murdock	Christopher C. & Mary J(Winters) Ky/In		HDOH	853	---
10 Jun 1823	Jacob Rose	Archibald & Nancy(Bruce) Ky/Ky		HSHE	660	1841
00 000 0000	John S. Sisson			SHGI	428	---
25 Apr 1850	James M. Stodghill	Martin & Louisa(Carr)	In/Henry	HDOH	923	---
23 Oct 1856	John R. Welch	Thomas & Ann	Ire/Ire	LGIN	833	1875
00 000 0000	John W. Wheeler			AJEN	47	1877

GARRARD COUNTY (SEE NEXT PAGE)

GARRARD COUNTY

BIRTHDATE	NAME OF BIOGRAPHEE	PARENTS/BIRTHPLACE/BIRTHDATE		SOURCE/PAGE		DATE
02 May 1810	Wesley Alverson	Pleasant & Nancy(Overstreet)	Va/Va	CLOW	871	----
20 Jan 1817	George Y. Atkison			BGAS	10	----
18 Nov 1818	Samuel W. Austin	John B. & Nancy(Van Hook)	Va87/Va88	BMON	215	----
19 Mar 1854	Dr. Charles T. Bronaugh	Robert N. & Mary(Taylor)	IN19/IN19	MONT	1128	----
10 Aug 1838	William F. Brown	Thomas L. & Elizabeth(Burroughs)	Va/02	BPUT	432	----
09 Feb 1802	Patience Bryan[Kemper]			MPRO	91	----
00 000 0000	Patience Bryant[Kemper]			EIND	F44	----
02 Oct 1828	Jesse W. Burton	Robert A. & Sarah(Williams)	Ky/Ky	HKDA	755	----
20 Apr 1838	Capt.Samuel M.Crandell	Joshua T. & Mary(Marksberry)	Ky/Ky	BHV I	718	1863
17 Jan 1845	James S. Dodds	Samuel & Margaret E(Ramsey)	Ky/Ky	HHHE	818	1850
00 000 0000	Mary E. Eads[Rudisill]			BPUT	366	----
10 Mar 1810	Joseph East	James & Lucy(English)	Va/Va	HWBJ	550	----
00 000 0000	Thomas Felkins	William & Jane(Williams)	Va/Ky	BWMB	301	1840
22 May 1793	William Hubbard			BPUT	435	----
00 000 0000	Arthur S. Kemper			EIND	F44	----
04 May 0000	Arthur S. Kemper			MPRO	91	----
17 Nov 1786	Robert Kennedy			BGAS	218	----
09 Jun 1809	George W. Leisure	Nathan & Sarah(Irvin)	Md/Va	RUSH	512	1829
27 Jan 1837	Willis McCoy	John & Mary	Ky/Ky	BPUT	448	c1849
10 Apr 1827	William O. Pinkston	John & Elizabeth		HGSU	804	1829
00 000 0000	Elizabeth Reynolds[Gilbert]			BHCL	485	----
00 000 0000	A. Smith			ADEA	72	1834
00 000 0000	William H. Smith			AKNO	61	1873
08 Feb 1836	Joseph L. Vaughan	Thompson & Elizabeth(Vaughan)	Ky/Ky	BPUT	446	----
00 000 0000	J.W. Vauter			ASOH	46	1829
27 Oct 1837	Mariah Warmouth	James & Margaret(Simpson)	Ky/Ky	BSCC	A246	1839
29 Nov 1796	John Wilson			BGAS	421	----
29 Nov 1796	John Wilson	Rev. James & Agnes(McKee)		DIND	1721	1821
20 Jan 1834	Alexander H. Wray	Eli & Paulina(Henderson)		JACK	732	1835

| 04 Apr 1797 | Abram Yater | | BGAS | 432 | 1821 |
| 00 000 0000 | J.L. Yater | | AJEN | 47 | 1869 |

G R A N T   C O U N T Y

BIRTHDATE	NAME OF BIOGRAPHEE	PARENTS/BIRTHPLACE/BIRTHDATE		SOURCE/PAGE	DATE
00 000 0000	Mary J. Brown			AGIP 16	1862
09 Nov 1835	James H. Caldwell	Thomas & Rebecca(Swineford)	Va/Ky	RUSH 682	----
23 Aug 1799	John S. McMurtry	Alexander & Polly(Smith)		BVPA 411	1825
22 Dec 1824	William K. Nation	Wesley & Jemima(Harrison)		GBRD 363	----
25 May 1858	George W. Rains	John & Mahala	Ky/Ky	JACK 671	----

G R A V E S   C O U N T Y

BIRTHDATE	NAME OF BIOGRAPHEE	PARENTS/BIRTHPLACE/BIRTHDATE	SOURCE/PAGE	DATE
00 000 0000	J.P. Hobbs		AHAR 46	1875
00 000 0000	Dr. R.R. Kime		AGIP 16	1862
01 Oct 1827	Mary A. Skaggs[Cox]		MPRO 182	----

G R A Y S O N   C O U N T Y

BIRTHDATE	NAME OF BIOGRAPHEE	PARENTS/BIRTHPLACE/BIRTHDATE		SOURCE/PAGE	DATE
00 000 0000	Benjamin K. Ashcraft	Jediah & Ann(Wilson)	94/97	SHGI 515	----
00 000 0000	B.K. Ashcraft			GIBS 236	1870
04 Apr 1840	Dr. Zachariah Carnes	William & Eliza(Decker)		HJOH 778	----
00 000 0000	J.S. Cunningham			AWAR 58	1866
19 Jan 1838	Champion Edwards	Jackson & Elizabeth(Decker)	**/**	HWSP 448	1862
00 000 0000	Louisa Elder[Headdy]			GIBS 243	1863

BIRTHDATE	NAME OF BIOGRAPHEE	PARENTS/BIRTHPLACE/BIRTHDATE		SOURCE/PAGE	DATE
00 000 0000	Louisa Heady			AGIP 13	1864
02 Jun 1874	Roscoe Keper	Rev. J.D. & Louisa(Fuller)		DIND 1575	----
29 Apr 1822	George Weedman	David & Nancy(Spurger)	Ky/Ky	HWSP 813	----
00 000 0000	J.W. Wilson			AGIP 17	1847
17 Apr 1817	John W. Wilson	Vincent & Annie(Davis)	Ky/Ky	HPDB 412	1860
00 000 0000	Dr. W. Wilson			FWAR 179	1873
24 Jan 1846	Dr. Wesley Wilson	Vincent & Annie(Davis)		HWSP 243	1860

G R E E N   C O U N T Y

BIRTHDATE	NAME OF BIOGRAPHEE	PARENTS/BIRTHPLACE/BIRTHDATE		SOURCE/PAGE	DATE
00 000 0000	John Baker	Frederick		HLOW 604	----
23 Apr 1820	Benjamin W. Balay	Obadiah & Nancy(Hilburn)	Tn/Ky	CLOW 950	1823
00 000 1810	Levi Carpenter			CLOW 930	1825
00 000 1792	Samuel R. Cavins			HGSU 337	----
17 May 1845	Thaddeus Dobbins	Charles G. & Catherine(Graham)	Ky/Ky	BSCC B138	----
11 May 1813	Thomas Durbin	Amos & Susan(White)	Md/x	HGLI 637	----
02 Mar 1834	Dr.Joseph F.Faulkner	William & Anna(Harned)	Ky/Va	HPDB 719	----
16 Nov 1852	Dr. Walter M. Ford	Thomas J. & Emily J(Thurman)	Ky/Ky	HSHE 673	----
29 May 1817	Greth J. Loyd	William		DIND 1878	1820
25 Dec 1841	Joseph H. Loyd	Greth J. & Phoebe Ann(English)		DIND 1878	----
04 Jul 1818	Charles D. Murray			BGAS 286	----
00 000 0000	Bland B. Whitaker	Levi & Margaret(Seaton)	Md/Md	CLOW 904	1827

G R E E N U P   C O U N T Y

BIRTHDATE	NAME OF BIOGRAPHEE	PARENTS/BIRTHPLACE/BIRTHDATE	SOURCE/PAGE	DATE

BIRTHDATE	NAME OF BIOGRAPHEE	PARENTS/BIRTHPLACE/BIRTHDATE	SOURCE/PAGE	DATE
00 000 0000	W.C. Irons		AGRE 53	1856
16 Sep 1810	James McLain	Archibald & Rhoda(Dewey)	HWAY B291	----
14 Aug 1824	William P. Walters	Samuel & Elizabeth(Lamb)	HGSU 761	1832

HANCOCK COUNTY

BIRTHDATE	NAME OF BIOGRAPHEE	PARENTS/BIRTHPLACE/BIRTHDATE		SOURCE/PAGE	DATE
00 000 0000	M.J. Alexander			ASPE 65	----
27 Oct 1857	Millard F. Babbitt	Stephen B. & Martha M(Nichols)	Pa/**	HWSP 754	----
00 000 0000	W.L. Bruner			AWAR 58	1862
12 Dec 1856	William J. Gabbert	Eli E.	Ky/Va	HWSP 518	----
00 000 0000	William Grimes			ASPE 67	1865
00 000 1812	John H. Huffman	George	Pa/x	ASPE 13	----
00 000 1812	John H. Huffman	George & Deliliah I(Stapleton)	Pa/Ky	HWSP 566	----
15 Oct 1820	John McFall	John & Elizabeth(Young)	Va/Ky	HWSP 790	1835
04 May 1859	Henry Mason	James & Nancy(Blincoe)	x/**	BVAN 95	----
03 Oct 1815	Dr. Adam F. Medcalf	Allan & Frances(Winkler)		HWSP 560	1828
14 Dec 1842	George J. Procaskey	George & Barbara(Lory)	Poland/Ger	HWSP 480	----

HARDIN COUNTY

BIRTHDATE	NAME OF BIOGRAPHEE	PARENTS/BIRTHPLACE/BIRTHDATE		SOURCE/PAGE	DATE
00 000 0000	Rachel E. Ales[Thompson]			GIBS 242	1861
00 000 1831	William L. Allen			ASUL 19	1837
08 Mar 1808	John Braselton			SHGI 552	----
29 Sep 1848	Samuel L. Bridwell	Henry L. & Amanda(Shy)	Ky/Ky	BHVI 688	1854
06 Jul 1843	Ira Broshears	Jeremiah & Ruth(Sullivan)	France/Tn	HWSP 496	----
00 000 1795	Isaac Chambers			BGAS 60	----
00 000 0000	A.H. Colvin			AHAR 46	1832
00 000 1813	Andrew H. Colvin			BSCC B132	1813

BIRTHDATE	NAME OF BIOGRAPHEE	PARENTS/BIRTHPLACE/BIRTHDATE	SOURCE/PAGE		DATE
11 Feb 1874	Edward G. Davis	Dr. J.T. Eng33/x	BHCL	443	---
00 000 1803	Justus Davis		BGAS	94	---
02 Aug 1834	David S. Dodson	John B. & Catherine(Ament) Ky/Holland	BMMB	250	---
07 Jul 1833	C.H. Dougherty	Samuel & Matilda(Brown)	HSTU	560	1850
00 000 0000	Samuel L. Duncan[Downing] Johnson		DGIN	859	---
00 000 0000	R.W. Dunn		AHAR	45	---
00 000 1842	John E. Enlow	Thomas K. & Amanda(Gwathmy) Ky11/In21	BHCL	760	---
07 Apr 1845	James W. Ford	David & Matilda(Jackson) Ky/Ky	HWSP	517	---
00 000 0000	Dorotha A. Foster[Carr]		HWSP	780	---
00 000 0000	R.G. Garden		AWAR	58	---
26 Nov 1826	Royal G. Gardner	William & Maria(Glass) Md/Ky	HWSP	188	1833
00 000 1821	Frank R.M. Gilbert		BHCL	485	1833
27 Oct 1823	Dr. Franklin R.M.Gilbert		BSCC	B14	---
00 000 0000	Gentry Giles		ASPE	65	1833
13 Apr 1843	Dr.Thomas J.Hargan	Daniel & Susan(Crandall) Ky/Ky	HWSP	157	1876
03 Feb 1822	Catherine Hayden[Stevens]	Daniel & Hannah(Shacklet)Pa00/x	SCWA	936	---
18 Oct 1886	Obed A. Irwin	Christopher C. & Mary J(Christman)	MONT	591	1888
29 Jan 1820	Smiley D. Irwin	Isaac & Ellen C(King) Va/x	BPUT	453	---
31 Dec 1839	James Jenkins	James A. & Susan(Irwine)	BSCC	B159	---
11 Jan 1801	Jacob Johns		EBOO	309	---
00 000 1813	Elizabeth Johnson[Johnson] Eliza	NC89/x	HPOS	559	---
00 000 1820	Joseph B. Jones		CSHE	780	---
10 Aug 1852	Peter G. Kamp	William H. & Ellen(Johnson)	CSHE	850	1858
00 000 0000	William A. Kandle		AHAR	45	---
00 000 0000	James Kelley	Gideon	BSCC	B160	---
31 Aug 1804	L.C. Kennedy	Peter & Rachel Pa/Pa	BMMB	330	---
22 Jan 1833	Capt.John W.Marshall	John W. & Margaret(Hughes) Ky/Ky	BSCC	B173	---
17 May 1816	Frederick W. Matthis		BGAS	266	---
00 000 0000	William K. Parent	David & Jane(Aubrey)	BVPA	365	1852

27 Sep 1817	John Pearman	Sebert	Ky/x	BVER	510	1829
00 000 0000	Nicholas Peckinpaugh			HPOS	517	1818
00 000 1796	James D. Piety	Thomas		BHVI	899	----
15 Sep 1820	William V. Reynolds	William R. & Sarah J(Tower)	RI/Ma	HWSP	792	----
04 Feb 1802	Jacob Richardson	Thomas & Elizabeth(Crouch)	Va/Va	HWSP	174	----
00 000 0000	William B. Richardson			ASPE	67	1829
09 Feb 1809	Hon. William B. Richardson Ebenezer		Md85/x	ASPE	16	----
06 Feb 1809	William B. Richardson			BGAS	329	----
00 000 1803	Jacob Riley			BVER	364	1827
09 Oct 1831	John Rogers	Shacklet & Elizabeth(Smith)		HGSU	737	1855
19 Mar 1829	John Rout	Richard & Levisa	Ky/Ky	HWSP	524	1845
08 Mar 1842	William C. Scifres	David & Permelia A(Padgett)	Ky/Ky	HWSP	218	----
00 000 0000	Eleanor Sheckell[Peckinpaugh]			HPOS	517	----
11 Jan 1807	John Stephenson			BGAS	370	1846
30 Sep 1845	Warder W. Stevens	Henderson & Catherine(Hayden)In24/**		SGWA	936	----
30 Sep 1845	Warder W. Stevens			EIND	C37	----
30 Sep 1845	Warder W. Stevens			HLOW	875	----
00 000 0000	Wardner W. Stevens			AWAS	49	1867
00 000 0000	D.B. Swan			AHAR	45	1843
16 May 1824	Alfred G. Thomas	Isaac & Mary(Watts)	Ky/Ky	BHVI	956	1829
00 000 0000	J.B. Thompson			GIBS	242	1868
24 Jun 1857	Elijah Vessels	Cornelius & Elizabeth	**/**	BVPA	380	----
04 Jun 1815	Thomas Walker			CLOW	414	1822
04 Mar 1804	Serrill Winchester			HJOH	674	----
00 000 0000	Robert E. Worley			ADEA	50	1840
00 000 0000	Jacob Young	Adam & Rachel(Uncel)		HWSP	495	----

H A R L A N   C O U N T Y   (N O N E)

BIRTHDATE	NAME OF BIOGRAPHEE	PARENTS/BIRTHPLACE/BIRTHDATE	SOURCE/PAGE	DATE
00 000 1806	Nancy W. Atchison[Edleman]		HHEN 694	1828
00 000 1823	John M. Austin	John B. Va88/x	BTWJ 406	---
12 Jan 1814	David Beaver	Michael & Margaret(Coon) Md/Md	RUSH 427	---
19 Aug 1818	Sampson Bowen		EBOO 236	---
14 Aug 1807	James Bowles	Robert & Elizabeth Va/Oh	RUSH 371	1835
00 00c 1809	James Bowles		KTCD 650	1830
13 Nov 1811	T.Jefferson Bowles	Robert & Mary(Harris) Scotland/Md	RUSH 352	1828
16 Nov 1802	Hervey Brown		BGAS 40	---
08 Apr 1801	Jonathan Brunson	Thomas	SIND 632	---
20 Jan 1805	Washington Burnes		BART 811	c1805
00 000 0000	Isaac H. Carbaugh		ADEA 44	1811
06 Oct 1817	Samuel Catherwood		BPUT 345	---
00 000 0000	J.T. Cleveland	SC/x	GIBS 241	1848
01 Jun 1808	Jane Craig[Van Hook]	John & Margaret(McIlvain)	BWON 208	---
11 Jun 1819	Robert C. Craig	Robert & Ann(Newell)	BWON 540	1825
00 000 1812	William Crane	Isaac	RUSH 353	---
00 000 0000	R. Dyson		AHAR 46	1868
13 Jul 1835	James H. Edelman	Leonard & Nancy W(Atchison) Tn/Fayette	HHHE 694	1836
14 Jul 1832	Anthony Egnew		HWSP 516	---
10 May 1811	James C. Endicott		BGAS 118	---
00 000 1794	Susan Endicott[Lowe]		HPOS 624	---
25 Dec 1816	William English	Robert & Patsy(Kenning) **/**	RUSH 507	1823
00 00c 1849	Thomas Erlywine		ASUL 61	1891
00 000 0000	John Garten		GIBS 235	1832
30 Aug 1820	Alexander Gosnell	Benjamin & Dorcas(Furinash) Md60/Va	GBRD 241	1826
06 Jun 1820	John W. Grubbs		BGAS 156	---
00 000 0000	A. Hall		ASPE 67	1832
23 Jul 1806	David D. Hamilton	Benjamin & Nancy(Dryden) Md70/x	SCWA 715	---
09 Dec 1817	David N. Hamilton	Joseph & Jane(Dills) Bourbon/x	GBRD 320	1835
02 Feb 1805	Reuben C. Harrison		BGAS 169	---

Date	Name	Parents/Spouse	Origin	Code	No.	Year
22 May 1868	Dr. Thomas C.Henry		SC/Ky	KTCD	1056	---
00 000 0000	Jackson Herring			HHHE	391	---
21 Sep 1791	Rebecca Holliday[McClintock]			NSPC	172	1829
00 000 1803	Rev. William A. Holliday Samuel			DGIN	1006	1812
00 000 1801	Rev. William A. Holliday Judge Samuel			NSPC	537	---
16 Jul 1803	William A. Holliday Samuel & Elizabeth(Martin)		Va/De	SIND	392	1806
00 000 1822	James Holmes James & Prudence(Klampet)			HDOH	764	1824
04 Sep 1807	Robert J.Hudelson			BGAS	195	---
00 000 1793	Jonathan G. Jacquess			HPOS	599	1815
00 000 0000	Cecilia Jennings[Wedekind]			FWWA	B689	---
00 000 1804	Hon. David Kilgore			KTCD	1069	---
03 Apr 1804	David Kilgore			BGAS	221	---
03 Apr 1804	Judge David Kilgore Obed & Rebecca(Cuzick)		Pa/x	EIND	F46	---
11 Aug 1806	William Kirkpatrick William & Anna(Mays)		Pa/Pa	RUSH	415	1812
02 Jan 1848	Dr.David Krausgrill Philip & Mary(Keller)			HPOS	673	---
00 000 1794	George Lowe			HPOS	624	---
01 May 1802	William McClure			HFUF	636	---
01 May 1802	William McClure -- & Phoebe(Eads)		Pa/x	EIND	D14	---
28 Oct 1815	Robert G. McDuffie Robert & Sarah(Taylor)			HSHE	690	---
00 000 0000	James B. Massie			AWAR	57	1833
00 000 1815	John Meek Samuel		Ky/x	RUSH	359	1827
21 Jan 1824	Thomas Miller Aaron & Polly(Ravencroft)			RUSH	724	1830
00 000 0000	Judge Robert Patterson			NSPC	532	---
11 Feb 1808	Joseph Peck			BGAS	310	---
14 Feb 1795	James Rariden			BGAS	322	---
22 Apr 1828	Zachariah T. Riley			BGAS	331	---
01 Aug 1801	Abner Robinson			RCAR	112	1811
00 Oc 1797	William C. Robinson			BGAS	336	---
00 Jan 1809	Ambrose S. Ruby			BGAS	340	---
21 Dec 1813	James H. Selby John & Annie(McCallie)		Md83/x	RUSH	488	1827
31 Jan 1795	James Seller			EWON	175	---
31 Jan 1796	James Seller			BGAS	348	---
20 Sep 1823	William A. Seller James & Mary D.		Va/Va	EWON	375	1827
15 Oct 1819	Stephen Sharp			MHMA	48	1850

BIRTHDATE	NAME OF BIOGRAPHEE	PARENTS/BIRTHPLACE/BIRTHDATE		SOURCE/PAGE		DATE
12 Jun 1827	William Sharp	Archibald & Elenor(McClure) **02/Bourb		RUSH	362	1832
13 May 1824	Catherine Smith[Nation]			GBRD	363	----
05 Mar 1826	Joel F. Smith	Paul & Christian(Jaquess)	Pa86/NJ86	RUSH	362	1836
00 00c 1810	Sarah Ann Smith[Bowles]			KTCD	650	1830
08 Nov 1822	Napoleon B. Snodgrass	Benjamin & Ursala(Evans)		HSHE	720	----
00 000 0000	Elizabeth Stagg[McGuire]			HJOH	791	----
20 Oct 1826	James W. Stewart	David B. & Margaret	**/Fayette	RUSH	552	1835
00 000 0000	S.M. Stockslager			AHAR	45	1842
28 May 1824	Adam C. Veach			BGAS	402	----
28 May 1824	A.C. Veach			CLOW	457	1852
15 Sep 1803	John Waggoner			RUSH	490	1826
00 000 1809	Milton L. Wagoner			CSHE	686	1826
01 Dec 1819	David Wilson	David & Jane(Guynn)	Ky/Ky	HHEN	740	----
18 Oct 1836	John Winans	John		BHOT	T293	----
00 000 0000	Isabella Worrell[Herring]			HHHE	391	----
00 000 1801	John S. Yoke			HJOH	503	----

H A R T   C O U N T Y

BIRTHDATE	NAME OF BIOGRAPHEE	PARENTS/BIRTHPLACE/BIRTHDATE		SOURCE/PAGE		DATE
08 Jan 1844	Thomas J. Brooks	James L. & Lucinda(Woodward)	Ky/Ky	BHOT	T351	1865
14 Jan 1846	Henry H. Devore	Philip	Ky/x	BSCC	A275	----
19 Nov 1820	Samuel Logsdon			HWSP	471	1833
16 Aug 1848	Dudley L. Pedigo	Jesse S. & Jane(Richardson)	Ky/Ky	HWSP	479	----
27 Sep 1850	James W. Pedigo	Jesse S. & Jane(Richardson)	Ky/Ky	HWSP	478	----
00 000 0000	George W. Self			AHAR	45	1864
22 Jul 1845	George W. Self			BGAS	348	----
00 000 0000	Jonathan Wheeler			AWAR	58	1866
27 Sep 1859	Dr. Ira C. Willan	Dr. Elzy B. & Carrie R(Murray) Ky/Ky		BWWB	259	1861

H E N D E R S O N C O U N T Y

BIRTHDATE	NAME OF BIOGRAPHEE	PARENTS/BIRTHPLACE/BIRTHDATE		SOURCE/PAGE		DATE
10 Feb 1856	Dr. Baxter Begley	John & Frances(Hughes)	Ire/Ky	GCEV	B253	---
00 000 0000	Dr. B.W. Begley			AVAN	72	1868
20 Mar 1850	H.T. Dixon		**/x	BVAN	47	---
02 Dec 1853	Jacob Franz	Andrew & Christina(Bohn)	Ger/Ger	HWSP	148	1870
00 000 0000	W.J. Hall			AGIP	13	---
19 Jun 1855	Jay Hardy	T.R. & Kate(Semonin)		HWSP	463	---
00 000 0000	C.L. Hollis			FWAR	176	1859
00 000 0000	Charles F. Hopkins			AWAR	58	1864
00 000 0000	Richard Hopkins			ASPE	66	1872
09 Mar 1827	Richard H. Hopkins	Richard & Elizabeth(Ellis)	Va/Va	HWSP	572	---
10 Aug 1809	Isham Kelley	David & Nancy	Va/Va	HWSP	233	---
00 000 0000	Lewis Lenn			AWAR	58	1814
24 Feb 1813	Lewis Lenn	James & Ruth(James)	Md/Pa	HWSP	233	---
25 Dec 1879	George A. Moorhead	James & Wilhelmina(Maurer)	Ky/In	DIND	1921	---
16 Jun 1844	Dr. John W. Powell	James M. & Matilda(Greene)	Ky/Va	HPOS	521	---
00 000 0000	Emma J. Seward			AVAN	72	1855
00 000 0000	W.H. Stone			FWAR	178	1849
09 Sep 1814	John A. Vann	Absalom & Rebecca(Rollison)		HWSP	193	1815
00 000 1838	John A. Vann			AWAR	58	---
01 Apr 1826	James W. Walden	James & Katherine(McDermitt)	**/Md	HWSP	194	---
22 Jan 1813	Nathan B. Walden	Nathan & Sarah(Lambert)	Va/Va	HWSP	193	---
00 000 0000	N.B. Walden			AWAR	58	1835

H E N R Y C O U N T Y

BIRTHDATE	NAME OF BIOGRAPHEE	PARENTS/BIRTHPLACE/BIRTHDATE	SOURCE/PAGE		DATE
00 000 0000	Elizabeth Abbett	James & Nancy(Brent)	EPUT	421	---
04 Oct 1819	Oliver H.P.Abbett		BGAS	1	---

BIRTHDATE	NAME OF BIOGRAPHEE	PARENTS/BIRTHPLACE/BIRTHDATE	SOURCE/PAGE	DATE
04 Oct 1819	Oliver H.P. Abbett	Va/Va	NSPC 267	---
05 Jun 1851	Capt.Joseph C.Abbott	John M. & Mildred(Garriott)Va03/Trimble	BSCC B203	---
11 Apr 1808	Hugh Adams	David & Polly(Kephart) Ire/Ger	BMMB 245	---
00 000 1795	Aaron M. Aten	Adrian	HJOH 580	---
00 000 0000	Mary Baker[Zaring]	John	HJOH 917	---
00 000 1785	Rev.Henry D. Banta	Daniel & Anna	HJOH 1188	1861
14 Aug 1811	Jacob Banta	Peter	HJOH 582	---
03 Oct 1821	Peter J. Banta	John P. & Catherine(List) **02/02	HJOH 587	1826
16 May 1831	Samuel Banta	Peter & Vooncha(Van Nuys) Ky/Ky	HJOH 587	1836
23 Mar 1851	Sallie Ann Beazley	Augustine & Sallie Ann(Webb)**05/**12	HJOH 770	1831
07 Sep 1818	Abraham Bergen	Garrett G. & Mary(Banta)	HJOH 590	---
00 000 0000	Levina Black[Shuck]	William & Sarah(List)	BHOT T370	---
00 000 1844	George Brent	Sanford	HHHE 647	---
09 Jan 1833	Dr. William M. Brent	Sanford & Nancy(Scott) Ky/Ky	HLOW 653	---
09 May 1852	Martha Burton[Baird]	Laban & Sarah(Harris) Va07/x	BHCL 877	1825
00 000 1812	George Byers		HJOH 597	---
16 May 1823	Henry Byers	Henry & Elizabeth(Wiley) Pa86/91	HJOH 597	---
01 Feb 1816	David Campbell	James & Sarah(Carter)	BHOT T380	1846
25 Jul 1820	James S. Chilton	Squire John & Eeleon(Stewart) Va/x	BTWJ 420	1842
18 Jul 1794	Isaac Clem	Philip & Phebe(Miller)	HJOH 819	---
24 Sep 1831	Nancy J. Clem[Vanarsdall]	Isaac & Nancy(Shepherd)**/Shelby	HJOH 823	97/92
16 Feb 1800	William Corn	George & Rhoda	MONT 928	1827
00 000 0000	Marion I. Cotton		DGIN 1026	---
07 Oct 1841	William Cox	Arvis & Nancy(Dickens) **/**	CLOW 422	1851
07 Apr 1827	Allen S. Cropper		TRAN 397	---
14 Jan 1815	Sarah Demaree[Banta]	David	HJOH 582	---
00 000 1794	Margaret Demott[Aten]	Abram	HJOH 580	---
21 Sep 1811	Julia F.Eddy[McBride]	William & Jane(Gillespie) Va/Va	HJOH 810	1827
21 Sep 1811	Julia F.Eddy[Prewett]	William & Jane(Gillespie) Va/Va	HJOH 810	1827
00 000 1815	Joseph Fitzgerald		MPRO 429	---

Date	Name	Parents	Origin	Code	No.	Year
00 000 1833	Mary Grimes[Stephenson]			HLOW	936	---
00 000 0000	Nancy Harden[Province] Daniel			HJOH	880	---
15 Aug 1825	Austin Herrell	William & Rachel(Wiley)		HnIA	583	1842
12 Jan 1853	Wickliffe B.Holsclaw	Joshua & Zerelda(Carpenter)	Pa35/Ky29	KTCD	751	---
03 Nov 1838	Dr.Milton L.Humston	Charles M. & Susan M(Tiplett)		HWBJ	759	---
23 Nov 1867	Edwin W. Hydron	William & Mary F(Schermerhorn)	In/Jeff	BHCL	503	---
00 000 1829	Elza Jones			BVPA	398	1830
17 Jul 1823	James Kephart	William & Elizabeth(Herrell)	Ky/Ky	BMMB	255	---
21 Oct 1826	John S. Kephart	Samuel & Jemima(Swift)	Ky/Ky	HJOH	708	1835
12 Feb 1825	James Kerlin	George & Rachel(Banta)	Ky/Ky	HJOH	624	---
22 May 1811	Enoch M. Lindsay			HDOH	723	---
04 Oct 1832	Albert List	Garrett & Elizabeth(Voris)	Ky08/Ky	HJOH	629	1834
00 000 0000	Fielding Mahoney			ARIP	50	1837
29 Jun 1822	Joseph C. Martin	William C. & Elizabeth(Randall)	Ire/Va	HWBJ	773	---
31 Jul 1833	Hon. John L. Megenity			HLOW	594	---
10 Apr 1802	Francis Miller	Ephraim & Jemima(Allen)	Va/Va	BART	658	1821
00 000 0000	B.H. Mitchell			ASPE	65	1883
06 May 1820	Robert H. Mitchell	Andrew & Dorcas(Hardwick)	Va/Va	HWSP	538	---
02 Nov 1816	Daniel Moore	William & Elizabeth(Roberts)	Pa/NC	CLOW	508	---
25 Sep 1829	John T. Morgan	Preston & Rhoda	Ky/Ky	CLOW	376	---
11 Nov 1826	Dandridge Oliver			BGAS	298	---
00 000 0000	Dr. Dandridge H.Oliver			NSPC	211	1835
28 Nov 1827	Truman H. Palmer			BGAS	304	---
28 Nov 1827	Truman H. Palmer	William & Permelia(Higgs)		EIND	123	---
07 Aug 1825	John A. Peters	Joseph & Frances(Cheatham)	c98/c04	BHVI	894	---
28 Jun 1838	Joseph T. Peters	Joseph & Frances(Cheatham)	c98/c04	BHVI	896	---
19 Dec 1840	Dr. W.M. Province	Samuel & Nancy(Harden)	Ire08/**	HJOH	880	---
18 Oct 1809	Aaron Rawlings			BGAS	322	---
19 Dec 1819	George Ringo	Major & Elizabeth(Bryan)		CLOW	456	---
23 Mar 1818	Morgan B. Ringo			BGAS	331	---
27 Dec 1820	William A. Robbins	John & Ruth(Anderson)		GBRD	322	---
00 000 0000	Moses Roberts	James & Sarah(Bishop)		HLOW	651	---
00 000 0000	Nepthfalum R. Ross	Willam & Susan(Paten)		KTCD	1034	---
00 000 0000	Elizabeth Roten[Ashmore]			CLOW	476	---

H E N R Y   C O U N T Y   (C O N T.)

BIRTHDATE	NAME OF BIOGRAPHEE	PARENTS/BIRTHPLACE/BIRTHDATE	SOURCE/PAGE	DATE
28 May 1834	William A. Shuck	Samuel & Sarah(Frazier)	Ky/Ky	BHOT T370	1872
22 Aug 1818	Francis P. Smith			BGAS 362	1850
08 Dec 1833	Sarah E Smith[Barlow]			HHHE 562	----
00 000 1810	Milton A. Spurgeon	William		BART 888	1834
07 Apr 1809	William Staton			BGAS 369	1835
00 00c 1833	Benjamin Stephenson			HLOW 936	----
00 000 0000	Charles W. Stillwell			JACK 627	----
08 Oct 1797	William P. Thomasson			BGAS 388	----
26 May 1819	Samuel Tucker	James & Mary(Kitcher)	Ire/Va	BMMB 213	1836
03 Mar 1824	William H. Utterback	Martin & Elizabeth(McDowel)		BMON 458	1830
02 Sep 1833	William T. Vories	John & Elizabeth(Shuck)	Ky/Ky	HJOH 836	----
27 Jan 1828	Jacob P. Walker	Samuel & Nancy(Young)	Ky/Ky	BMMB 791	1839
28 Jan 1821	Fannie Webf[Brewer]			HJOH 773	----
00 000 1809	William Wells			BART 761	1840
21 Dec 1821	Elizabeth Wheeler[Draper] William & Elizabeth(Van Horn)			HJOH 784	----

H I C K M A N   C O U N T Y

BIRTHDATE	NAME OF BIOGRAPHEE	PARENTS/BIRTHPLACE/BIRTHDATE	SOURCE/PAGE	DATE
00 000 0000	E.T. Bugg		AGIP 9	1845
00 000 0000	Hugh McCammon		WHSU A64	1817

H O P K I N S   C O U N T Y

BIRTHDATE	NAME OF BIOGRAPHY	PARENTS/BIRTHPLACE/BIRTHDATE	SOURCE/PAGE	DATE
00 000 0000	Harrison Ashby		GIBS 240	1867

BIRTHDATE	NAME OF BIOGRAPHEES	PARENTS	BIRTHPLACE	SOURCE/PAGE	DATE
10 Aug 1859	Duncan C. Givens	Judge M.C. & Kate H.	Ky/Ky	BVAN 135	----
01 000 0000	L.L.L. Hanks			AGIP 9	1874
01 Aug 1795	Mason J. Howell			BGAS 193	----
00 000 0000	Dr. A.M. Owen			AVAN 72	1870
19 Mar 1849	Dr. Abraham M. Owen	Abraham B.	Va/x	BVAN 8	----
19 Mar 1849	Dr. Abraham M. Owen	Abraham B.	Va/x	HVAN 241	1870
01 Oct 1854	Dr. John E. Owen			HVAN 255	1875
01 Oct 1854	Dr. John E. Owen	Abraham B.	Va/x	BVAN 29	----
13 May 1809	L.P. Parker	Thomas & Nancy(Stanton)	**/**	HWSP 203	----

J A C K S O N   C O U N T Y   (N O N E)

J E F F E R S O N   C O U N T Y

BIRTHDATE	NAME OF BIOGRAPHEES	PARENTS/BIRTHPLACE/BIRTHDATE	SOURCE/PAGE	DATE
00 000 1857	Annie Applegate(Coons)	J.D.	HJOH 721	----
11 Apr 1857	James D. Applegate	John D. & Mary A(Applegate) In/**	BHCL 762	----
19 Apr 1822	Peter N. Applegate	Samuel & Cassandra(Newkirk)	CLOW 959	1826
23 Sep 1873	Dr James W. Arnold	William Z. & Prudence(Moore)**37/Ky45	KTCD 915	----
00 000 0000	F.W. Ashby		ASPE 66	1864
30 May 1830	Fielding W. Ashby		BGAS 9	----
00 000 0000	James S. Ashby		LGIN 1061	----
15 Sep 1795	John Bailey		WHSU A35	----
00 000 0000	James Batman		HLOW 242	1816
11 Nov 1846	George W. Bence		BGAS 22	----
11 Nov 1846	George W. Bence		BPUT 459	1853
00 000 0000	William Benson		AHAR 45	1834
24 Jan 1843	William Bersman	William & Mary B. Ger/Ger	HWSP 514	----
30 Oct 1837	J.L. Berry	William A. & Lucinda(Millison) Va/Ky	HGSU 716	1840
17 Sep 1840	John T. Blair	Robert & Sarah E(Moore)	BHVI 682	----
14 Oct 1863	Donald D. Blanchard	John L. & Sallie H(McDonald) Ky/x	BSCC B69	----

BIRTHDATE	NAME OF BIOGRAPHEE	PARENTS/BIRTHPLACE/BIRTHDATE	SOURCE/PAGE	DATE
00 000 0000	Andrew Blunk		BSCC B128	----
00 000 1798	Jacob Booker		WHSU A39	c1819
00 000 0000	William Borgman		ASPE 65	1871
15 Sep 1851	William P. Bremer	Simeon & Mary K(McPherson) Ky/Ky	BWER 416	----
00 000 1827	A.J. Brentlinger		ASUL 37	1860
04 Jul 1793	Andrew J.Brentlinger		WHSU B127	----
00 00c 1807	Rosanna Brentlinger[Hoke]		WHSU B111	----
00 000 0000	Rosanna Brentlinger[Hoke]		MPRO 177	----
00 000 0000	Hudson Burrows		HKDA 800	----
24 Apr 1878	Edward B. Cain	Edward A. & Addie(Byron) In/**	BHCL 484	----
16 Nov 1798	John Callahan	James & Elizabeth(Phillips) Va/Va	HDOH 656	----
00 000 0000	George W. Carico		BVPA 195	----
00 000 1809	Adam Carrithers		HGSU 767	1818
14 Aug 1855	John J. Casey	William & Mary(Bryan) Ire/Ire	HVAN 436	----
24 Nov 1830	Martha J. Chamberlain[Welman]		WHSU B288	----
00 000 0000	J.E. Chappell		AGIP 9	1858
16 Mar 1813	Benjamin Cleaveland	Adin & Mary(Conyers)	HGSU 787	1838
00 000 1804	David Coats		BART 676	----
06 Nov 1835	Edward J. Collins	William Md99/x	WHSU B598	----
00 000 1835	E.J. Collins		ASUL 48	1837
21 Feb 1826	James O. Collins	William S. & Mary(Hoke)	HGSU 749	1837
03 Jul 1827	B.H. Cornwell	William & Mary(Swan) Va/Va	BVPA 207	----
03 Jul 1819	B.H. Cornwell	William & Mary (Swan) Va/Va	BHVI 714	----
00 000 1809	Edward Cornwell	William & Mary F(Swan) Va/Md	HLOW 583	----
10 Oct 1842	Capt.George W.Coward	Milton & Charlotte(Ellingsworth)Tn/Tn	BHCL 471	----
21 Oct 1841	Abraham E. Curlee	Samuel M. & Susan S(Little) SC/c20	BHOT H456	----
00 000 0000	Adam Danner		ADEA 50	1843
30 Jun 1835	Alexander W.C. Dickerson John S. & Mary(Bostwick) Ky/Ky		WHSU B335	c1840
00 000 0000	Joseph P. Doubet	Peter Fr/x	BHCL 520	----

Date	Name	Parents/Notes	Origin	Code	No.	Year
09 Feb 1830	John Doup	John & Kitura(Shadburn)		BART	687	---
24 Dec 1849	Louis P. Dupaquier	John & Mary(Shopple)	Fr/Switz	HWSP	822	---
26 Oct 1815	John Edwards			BGAS	114	---
26 Dec 1820	William K. Edwards			BGAS	114	---
04 Jul 1857	C.H. Ellert	B.J. & E.M(Rogge)		HVAN	454	1880
00 000 0000	Samuel Enochs			ASUL	60	1830
00 000 0000	J.H. Eurton			AHAR	46	1847
08 May 1816	Daniel C. Far			BWMB	183	1822
28 Feb 1853	John J. Farrar	John M. & Caroline J(Jarvis)Oh25/Eng32		HVAN	414	---
07 Nov 1805	Nathaniel Field			BGAS	125	---
07 Nov 1805	Dr. Nathaniel Field			GIND	668	---
07 Nov 1805	Dr. Nathaniel Field			EIND	C17	1829
29 Aug 1841	Andrew Fife	John & Elizabeth(Wright)	Ind/Ger	BSCC	B146	---
23 Jan 1816	Thomas Forsyth	James & Jane(Sturgeon)	Va/Va	HJOH	883	---
00 000 0000	John V. Foster			AWAR	58	1833
23 Jan 1815	Martha Gamble[Dunlap]			HJOH	480	---
01 May 1858	Dr. Charles H. Gilbert	Rev.Alfred M. & Rosanna G(Endress)		RUSH	696	---
00 000 0000	Jeanette Graumer[Cohen]			BHCL	614	---
27 Jan 1817	Bennett Grigsby	William & Anne(Cornwell)	SC/x	HLOW	643	---
23 May 1852	Samuel J. Groom	William H. & Louisa(Stowers)	Va/x	HWSP	816	---
00 000 0000	Paul Haller			GIBS	243	1876
28 Apr 1850	Richard M. Hartwell	Samuel A. & Charlotte(Meldrumm)		BHCL	663	---
00 000 0000	Napoleon B. Hayward	James	Eng/x	GCEV	B410	1869
00 000 0000	V.A. Hayward			AVAN	64	1879
00 000 0000	P. Hessemer, Jr.			AHAR	45	---
00 000 0000	Louisa Hild[Cook]			GCEV	B69	---
00 000 0000	Edward N. Hill	Frank & Alice(Newland)	**/**	GCEV	B363	---
07 Feb 1818	James W. Hinkle	Philip & Martha(Reed)		HGSU	728	1819
26 Aug 1844	Emily Hobbs[Haddan]	James & Elizabeth		EPUT	329	1852
14 Jul 1868	Henry E. Hodkins	Joseph & Margaret	Pa/Pa	GCEV	B220	---
00 0c 1810	Jacob Hoke			NPRO	177	---
30 Jun 1809	Jacob Hoke			WHSU	A60	---
00 000 0000	Jacob Hoke			WHSU	B11	---
09 Aug 1870	Jacob F. Hoke			ASUL	6	1891
00 000 0000	Jacob F. Hoke	Andrew J. & Mary(Snyder)		DIND	1943	---

BIRTHDATE	NAME OF BIOGRAPHEE	PARENTS/BIRTHPLACE/BIRTHDATE		SOURCE/PAGE	DATE
00 000 1797	Mary Hoke[Brentlinger]			WHSU B126	----
12 Mar 1804	Sarah Hoke[Brentlinger]			WHSU B127	1836
22 Feb 1822	William Hollick	Martin & Sophia(Bramble)	Md/Md	CLOW 893	----
00 Mar 1826	James Howard	George & Catherine(Hoke)	Md/x	BHCL 892	1836
00 000 0000	Rual Howard	Joseph		WHSU B351	1831
00 000 0000	Esther Howes[Smith]	Mitchell P.		---- --	----
00 000 0000	Stephen T. Hughes			HWSP 741	1846
00 00c 1780	John Johnson			BGAS 208	----
28 Feb 1796	John Kelly			BGAS 216	----
16 Oct 1852	Charles A. Korby	Charles	Ger/x	DIND 1640	----
08 Oct 1856	Dr.Charles W. Ladd	W.W. & Mary E(Steele)		HWSP 761	----
18 Aug 1847	James N. Langworthy	George W. & Emily B(Baker)	NY/Pa	CLOW 434	----
00 000 0000	J.H. Lehmeyer			AHAR 45	1843
12 Jan 1835	David F. Lennell	John & Margaret	Ger91/Ger93	BSCC B164	----
16 Oct 1852	Jacob E. Lidikay	Jacob & Catherine(Yenawine)		MONT 1225	----
00 000 0000	John H. Lorenz			AVAN 72	1860
00 000 0000	Charles F. Lurton			AJEN 48	1881
00 000 0000	Fannie T.McFadin[Montgomery]			GIBS 243	1877
00 000 0000	H. McGravin			AHAR 45	1849
00 000 1831	John MacKay			BHCL 629	1848
00 000 0000	Sarah Mallott[Coburn]	William & Leah P(McKeown)		EIND G249	----
00 000 0000	Volney T. Mallott	William H. & Leah P(McKown)		DIND 1585	----
09 Sep 1838	Volney T. Mallott			MPRO 454	1841
00 00c 1813	William H. Mallott	Hiram		DIND 1586	----
10 Apr 1796	Elijah Malott			HPDB 444	c1816
28 Jan 1837	James H. Malott	Benjamin & Louisa(Malott)	Ky/Ky	HLOW 296	----
00 000 0000	Maria Malott[Batman]			HLOW 242	1816
00 000 0000	Michael A. Malott	Hiram & Mary(Hawes)		DIND 1751	----
25 Mar 1809	Michael A. Malott			BGAS 259	----

Date	Name	Parents	Place	Ref	Code	Year
00 000 0000	Sarah Malott[Coburn]	William H. & Leah(McKown)		TBAB	282	---
09 Sep 1838	Volney T. Malott	William H. & Leah(McKown)		SIND	223	1841
09 Sep 1838	Volney T. Malott	William H. & Leah(McKown)		EIND	G229	1841
09 Sep 1838	Volney T. Malott	William H. & Leah(McKeown)	Ky13/In	DGIN	1049	---
00 000 0000	Elizabeth Means[Myers]	Edward & Sarah		BHCL	581	---
00 000 0000	Hugh F. Meikle	Thomas & Margaret(Fulton)	Scot/Scot	BELA	206	---
00 000 0000	Frederika Mellin			HWSP	771	---
07 Oct 1859	Peter Metzger	Silas & Anna Mary(DePrez)	Ger/x	CSHE	368	---
00 000 0000	J. Miller			AHAR	45	1856
11 Apr 1805	Lucinda Millon[Berry]			WHSU	B122	---
18 Mar 1860	Charles Moenkhaus	William & Frederica(Ramsbrok)	Ger/Ger	HPDB	638	---
00 000 0000	M. Mollenkamp			ARIP	59	1872
02 Dec 1824	Henry Monyhan	Turn & Nancy(Bateman)	Ire/x	HLOW	636	---
14 Feb 1838	John H. Moore	Joseph & Mary(McHenry)	x/Va	HVAN	204	---
14 Oct 1832	John W. Moore	Eleven & Elizabeth(Tyler)	Md/Ky	BHVI	867	---
00 000 0000	Mary Murray[Harris]	Samuel & Ellen(Allison)	Ky/Ky	FDAV	502	---
22 Jun 1854	T.C. Murray	Dennis & Margaret(Coughlin)	Ire/Ire	HGSU	348	1856
10 Dec 1847	Samuel D. Oglesby			BSCC	B33	---
00 000 0000	George F. Penn	James C. & Jane(Floyd)	Va/ky	BSCC	B107	---
11 Oct 1807	John S. Perry	Sylvester & Elizabeth(Stewart)	Vt73/x	BPUT	475	---
00 000 0000	Thomas J. Piers	Joseph & Margaret(Gregory)		BHCL	658	---
00 000 1808	Thomas J. Plumoner	John & Altha(Banfield)	Md/Md	JACK	640	1820
27 Feb 1835	Henry Pollock	William & Judith(Merritt)	Ire98/Ky04	BSCC	A273	---
23 Jun 1822	Thomas N.Postlethwaite	William & Mary(Neal)	Ger/Ger	JACK	710	1867
20 Aug 1839	Dr.William A.Pottorff	Simeon & Eliza A(McKewen)	**/**	BWMB	312	---
00 000 0000	Frances Rademacher	Charles & Catherine		HPDB	681	---
15 Aug 1856	John Rau	Frederick G. & Rebecca(Schneider)	Ger/In	DIND	1970	---
19 Feb 1794	James B. Ray			BGAS	322	---
13 Jun 1832	John O. Reay	William & Caroline(Meriwether)	Va/ky	HWSP	481	---
00 000 0000	John Redick			AHAR	45	1850
31 Mar 1846	John Redick	Philip & Mary(Fleshman)	Ger/Ger	BSCC	B180	1850
08 Jun 1880	Charles R. Rigsby	Thomas D. & Lida(Latta)		BHCL	553	1885
13 Jan 1822	Charles W. Risinger	Daniel & Sarah(Miers)	Ky/ky	WHSU	B60	1839
00 000 0000	M.L. Risinger			ASUL	132	---

J E F F E R S O N   C O U N T Y   (C O N T.)

BIRTHDATE	NAME OF BIOGRAPHEE	PARENTS/BIRTHPLACE/BIRTHDATE		SOURCE/PAGE	DATE
00 000 0000	J.H. Rochner			AHAR	46	1848
00 000 1831	W.A. Rooksberry			ASUL	134	1851
11 Jul 1878	Edward P. Rucker			DTCE	736	---
00 000 0000	Frances Sanders[Stewart]			SHGI	714	---
00 000 0000	Jennie J. Saunders			HWSP	816	---
00 000 0000	J. Schumann			AHAR	45	1839
28 Apr 1808	Allen R. Seaton	George & Sarah(Drake)	Va/Ky	BMMB	346	---
25 Apr 1821	Adam R. Shake	George & Christian(Donaldson)	**/**	BMMB	318	---
00 000 0000	George W. Shake			BMMB	346	1835
18 Mar 1830	William L. Shallcross	John & Mary(Lewis)	Eng/x	HWSP	764	---
00 000 1825	John Shannon	Samuel & Mary A	Pa/Ire	JACK	736	1837
30 Mar 1831	Jesse Sheridan	Jesse & Elizabeth(Goodman)	Pa/**	BHV I	925	1868
00 000 0000	George D. Smith	Peter		BHCL	551	1878
10 Nov 1826	William E. Smith	George W. & Sabina(Tubbs)		HLOW	341	---
10 Aug 1841	William W. Smith	Henry W. & Permelia(Garr)		BHOT	H494	---
00 000 0000	R.H. Snapp			AHAR	46	1850
00 000 1820	G.W.G. Sparks			BVPA	395	1835
00 000 0000	Benjamin Stafford			AGRE	54	1848
00 000 0000	Benjamin Stafford	Benjamin & Eva(Caress)		HGSU	416	1818
31 May 1809	Isaac Stewart			BGAS	372	---
03 Apr 1792	Dr. J.H. Stewart			HCAR	233	---
27 Mar 1809	Thomas P. Stewart	James	Ga/x	SHGI	714	---
00 000 0000	John M. Stucky			BGAS	377	1848
15 Jun 1825	Dr. John M. Stucky	Frederick & Louisa(Meyers)	Ky/Ky	EIND	B446	---
15 Jun 1825	Dr. J.M. Stucky	Frederick & Louisa H(Myers)	Ky/Ky	CLOW	900	---
00 000 0000	George R.C. Sullivan			BGAS	378	1809
20 Sep 1837	Joseph F. Sulzer			BGAS	379	---
20 Sep 1837	Hon.Joseph F.Sulzer	Samuel & Magdalene(Herman)		HWSP	765	---
27 Sep 1843	George T. Summers	George G. & Diana(Gilliland)	Ky/Ky	BMMB	322	---
25 Aug 1845	James S. Summers	George G. & Diana(Gilliland)	Ky/Ky	BMMB	322	---

BIRTHDATE	NAME OF BIOGRAPHEE	PARENTS/BIRTHPLACE/BIRTHDATE		SOURCE/PAGE		DATE
00 000 1867	John H. Talge	John B.	35/x	DGIN	1002	1876
23 Mar 1848	William H. Tapp	James P. & Eliza J(Clark)	Ky/Ky	HLOW	301	1863
24 Aug 1799	David Tate	Samuel & Nancy(Johnson)	Pa/Pa	HWSP	795	----
14 Jan 1822	James Taylor			MPRO	590	1831
14 Jan 1822	James Taylor			DGIN	1175	1831
07 Apr 1811	Henry G. Todd			BGAS	393	----
00 000 0000	Preston F. Tulay			BGAS	396	c1815
24 Sep 1838	Lou J. Tyler[Kerlin]	Milton W. & Mary(Seaton)	Ky/Ky	HJOH	624	----
15 Oct 1876	Capt.John R.Van Liew	Dennis & Blanche(Weaver)		BHCL	595	----
00 000 0000	Jane A. Watson[Ashby]			DGIN	1061	----
04 Jul 1858	Charles A. Weaver	Joseph & Gertrude(Kinsey)	Ger/Ger	HVAN	426	----
05 Jun 1848	August J. Weber			GCBV	B230	----
01 Jan 1820	E.A. White	Simon & Mary(Funk)		BMON	168	1824
00 000 0000	J.M. White			AGIP	17	1856
20 Jun 1847	George L.T.Widerin	Christian & Mary Ann(Meder)		BSCC	B286	----
00 000 0000	Rev. G.L. Widerin			AGIP	12	1877
00 000 0000	John R. Williams	William & Elizabeth(Hethington)	Ire/Ire	FDAV	527	----
00 000 1818	John Wilson	John & Nancy(Grate)	Ky/Ky	HLOW	346	----
31 Mar 1857	Frank Woerner	Conrad & Mary(Zwirman)	Ger/Ger	BHCL	570	----
27 May 1821	Jefferson Wooden	Robert M. & Malinda	Ky/Ky	BWMB	352	----
25 Dec 1848	Martha Yates[Padgett]	William & ---(Shake)	Ky/Ky	WHSU	B124	----

J E S S A M I N E   C O U N T Y

BIRTHDATE	NAME OF BIOGRAPHEE	PARENTS/BIRTHPLACE/BIRTHDATE		SOURCE/PAGE		DATE
12 Sep 1847	Wiley F.Ackman			BGAS	1	----
00 000 0000	Sarah Boatman[Willis]			WHSU	B405	----
00 000 0000	Elijah Bourn			BWMB	297	----
23 Sep 1807	Elijah Bowen	Elijah & Nancy	Va/Va	BWMB	285	----
01 Jan 1818	Tavner Bowen			WHSU	A40	1836
29 Aug 1811	William W.Chisham	Daniel & Elizabeth(Beckham)	Va77/Va75	HLOW	605	----
08 Apr 1827	Elizabeth Corbin[McConnell]			WHSU	B407	1836

BIRTHDATE	NAME OF BIOGRAPHEE	PARENTS/BIRTHPLACE/BIRTHDATE		SOURCE/PAGE	DATE
28 Apr 1845	Rebecca Corbin[Jackson]	Martin & Amanda	Va/Va	----	--	c1850
28 Jun 1817	James M. Darnall			BGAS	92	---
28 Jun 1827	James M. Darnall	Zenas & ---(Bridges)		EIND	K12	---
28 Jun 1817	Dr. James M. Darnall	Zenas & Agnes(Bridges)	Ky/Ky	BHOT	H317	1822
14 Oct 1837	William M. Davis			DGIN	1025	---
09 Mar 1836	Patrick H. Dean			TRAN	311	---
17 Nov 1815	Robert Doak	James W. & Mary(Irwin)		HLOW	662	---
21 Aug 1807	Perret Dufour	John F. & Polly(Crutchfield)	Switz83/x	BGAS	107	---
21 Aug 1807	Perret Dufour	John F. & Polly(Crutchfield)	Switz/NC	EIND	D21	1809
00 000 1822	William E.Featherston			NSPC	551	1828
04 Mar 1820	James A. Frost	Simeon & Mary(Beckham)	**92/Va92	HLOW	608	1826
14 Oct 1792	James Land			WHSU	A62	1821
21 Feb 1817	Isaac McCune	James & Kirich(Dean)	Ky/Ky	HLOW	654	---
00 000 1812	William E. Martin	Moses & Sarah(Singleton)		SCWA	739	1833
29 Mar 1805	Joseph R. Morris	Joseph & Sarah(Rodman)	Va/Va	HHEN	628	---
01 Dec 1844	William M. Neal	Moses H.	NC/x	HJOH	643	1854
01 Dec 1811	David D. Nicholdson			BGAS	293	---
01 Dec 1811	D.D. Nicholdson	Benjamin & Jemina(Stars)	Va/x	BMON	467	1812
03 Jan 1819	Dr. John A. Ritter	John & Agnes(Butler)	Ky/Va	HLOW	630	---
00 000 0000	Lewis T. Rogers			GIND	665	---
15 Mar 1815	Benjamin W. Sisson			WHSU	B290	---
27 Aug 1825	Caroline Snider	John		WHSU	B112	---
03 Dec 1827	John C. Snider	John & Elizabeth(Cravens)		HGSU	758	1836
04 Mar 1827	Dr. Robert N. Todd			NSPC	539	---
13 Mar 1814	William S. Todd	David & Sallie D(Smith)	Tn/Tn	HMIA	480	1829
00 000 0000	Lucy True[Wells]			HLOW	664	1829
00 000 0000	David Walter			ASPE	67	1820
18 Jan 1824	Joel O.Walters	Luke & Evarilla(Lamb)	Va/Va	WHSU	B116	1830
27 Apr 1849	John A. Welch	Thomas D. & Elizabeth(Springer)	Ky16/Ky	BVPA	398	---
00 000 0000	Abraham Wells			HLOW	314	1829

BIRTHDATE			SOURCE/PAGE		DATE
00 000 1791	Jacob Wells		JACK	731	1816
00 000 1788	Sarah Wells		JACK	731	1816
08 Jun 1826	David M. Whitmire	John	WHSU	B112	---

J O H N S O N   C O U N T Y

BIRTHDATE	NAME OF BIOGRAPHEES	PARENTS/BIRTHPLACE/BIRTHDATE	SOURCE/PAGE		DATE
00 000 0000	William Fairchild		GIBS	243	1881

K E N T O N   C O U N T Y

BIRTHDATE	NAME OF BIOGRAPHEE	PARENTS/BIRTHPLACE/BIRTHDATE		SOURCE/PAGE		DATE
09 Sep 1830	George B. Colt	John D. & Frances(Mills)	Ct/Mason	HDOH	672	---
00 000 0000	William Colven			ASOH	45	1870
00 000 0000	J.W. Curtis			ADEA	68	1824
14 Dec 1843	John H. Dannettell1			HVAN	199	---
00 000 0000	J.T. Dickson			AGIP	9	1870
11 Mar 1840	Harry Fisk	William B. & Cynthia(Stevens)	Me/Ky	HDOH	711	---
00 000 0000	Fisk Brothers			ADEA	44	1856
00 000 0000	Kate Fledderman[Langfermann]			WFUF	1053	---
25 Dec 1839	Peter Foulks	Redland & Nancy(Ellis)	Ga/NY	HWBJ	555	---
00 000 0000	John D. Frazer			ADEA	68	1822
00 000 0000	W.W. Hill			MHMA	47	1843
06 Feb 1830	William W.Hill	Jordan & Denisa(Hawkins)	Fayette/x	MHMA	110	---
13 Jun 1807	Joel Hume			BGAS	197	---
03 Apr 1824	Robert T. Kercheval	-- & --(Longly)	Va/x	EIND	A28	---
19 Mar 1851	George L. Klein	George J. & Rosina(Dollman)	Oh/Oh	WFUF	743	---
00 000 0000	Gerhard Ludiker			ARIP	49	1852
00 000 1826	James B. Mann			NSPC	323	1836
00 000 0000	Philip Martin			AVAN	64	1866

K E N T O N   C O U N T Y   (C O N T.)

BIRTHDATE	NAME OF BIOGRAPHEE	PARENTS/BIRTHPLACE/BIRTHDATE	SOURCE/PAGE	DATE
02 Jul 1850	Dora V[Monroe]		CSHE 774	---
02 Mar 1801	George Noble	Thomas	NSPC 203	---
00 000 0000	Norval W. Perry		AJEN 47	1871
00 000 0000	H. Reape		ASOH 46	1848
02 Jul 1850	Dora V[Riggs]		CSHE 774	---
00 000 1800	Norval Sparks		HDOH 916	1806
00 000 0000	Simeon Stansifer	John & Sarah(Herod)	EIND 842	---
22 Jan 1826	Col.Simeon Stansifer	John & Sarah(Herod) Va75/Va99	BART 746	1851
15 Nov 1819	Ausburn T. Stephens	James & Sarah(Trail) Va80/Md96	HPOS 574	1855

K N O T T   C O U N T Y   (N O N E)

K N O X   C O U N T Y

BIRTHDATE	NAME OF BIOGRAPHEE	PARENTS/BIRTHPLACE/BIRTHDATE	SOURCE/PAGE	DATE
25 Jan 1824	Ambrose Arthur	Joseph & Mary(McFarland) Tn01/Ky03	HKDA 471	---
11 Sep 1855	Jesse Cope	Andrew J. & Winnie(Lewis) Ky/NC	HPDB 758	1862
00 000 1803	Josiah Shewmaker	Leonard & Unis(Richie)	JACK 641	1814
00 000 1810	Hiram Thomas		HHAN 407	1811

L A R U E   C O U N T Y

BIRTHDATE	NAME OF BIOGRAPHEE	PARENTS/BIRTHPLACE/BIRTHDATE	SOURCE/PAGE	DATE
00 000 1801	George Dunee		BVPA 247	---
07 Mar 1845	Frances M. Matherly	Henry B. & Melvina P(Miller) Va/Ky	BHVI 853	1865
00 000 0000	N.B. Wilson		AGIP 9	1876

L A U R E L   C O U N T Y

BIRTHDATE	NAME OF BIOGRAPHEE	PARENTS/BIRTHPLACE/BIRTHDATE	SOURCE/PAGE		DATE
27 Aug 1820	John Cromer	George & Jane(Walker)	HLOW	886	---
00 000 0000	Ralston Ferguson		HLOW	308	---
14 Apr 1835	Andrew McHargue	James & Phebe	BVPA	390	1851
16 Jan 1823	Dr.Jackson L.Moore	Uriah & Amanda(Sellers)	EIND	B24	1836
02 Feb 1826	J.M. Sellers	Edward & Amelia(Staton)	HLOW	313	1830
29 Mar 1808	Asbury Sims	Starlin	FDAV	514	1820

L A W R E N C E   C O U N T Y   (N O N E)

L E E   C O U N T Y   (N O N E)

L E S L I E   C O U N T Y   (N O N E)

L E T C H E R   C O U N T Y   (N O N E)

L E W I S   C O U N T Y

BIRTHDATE	NAME OF BIOGRAPHEE	PARENTS/BIRTHPLACE/BIRTHDATE	SOURCE/PAGE		DATE
00 000 0000	B.T.W.S. Anderson		ADEA	66	1816
00 000 1837	J.P. Beckett		ASUL	29	1854
05 Oct 1807	Ryland T. Brown		MONT	905	---
05 Oct 1807	Ryland T. Brown		NSPC	418	---
12 Feb 1833	Leander M. Campbell	Lewis & Susan	HHHE	455	1852
11 Mar 1804	Rebecca Cox[Miller]		HMIA	778	---

L E W I S   C O U N T Y   (N O N E)

BIRTHDATE	NAME OF BIOGRAPHEE	PARENTS/BIRTHPLACE/BIRTHDATE	SOURCE/PAGE	DATE
25 May 1816	William K. Davis	Waller & Catherine(Putnam) Va/Va	HJOH 887	----
19 May 1838	Samuel H. Doyal	John W. & Matilda	TBAB 752	1838
19 Dec 1813	Edward B. Hains	Joseph & Elizabeth(Wellingsford)Ky/In	HWSP 501	----
00 000 0000	H.W. Miller		MHMA 47	1848
28 Feb 1818	Jacob Miller	Jacob & Barbara(Fried) Ger/Md	BWER 425	1831
24 Nov 1820	John S. Myers	Henry & Hannah(Salisbury) Pa/Ky	RUSH 441	1831
00 000 0000	Moses Orme		SIND 589	1827
00 000 0000	Nicholas Orme		BJOH 149	1829
00 Dec 1819	Charles Ormes	Moses	NSPC 236	1828
10 Apr 1829	Richard D. Pell	John & Rebecca(Ales) Va/NJ	CLOW 470	1838
20 Apr 1825	William F. Pell	John & Rebecca(Ales) Va/Ky	CLOW 470	1839
15 Jul 1794	Hannah Salisbury[Myers]		HJOH 833	----
15 Jul 1794	Hannah Salisbury[Myers]		HJOH 493	----
00 Nov 1805	George Thomas	Daniel & Mary(McQueen)	RUSH 756	1832
00 000 0000	George Thomas		RUSH 850	1832
25 Jan 1823	James F. Wiley	James & Martha K(Looney) Pa90/**98	HJOH 833	1826

L I N C O L N   C O U N T Y

BIRTHDATE	NAME OF BIOGRAPHEE	PARENTS/BIRTHPLACE/BIRTHDATE	SOURCE/PAGE	DATE
00 000 1815	William Applebay	Philip & Mary(Walker)	HHHE 528	----
00 000 1825	David C. Atherton	John & Susan(Boatman) x/Ky	BWPA 508	1827
20 Jan 1808	William Berry		BGAS 24	----
07 Sep 1804	John W. Blankenship	Noel & Amy	BMON 598	1834
27 Oct 1782	William C. Bramwell		BGAS 35	----
00 000 0000	William S. Bridwell		AGRE 53	1843
15 Jan 1809	Harry Bright	Henry & Elizabeth(Pope)	HLOW 347	1865
00 000 0000	Jesse Corn		HPDB 588	1819

12 Jan 1816	William Crow	Benjamin & Susanna(Sullivan)	Ky90/Tn93	HWBJ	189	1820
00 000 0000	Charles DePauw			BGAS	99	----
11 Mar 1785	John DePauw			BGAS	99	----
20 Mar 1802	John Y. Dodd	John & Nancy(Young)		HGSU	810	1828
00 Aug 1816	John H. Elder	James	Va/x	GBRD	242	----
00 000 0000	Elisha Embree	Joshua		SHGI	472	1811
28 Sep 1801	Elisha Embree			BGAS	118	----
28 Sep 1801	Elisha Embree	Joshua & Elizabeth		EIND	A19	1811
00 000 1811	Jesse Emerson	Reuben & Elizabeth(Logan)	Va/Va90	GIBS	173	----
00 000 0000	Polly Emerson[Harris]			GIBS	243	1811
16 Nov 1794	William Evans	Thomas & Ann(Crow)		SCWA	780	----
31 May 1812	George Fleece			BGAS	128	----
03 Jan 1828	Samuel G. Gash	Thomas & Eliza(Wilson)	Ky/Ky	BMMB	302	----
04 Jul 1829	William H. Hammonds	Joseph & Fannie(Pendlay)	Va/Va	HLOW	319	----
00 000 0000	John Herron			SIND	552	1828
00 000 1800	William Hert	William	Va69/x	MPRO	248	----
15 Oct 1801	William Hixson			BVPA	339	1805
00 000 0000	Jacob Johnson	Luke & Susan(Stines)	Md/x	HLOW	635	----
00 000 0000	Isaac Kelly			SIND	586	1827
14 Feb 1814	Levi D. Laney	James & Elizabeth(Davis)	NC/90	BVPA	318	1830
09 Sep 1858	William S. Leffew	Samuel & Arah Belle		BTWJ	51	----
19 Dec 1831	Marion W. McFerran	Thomas & Lucinda(Hendricks)	Ky/Ky	HSHE	658	1835
00 000 0000	Artemas B. McRoberts			GIBS	237	1848
00 000 0000	J.M. Martin			AGRE	54	1865
20 Dec 1806	George May, Jr.			BGAS	267	----
21 Apr 1805	James G. May	Jacob & Eleanor(McDonald)		SCWA	965	----
21 Apr 1805	Prof. James G. May	Jacob & Eleanor(McDonald)		HLOW	868	----
10 Apr 1808	Samuel May	David	Md/x	SCWA	673	----
18 Jul 1813	David Mull	David & Annie(Stites)	NC/x	CLOW	882	----
01 Jun 1831	John Pendlay	Joshua & Jane A(Darter)	Va/Va	HPDB	769	----
00 000 0000	William Peyton	Martin & Rachael(Arbuckle)	Va/Va	HLOW	596	1816
04 Aug 1813	Lovell H. Rousseau			BGAS	339	----
01 May 1834	Solomon Scott	Elijah & Elizabeth(Duddevar)	**/**	HLOW	598	----

BIRTHDATE	NAME OF BIOGRAPHEE	PARENTS/BIRTHPLACE/BIRTHDATE		SOURCE/PAGE	DATE
07 Jul 1827	Gen.James M.Shackelford			HVAN 376	----
00 000 0000	J.M. Shackelford			AVAN 72	1864
11 Sep 1818	William H.H. Stipe	Henry & Jennie(Adams)	Ky/Ky	HKDA 467	1824
16 Nov 1815	John L. Stone			BGAS 374	1822
00 000 0000	Mary G. Thickstan			AHAR 46	1849
22 Feb 1841	Strother P. Vaughan	Thompson & Elizabeth	Ky/Ky	BPUT 471	1862
10 Jan 1826	Edward Willis	Richard		WHSU B119	1832

L I V I N G S T O N   C O U N T Y

BIRTHDATE	NAME OF BIOGRAPHEE	PARENTS/BIRTHPLACE/BIRTHDATE		SOURCE/PAGE	DATE
09 Nov 1835	John H. Bass	Sion	NC/SC	HALL 133	----
09 Nov 1835	John H. Bass	Sion & Jane(Dodd)	Va/Va	MPRO 242	----
00 000 0000	John H. Bass	Sion & Jane(Todd)	Va02/SC02	DIND 1444	1866
00 000 0000	Thomas Campbell			GCEV B42	----
05 Apr 1804	Samuel W. Dunn	John & Margaret K(Karm)	Va/Ky	CLOW 835	----
30 Jan 1817	Fidelo T. Hodge	Thomas & Harriet(Barnes)	NC/NC	HVAN 451	----
00 000 0000	Comfort S. Knowles[Marvel]			GIBS 235	1813
03 Jul 1810	William Ritchie	Simpson & Mary(Bowling)	NC/Md	HVAN 593	----

L O G A N   C O U N T Y

BIRTHDATE	NAME OF BIOGRAPHEE	PARENTS/BIRTHPLACE/BIRTHDATE	SOURCE/PAGE	DATE
27 Sep 1814	James M. Barnett	John & Sallie(McNeely)	HWSP 441	1816
21 Apr 1849	William M. Blakey	George T. & Sarah E(McLean)	HVAN 380	----
17 Nov 1854	Thomas C. Clark	John A. & Amerial O(Hawkins)Shel/Merc	BVPA 270	12/16

BIRTHDATE	NAME		SOURCE/PAGE		DATE
00 000 0000	J.M. McCormick		AGIP	12	1854
19 Feb 1806	Hon. Finis E. McLean Epraim		EPUT	476	---
10 Mar 1802	Urban Marrs		HPOS	684	1809
10 Mar 1802	Urbin Marrs		BGAS	260	---
00 000 0000	Elizabeth Page[Cunningham]		KTCD	1029	---
00 000 0000	Maria J. Perry[McCormick]		GIBS	241	1854

L Y O N   C O U N T Y   (N O N E)

Mc C R A C K E N   C O U N T Y   (N O N E)

Mc C R E A R Y   C O U N T Y   (N O N E)

Mc L E A N   C O U N T Y

BIRTHDATE	NAME OF BIOGRAPHEE	PARENTS/BIRTHPLACE/BIRTHDATE		SOURCE/PAGE		DATE
00 000 0000	Jane Arpy[Bell]			GIBS	242	1851
00 000 1832	Rev. Byram Condit			GCEW	B407	1848
12 Mar 1836	Judge Azro Dyer	Dillis	Ct/x	HVAN	370	---
03 May 1846	Dr.Edward Linthicum	Rufus & Sarah(Hicks)		HVAN	259	---
03 May 1844	Dr.Porter Linthicum	Rufus & Sarah(Hicks)		DIND	2175	---
28 Feb 1835	Samuel F. McLaughlin	Thomas & Susan(Reaves)		HWSP	548	1845
00 000 0000	B.C. Mosley			ASPE	65	1861
00 000 0000	Benjamin Murgrave			AWAR	57	1832

MADISON COUNTY

BIRTHDATE	NAME OF BIOGRAPHEE	PARENTS/BIRTHPLACE/BIRTHDATE		SOURCE/PAGE		DATE
19 Jan 1827	John W. Barnes	Noah & Mary(Wheeler)	Md/**	HSHE	757	1832
00 000 0000	Julia Barnes[Moberly]			HSHE	595	---
16 Apr 1805	Polly Batterson[Wheeler]			HSHE	779	1827
00 000 0000	Elizabeth Boyd[Martindale]			MPRO	162	---
29 Jun 1794	Samuel K. Boyd	Samuel & Isabel(Higgins)		HWAY	B324	1811
24 Jan 1804	Thomas Burnside	John & Mary(Denton)	Pa/x	BVPA	433	1830
00 000 1801	William Burnside			BVPA	431	1813
27 Jan 1816	Robert Clark	Woodson		KTCD	698	1831
16 Nov 1824	Wesley Cobb			HJOH	748	---
07 May 1817	James E. Dunn	Nathan A.	Boyle90/x	BMON	170	---
00 000 1822	James M. Elder	Alexander		BVPA	406	1825
00 000 1810	Mary A. Evans[Harrison]			HPDB	443	---
02 Apr 1808	David Gentry			HWAY	B335	---
27 Jan 1811	Eli Green	John & Rebecca(Snider)		RUSH	479	1813
00 000 0000	Millicent Griggs[Thompson]			HHHE	760	---
00 000 1807	Otho Harrison			HPDB	443	---
01 Sep 1824	Sarah Holman[Radcliff]	Daniel & Rebecca)	Va/Va	BMMB	360	---
25 Jan 1794	Sophia W. Irvine[Dunn]	Benjamin	Va/x	BMON	170	---
00 000 0000	Charles K. Lendrum			GIBS	239	1880
02 May 1809	William R. McCord			HKDA	368	---
11 Jun 1821	R.C. McWilliams	John C. & Nancy(Hockaday)	Va/x	BVPA	416	1845
19 May 1815	William M. Mason			BGAS	264	---
19 May 1815	William M. Mason	Edwin & Nancy J.		BMMB	766	---
00 000 0000	Thomas Moberly			HSHE	595	---
20 Jan 1821	Thomas Moberly	William & Martha(Robertson)	NC/**	HSHE	774	1825
20 Jan 1821	Thomas Moberly	William & Martha(Robertson)	Ky/Ky	CSHE	350	---
20 Jan 1821	Thomas Moberly	William & Martha(Robertson)	NC/NC	CSHE	682	---
09 May 1847	T.S. Moore	Walker & Sarah(Fitzpatrick)	Ky/Ky	BHVI	868	1852
00 000 0000	William Noland			HHHE	267	1839
00 000 0000	H.C. Owen			AGRE	53	1839
00 000 0000	Henry C. Owen	William & Sally(Crook)		HGSU	410	1819

BIRTHDATE	NAME OF BIOGRAPHEE	PARENTS/BIRTHPLACE/BIRTHDATE		SOURCE/PAGE	DATE
00 000 0000	Edmond Parrish		Scot/x	CSHE 696	----
03 May 1805	Joseph Plough	Henry & Ann(Palsey)	Pa/Va	RUSH 551	1807
13 Nov 1821	John W. Robertson	James & Nancy(Wheeler)	**91/**96	HSHE 532	----
14 Apr 1823	Martin Scott	Elias & Jemima(Green)		CLOW 961	----
17 Apr 1809	Rev.J.C. Smith			NSPC 280	1820
00 000 1817	James H. Swope			HDOH 940	----
15 Sep 1815	William E. Tennant	Richard S. & Elizabeth(Cahill)		BPUT 493	----
00 000 0000	Squire Thompson	Jesse & Mary(Little)		HHHE 760	----
20 May 1826	William S. Turner			BGAS 398	----
10 Jan 1803	Reason Wheeler			HSHE 779	1827
15 Jan 1801	Tilson Wheeler	John & Susanna(Tivis)	Md/Md	HSHE 743	----

M A G O F F I N   C O U N T Y   (N O N E)

M A R I O N   C O U N T Y

BIRTHDATE	NAME OF BIOGRAPHEE	PARENTS/BIRTHPLACE/BIRTHDATE		SOURCE/PAGE	DATE
00 000 1851	Robert Able			ASUL 16	1865
00 000 1821	S.W. Asbury			ASUL 21	1837
30 Sep 1823	Hon. E.H. McBerry	Holesworth & Mary(Stevenson)	**94/**	RUSH 678	----
22 Mar 1846	John T. Clark	Elisha & Emily Jane(Durham)	Ky/Ky	CLOW 525	----
00 000 0000	Lorinda Conwell[Harlan]			TBAB 383	----
00 000 0000	William Cravens			AWAR 58	1847
00 000 0000	G.T. Dearing			AGIP 16	1860
02 Mar 1831	William H. Forsythe	Joseph & Jane(Pierce)		HWSP 501	----
00 000 0000	Austin Harlan			TBAB 383	----
00 000 0000	J.W. Jackson			ASUL 85	1837
13 Oct 1836	James W. Jackson	John T. & Mary L(Pirtle)	Ky10/Ky13	WHSU B323	----
07 Jul 1810	John T. Jackson	John		WHSU B329	1836
08 Feb 1819	George Little	Reynold & Sarah(Prather)	Ger/Md	HWSP 335	----
00 000 0000	John W. Pearce			AWAR 58	1858

BIRTHDATE	NAME OF BIOGRAPHEE	PARENTS/BIRTHPLACE/BIRTHDATE		SOURCE/PAGE		DATE
00 000 1833	G.R. Railey			ASUL	129	1842
28 May 1843	Joseph C. Ridge	Isaac & Margaret H(Nelson)	Md/Ky	HPDB	406	----
00 000 0000	J.T. Scanland			AGIP	16	1858
28 Oct 1848	Clinton K. Tharp	Callen & Bernece(Rowlins)	Ky/Ky	LLDM	B26	----
28 Oct 1848	Clinton K. Tharp			BGAS	387	----
20 Sep 1834	James Woodward	William & Julia(Dyer)	Va/Md	BSCC	B194	1845

M A R S H A L L   C O U N T Y   (N O N E)

M A R T I N   C O U N T Y   (N O N E)

M A S O N   C O U N T Y

BIRTHDATE	NAME OF BIOGRAPHEE	PARENTS/BIRTHPLACE/BIRTHDATE		SOURCE/PAGE		DATE
26 Dec 1790	Archibald Alexander			BGAS	4	----
08 Nov 1818	Sarah A.Applegate[McNary]	Peter W. & Ellen(Tenness)		BPUT	408	c1830
00 000 0000	James W. Barclay			AJEN	48	1876
15 Apr 1834	James W. Barclay			WHSU	B110	----
18 Nov 1818	William M. Bell	--- & Mary(Early)		BVER	500	----
00 000 0000	Reason Bicks			BPUT	475	1833
00 000 1859	F.J. Bolinger			ASUL	32	1865
09 Jul 1854	James S. Bolinger	William H. & Victoria(Close)	**21/x	WHSU	B85	1865
24 Jul 1821	William H. Bolinger	William H. & Susan	Ger/Ger	WHSU	B85	1865
21 Jul 1821	William H. Bolinger	Henry & Susan	Pa/Pa	HGSU	717	1865
09 Sep 1849	C.B. Bollinger	W.H. & Victory(Close)	**21/Fr	HGSU	765	1864
17 Jan 1825	Thomas Branigin	John & Lucy F(Branch)	Va/Va	HJOH	591	1833

Date	Name	Parents/Spouse	Origin	Code	Page	Year
00 000 1810	John Brayfield	John		BHCL	804	---
00 000 1828	James T. Brewer	George & Ann(Carrico)		HKDA	811	---
15 Aug 1805	William J. Brown			NSPC	394	---
15 Aug 1805	William J. Brown			BGAS	42	---
11 Dec 1823	Isaac Browning	Edmund & Hannah	Va/NJ	BPUT	344	1836
00 000 1795	Dr. William Bunel			HWAY	B382	---
22 Mar 1837	James W. Burgess	Mordecai & Sally(Ryan)	Md/Md	BJAY	587	---
01 Dec 1800	John L. Burgess			BGAS	46	---
12 Feb 1833	Leander M. Campbell			BGAS	53	1820
00 000 0000	John Collins			SIND	547	---
00 000 0000	Zachariah Collins			SIND	628	1821
15 Nov 1820	John Conway	Miles & Catherine(McShirley)	Ky/Ky	HHEN	723	---
04 Apr 1810	Rev.W.H. Cornelius			WHSU	B205	---
04 Jul 1819	Elisha P. Cowgill	Elisha & Ann S(Tarvin)	Va/Va	BPUT	328	---
25 Dec 1818	Joseph Cox	Joseph		HCAR	250	---
08 Jun 1806	Jacob Crosby	William & Catherine		BPUT	363	1834
22 Oct 1819	John H. Culbertson	Robert & Nancy(Hunter)	Ky/Ky	RUSH	688	1851
18 Dec 1818	Margaret Davidson[Wisehart]			FMWA	B476	1826
18 Dec 1818	Margaret Davidson[Wisehart]			HHHE	743	1826
12 Jan 1817	David J. Davis			BGAS	93	---
18 Sep 1820	Enoch Dicks	John & Mary	Ky/Ky	BPUT	518	1835
04 Jul 1823	Rebecca Dicks[Wysong]	John & Mary(Patterson)		BPUT	390	---
31 Jul 1818	James Duzan	William	**/x	BVER	452	1835
15 Oct 1849	Charity Dye			DIND	1694	---
00 000 0000	C.V. Efner			ASOH	45	1852
07 Apr 1803	George W. Finch			BGAS	126	---
18 Dec 1807	Hon. James B. Foley	--- & Mary(Bradford)		GBRD	239	---
18 Dec 1807	Hon. James B. Foley	--- & Mary(Bradford)		EIND	D23	---
21 Jun 1830	John J. Foley	James B. & Martha(Carter)	**07/x	GBRD	241	---
04 Oct 1824	Ephraim S. Frazee			BGAS	134	---
04 Oct 1824	Ephraim S. Frazee	Ephraim & Susan(Doniphan)	92/x	RUSH	430	---
00 000 0000	William D. Frazee			BJAY	207	1847
25 Aug 1812	John T. Fyffe			BPUT	436	---
27 Oct 1814	Thomas Fyffe	Jonathan	Md/x	BPUT	353	1836

BIRTHDATE	NAME OF BIOGRAPHEE	PARENTS/BIRTHPLACE/BIRTHDATE		SOURCE/PAGE	DATE
16 Feb 1822	Lemira Gifford	Elisha & Nancy		BPUT 407	1829
23 Apr 1814	William H. Gifford			BGAS 141	---
23 Apr 1814	Dr.William H.Gifford	Elisha & Ann(Tennis)	NJ/Pa	CLOW 353	---
04 Mar 1809	George S. Green			BGAS 151	---
04 Mar 1809	Judge George S.Green			HPOS 495	c1837
00 000 1801	Henry C. Guffin			NSFC 393	1822
21 Feb 1834	John F. Gulick	John H. & Sarah(Crockrell)	Pa/Va	BHVI 774	1852
00 000 0000	Bowen Hale	John	Md/x	MPRO 404	---
26 Oct 1803	Ambrose D.Hamrick			BGAS 162	---
00 000 0000	James Havens			RUSH 705	---
27 Nov 1803	Jefferson Helm			BGAS 176	---
00 000 0000	Sarah Hill			DGIN 647	---
00 000 0000	Nancy Holton[Robinson]			HSHE 645	1832
24 Nov 1835	Francis T. Hord			BGAS 190	---
00 000 0000	Francis T. Hord			EIND E18	---
24 Nov 1835	Judge Francis T. Hord	Francis T. & Elizabeth S(Moss)		MPRO 364	---
24 Nov 1835	Hon. Francis T. Hord	Francis T. & Elizabeth S(Moss)	Va/Va	BART 699	---
00 000 0000	Francis T. Hord	Elias	Va/x	TBAB 744	---
24 Nov 1835	Francis T. Hord	Francis T.		TBAB 637	1857
20 Oct 1840	Kendall M. Hord	Francis T. & Elizabeth S(Moss)	**/Va	TBAB 744	1863
20 Oct 1840	Kendall M. Hord	Francis T. & Elizabeth S(Moss)	**/Va	HSHE 494	---
20 Oct 1840	Judge Kendall M.Hord	Francis T. & Elizabeth S(Moss)	Va/Va	CSHE 341	---
00 000 0000	Oscar B. Hord			SIND 214F	1849
31 Aug 1829	Oscar B. Hord	Francis T.		TBAB 238	1849
09 Mar 1807	Aaron Houghton	William & Celia A(McKay)		LLDM B49	1819
00 000 1809	William H. Houghton	William & Celia A(McKay)		LLDM B53	1819
00 000 1801	John Howard			EBOO 304	1837
00 000 0000	Clarissa Hubanks[Zink]			WHSU B193	---
00 000 1810	Theodore Hudnut			BHVI 798	---
15 Jul 1810	Theodore Hudnut	Joseph & Catherine(Dalton)	Ky/Va	HPOS 499	---
15 Jul 1810	Theodore Hudnut	Joseph & Catherine(Dalton)		EIND H56	---

Date	Name	Parents	Place	Code	No.	Year
04 Oct 1809	Elisha Hyatt	Thomas & Margaret		HKDA	774	--
00 000 1809	Elisha Hyatt	Thomas & Margaret(McTerren)	Pa/x	EIND	B18	--
04 Sep 1814	John Hyatt			BGAS	201	--
04 Sep 1814	Hon. John Hyatt	Thomas & Margaret(McPharson)	Md/Pa	HKDA	775	--
12 Mar 1807	Leander Jacobs	Samuel & Mary		HCLI	913	--
19 Jul 1819	Stanfield P. James	Thomas & Harriet	Ky/Ky	BPUT	407	1822
10 Jun 1812	Harrison Jones	William & Lucy(Thompson)	Ky/Ky	HDEK	575	--
29 May 1832	Col. John A. Keith	Isham & Diadema(Frazee)		EIND	B20	--
30 Nov 1837	SquireI. Keith	Isham & Diadema(Frazee)		EIND	E21	1842
00 000 0000	Francis M. Knetzer	Charles & Catherine	Md/Ky	BPUT	505	--
08 Jul 1824	William Knowles			BGAS	225	--
04 Sep 1850	John H. Lamar	William W. & Elizabeth(Blake)		EIND	D41	--
07 Apr 1821	James Leachman	William & Mary(Reeves)	Va/Ky	BPUT	408	1830
00 000 1809	John Lee	Gashum	NJ/x	FDAV	554	--
19 Dec 1796	Abner H. Longley			BGAS	240	--
00 000 0000	Nancy[Lytle]			HHEN	501	--
26 Oct 1810	John McCord			BGAS	247	--
00 000 1811	Anna McCoy[Lee]			FDAV	554	--
00 000 0000	Mary McCullin[Brookie]David & Elizabeth			HCLI	634	--
00 000 1844	William McDaniel			ASUL	105	--
04 May 1814	John W. McNary	John & Sarah	Va/Pa	BPUT	407	1826
20 Dec 1830	James Mahan	Jerry & Jemina(Browning)	Ky/Ky	WHSU	B293	--
00 000 0000	John Mahin			HHEN	501	1828
00 000 1889	Frank R.Manning	B.P. & Lettie(Horton)		DIND	1689	1903
31 Apr 1823	Milton Marmaduke		Va/Ky	HKDA	788	1824
18 May 1807	Jesse Marvin			BGAS	264	--
00 000 0000	James Mattingly			LLDW	B17	--
00 000 0000	James Mattingly			FDAV	317	--
27 Feb 1813	William Merrett	Reuben & Sarah(Helm)		WFUF	625	1837
11 Jun 1809	Hamilton Miller	James & Nancy(Robinson)	Pa70/**	RUSH	439	1835
20 Sep 1794	Jesse Morgan			BGAS	282	--
17 Dec 1846	W.T. Murray	Jeremiah & Malinda(Steele)	Ire/x	WFUF	767	1804
00 000 0000	Thomas H. Nelson	Dr. Thomas W. & Frances(Doniphan)		BHVI	877	--
00 Apr 1828	William W. Owens			BGAS	303	--

BIRTHDATE	NAME OF BIOGRAPHEE	PARENTS/BIRTHPLACE/BIRTHDATE	SOURCE/PAGE	DATE
26 Mar 1853	Evan L. Patterson		BGAS 308	---
17 Oct 1832	John R. Peed	William & Elizabeth Ky/Ky	HHEN 518	1857
00 000 1825	James F. Peyton	Anthony & Margaret(Wellington) Va/Ky	BVPA 430	1827
00 000 0000	James Reed		ASOH 45	1845
24 Feb 1821	George W. Reeve	Elder Benjamin F. Va98/x	RUSH 443	1833
20 Feb 1802	John Reeves	James & Sarah(Holton) Ire/Md	BMMB 333	---
00 000 0000	Barney Relley	James Scothland/x	LLDM B55	1818
17 May 1795	John Relley		BGAS 326	---
00 000 0000	Osman Robinson		HSHE 645	1832
00 000 0000	Judson Ross		BPUT 446	---
02 Apr 1820	John E. Rumsey	Charles	BGAS 341	---
02 Apr 1820	John E. Rumsey	David L.	BHCT T256	1833
31 Jul 1802	Daniel Runyon	NJ/x	BVER 350	---
10 Sep 1848	John W. Russell	Jonathan & Sarah(Hite) Va18/Va16	HJOH 907	1856
11 Feb 1829	Tabitha Sanford[Small]	Hamilton & Tabitha Ann(Clark) Ky/Ky	FDAV 575	---
20 Nov 1823	John F. Shelton	John Va97/Ky98	HFOS 612	1824
00 000 1832	Robert C. Shofstall		ASUL 137	1865
04 Oct 1801	Daniel R. Smith	Hezekiah & Mary Ann	SIND 626	---
28 Oct 1800	Matthew R. Southard		BGAS 366	---
29 Jun 1806	David W. Stark	David W. & Martha(Rogers)	BVPA 116	---
01 Jan 1814	Asbery E. Steele		BGAS 370	---
01 Jan 1814	Col. Asbury Steele	Joseph & Susannah(Fields)	EIND K47	---
03 Dec 1829	James Stewart	William Pa71/71	KTCD 1065	---
30 Jun 1817	Jonah Sullivan	Lewis & Elizabeth(Bennett) Ky/Ky	HMIA 810	---
00 000 1822	Dr. W.H. Sullivan	Austin & Catherine(Hiles) **71/**	HDOH 924	---
24 Mar 1822	Dr. Robert H. Tarleton		BMMB 209	---
01 Feb 1805	John G. Tennant	Richard S. & Elizabeth(Cahill)NJ65/NJ	BPUT 410	65/79
06 Nov 1837	George H. Thompson		BGAS 389	1840
00 000 1802	Brazzle Tracy	John & Nancy	BMON 593	1826
00 000 0000	Lydia Ann Voriss[Vall]		BJAY 456	---

BIRTHDATE	NAME OF BIOGRAPHEE	PARENTS/BIRTHPLACE/BIRTHDATE		SOURCE/PAGE		DATE
09 Jul 1813	Zachariah Walker			BGAS	405	----
21 Jan 1840	Abraham Weaver	Jacob & Charlotta(Kinneman)	Pa/Pa	FDAV	675	----
00 000 1804	Robert Wells			SIND	546	1827
13 Oct 1799	John Wilkes	John		HJOH	916	1830
08 Feb 1810	Watson Williams		Ky/x	HKDA	806	----
00 000 0000	Benjamin Wilson			ADEA	72	1805
00 000 0000	William T. Wilson			HSHE	548	1829
15 Feb 1790	James S. Wood			BGAS	426	1818
00 000 1815	John M. Wood	John	Ky/x	DGIN	813	1832
25 May 1815	John M. Wood			NSPC	303	1834
00 000 0000	Seralda J.Youngman[Adams]	Jesse & Amy(Dix)	Va/Pa	BPUT	387	1832

M E A D E   C O U N T Y

BIRTHDATE	NAME OF BIOGRAPHEE	PARENTS/BIRTHPLACE/BIRTHDATE		SOURCE/PAGE		DATE
00 000 0000	J.D. Armstrong			ASPE	67	1857
27 Feb 1837	Joseph D. Armstrong			ASPE	22	----
27 Feb 1837	Joseph D. Armstrong			HWSP	437	----
27 Feb 1837	Joseph D. Armstrong	James F. & Frances(Brown)Fay/Bullitt		EIND	A1	----
00 000 0000	E.B. Berry			AHAR	46	1857
00 000 0000	Philip Brandenburg	Jonathan	Va/x	BSCC	B130	1816
00 000 0000	Lydia Charley[Brandenburg]	George	Va/x	BSCC	B130	1811
00 000 0000	C.P. Dalton			AHAR	45	1873
00 000 0000	C.M. Dawson			AHAR	45	1837
24 Jan 1831	Joel E. Drake	Greenberry & Nancy(Lane)	Va/Va	CLOW	399	----
00 000 0000	S.B. Hatfield			FWAR	176	1876
30 Jan 1842	Sidney B. Hatfield	William & Jane(Debolt)	Oh/Oh	HWSP	155	----
00 000 0000	Mary K. Hill			ASPE	65	1852
17 Feb 1828	John S. Huffman	Adam S. & Rebecca(Stoptaugh)		HWSP	546	----
00 000 0000	John E. Jenkins			GIBS	233	----
05 Mar 1841	Jesse W. Kincheloe	Allen L. & Susan(Marlay)		HWSP	468	----
23 Feb 1837	F.C. Lutes	Wilson B.	Bullitt/x	LLDM	B15	----

M E A D E   C O U N T Y   (C O N T.)

BIRTHDATE	NAME OF BIOGRAPHEE	PARENTS/BIRTHPLACE/BIRTHDATE	SOURCE/PAGE		DATE
14 Apr 1827	George M. McCarty	William T. & Sophia(Bentley) Ky/Pa	BSCC	B173	----
00 000 0000	Alexander Maddux		AVAN	72	1850
07 May 1820	Alexander Maddux	Thomas W/x	HVAN	636	1834
11 Aug 1833	Michael Mogan		HWSP	819	----
00 000 0000	D.A. Mounts		AHAR	47	1864
07 Dec 1851	Dr. Henry H. Selser	Harvey G. & Mary(Popham) Ky/Ky	BSCC	B62	----
00 000 1800	Merise Shelby[Cobb]		HKDA	326	----
00 000 0000	Col. Samuel Smith		AHAR	47	1865
10 Apr 1807	Enoch S. Taber		BGAS	382	1849
16 Jan 1840	Thomas H. Woolfolk	John F. & Mahala(Harris)	HWSP	512	----

M E N I F E E   C O U N T Y   (N O N E)

M E R C E R   C O U N T Y

BIRTHDATE	NAME OF BIOGRAPHEE	PARENTS/BIRTHPLACE/BIRTHDATE	SOURCE/PAGE		DATE
00 000 0000	John M. Agan		ASPE	66	1848
15 Sep 1837	Henry Alfrey	Ky/Ky	MONT	869	----
15 Sep 1837	Henry Alfrey	Moses & Anna(Baunty) KyOl/Ky	MONT	602	----
07 Feb 1819	Abner W. Allen	Eli & Elizabeth(McDonald)	HLOW	647	1819
25 Dec 1825	George W. Allison		BGAS	5	----
00 000 0000	Andrew Anderson		HPDB	449	1816
00 000 0000	Mary[Anderson]		HPDB	449	----
07 Jun 1822	Edward Barnes	William	BVPA	410	1828
01 Jan 1821	George M. Bishop	Valentine & Mary E(Horine)	HJOH	400	----
27 Apr 1804	Thomas Bonnell	Va/Va	BART	770	1820
26 May 1822	John Brazalton	Jonathan & Rebecca(Dean)	BGAS	36	----

	Name	Parents	Codes	Loc	No.	Year
18 Jun 1814	Daniel Brewer	Daniel & Theodocia(Derland)		HJOH	770	1833
00 000 0000	Daniel Brewer	Daniel & Theodocia(Derland)		HJOH	592	---
00 000 1825	Henry Brewer			SIND	588	---
00 000 1796	John Brewer			WHSU	B203	1807
08 Jan 1820	John C.Brewer	Abram	90/x	WHSU	B98	---
20 May 1807	John C.Brewer	Daniel & Theodocia(Derland)	NJ70/**	HJOH	771	1831
19 Apr 1819	Mary A.Brewer[Banta]			HJOH	587	1814
00 000 1795	James T. Brown			HDOH	153	1821
25 Nov 1813	Alexander Buchanan			BVPA	405	---
00 000 1818	Henry H. Bunten	William & Leanna(Wilson)		HHHE	274	---
10 Sep 1798	W.D. Burford			BVPA	406	1827
00 000 0000	George Byers			AGIP	12	1823
12 Apr 1819	Abraham Canary	Michael & Elizabeth(Gashwooller)Ky/Ky		BWMB	785	---
07 May 1792	Christian Canary			WHSU	A42	---
29 Apr 1836	Margaret Canary	Henry & Elizabeth(Terhune)		HJOH	882	1844
09 Apr 1812	Jacob D. Cassatt			BGAS	58	---
04 Jan 1845	Matthew Colvin	Elisha & Margaret(Curry)	Ky/Ky	BHCL	630	---
29 Mar 1825	Ann Comingore[Brewer]Henry R. & Elizabeth(Smock)		**/**	HJOH	774	---
29 Mar 1825	Ann Comingore[Brooks]Henry R. & Elizabeth(Smock)		**/**	HJOH	774	---
22 May 1813	Henry Comingore			HLOW	583	1825
03 Sep 1805	William Conner			HHSJ	997	---
04 Dec 1821	Joseph V. Covert	Daniel & Rachel(Voorhies)	**99/**97	HJOH	601	---
08 Apr 1810	William V. Covert	John	82/x	HJOH	875	---
00 000 0000	Martin Crow			DTCE	525	---
29 Mar 1825	Anna Cummingoer[Brewer]			WHSU	B98	---
00 000 1812	Elizabeth Cunningham[Rynerson]		Ky/Ky	HHHE	450	---
12 Jan 1814	Bedial J. Davis[Harris]			HHHE	747	1833
21 May 1844	Dr. John E. Davis	Achilles E. & Melinda(Moore)	**/**	GPLA	642	---
09 Dec 1829	Thomas F. Davis	Thomas S. & Martha(Robinson)	Ky/Ky	HWSP	142	---
00 000 0000	W.R. Davis			AWAR	57	1839
09 Sep 1827	William R. Davis	Rev. Thomas S. & ---(Robinson)		FWAR	156	---
17 Oct 1803	John Day	Edmond & Nancy		BART	881	1820
00 000 0000	Elias Dayhoff			AGRE	54	1824

BIRTHDATE	NAME OF BIOGRAPHEE	PARENTS/BIRTHPLACE/BIRTHDATE		SOURCE/PAGE		DATE
27 Nov 1813	Abraham Debaun	Samuel & Mary(Devine)	Va76/x	WHSU	B18	1831
25 Nov 1821	John Debaun			BVPA	471	1830
14 Jan 1820	Samuel Debaun	Joseph		WHSU	B81	---
00 000 1798	John Delard	Etienne	SC67/x	HKDA	310	---
29 Mar 1812	George W. Demaree			HJOH	876	---
17 Mar 1798	James Denny			BGAS	99	---
00 000 0000	James H. Denny			DGIN	675	1850
00 000 1802	James H. Denny	John	Va/x	TBAB	309	---
00 000 1813	Harrison Durham	Jesse B.		JACK	647	---
25 Nov 1820	Jesse Y. Durham			BGAS	111	---
16 Dec 1805	Miranda Durham[Tucker]	Thomas & Frances(Moss)	Va/Md	HHHE	657	---
04 Mar 1820	G.D. Eccles	Samuel	Va/x	HJOH	606	---
08 Mar 1820	Garrard D. Eccles	Samuel & Jane(Darland)	W88/Pa85	HJOH	789	1835
28 May 1846	George W. Epperson	Samuel P. & Eliza J(Bregle)	Ky/Ky	BHOT	T384	1850
14 Mar 1815	Samuel P. Epperson	David & Anna(Cox)		BHOT	T384	---
07 Dec 1810	Julia Ann Franklin[Boles]			WHSU	B365	1830
00 000 1801	Eleanor Frary[Jones]			HJOH	622	---
14 Jul 1829	Dr. J.S. French	Simon & Mary(Smock)	NJ00/05	EMON	258	---
19 Oct 1801	D.W. Galey	Benjamin & Elizabeth(Woods)	SC/x	EMON	347	---
27 May 1809	Squire John C.Gilkeson	Thomas & Nancy(Buchanan)	Va/Va	BVPA	233	1821
00 000 1808	Lloyd Glazebrook			BGAS	143	---
00 000 1808	Hon. Lloyd Glazebrook Clifford			EPUT	443	---
04 Feb 1827	Abraham Godfrey	William & Rosa(Ray)	Va/Ky	CLOW	401	---
11 Oct 1814	David W. Haines	Wesley & Adaline		EPUT	368	1821
00 000 0000	John Hamner	John & Mary(Neubary)	Va/Va	HJOH	419	1823
00 000 0000	Martha W. Hanna[Glenn]			EMON	356	1827
29 Sep 1810	Nicodemis Harris			HHHE	747	1833
00 000 0000	William Hart			FWAR	123	---
00 000 0000	William Hart			HWSP	158	---

Date	Name	Parents/Spouse	Origin	Code	No.	Year
00 000 0000	Dr. Andrew Hay			EIND	C23	1815
01 Dec 1790	Andrew P. Hay			BGAS	173	----
28 Aug 1833	Daniel J. Hayden	John W. & Mary A(Carey)	KyOl/Ky04	HGSU	801	1860
00 000 0000	Malinda W. Hayden[Woner]			WHSU	B239	----
09 May 1827	James Hendrickson	James & Elizabeth(Nayles)	Va/NC	HSHE	728	1827
00 000 0000	Jesse J. Hungate			AWAS	49	1819
27 Jun 1819	William H. Jennings			BGAS	205	----
27 Jun 1819	William H. Jennings	William & Mary		HJOH	618	----
14 Dec 1819	Grafton Johnson	James & Mary(Taylor)	NC/Va	HJOH	794	----
00 000 1818	Mary J. Johnson[Waldren]			HJOH	670	----
20 Jan 1836	Mary Jane Kallams[Husk]			FWAR	143	----
26 Mar 1826	John Hungate			BGAS	198	----
00 000 1799	William M. Kenton			BGAS	219	----
00 000 0000	Ann Lagrange[Voorhies]			HJOH	667	----
09 Feb 1826	Daniel C. Lagrange	Peter & Lemima(Covert)	NJ/NJ	HJOH	627	1826
00 000 1802	Peter D. Lagrange		Va/x	HJOH	627	1826
00 000 1797	Elizabeth Luyster[Hamilton]			HJOH	877	1834
16 Aug 1813	Harvey S. Lyons	Robert & Jane(Vanarsdall)	Va/**92	HJOH	903	----
29 Oct 1818	John M. Lyons	Robert & Jane(Vanarsdall)	Va/**92	HJOH	903	----
23 Jan 1801	Alexander McCaslin			HJOH	633	----
00 000 1797	David McCaslin			HJOH	635	1827
01 Nov 1819	James McDonald	Daniel & Catherine(Vannest)	Va/Ky	HLOW	620	----
00 000 1802	William J. McIntosh			BEGR	88	1822
00 000 0000	James B. Mann	Josiah T.	Va/x	WHSU	B243	1819
05 Oct 1816	James B. Mann	Josiah & Elizabeth(Schooling)		HGSU	803	1819
29 Jan 1816	Dr. George Manners	James & Letice(Hight)	Ky/Ky	BMON	498	----
00 000 1849	Jonathan Milburn			ASUL	108	----
06 Oct 1828	Ezra A. Olleman			BGAS	298	----
06 Oct 1828	Ezra A. Olleman	James & Mary(Tsinger)	Va/NC	BMMB	355	----
00 000 0000	Mary R. Parish[Courtney] Charles J. & Elizabeth Ann(Seths)			CSHE	621	1855
13 Apr 1848	Sarah Poulter[Haymaker] William R. & Louisa Ann(McRae)			HJOH	614	----
24 Dec 1832	Jackson Powell	John & Mary(Thompson)	Va/Ky	HJOH	651	1857
07 Dec 1841	John Powell	John & Mary(Thompson)		HJOH	651	----
10 Mar 1819	Reuben S. Ragan			BGAS	321	----

BIRTHPLACE	NAME OF BIOGRAPHEE	PARENTS/BIRTHPLACE/BIRTHDATE	SOURCE/PAGE	DATE
00 000 1806	Patsy M. Ransdell[Lagrange] Wherton		HJOH 627	----
00 000 1801	Lewis A. Rose	Charles & Mary(Reese) 78/79	HHHE 294	1827
11 Oct 1836	James G. Ryan	Patrick D. & Permelia A(Grayham)Va/Ky	BMMB 316	----
04 Oct 1814	Isaac N. Rynerson		BGAS 342	----
00 000 1795	John Rynerson		HHHE 450	----
07 May 1817	John Rynerson	Isaac Ky87/Ky97	BVPA 497	1824
00 000 0000	Samuel D. Sandefur		HSHE 662	1823
13 Feb 1796	William R. Sanford		EBOO 359	----
00 000 0000	Elizabeth Shipp[Sandefur]		HSHE 622	1823
00 000 0000	Elizabeth Smock[Comingore] Jacob & Ann(Banta) Pa/**		HJOH 774	----
08 Mar 1797	Jacob Smock		SIND 590	1823
00 000 0000	John B. Smock		BJOH 152	1823
08 Oct 1792	Simon Smock		SIND 584	----
31 Dec 1808	Thomas C. Smock		SIND 584	1825
03 Nov 1811	Jeremiah S. Tanner		BGAS 383	----
03 Feb 1821	James Terhune	Garret & Nancy(Davis)	HJOH 661	----
22 Apr 1817	Isaac Smock		DGIN 779	----
00 000 0000	Isaac Smock		BJOH 152	1823
08 Mar 1797	Jacob Smock		6IND 588	----
25 Sep 1797	Benjamin Thornburg		BMMB 211	----
25 Sep 1797	Benjamin Thornburg		BMMB 242	1808
03 Oct 1823	Cornelius Vanarsdall Simon & Catherine(Whitenack)		HJOH 823	----
17 Aug 1792	Jane Vanarsdall[Lyons]		HJOH 902	1825
10 Mar 1848	John W. Vanarsdall	John & Catherine **/**	HSHE 628	----
22 Dec 1799	Simon Vanarsdall	Cornelius A.B. & Mary(Brewer) **/**	HJOH 823	1827
00 000 0000	Elizabeth Vandiver[Byers]		HJOH 597	----
13 Feb 1823	James H. Vandiver	Peter & Sarah(Garshwiler) NJ87/Ky88	HJOH 881	1826
00 000 0000	Susan Vanmuys[List]		HJOH 629	1838
00 000 1813	Thomas J. Vanosdol	Jacob	BSCC B298	1818
05 Apr 1800	Samuel A. Verbrike		BGAS 403	1831

BIRTHDATE	NAME OF BIOGRAPHEE	PARENTS/BIRTHPLACE/BIRTHDATE		SOURCE	PAGE	DATE
09 Sep 1823	George Vermilion	Cornelius & Elizabeth(Sanford)	Va/Va	BHVI	975	----
07 Jun 1822	--- Vermillion	Cornelius & Elizabeth(Sanford)	Va/Ky	BVPA	448	1825
23 Sep 1827	Thomas S. Vermillion	Joel & Martha(Shaw)		BPUT	384	----
00 000 1798	Stephen Voohres			EIND	H50	----
00 000 1798	Stephen Voorhees	Peter & ---(Vanarsdale)	NJ/x	BHVI	979	----
00 000 0000	Andrew C. Voorhies			HJOH	667	----
10 Aug 1801	Isaac B. Vorhies	Jacob & Margaret		HJOH	825	1827
27 Sep 1829	Harrison R. Voris	Isaac & Jane(Vaharsdale)	04/Ky07	HJOH	668	1829
00 000 0000	David Westerfield	James	NJ/x	HHHE	679	----
27 Sep 1847	Melinda M. White[Hubbard]	Burr & Lucinda(Salter)	Ky/Ky	BPUT	436	1851
08 Feb 1806	Peter Whitenack	John & Ann(Debon)	NJ/NJ	HJOH	831	----
28 Sep 1801	Rachel B. Whitenack[Vorhies]	Abram & Ann		HJOH	825	1827
18 Jan 1782	Walter Wilson			BGAS	423	c1787
18 Jan 1782	Gen. Walter Wilson			EIND	J46	----
00 000 0000	G.W. Wolfe			AHAR	47	1819

M E T C A L F E   C O U N T Y

BIRTHDATE	NAME OF BIOGRAPHEE	PARENTS/BIRTHPLACE/BIRTHDATE		SOURCE	PAGE	DATE
07 Aug 1843	David T. Evans	Robert & Lucy(Button)		BWMB	353	1861
00 000 0000	B.T. Pace			AWAS	49	1866
00 000 0000	Isaac B. Vorhies			BJOH	150	1828
00 000 0000	J.W. Wisdom			FWAR	179	1877

M O N R O E   C O U N T Y

BIRTHDATE	NAME OF BIOGRAPHEE	PARENTS/BIRTHPLACE/BIRTHDATE		SOURCE	PAGE	DATE
00 000 0000	J.A. Conlee			AHAR	45	1828
00 000 0000	Louise Curtis[Evans]			HPDB	419	----
08 Aug 1816	Henry Dickerson	John R. & Mary(Grider)	Md/Md	BPUT	332	----

BIRTHDATE	NAME OF BIOGRAPHEE	PARENTS/BIRTHPLACE/BIRTHDATE	SOURCE/PAGE	DATE
08 Jan 1829	Andrew J. Harland	Joel W. & Mary(Mulkey) 94/**	HCLI 835	---
00 000 1830	Nancy[Miller]		ASUL 108	---
00 000 1798	Polly Mulkey[Harland]		HCLI 563	---
00 000 0000	William B. Nichols		ASPE 65	1878
27 Dec 1810	Thomas H. Wiley	John & Mary(Sims)	HSTJ 748	---

BIRTHDATE	NAME OF BIOGRAPHEE	PARENTS/BIRTHPLACE/BIRTHDATE	SOURCE/PAGE	DATE
10 Mar 1841	George T. Allen	James **/x	BPUT 366	---
00 000 0000	James I. Allen		BPUT 374	1829
00 000 0000	Zeralda Allen[Fyffe]	Robert	BPUT 353	---
09 Dec 1816	Dulcena Badger	David & Elizabeth(Miller) Pa/Va	BPUT 369	---
09 Jan 1819	Elder Oliver P. Badger	David & Elizabeth(Miller) Pa/Va	BPUT 504	1833
06 Mar 1847	George M. Black	Miller & Margaret(Whittsitt)**00/**12	BPUT 507	1852
28 Sep 1833	William Bridges	Charles C. & Rachel(Lockridge)	BPUT 393	---
22 Feb 1844	Lucy W. Chism[Shoptaugh]	Samuel & Sarah	BPUT 521	1852
08 Jun 1812	Thomas Cole	Robert & Martha(Ward) Va/Va	BHOT T337	1827
10 May 1818	Samuel Colliver		BGAS 73	---
07 Nov 1821	John G. Crain		BGAS 83	---
00 000 0000	Johnson Darnell		BPUT 358	1833
00 000 0000	Salinda Darnell[Ferguson]		HHHE 451	---
09 Dec 1804	Samuel Darnell	Daniel & Nancy(Turpin) Md/Md	BPUT 325	---
11 Mar 1830	Catherine Davis[Tucker]	Nathan & Nancy(Kidd) Ky/Ky	HH4E 657	1835
00 000 0000	James Davis	Matthias & ---(McClellan)	GBRO 425	---
00 000 0000	Jesse Davis	Enoch & Nancy(Hart)	HHHE 783	---
30 Nov 1817	John Davis		BGAS 94	---
12 Dec 1822	Walter Davis	Nathan & Nancy(Kidd) Ky/Ky	HHHE 260	1834

BIRTHDATE	NAME OF BIOGRAPHEE	PARENTS/BIRTHPLACE/BIRTHDATE	SOURCE/PAGE	DATE
00 000 0000	Dillard C. Donnohue		BPUT	1840
06 Jan 1803	Francis Dunlavy	Daniel & Martha(Yocom) 65/83	HJOH	1825
15 Jul 1804	John Y. Dunlavy	Daniel & Martha(Yocum) Pa/Ky	HLOW	1826
11 Aug 1819	David P. Farrow	Alexander S. & Elizabeth(Nelson)Ky/Ky	BPUT	---
25 Oct 1815	Henry H. Gooder	John H. & Mary Va/Va	MONT	1237
01 May 1822	Thomas M. Hamilton		BGAS	162
11 Sep 1826	Jack R.M. Hamrick	Thomas	BPUT	514	1836
00 000 1809	Silas Hardwick	Charles & Elizabeth(Crook)	HHHE	669	1832
07 Oct 1817	Emily Hensley[Gardner]	John W. & Mary A(Hall)	BPUT	509	1829
00 000 1816	Johnson Hunt		HHHE	782	---
24 Feb 1811	Henry S. Lane		EIND	H30	---
24 Feb 1811	Henry S. Lane		BGAS	228	---
24 Feb 1811	Hon. Henry S.Lane		MONT	577	---
09 Jul 1812	Higgins Lane		BGAS	228	---
00 000 0000	Higgins Lane		BPUT	365	1844
00 000 1818	R.H. Lane	Robert G. & Elizabeth(Hackley) Va/Ky	EWON	455	1842
30 Mar 1814	Andrew M. Lockridge	Robert & Elizabeth(Malone) Va84/NC86	EIND	E23	---
03 Jun 1825	Dulcenia Lockridge	Robert & Elizabeth(Malone) 84/86	MONT	1026	---
30 Oct 1829	Dr. F.B. McCullough		CLOW	452	1830
00 000 0000	J.H. Means		ASOH	45	1837
15 Aug 1823	William Mitchell	John F. & Enfield(Ralls) Mason91/x	EIND	G150	---
04 Dec 1820	Hiram Myers	Lewis & Catherine(Cooper) Ky/Va	CLOW	897	1824
11 Feb 1821	Franklin P. Nelson	James L. & Paulina(Yeates) **95/Ky03	BPUT	413	---
00 000 0000	James I. Nelson		BPUT	374	1829
05 Jul 1804	James E.M. O'Hair	Michael Ire/x	BPUT	442	---
07 Sep 1823	William B. Owens	John & Mary(Ewen)	HWBJ	191	---
12 Sep 1799	Brannock Phillips		BGAS	313	---
00 000 0000	Narcas Pleak		GBRD	404	1818
30 Jun 1808	David Priest	Powell Va/x	RUSH	740	1820
10 Feb 1822	George W. Priest		BGAS	319	---

MONTGOMERY COUNTY (CONT.)

BIRTHDATE	NAME OF BIOGRAPHEE	PARENTS/BIRTHPLACE/BIRTHDATE		SOURCE/PAGE		DATE
26 Aug 1816	Cornelius G. Raines	Walter & Tabitha	Va/Va	BPUT	336	1829
00 000 0000	Rev. Edwin Ray			NSPC	195	---
02 Apr 1837	Elizabeth Scobee[Hillis] William & Nellie J.			BPUT	349	---
00 000 1802	Robert Scobee	William	Clark/x	BPUT	517	1851
21 Dec 1823	Kenneth W. Self	Presley & Helen(Wilson)	Va87/WV87	WHSU	B200	---
00 000 0000	Elizabeth Slavens[Heady]			CLOW	402	---
01 Mar 1811	Dr. John Slavens	Reuben		BPUT	447	---
00 000 0000	Martha Smothers[Davis] Hugh		Ire/x	GBRD	425	---
00 000 0000	J.H. Stewart			AJEN	48	1840
07 Jun 1822	Stephen Stewart			BHOT	T288	---
13 Nov 1801	Hezekiah Strange	Stephen & Ann(Crook)		HCLI	644	---
00 000 1801	Hezekiah Strange			HCLI	462	1829
22 Mar 1822	Thomas M. Stringer			BGAS	376	1834
08 May 1815	Lucinda Tateman[Wills]			HHHE	453	1831
09 Nov 1844	James F. Taylor	Augusta & Ormilda(Allen)		MONT	1019	---
00 000 0000	Elizabeth Thompkins[Howlett]			BPUT	388	1822
00 000 0000	Mahala Tipton[Donnohue]			BPUT	466	1840
18 Jan 1823	J.G.W. Traylor	Nicholas & Mary(Trimble)	NC/Va	JACK	726	1830
00 000 1809	Amos S. Wills			HHHE	452	1831
03 Jan 1838	Henry C. Wilson	Henry H. & Mary	Va/Ire	BPUT	461	1840
20 Nov 1809	James E. Wilson			BGAS	421	1815
29 Jan 1830	Dr. J.B. Wilson	Henry		BMON	456	1834
05 May 1813	Nathan H. Wilson	Moses & Nancy(Dean)		BART	861	1818
06 Dec 1807	Francis B. Yocum			BGAS	432	1832
02 Oct 1813	William M. Young	Thomas	**/x	BPUT	482	---

M O R G A N   C O U N T Y

BIRTHDATE	NAME OF BIOGRAPHEE	PARENTS/BIRTHPLACE/BIRTHDATE	SOURCE/PAGE	DATE
00 000 1816	Frances[Roach]		BMON 239	----

M U H L E N B U R G   C O U N T Y

BIRTHDATE	NAME OF BIOGRAPHEE	PARENTS/BIRTHPLACE/BIRTHDATE	SOURCE/PAGE	DATE
00 000 1817	Lenhart Abbot		HPDB 449	----
00 000 0000	C. Arnold		AGIP 17	1817
00 000 0000	S.J. Cates		ASPE 66	1865
08 Sep 1807	Jane M. Clark[Robison]		HJOH 496	----
00 000 0000	Joseph Cross		AGIP 17	1829
00 000 0000	Azro Dyer		AVAN 69	1864
00 000 0000	J. Heck		AGIP 13	1830
26 Feb 1849	Dr. Oscar F.Howard	Nathaniel & Eliza(Fintress)	HWSP 464	----
00 000 0000	Dr. Thomas M. Howard		AWAR 57	1874
00 000 0000	I.W. Little		AGIP 16	1870
27 Sep 1815	Benjamin Musgrave	Samuel & Rebecca(Davis) Pa/Ky	HWSP 168	----
00 000 0000	J.A. Newton		AWAR 57	1868
00 000 1809	Jemima Smith[Smith]		HPOS 635	----
00 000 1811	William Smith		HPOS 635	----
00 000 0000	Mary Stembridge	--- & Mary Ann(Akers) x/Christian	DIND 2075	----
26 Mar 1843	Ephraim Whitmer	Michael & Barbara Ann(Shaver) Ky/Va	HWSP 182	----

N E L S O N   C O U N T Y

BIRTHDATE	NAME OF BIOGRAPHEE	PARENTS/BIRTHPLACE/BIRTHDATE	SOURCE/PAGE	DATE
07 Feb 1822	George T. Albin	George & Nancy(Foxworthy) Ky/Ky	BHVI 657	----

BIRTHDATE	NAME OF BIOGRAPHEE	PARENTS/BIRTHPLACE		SOURCE/PAGE	DATE
14 Feb 1818	James L. Allan			WHSU A34	1835
00 000 0000	Harvey Atkins			BSCC B66	----
00 000 1804	William E. Beard			WHSU A36	1826
02 Mar 1804	William Beard			HGSU 796	1826
06 Jan 1815	Richard A. Bland			WHSU A41	----
17 Oct 1796	Levi Bogard			BVPA 486	1820
13 Sep 1825	Hayden Bridwell	Noah & Nancy(Cuppy)		HLOW 350	----
09 Dec 1809	Azariah D. Brown			BVPA 342	1824
20 Dec 1807	Cadmus V. Brown	Richard & Nancy(Hughes)	Pa/x	HWSP 445	1818
00 000 0000	C.V. Brown			ASPE 67	1817
20 May 1833	Benjamin F. Burkhart	J. & Mary(Wilkinson)	Ky/Ky	HWSP 516	----
29 Jan 1808	Reed Case	William		HCAR 251	1808
00 000 0000	Cornelius Clark	Thomas	Va/x	SHGI 669	----
07 Feb 1820	William H. Combs	John & Catherine(Lemons)	Pa77/x	EBOO 257	----
20 Aug 1810	Robert G. Cotton			BGAS 80	----
00 000 1803	Henry Drake	William	Ky/x	BHVI 738	----
25 Feb 1835	Thomas Eastham	Isaac N. & Eliza(Sweets)	Ky/Ky	HKDA 321	1851
05 Mar 1837	Philip A. Elkin	Benjamin & Eliza(Williams)	Ky/Ky	CLOW 399	1848
05 Mar 1821	Catherine J. Gardiner[Oliver]	Luke & Hannah		BPUT 502	----
00 000 1810	William M. Gibson	William		BHCL 679	----
00 000 0000	Mary E. Gordan[LeGrange]			GIBS 240	1840
11 Mar 1791	John W. Graham			BGAS 149	----
11 Mar 1791	Hon. John W. Graham			HWSP 455	----
24 Jan 1813	J.M. Halbert	John & Elizabeth(Marks)	Va/Va	CLOW 526	1820
00 000 0000	Samuel Harding			HWSP 786	----
00 000 1811	Waller Harrell	Isaac & Elizabeth(Watkins)	Va/Va	JACK 649	1815
22 Oct 1817	William C. Halbert	Thomas & Margaret(Woodsmall)	Va/Va	CLOW 891	1822
00 000 0000	G.W. Harris			ASPE 65	1843
00 000 0000	J.N. Hopkins			AWAR 58	1860
00 000 0000	A.E. Houghland			AWAR 58	1829

Date	Name	Parents/Spouse	Origin	Code	No.	Year
11 Nov 1803	David Huston			BGAS	200	---
21 Jan 1814	Samuel M. Huston		Pa/Pa	HLOW	339	1825
23 Nov 1820	Abel H. Isbell		NC/Va	BVPA	467	---
04 Jul 1800	Enoch R. James			BGAS	204	---
00 000 1826	J.N. Johnson	Elias & Sarah(Whitehead)	NC92/NC96	HPOS	558	1832
00 000 1790	William S. Jones			BART	798	c1820
27 Oct 1828	Humphrey S. Joseph	Simon S. & Lydia(Sapp)	Ky/Ky	BVPA	269	---
00 0oc 1797	Robert Kirkham			WHSU	A62	1832
10 Feb 1823	Henry Kurtz			HHHE	660	1823
00 000 0000	Richard Legrange			GIBS	240	1819
00 000 0000	John T. McDaniel	John W. & Susan(Anderson)	Ky/Ky	HWSP	522	1846
21 Feb 1827	Preston McDonald			WHSU	B335	---
00 000 0000	Dr. John McGown			AWAS	49	1870
00 000 0000	Isabel McKune[Harris]			HPDB	457	---
19 Oct 1808	James Marks			BVPA	358	1829
08 Apr 1854	James B. Napier	Henry C. & Sally Ann(Jewell)	Va/x	FMWA	B200	---
05 Nov 1808	Thomas Nichols			BGAS	292	---
31 Oct 1841	Joseph W. Nourse	Charles & Rosanna(Logan) **92/Shelby		HWSP	476	92/05
20 Nov 1825	Thomas Osburn	John & Sallie(Gardner)	Ky89/Ky92	HGSU	734	1826
00 000 0000	A.H. Polk			AGIP	12	1839
00 000 0000	Elizabeth Polk[Spencer]			BSCC	B119	---
07 Jan 1816	George W. Polk	James & Nancy	Pa/x	HJOH	808	---
00 000 1829	John A. Polk			BGAS	316	---
11 Oct 1796	Richard Polk			BGAS	316	---
08 Nov 1849	John S. Railsback	Lewis D. & Delitha J(Reynolds)	Ky/Ky	WHSU	B174	---
07 Nov 1816	Joseph C. Richardson	John & Nancy(Castleman)	WP83/Ky83	HWSP	482	---
26 Jan 1826	E.C. Russell	Andrew & Cynthia	Ky/Ky	BVPA	416	1845
00 0oc 1805	Isaac Sands			BGAS	343	---
00 000 1815	Samuel Sands			BGAS	344	---
00 000 0000	Eliza Settles[Smith]			HLOW	903	---
28 May 1815	Cinderella Shirley[Cole]	Isaac & Catherine(Hendrickson)Ky/Ky		BHOT	T337	---
00 000 1792	James B. Slaughter			EIND	A51	---
00 000 0000	Henry G. Smith			HLOW	903	---
00 000 0000	Capt. Spear Spencer			BSCC	B119	---
18 Mar 1838	Elizabeth Tabor[Radford]	Enoch S. & Sarah(Dugan)		EWMB	361	---

N E L S O N   C O U N T Y   (C O N T.)

BIRTHDATE	NAME OF BIOGRAPHEE	PARENTS/BIRTHPLACE/BIRTHDATE	SOURCE/PAGE		DATE
00 000 0000	William H.H. Taylor		ASPE	65	1865
02 Mar 1840	Charlotte J.Terrell[Hamilton]	Henry H. & Nancy(Foster)Ky/Ky	HJOH	877	c1854
24 Mar 1820	Daniel N. Tichenor	Ebenezer & Susan(Bull) **/**	SHGI	533	1833
00 000 0000	H.T. Tichenor		AGIP	12	1837
00 000 0000	T.N. Tichenor		GIBS	236	1847
00 000 0000	William N. Tichenor		AGIP	12	1837
00 000 0000	William N. Tichenor		GIBS	234	1837
25 Dec 1826	William N. Tichenor	Daniel & Jane(Glover) **02/**99	SHGI	656	---
25 Dec 1826	William N. Tichenor	Daniel & Jane(Glover)	SHGI	535	---
00 000 0000	Margaret VanWinkle[Harding]		HWSP	786	c1820
03 Dec 1827	James M. Watson	Scarlet & Kiziah(Walker) Va01/Ky05	BHVI	989	---
03 Apr 1800	Joseph White	James	FMWA	B638	1810
14 Jun 1792	Judge Samuel Wible		HLOW	664	---
14 May 1836	James W.Wilkinson	John G. & Eliza(Bishop) **/**	HWSP	236	---
20 Oct 1818	Asa C. Williams	Urbane & Nancy(Johnson) Va/NC	HPOS	542	1828
22 Sep 1802	George P.R. Wilson		BGAS	421	---
00 000 0000	George P.R. Wilson		BSCC	B119	---
00 000 0000	John D. Wiseheart	Jacob & Mary Elizabeth	HHHE	816	---

N I C H O L A S   C O U N T Y

BIRTHDATE	NAME OF BIOGRAPHEE	PARENTS/BIRTHPLACE/BIRTHDATE	SOURCE/PAGE		DATE
00 000 1799	Solomon Adams	Thomas	HHHE	344	---
00 000 0000	Solomon Adams		HHHE	276	c1825
00 000 1798	Joseph Allfrey		BSCC	B203	---
24 Jul 1809	Ambrose D. Barnett	John P. Va/x	HJOH	588	c1821
15 Nov 1841	Elder William F.Black		NSPC	324	---
20 May 1834	William W.Boardman	James R. & Sally(Hazelrigg) Ky/x	EPUT	385	1854

Date	Name	Parents/Spouse	Origin	Code	No.	Year
25 Apr 1822	Robert F. Boyd			BGAS	33	---
07 Jul 1841	William M. Brooks	Mosley & Susanna(Geohegan)	**05/**03	RUSH	427	1849
12 Sep 1808	Elijah Buntin	Andrew & Elizabeth(Lothridge)	Ky/Ky	HCLI	635	1829
10 Oct 1805	John L. Buntin			EBOO	235	---
22 Mar 1817	Greenbury Bunton			EBOO	234	---
18 Jul 1820	Andrew Burns			EBOO	238	---
30 May 1847	Dr. Samuel O. Burris	James D. & Rebecca(Miller)	Md12/Pa18	---	---	1862
00 000 0000	Alexander Clark			SIND	588	---
21 Mar 1817	Barton Coldwell	John & Clarissa(Pauly)		EBOO	252	---
23 Mar 1838	David Coldwell	John & Elizabeth		EBOO	253	1832
21 Mar 1804	David A. Coldwell	Thomas & Sarah	Pa78/Pa	EBOO	249	---
06 Jan 1819	William Coldwell			EBOO	253	---
25 Feb 1801	Rachel L. Cowar[Hill]			EBOO	301	---
25 Feb 1791	Jonathan Crose			EBOO	247	1830
17 Jun 1811	Abraham Deupree			HJOH	412	---
00 000 0000	Jacob Downey			RUSH	505	1830
16 Mar 1805	James Downey	Archibald & Sarah(Cook)	Pa/Pa	RUSH	412	1831
00 000 1806	Dorcas[Early]			SHMI	362	---
00 000 1803	James Early			SHMI	362	---
04 Aug 1816	Dorsey O. Elliott	William & Sarah(Turner)	Ky/Md	CLOW	463	1819
00 000 1806	Dorcas Edward			HMIA	642	1831
00 000 1803	James Edward			HMIA	642	1831
16 Jun 1818	Orlando E. Foster	James M. & Rachel(Nesbit)	Ky/Ky	CLOW	933	1835
00 000 0000	Henry Glenn			BJOH	146	1823
00 000 0000	Sarah Glenn[Clark]			SIND	588	---
00 000 0000	Archibald Green			BJOH	133	1822
20 Sep 1819	Philander Hamilton			BGAS	162	---
22 Jul 1821	Robert A. Hamilton	James E. & Jane(McCoy)	95/x	GBRD	262	1822
27 Jul 1810	Franklin Hardin			BGAS	166	---
27 Jul 1810	Judge Franklin Hardin Henry			NSPC	145	---
27 Jul 1810	Judge Franklin Hardin Henry & Catherine			HJOH	899	---
16 Jul 1801	Gilbert T. Harney			BMON	466	---
20 Sep 1809	James Hazlett	Samuel & Mary(Stephenson)	Pa/x	EIND	117	---

BIRTHDATE	NAME OF BIOGRAPHEE	PARENTS/BIRTHPLACE/BIRTHDATE	SOURCE/PAGE	DATE
24 Aug 1820	John C. Hedelson	James & Esther(Craig)	HHEN 491	1831
00 000 0000	James Hill		HSHE 656	1822
04 Apr 1801	William Hill		EBOO 301	----
00 000 0000	Margaret Hinkston[Smart]		SIND 582	----
04 Apr 1821	Hon.Milton B.Hopkins		BHOT H334	----
14 Jun 1825	James Hudelson	James & Esther(Craig) Ky88/Tn97	HHEN 818	1831
24 Aug 1820	John C. Hudelson	James & Esther(Craig) Ky/Ky	HENR 1139	----
14 Nov 1823	William Hudelson	James & Esther(Craig) Ky/Ky	HHEN 819	1831
00 000 0000	William Hudelson		RUSH 382	----
00 000 1808	Joel Hufford		HHHE 350	1832
00 000 0000	Matilda Hunt	Lemuel	HHAN 460	1826
00 000 1786	Abraham Kern		HLOW 310	1816
12 Apr 1802	Thomas Kersey		EBOO 314	----
00 000 1796	Francis P. McClain	Alexander & Elizabeth(Caldwell)	SIND 634	----
16 Nov 1818	Thomas McClintock		HGSU 784	1829
00 Jan 1787	Jesse C. McCoy		NSPC 172	1829
09 Oct 1815	James A. McDonald		BPUT 440	----
08 Aug 1824	Samuel McGinnis		EBOO 333	----
01 Apr 1795	Charles McKenzie	William Ire/x	RUSH 485	----
00 000 1822	J.J. Metcalfe	James Md/x	TRAN 459	----
00 000 0000	James Morgan		ADEA 44	1873
09 Jan 1802	John D. Morris		GBRD 350	----
18 Sep 1815	Thomas A. Morris	Morris	NSPC 134	1821
26 Dec 1811	Thomas A. Morris	Morris & Rachel Va80/x	MPRO 202	----
26 Dec 1811	Gen.Thomas A.Morris	Morris & Rachel(Morris) Va80/x	EIND G258	----
26 Dec 1811	Gen.Thomas A.Morris	Morris & Rachel	SIND 301	1821
26 Dec 1811	John Morrison	Morris	NSPC 119	1821
26 Mar 1796	Nancy Orr[Saxon]	William & Sally	GBRD 367	1823
00 000 0000		John & Susan	KTCD 1060	1836

-166-

BIRTHDATE	NAME OF BIOGRAPHEE	PARENTS/BIRTHPLACE/BIRTHDATE		SOURCE/PAGE	PAGE	DATE
00 000 1780	Isaac Powell			EBOO	347	1835
05 Nov 1824	John M. Powell	John & Sarah	Va/Ky	RUSH	422	1832
15 Mar 1796	James Saunders			BGAS	344	---
00 000 1818	Adam Sears	David & Anne(Kern)	NC92/x	HLOW	313	---
15 May 1845	William T. Shrout	A.W. & Sarah(Highland)Bourb25/Bourb1?		CSHE	693	---
00 000 0000	Hezekiah Smart			SIND	582	---
00 000 0000	John Smart			SIND	582	---
17 Sep 1840	Jetson W. Smith	Jetson & Mary A(James)	Ky/Md	RUSH	363	---
25 Jul 1817	Marquis Linday Smith	Hezekiah & Mary Ann		EIND	M58	---
16 Jul 1816	Dr. W.C. Smydth			BBGR	94	1818
00 000 1783	Robert Stephenson			EBOO	367	---
25 Oct 1805	William S. Thomas			SIND	552	1828
26 May 1799	James A. Thompson			EBOO	383	1830
12 Jul 1848	James H. Throop	George A. & Abigail(Milton)		CLOW	474	---
00 000 0000	Col. John Wishard			BJOH	143	1825
00 000 0000	Capt. Robert C. Wishard			BJOH	145	1823
17 Jan 1816	Dr. William H. Wishard	John & --(Oliver)	Pa/x	EIND	G242	---
17 Jan 1816	Dr. William H. Wishard	John & Agnes H(Oliver)	Pa/Ky	DGIN	1244	1825
17 Jan 1816	Dr. William H. Wishard	John & Agnes H.		SIND	594	1825
00 000 1816	Dr. William H. Wishard	Col. John		MSPC	143	1825
00 000 1809	Caleb Wood	John & Susan	Va/Va	BHOT	T332	1841
18 Jul 1830	John Younger	Lewis & Nancy(Crose)	Ky/Ky	HLOW	276	1832
03 Jul 1832	Michael Younger	Lewis & Nancy(Crose)	Ky/Ky	HLOW	277	1832
23 Mar 1828	William P. Younger	Lewis & Nancy(Crose)	Ky/Ky	HLOW	276	1832

O H I O   C O U N T Y

BIRTHDATE	NAME OF BIOGRAPHEE	PARENTS/BIRTHPLACE/BIRTHDATE		SOURCE/PAGE	PAGE	DATE
22 Jun 1843	Dr. H.L. Ambrose	Jacob & Marie(James)	Ky/Ky	HWSP	437	---
00 000 0000	Dr. H.L. Ambrose			ASPE	67	1869
00 000 0000	David J. Axton			ASPE	66	1858
20 Apr 1832	David J. Axton	Bayless E. & Elizabeth(Terry)		HWSP	543	---
12 May 1824	Robert J. Axton	Bayless E. & Elizabeth(Terry)	NC/NC	HWSP	543	---

BIRTHDATE	NAME OF BIOGRAPHEE	PARENTS/BIRTHPLACE/BIRTHDATE		SOURCE/PAGE	DATE
00 000 0000	L.J. Bannon			ASPE 66	1850
00 000 0000	William Blancet			GIBS 243	1856
00 000 0000	A.F. Breshears			AWAR 57	1857
00 000 0000	J.M. Brite			AVAN 64	1867
04 Feb 1839	Benjamin O. Brooks	William & Maria F(Brown)	Va/Va	HWSP 231	----
16 Feb 1836	William M. Brooks	William & Maria F(Brown)	Va/Va	HWSP 231	----
00 000 0000	William M. Brooks			AWAR 58	1869
00 000 0000	A.F. Broshears[Hougland]	Manuel & Margaret(Humphrey)	Ky/Ky	FWAR 174	1857
16 Aug 1855	Dr.Alvis P. Brown	James F. & Marinda L(Addington)		HWSP 161	----
00 000 0000	J.F. Brown			AWAR 58	1864
00 000 0000	William H. Brown			AWAR 58	1849
00 000 0000	C.H. Cooper			AWAR 58	1836
03 Jul 1833	Cornelius H. Cooper	Alexander & Sallie(Miller)	Md/Ky	HWSP 224	1837
00 000 0000	W.H.T. Davis			FWAR 175	1834
13 Apr 1834	Thomas J. Downs	William		EIND A18	1855
13 Apr 1834	Thomas J. Downs	William		FWAR 125	----
13 Apr 1834	Thomas J. Downs	William		HWSP 145	----
00 000 0000	N.G. Dubois			AWAR 57	1833
16 Mar 1821	Nelson G. Dubois	Stephen & Rebecca	SC/Va	HWSP 187	----
00 000 0000	Margaret Forman[Lendrum]			GIBS 239	1880
00 000 0000	W.H. Graves			FWAR 176	1872
00 000 0000	W. Grigsby			ASPE 66	1815
00 000 0000	James H. Haynes			AWAR 58	1864
12 Aug 1833	William J. Hedges	Peter & Sarah A(Tanner)	Ky/Ky	HWSP 244	----
09 Dec 1800	James Hinman	Samuel & Nancy(Hedges)	NY/Md	HWSP 198	1814
00 000 0000	John Hull			AWAR 58	1839
00 000 0000	Asa Iglehart			AVAN 69	1849
08 Dec 1816	Asa Iglehart	Levi & Annie(Taylor)		BVAN 115	1823
08 Dec 1816	Asa Iglehart	Levie & Anne(Taylor)	Md86/x	HVAN 355	----
08 Dec 1817	Asa Iglehart	Levi & Anne(Taylor)	Md86/x	TBAB 393	----

BIRTHDATE	NAME OF BIOGRAPHEE	PARENTS/BIRTHPLACE/BIRTHDATE		SOURCE/PAGE		DATE
00 000 0000	David B. Kelley			HWSP	546	---
00 000 0000	William M. Leach			AWAR	58	1828
05 May 1813	Christopher J. Mason	John H. & Elizabeth(Jackson)	Va/x	HWSP	472	---
19 Nov 1825	D.L. Miller	Jesse B. & Janet(Iglehart)	WOO/Md04	HWSP	211	---
00 000 0000	R.B. Pattie			ASPE	67	1864
09 Mar 1834	Robert B. Pattie	John & Mary E(Maxwell)	Ky/Ky	HWSP	550	---
06 Aug 1802	Ezekiel Perigo	Romey & Rhodia(Hinman)	Md/x	FWAR	80	1819
00 000 0000	E. Perigo			AWAR	57	1819
06 Sep 1818	Robert Perigo	Jonathan & Isabella		FWAR	114	1819
00 000 0000	Robert Perigo			AWAR	57	1819
06 Sep 1818	Robert Perigo			BGAS	311	---
06 Sep 1818	Hon. Robert Perigo	Jonathan & Isabella(McGill)	Ky/Ky	HWSP	172	---
06 Feb 1824	Benjamin K. Salle	Oliver P. & Elizabeth(Johnson)	Va/Va	HWSP	484	---
31 Dec 1841	Dr. Andrew Smith	Benjamin & Katherine W.		EIND	A51	1829
00 000 0000	John T. Wallace			GIBS	239	---
17 Oct 1845	Charles L. Wedding	Mark & Nancy J(Hale)		HVAN	372	---
17 Oct 1845	Charles L. Wedding			ASPE	16	---
17 Oct 1845	Charles L. Wedding			BVAN	67	---
17 Oct 1845	Charles L. Wedding			EIND	A56	---
02 Dec 1852	Columbus V. Wedding	Mark & Nancy J(Hale)		HVAN	258	---
13 May 1856	Dr. Milliard F.Wedding	Mark & Nancy J(Hale)	Va/19	HWSP	798	---

O L D H A M   C O U N T Y

BIRTHDATE	NAME OF BIOGRAPHEE	PARENTS/BIRTHPLACE/BIRTHDATE		SOURCE/PAGE		DATE
29 Oct 1863	Thomas C. Ahern	John & Catherine	Ire21/Ire33	BART	661	1865
22 Jul 1833	Joseph H. Allison	Elijah & Margaret(Frederick)	Ky/Ky	BMMB	270	1834
00 000 0000	W.J. Ballard	Camdon & Lavinia(Raley)	**/Ky	DIND	2218	---
00 000 0000	Dr. W.H. Bright			AWAS	49	1839
13 Sep 1831	Dr. William H.Bright	James H. & Susannah(Truman)	Md/Md	HLOW	921	---
06 Feb 1821	John A. Brookie	William & Mary(Dougherty)	Ky/Ky	HCLI	634	---
27 Jan 1819	Rice E. Brown	William & Elizabeth(Wilson)	Va/Va	BMMB	342	---

OLDHAM COUNTY (CONT.)

BIRTHDATE	NAME OF BIOGRAPHEE	PARENTS/BIRTHPLACE/BIRTHDATE	SOURCE/PAGE	DATE
09 May 1826	John Clore	James & Sarah(Keller)	HJOH 886	---
00 000 0000	Sarah Coons[Guyton]		HJOH 496	---
03 Dec 1844	Benjamin Cornwell	John & Minerva(Williams) Ky/Ky	BMMB 243	---
20 Apr 1811	Lucy E. Dawson[Tomlinson]	Daniel & Keziah(Tanner)	SIND 596	---
08 Mar 1815	William P. Enochs	Garrard & Sarah(Johnson)	HLOW 900	1824
07 Aug 1828	David F. Featherngill	Joseph & Mary(Forsyth)	HJOH 606	1829
27 Mar 1822	John H. Featherngill	Joseph & Mary(Forsyth)	HJOH 607	---
29 Oct 1827	William J. Fisher	Brandes Shelby97/x	BMON 265	---
15 Jan 1842	Abner Hardin	Henry & Emma(Ritter) Ky16/Ky17	HJOH 750	1852
13 Jan 1805	Cornelius Howard	Joseph & Sarah NC/NC	WHSU B72	1820
01 Oct 1826	Anderson B. Hunter	Ralsamon	HJOH 94	1840
01 Oct 1826	Anderson B. Hunter	Ralsamon	TBAB 671	---
00 000 0000	James Ingram	Jeff	BSCC B17	1816
07 Jul 1833	Elijah T. Keightley		BGAS 215	---
12 Dec 1826	John W. Keightley		BGAS 215	---
11 Jan 1820	William Law	John & Mary(Tracy) **/**	HJOH 799	1841
10 Aug 1818	Jeptha McQuinn	Ezekiel & Elizabeth(Coons)	HJOH 755	1834
07 Oct 1818	David P. Monroe		BGAS 277	---
03 Apr 1824	William Y. Monroe		BGAS 277	---
04 Oct 1825	Eusebia N. Nay[Terhune]	Asa B. & Lucinda(Whitesider)	HJOH 662	---
21 May 1819	Gabriel M. Overstreet		BJOH 93	1834
21 May 1819	Gabriel M. Overstreet		TBAB 667	---
00 000 0000	Catherine H. Pruitt[Shake]		BMMB 346	---
03 Dec 1823	Daniel Pruitt	Eli] & Nancy(Williams) NC/Ky	BMMB 312	---
28 Aug 1816	Mary Ragsdale[Forsyth]		HJOH 883	---
00 000 0000	John Redding		BHGL 678	---
00 000 0000	David Shake		WHSU A37	---
08 Jan 1814	John Shake	Jacob & Nancy(Donelson)	HGSU 795	1830
20 Nov 1828	Lemuel H. Shake	David & Artemisia(Blevins)	HGSU 757	1856
15 Aug 1845	Venalia Shake	J.B. & Sarah Ann(Sturgeon) Ky/Ky	HJOH 711	1830

BIRTHDATE	NAME OF BIOGRAPHY	PARENTS/BIRTHPLACE/BIRTHDATE	SOURCE	PAGE	DATE
06 Sep 1836	William S. Sherley	Lawrence & Laurenda M(Overstreet)	BGAS	352	----
06 Sep 1836	William S. Shirley	Lawrence & Laurenda M(Overstreet)	TBAB	653	Va/**
00 000 0000	Rebecca Snyser[Musselman]	Joseph & Elizabeth(Deadman) Pa/Ky	HJOH	710	----
20 Mar 1834	Capt.Wm.T. Swift	John & Elizabeth A(Dawkins)	HLOW	656	----
00 000 0000	Ruth Webb[Fitzpatrick]		HJOH	483	----
10 Jun 1831	Jeremiah L. Welman	Andrew N. & Elizabeth(Williams) Va/Ky	BMMB	280	1845
02 Jun 1806	Lucinda Whitesides	Joseph & Elizabeth(Button)	HJOH	662	----
16 Jun 1824	Aaron L. Wilhite	Lamech & Mary(Koebler) Va/Va	BMMB	350	1836
09 Oct 1831	Thomas Wilhite	Noah & Polly(Williams) Va/Ky	BMMB	349	1835
27 Dec 1825	Franklin Woodard		BGAS	427	1837
01 Jan 1796	Robert M. Wooden		BGAS	427	----
29 Jul 1829	John T. Yager	William & Nancy(Overstreet) Ky75/**80	HJOH	725	----
18 Feb 1838	John S. Zaring	Lewis & Nancy(Logan) **08/x	HJOH	917	----
04 Dec 1808	Lewis Zaring	Benjamin & Nancy(Baker)	HJOH	917	----

O W E N   C O U N T Y

BIRTHDATE	NAME OF BIOGRAPHY	PARENTS/BIRTHPLACE/BIRTHDATE	SOURCE	PAGE	DATE
24 May 1824	John H. Akers		BHOT	T267	1850
31 Dec 1818	Fannie Alexander[Hollingsworth]		EBOO	300	----
15 Jan 1838	Thomas J. Allnot	Ninian & Mary Ann Ky82/Tn92	MONT	1143	----
07 Oct 1864	James W. Brissey	James M. & Sarah(Osburn) Ky/Ky	KTCD	690	1865
30 Sep 1827	Morgan Chandler		BGAS	61	----
30 Sep 1827	Morgan Chandler	Uriah & Lydia Va/NC	EIND	G19	----
30 Sep 1827	Morgan Chandler		HHAN	377	1851
00 000 1825	Jesse Cox	John & Lurana(Osborn) Va/NC	JACK	657	1833
17 Apr 1848	Lycurgus Dalton		BGAS	91	----
02 Dec 1873	Albert D. Gayle	James & Sally(Green) Ky/Ky	FMWA	B15	----
10 Dec 1827	John E. Greer		BGAS	152	----
00 Jun 1818	James W. Haddan	John & Rebecca	BPUT	329	1824
00 000 0000	Jesse S. Harper		ADEA	66	1858

OWEN COUNTY (CONT.)

BIRTHDATE	NAME OF BIOGRAPHEE	PARENTS/BIRTHPLACE/BIRTHDATE	SOURCE/PAGE	DATE
04 Apr 1845	George W. Jackson		WHSU B211	1878
00 000 0000	James R. Kendall		BVPA 338	----
00 000 0000	Fieldea Lett		AJEN 48	1827
00 000 0000	G. Lewis		ASOH 45	1849
03 Jan 1830	Sarah E. Mothershead[Graves]	Alvin 89/x	HVAN 410	----
24 Dec 1879	John C. New	William J. & Elizabeth(Claxon)Gall/**	FMWA B201	37/39
27 Mar 1852	E. Perry	Lewis & Orphy E(Said) Ky/Ky	BHOT T321	1852
00 000 0000	Dr. F.H. Sale		ADEA 50	1850
17 May 1828	Dr. F.H. Sale	James H. & Elizabeth T(Elliston)Va/**	HDOH 891	93/01
24 Oct 1857	Yula Satterwhite[Jackson]		WHSU B211	1878
00 000 0000	Catherine Titus[Wingate]		HSHE 548	----
12 Jun 1815	Martin S. Toon	John & Malinda(Stafford) De/Ky	SIND 534	----
08 Oct 1817	John West	Van & Sarah(Bourn) 88/98	HJOH 826	1838
00 000 0000	Smith Wingate		HSHE 548	----
16 Nov 1825	William S. Woodfill	Gabriel Shelby00/x	GBRD 369	----
00 000 0000	J.A. Works		ASOH 46	1848
08 Sep 1820	James A. Works	Andrew & Rachel(Ireland)	HDOH 1281	----

OWSLEY COUNTY (NONE)

PENDLETON COUNTY

BIRTHDATE	NAME OF BIOGRAPHEE	PARENTS/BIRTHPLACE/BIRTHDATE	SOURCE/PAGE	DATE
00 000 1833	Rev. Walter M.Benson	John & Mary Ellen(Minor)	HHHE 806	1835
30 Sep 1844	George W. Bryan	Hampton & Margaret(Gosney)Campb/Camp	HSHE 606	96/03
00 000 0000	Luke Bryan	Samuel & Mary(Boone) NC/NC	SIND 583	----
20 Mar 1846	John M. Golden		BGAS 145	----

BIRTHDATE	NAME OF BIOGRAPHEE	PARENTS/BIRTHPLACE/BIRTHDATE	SOURCE/PAGE	DATE
10 Aug 1811	John A. Hendricks		HSTJ	----
10 Aug 1811	John A. Hendricks		BGAS 179	----
11 Dec 1813	John H. Herod	Bailey & Sarah(Hart) Va/Va	BPUT 486	1833
00 000 1845	W.B. Herod	Luther	BMON 473	1851
13 Jun 1824	Alfred C. Lightfoot	William B. & Elizabeth(Colvin) Ky/Ky	RUSH 866	1830
19 Mar 1829	P.H. McCann	Patrick & Elizabeth(Iles) Ire/x	BHOT H387	----
02 May 1819	James McColley	George	BHOT T282	----
00 000 0000	William Monroe		SIND 581	----
00 000 0000	H.M. Pettit		ARIP 49	1876
22 Dec 1802	Greenberry Rush		BGAS 341	----
04 Feb 1812	Woodson W. Thrasher		BGAS 392	----
31 May 1834	Dr. B.F. Tomlin	Simeon & Elizabeth(Clements) Va/Va	BHVI 969	----
17 Sep 1823	Hayden Yelton	Charles & Millie(Gosney) Va/Va	HHEN 681	----

PERRY COUNTY

PIKE COUNTY (NONE)

BIRTHDATE	NAME OF BIOGRAPHEE	PARENTS/BIRTHPLACE/BIRTHDATE	SOURCE/PAGE	DATE
00 000 0000	Nancy Brown[Kelley]		BMON 404	1829
00 000 0000	William Kelley		BMON 404	1829
00 000 0000	G.G. Lee		FWAR 177	1842

POWELL COUNTY (NONE)

PULASKI COUNTY

BIRTHDATE	NAME OF BIOGRAPHEE	PARENTS/BIRTHPLACE/BIRTHDATE	SOURCE/PAGE	DATE
17 Sep 1802	Harvey Blacklidge		WFUF 657	c.1813

P U L A S K I   C O U N T Y   (C O N T.)

BIRTHDATE	NAME OF BIOGRAPHEE	PARENTS/BIRTHPLACE/BIRTHDATE		SOURCE/PAGE	DATE
20 Feb 1802	Noah Boone			BGAS 32	----
19 Apr 1819	Elisha Bradley	Reuben & Elizabeth(Ping)	Va/Va	BART 809	1832
26 Jun 1800	John Cooper			HCLI 854	----
25 Aug 1816	Mary A. Cooper[McKinney]			HCLI 860	----
13 May 1808	Stanley Cooper			BGAS 78	----
28 Mar 1815	Elizabeth Gasteneau	Joab & Sallie		BPUT 508	----
26 Aug 1827	Rachel Gastineau[Newman]	Joab & Sarah(Hayes)		BPUT 395	----
29 Nov 1799	John Hargrove			BGAS 166	----
29 Nov 1793	Hon.John Hargrove	William & Sallie(Jasper)	SC/x	GIBS 194	----
00 000 0000	James Harman			SIND 598	1820
16 Oct 1826	Levi Hasty	Levi & Lydia	De/Ky	BPUT 498	----
10 Mar 1810	Jesse Herrin			SIND 558	1831
29 Nov 1799	Allen Hill			BGAS 184	----
23 Aug 1810	James Hill			BGAS 184	----
13 Apr 1812	Noah Lee	Charles & Nica		BPUT 508	----
00 000 0000	Sarah[Lemasters]			GCEV B400	----
29 Aug 1825	Harvey McDaniel	Spencer & Martha(McDaniel)	Va/Tn	BWMB 195	----
00 Jan 1834	John McDaniel	John & Unia E(LittleJohn)	Ky/Ky	BWMB 367	----
00 000 1794	Samuel McGowan	David & --(McClelland)		GIBS 217	----
13 Oct 1813	William V. McKinney			HCLI 859	----
00 000 0000	John C. Mayfield	Pleasant W. & Jane(Buchanan)	Ky/Va	CLOW 895	c1830
06 Apr 1821	Dr. Granville Newby	Edmund & Mary(Tumbleson)	Va/Ky	BHOT T445	c1828
16 Mar 1826	William Owen	Jonathan & Louisa(Taylor)	NC/NC	CLOW 437	----
06 Dec 1819	Rev. G.C. Price	Shadrach & Nancy	Va/Va	BVPA 125	1830
04 Jun 1815	Elias Ranard	Benjamin & Elizabeth(Massey)	NC/Ky	CLOW 942	1875
00 000 0000	Dr. J.A. Randolph			AKNO 60	----
18 May 1807	Milton Short	Wesley & Rebecca(Owen)	Va80/x	HJOH 655	----
03 Aug 1798	Judge Jesse Williams			HWAY B368	1815
00 000 0000	Thomas Wilson			AWAR 58	1833
02 Dec 1811	Thomas W. Wilson	James & Elizabeth(Fox)		HWSP 239	1833

R O C K C A S T L E   C O U N T Y

BIRTHDATE	NAME OF BIOGRAPHEE	PARENTS/BIRTHPLACE/BIRTHDATE		SOURCE/PAGE		DATE
07 Feb 1819	William M. Brush	John & Mary	Ky/Ky	CLOW	533	1831
30 May 1826	Elijah Church	Joel & Cynthia(Landford)	Ky/Ky	CLOW	419	1829
02 Sep 1808	William B. Endicott			HEOS	591	1814
07 Mar 1823	Josiah Henderson	Joseph & Elizabeth(Vance)	Va/Pa	BVER	493	1839
29 May 1810	James Hill	William & Elizabeth(Jones)	Madison/Ky	GPLA	649	---
20 Dec 1808	James King	William	Va/x	HCLI	680	---
19 Feb 1831	John J. Lasswell	William & Susannah(Kamp)	Va96/Va94	HKDA	508	---
00 000 0000	Robert N. Owens	William & Kate(Tyree)	**/**	SCWA	766	---
08 Feb 1815	Levi Smith	Jonathan & Barbara	Va/Va	HELK	964	---
16 Feb 1870	Charles R. Sowder	Daniel R. & Eliza(Cummins)	**/**	DGIN	679	1841
00 000 0000	Allen Williams	Hezekiah & Nancy(Owens)	**/x	BVPA	325	1841
15 Dec 1849	James C. Williams			MONT	947	1852

R U S S E L L   C O U N T Y

BIRTHDATE	NAME OF BIOGRAPHEE	PARENTS/BIRTHPLACE/BIRTHDATE		SOURCE/PAGE		DATE
24 Feb 1822	Amos Allison	Matthew & Mary(Richardson)	Va92/x	RUSH	477	1822
12 Sep 1830	James W. Cabbage	John & Nancy		FWAR	146	1832
12 Sep 1830	James W. Cabbage			BGAS	51	---
28 Oct 1820	Greenbury C. Cannon	John & Laurena		EIND	C7	---
00 000 0000	Cyntha Houghland			AWAR	58	1851
03 Jul 1840	Christopher C.H. Kerns	Isham & Louise(Hall)	Ky/x	BSCC	B160	---

RUSSELL COUNTY (CONT,)

BIRTHDATE	NAME OF BIOGRAPHEE	PARENTS/BIRTHPLACE/BIRTHDATE		SOURCE/PAGE		DATE
00 000 0000	D.J. McKinney			AGIP	17	1859
30 Oct 1835	Judge J.T. Pierce	Dr. J.S. & Eveline(Moore)		EIND	B27	---
00 000 0000	P.W. Shepard			AGIP	17	1851
08 Jun 1845	Thomas M. Smith			BGAS	364	---
20 Apr 1825	George M. Spurgeon	Ell & Rachel(Newcomb)	NC/Md	HLOW	911	1828
00 000 0000	Josiah Stephens			AWAR	58	---
18 Mar 1827	Aaron Wilson	James & Elizabeth(Fox)	Va/NC	HWSP	182	---
00 000 0000	Henry Wilson			AWAR	58	1854
09 Apr 1839	James W. Wilson	John & Justina(Gossar)	**/**	HWSP	240	1848
00 000 0000	J.W. Wilson			AWAR	58	1849
13 Dec 1840	Rice Wilson	John & Jestina(Gossar)	Ky16/x	HWSP	182	---
00 000 0000	Rice Wilson			FWAR	179	1848
00 000 0000	Rice Wilson			AWAR	54	1848
00 000 0000	William R. Wilson			AWAR	58	1849

SCOTT COUNTY

BIRTHDATE	NAME OF BIOGRAPHEE	PARENTS/BIRTHPLACE/BIRTHDATE		SOURCE/PAGE		DATE
21 Aug 1822	Edward P. Adams	Isaac & Nancy Ann		RUSH	495	1825
15 Jan 1820	James M. Adams	Isaac & Nancy(Polk)	**/**	HSHE	697	1825
00 000 0000	William Baird			BGAS	11	---
01 Apr 1818	Harvey R. Barlow			HHHE	562	---
00 000 0000	Ruth Betts[Campbell]			EBOO	255	---
14 Jul 1814	Robert Braden	William & ---(Jackson)	Ire/Ire	GBRU	291	---
20 Feb 1826	Alexander K. Branham			TRAN	436	---
06 Jul 1819	Greenbury F. Burgess	Edward & Sarah(Fields)	Va/Md	CSHE	676	---
27 Dec 1803	Michael D. Campbell			EBOO	255	---
00 000 0000	James Cumming			ADEA	44	1831

Date	Name	Parents/Spouse	Place	Code	No.	Year
00 000 0000	Sarah Davis[Reese]			HSHE	659	---
09 Nov 1837	William H. English	Samuel & Eleanor(Taylor)	Ky/Ky	HHSJ	810	1840
02 Sep 1812	Christopher Greenup	John & Mary A(Holland)	Md/Ky	HCAR	338+	1832
03 Oct 1816	John W. Greenup	John & Mary A(Holland)	Md/Ky	HCAR	338+	1832
30 Aug 1818	Samuel G.Greenup	John & Mary A(Holland)	Md/Ky	HCAR	338+	1832
11 Jan 1830	Samuel Gregg	George W. & Mary(McMurtry)	Ky/Ky	HJOH	792	1830
03 Nov 1805	William Griffith	Thomas & Hannah(Richeson)	De/x	HJOH	485	1818
05 Jun 1812	Augustus C. Handy			BGAS	163	---
00 000 0000	William Handy			BGAS	163	---
26 Jul 1799	Col. Hugh Hanna			EIND	K21	---
18 Oct 1797	Samuel Hanna	James		EIND	L32	---
00 000 1818	Salathiel Jackson			WHSU	B149	---
19 Jan 1813	Robison Johns	Abram & Elizabeth	x/68	HHAN	403	1823
30 Sep 1849	James E. Kackley	Elias & Lucy(Burke)		HKDA	355	---
00 00c 1792	John M. Lemmon			BGAS	233	---
30 Oct 1818	Dr. D.F. Lindsay	Joseph & Eleanor(Montgomery)	Ky/Pa	BHOT	T342	1825
20 Oct 1813	William McLane	Robert & Elizabeth(Van Zant)		HLOW	636	---
06 Sep 1806	Alphonso B. Marlow	George & Mary(Reid)	Va/Va	RUSH	548	1821
16 Sep 1814	Robert Miller	John & Margaret	SC/Ire	HMIA	778	1818
00 000 0000	Scott Miller	Henry		HJOH	642	1830
04 Jul 1812	Joseph Montgomery	William		HSHE	620	1824
02 Oct 1810	Mary H. Morris	William & Mary(Beacham)		RUSH	516	1830
19 Dec 1824	Theodore Morris	John & Mary(Miller)	Ky/Ky	RUSH	417	1828
08 Jan 1808	Dr. John L. Mothershead Nathaniel		Va55/x	SIND	278	---
04 Oct 1845	Charles G. Offutt			BGAS	297	---
04 Oct 1845	Charles G. Offutt	Lloyd & Elizabeth	Md/Ky	EIND	G163	---
04 Oct 1845	Hon.Chas.G.Offutt	Lloyd & Elizabeth	Md/Ky	HHAN	469	---
27 Dec 1828	William R. Poynts	James & Rebecca(Ross)		BMON	274	---
26 Jul 1829	Sidney S. Pullan	Gonel B. & Ann	Ky/Ky	CLOW	378	1832
01 Jul 1827	Dr. F.J.C. Rawlins	John & Patsey	De/De	HHEN	897	---
00 000 0000	Benjamin Reese			HSHE	659	---
10 Apr 1813	John Roberts	Billingsley & Nancey(Jewell)		DIND	2198	1828
00 000 0000	Martha[Scott]			BMON	357	c1825
00 000 1866	Capt.Francis B.Shepherd	Phillip B. & Catherine(Lee)Meade/x		BHGL	574	---

BIRTHDATE	NAME OF BIOGRAPHEE	PARENTS/BIRTHPLACE/BIRTHDATE	SOURCE/PAGE	DATE
00 000 0000	Dr. D.J. Shirley		DGIN 696	----
00 000 1817	Dr. D.J. Shirley		MPRO 168	1834
29 Aug 1803	Rhoda Smith	Berryman Va/x	BVER 437	----
28 Oct 1819	Shelby Stafford	James & Mary(Leach) Va/Md	HSHE 742	1831
27 Nov 1816	Joseph Stapp	Elias & Susan(Branham) **87/**86	HDOH 919	----
00 000 0000	Joseph Stapp		ADEA 44	1848
14 Jul 1792	Milton Stapp		BGAS 369	----
00 000 1819	Elizabeth Steers[Montgomery] William	Ky/x	HSHE 620	----
30 Aug 1809	Hanson Talbot	Gassaway & Sarah(Gillums) Md/Md	HLOW 661	----
07 Sep 1814	Leland Tansell	Francis & Catherine(Cook) Fr/x	EBOO 377	----
11 Feb 1811	Joseph M. Tilford		NSPC 423	1816
17 Feb 1811	Joseph M. Tilford	Alexander & Eleanor(McCullough)Va75/x	EIND G229	----
17 Jun 1820	Job D. Tindall		CSHE 443	1835
00 000 1815	Mahala Turpin[Eaton]	Jacob & Martha(Taylor) Md85/86	HHHE 764	1820
03 Nov 1806	Smith Vawter		BGAS 402	----
12 Mar 1833	R.R. Washburn	Isaac & Maria(Bratton) Oh/Oh	HSHE 694	1833
17 Oct 1809	Jerry Weakley	Conrad & Sarah(Miller) Pa/Scotland	HSHE 543	1833
00 000 0000	Calton Wiggens		AWAR 58	1856
17 Oct 1809	Lt.Col. Joel Wolfe	Conrad & Sarah(Milller) Pa/Scotland	RUSH 764	1833
12 Jan 1809	William Wolfe	Jacob & Euphemy(Cannon) Md79/De79	HSHE 649	1828

S H E L B Y   C O U N T Y

BIRTHDATE	NAME OF BIOGRAPHEE	PARENTS/BIRTHPLACE/BIRTHDATE	SOURCE/PAGE	DATE
27 Mar 1827	Hon. James M. Allen	William & Elizabeth(Youel) Va/Va	BHVI 659	1831
00 000 0000	Jane Allen[Logan]		HCLI 756	----
19 Mar 1808	Joseph Allen		BGAS 5	----
28 Mar 1814	Robert Allen	Josiah & Nancy(Biby) Va/Va	BHVI 660	----

Date	Name	Parents/Spouse	Code	Origin	No.	Year
16 Aug 1799	Sarah B. Allen[Corn]		MONT		928	1827
10 Dec 1825	William Allen	James & Sarah(Conley)	BPUT	Va/Ky	377	1834
00 000 0000	James Ashby		AKNO		64	1845
25 Dec 1828	S.F. Ashby	S. & Nancy(Radford)	BMON	**87/**97	452	---
25 Aug 1818	Thompson V. Ashby		MONT		1026	---
00 000 0000	David Avis		AGIP		13	1832
04 Feb 1805	Thomas D. Baird		BGAS		11	---
13 Oct 1868	Hon.Curtis W.Ballard	William J.	BHCL	Ky/x	788	---
13 Oct 1868	Curtis W. Ballard	W.J. & Mary(Moody)	DIND	Oldham47/**47	2218	---
00 000 0000	James F. Ballard		AGRE		54	1836
00 000 0000	J.D. Banta		ASOH		45	1824
06 Aug 1804	Thomas Bedsler	John & Polly(Southern)	HLOW	NC/Ky	657	---
08 Nov 1817	Abram Bird	Henry	SIND	Va/x	155	---
09 Feb 1839	John B. Bishop	Byron & Elizabeth(Turner)	BPUT		455	---
12 Nov 1817	Abner Bohannon	John & Mary(Sacrey)	CLOW	Ky/Md	396	---
00 000 1833	Isaac Brown		ASUL		36	1883
08 Apr 1828	Samuel Brown	James	HJOH	Ky/x	593	1846
01 Mar 1807	Blakely Brush		BMON	Va/Va	348	1825
00 000 1816	Mary A. Brush[McCormick]		BMON		357	---
00 000 0000	Isabella H. Bryan	Thomas & Elizabeth	HJOH		636	---
26 Oct 1842	James H. Campbell	John S. & Julia A(Miles)	CLOW	Pa/**	398	1852
11 Aug 1824	H. Rice Canine		BMON		192	1825
25 Dec 1815	William Canine		BMON		347	1825
19 Jun 1832	W.B. Canine	Abraham & Sarah(Leffler)	HWBJ	Ky/Ky	752	1832
00 000 0000	William N. Carman	Isaac & Mary(Hughes)	MONT		1011	---
00 000 0000	Elizabeth Carter[McClure]		MONT		1276	---
00 000 1795	John Chambers		BGAS		60	---
00 000 1813	G.W. Clark	William & Betsy(Blades)	BMON	Ky/Ky	453	1825
28 Oct 1829	G.W. Clark	Allen W. & Martha	HWBJ	Va93/Va03	798	---
21 May 1810	Marvin Cleveland	Ezer & Martha(Wadkins)	HLOW	NY/Tn	287	1814
29 May 1819	Archibald Collings	Abraham & Nancy(Nutgrass)	BPUT	Ky/96	360	1831
03 Jan 1847	Edwin M. Coots	R.M. & Elizabeth(Morton)	BSCC	**/**	B6	---
00 000 0000	Elmira Cowher[Lee]		HWBJ		343	---
18 Feb 1797	John P. Cox		BGAS		82	---

BIRTHDATE	NAME OF BIOGRAPHEE	PARENTS/BIRTHPLACE/BIRTHDATE		SOURCE/PAGE		DATE
12 Jan 1820	Jesse M. Crim	Moses & Sarah(Jacobs)	Ky/x	BSCC	B7	---
15 Apr 1825	Edward H. Crow	Joseph & Cassandra	Md/Va	BPUT	451	---
23 Jul 1819	Samuel Crowe			BGAS	86	---
23 Jul 1819	Col.Samuel S.Crowe	John F. & Esther(Alexander)		EIND	C8	1823
27 Jan 1843	Joseph Daniels	William & Eliza(Hite)		CLOW	932	---
00 000 1824	Warren Davis	Warren		MONT	751	---
29 Mar 1828	Joel G. Deere			DIND	1295	---
09 Jan 1796	Peter Demaree	David & Rachel(Bruner)		HJOH	786	---
10 Feb 1828	William W. Demaree	Peter & Mary(Johnson)	**/**	HJOH	786	---
21 Oct 1802	Elizabeth Elliott[Shaw]			BVER	280	1822
22 Dec 1812	Joseph Ellis	Joseph & Fannie		BPUT	461	---
28 Oct 1816	Daniel Epperson	Francis & Tabitha(Redding)	Ky/Ky	BPUT	368	---
15 Apr 1791	Joseph F. Farley			BGAS	122	---
00 000 0000	William H. Figg	Asbury		HHHE	289	---
23 Jun 1833	Elizabeth Fisher[Harrison]	James & Elizabeth(Briscoe)		BVER	477	1834
00 000 0000	Samuel D. Fitzpatrick			HJOH	790	---
12 Apr 1846	Enos M. Fitzsimmons	Richard & Martha(Miles)	Ky/Ky	BHOT	T356	1850
00 000 1808	Lucinda Fulenwider[Mount]			MPRO	59	---
05 Feb 1802	Eleazar Fullen wider	Jacob & Katie(Winters)		MONT	950	1830
31 Aug 1803	William W. Galey			BMON	164	1823
00 000 0000	Thomas B. Glover			NSPC	454	---
08 Oct 1805	Thomas G. Glover	Uriah & Priscilla(Gaddis)	NJ/x	HLOW	635	---
01 Oct 1818	Granville C. Gordon	David	NC/x	BPUT	463	1829
00 000 1806	William Gott			MPRO	148	1829
00 000 1806	William Gott	Robert		MONT	745	---
00 000 1806	William Gott			BMON	317	1829
06 Jun 1809	James H. Graham			HJOH	674	---
14 Oct 1798	James Green	Thomas & Margaret(Johnson)	Pa/Pa	CLOW	936	---
13 Sep 1812	H.H. Hall			BMON	382	---
08 Sep 1828	Samuel Q. Hall	Bainbridge & Polly(Nichols)		BMON	382	---

Date	Name	Parents / Spouse	Place	Code	No.	Year
00 000 1827	James H. Hammond			ASUL	76	1883
11 Oct 1818	Gilbert Hankins	William & Mary	Va/Ky	CLOW	465	c1840
05 Jul 1805	William Hanna			BMON	349	---
07 Sep 1835	John A. Hardins			MONT	964	---
01 Mar 1824	James F. Harney	Josiah & Elizabeth(Miller)	Md01/x	BGAS	167	---
01 Mar 1824	James F. Harney	Rev.Gilbert T. & Charlotte(Kyle)x/Va G.T.		MPRO	336	1835
07 Dec 1807	Hon.James H.Harrison	Joshua & Sarah(Paris)	Md/Tn	BMON	380	---
10 Feb 1828	Reuben T. Harrison	Reuben & Rhoda(Paris)	Md/Ky	HWSP	786	---
08 Jun 1824	Thomas J. Harrison			BGAS	170	---
00 000 1849	Philip T. Hartford	William & Betsey(Hamilton)	Va/Va	HDOH	1223	---
00 000 0000	Irmi Heady			CLOW	402	---
00 000 0000	James Henderson			EIND	G89	---
00 000 0000	James C.Henderson			BMWB	190	1831
00 000 0000	Hollingsworth Bros.			AVAN	69	1849
22 Oct 1834	James A. Hope	Isaac & Susan(Ellis)	Md/Ky	BPUT	361	1835
00 000 1800	Walter Houseman			FMWA	B808	---
15 Jan 1798	Henry Hunter	Samuel & Elizabeth	Ky/Ky	BPUT	509	1865
00 000 1820	Fielden Jeffries			ASUL	86	---
00 000 1810	Daniel Ketcham			HKDA	845	---
00 000 0000	Henry Lee			HWBJ	343	1816
10 Dec 1801	William Lee	John & Elizabeth(Mitchell) Va77/Va77		BPUT	482	---
01 Feb 1804	John Lemmon			BGAS	233	---
22 Mar 1799	Anna Lewis[Jones]			HJOH	621	1836
00 000 0000	Amzi Logan			HCLI	756	---
01 Nov 1832	Marcus D.L.Long	William D. & Rhoda H(Clark)		BMON	421	1854
12 Oct 1816	Thomas Long	Thomas & Nancy(Jackson)	Va/x	BPUT	327	1829
00 000 1820	W.D. Long			CLOW	364	---
30 Sep 1818	Allen McCaslin	David & Mary(Marrs)	Va67/Pa77	HJOH	632	---
09 Mar 1808	James McClain	Jacob & Catherine(Lacefield)Mercer/82		HJOH	491	1828
00 000 1803	Nancy McCook[Strange]			HCLI	463	1810
12 Nov 1809	Andrew McCormick	John & Martha Jane(Todd)	Va/x	BMON	351	
00 000 1807	Preston McCormick			BMON	357	
17 Nov 1807	John McIndoo	Jacob & Margaret(McDowell)	Pa/Ky	CLOW	880	

S H E L B Y   C O U N T Y   (C O N T L.)

BIRTHDATE	NAME OF BIOGRAPHEE	PARENTS/BIRTHPLACE/BIRTHDATE		SOURCE/PAGE	DATE
27 Dec 1846	Delilah Maddox[Todd]	Elijah & Emily(Todd)	Ky12/Ky14	MONT 1185	----
31 Mar 1812	A.C. Martin	William & Mary A(Wayman)	Va/Va	HLOW 925	----
00 000 1801	Edmund W. Martin	Abner & Mary(White)		HLOW 924	1814
00 000 1812	Jonathan J. Martin			ASUL 101	----
00 000 1816	Manoah Martin	Lewis	Va/x	BSCC B174	----
13 Jun 1810	John Mathes			BGAS 265	1814
07 Jan 1837	Catesby J.Mayfield	Southerland & Amelia	Ky/Canada	HPDB 728	----
00 000 0000	Elhanan Miles	James & Susan(Simmons)	Oh/Ky	BHOT T363	----
03 Dec 1827	Harvey Miller	James & Nancy(Lee)	Va/Va	MONT 1092	1831
10 Apr 1818	William Minter			WHSU B236	----
29 Sep 1834	James L.Mitchell	P.L.D. & Mary A(Ketcham)		EIND G151	----
29 Sep 1834	Maj.James L.Mitchell	Pleasant L.D. & Mary A(Ketcham)	Va/Va	TBAB 324	----
08 Dec 1809	Pleasant L.D. Mitchell			BGAS 276	----
21 Apr 1817	Jacob B. Moss	George & Lydia(Vuilderback)	Ky/Ky	CLOW 483	----
12 Aug 1817	Matthias Mount	P.J. & Elizabeth P(Woodward)	Ky/Ky	HSHE 732	----
22 Feb 1846	James Nutgrass	William & Mary(Page)		BPUT 452	1850
00 000 0000	John Parkhurst			HJOH 753	----
07 Jun 1825	Bennet Payne	Robert H. & Sarah(Whitecotten)	Va/Tn	CLOW 509	1831
14 Dec 1799	John W. Payne			BGAS 309	----
13 Mar 1829	S.H. Pearcy	William & Mary(Holly)	Va/Pa	BMMB 360	----
00 000 0000	James H. Pebworth			HHHE 631	----
03 Dec 1808	John W. Penn	Ephraim & Mary	Ky/Ky	HCAR 306+	1816
00 000 0000	John H. Perkins			ARIP 51	1825
00 000 0000	Mary Pierce[Henderson]			BMMB 190	1831
00 000 0000	Mary Piercy[Henderson]			EIND G89	----
00 000 0000	Allison Pollard			EIND K39	----
00 000 0000	Mary[Pollard]			EIND K39	----
28 Mar 1848	Jeptha D. Porter	Samuel & Etheelenda(Brown)	Ky/Ky	CLOW 544	1864
11 Sep 1833	William Radford	William & Nancy(Pearcy)	**09/**06	BMMB 361	----
28 Apr 1829	J.T. Ragsdale	Frederick & Sarah(Hunter)	Ky/Ky	HJOH 714	1834

Date	Name	Parents/Spouse	Origin	Place	No.	Year
24 Nov 1823	Lewis N. Rice	Jesse & Martha(Wilcoxson)	Va/Va	CLOW	409	---
00 000 0000	Cassandra Robertson			BSCC	B118	---
09 Aug 1793	John G. Ryker	Gerardus	NJ/x	BSCC	B264	1851
19 Mar 1843	George W. Scearce	Ezra W. & Martha(Shepherd)	Ky08/Ky09	HHHE	200	---
00 000 1815	William Schwindler	Jonathan & Letitia(Mount)	Va/Va	MONT	694	---
07 Apr 1798	David Scott			BGAS	347	---
00 000 0000	Abigail Sellers[Parkhurst]			HJOH	753	1827
00 000 1801	Polly Sellers[McCaslin]			HJOH	635	1831
04 Mar 1831	William T. Servies	William A. & Eliza(Pilcher)		MONT	1081	1830
04 Mar 1830	William T. Servies	William A. & Eliza(Pilcher)		BWON	418	1828
07 Sep 1827	Thomas B. Shannon	Alexander & Agnes(Brown)	Va/Pa	BHOT	T407	1864
01 Aug 1828	James S. Shelburne	Benjamin & Johanne(Webb)	Va/Ky	BVPA	220	---
17 Mar 1791	Nancy Shepherd[Clem]			HJOH	819	---
13 May 1845	Fannie E. Shipman[Fullenwider]			MONT	951	---
00 000 1806	Lucinda Smith[Glazebrook]			BPUT	443	---
00 000 0000	Deliah Spencer[Slaughter]	Capt. Spier		EIND	A51	---
00 000 0000	George Still	Murph D.	Eng/x	HLOW	600	---
14 Jul 1796	Jeremiah Stillwell			BWON	241	---
00 000 1836	Dr. W.O. Stone			ASUL	146	1881
12 Apr 1810	Nathaniel S. Straughan	John & Obedience(Scott)	Va/Ky	BPUT	401	1831
00 000 1813	Rhoda A. Swindler			MPRO	149	1829
11 Aug 1817	Dr. E.P. Talbott	Othoniel & Elizabeth(Fitzwalter)Md/**		CLOW	411	---
28 Apr 1831	J.E. Talbott	Lorenzo & Hester(Scott)		BPUT	479	1831
13 Apr 1813	Columbus Tegarden			HLOW	614	---
31 Jul 1798	John Tegarden	Basil & Annie(Todd)		HLOW	638	1816
24 May 1809	Hezekiah Thomas	William & Mary(Seyfres)	Va/Pa	JACK	723	---
00 000 0000	Huldah Thomas[Boothe]			CLOW	396	---
12 Nov 1794	Elizabeth Threlkeld[Sanford]			EBOO	359	---
00 000 1846	Joe Tilley			ASUL	152	---
00 000 1809	Johnson Todd			MONT	1185	---
00 000 1809	Johnson Todd			BWON	354	---
01 Mar 1826	Franklin Underwood	John		HHHE	316	1834
00 000 1824	William Underwood	John & Rebecca(Radford)		HHHE	648	---
18 Oct 1824	Cornelius D. Vannuys	Tunis & Catherine		HJOH	666	---

BIRTHDATE	NAME OF BIOGRAPHEE	PARENTS/BIRTHPLACE/BIRTHDATE		SOURCE/PAGE	DATE
03 Nov 1829	Rev.Hervey L.Vannuys	Tunis & Kate(Demaree)	NJ75/Pa	PBES 457	----
16 Aug 1820	John H. Vannuys	Tunis & Catherine(Demaree)	NJ72/Pa	HJOH 667	1836
00 000 1803	Samuel Vannuys			HJOH 666	----
00 000 0000	Rebecca Vontrece[McKnight]			HLOW 261	----
10 Apr 1814	Catherine Wasson[Hall]	Alexander & Jane		----	----
00 000 0000	David T. Weir			BSCC B117	----
00 000 0000	William M. Weir			BSCC B118	----
17 Dec 1797	Bland B. Whitaker	Levi & Margaret(Seaton)	Md/Md	CLOW 904	1827
00 000 1830	George B. White			TBAB 682	1843
00 000 1827	Dr. S.T. Whittington	Littleton & Frances		BMON 358	----
17 Dec 1825	William Whittington			DIND 1295	----
14 Oct 1836	Henry Williams	Garland & Harriet(Mitchell)	**/x	MONT 876	----
19 Aug 1801	John Williams	John & Sarah(Kirkendall)	Pa/Pa	BMWB 351	----
29 Mar 1814	Abel Wilson	Alexander & Sarah(Lucas)	Ky/Ky	BPUT 364	----
17 May 1826	Dr. John L. Wooden	Levi & Frances(Weyman)	**/Ger	GBRD 400	1821
00 000 1800	Gabriel Woodfill	Andrew & --(Mitchell)	Pa/x	GBRD 369	----
06 Sep 1804	Gabriel Woodfill	Andrew	Pa81/x	EIND D76	----
00 000 0000	William H. Young	Jacob & Rachel(Goodnight)	Ky/Va	JACK 661	----
03 May 1828	Jonathan Yount			HJOH 706	----

S I M P S O N   C O U N T Y

BIRTHDATE	NAME OF BIOGRAPHEE	PARENTS/BIRTHPLACE/BIRTHDATE		SOURCE/PAGE	DATE
12 Aug 1836	David M. Kelley	Joseph & Dosha(Holcomb)	NC/NC	HWSP 547	----
00 000 0000	Col. Ledgerwood			BVPA 352	1803
00 000 0000	W.L. Wilson			GIBS 237	1865
00 000 0000	W.L. Wilson			AGIP 13	1865

SPENCER COUNTY

BIRTHDATE	NAME OF BIOGRAPHEE	PARENTS/BIRTHPLACE/BIRTHDATE	SOURCE/PAGE	DATE
28 Mar 1814	Robert Allen		WHSU B80	---
10 Jun 1850	Charles B. Anderson	Charles W. & Mary A(Brown) Ky/Ky	HWSP 495	---
05 Jan 1830	John P. Baird		BGAS 11	---
22 Sep 1831	L.M. Baird	Va/x	HVAN 156	---
00 000 0000	Stephen C. Beard	Stephen & Sarah(McDonald)	BHV I 672	1818
00 000 1841	Isaac W. Beauchamp		BGAS 19	---
00 000 1848	James M. Boston		ASUL 33	1851
23 Oct 1837	M.S. Boston	Edward & Sarah(Stout) Md/Ky	BHV I 685	1840
10 Jan 1802	Arthur Boyll		BHV I 688	---
10 Feb 1807	Culbertson Boyll	Henry & Sarah(Park) Va/Jefferson	BHV I 687	---
16 Feb 1822	Perry Brown		HGSU 797	1831
00 000 0000	P.A. Buskirk	Alfred & Letitia(Dayhoff)	HGSU 440	1823
26 Jun 1811	Catherine Carr[Boyll]		BHV I 688	---
22 Sep 1833	Dr. William O. Collins	Archibald & Susan(Ware) Ky/Ky	BHV I 708	---
00 000 1847	William M. Cook		ASUL 48	1890
00 000 0000	J.F.[Dicers]		ASUL 55	1862
27 Feb 1825	James G. Foreman	Joseph & Susannah(Cox) Ky/Ky	CLOW 536	1855
19 Jan 1821	Rhoda Ann Hatfield[Francis]	William & Elizabeth(Gregory)Eng	HSHE 745	---
11 Nov 1796	Isaac Hoagland		BGAS 185	---
26 Dec 1841	D.S. Howard	John & Phila(Summers) NC/x	BVPA 167	1855
00 000 1840	V. Jewell		ASUL 86	---
14 Oct 1839	N.B. Kennett	Joseph H. & Rhoda(St. Clair)	BVPA 440	1851
03 Nov 1832	Isaac N. Kesler		BGAS 221	---
01 Sep 1795	Ephram Kester	William	BHV I 812	1822
00 000 1825	Thomas I. Kinnett		BVPA 488	1850
00 000 1804	John Lemmon		BSCC B164	---
00 000 0000	Rebecca McGrew[Miller]		BHV I 708	---
00 000 1829	M.J[McKinney]		ASUL 106	1836
14 Jul 1822	Martha Maddox[Long]	Nelson & Martha(Beauchamp)	BPUT 327	---
00 000 1807	John L. Menaugh		BSCC A271	---

BIRTHDATE	NAME OF BIOGRAPHEE	PARENTS/BIRTHPLACE/BIRTHDATE		SOURCE/PAGE	DATE
00 000 0000	David Miller			BHVI	708	---
24 Apr 1820	Charles W. Moss	George & Lydia(Vuilderback)	Va/Ky	CLOW	482	---
17 Dec 1805	James G. Norman			BVPA	472	1846
13 Jul 1826	Allen F. Payne	J.C. & Rebecca(Mercer)	Va92/**97	CLOW	454	1828
14 Mar 1823	William Payne	Robert H.		CLOW	509	---
15 Aug 1837	James M. Polk	William & Sarah(Stoptaugh)		HJOH	809	1856
28 Nov 1831	Harvey M. Pound	David & Massie(Sparks)	Ky/Ky	BHVI	900	1826
11 Jan 1826	Spencer Russell	James & Mary(McKinley)		HGSU	778	1830
00 000 1824	James H. Scott			ASUL	136	---
00 000 1824	James H. Shaw			ASUL	139	---
17 Oct 1808	Mahala Shively[Pierce]			HLOW	659	---
07 Mar 1825	J.C. Slout			BVPA	430	1826
01 Aug 1823	Reuben Smith	Morgan & Elizabeth(Jeems)		MGSU	422	1825
00 000 1822	S.W. Snyder			ASUL	143	1851
00 000 0000	C. Stark			ASUL	147	---
14 Sep 1811	Elijah M. Stout	William & Mary(Van Dyke)	Va/Va	CLOW	547	1835
00 000 1827	Elizabeth[Stout]			ASUL	147	---
01 Jan 1829	George W. Stout	Robert & Martha(VanDyke)	Ky/Ky	BHVI	946	---
03 Dec 1852	J.W. Stout	James & Arsula(Taylor)	Ky/Ky	BHVI	947	1855
00 000 1827	James Stout			ASUL	147	1855
00 000 0000	Nancy Thurman[Hedges]			BHVI	687	---
07 Oct 1826	Richard Watson	Scarlet & Kizzia(Walker)	Va/**	BVAN	497	1828
14 Nov 1820	Louis L. Weeks	William L. & Nancy(Kester)	Va/Ky	BHVI	994	---
00 000 0000	Elizabeth Wells[Beard]			BHVI	672	---

T A Y L O R   C O U N T Y

BIRTHDATE	NAME OF BIOGRAPHEE	PARENTS/BIRTHPLACE/BIRTHDATE	SOURCE/PAGE	DATE

BIRTHDATE	NAME OF BIOGRAPHEE	PARENTS/BIRTHPLACE/BIRTHDATE		SOURCE/PAGE	DATE
18 May 1800	William H. Craig			BGAS	83	----
16 Nov 1824	John Hogeland	John & Nancy(Shipp)	Pa/x	HJOH	705	1832

T O D D   C O U N T Y

BIRTHDATE	NAME OF BIOGRAPHEE	PARENTS/BIRTHPLACE/BIRTHDATE		SOURCE/PAGE	DATE
00 000 0000	Dr. James Allison			AWAR	58	1877
00 000 0000	Rev.Patterson B.McCormick			GIBS	241	1842
00 000 0000	John T. Simpson			AWAR	58	1826
16 Dec 1831	James P. Utley	David H. & Ellen(Heltsley)	NC/Ky	HPOS	656	c1833
14 Jun 1853	George B. Welty	John & Frances E(Bynch)	Pa14/Tn17	MONT	661	----

T R I G G   C O U N T Y

BIRTHDATE	NAME OF BIOGRAPHEE	PARENTS/BIRTHPLACE/BIRTHDATE		SOURCE/PAGE	DATE
06 Nov 1851	Hilary E. Bacon	Charles A. & Margaret(Gibson)	Va/Al	DIND	2168	----

T R I M B L E   C O U N T Y

BIRTHDATE	NAME OF BIOGRAPHEE	PARENTS/BIRTHPLACE/BIRTHDATE		SOURCE/PAGE	DATE
05 Dec 1819	Dr. William C.A. Bain	Leroy & Elizabeth(Baker)		EIND	C1	----
00 000 1831	William E. Ball	Henry & Nancy(Wise)	Ky/Ky	BVPA	426	1837
00 000 0000	G.H. Barringer			AJEN	47	1879
00 000 0000	Rev. Henry Brenton			SIND	580	1822
06 Oct 1818	Alexander B. Conduitt	Willis G. & Matilda(Moreland)	Tn/x	NSPC	265	1826
06 Oct 1818	Alexander B. Conduitt			BGAS	74	----
17 Aug 1836	J. Randolph Conway	John & Emily(Hoagland)	Ky00/Ky03	BSCC	B217	1840
17 Aug 1836	J. Rodolphus Conway	John & Emily(Hogland)	Ky00/Ky03	BSCC	B218	1840

T R I M B L E   C O U N T Y   (C O N T.)

BIRTHDATE	NAME OF BIOGRAPHEE	PARENTS/BIRTHPLACE/BIRTHDATE	SOURCE/PAGE	DATE
00 000 1824	Thomas D. George	Milton	BSCC B227	----
26 Jan 1817	Oliver P. Gilham		BGAS 142	----
00 000 0000	H.D. Green		AJEN 47	1822
00 000 1824	Margaret M.Hunter[Peggs]		HJOH 879	----
00 000 0000	Thomas Kirk		ARIP 50	1839
21 Feb 1818	James H. McClellan	William Va/x	HJOH 635	----
00 000 1808	John Mathis	William & Mary(Warden)	BSCC B243	----
00 000 0000	Francis Mayfield		HJOH 428	----
29 Apr 1818	Francis F. Mayfield		BGAS 267	----
29 Apr 1819	Francis F. Mayfield	Joshua & Lucinda(Ouseley) Ky/Ky	BSCC B245	----
00 000 0000	Lewis Metesser		AKNO 64	1875
00 000 0000	John L. Miles		ARIP 50	1860
17 Jan 1853	Grafton Peak	William A.J. & Susannah(Johnson)	HJOH 806	----
14 Sep 1814	Evan O. Peggs	Joseph & Nancy(Cunningham) Ire/Pa	HJOH 879	----
23 Dec 1825	Isabella Peggs[Jones]Jacob	94/x	HJOH 622	----
24 Oct 1807	Joseph Peggs	Joseph & Nancy(Cunningham) Ire/Pa	HJOH 807	1842
15 Jan 1832	Harvey Satterwhite		BGAS 344	----
17 May 1824	Hannibal Trout		BGAS 396	----
06 Nov 1803	Thomas Wilson		HDOH 977	----

U N I O N   C O U N T Y

BIRTHDATE	NAME OF BIOGRAPHEE	PARENTS/BIRTHPLACE/BIRTHDATE	SOURCE/PAGE	DATE
27 Nov 1855	Dr. William Alexander	William & Augusta(Boetinger) Ire/Ger	HVAN 263	1856
00 000 0000	Sarah Curry[McClure]		WHSU B263	----
13 Jul 1861	William M. Dunham	Dr. William & Susan(Hardin) Va/Ky	EVAN 80	----
00 000 1860	Charles B. Harris	Addison J. & Catherine(Bosley) Ky/Md	EVAN 35	1885
31 Aug 1851	Anthony C. Hawkins	Anthony S. & Elizabeth J(Hopgood)Ky/Ky	HVAN 91	14/16

				WHSU B263	----
00 000 0000	Samuel McClure	James W. & Jane(Leach)	NCc10/Tn08		
01 Mar 1848	Dr.Thomas E.Powell	James & Jane(Leach)	NCc09/Tn13	EVAN 39	----
01 Mar 1848	Dr. T.E. Powell			HVAN 261	----

W A R R E N   C O U N T Y

BIRTHDATE	NAME OF BIOGRAPHEE	PARENTS/BIRTHPLACE/BIRTHDATE		SOURCE/PAGE	DATE
00 000 0000	Elizabeth Allen[Williams]			HPOS 615	----
18 Sep 1832	John J.W. Billingsley			BGAS 25	----
00 000 0000	Annie Carter[Eskew]			SHGI 728	----
00 000 0000	George W. DePriest	William & Nancy		SHGI 845	----
25 May 1805	Joseph Devin			BGAS 100	----
20 Nov 1856	John W. Dillard	Henry & Mary(Combs)	Ky/Ky	FDAV 398	----
00 000 0000	J.S. Epperson			AGIP 12	1839
04 Feb 1830	James S. Epperson	Charles & Elizabeth(Smith)	Va72/x	GIBS 170	----
00 000 0000	James S. Epperson			GIBS 233	1840
00 000 0000	John Eskew			SHGI 728	----
27 Jul 1811	John Hall			BGAS 160	----
00 000 0000	John H. Harpole			AWAR 57	1821
16 Aug 1819	Thomas J. Hudspeth	Thomas	Vac93/x	EIND A25	----
25 Dec 1851	Willis F. McCoy	Stark & Marinda(Kelsey)	** c28/**	HPDB 425	----
00 000 0000	Nathan Pryatt			AWAR 57	1831
25 Nov 1807	Nathan Pyeatt			BGAS 320	----
18 Sep 1812	Miles Rice	Joseph & Frances(Broadwell)	Tn/x	HWSP 203	----
00 000 0000	Lewis A. Rose			HHHE 640	----
25 Jan 1806	Thomas Shoulders			BGAS 355	----
23 Aug 1841	Dr.Walter R.Temple	Jonathan C. & Sarah F(Brashear) Ky/Ky		HWSP 228	----
00 000 0000	Marion Thompson			AWAR 58	1836
00 000 0000	T. Woolsey			AGIP 16	1835

WASHINGTON COUNTY

BIRTHDATE	NAME OF BIOGRAPHEE	PARENTS/BIRTHPLACE/BIRTHDATE		SOURCE/PAGE		DATE
31 Jan 1828	James P. Arvin	Harry	Md87/x	HKDA	873	----
17 Feb 1813	C. Barlow	John & Priscilla(Burris)	Ky/Ky	BHOT	T334	1829
00 000 0000	Dr. J.W. Bradbarn			AHAR	46	1879
16 Sep 1807	John Calvert			WHSU	A44	1814
00 000 0000	Betsey Carter[Westerfield]			HHHE	679	----
25 Jun 1827	Daniel Cass	James & Elizabeth(Plew)		HGSU	809	----
21 Feb 1818	William E. Catlin			WHSU	A45	----
17 Nov 1811	Oliver Cromwell			BGAS	86	----
25 Jun 1820	Samuel Cutsinger			HJOH	408	1822
06 Apr 1818	James M. Dearing	John & Polly	Va/Ky	HPDB	451	----
20 Dec 1812	George G. Dunn			BGAS	109	----
00 000 1836	J.F. Gritton			ASUL	70	1871
16 Mar 1792	Ede Harding	Robert & Martha	Pa/Pa	SIND	650	1805
00 000 1798	Israel Harding	Robert & Martha	Pa/Pa	SIND	650	1805
16 Jan 1798	Israel Harding			BGAS	166	----
10 Sep 1795	Samuel Harding			BGAS	166	----
00 000 1795	Samuel Harding	Robert		SIND	650	1805
23 Jan 1835	William A.Jackson	John T. & Mary(Pirtle)	Ky/Ky	HGSU	415	1839
28 Jul 1810	Rev. John Keeling	James & Mary		HSHE	731	----
12 Jun 1844	John H. Kidwell			HKDA	784	----
00 000 0000	Jane S[Kirkman]			GIBS	233	1825
10 Apr 1808	Anthony S. Mason	James & Rebecca(Sandusky)		HGSU	784	----
00 000 0000	John S. Morgan			AKNO	60	1863
16 Sep 1804	Nathan Nichols	Nathan & Nancy(Gresham)	NC/Va	BMMB	345	----
00 000 1852	W.M. Plew			ASUL	123	1856
10 Jun 1810	Green B. Reed			HPDB	445	1818
11 Sep 1824	John J. Reinhart	Caleb & Eunice(Farris)	Pa/Ky	LLDM	B49	----
00 000 0000	L. Robinson			AGIP	16	1839
00 000 0000	Hillary Spalding			HKDA	800	----
00 000 1802	William Stevens			SCWA	936	----

BIRTHDATE	NAME OF BIOGRAPHEE	PARENTS/BIRTHPLACE/BIRTHDATE		SOURCE/PAGE		DATE
00 000 0000	Mary Strange[Spalding]			HKDA	800	---
00 000 0000	J.R. Summers			AHAR	46	1844
17 Jul 1841	John F. Thomas	James & Mary(Trotter)	Va/NC	HPDB	428	1824
23 Jun 1820	John W. Thompson			NSPC	357	---
03 Apr 1817	William Thompson			BGAS	391	---
13 Jun 1816	James Wade	Evan & Ellen(Brewer)		HKDA	891	---

W A Y N E   C O U N T Y

BIRTHDATE	NAME OF BIOGRAPHEE	PARENTS/BIRTHPLACE/BIRTHDATE		SOURCE/PAGE		DATE
07 Jul 1805	Linzy Ballu	Linzy & Agnes(Repley)		BHOT	T334	1827
00 000 0000	Dr. A.H. Bryan			AVAN	69	1876
22 Aug 1832	Dr. Anthony H.Bryan	Edmund & Lettice(Pierce)	Va96/Boyd05	BVAN	75	---
22 Aug 1832	Dr. Anthony H.Bryan	Edmund	96/x	EIND	A9	---
13 Nov 1823	Daniel W. Cooper	Abraham & Elizabeth(Collett)	Ky/Ky	HJOH	702	1833
00 000 0000	E. Cowes			AGRE	53	1848
00 000 1840	James Dyke	William	Eng/x	FDAV	340	---
12 Apr 1820	James H. Ellers	John & Susan(Smith)		CLOW	932	---
00 000 1797	Abraham Fox	Abraham		HGSU	769	---
02 Apr 1823	John Gibbs	James & Mary	Ky00/Ky	BWMB	185	1830
13 Jan 1815	James Hamilton	John & Elender(Collett)	NC/NC	BWMB	251	---
00 000 0000	Mary Haynes[McGowan]	John & Margery		GIBS	217	---
22 Jan 1855	Dr. J.W. McGowan	Dr. W.J. & Delila J(Ramsay)	**/**	SHGI	896	---
00 000 0000	J.W. McGowan			AGIP	9	1863
00 000 0000	William J. McGowan			AGIP	9	1863
00 000 0000	Dr. William J.McGowan			GIBS	238	1863
13 Sep 1820	Owen W. Owens	Andrew & Sarah(Brown)	Ky/x	HLOW	352	1820
00 000 0000	D.J. Ramsey[McGowan]			GIBS	238	---
26 Jan 1830	John F. Ray	John & Polly		BWMB	203	1830
00 000 0000	Samuel J. Scott	Thomas J. & Elizabeth(Kennedy)		HKDA	831	---
00 000 0000	Nelson Sinclair			AGRE	53	1833
00 000 0000	Nelson Sinclair		Va/Va	HGSU	404	---

WAYNE COUNTY (CONT.)

BIRTHDATE	NAME OF BIOGRAPHEE	PARENTS/BIRTHPLACE/BIRTHDATE		SOURCE/PAGE	DATE
17 Jul 1828	Dr. James Turpin	George & Jennie(McDonald)	Ky/Ky	HWSP 488	---
29 May 1828	James Warren	Reuben	Va/x	HLOW 639	---
00 000 0000	Isaac West	Alexander & Sarah		HHHE 648	---
14 Feb 1803	West Lee Wright	William	NC/x	JACK 643	1809

WEBSTER COUNTY

BIRTHDATE	NAME OF BIOGRAPHEE	PARENTS/BIRTHPLACE/BIRTHDATE		SOURCE/PAGE	DATE
17 Aug 1873	Floyd J. Biggs	Alonzo C. & Charlotte J(Hall)		SHGI 458	---
17 Nov 1864	George K. Denton	George M. & Emma(Kirkpatrick)		DIND 2259	---
00 000 0000	L.P. Hobgood			AGIP 12	---
06 Mar 1838	Laban M. Rice	James R. & Elizabeth(Nichols)NC/Caldw		HVAN 161	90/07

WHITLEY COUNTY

BIRTHDATE	NAME OF BIOGRAPHEE	PARENTS/BIRTHPLACE/BIRTHDATE		SOURCE/PAGE	DATE
04 May 1806	Andrew Campbell	William & Mary(Gilless)	Va/Va	HGSU 430	---
00 000 0000	C.G. Lovitt			AGIP 9	1861
25 Mar 1852	John A. McFarland	Presley & Nancy(Winkler)	Ky27/Va27	BVPA 393	---
25 Aug 1828	Calvin Pruett	Michael	Tn03/04	BVPA 381	---
06 Sep 1821	William Pruett	William & Sarah(DeMoss)	Ky/Ky	HLOW 661	---
26 Jan 1830	Samuel Ramsey			BGAS 321	---

WOLFE COUNTY

BIRTHDATE	NAME OF BIOGRAPHEE	PARENTS/BIRTHPLACE/BIRTHDATE		SOURCE/PAGE	DATE
02 Sep 1886	Fred Creech	Frank L. & Nancy(Riggs)	Va/Va	HHHE 233	----

W O O D F O R D   C O U N T Y

BIRTHDATE	NAME OF BIOGRAPHEE	PARENTS/BIRTHPLACE/BIRTHDATE		SOURCE/PAGE	DATE
00 000 1824	Elisha Baker			BVPA 394	1832
29 Mar 1814	Dr. James Baker			HLOW 662	----
00 000 1812	John Baker	James	Va85/x	HKDA 310	----
11 Jun 1826	Robert A. Brookie	William & Mary(Dougherty)		HCLI 635	1834
00 000 0000	Nancy Buchanan			HHHE 843	----
12 Apr 1792	Joseph Dale	George	**/x	WFUF 541	1806
01 Mar 1832	Walter Elkin	Merryman & Susan A(Bailey)	Ky/Ky	CLOW 425	----
00 000 0000	Martha T. Elliott[Moore]			HJOH 828	----
20 Apr 1829	J.H. Faris	John & Emily(Redmond)	Ky00/Ky	HKDA 477	----
08 Feb 1818	John L. Ford			BGAS 130	----
00 00c 1808	Thomas Glenn			BMON 356	1827
00 000 1798	Patsy Harper[Shepard]			HKDA 462	----
01 Aug 1795	Mason J. Howell			EIND A25	c1800
30 Jun 1792	Samuel Jack			BGAS 202	----
26 Oct 1823	David Long	John & Elizabeth(Martin)	Va96/**	HLOW 259	1829
00 000 0000	Edward McGuire			HJOH 791	----
26 Oct 1804	Isaac Miles			HDOH 842	----
00 000 1810	Jane Rankin[Field]			HLOW 293	----
00 000 1820	W.T. Ross			GIND 659	----
25 Jan 1808	William T. Ross			BGAS 339	----
03 Sep 1834	Ignatius F. Shannon	David A. & Nancy(Alexander)		BPUT 381	1835
00 000 1799	Horace B. Shepard			HKDA 466	----
14 Apr 1799	Horace B. Shepard			BGAS 352	----
27 Jan 1821	James H. Smith	William & Anna M(Tull)		BSCC B274	----
01 Sep 1814	Granville T. Smitha	John		BSCC B274	----
21 Nov 1802	Alexander C. Stevenson			BGAS 372	----

BIRTHDATE	NAME OF BIOGRAPHEE	PARENTS/BIRTHPLACE/BIRTHDATE	SOURCE/PAGE	DATE
17 Aug 1788	Wilson Thompson		BGAS 391	----
01 Sep 1800	Greenberry Ward	Va70/Va70	BVPA 113	1821
22 Nov 1806	Mahala Webb[Fisher]		HSHE 655	1821
29 May 1834	Jacob Wilhoit	Abram & Frances(Mosby) Ky/Va	HPDB 617	1838

C O U N T Y   N O T   G I V E N

BIRTHDATE	NAME OF BIOGRAPHEE	PARENTS/BIRTHPLACE/BIRTHDATE	SOURCE/PAGE	DATE
04 Sep 1824	Abraham Abbett		HWBJ 523	----
11 Feb 1825	Sarah A[Abbett]		HWBJ 523	----
00 00c 1815	E.N.H. Adams		HJOH 719	----
02 Feb 1804	Henry Adams		BMMB 359	----
00 000 0000	Henry Adams		BMMB 245	----
00 000 0000	Henry Adams		BMMB 246	----
00 000 0000	Jacob Adams		BMMB 246	----
00 000 0000	John Adams		BPUT 387	----
00 000 0000	Peter Adams		HWSP 777	----
00 000 0000	Joseph Albin		BPUT 399	1832
00 000 0000	Mary Ann Alcorne[Burton]		HHEN 751	----
00 000 0000	Mary Alcorne[Burton]		HENR 721	----
00 000 0000	J.M. Alexander[Ward]		BMMB 784	----
00 000 0000	Nancy Alexander[Spencer]		BMMB 782	----
00 000 0000	William Alexander		HPOS 647	----
00 000 0000	Hugh Allen		HWAY B377	----
00 000 0000	Mary Allen[Gardner] James & Martha(Braton)		BPUT 457	----
00 000 0000	Nancy Allen[Cain]		BHOT H375	----
00 000 0000	Nancy Allen[Hargis]		HWSP 787	----

Date	Name	Parents	Place	Code	Ref	Year
00 000 0000	Robert N. Allen			TBAB	377	c1825
00 000 0000	Sarah Alkire[Hurst]			HMIA	522	1845
00 000 0000	Charles Allison			SIND	625	1819
00 000 0000	David Allison			SIND	625	1819
00 000 0000	Thomas Almon			HPOS	581	1790
00 000 0000	Thomas Alverson			CLOW	926	---
00 000 0000	Catherine Ament[Dodson]			FMWA	B132	---
00 000 0000	Christiana Amos[Pruden]			BAWE	294	---
00 000 0000	James Anderson			HPDB	735	---
00 000 0000	James Anderson			BWMB	295	---
00 000 0000	Joel Anderson			HWBJ	716	---
00 000 0000	John Anderson			HPDB	736	---
00 000 0000	Sarah C. Anderson[Johnson]			GIBS	235	1858
00 000 0000	Vincen Anderson			CLOW	522	---
00 000 0000	William Anderson	Nathan & Elizabeth(Fortner)	Ky/Ky	FMWA	B519	1819
00 000 0000	Abraham Annis	John		WHSU	B102	1832
00 000 0000	Nancy Applegate(Tolle)			BHOT	T348	---
00 000 0000	Elizabeth Armstrong[Anderson]			HPDB	736	---
00 000 0000	Elizabeth Armstrong[Kelly]			HSHE	671	---
00 000 0000	John Armstrong			HLOW	885	---
00 000 0000	Margaret Armstrong			WHSU	B40	---
00 000 0000	Mary Armstrong[Taylor]			BWMB	209	1809
00 000 0000	Robert A. Armstrong			BHOT	H409	---
00 000 0000	Levin Arnett			WHSU	A35	---
00 000 0000	Rachel Arnold[Coats]			CLOW	909	---
01 Aug 1805	Richard Arnold	Richard & Rebecca	Ky65/Ky73	HHHE	692	1818
00 000 1795	Alexander Arrasmith			BVER	280	1816
00 000 0000	Elizabeth Ash[Cox]			HLOW	653	1861
25 Jan 1829	Robert Ash	Benjamin & Hannah(Fig)	Ky/Ky	HWSP	814	---
00 000 0000	Julia Ashby[Dillon]			HHHE	710	---
00 000 0000	Milanda Ashbrook[Cofer]			HHHE	296	---
00 000 0000	Melinda Asher[Alexander]			CLOW	886	1816
00 000 0000	John Askren			BHVI	661	---
00 000 0000	Lydia Atkins[Benbow]			HHHE	251	---
00 Feb 1814	Philip A. Atkinson			BGAS	10	---

BIRTHDATE	NAME OF BIOGRAPHEE	PARENTS/BIRTHPLACE/BIRTHDATE	SOURCE/PAGE	DATE
24 May 1847	Lucinda Aust[McCoy]		HPDB	425	---
00 000 0000	Mary E. Austin[Hillman]		GIBS	237	1871
00 000 0000	Minerva Awings[Cassady]		CLOW	918	---
00 000 0000	Joseph Bacon		FDAV	436	---
00 000 1820	Sarah A. Baer		HCAR	164	1836
00 000 1778	Mary Baird[Thompson]		HKDA	442	1802
10 Jun 1828	I.C. Baker	James H. & Nancy(Kemper) Ky/Ky	BWMB	283	---
18 Dec 1827	John Baker	Isaac & Patsy(Sparks) Ky01/02	MONT	1100	---
00 000 0000	Mary Baker[Burns]		BWMB	774	---
00 000 0000	Mary Baker[Riddle]		HWSP	820	---
00 000 0000	William Baker		BWMB	363	1822
04 Jul 1804	Rev.William Baker		HLOW	632	1811
00 000 0000	Eliza Baldon[Pickens]		DGIN	850	---
05 Jul 1867	James M. Baldwin	William & Malissa(Green) A1/A1	WHSU	B393	1900
12 Jun 1812	John L. Bales		BGAS	17	---
00 000 0000	Beverly Ballard		HHHE	503	---
18 May 1832	John Ballard	Taylor & Nancy(Fitzpatrick) 01/06	HJOH	475	---
00 000 0000	Polly Ann Ballard[Brown]		CLOW	533	---
00 000 0000	Cornelius Banta		BWMB	295	---
00 000 1786	Henry Banta		HKDA	809	---
00 000 0000	Henry Banta		EIND	J3	---
00 000 0000	Jacob Banta		TBAB	675	1832
00 000 0000	Nancy Banta[Carmine]	Abram & Mary(Demaree)	HJOH	775	---
14 Mar 1800	Rachel Banta[Kerlin]		HJOH	878	1831
00 000 0000	Lucy Barbee[Young]		HKDA	558	---
00 000 0000	Nancy Barker[Grigsby]		HWSP	518	---
23 Dec 1807	Harmon G. Barkwell		HWSP	440	---
00 000 0000	John Barlow		HSHE	666	---
00 000 0000	Ruth Barlow[Runkle]		HJOH	439	---
00 000 0000	Anna Barnes[Devore]		CLOW	95	---

Name	Parent / Notes	Origin	Date	Ref	No.	Year
Mary Barnes[Law]			00 000 0000	HJOH	424	1836
Phebe Barnes[DeCoursey]			00 000 1807	HJOH	411	1832
James F. Barnett			00 000 1815	BVER	245	1837
John Barr	James		00 000 0000	FDAV	383	1816
James Barrow			00 000 1808	HKDA	747	c1816
Catherine Bartholomew[McNaught]			00 000 0000	BHOT	T297	---
George Bartlett			00 000 0000	CLOW	881	1814
Lucinda Bartlett[McKee]			00 000 0000	HKDA	473	---
Winston Barton	Thomas & Susan(Alexander)		00 000 1813	CLOW	923	---
Joseph S. Basinger			00 000 0000	HWSP	136	---
J.H. Bass			00 000 0000	HPDB	461	1852
Josiah H. Bass			00 000 0000	HALL	182	---
Nancy Bass[Gray]			00 000 0000	BWMB	217	---
Nancy Bass[Gray]			00 000 0000	BWMB	786	---
Thomas W. Bass	Nathan & Ruhama(Price)	Va75/NJ77	29 Jul 1819	HWSP	208	---
Alford Batts			00 000 1844	DGIN	1119	1861
America Baty[Swindler]			00 000 0000	ASUL	21	---
Permelia[Baumgarden]			00 000 0000	BMON	418	---
Ellen Beasley[Herring]			00 000 0000	BHOT	410	---
T.J. Beauchamp			00 000 1843	HHHE	761	1813
James Beck			00c 1803	ASUL	25	1830
Phillip W. Beck			00 000 0000	HELX	362	1813
Simeon Beck			00 000 0000	ASUL	25	---
Clayborn Bedwell			00 000 1825	TCMA	605	---
Elisha Bedwell			00 000 0000	HKDA	313	---
Robert Bedwell	Thomas		00 000 0000	WHSU	A36	---
Enoch Beem			00 000 0000	WHSU	B160	---
Levi Beem			00 000 0000	CLOW	872	1810
Levi Beem	Daniel	03/x	00 000 1803	CLOW	826	1810
William Behymer			00 000 0000	TBAB	660	---
Elizabeth Bell[Duret]	Major Daniel		00 000 0000	BHOT	T298	1826
Henry Bell			00 000 1819	HMLA	416	1835
Mary A. Bell[Davis]	Samuel	Ky/x	00 000 0000	SIND	556	---
				BSCC	B138	---

BIRTHDATE	NAME OF BIOGRAPHEE	PARENTS/BIRTHPLACE/BIRTHDATE	SOURCE/PAGE	DATE
00 000 0000	M.A. Benham		HCAR 352	----
00 000 0000	Dr. A.T. Bennett		ASPE 65	1866
00 000 1812	John Bennett		BSCC B127	----
20 Mar 1851	Mary C. Bennett[Galey]John & Sarah		MONT 1240	----
00 000 0000	William Bennett		HLOW 648	----
00 000 0000	William Benson		DIND 2241	----
00 000 0000	Charles E. Bentley		BHVI 678	----
19 Sep 1815	Margaret Bergen[Covert]		HJOH 875	----
00 000 0000	Mary J. Berkshire[Hopping]		MONT 1015	----
26 Aug 1846	John Betz	John & Elizabeth(Mehringer) Ger/Ger	HPDB 585	----
00 000 0000	Jesse Bicknell		WHSU A38	1829
00 000 0000	Nancy Biggs[Crist]		CLOW 535	1831
17 Oct 1819	Asa J. Bishop		BPUT 454	----
00 000 0000	Cassandra Black[White] John & Virginia(Campbell)		HHHE 759	----
00 000 0000	Robert Black		FMWA B251	1813
00 000 0000	Robert Black		FMWA B384	----
00 000 0000	Robert Black	James	HWAY B324	1813
12 Aug 1812	Sarah Blackburn[Posey]		TBAB 404	----
22 Nov 1804	Martha Blair[Thompson]		EBOO 383	1830
00 000 0000	Samuel Blair		BHVI 867	----
00 000 0000	George W. Blakemore		BGAS 28	----
00 000 1802	Animy Blankenbeker[Tyler]		HWBJ 785	----
00 000 1811	Allen S. Blann		HKDA 449	c1832
00 000 0000	John Blanton		HHHE 674	----
00 000 0000	Daniel Bledsoe		BHVI 682	----
00 000 0000	Rhoda Blevence[Walker]		HKDA 468	c1827
00 000 1806	Jane Blockford[Kennedy]		BWMB 193	----
00 000 0000	Sarah Blunk[Brindley]		BVER 323	1828
00 000 0000	Melinda Boatman[Plummer]		WHSU B119	1868
00 000 0000	Sarah Bogan[Scales]		FWAR 132	----

Date	Name	Parents/Spouse	Birthplace	Code	No.	Year
00 000 0000	Elizabeth Bogard[Sills]			WHSU	B187	---
00 000 0000	Daniel Bohannon	Booten & Nancy(Claten)	Va/Va	HVAN	584	---
00 000 0000	George Bohannon	Booten & Nancy(Claten)	Va/Va	HVAN	584	---
00 000 0000	Henry Bohannon	Booten & Nancy(Claten)	Va/Va	HVAN	584	---
00 000 0000	James Bohannon	Booten & Nancy(Claten)	Va/Va	HVAN	584	---
00 000 0000	Susan Bohannon	Booten & Nancy(Claten)	Va/Va	HVAN	584	---
00 000 0000	F.M. Boling			ASUL	33	---
00 000 1849	C.B. Bolinger			ASUL	32	1864
00 000 1854	J.S. Bolinger			ASUL	32	1856
00 000 1815	W.H. Bolinger			ASUL	32	---
00 000 1853	W.T. Bolinger			ASUL	32	---
00 000 0000	Malinda Bolton			BSCC	B176	---
00 000 0000	Martha Bond[Wilkinson]			HMIA	811	1848
00 000 0000	H.A. Bondurant			MHMA	153	---
00 000 0000	John Bone			FWAR	149	---
00 000 1783	George Boon			BGAS	31	---
00 000 0000	Mecca Boon[Woods]			BHOT	H483	---
19 May 1796	Benjamin Boone			BGAS	32	---
00 000 0000	Moses Boone Squire			BPUT	330	1805
00 000 0000	Abigail Booth[McGinnis]			CLOW	894	1811
00 000 0000	George Borude			MHMA	91	---
00 000 1844	J.W. Boston			ASUL	32	---
00 000 0000	Mary T. Boswell[Allison]			CLOW	824	1817
00 000 0000	Fletcher Bottorff			BHCL	815	---
00 000 1824	W.C. Bourn			ASUL	34	1843
20 Dec 1846	Martha J. Bourne[Vermillion] Ambrose			BPUT	384	1831
00 000 0000	Anthony Bowen			BPUT	344	---
00 000 0000	Samirah Bowman[Watson]			BWMB	340	---
00 000 0000	Eliza Bowers[Hume]			DGIN	724	---
24 Oct 1796	Robert Boyd			HHEN	721	---
00 000 1791	William Boyd			HWAY	548	1811
04 Jan 1792	John Boyle			HPOS	582	---
00 000 0000	David Boyll			BHVI	687	1830
00 00c 1805	Hugh J. Bradley			BGAS	34	---

BIRTHDATE	NAME OF BIOGRAPHEE	PARENTS/BIRTHPLACE/BIRTHDATE	SOURCE/PAGE		DATE
00 000 0000	Gideon Braiser		BWMB	297	---
00 000 0000	Abraham J. Brand		HWSP	444	---
00 000 0000	John W. Branch		BWMB	175	---
00 Feb 1815	N.S. Branigin		HJOH	591	1836
00 000 1846	Martha A. Brannigin[Featherngill]		HJOH	607	---
00 000 0000	Thomas Branigin		HJOH	764	---
00 000 0000	Nancy Bray[Culver]		CLOW	931	---
00 000 0000	Rebecca Breckinridge[Carpenter]		PBES	187	---
00 000 0000	Martha A. Brener[Michael]		HMIA	649	---
00 000 1803	Elizabeth Brent[Richardson]		HJOH	754	1836
00 000 0000	Christina Brentlinger[McCormick]		BHCL	813	---
00 000 0000	Joseph Brentlinger		WHSU	B126	---
00 000 0000	Martha Brenton[Mack]		BHVI	848	---
00 000 0000	Garret Brewer		CLOW	944	---
00 000 0000	Samuel Brewer		SIND	585	---
00 000 1800	George Bridges		HJOH	592	1829
04 May 1800	George Bridges		HJOH	697	1829
00 000 1800	George Brindley		BVER	258	1828
20 Jun 1800	George Brindley		BVER	323	1828
00 000 0000	Annie Brinkley[Allen]		HLOW	851	---
00 000 0000	John Bristow		HWBJ	339	---
05 Nov 1803	Mirian Brooks[Finley]		HLOW	607	---
00 000 0000	Ira Broshears		ASPE	65	1860
00 000 0000	Elizabeth Brown[Smith]		BWMB	348	---
00 000 0000	Daniel Brown		CLOW	533	---
00 000 0000	George W. Brown		ASPE	66	1853
00 000 0000	Isaac Brown		BWON	580	---
06 Jun 1833	James M. Brown	Francis O. & Mary E(Wright)	BWMB	285	---
00 000 0000	James Brown		DGIN	1177	---
00 000 0000	John C. Brown		HWSP	223	---

Date	Name		Code	No.	Year
00 000 1797	Mary A[.Brown]		BTWJ	326	---
00 000 0000	Oliver H. Brown		BWMB	342	---
30 Jan 1847	Robert S. Brown	Robert & Lucy J(Pemberton)	HWSP	230	1854
00 000 1801	Thomas J. Brown		EVER	259	1830
00 000 0000	William A. Brown		BMON	376	1828
00 000 0000	Kate Brownlee[Montgomery]		HPDB	639	---
00 000 0000	Phoebe J. Brumfield[Grainger]		HVAN	635	---
00 000 1808	Sarah Bruner[Key]		SHGI	912	1825
22 Feb 1797	Robert Brunson		SIND	632	---
00 000 0000	Thomas Bryan		SIND	583	---
00 000 0000	Dr. James H. Bryant		HWSP	515	---
00 000 0000	James M. Bryant		HCLI	542	---
29 May 1832	Mary Ann Buckner[Vandiver] Avery & Margaret(Sturgeon)		HJOH	882	---
00 000 1806	William H. Buford		HGAR	163	1832
00 000 1806	William H. Buford		RGAR	59	1832
00 000 0000	Sarah Bull[Robinson]		BHOT	T346	1828
00 000 1807	Isaac N. Billington		EVER	245	1835
00 000 0000	Nancy Bunnell[Reed]		HWAY	B590	---
00 000 1818	John Bunten William		HHHE	441	1823
00 000 0000	Anna Buchannon[Lawler] Levi		HHHE	557	---
00 000 0000	James Burcham		HLOW	899	---
00 000 0000	Dawson Burgess[Griggs]		EWMB	298	---
00 000 0000	John L. Burgess		HWAY	B550	---
00 000 0000	Isaac Burnett		EPUT	367	---
13 Sep 1809	Jacob Burnett		WHSU	A42	---
00 000 0000	Emeline Burns		RGAR	60	1834
00 000 0000	Emeline Burns		HGAR	163	1834
06 May 1816	John M. Burns		EBOO	238	---
00 Oct 1801	Torrance Burns		HELK	362	1834
00 000 0000	Wiley Burns		BWMB	774	---
00 000 1799	James Burnside		EPUT	397	---
00 000 0000	James Burnside		EVER	516	---
00 000 0000	Julie Burris[Barr]		HKDA	747	---
00 000 0000	Robert Burris		FDAV	384	---

BIRTHDATE	NAME OF BIOGRAPHEE	PARENTS/BIRTHPLACE/BIRTHDATE	SOURCE/PAGE	DATE
00 000 0000	Henry Burton		HENR 721	c1801
00 000 0000	Lucinda Bush[Christie]		HHHE 465	----
00 000 0000	George Butler		BWMB 248	----
00 000 0000	Jane Buzan[Butler]		BHOT T299	----
12 May 1850	Dr. L.S. Byers		CLOW 446	----
00 000 0000	Phillip Byers		BHOT H410	----
00 000 0000	William Byrd		CLOW 338	1829
00 000 0000	Barnabas Cain		CLOW 873	----
00 000 0000	Wallace Caldwell		BHVI 695	----
00 000 0000	William Caldwell		BJAB 541	----
00 000 0000	John Call		HHHE 441	----
16 May 1799	William Callon		SIND 645	----
00 000 0000	Preston Calvert		HCAR 351	1836
00 000 0000	Robert Calvert		WHSU B76	----
00 000 0000	Joseph Campbell		CLOW 828	----
00 000 1796	Joseph Campbell		BGAS 53	----
20 Apr 1804	William Campbell		BHOT T352	----
00 000 0000	Barbara Canary[Creager]		WHSU B109	----
00 000 0000	Sarah Cannatsay[Anderson]		BWMB 773	----
00 000 0000	Tracy Capp[Harp]		HWSP 817	----
00 000 0000	Simon Caress		FDAV 500	----
00 000 0000	Thomas Carle		SIND 582	c1825
17 Feb 1840	Dr. Simeon B. Carleton Henry & Martha(Williams)	Va/Va	HPDB 391	----
00 000 0000	Robert Carnahan		FDAV 315	----
00 000 0000	Andrew Carmine	Andrew & Lydia(Bice)	HJOH 775	----
00 000 0000	Hiram Carr		HWSP 779	----
11 Jul 1796	Moses Carr		BHVI 900	----
00 000 0000	Ruth Carr[Boyll]		BHVI 687	----
00 000 1807	Anne Carrico		HKDA 811	----

Date	Name		Code	No.	Year
00 000 0000	George G. Carrico		HKDA	812	1818
00 000 1843	E.S. Carrithers		ASUL	42	1873
00 May 1800	George Carrithers		WHSU	A44	1817
18 Aug 1807	Elizabeth Carruther[Smock]		WHSU	B83	---
00 000 0000	Betsey Carter[Brown]		BWMB	342	---
00 000 0000	Elizabeth K. Carter[Conder]	Ky01/Ky02	HLOW	583	---
23 Aug 1827	James Carter Jesse & Sarah(Elder)		HPDB	417	---
00 000 0000	Joseph Carter		HWSP	140	1848
01 Jul 1877	Bertha Carty[Walters] Augustus		WHSU	B387	1878
00 000 0000	James Case		WHSU	B91	---
00 000 0000	John S. Case		HCAR	164	1838
00 000 0000	James J. Cassady		CLOW	918	---
00 000 0000	Thomas Cassidy		HPDB	588	---
00 000 0000	Mary[Cassity]		BVAN	93	---
00 000 0000	Sarah Caughey[Fleming]	Ire/x	BTWJ	525	---
00 000 0000	Susan Cavender[Dorsey]		HWSP	144	---
00 000 0000	Susan Cavender[Dorsey]		HWSP	231	---
00 000 1804	Martha Cawthorn[Johnson]		HJOH	502	---
00 000 0000	James Chafin		BWMB	758	c1843
00 000 0000	Matilda Chamberlain[Galey]		HWBJ	551	---
00 000 0000	George Chambers		HPDB	464	---
28 May 1795	Capt.Isaac Chambers		BSCC	A211	---
00 000 0000	Joseph Champ		HMIA	510	---
25 Dec 1830	William M. Chanley George W. & Malinda(Baysinger) Tn/Ky		HPDB	717	---
00 000 0000	Barnett Chastain William Va/x		SCWA	697	---
00 000 0000	Cynthia[Chastain]		SCWA	698	---
17 Dec 1793	Isaac Chenoweth		BGAS	62	---
00 000 0000	Joseph Chenoweth		LLDW	B33	---
00 000 0000	John Cherry		HWSP	140	---
00 000 0000	Benjamin Chesnut		HKDA	885	---
00 000 0000	Martha Chinn[Gates]		BHOT	T428	---
00 000 0000	Ella Christie[Underwood]		HHHE	316	---
15 Jan 1816	John Christie		HHHE	465	---
00 000 0000	Lucinda Churchill[Crim]		HLOW	893	---

BIRTHDATE	NAME OF BIOGRAPHEE	PARENTS/BIRTHPLACE/BIRTHDATE	SOURCE/PAGE	DATE
00 000 1806	Catherine Cissell[Shircliff]		HKDA 832	----
00 000 0000	Elizabeth Cissell[Carrico]		HKDA 812	1812
00 000 0000	Allen Clark		HJOH 879	1832
00 000 0000	Darmis Clark[Sharp]		GIBS 236	1826
00 000 0000	James Clark		HLOW 324	----
00 000 0000	Mary Clarke[Harmon]		HPDB 760	----
00 000 0000	Mary Clarkston[Stuteville]		HWSP 486	----
00 000 0000	Jeremiah Claxton Joshua		HLOW 582	1830
00 000 0000	America Clem[Peed]		EIND M51	----
00 000 0000	John N. Clements		HHHE 683	----
10 May 1817	John Click		WHSU A45	1865
25 Mar 1816	Allen W. Clifford		HPDB 468	c1829
00 000 1796	Elizabeth Clifford[Houchin]		HPDB 422	----
22 Feb 1837	John J. Clifft Thomas & Melinda(Jones) Tn/Ky		HGSU 339	1838
00 000 0000	J.N. Cline		HCAR 352	1834
00 000 0000	Joseph Clinton		SIND 618	----
00 000 1819	Howard Clore Israel & Frances(Deer)Ma79/Madison83		BVPA 462	----
00 000 1821	Simeon Clore		MONT 1141	----
00 000 0000	David Cloyd		BHVI 703	----
00 000 0000	Van B. Cobb		BWMB 177	----
00 000 0000	Hugh Cochran		HWBJ 340	----
00 000 0000	Stephen Cofer		HHHE 296	1831
00 000 0000	Lewis Coffey		BWMB 248	----
00 000 0000	Catherine Coghill[Smith]		HWBJ 561	----
00 000 0000	Elizabeth Coleman[Mitchell]		GSHE 665	----
00 000 0000	Martha Coleman[Black]		SHGI 786	----
00 00c 1820	Sims A. Colley		BGAS 72	----
00 000 0000	J.O. Collins		WHSU B24	----
00 000 0000	W.S. Collins		WHSU A36	1837
00 000 1828	Susan A. Colville[Pattison]		HHHE 460	----

Date	Name	Parents/Spouse	Origin	Code	No.	Year
18 Apr 1793	Boswell Colvin			BHOT	T423	---
00 000 0000	Elisha Colvin	Abraham J. & Sarah	Ky/Ky	BHCL	630	---
00 000 0000	Elizabeth Colvin[Cochran]			HKDA	328	---
00 000 1811	Thomas J. Colvin			FMWA	B290	---
00 000 0000	Cynthia Comingore[Brewer]			HJOH	592	---
00 000 1797	Samuel Cominger	John A.	Ger/x	SIND	284	---
00 000 0000	James Conaway			BHVI	709	---
00 000 0000	John Conder			HLOW	583	---
00 000 0000	Alexander B. Conduitt			DIND	1707	---
00 000 0000	Alexander B. Conduitt			DGIN	809	---
00 000 0000	Melissa R[Conduitt]			DIND	1707	---
00 000 0000	Mary Conley[Kellams]			HPDB	761	---
00 000 0000	Thomas Conley	John		WHSU	B400	---
30 Mar 1813	Daniel Conner	Rubin & Nancy		KTCD	871	---
00 000 0000	Daniel Conner			BWAB	333	---
00 000 1799	A.G. Connolly			HGAR	164	1835
00 000 1817	Thompson Conrad	Joseph & Rachel	Pa/Va	BWON	576	---
00 000 0000	Elizabeth[Conway]			EIND	D11	---
00 000 0000	Richard Conway			BHOT	T301	---
00 000 0000	William Conway			EIND	D11	---
00 00c 1823	George Coons			HJOH	720	---
00 000 0000	John Cooper			HWBJ	563	---
02 Jun 1818	John J. Cooper	John & Polly(Wilson)		CLOW	833	---
00 000 0000	Millie Cooper[Allen]			HWSP	514	---
00 000 0000	Polly Cooper[Dolson]			BHVI	735	---
00 000 0000	Stanley Cooper			BHOT	314	---
00 000 0000	Elizabeth Corn[Stewart]			BHOT	H491	---
00 000 0000	John Corn			BHOT	T355	---
00 000 0000	Dolly[Cory]			BKOS	489	---
00 000 0000	Phebe Cotton[Dewit]			HSHE	763	---
15 Jan 1793	William Cotton	William & Elizabeth		HSHE	760	1855
00 000 1842	Sanders Courtney	James		CSHE	621	---
00 000 0000	Eliza Cover[Kelly]			HWSP	163	---
00 000 0000	Harriet Coward			HLOW	632	---
00 000 0000	Margaret Cowen[Blair]			BKOS	399	1835

BIRTHDATE	NAME OF BIOGRAPHEE	PARENTS/BIRTHPLACE/BIRTHDATE	SOURCE/PAGE	DATE
00 000 1813	Amy Cox[Miller]		HMIA 777	----
00 000 0000	James Cox		HPDB 717	----
00 000 1818	Joseph Cox		HCAR 163	1829
00 000 1815	Joseph Cox		RCAR 26	1831
00 000 0000	Levi Cox		HWSP 141	----
00 000 0000	Polly Cox[Flick]		HLOW 654	----
00 000 0000	Samuel F. Cox		CSHE 683	----
00 000 0000	Margaret Coy[Anderson]		BWMB 295	----
13 Oct 1794	Elizabeth Cracraft[Rinker]		BHVI 267	----
00 000 0000	Georgia Craig		BHVI 682	----
00 000 0000	Merit S. Craig		BGAS 83	----
23 Jul 1803	William A. Crawford		BTWJ 334	----
00 000 0000	Thomas J. Creager		WHSU B108	----
00 000 0000	William Creager		WHSU A46	----
00 000 0060	Jesse Crim		HLOW 893	1818
00 000 1815	Martin D. Crim		BGAS 85	----
27 Nov 0000	Anna Crisenbury		HALL 179	1826
00 000 1826	Mary[Crist]		ASUL 49	1831
00 000 0000	Nicholas Crist		CLOW 535	----
00 000 1818	Shellim Crockett	Robert	DIND 1331	----
00 000 0000	Shellin Crockett		PBES 66	----
00 000 0000	Owen D. Cromwell		CLOW 423	1819
12 Aug 1822	James M. Crooke	Olly & Nancy(Cruse) Ky98/x	HKDA 840	----
00 000 0000	William Crooks		HCAR 163	----
00 000 0000	William Crooks		RCAR 46	----
00 000 0000	Daniel Cropper		TRAN 397	----
00 000 0000	Joseph Cross		HPDB 418	1829
00 000 0000	Nathaniel Crowder		HWSP 544	----
00 00c 1794	Marks Crume		BGAS 87	----
00 000 0000	Emila Cruse[Nelson]		WHSU B96	1823

Date	Name	Parents/Notes		Code	No.	Year
00 000 1812	Elizabeth Cunningham[Woods]			BHVI	1002	---
00 000 0000	James Cunningham			BWMB	181	---
00 000 0000	William N. Cunningham			BWMB	181	---
25 Aug 1783	Jane Curry[McClure]			HKDA	458	---
00 000 0000	William Curry			WHSU	A43	1817
00 000 0000	James A. Curtner			WHSU	B50	---
00 000 0000	John Cutsinger	George & Rebecca	Ger/Ger	CSHE	707	---
00 000 0000	Elizabeth Dailey[Holder]			WHSU	B229	---
00 000 1812	Catherine Dale[Kaler]			WFUF	1046	---
00 000 0000	Thomas Daley			HVAN	593	---
00 000 1809	Patience Dalton[Griffith]			CLOW	537	---
00 000 0000	David S. Danaldson			GIND	649	---
00 000 0000	Jane E. Dannells[Scott]			HWBJ	367	---
00 Dec 1806	James Danner			BGAS	91	---
00 000 0000	Kilen Darcas[Hoback]			BHOT	T340	1834
00 000 0000	John F. Darnell			HHHE	400	---
00 000 0000	James Daughtery			HHHE	687	1830
00 000 1828	James T. Davidson	Judah & Mary(Steele)		TBAB	729	---
26 Oct 1826	Robert P. Davidson	Judah & Mary(Steele)		TBAB	729	---
26 Oct 1826	Robert P. Davidson			EIND	19	---
00 000 1800	Abner M. Davis			BGAS	93	---
00 000 1823	George W. Davis			BSCC	B138	---
00 000 0000	Jeremiah Davis			CLOW	951	---
00 000 0000	John Davis			BSCC	B138	---
00 000 0000	John Davis			HPOS	585	---
00 000 0000	Julia Ann Davis[Gobbel]			HPDB	722	---
00 000 0000	Mary E. Davis[Smith]			CLOW	899	---
05 May 1825	Rebecca Davis[Miles]			MONT	1219	---
00 000 0000	Sarah Davis[Askren]			BHVI	661	---
29 Jul 1800	William Davis	William & Charlotte	73/x	DIND	1563	---
00 000 0000	Jane Dawson[Peer]			BVER	502	---
00 000 0000	Jane Dawson[Peer]			BVER	486	---
00 000 1798	Joseph Dawson			MHMA	91	---
00 000 0000	Ambrose Day			BPUT	489	1829

BIRTHDATE	NAME OF BIOGRAPHEE	PARENTS/BIRTHPLACE/BIRTHDATE	SOURCE/PAGE	DATE
00 000 0000	Joanna[Day]		EPUT 489	---
00 000 1796	John N. Day	John	HWBJ 192	1802
00 000 0000	James Dean		BHOT T303	---
31 Mar 1842	John B.T.Dearing	William & Elizabeth(Morton)	HPDB 419	c1844
00 000 0000	William L.Dearmond		BWAB 548	1822
00 000 1813	Abraham Debaun		ASUL 53	1831
00 00c 1827	Charity Debaun[Frakes]		WHSU B334	---
00 000 0000	Simon Debaun		WHSU B345	---
00 000 0000	John DeCoursey		HJOH 411	1832
00 000 0000	William Dedman		HPDB 419	1820
06 Nov 1783	Elizabeth Deem[Black]		HMIA 772	---
00 000 0000	Elizabeth Defoe[Bush]		CLOW 534	---
01 Aug 1834	James T. Demaree	Samuel & Frances(Cropper) Ky03/Ky06	HPGS 587	---
00 000 0000	Sarah Demaree[Banta]		TBAB 675	1832
00 000 0000	William U.Demaree		BSCC B221	1812
22 Nov 1816	Ann Demott[French]		SHGI 570	---
09 Dec 1802	Mary Demott[Henderson]		HJOH 615	---
00 000 1809	John W.S. Denney	William	WHSU B90	---
00 000 0000	Elizabeth Denny		BHOT T297	---
00 000 1802	William Denny	James & Catherine	HKDA 331	1804
00 000 1804	James DePauw		BGAS 99	---
00 000 0000	John DePauw	Charles Fr/x	DIND 1355	---
00 000 0000	Elizabeth DePew[Kirk]		BMMB 330	---
00 000 0000	Elizabeth Depew[Kirk]		BMMB 344	---
00 000 0000	Thomas Deupree	William	CSHE 562	c1821
00 000 0000	Peter Dewit		HSHE 763	---
00 000 0000	Thomas Dewitt		ASPE 65	1865
00 000 0000	William Dickerson		SIND 548	1825
00 000 0000	Joel Dickin		BVER 257	1821

Date	Name		Code	No.	Year
00 000 0000	Jonathan Dilley		WHSU	B344	---
00 000 0000	Jonathan R. Dilley		WHSU	B91	---
00 000 0000	Luke Dillon		HHHE	710	---
00 000 0000	John Dills		BPUT	431	---
00 000 0000	Jacob Dinsmore		EBOO	259	---
00 000 0000	Martha Dinwiddie[Ramsay]	Ky/Ky	SIND	163	---
20 Mar 1850	Dr. H.T. Dixon C.C. & Isabella(Clay)		HVAN	262	---
00 000 0000	Barthenia P. Dobbs[Parker]		BWMB	310	---
00 000 0000	John Dodd		WHSU	B204	---
00 000 1802	John Y. Dodds		WHSU	A49	---
00 000 1809	William F. Dodds		WHSU	A50	---
00 000 0000	John B. Dodson		FMWA	B132	---
00 000 0000	Martha J. Dooley Moses & Elizabeth(Bohannon)	Va99/x	HHHE	653	---
00 000 0000	Harrison[Dorothy]		WHSU	B194	---
00 000 0000	Greenberry Dorsey		HWSP	231	---
00 000 1817	Greenberry W. Dorsey		HWSP	144	c1824
00 000 0000	William W. Doss		BVER	259	1830
00 000 1815	Rev. A.R. Downey		EIND	A18	c1830
00 000 0000	Rev. James Drake		HFOS	588	---
00 000 0000	Nancy Drake[Adkins]		BMON	401	---
21 Dec 1803	Robert Driskell		HLOW	881	1810
00 000 0000	James J. Duckworth		HHHE	794	---
00 000 0000	Jane[Duke]	Ire/Ire	BHOT	H321	---
00 000 0000	Pressley S. Duckworth		HHHE	198	1850
00 000 0000	William Duncan		HLOW	657	1805
00 000 0000	Margaret Dungan[Hornback]		BFWJ	364	---
18 Apr 1804	Elizabeth Dunham[Wilkes]		HJOH	916	1830
00c 1813	David Dunlavy		BGAS	108	---
00 000 0000	Martha A. Dunlavy[Casteel]		CLOW	344	---
00 Dec 1812	Hon. George G. Dunn		HLOW	246	---
00 000 0000	Joseph Dunn		HKDA	553	---
00 000 1781	Williamson Dunn		GIND	646	---
00 000 1844	Dr. J.L. Durham		ASUL	57	1879

COUNTY NOT GIVEN (CONT.)

C O U N T Y   N O T   G I V E N   (C O N T.)

BIRTHDATE	NAME OF BIOGRAPHEE	PARENTS/BIRTHPLACE/BIRTHDATE	SOURCE/PAGE	DATE
01 Jan 1799	Jacob D. Early		BVPA 203	1817
00 000 0000	Sarah Earlewine[McGinnis]		HCLI 690	---
00 000 0000	George W. Earlywine		BMMB 775	---
00 000 0000	Mahala J. Earlywine[Davison]		HWBJ 526	---
00 000 0000	Mahala Eastin[English]	Lt. Philip & Sarah(Smith)	DIND 2154	---
00 000 0000	Rebecca Eckles[Banta]		BMMB 295	---
00 000 0000	Sarah Edmondson-Chenoweth[Edwards]		HWBJ 721?	---
00 000 1804	James Edwards		HWBJ 721	---
00 000 0000	Frances Egnew[Varner]		HWSP 525	---
00 000 0000	James H. Egnew		HWSP 517	---
00 000 0000	Ann Elder[Jabboe]		CLOW 360	1832
00 000 0000	Mary Elliott[Galloway]		HDOH 718	1817
00 000 0000	Zulina[Elliott]		BPUT 498	---
00 000 0000	Catherine Ellis[Edwards]		MONT 615	---
12 May 1805	Charles R. Ellis		HLOW 887	---
00 000 1809	Edward Ellis		HLOW 684	---
00 000 1801	Nancy Ellis[Kendall]		HKDA 820	1817
00 000 1801	Jonas Elson		RCAR 47	1832
00 000 0000	Jonas Elson		HCAR 163	1832
00 000 0000	Nicholas Elson		BHOT H323	---
00 000 0000	Jesse Emerson	Reuben	SHGI 579	---
00 000 0000	Reuben Emerson		SHGI 562	---
00 000 0000	Lemuel Emmerson	Jesse	SHGI 667	1809
00 000 0000	Maj. Elisha G. English		NSFC 377	1818
00 000 0000	Lydia Engle[Riggs]		WHSU B303	---
00 000 1801	Edna Ennis[Skaggs]		BMMB 363	---
17 Jan 1829	E.R. Eskridge	Joseph W. & Fannie(Robinson) Va/Va	HKDA 762	---
00 000 0000	Cassandra Evans[McNab]		BMMB 229	---
00 000 0000	Hannah Evans[Williams]		BVAN 127	---
00 000 1803	Harmon Evans		HKDA 814	---

Date	Name	Parents/Spouse	Place	Code	No.	Year
00 000 0000	Keziah Evans[Mavity]			HLOW	594	---
00 000 0000	Rachel Evans[Burcham]			HLOW	899	---
00 000 0000	Richard Evans			GIND	673	---
00 000 0000	Nancy Everman[Gardner]			BPUT	478	---
22 Feb 1808	Robert W. Ewing	Robert & Elizabeth(Booker)	Va/Va	HVAN	631	---
00 000 0000	James C. Faris			BHVI	750	1811
00 000 0000	Joshua Farnsley	James		BSCC	B142	---
00 000 0000	Martha A. Fear[Gartin]			BJAB	772	---
00 000 0000	Rev. Jeremiah Featherston			SIND	581	---
00 000 0000	John W. Ferguson			BGAS	124	---
17 Jan 1807	Mary Ferree[Pirtle]			WHSU	B296	---
00 000 0000	Fannie K. Fidler[Mugg]			CLOW	941	---
00 000 0000	Sarah Field[Campbell]			HLOW	582	---
27 Dec 1793	Abraham Fields	Keen & Anna(West)	Ky/x	GIES	188	---
00 000 0000	William Fields			BHVI	755	1848
00 000 1837	Robert P. Figg	Francis		HHHE	532	---
00 000 0000	G.W. Finch			SHGI	763	---
00 000 0000	Phillip Finch			HWSP	783	---
00 000 0000	Christine Finke[Storke]			GCEV	B345	---
16 May 1805	Jefferson Finley	David & Elizabeth	54/x	HLOW	607	1833
00 000 1822	James R. Finnell			BVER	244	---
00 000 0000	Hortense Fisher[Watts]			CLOW	442	---
00 000 1808	J.S. Fisher			BVER	244	1833
00 000 0000	James Fisher			HJOH	483	---
00 000 1824	Susan H[Fislor]			JACK	659	1844
00 000 0000	Mary Flack[Cox]			CSHE	684	---
00 000 0000	Susan Fleece[Clay]			DGIN	1137	---
14 Sep 1824	Erastus L. Floyd			BGAS	130	---
00 000 1804	James P. Foley			FMWA	B603	---
00 000 0000	Susan Ford[Smith]			HHHE	522	---
06 Jul 1813	James Forsyth	J. & Jane(Sturgeon)		HJOH	703	1830
00 000 0000	David Forsythe			FDAV	323	---
03 Jun 1806	Matilda Forsythe[Bridges]			HJOH	592	1829
00 Mar 1825	Sarah J. Forsythe[Branigin] David			HJOH	591	1832

BIRTHDATE	NAME OF BIOGRAPHEE	PARENTS/BIRTHPLACE/BIRTHDATE	SOURCE/PAGE	DATE
00 000 0000	W.H. Forsythe		ASPE 65	1834
00 000 0000	Elizabeth Fowler[Masters]		HPDB 467	c1819
00 000 0000	Greyson Frakes		HWSP 824	---
00 000 1804	John Frame		GPLA 393	---
27 Nov 1817	William Frame	William & Susan(Davis)	BWON 464	---
00 000 1804	John Frames		GPLA 393	---
00 000 0000	Hannah Francis[Hamilton]		BWMB 251	---
00 000 1809	Lucinda Francis[Rouse]		HJOH 479	---
00 000 0000	Catherine Frank[Miller]		HWSP 474	---
00 000 0000	Nancy Frazee[Dailey]		HWBJ 353	---
00 000 0000	E.L. Frazier		GSHE 805	---
02 Nov 1802	James Frazier		HCLI 670	---
00 000 1792	Doris French		HPOS 648	1807
00 000 0000	Dovinda Fresh[Leisure]		HSHE 638	1835
00 000 0000	Elizabeth Friedley[Edmondson]		CLOW 425	---
00 000 0000	Nancy[Friend]		HCLI 621	---
00 000 0000	John Fry	George Va/x	BHCL 735	---
17 Aug 1799	Sarah Fry[Bottorff]		BHCL 633	---
00 000 0000	Jane Fulton[Banta]		HKDA 809	---
00 000 0000	John Fuquay		HWSP 197	1820
00 000 0000	Charles D. Gabbert		AWAS 50	1855
00 000 0000	Charles D. Gabbert		HLOW 586	---
00 000 0000	Margaret Galbreath[Vickery] David	Scotland/x	HHEN 831	---
00 000 1811	Eliza[Galey]		MONT 1240	---
00 000 0000	Samuel Galey		HWBJ 551	---
00 000 1810	Samuel S. Galey		MONT 1240	---
00 000 0000	Sarah Galliher[Hughes]		CLOW 928	---
00 000 0000	Juliette Galway[Richards]		CLOW 912	---
00 000 0000	Morgan Gambill Morgan		WRSU B320	---
00 000 0000	Hannah Gannon[Pennington]		BHVI 893	---

Date	Name			Code	No.	Year
10 Oct 1830	H.W. Garnell			BPUT	452	---
00 000 1828	Harrison B. Garner	Solomon & Deborah		HHHE	341	1832
00 000 0000	Solomon Garner			HHHE	395	---
00 000 0000	Elizabeth Garr[Clements]			HLOW	582	---
14 Dec 1811	O.W. Garrett			HJOH	704	c1841
00 000 0000	William Garrison			BWMB	184	---
00 000 1805	Nancy Garshwiler[Hunt]			HJOH	617	---
00 000 0000	Sarah Garwood[Spain]			BHVI	936	---
00 000 0000	Samuel Gasaway			ASPE	65	---
00 000 1836	S.A. [Gaskins]			ASUL	66	---
00 000 1866	Walter S. Gayle			FWWA	B16	---
00 000 0000	Josephus Geary			BWMB	763	---
00 000 0000	Garland Gentry			BWMB	302	---
00 000 1812	Joseph Gentry	James & Elizabeth(Hornback)	NC/NC	HWSP	588	---
00 000 1827	W.J. George	Milton	Va/x	HJOH	609	---
11 Jan 1818	Elizabeth Gillaspie[McCracken]			GBRD	391	---
00 000 0000	Dr. Henry H. Gillen			BWAB	402	---
00 Jan 1802	Robert A. Gilkinson			WHSU	A53	1816
00 000 1822	Daniel Giltner			BHCL	880	---
00 000 0000	Enoch Giltner			BHCL	882	1826
00 000 1802	Rosann Ginn[McKnight]			HKDA	824	---
00 000 1821	Sarah Jane Gish[Drake]			HPGS	588	---
00 000 1809	James Gladish			HPDB	442	1810
00 000 0000	Nettie Glove[Ward]			HMIA	590	---
00 000 0000	Lovina E. Glover			HHHE	240	---
00 000 1786	Ruth Glover[Reed]			HLOW	637	---
00 000 0000	Thomas G. Glover			HLOW	293	---
00 000 0000	Ware Glover			HLOW	253	1810
00 000 0000	William Gobin			WHSU	B149	---
00 000 0000	Phoeba Godfrey[Hart]			TRAN	370	---
00 000 0000	Joseph Godwin			FDAV	367	---
00 000 0000	David Goff			BHVI	853	---
00 000 0000	Sarah Goff			BHVI	853	---
28 Dec 1791	George Golding			HDOH	731	1814

BIRTHDATE	NAME OF BIOGRAPHEE	PARENTS/BIRTHPLACE/BIRTHDATE	SOURCE/PAGE	DATE
00 000 0000	Sarah Goodright[Coffey]		CLOW 832	----
20 Jan 1824	Judge David S. Gooding Asa & Matilda		EIND G227	1879
00 000 1840	M. Goodman		ASUL 69	----
00 000 0000	Elizabeth Goodpaster[Spurlen]		HSHE 680	----
00 000 0000	David Goodpasture		HLOW 900	----
00 000 0000	Solomon Goodpasture John	Ky/x	KTCD 1067	c1850
19 Jun 1812	James Goodwine James & Elizabeth(Snyder)		HWBJ 171	----
00 000 1780	James Goodwine		HWBJ 192	----
00 000 0000	Mehitabel Goodwine Samuel		BSCC B214	----
10 Aug 1810	Thomas Goodwine James & Elizabeth(Snyder)		HWBJ 170	----
00 000 0000	Thomas Gootee		LLDM B48	----
00 000 0000	Thomas Gootee		BGAS 147	----
00 000 0000	James Gordon		GIBS 235	1840
10 Jul 1795	William Gordon		BSCC B223	----
00 000 0000	John Gosnell		BHVI 768	1828
00 000 0000	Eliza Graham[Carnahan]		FDAV 315	----
06 Jun 1809	James H. Graham		HJOH 610	c1830
00 000 0000	Mary Graham[Campbell]		FDAV 828	----
00 000 0000	Melinda Graham[Crawford]		HLOW 347	c1815
01 Dec 1806	Thomas B. Graham James & Jane(Mitchell)	De/Pa	HKDA 766	----
00 000 0000	Tilghman Graham		CSHE 893	----
21 Mar 1803	Mary Grant[Osburn]		HWBJ 207	----
00 000 0000	Andrew Gray		BMMB 786	----
00 000 0000	Andrew Gray		HWSP 208	----
00 000 0000	Samuel Gray		HLOW 909	1812
00 000 0000	William Gray		CLOW 427	----
00 000 0000	Zeralda Gray[Wallace]		DGIN 1167	----
00 000 0000	George Greathouse		LHDP 118	----
00 000 0000	Stephen Green		EIND D29	----
00 000 0000	S. Green		AWAS 50	1863

Date	Name		Code	No.	Year
00 000 1821	William H. Green		HPDB	740	c1822
00 000 1818	Henry H. Greenup		RGAR	59	1832
00 000 1818	Henry H. Greenup		HCAR	163	1832
00 000 1817	John Greenup		HCAR	163	1832
00 000 1817	John Greenup		RGAR	59	1832
00 000 0000	Louisa Greenup		HCAR	163	1832
00 000 0000	Louisa Greenup		RGAR	60	1832
00 000 1819	Samuel Greenup		HCAR	163	1832
00 000 1819	Samuel G. Greenup		RGAR	59	1832
00 000 1816	William Greenway		HPDB	433	--
00 000 0000	Martha Gregg[Whitaker]		BWMB	340	--
00 000 0000	Joel Gregory		HSHE	728	--
00 000 0000	Rebecca Grider[High]		BHVI	792	1830
00 000 0000	Bartlett Griffith		CLOW	537	--
00 000 0000	James Griffith		HJOH	485	--
00 000 1795	Jane Griffith		HCAR	163	1827
00 000 1795	Jane Griffith		RGAR	59	1837
00 000 0000	Reuben Grigsby		HWSP	518	--
00 000 0000	Mary Grimes[Stephenson]		SCWA	944	--
00 000 0000	Nancy Grimes[Pruitt]		HPDB	731	c1840
00 000 0000	James A. Groves		BHOT	328	--
00 00c 1799	Jeremiah Grover		BGAS	156	--
00 000 0000	Mary Groves[McMains]		MONT	670	--
00 000 0000	James T. Gribbs	James T. & Eliza P(Prentiss)Va96/Fayet	HJOH	486	--
00 000 1829	Naomi Gunn[White]		WHSU	B282	--
31 May 1813	Thomas S. Gunn		BGAS	157	--
08 Jun 1821	Louisa J. Gunynn[Mason]		WFUF	538	--
00 000 0000	Margaret M.Halbert[Goss]	Va/Va	CLOW	960	1822
22 Apr 1811	Bluford Hall	William & Polly(Thixton)	HLOW	929	1818
00 000 0000	Sarah Hall[Chafin]		BWMB	758	c1843
00 000 0000	William L. Hall		BHOT	T431	1854
00 000 0000	P. Haller		AGIP	9	1877
00 000 0000	Dorothy Hamilton[Hickman]		BWMB	364	--
00 000 0000	H.H. Hamilton		AWAS	50	1817

BIRTHDATE	NAME OF BIOGRAPHEE	PARENTS/BIRTHPLACE/BIRTHDATE	SOURCE/PAGE	DATE
00 000 0000	James H. Hamilton		EMMB 251	----
00 000 1801	Nathaniel Hamilton		WHSU B365	1814
00 000 0000	William Hamilton		WHSU B199	----
00 Oct 1816	John Hammond		WHSU A56	----
00 000 0000	William Hance		HCAR 306	----
00 000 1796	William Hance		HCAR 58	1828
00 000 1795	William Hance		RCAR 163	1828
00 000 0000	James T. Hancock		BHOT T231	c1831
00 000 0000	Orpha Hancock[Hankins]		MONT 996	----
00 000 0000	Sandora Hancock[Butcher]		BHOT H494	----
00 000 0000	William Hancock		BHCL 774	----
00 000 0000	William Handy		HSHE 635	----
00 000 0000	James W. Hanes		HFOS 622	----
00 000 0000	Thomas Hanks		TCMA 622	----
00 000 0000	Jane Hansford[Fields]		BHVI 755	----
12 Feb 1803	James P. Harbison		HPDB 659	1827
00 000 0000	Isaac Harbit		BHOT T432	1837
00 000 1809	Hettie Hardin[Blann]		HKDA 449	c1832
00 000 0000	Isaac J. Hardin		HHHE 506	----
00 000 0000	Lucinda Harding[Bristow]		HWBJ 339	----
00 000 0000	Rush Harding[Hopkins]		HHHE 641	----
00 000 0000	Melissa R. Hardwick[Conduitt]		DGIN 809	----
06 Feb 1823	J.J. Hardy Benjamin & Amy(Pedigo) Fr/Va		HGSU 342	1832
00 000 0000	John Hargis		HWSP 787	----
29 Nov 1793	Hon.John Hargrove William		HPDB 465	----
00 000 0000	J.M. Harlan		GIBS 235	1861
00 000 0000	Lucinda Harlan[Anderson]		FMWA B519	1819
00 000 1792	Joel W. Harland		HCLI 563	1831
00 000 0000	Susan Harland[Fowler]		SHGI 699	----
00 000 0000	Susan Harmon[Pinnick]		HLOW 635	----

Date	Name	Notes	Origin	Code	No.	Year
00 000 0000	Elizabeth Harp[Talbot]			BWON	233	---
00 000 0000	Martha Harper[Shepard]			HKDA	389	---
00 000 0000	Nancy W. Harrah[Cox]			BPUT	420	---
00 000 0000	Eliatha Harris[Miller]			HWBJ	395	---
00 Sep 1820	Elizabeth Harris[Cutsinger]			HJOH	408	---
00 000 0000	James Harris			HKDA	816	1819
00 000 0000	Dr. James Harris			TCWA	620	---
00 000 0000	James M. Harris			HWBJ	374	---
00 000 0000	James M. Harris			BWMB	287	---
00 000 1818	John Harris		Ky/x	HJOH	612	c1824
00 000 0000	Mahala Harris[Pugh]			WHSU	B97	---
00 000 0000	Masterson Harris			HWSP	519	---
27 Jun 1811	Sophia Harris[Rice]	William & Nancy(Barrett)		HHHE	356	---
00 000 0000	Carter Harrison			BWMB	765	1839
00 000 0000	Reuben C. Harrison			HMIA	598	---
00 000 0000	William Harrod			HLOW	861	---
00 000 0000	Martha L. Harter[Talbott]			EHVI	953	---
00 000 0000	Nancy Hartman[Siner]			CLOW	512	---
00 000 0000	Ellen Nancy Harvey[Beeson]	Benjamin & Nancy(Sellars)		WFUF	735	1816
00 000 1813	John C. Hash			WHSU	B361	---
15 Aug 1841	George Hasenour	Martin & Tharsila	Ger/Ger	HPDB	761	---
00 000 0000	Mary E. Haskins[Clements]			HLOW	654	1830
00 000 0000	William Haskins			HPDB	600	---
00 000 0000	John Hatfield			HLOW	659	---
00 000 0000	Thomas Hatfield			HWAY	B389	1812
00 000 1821	Henry Hawkins			ASUL	74	1842
00 000 0000	Margaret Hawkins[McCarty] Rev. Jameson			DGIN	673	---
00 000 0000	Mary Hawkins[Mayhall]			BPUT	471	---
00 000 1807	Dr.A.B. Hayden		Va/Va	HVAN	249	---
00 000 0000	John Haynes			HDKA	770	1849
00 000 0000	John Haynes		NC/x	HKDA	887	---
00 000 0000	Maj. H.G. Hazlerigg			EBOO	296	---
00 000 1817	John W. Hazelrigg	William & Elizabeth	94/95	WHSU	B275	1840
26 Sep 1810	Almond Heady	Thomas & Rebecca(Goodwin)	Pa80/Pa83	EBOO	303	---

BIRTHDATE	NAME OF BIOGRAPHEE	PARENTS/BIRTHPLACE/BIRTHDATE		SOURCE/PAGE	DATE
23 Dec 1804	Martha Heady[Jackson]			EBOO 313	----
00 000 0000	Martha Heavern[Williams]			HWAY B368	----
00 000 0000	Louvisa Heflin[Groover]			BHOT T430	----
00 000 0000	Charlotte Helm[Thomas]			DGIN 655	----
27 Nov 1803	Dr.Jefferson Helm	William & Elizabeth(Drummond)		RUSH 709	1811
00 000 0000	Emeline Henderson[Wolf]			HSHE 651	----
00 000 0000	Hezekiah Henderson			BHVI 788	----
00 000 0000	Mary J.Henderson[Myers]			BVER 514	----
00 000 1820	Parth.M. Henderson			MHMA 91	----
00 000 1790	George F. Hendrick			HKDA 875	----
13 May 1808	Nancy Hendrick[Frazier]			HCLI 670	----
00 000 0000	Ambrose Hendricks			BMON 520	----
00 000 0000	George Hendrix			HWAY B287	----
00 000 0000	Adeline Henry[Dilley]			WHSU B91	----
00 000 0000	Adeline Henry[Dilley]	Elijah	Ky/Ky	WHSU B344	----
00 000 0000	Hamilton Henry			ENMB 364	1830
07 Dec 1829	J.W. Hensley	William & Sarah(Peterson)	Ky/NC	KTCD 1075	1813
00 000 0000	Nancy Hensley[Shepherd]			HLOW 897	----
00 000 0000	Mahala Hensley[McNutt]			BHVI 845	----
00 000 0000	William Hensley	James & Sally(Icenangoe)		KTCD 1075	1830
28 Dec 1815	Rev. E.D. Herod			HJOH 616	----
00 000 0000	Azariah Herring			HHHE 761	----
00 000 0000	Thurza Hess[Sheppard]			ENMB 205	----
00 000 0000	Margaret Hesson[Brand]			HWSP 444	----
00 000 0000	Nancy Hesson[Tuley]			HWSP 556	----
00 000 0000	Frances Hiatt[Overturf]			WFUF 1067	----
00 000 1800	Jeremiah Hibbs			HJOH 750	----
00 000 0000	James T. Hickman			ENMB 253	----
00 000 1847	Dr. C. Hicks	James & Ann(Reed)	NC20/x	HPOS 684	----
11 Jun 1810	Jefferson Hicks			EMON 460	1831

00 000 0000	Polly A. Higby[Nave]		HSHE	708	1824
00 000 0000	Henry Higgins		HSHE	493	---
00 00c 1806	Tillman High		BHVI	792	1830
00 000 0000	Mary Hight[Legge]		BWMB	778	---
00 000 0000	George G. Hikes	Pa/x	BHCL	800	1812
00 000 0000	Nancy Hilburn[Balay]		CLOW	950	---
29 May 1810	James Hill Capt. William		BELA	96	---
00 000 0000	Nancy Hill[Henderson]		BHVI	788	---
00 000 0000	Sarah Hill[Fletcher]		CLOW	837	---
00 000 0000	James Hillis		BTWJ	189	---
00 000 0000	Daniel Hillman		SHGI	1066	---
00 000 0000	Elizabeth Hillman[Colvin]		HPDB	465	---
00 000 1839	J.S. Hinkle		ASUL	78	---
00 000 1812	Jackson Hinkle		WHSU	A58	1819
00 000 0000	James S. Hinkle		WHSU	B133	---
00 000 1820	Margaret A. Hinkle John & Elizabeth		WHSU	B355	1830
00 000 0000	Mary Hinkle[Rankin]		DGIN	1028	---
00 000 0000	Philip Hinkle		WHSU	A57	1819
00 000 1824	Mary Hinton[Riley]		DIND	1352	---
00 000 0000	John Hoback		BHOT	T340	1834
00 000 1805	Joseph E. Hocker		BGAS	186	---
00 000 0000	Perlina Hodge[Rhodes] Jesse & Rebecca(Fisher)	Va/Ky	HSHE	711	1809
00 00c 1799	John Hodges		BGAS	186	---
00 000 0000	Mary M. Hoggegg[Naugle]		BPUT	412	---
00 000 1827	S. Hoggett		ASUL	82	1865
00 000 0000	Mary Hoke[Collins]		WHSU	A36	1837
00 000 0000	Catherine Holbert[Burgess]		BWMB	298	---
20 Dec 1820	Capt.James Holdson		WHSU	B307	1824
00 000 0000	J.M. Holeman		HJOH	706	---
00 000 0000	Eliza Hollcraft[Stratford]		BHOT	T373	---
00 000 1807	Anna Hollis[Weaver]		HHHE	587	1836
00 000 0000	Joseph Holman George		HMIA	434	1820
00 000 0000	Jacob Holmes		BWMB	304	---
00 000 1814	Vine Holt		RCAR	46	1829
00 000 1814	Vine Holt		HCAR	163	1829

COUNTY NOT GIVEN (CONT.)

BIRTHDATE	NAME OF BIOGRAPHEE	PARENTS/BIRTHPLACE/BIRTHDATE	SOURCE/PAGE	DATE
00 000 0000	Martha Holtzclaw[Ellis]		HLOW 634	----
12 Dec 1811	George H. Hon		BGAS 188	----
00 000 0000	Thomas Hooton		DGIN 681	----
00 000 0000	James Hoover		HALL 187	1863
00 000 0000	Abigail[Hope]		HPDB 660	----
09 Nov 1789	James Hope		HPDB 660	----
00 000 0000	Armilda Hopewell[Annis]		BHVI 934	----
00 000 1830	Armilda Hopewell[Annis]		WHSU B102	----
00 000 0000	John Hopewell		WHSU B309	----
00 000 0000	James A. Hopper		BWON 556	----
00 000 0000	Adam Hornback	Isaac & Margaret(Funk) Ky/Ky	BTWJ 364	----
00 000 0000	Joseph Hoskins		BPUT 500	1818
17 May 1798	Jesse Houchin		HPDB 422	----
00 000 1828	J.J. Houck		ASUL 80	----
00 000 0000	Abraham Houghland		HWSP 161	----
25 Jan 1824	John Houk	William & Lydia(Fisher) Va/NC	CLOW 402	1826
00 000 0000	Jemima House[Mean]		HSHE 514	----
00 000 0000	Sarah Houston[Tucker]		HLOW 877	----
00 000 1813	Eliza K. Houts[Barber] George & Jennie(Graham)		FDAV 541	----
21 Aug 1795	Aaron Howard		CSHE 746	----
00 000 1805	C. Howard		ASUL 82	1835
00 000 0000	John W. Howard		HJOH 792	----
00 000 0000	Mahala Howard[Chesnut]		HKDA 885	----
00 000 0000	Rual Howard	Joseph NC/x	WHSU B349	1831
03 Mar 1806	Lucinda Howe[Stewart]Robert		GIBS 189	----
00 000 0000	Elizabeth[Howlet]		BPUT 438	----
00 000 0000	George W. Howlet		BPUT 438	----
00 000 0000	Mary Hubbard[McHenry]		CLOW 880	----
00 000 0000	William Hubbard		HKDA 844	----
06 Sep 1826	Fielding Huddleston William & Susan(Phillips)		HHHE 824	----

Date	Name	Parents/Spouse	Origin	Ref	No.	Year
00 000 0000	Margaret Huff[Powell]			EIND	F65	---
00 000 1812	William Huff			BVER	259	1835
00 000 0000	Lucy J. Huffman[Harlan]			GIBS	235	1861
00 000 0000	C.K. Hughes			ASPE	65	1853
08 Dec 1823	George N. Hughes			HJOH	752	---
00 000 0000	Hethindar Hughes[Woten]			BJAB	440	1805
00 000 0000	Jacob Hughes			CLOW	928	---
00 000 0000	James B. Hughes			MONT	1197	---
00 000 1803	Mary Hughbanks[Lee]			CSHE	593	1824
00 000 0000	John Hulet			BWON	560	---
00 000 0000	Rev. Madison Hume			DGIN	724	---
00 000 1802	John R. Hunt Meshack		NC/x	WHSU	A59	c1822
00 000 1802	Joseph Hunt Simeon			HJOH	617	---
00 000 1805	Joshua P. Hunt			MPRO	360	---
00 000 0000	William R. Hunt			HJOH	641	1826
00 000 1826	Eliza C. Hunter[Barrows]			HKDA	472	---
00 000 1809	Matilda Hurst[Gullaway]			BAWE	551	---
18 Mar 1815	St. Clair Hurst	William & Mary(Emmons)		RUSH	843	1848
00 000 0000	John Huser			ASPE	65	1860
00 000 0000	Margaret Hutchison[DeCamp]			WHSU	B337	---
00 000 0000	William Hutchison			WHSU	B337	---
00 000 0000	William Hutson			BHOT	H488	---
00 000 1810	Albert G. Hutton			BGAS	201	---
00 000 0000	Elisha Hyatt		Ky/Ky	FDAV	381	---
08 Dec 1817	Asa Iglehart	Levi & Anne(Taylor)	Md86/x	DIND	1986	---
00 000 0000	Thomas Iles			DIND	1920	---
00 000 0000	Abraham Inlow			BWON	384	1828
13 Nov 1813	Martha Irvin[McLane] William & Polly			HLOW	636	---
00 000 0000	Mary Isgregg[Holliday] John & Mary			WFUF	810	---
00 000 0000	Peter Jabboe			CLOW	360	1832
00 000 0000	Catherine Jackson[Hancock]			BHOT	T237	c1831
17 Dec 1832	Lt.James H. Jackson William & Martha(Clemens)			HWBJ	771	---
00 000 0000	J.H. Jackson			WHSU	B198	---
00 000 1797	John H. Jackson William		Va/x	GERD	418	---

COUNTY NOT GIVEN (CONT.)

BIRTHDATE	NAME OF BIOGRAPHEE	PARENTS/BIRTHPLACE/BIRTHDATE	SOURCE/PAGE	DATE
00 000 0000	John Jackson		BVER 351	----
07 Jul 1810	John T. Jackson	John	WHSU B323	----
05 Mar 1792	Jane Jackson[Golding]		HDOH --	----
00 000 0000	James Jacobs		HJOH 753	----
00 000 0000	John W. Jamison	John	BTWJ 432	----
00 000 1812	Asbury C. Jacquess	Jonathan & Rebecca(Fraizer)	HPOS 623	----
00 000 0000	Julia Jarred[Vanhoutin]		BHVI 974	----
00 000 0000	James Jeffres		CLOW 538	----
00 000 0000	Francis Jeffries		BKOS 292	----
00 000 0000	Harvey Jeffries		MONT 1208	1820
00 000 0000	Margaret[Jeffries]		BKOS 292	----
00 000 0000	Jane Jenkins[Pruett]		HLOW 630	1824
00 000 0000	L. Jenkins		AGIP 13	1847
00 000 0000	Richard Jenkins		HVAN 87	----
00 000 0000	Elizabeth Jett[Smoot]		HKDA 869	----
00 000 0000	Alfred Johnson		BWON 426	----
00 000 0000	Catherine Johnson[Roe]		HSHE 660	1827
00 000 1800	Cornelius Johnson		CLOW 920	1816
00 000 0000	Edward H. Johnson		FDAV 397	----
00 000 1793	Elijah Johnson		BFUT 427	----
00 000 1798	Hannah Johnson[Jones]		HKDA 864	----
00 000 0000	Harriett Johnson[Sparks]	John	CSHE 979	----
00 000 1802	Hiram Johnson		HKDA 863	----
00 Mar 1803	James Johnson	Daniel & Sarah(Grubbs)	CLOW 961	----
00 000 1800	James L. Johnson		HWBJ 161	----
00 00c 1802	Jas. Johnson		HJOH 502	----
00 000 0000	John Johnson		SIND 634	----
01 Jan 1798	John Johnson	Jeremiah	SIND 646	----
00 000 0000	Lewis Johnson		CLOW 921	----
00 000 1814	Malinda W.Johnson[Threlkeld]		HKDA 443	----
00 000 0000	Mary A. Johnson[Stalling]		HPOS 577	----

-222-

Date	Name	Parents	Code	Repository	No.	Year
00 000 0000	Nancy Johnson[Dilley]			WHSU	B340	---
00 000 0000	Parmelia Johnson[Griffin]			BWMB	764	---
00 000 0000	Sarah Johnson[Mitchell]			BHOT	315	---
00 00c 1795	Thomas B. Johnson			BGAS	209	---
00 000 0000	Thomas F. Johnson			HWSP	559	---
01 Mar 1802	William Johnson	Thomas	Va/x	BSCC	B236	---
20 Dec 1822	William Johnson	William & Mary(Alvis)	Ky/Va	HLOW	910	1832
00 000 0000	Berryman Jones			HWBJ	590	---
00 000 0000	Craig Jones			SIND	602	---
00 000 0000	John Jones			CLOW	958	---
00 000 1810	Joseph Jones			BVER	244	1831
00 000 0000	Martha J. Jones[Carnahan]			HWBJ	351	---
00 000 0000	Nancy C. Jones[Servies]			MONT	932	---
00 000 0000	Sarah Jones[Brasier]			BWMB	297	---
00 000 0000	Sarah A. Jones[Hilton]			BWMB	191	---
00 000 0000	Thomas M. Jones			HWSP	199	---
00 000 0000	William W. Jones			BWMB	344	---
00 000 1793	Margaret Jordan[Beckes]			HKDA	543	---
00 000 0000	Dorothy Jubinal[Beauchamp]			BVER	436	1826
00 000 1794	Benjamin Judy			HWBJ	190	---
00 000 0000	Martha Karney[Johnston]			HDOH	782	---
00 000 1821	Alexander C. Keach			JACK	659	1844
00 000 0000	Louisa Keach[Swaim] Rev. John R. & Hannah(Meade)			SCWA	832	---
00 000 0000	Eliza Kearby[Dillard]			HLOW	648	1811
00 000 1806	William Kearns			BVER	243	1826
00 000 0000	Jane Keeney[Hamilton]			MONT	792	---
00 000 1788	George H. Keith			FDAV	390	---
00 000 0000	Rachel Keith[Chambers]			TBAB	291	1830
00 000 0000	W. Keith			HKDA	523	1819
01 Oct 1835	Dr. Francis H. Kelley Robert & Charlotte(Walton)		Va97/x	HPOS	600	---
00 000 0000	Isaac Kelley			SCWA	810	---
00 000 0000	Perry Kelley			WHSU	B79	---
00 000 0000	Isham Kelly			HWSP	163	---
00 000 0000	Matthew Kelly			HSHE	671	---

BIRTHDATE	NAME OF BIOGRAPHEE	PARENTS/BIRTHPLACE/BIRTHDATE	SOURCE/PAGE	DATE
00 000 0000	Mary J. Kelly[Wells]		HVAN 200	---
00 000 0000	Mary Kelsey[Hays]		WFUF 818	---
00 000 0000	James Kemp		BMMB 254	---
00 000 0000	Nancy Kemper[Baker]		BMMB 283	---
00 000 1805	John R. Kendall		HKDA 820	1817
00 000 1823	Lucinda Kendall[Herod]		HJOH 616	---
00 000 0000	Mary Kendall[Melton]		HLOW 650	---
00 000 0000	Cynthia Kennard[Diltz]		HWBJ 373	---
00 000 0000	Luke C. Kennedy		BMMB 193	---
00 000 1808	Catherine Kennerly[Cushman]		WHSU B240	---
00 000 0000	Matilda Kenton[Parkison]		HWBJ 534	---
00 000 0000	Amy[Adams] Kephart		BMMB 245	---
00 000 0000	Hannah Kephart[Mitchell]		HJOH 756	---
19 Jan 1790	George Kerlin	James & Margaret(Smith)	HJOH 878	---
00 000 0000	William Kerns		BVER 404	1825
00 000 0000	Elizabeth Kester[Beauchamp]		BHVI 946	---
13 Dec 1794	Rebecca Kester[Carr]		BHVI 900	---
00 000 0000	John L. Ketcham	John Ky/x	DGIN 1143	---
00 000 1804	Sarah A. Ketcham[Fraley]		MONT 1211	---
00 000 1794	William Key	William & Hannah(Level)	SHGI 912	---
00 000 0000	J. Kidwell[Mattingly]		HKDA 821	---
00 000 0000	W.W. Kilgore		HMIA 444	1868
00 000 0000	Fountain Kimberlain		SIND 542	1820
00 000 1803	Jacob Kimberlain	Henry	SIND 532	1821
00 000 1800	John Kimberlain		SIND 632	1821
00 000 1797	John C. Kimberlain	Henry	SIND 632	---
28 Nov 1813	John J. Kincaid	John Tn75/x	GBRD 353	---
00 000 0000	Benjamin King		BPUT 466	---
00 000 0000	Isaac King		HPDB 726	---
00 000 1812	James King		HWAY B346	1824

			Name	Parents/Notes		Code	No.	Year
00	000	1819	James King			CSHE	823	1828
00	000	0000	James W.D. King	John & Judith(Roundtree)		FMWA	B494	---
00	000	0000	Jesse King			FMWA	B464	1826
07	Jul	1821	Joseph King			FMWA	B296	1828
07	Jul	1821	Joseph King	John & Judith(Roundtree)		HWAY	B347	---
00	000	0000	Lucinda King[Pinnick]			HLOW	655	---
00	000	0000	Mary King[Jones]			FMWA	B290	---
00	000	0000	Melinda King[Jeffries]			MONT	1208	1820
00	000	0000	Rachel King[Kirts]			BWMB	766	---
00	000	0000	Rebecca King[Culbertson]			FMWA	B578	---
00	000	0000	Robert King			HLOW	650	---
00	000	0000	Sarah King[Rector]			BHOT	T403	---
05	Sep	1823	William King	John & Cynthia	Va83/Ky89	FMWA	B34	---
05	Sep	1823	William King	John & Judith(Roundtree)	Va83/Ky89	WFUF	598	1828
00	000	0000	Jane Kinsley[Kilgore]			HMIA	444	---
00	000	0000	Edmond Kirk			HKDA	539	---
00	000	0000	Martha Kirk[Lankford]			BWMB	331	---
00	000	0000	William H. Kirk	David		BWMB	330	---
00	000	0000	William H. Kirk			BWMB	344	---
09	Sep	1809	Joseph Kirkman	James		GIBS	176	1813
00	000	0000	David Kirkpatrick			MPRO	434	---
00	000	1812	John S. Kirkpatrick			BVER	290	1832
00	000	0000	Moses Kirkpatrick			BGAS	224	---
00	000	0000	Elijah Kirtley			BHOT	T309	---
04	Apr	1848	John W. Kirtsinger	Harrison & Sarah		HSTJ	743	1859
00	000	0000	Mary Kitchen[Risk]			BPUT	412	---
00	000	0000	R.H. Kite			HCAR	352	1880
00	000	0000	William Knowland			HKDA	560	---
00	000	0000	Julia A. Koleapple			BPUT	357	---
00	000	0000	Charles A. Korbly		Ger/x	DGIN	818	---
00	000	0000	Henry F. Kurtz			HHHE	480	---
00	000	0000	Aaron Lagrange			HJOH	626	---
00	000	0000	Isaac Lamaster			BHOT	H489	---
00	000	0000	Mary P. Lamb[Wilson]			WHSU	B113	---

COUNTY NOT GIVEN (CONT.)

BIRTHDATE	NAME OF BIOGRAPHEE	PARENTS/BIRTHPLACE/BIRTHDATE		SOURCE/PAGE	DATE
00 Feb 1817	Charles Lane	Joel	Ky/x	WHSU B87	---
00 000 1811	Henry S. Lane			GIND 645	1833
24 Dec 1810	John F. Lane	Amos & Mary		HDOH 806	---
00 000 0000	James Lang			BSCC B162	---
00 000 1851	Dr. R.G. Langsdale			HDOH 808	---
07 Jun 1807	Lucretia Lanier[Williams]			KYCD 760	---
00 000 0000	Belinda Lankford[Cooprider]			CLOW 420	---
00 000 0000	Larkin Lankford			CLOW 434	---
00 000 0000	Melinda Lankford[Cooprider]			CLOW 422	---
00 000 0000	John O.M. Laughlin			HKDA 846	---
00 000 0000	Charlotte Laville[Blacklidge]			WPUF 657	---
00 000 0000	William Law			HJOH 424	1836
07 May 1820	Elizabeth Lawrence[Riley]			HFDB 747	---
00 000 0000	Rev. Alfred Layman			CLOW 853	---
00 000 0000	Dr. J.H. Layman			AWAS 49	1844
00 000 0000	Rev. John Layman			HCLI 754	1827
10 Apr 1813	Rev. Alfred Laymon	John & Jennie(Steele)	Va/Ky	CLOW 878	1815
00 000 1827	Dr. P.M. Layne	Elisha	Va/x	MONT 847	1830
00 000 0000	Enos Leach			HHHE 311	---
00 000 0000	John A. Leach			EMMB 256	---
00 000 0000	Sarah Leach[Leak]			HHHE 526	---
00 000 1816	James L. Leak			HHHE 298	1834
00 000 1818	Landrum Leak			HHHE 526	1835
00 000 1811	James M. Leathers			DGIN 645	1833
00 000 0000	William Ledgerman			WHSU B511	1793
00 000 0000	David S. Lee			BHOT T342	---
00 000 0000	Henry Lee			BGAS 231	---
26 Jan 1789	Isaac Lee			HLOW 340	1814
00 000 1802	James N. Lee			CSHE 593	1824
00 000 0000	Spencer Lee			HLOW 258	c1815

	Name	Notes		Code	No.	Year
00 000 0000	Catherine[Lefler]			BSCC	B131	---
00 000 0000	Peter Lefler			BSCC	B131	---
00 000 0000	William A. Legge			BWMB	778	---
00 000 0000	Richard LeGrange			SHGI	736	---
00 000 0000	Joseph P. Leisure			HSHE	638	1835
00 00c 1822	Zachariah Lemaster			SIND	583	---
00 00c 1803	Thirza LeMasters[Hudson]			CLOW	466	---
00 000 0000	John Lemmon			HPDB	535	1802
00 000 0000	John Lemmon			HPDB	743	---
00 000 0000	William P. Lemmon			BWMB	366	1818
00 000 0000	Barbara Letherman			HLOW	340	---
29 Jan 1798	David S. Lewis			BGAS	234	---
00 000 0000	Frankie Lewis[Hutson]			BHOT	H488	---
00 000 0000	Gideon Lewis			BWMB	331	---
11 Sep 1809	John A. Lett	Randall & Sarah(Tyndall)	Ga/Ga	HEDB	458	1813
00 000 1839	George E. Lidikay			MONT	965	---
31 Dec 1792	Isaac Limpus	John		NFUF	980	---
00 000 0000	Leonard Lincoln			SHGI	688	---
00 000 1793	Thomas Lindsay			HDOH	813	1811
00 000 0000	Elizabeth Lindsey[Alexander]			HPDB	384	1836
00 000 0000	T.T. Linn			MHMA	153	---
00 000 0000	Katherine Lisman[Hopewell]			WHSU	B309	---
00 000 0000	Anna List			HJOH	666	---
00 000 1797	Theodore List			HJOH	629	1838
00 000 0000	Polly Little[Wheeler]			HLOW	884	---
00 000 0000	Hannah Livingston[King]			HLOW	650	---
00 000 0000	Huldah Lizenby[Cunningham]			BWMB	181	1826
00 000 1817	Elizabeth Lloyd[Hazelrigg]			WHSU	B275	---
00 000 0000	James M. Lloyd			CLOW	405	---
00 000 1832	John G. Lloyd	Philip & Anna		WHSU	B101	1835
00 000 0000	Jorman Lockhart			HHHE	496	---
00 000 0000	Judith Lockhart[Warner]			BWMB	215	---
00 000 0000	Susan Lockhart[Hatfield]			HLOW	657	---
00 000 1805	Robert Lockridge			BVPA	198	1805

BIRTHDATE	NAME OF BIOGRAPHEE	PARENTS/BIRTHPLACE/BIRTHDATE		SOURCE/PAGE	DATE
25 Feb 1796	Ezekiel D. Logan			BGAS 239	----
00 000 0000	Elizabeth Long[Forward]			BHCL 848	----
00 000 0000	Richard Loring			BSCC B242	----
00 000 0000	Joseph D. Losley			BPUT 485	----
00 000 0000	Margaret Lovelace[Lisman]			WHSU B146	----
00 000 1803	Jonathan Lowe			HSHE 731	----
01 Dec 1823	Lawrence Lowe	Elijah & Kate(Voris)	c98/c98	HJOH 489	1828
00 000 1812	Littleton Lowe			SHGI 609	c1824
00 000 1811	Simon P. Lowe			BGAS 242	----
00 000 0000	Mary A. Lowery[Hite]			BHOT H377	----
29 May 1817	Joseph H. Loyd	William & ---(Polter)		GBRD 332	1820
00 000 0000	J.S. Lynam			ASPE 65	1861
00 000 0000	Delilah Lynch[Turner]			HWSP 827	----
00 000 0000	Mary J. Lyon[Anderson]			CLOW 522	----
00 000 1794	Daniel McAtee			HKDA 822	----
00 000 0000	Eliza J. McCammon[Stillwell]			BHOT T410	----
00 000 0000	Benjamin McCart			HWBJ 553	----
00 000 0000	Margaret McCartey			CLOW 926	----
00 000 0000	Thomas McClain			HJOH 822	----
00 000 0000	James McClaskey			BWON 543	----
16 Jun 1822	Joel C. McClellan	William & Elizabeth(Cline)		BWMB 279	1836
00 000 0000	Elizabeth McClery[Watts]			BWMB 771	----
00 000 1788	Thomas McClintock	Joseph	Md/x	SIND 634	1829
13 Mar 1813	William H. McClintock	Joseph	Md/x	SIND 635	1829
15 Jul 1847	Louisa McClure[Steele]	Martha & Teressa(Gudgell)		BWON 310	----
00 00c 1779	Margaret McClure[Holmes]			HKDA 428	----
01 Jun 1784	Samuel McClure			HKDA 458	----
00 000 0000	Narcissus McCollins[Rice]			MONT 1224	----
09 Mar 1796	John McCollum			SIND 587	----
00 000 0000	Hon. James H. McConnell			FMAD 507	----

	Name	Parents	Place	Code	No.	Date
00 00c 1796	Samuel H. McCord			BGAS	248	c1796
00 000 0000	Mathew S. McCorkle	William & Margaret(Allen)		EPUT	405	1825
06 Mar 1824	J.A. McCord		Pa/x	HKDA	879	---
00 000 1793	Phillip McCormick			BGAS	248	---
00 000 0000	Elizabeth McCowan[Crews]			BHVI	721	---
00 000 0000	A.H. McCoy			HWSP	535	---
00 000 0000	John McCoy			HVAN	256	---
00 000 0000	John McCracken	James & Sally(Meek)	Ky/x	GBRD	319	---
00 000 0000	Margaret[McCullough]			BWON	167	---
00 000 0000	William M. McCulloch	William & Druzilla(Morgan)		GBRD	407	---
07 Mar 1829	Thomas McCune	James & Keziah		HPDB	767	1832
00 000 0000	John McDaniel			BWON	213	---
00 000 0000	Sarah McDonald[Berry]			EIND	11	---
00 000 1820	Robert McDonald			BVER	245	1834
00 000 0000	Abigail[McElfresh]			HDOH	831	---
00 000 0000	Samuel McElfresh			HDOH	831	---
05 Jan 1801	Jane McFarland[McCollum]Benjamin			SIND	587	---
19 Dec 1831	Marion W. McFerran	Thomas & Lucinda(Hendricks)	Ire/Ky	CSHE	551	1835
00 000 0000	Harrison McGary			SHGI	738	---
00 000 0000	Harrison D. McGary			SHGI	944	---
00 000 1804	Michael McGaughey			MONT	1133	---
00 000 0000	Elisha McGinnis			CLOW	894	---
00 000 1820	Joseph T. McGinnis			EPUT	448	---
00 000 0000	Samuel McGinnis			HCLI	690	---
00 000 1817	William F. McGinnis			BGAS	252	---
00 000 0000	Christina McGowan[Kemp]			BWMB	254	---
00 000 0000	Rebecca McGrew[Miller]			WHSU	B338	---
00 000 0000	Sarah McGuire[Thompson]			HWSP	205	1835
00 000 0000	William McHaley			CLOW	855	c1823
00 000 0000	George A. McHenry			CLOW	880	---
00 000 1794	Phoebe McIntire[Bruce]			HDOH	643	---
00 000 0000	Amanda McIntyre[Butcher]			MONT	711	---
00 000 0000	Joseph McKee			CLOW	923	---
00 000 1798	Nancy A. McKee[Hollingsworth]			HKDA	427	---

BIRTHDATE	NAME OF BIOGRAPHEE	PARENTS/BIRTHPLACE/BIRTHDATE	SOURCE/PAGE	DATE
01 Jan 1803	Benjamin McKeen		BHVI 840	----
00 000 0000	Sarah McKenney[Thrailkill]		HWSP 551	----
00 000 0000	Catherine McKinley[Gray]		HLOW 909	1812
00 000 0000	Mary A. McKinley[Ringo]		CLOW 517	----
00 000 1803	Thomas R. McKinney		WHSU A67	1815
00 000 1796	James McKnight		HKDA 824	----
00 000 0000	John McLain		NSPC 308	1826
00 000 0000	Hugh A. McLary		BMMB 778	----
00 000 0000	Oliver McLoed		MONT 1200	1843
22 Apr 1818	Oliver McLoed		MONT 731	----
00 000 0000	Robert McMains		MONT 670	----
00 000 0000	Catherine McMullen[Archer]		SHGI 498	----
00 000 0000	Mary McMullen[Hitch]		SHGI 511	----
00 000 0000	Henry McNab		BMMB 229	----
00 000 1800	Fannie McQuaid[Bartlett]		HKDA 473	----
00 000 1815	Martin McQuinn		HJOH 756	----
00 000 1822	Artemus McRoberts		SHGI 1006	----
00 000 0000	Catherine[McTaggart]		HWAY B583	----
00 000 0000	John W. Maddox	John	BGAS 258	----
08 Apr 1787	Mathew Magill	Va/x	HCLI 758	----
13 Jan 1832	Caroline Mahan[Branson]	Jeremiah & Jemima(Browning) Ky/Ky	WHSU B172	1834
00 000 0000	Mary Mahan[Read]		EIND C32	----
00 000 0000	Marly Mahoney[Fisher]		HJOH 483	----
00 000 0000	Morgan D. Mahorney		BMMB 306	----
00 000 0000	Amanda Manchester[Dye] Hiram		DIND 1805	----
00 000 0000	Della Manley[Baker]		BMMB 363	----
05 Oct 1816	James B. Mann	Josiah & Elizabeth(Schooling)	WHSU B257	----
00 000 1803	William Mansfield		BGAS 259	----
00 000 0000	Rebecca Mappin[Powell]		BHOT H474	----

00 000 0000	Aletha March[Howard]	HJOH	792	---
00 000 1819	William Marlow	ASUL	102	1831
00 000 0000	Ambrose Marshall	WHSU	B194	---
23 Dec 1807	Hannah Marshall[Preble]	BHOT	H361	---
00 000 0000	Ison Marshall	CLOW	541	---
00 000 0000	Enoch Martin	SCWA	886	---
00 000 1813	Jane Martin[Lane]	HKDA	846	---
00 000 0000	John Martin	HLOW	935	---
00 000 0000	Joseph W. Martin	HLOW	296	---
00 000 0000	Lucy Martin[Scroggan]	HLOW	269	1828
00 000 1805	Maria Martin[Johnson]	HKDA	863	---
00 000 0000	Patsy Martin[Martin]	HLOW	935	---
05 Aug 1813	Thomas Martin	HPDB	424	---
00 000 1811	William D. Martin	HKDA	457	---
00 000 0000	Margaret Martindale[Long]	HMIA	777	1812
00 000 0000	James M. Mason	BHVI	853	---
00 00c 1797	John Mason	HWSP	789	---
00 000 1806	Lincoln Mason	BSCC	B174	---
00 000 1825	Mary Mason[Wheat]	BJAY	451	---
00 000 0000	Rankin Mason	FDAV	607	---
00 000 0000	Rev. William F. Mason	DGIN	768	---
00 000 0000	William M. Mason	BWMB	767	---
00 000 0000	Elizabeth Massey[Ranard]	CLOW	942	---
00 000 0000	Rachael Massey[Disbrow]	BHOT	T356	---
00 000 0000	Elizabeth Massie[McCulla]	HWSP	169	---
00 000 0000	Richard Masters	HPDB	467	c1819
00 000 0000	Julia Masterson[Sudwell]	HWSP	509	---
22 Mar 1833	Louisa J. Masterson[Smith]	HWSP	541	---
00 000 1808	Francis A. Matheny	BGAS	265	---
08 Jul 1808	Elder J.M. Mathes	CLOW	856	1818
00 000 0000	Richard Mathews	BSCC	B244	1818
00 000 0000	Polly Matthews[Young]	BWMB	294	---
00 000 1804	Henry Mattingly	HKDA	821	---
00 000 0000	Thomas Mattingly	HWSP	547	---

BIRTHDATE	NAME OF BIOGRAPHEE	PARENTS/BIRTHPLACE/BIRTHDATE		SOURCE/PAGE		DATE
00 000 0000	Milford Mattox			AWAS	50	1826
00 000 1828	Martha A. Mauzy[Wilson] Peter & Sarah(Gooding)	Ky/Ky		HSHℓ	547	1829
00 000 0000	James Mavity John & Dorothy(Reel)			HLOW	594	----
19 May 1793	Edward R. Maxwell			BGAS	266	----
00 000 0000	Lucinda Maxwell[Wiley]			MPRO	420	1811
00 000 1809	George May			BGAS	267	----
00 000 1839	George A. May			MONT	933	----
00 000 0000	Clarinda Mayfield[Hendricks]			BMON	520	----
00 000 0000	Jeptha Mayfield			BSCC	B245	----
00 000 0000	Joshua Mayfield			BSCC	B246	----
00 000 0000	W.C. Mayfield			ASUL	101	----
00 000 0000	John B. Mayhall			BFUT	471	----
00 000 0000	Mahala Mayhall[Turpin] William	Ky/x		SHGI	530	1830
00 000 1808	Martha Meadley[Ganoe]			HKDA	423	----
00 000 1821	Elizabeth Meadows[Hornaday]			HKDA	876	----
00 Oct 1814	John Meek Samuel	82/x		GBRD	396	----
00 000 1818	Joseph Meek			HGAR	164	1844
00 000 1816	Lavina Meek[Cromwell]Edwin & Rachel	Ky/Ky		BSCC	B135	----
00 Oct 0000	Mary Ann Megee[Ensminger]			HHHE	291	----
10 Nov 1853	John Mehne John & Barbara(Price)	Ger/Ger		HPDB	709	----
00 000 0000	Martha Melton[Wilson]			DGIN	1092	----
00 000 0000	Elizabeth Ann Menefee[Walker]			HHHE	762	1862
00 000 0000	Ambrose Milam			WHSU	B214	----
00 000 0000	Henry R. Milam			WHSU	A67	c1814
24 Oct 1832	Richard F. Milburn Francis & Mary(Inman)			HPDB	709	----
00 000 0000	Sarah Mile[Weddle]			BHVI	992	----
07 Oct 1825	Franklin Miles			MONT	1219	----
00 000 0000	Samuel Miles			CLOW	407	----
00 000 0000	Mary Miley[Harrell]			HPDB	397	1818
00 000 0000	Abigail Miller[Leach]			EMMB	256	----

Date	Name	Parents / Notes		Code	Number	Year
00 000 0000	B.W. Miller			MHWA	152	1848
00 000 0000	C.I. Miller			HWBJ	395	---
00 000 0000	David Miller			WHSU	B338	---
00 000 1805	Francis M. Miller	George & Elizabeth		HVAN	197	1809
00 00c 1795	Jacob Miller	David & Abigail(Morgan)		PBES	596	---
00 000 1818	Jacob Miller			BVER	244	1818
00 00c 1805	James F. Miller			BGAS	273	---
00 00c 0000	John W. Miller			HLOW	262	c1835
08 Dec 1813	Louisa Jane Miller[Hufford]			---	---	1832
00 000 0000	Matilda Miller[Potter]			BHCL	743	---
00 000 0000	Nicholas Miller			HWSP	474	---
00 000 0000	Sarah Miller[Farr]			BMMB	364	---
00 000 1813	Benjamin Mills			BVER	244	1833
17 Sep 1819	John A. Mills			HWSP	234	---
00 000 1806	Mary Ann Mills[Daugherty]			HHHE	687	1830
00 000 0000	Col. William Minter			WHSU	A69	1840
00 000 0000	Aaron Mitchell			HJOH	756	---
00 000 0000	Paul Mitchell			BCHE	665	---
21 Aug 1803	Robert Mitchell	Thomas & Elizabeth(Harmon)	76/80	HLOW	870	---
00 000 0000	Silas Mitchell			BHOT	T315	1830
00 000 1814	Thomas J. Mitchell			BVER	289	---
00 000 0000	James Montgomery			SHGI	460	---
00 000 0000	John R. Montgomery			HPDB	639	---
19 Dec 1822	Margaret Montgomery[Green]			CSHE	688	---
00 000 0000	Jane Moore[Gurton]			HWAY	B286	---
00 000 0000	Mary Moore[Mitchell]			BMMB	198	1810
00 000 0000	Mary Moore[Mitchell]			BMMB	230	---
00 000 0000	Mary Moore[Mitchell]			EIND	E29	---
00 000 0000	Nancy Moore[Peck]			BPUT	380	1822
00 000 0000	S.H. Moore			BHOT	H353	---
00 000 0000	Agnes Moreland[Dills]			BPUT	431	---
00 000 1824	William H. Morgan			HHHE	597	1855
00 000 1818	Joshua Moore	Lee & Mary(Law)	Md/Md	HSHE	640	1827
00 000 0000	Isabella Mosby[Anderson]			HPDB	735	---

BIRTHDATE	NAME OF BIOGRAPHEE	PARENTS/BIRTHPLACE/BIRTHDATE	SOURCE/PAGE	DATE
00 000 0000	William H. Moss		GIBS 235	1880
12 Mar 1798	William Mount		EMON 166	1823
00 000 0000	Garrard Mounts		SHGI 717	----
00 000 0000	Sarah Mouser[Brown]		CLOW 887	----
00 000 0000	John Mugg		CLOW 941	----
00 000 0000	William Mugg		BHOT H415	1845
00 000 1817	Catherine Mullen[Stafford]		TCMA 577	c1837
00 000 0000	James Mundell		HCLI 643	----
00 000 1838	Elizabeth M. Murdoch[Gates]		DGIN 974	----
00 000 0000	Mary A.C. Murphey[Sims]		HJOH 443	----
00 Nov 1802	Thomas Murphey	Kanlum & Nancy(Sicklesworth)	CLOW 961	----
00 000 1810	Aaron Murphy		HPOS 604	1813
00 000 0000	Nancy Murphy[Johnson]		FDAV 397	----
00 000 0000	Nancy Murphy[Johnson]		FDAV 397	----
00 000 1813	Benjamin Musgrave		BVAN 54	----
00 000 0000	Henry Musselman		HJOH 710	1822
00 000 0000	John Myers		SIND 582	----
00 000 0000	Thomas Myers		BVER 514	----
00 000 0000	Marvel W. Nash		WHSU B259	----
00 000 0000	Marvel W. Nash		WHSU A37	c1825
00 000 0000	Elizabeth Nave[Woodard]		HSHE 743	1827
00 000 0000	Solomon Nave		HSHE 708	1824
00 000 0000	Charles B. Naylor		BGAS 288	----
00 000 1818	Asa Neal		FDAV 582	----
27 Sep 1844	George W. Neal	Robert H. & Lucy Ann(Wells) **17/**23	HSHE 518	1862
30 Aug 1812	Matilda Neal[Wilson]		HDOH 978	----
00 000 1795	Elias Nelson	Charles & Nelly(Crouch) Ky/Ky	BAWE 527	1842
00 000 0000	James Nelson		HWSP 506	----
00 000 0000	John J. Nelson		WHSU B96	1823
00 000 1821	Joseph A. Nesbit	John & Mary	SIND 634	----
26 Dec 1825	William O. Nesbit		WHSU B273	----

	Name	Parents / Notes	Code	No.	Year
00 000 0000	Melinda Newkirk[Briley]		CLOW	532	-----
13 Nov 1806	Richard Newlon	William & Nancy	HLOW	9111	c1818
00 000 0000	John Nicholas		EMMB	309	-----
00 000 0000	Abigail Nicholson[Caldwell]	NC/x	BHVI	695	-----
00 000 0000	Edward W. Nicholson James		DGIN	653	-----
00 000 0000	Edward W. Nicholson James		DIND	1527	-----
00 000 0000	Jesse C. Nicholson		BMON	315	-----
00 000 0000	William W. Nicholson		GIND	646	1822
00 0c 1792	Joseph B. Nickell		BGAS	293	-----
00 0c 1797	William T. Noel		BGAS	294	-----
12 Aug 1822	Benjamin F. Norris Benjamin & Priscilla(Norris)		RUSH	442	1834
00 000 0000	Phebe Norris[Garrison]		EMMB	184	-----
00 000 0000	John Northcott		FWWA	B549	-----
00 000 0000	John Nowels		HWBJ	532	-----
00 000 1809	Silas Nowlin Zachariah & Mary E(Pride) Va/Ky		HDOH	858	1818
01 Apr 1808	William Oakerson John & Elizabeth(Todd)		TRAN	481	-----
29 Jul 1824	Presley N. O'Bannon William Breckinridge/x		DIND	2284	-----
00 000 1804	Sylvester O. O'Bryan		FDAV	409	-----
00 000 0000	Joses Oldham		HSHE	709	-----
00 000 0000	Ellen Ollis[Marshall]		CLOW	541	-----
00 000 0000	John H. Ooley		CLOW	941	-----
00 000 0000	Eleanor Osborn[Crosby]		EPUT	363	1834
00 000 1789	John Osborn		WHSU	A70	-----
00 0c 1811	John Osborn		BGAS	301	c1811
00 000 1818	M[Osborn]		ASUL	115	1829
00 000 0000	Sarah Osborn[Cooper]		HWBJ	563	1843
00 000 1794	Silas Osborn		BGAS	301	-----
00 000 1825	Thomas Osborn		ASUL	115	1829
00 000 0000	Elizabeth Osborne[Dodd] Isaiah		WHSU	B204	-----
04 Oct 1828	John J. Osborne		MONT	1273	-----
00 000 1803	Philip W. Osmon		BVER	258	1826
00 000 1803	Philip W. Osmon		BVER	479	-----
00 000 0000	Lucinda Ouseley[Mayfield]		BSCC	B246	-----
00 000 0000	James Overture		WFUF	1067	-----
00 000 1819	William Owens		ASUL	116	-----

BIRTHDATE	NAME OF BIOGRAPHEE	PARENTS/BIRTHPLACE/BIRTHDATE	SOURCE/PAGE	DATE
00 000 0000	Ebenezer Paddock		HJOH 905	---
00 000 0000	Isaac Painter		HWSP 523	---
00 000 0000	Mary A[Painter]		HWSP 523	---
00 000 0000	Nancy Parker[Pratt]		CLOW 882	---
00 000 0000	Nancy Parker[Toner]		BMMB 212	---
00 000 0000	Robert Parker, Sr.		HWBJ 547	---
00 000 0000	Daniel Parkhurst		HJOH 723	1836
00 000 0000	John Parkison		HWBJ 534	---
00 000 0000	James O. Parks		MHMA 47	1836
00 000 0000	J.O. Parks		MHMA 153	1836
23 Dec 1832	James Farmer	Isaac & Sarah(Wishard) Md01/05	HJOH 494	1835
00 000 0000	Margaret Patten[McCorkle]		BPUT 405	1825
00 000 0000	William B. Pattison		HHHE 460	---
00 000 1833	William Pauley		SHGI 1010	1850
13 Jan 1816	Benjamin Pauly		EBOO 345	1835
00 000 1823	A.M. Payton		BVER 244	1830
00 000 0000	Jacob Payton		BJAB 772	---
00 000 1800	James L. Payton		BVER 244	1830
00 000 0000	John Peake		BSCC B107	---
00 000 0000	Henry Pearcy	Robert Ky/x	BMMB 201	---
00 000 0000	James Peed		HHEN 517	---
00 000 0000	Anna M. Peniston[Beatly]	Eng/Eng	SCWA 737	---
08 Apr 1804	Charlotte Penn[McLoed]		MONT 731	---
00 000 1813	Huldah Penn		HCAR 163	1833
00 000 1809	John W. Penn		HCAR 163	1833
00 000 0000	Isaac Pennington		HHHE 397	---
00 000 0000	Samuel H. Perigo		HWSP 227	---
00 000 0000	Abbariller Perkins[Keith]		HKDA 783	---
00 000 1795	Abbie Perkins[Keith]		FDAV 390	---
00c 000 1791	John R. Peters	Jonathan & Mary(Tatum) Ky/NC	BSCC B108	---

Date	Name	Parents/Spouse	Code	No.	Year
00 000 0000	Elizabeth Phillips[Becks]		BWMB	795	---
00 000 0000	M. Phillips[Reed]		HWSP	234	1816
00 000 0000	Samuel Pickens		DG1N	850	---
31 Jan 1797	John Pierce		BWMB	360	---
00 000 1796	Hannah Percy[Ross]		BPUT	506	---
00 000 0000	Moses Pierson		BHVI	898	1825
23 Nov 1823	John J. Piles	William & Elizabeth(Haydon) Henry/x	BSCC	B255	---
00 000 0000	Christina[Ping]		BWMB	796	---
00 000 0000	Job Ping		BWMB	796	---
00 000 0000	John A. Pinkston		HWSP	539	---
00 000 1829	W.O. Pinkston		ASUL	125	1829
00 000 0000	Catherine J. Pipe[Survant]		HPDB	454	---
00 000 1810	Alford Pirtle		ASUL	124	1815
00 000 0000	Mary Pirtle[Nosler]		BWMB	332	---
00 000 0000	John Plake		TCWA	506	---
00 000 0000	Elizabeth Plasters[Higgins]		HHHE	222	---
00 000 0000	Jonathan Plunkett		BWON	490	---
00 000 0000	Nancy Poague[McClaskey]		BWON	543	---
00 000 0000	Mary Ann Poe[Jones]		BWMB	344	---
00 000 0000	Clayborn Polk		SHGI	950	---
00 000 0000	Mary Polk[Ellison]		HWSP	146	---
00 000 0000	Thomas Polk		HWSP	791	---
02 Feb 1822	Squire W. Polk		MONT	1262	---
00 000 0000	Elizabeth Porter[Steele]		BHOT	T328	---
00 00c 1803	William M. Porter		BGAS	317	---
00 000 0000	John T. Potter		BHCL	743	---
00 000 0000	Eunice Pound[Goble]		CLOW	537	---
00 000 0000	John Powell		EIND	F65	---
00 000 0000	John Powell		BHOT	H474	---
00 000 0000	Isaac Powers		HWSP	218	---
00 000 0000	Artemas Pratt		CLOW	883	1834
07 Feb 1805	M.M. Preble	Benjamin B. & Lucretia(Marshall)	BHOT	H361	1807
14 Feb 1801	John Pressel	Daniel & Motley(Larndy)	HHEN	734	---
00 000 0000	Phoebe Preston[Adams]		BPUT	387	---

BIRTHDATE	NAME OF BIOGRAPHEE	PARENTS/BIRTHPLACE/BIRTHDATE		SOURCE/PAGE		DATE
00 Jun 1811	D.S. Prichard	C.G. & Isabelle(Spears)		BHOT	T399	1820
00 000 0000	Margaret Priestland[Frakes]			BSCC	B147	----
16 Sep 1804	David P. Pritchard			HJOH	761	----
00 000 0000	Margaret Pritchard[Forsythe]			FDAV	323	----
00 000 0000	Walker Pritchard			BHOT	T400	----
00 000 0000	Elisha Pritchett			SHGI	802	----
00 000 0000	Nancy Pritchett[Jones]			CLOW	958	----
00 000 0000	Hannah Pruitt[Wilson]			BMMB	351	----
00 00c 1840	John Pruitt			HPDB	731	----
00 000 0000	Augustus Purcell			HWSP	576	----
01 Jul 1815	William Pursell	Thomas & Melinda	Va/Va	BPUT	428	1823
00 000 0000	Eli Putoff	John & Mark(Hoke)		SGWA	840	----
00 000 0000	Field Rabourn			HWBJ	174	----
00 000 0000	Abner Ragan			HHHE	742	----
00 000 0000	James M. Ragan	Abner & Mary(MacCoun)		HHHE	742	----
00 000 1825	Delilah Ragland[Blanton]			HHHE	674	----
00 000 0000	Elizabeth Ragland[Stevenson]			HHHE	482	----
01 May 1811	Lucinda Ragsdale[Hicks]			BMON	460	----
00 000 0000	Malinda Ragsdale[Fendley]			HJOH	893	1820
00 000 1824	Daniel L. Railsback			ASUL	128	1853
00 000 1851	B.D. Railsback			ASUL	128	1854
00 000 0000	Nancy Rains[Adams]			HWSP	777	----
00 000 0000	Jane Rairden[Walker]			BMMB	791	----
00 000 0000	Henry Rairdon			HJOH	826	----
00 000 1804	Robert M. Ramsey			BMON	221	----
26 Jan 1830	Judge Samuel Ramsey	William & Mary		EIND	C31	c1832
00 000 0000	Samuel C. Randolph			ASPE	66	1861
00 000 1809	James Raney			HKDA	830	1818
00 000 0000	George I. Rankin			DGIN	1028	----
00 000 0000	Lovisa Rankin[Wood]			CLOW	885	1826

Date	Name	Parents/Notes	Code	No.	Year
29 Aug 1795	Martin M. Ray		BGAS	323	---
00 000 1793	James G. Read		BGAS	323	---
00 000 0000	James G. Read		EIND	C32	---
00 000 0000	Alexander D. Reading		MPRO	359	c1838
00 000 0000	John Rector		BHOT	T403	1826
00 000 0000	Minerva Redman[Mounts]		GIBS	235	---
20 Mar 1805	Armer Reed		BGAS	324	---
00 000 0000	A. Reed		HWSP	234	1815
00 000 0000	Ila Reeves		HHEN	897	1828
00 000 1801	James Reeves		TRAN	488	---
00 000 0000	Mary Reeves[Sharp]		CLOW	925	---
00 000 0000	Abraham Renbarger		BJAB	589	---
04 Sep 1826	J. Reynolds	William & Mary	BMON	352	1832
00 000 0000	Margaret Reynolds[Bodine]		BHVI	684	---
00 000 0000	Benjamin Rhoades		HWSP	174	---
26 Jun 1829	Issac H. Rhoades	Samuel & Susan(Wishard) Md86/Ky03	HJOH	907	---
00 000 0000	John Rice		BVER	474	---
08 Jan 1806	Lewis Rice		HHHE	356	1827
00 000 0000	Lucinda Rice[McHaley]		CLOW	855	c1823
00 000 0000	Philena Rice[Powers]		HWSP	218	---
00 000 0000	William A. Rice		MONT	743	---
29 Dec 1838	William A. Rice		MONT	931	1852
00 000 0000	Phebe Richards[Beem]		CLOW	872	---
00 000 0000	Rebecca Richards[Metsker]		HWBJ	200	---
00 000 0000	Samuel Richards		CLOW	912	---
00 000 0000	Anna Richardson[Tucker]		BHVI	972	---
00 000 1799	Dudley Richardson		HJOH	754	1836
00 000 1809	John Richardson		HPDB	451	---
00 000 0000	Mary[Richardson]		HPDB	451	---
00 000 0000	Mary Richardson[Egnew]		HWSP	517	---
00 000 0000	Rhoda Richardson[Portwood]	Basil & Amy(Thompson) Ky/Ky	HHHE	841	---
00 000 0000	Jonathan Ricketts		HDEK	542	---
00 000 0000	Samuel Right		HDOH	886	---

BIRTHDATE	NAME OF BIOGRAPHEE	PARENTS/BIRTHPLACE/BIRTHDATE	SOURCE/PAGE	DATE
00 000 1823	Noble S. Riley	Edward	DIND 1352	c1840
00 000 0000	Walter B. Ringo		CLOW 517	---
00 000 0000	Mariah Risinger[Chenoweth]		BMMB 299	---
00 000 1800	Elswie Risk		BPUT 412	---
00 000 0000	Huldah Risley[Cromwell]		CLOW 423	1819
19 Jan 1807	Benjamin T. Ristine	Henry & Nancy(Gray) NY/Va	BMON 194	1808
00 000 0000	Sarah Ritter[Franklin]		CLOW 934	---
00 000 0000	Elizabeth Rivers[Hunt]		HJOH 752	---
00 000 1836	Sarah[Robbins]		ASUL 133	1855
00 000 1804	Andrew W. Robertes	Minor & Jemima(Corn) Va/Va	MHMA 117	1808
00 000 0000	Elizabeth Roberts[Zuck]		BSCC B299	---
00c 1803	John H. Roberts		BGAS 334	---
00 000 0000	Parmelia Roberts[Ellis]		HPDB 760	---
23 Feb 1811	Robert Roberts		BWEL 373	---
13 Mar 1834	William R. Roberts	Reden & Israel Nicholas/Nicholas	EBOO 355	---
00 000 0000	Elizabeth Robertson[McKnight]		HLOW 914	---
00 000 0000	George W. Robertson		BSCC B61	---
00 000 0000	Margaret Robertson[Mogan]	Addison & Eliza	BSCC B176	---
00 000 0000	T.B. Robertson		HCAR 350	1848
00 000 1825	William Robertson		ASUL 132	1865
00 000 1784	William Robins		BSCC B249	1784
00 000 1801	Abner Robinson		HCAR 163	1824
00 000 1816	Elijah G. Robinson		HKDA 868	---
00 000 0000	Elizabeth Robinson[Bass]		BMMB 217	---
00 000 0000	Emma Robinson[Smitha]		BSCC B38	---
25 Dec 1830	George W. Robinson	William & Sarah(Lyon) NY74/NY64	BSCC B180	---
00 000 0000	Martha J[Robinson]		ASUL 133	---
00c 1803	Osmyn Robinson		BGAS 336	---
12 Dec 1808	Ozias Robinson		EBOO 354	---
00 000 0000	Martha Rodgers[Heath]		BHOT T339	---

00 000 1801	Amanda F. Rogers[Brookie] Alexander	HCLI	635	1801
00 000 0000	Asa L. Rogers	BPUT	450	---
00 000 0000	Mary[Rogers]	BPUT	450	---
00 000 0000	Sarah Rogers[Bohannon] George & Elizabeth(Pearson)	CLOW	396	---
00 000 1772	Joseph Rooks	TRAN	469	---
11 Jul 1831	J.B. Rose Walker & Edith(Kemper)	HPDB	747	---
00 000 0000	Mary R. Rose[Warner]	HHHE	328	---
00 000 0000	John Ross	GBRD	232	---
23 Oct 1823	Nancy J. Roswell[Graham]	CSHE	893	---
09 Apr 1789	Judith Roundtree[King]	FMWA	B34	1824
00 000 1799	Nathaniel Rouse	HJOH	497	---
00 000 0000	Richard Royal	HWSP	794	---
09 Jun 1787	Martin Royse	HLOW	892	---
00 000 1801	Phena Royster	HCAR	163	1824
00 000 1807	James Ruby	TRAN	224	---
00 000 0000	James Rudder	HLOW	929	1842
00 000 0000	Cynthia Ruggles[White]	BWMB	243	---
00 000 1808	Morrison Rulon	BGAS	340	---
00 000 1796	William P. Rush	BGAS	341	---
00 000 0000	Cynthia Rusher[Harris]	HWSP	519	---
00 000 1830	J.W. Russell	ASUL	135	1830
00 000 0000	Wilson Ryan	HLOW	645	---
00 000 0000	Elizabeth Ryman[Parson]	MPRO	191	---
00 000 0000	W.D. Sadler	CLOW	866	---
00 000 0000	John St. Clair	ARIP	50	1866
00 000 0000	Julia St. Clair[Harrison]	BWMB	765	---
00 000 0000	Clayton Sale Samuel	BFWJ	310	1832
00 000 0000	Hannah Salisbury[Myers]	HJOH	792	---
00 000 0000	Eliza Sallerfield	HKDA	906	---
00 000 1809	Nancy Sample[Welliver]	HJOH	672	---
00 000 1792	Robert Sample	BHCL	737	---
00 000 1813	Rebecca Sanders[Epperson] Thomas & Sally(Morton)	BPUT	368	---
07 Nov 1807	Martha Sands[Sloan]	BSCC	B62	---
00 000 0000	Lucretia Sanford[Robinson]	HKDA	868	---

BIRTHDATE	NAME OF BIOGRAPHEE	PARENTS/BIRTHPLACE/BIRTHDATE	SOURCE/PAGE	DATE
00 000 0000	Joseph Schonling		BGAS 346	----
00 000 0000	Nancy Scott[Underwood]		HHHE 620	1828
00 000 0000	Samuel Scroggan		HLOW 269	----
00 000 1809	John H. Scrogin		HKDA 441	----
00 000 0000	William Seay		CLOW 942	1835
00 000 1801	Polly Sellers[McCaslin]		HJOH 635	1827
00 000 0000	Jane Sentemay[Short]		MPRO 485	----
00 000 0000	Sarah J. Seright[Riffe]		BHOT T324	----
00 000 0000	William T. Servies		MONT 932	----
00 000 0000	Enoch Sexton		CSHE 956	1833
00 000 0000	E.C. Shaffer		AVAN 72	1852
00 000 1843	J.P. Shake		ASUL 137	----
00 000 1852	William F. Shake		ASUL 137	1865
00 000 0000	Elizabeth[Shanklin]		EMON 437	----
00 000 0000	John Shanklin		MONT 599	1828
00 000 0000	Johnson Shanklin		EMON 437	----
00 000 0000	Hubbard Sharp		CLOW 925	----
00 000 0000	Stephen Sharp		MHHA 153	1850
00 000 0000	Benjamin Shaw		BVER 280	----
00 000 0000	Rosanna Sheeks[Albin]		EPUT 399	1832
00 000 1808	John Shelburn		EBOO 362	----
00 000 0000	Mercy Shelby[Cobb]		EIND B10	1816
07 Oct 1819	Otis Shepard	George & Mary(McQuigg)	HWBJ ---	----
00 000 1808	Benjamin Shepherd		BVER 258	1828
00 000 0000	Daniel Shepherd		AWAS 49	1818
12 May 1813	David Shepherd	Thomas & Nancy(Hensley) Ky/Ky	HLOW 926	1818
00 000 0000	Horace B. Shepard		HKDA 389	1820
04 Aug 1816	James Shepherd		HLOW 926	1818
00 000 0000	Stephen Shepherd		CLOW 546	----
00 000 0000	Thomas Shepherd		HLOW 897	1813

Date	Name	Parents	Loc	Code	No.	Year
00 000 0000	Samuel M. Shewmaker			BHVI	926	---
00 000 1799	William Shields		Va/x	DIND	1465	---
00 000 0000	Mary Ship[Shepard]			HKDA	462	---
00 000 0000	Dr. D.J. Shirley			BHOT	H367	---
00 000 1803	James W. Shirley			HHHE	183	c1830
00 000 0000	Mary A. Shirley[Dailey]			HJOH	409	---
00 000 0000	Eliza Jane Shively[Bretz]			HPDB	586	---
28 Nov 1818	Fannie S. Shoemaker[Bailey]			BHVI	663	---
00 000 0000	Jacob Shoptaugh			BPUT	521	1828
00 000 0000	Ezekiel Short	John		MPRO	485	---
15 Oct 1798	Morgan Shortridge		56/x	BGAS	355	---
00 000 0000	Alice Shouse[Mason]			BPUT	414	1827
22 Feb 1856	Fannie Shryock[Justus]	Hillery & Mary(Lewis)	Ky/Ky	HJOH	796	---
28 Jan 1824	Hugh C. Siddens	James & Sarah		HWBJ	383	---
00 000 0000	Joseph Sidewell			HWSP	509	---
00 000 0000	Elizabeth Sill[Smyth]			BPUT	402	---
00 000 1833	John M. Sills			ASUL	140	1835
00 000 0000	Nancy Silvers			LLLM	B48	---
00 000 0000	Elizabeth Simmons[Lemmon]			HPDB	743	---
00 000 0000	Hiram W. Simmons			HWSP	795	---
00 000 0000	Samuel Sinclair			HWBJ	742	---
00 000 1815	Hunley Singleton	William & Nancy(Tolbert)	Ky/Ky	FDAV	596	1837
16 Oct 1800	Benjamin Sisson			ASUL	141	---
01 Oct 1827	John Skaggs			BMMB	363	---
00 000 0000	Mary A Skaggs[Cox]			BHOT	T232	---
30 Jul 1825	Mary A. Skaggs[Cox]			HMIA	409	---
00 000 1781	James A. Skelton			BMON	419	1832
00 00c 0000	Mary Slusher[Coghill]			HWBJ	197	---
00 000 0000	Allen Smiley			BGAS	360	1822
00 000 1814	Catherine Smith[Rice]			BMMB	348	---
25 May 1802	Elizabeth Smith[Thompson]			BVER	474	---
00 000 0000	Hannah Smith[Butler]	John & Mary		CSHE	722	1833
	James Smith			BPUT	331	---
				HWBJ	561	---

BIRTHDATE	NAME OF BIOGRAPHEE	PARENTS/BIRTHPLACE/BIRTHDATE	SOURCE/PAGE	DATE
00 000 0000	John P. Smith		HHEN 737	----
00 000 0000	Louisa Smith[Sullivan]		HMIA 475	----
00 000 0000	Lucy A. Smith[Ragan]		HHHE 742	----
00 000 1843	M.L. Smith		MHMA 154	----
00 000 0000	Manoah Smith		GIBS 178	1830
00 000 0000	Peter Smith		HLOW 270	----
00 000 1829	Richard Smith		ASUL 142	----
00 000 0000	Sarah J. Smith[Barlow]		HHHE 387	----
26 Jul 1805	Temple Smith		TRAN 389	----
00 000 0000	Thomas D. Smith	Isaac NC/x	HHHE 522	----
14 Feb 1841	William A. Smith		MONT 727	----
16 Nov 1822	William B. Smith		HWSP 541	----
00 000 0000	W.B. Smitha		BSCC B38	----
00 000 0000	John Smither		DIND 1,577	c1825
00 000 0000	Abraham Smock		BWMB 207	----
00 000 0000	Cornelius Smock		BHVI 934	----
00 000 0000	Ruth Smock[Ballard]		BHOT T419	----
00 000 0000	William P. Smoot		HKDA 869	----
00 000 0000	Ebenezer Smyth		BPUT 402	----
00 000 0000	William Snider		BWMB 782	----
00 000 0000	William H. Snider		BHVI 934	----
00 000 0000	Dr. James B. Sparks		CSHE 979	----
00 000 0000	Massa Sparks[Pound]		BHVI 708	----
00 000 0000	Susan Sparks[Inlow]		EMON 384	1828
00 000 0000	Edward Smythe		MPRO 115	----
20 Nov 1817	Nancy Spears[Campbell]		BHOT T352	----
00 000 0000	Sophia Spears[Pritchard]		BHOT T400	----
20 Jun 1808	A.B. Spear	Moses & Ann(Voris) Md/Md	HLOW 661	----
00 000 0000	Jarred Spencer		HWSP 820	----
00 000 0000	James W. Spencer		BWMB 782	----

Date	Name	Code	No.	Year
03 Sep 1863	H.M. Speyer Henry & Margaret(Pickens)	TCMA	513	---
00 000 0000	Narcissus Spilman[Tyner]	HWSP	182	---
00 000 0000	Francis X. Spink	EIND	B34	1822
00 000 1822	A.W. Springer	ASUL	144	1828
00 000 0000	Priscilla Springer[Stewart]	HCLI	764	---
07 Aug 1846	John Spry John & Malvina(Kimbrell) SCcO7/Ky11	BELA	449	1879
31 Oct 1805	Athel Staggs	BGAS	368	---
00 000 0000	Phoebe Stansberry[Sexton]	CSHE	956	1833
00 000 0000	Malinda Stark[Phillips]	HWSP	554	---
00 000 0000	James T. Staube	ASPE	66	1859
00 000 0000	James Steele	DGIN	792	---
00 000 0000	Jemima Steele[Layman]	HCLI	754	1827
00 000 0000	John Steele	BHOT	T328	---
24 Jan 1809	William S. Steele Thomas & Catherine(McClure) Va/SC	BMON	310	1827
00 000 0000	Basil Steeley	HWBJ	208	---
00 000 0000	James F. Stephens	ASPE	66	1850
00 000 0000	James F. Stephens	HWSP	510	---
21 May 1832	Armilda A. Stephenson[Jackson] John	EBOO	311	1832
18 Jun 1824	Benjamin Stephenson	SCWA	944	---
00 000 0000	Frankie Stephenson[Reeves]	HHEN	897	---
00 000 0000	Madison Stephenson	CLOW	925	---
00 000 0000	Thomas Stephenson	HWSP	509	---
00 000 0000	Stephen C. Stevens	BGAS	371	---
00 0c 1793	James D. Stevenson	DGIN	856	---
00 000 0000	Morgan Stevenson Payton & Sarah	HHHE	719	---
00 000 1798	Patton Stevenson	HHHE	482	---
00 000 0000	Elizabeth Steward[Watson]	BMMB	792	c.1834
00 000 1809	James H. Stewart	HCAR	163	1830
00 000 0000	Joseph Stewart	HCLI	764	---
00 000 0000	William Stewart Asa Va/x	BTWJ	414	---
00 000 0000	James Stillwell	BHOT	T410	---
00 000 0000	Jeremiah Stilwell	BMON	162	---
00 000 0000	Frances Stogsdale[Holmes]	BMMB	304	---
00 000 0000	Dudley Stone	HKDA	524	---

BIRTHDATE	NAME OF BIOGRAPHEE	PARENTS/BIRTHPLACE/BIRTHDATE	SOURCE/PAGE	DATE
00 00c 1806	Joseph P. Stone		BGAS 375	1817
00 000 0000	Elizabeth Storm[Keith]		HKDA 523	---
00 000 1825	James Story		ASUL 147	---
00 000 0000	Elizabeth Stout[Shirk]		HMIA 467	---
00 000 0000	Jane C. Stout[Lanning]		CLOW 540	---
00 000 0000	Robert Stout	Peter & ---(Sherwood)	BHVI 946	---
00 000 0000	William Strain		BVER 422	---
00 000 0000	Joshua Stratford		BHOT T373	---
00 000 0000	Elizabeth Street[Holeman]		HJOH 706	---
00 000 0000	Susan Stringer[Gentry]		BWMB 302	---
00 000 0000	Betsey Stump[Geary]		BWMB 763	---
00 00c 1791	Robert Sturgus		BGAS 378	---
00 000 0000	John A. Stuteville		HWSP 486	---
00 000 0000	Anna Suffield[Carl]		HMLA 509	---
00 000 0000	Jonah Sullivan		HMIA 475	1840
00 000 0000	William C. Sullivan	Dennis Md/x	BHCL 886	---
00 000 0000	Moriah Summerville	Joseph	BSCC A240	---
13 Apr 1827	James Survant	William & Jane Ky/Ky	HPDB 454	---
00 000 1817	John Swallow		FMWA B575	---
00 000 0000	Mary A. Sweat[Casper]		HWSP 838	1824
00 000 1804	James Switzer	John	MONT 1279	c1822
00 00c 1786	Elisha Tadlock		BGAS 382	c1811
00 000 1832	V.T. Tague		ASUL 149	1833
00 000 1817	Elizabeth Talbott[Allen]		TBAB 377	c1825
29 Mar 1817	Washington H. Talbott	William & Mary(Houston)	SIND 162	---
00 000 1821	Peyton Tansel		HHHE 365	1829
00 000 0000	William Tapp		WHSU B261	---
00 000 0000	Rachel Taylor[Tom]		BJAB 630	---
00 000 0000	Elizabeth Tegarden[Lee]		HLOW 258	c1815
00 000 0000	Mary Tencher[Knowland]		HKDA 560	---

Date	Name		Code	No.	Year
00 000 0000	Miranda Tennell[Dean]		BHOT	T303	---
01 Dec 1820	Ann Terhune[Smock]		DGIN	779	---
00 000 0000	Callen Tharp Perry		LLDM	B26	---
00 000 0000	Alvin Thomas		BWMB	363	---
00 000 0000	Catherine Thomas[Clough]		BWON	513	---
00 000 0000	Elizabeth Thomas[Whisler]		BHOT	T448	---
00 000 0000	Fountain Thomas		CLOW	867	---
00 000 1810	Frances Thomas[Smith]		EBOO	366	---
00 000 0000	James Thomas Thompson		CLOW	412	---
00 000 0000	Joel Thomas		EPUT	456	1832
17 Nov 1822	John F. Thomas		HWSP	488	---
00 000 0000	Malinda Thomas[McGowen]		BWMB	196	---
00 000 0000	Philemon Thomas		BHVI	957	---
00 000 0000	Sarah F. Thomas[Cockrum]		SHGI	916	---
20 Jan 1816	Arthur Thompson James & Mary(English)	Ire/x	HPDB	427	c1820
00 000 0000	Frances Thompson[Wheeler]		CLOW	392	1827
00 000 1818	Hamilton Thompson		RCAR	46	1827
00 000 1808	Hamilton Thompson		HCAR	163	1827
00 000 1813	James W. Thompson		WHSU	B368	---
00c 1792	John D. Thompson		CLOW	413	---
00 000 0000	Louisa Thompson[Hamilton]		MONT	1024	---
00 000 0000	Lucinda Thompson[Sandy]		BWMB	291	---
00 000 0000	Mary Ann Thompson[Harvey] James L.		HHHE	616	---
00 000 0000	Nancy Thompson[Hoskins]		EPUT	500	---
00 000 0000	Richard Thompson		HWSP	205	1835
00 000 0000	Robert Thompson	Va/x	HJOH	664	---
00 000 1807	Sam Thompson		RCAR	68	1826
00 000 1807	Samuel Thompson		HCAR	163	1826
00 000 1812	Thomas Thompson		HCAR	163	1831
00 000 1812	Thomas Thompson		RCAR	63	1831
00 000 1812	Thomas Thompson		BGAS	391	---
00 000 1836	W.E. Thompson		MHMA	154	---
04 Jun 1825	Wilson Thompson Joseph & Susan(Wilson)		CLOW	868	---
00 000 1802	Sarah Thornton[Howard]		HDOH	731	---

BIRTHDATE	NAME OF BIOGRAPHEE	PARENTS/BIRTHPLACE/BIRTHDATE	SOURCE/PAGE	DATE
00 Nov 1831	Dennis Threlkield	George	EBOO 382	----
21 Jul 1829	Angeline Thurman[Low]	Elijah	HCLI 860	----
00 000 0000	Hannah Tichenor[LeGrange]		SHGI 736	----
00 000 0000	Eleanor Tilley[McCoy]		BPUT 440	----
00 000 1814	William L. Tincher		BVER 259	1830
07 Nov 1783	Isaac Tindall		CSHE 527	----
00 000 1800	Eliza Todd[Bohanon]		HLOW 287	----
00 000 0000	Jane Todd[Wilson]		HJOH 831	----
00 000 0000	John M. Todd		BVER 464	----
00 000 0000	Dr. Robert N. Todd		DIND 1661	----
00 000 0000	Uriah Town		BJAB 630	----
00 000 0000	Joseph Townsend		HJOH 454	----
00 000 1812	Mary H.D. Townsend[Layman]	James Md/x	---- ---	----
00 000 0000	Andrew Tipton		BVER 280	1822
00 000 0000	Sarah F. Tracy[McClain]		HJOH 822	----
24 Oct 1815	Edward H. Trester		HDOH 952	----
00 000 1808	Samuel Trester		HDOH 952	----
28 Dec 1848	Leander M. Tribby	William & Mahala(Myers) Ky/Ky	MONT 1114	----
00 000 0000	James Trimble		WHSU A37	c1822
00 000 1808	William Trosper		BVER 290	1832
00 000 0000	Jane Trowsel[Armstrong]		BHOT H409	----
00 000 0000	Franklin Tucker		BHVI 972	1831
00 000 1811	Maria S. Tucker[Jones]		HJOH 623	----
00 000 0000	Elizabeth Tuley[Hesson]		HWSP 553	----
00 000 0000	John Tuley		HWSP 556	----
00 000 0000	John Turner		FMWA B402	----
00 000 0000	D. Turnham		ASPE 65	1819
00 000 0000	D. Turnam		ASPE 65	1819
00 000 0000	Alfred Turpin		SHGI 530	----
00 000 0000	Delilah Turpin[Coffey]		BMMB 248	----

Date	Name		Orig	Code	No.	Year
00 000 0000	George Tyler			HWBJ	785	---
00 000 0000	George Underwood			HHHE	620	---
00 000 0000	Mary Underwood[Wildman]			HMIA	512	---
00 000 0000	Lucy Utterback[Vandiver]			HJOH	764	---
00 000 0000	Susan Utterback[Crose]			EBOO	247	1830
00 000 0000	Susan J. Utterback[Miller]			HLOW	262	---
00 000 1796	Elizabeth Vance[Lowe]			HSHE	731	---
00 000 1810	James Vancleave			HLOW	937	---
17 Jul 1823	Ruth A. Vancleave[Todd]			MONT	1185	---
00 000 1812	Elizabeth Vandaveer[Murphy]			HPOS	605	---
00 000 1800	Mary Vandiver[Luyster] Henry			HJOH	630	---
00 000 0000	John Vanlue			HSHE	603	---
00 000 1787	Solomon Van Nada Martin	Ger/x	GIBS	178	---
00 000 0000	Margaret Van Nice[Kurtz]			HHHE	480	---
03 Nov 1829	Rev. H.I. Vannuys Tunis & Kate(Demaree)	NJ/Pa	HELK	968	1852
00 000 1862	Amanda Vansant[Bowen]			BPUT	344	1831
00 000 1801	L.T. VanScholack			MHWA	154	---
00 000 0000	William Vantress			HKDA	517	---
00 000 0000	H.C. Vaught			AJEN	47	1878
00 000 1811	Elizabeth Vawter[Stott] Rev. William		HJOH	659	---
07 Apr 1803	Sarah Vest[Hubbard]			BPUT	435	1840
00 00c 1810	Irwin Vinson			HELK	364	1831
00 000 0000	Rebecca Virt			BHOT	H417	---
00 000 0000	Stephen Voorhees Peter	NJ/x	PBES	495	---
00 Jan 1822	Hervey Vories John			HJOH	668	1830
28 Jan 1821	John Vories			HJOH	718	---
00 000 0000	Nancy Wakeland[Fowler]			SHGI	698	---
00 000 0000	Charles H. Walker			BWWB	791	---
00 000 0000	Robert Walker			HHHE	761	1862
00 000 0000	Elvira Wallace[Gudgel]			GIBS	238	---
00 00c 1808	Thomas Wallace			HJOH	764	---
00 000 0000	Zeralda G[Wallace]			MPRO	418	---
00 000 0000	John W. Waller			FDAV	385	1817

BIRTHDATE	NAME OF BIOGRAPHY	PARENTS/BIRTHPLACE/BIRTHDATE	SOURCE/PAGE	DATE
00 000 0000	Beverly R. Ward		HMLA 590	----
00 000 0000	Lucinda Ward[Cooper]		BHOT H314	----
00 000 0000	Susan Ward[Houghland]		HWSP 161	----
00 000 0000	Anna R. Warfield[Gordon]		BSCC B223	----
00 000 0000	Andrew J. Warner		BWMB 215	----
00 000 1841	J.W. Warner		ASUL 167	186?
00 000 0000	Harmon Warrum		HHAN 66	----
00 000 0000	James Washburn	Oh/x	CSHE 396	----
01 Jul 1830	Robert D. Washburn	James W. & Matilda(Dean)	CLOW 903	1858
00 000 0000	Jonathan Watson		BWMB 792	c1834
00 000 0000	Sarah Watson[Gear]		EIND F30	----
00 000 0000	Fielden C. Watts		CLOW 442	----
00 000 0000	William Watts		CLOW 442	----
00 000 1842	Sarah J[Weaver]		ASUL 159	----
00 000 1805	Thomas J. Weaver		HHHE 587	1836
00 000 0000	Martha Webb[Clark]		HJOH 879	----
09 Apr 1808	Zachariah Webb		HJOH 501	----
00 000 0000	Thompson Weddle		BHVI 992	----
00 000 0000	Sarah Welborn[Stephenson]		CLOW 925	----
00 000 0000	Elizabeth Welch[Mitchell]		BHVI 865	----
00 000 1804	Isaac Welliver		HJOH 672	----
00 000 1815	Frank Wells		ASUL 159	----
11 Sep 1801	Lemuel Wells		EIND G241	----
00 000 0000	Mary Wells[Carson]		HSHE 609	c1828
00 000 0000	Mary Welsh		HWBJ 328	----
29 May 1825	Samuel West		EBOO 389	1834
09 Sep 1800	William West		EBOO 387	1835
00 000 0000	Mary C. Wharton[Sadler]		CLOW 866	----
00 000 0000	Jesse Wheeler		HLOW 884	----
00 000 0000	Thomas Wheeler		CLOW 392	c1820

Date	Name	Parents / Notes	Origin	Code	No.	Year
00 000 0000	Elizabeth Whetstine[France]			HWSP	148	---
00 000 0000	Grafton Whitaker			BWMB	340	---
00 000 0000	Elias White			AKNO	60	1833
00 000 1814	Enoch White			BVER	243	1821
00 000 0000	Mary White[Cooprider]			CLOW	422	---
00 000 0000	Vincent White	Asa & Margaret(Hunter)		HHHE	759	---
00 000 0000	Thomas Whiteaker			HWBJ	748	---
00 000 0000	Mary Whitecotton[Losley]			BPUT	485	---
00 000 0000	John Whitesides			HJOH	674	---
00 000 0000	Margaret Whitmore[Bean]			BSCC	B210	---
00 000 1858	J.W. Whitlock			ASUL	161	1865
00 000 0000	David Whittinghill		Ky/x	HWSP	229	c1820
00 000 0000	Joseph F. Wiggins David			HHEN	834	---
00 000 1844	H.R. Wiggs			ASUL	165	---
18 May 1818	Elizabeth Wikoff[Burgess]			CSHE	677	---
10 May 1855	Jerry W. Wilbern	Andrew & Sarah(Walker)	Tn/Va	HWSP	511	---
25 Oct 1793	Elizabeth Willard[Barker]			HPDB	439	---
00 000 0000	John H. Wiley			BHVI	997	---
00 000 0000	William Wiley			BWEL	171	---
26 Feb 1814	Baylis Williams			FWWA	B335	---
25 Aug 1820	Charles H. Williams	Thomas & Mary(Arnold)	Md/Va	HPDB	430	1894
00 000 1827	Jeff Williams			ASUL	164	---
00 000 0000	John Williams			CLOW	949	---
00 000 0000	Liona Williams[Crabb]			BHVI	716	---
00 000 0000	Matilda Williams[Clearwater]			BHVI	702	---
00 000 0000	Robert Williams Rememberance			BSCC	B288	---
00 000 0000	Thomas Williams			BVAN	127	---
00 000 0000	William Williams			HPDB	654	---
00 000 1822	Z.G. Williams			ASUL	163	---
00 000 1828	A.J. Willis			ASUL	161	1833
00 000 1829	J.W. Willis			ASUL	161	1831
00 000 0000	Abel Wilson			BPUT	357	---
00 000 1804	Benjamin Wilson	Benjamin & Margaret(Armstrong)	Pa/Pa	HDOH	978	1805
00 000 0000	Elizabeth J. Wilson[McClelland]			HHHE	633	---

BIRTHDATE	NAME OF BIOGRAPHEE	PARENTS/BIRTHPLACE/BIRTHDATE	SOURCE/PAGE	DATE
00 000 0000	Elizabeth Wilson[Oldham]		HJOH 832	----
29 Jan 1812	James Wilson	David & Margaret	HHEN 740	----
00 000 0000	John Wilson	Va/Va	TBAB 726	----
00 000 0000	John F. Wilson		BMMB 760	----
25 Jan 1824	John W. Wilson		CSHE 514	----
00 000 0000	Letitia Wilson[Cornelius]		BMMB 760	----
00c 1818	Loretta Wilson		HJOH 764	----
00 000 0000	Susan Wilson[Smith]		BHOT T327	----
00 000 0000	Thomas Wilson		BMMB 369	----
00 000 0000	Urias Wilson		AWAR 58	1860
00 000 1826	W.P. Wilson		ASUL 162	1828
00 000 0000	Smith Wingate		CSHE 428	1823
00 000 0000	Albena Wise[Stevenson]		GIBS 238	----
00 000 1794	James L. Wishard		BVER 244	1830
00 000 1805	John O. Wishard		BVER 244	1834
00 000 0000	Lucinda Witham[Harris]		CLOW 429	----
00 000 0000	David Wolf	George Pa/x	BSCC B119	1811
00 000 1829	Lewis W. Wood		HCAR 164	1829
00 000 0000	William G. Wood		BKOS 421	1844
00 000 0000	Willis Wood		CLOW 885	1826
00 000 0000	Susan Wooden[Fritts]		CLOW 889	----
00 000 0000	Benjamin Woods		BHOT H483	----
00 000 1808	James Woodward		HCAR 164	1835
19 Nov 1806	Milton Woollen		MPRO 160	c1835
00 000 0000	Milton Woollen	Leonard & Sarah(Henry) Md74/x	DIND 2256	----
00 000 0000	Milton Woollen		TBAB 379	----
00 000 1818	David Worrell	Robert & ---(Pickens)	HLOW 640	----
00 000 1855	William Worthington		MHMA 154	----
00 000 0000	Joel Wright	Jonathan & Rachel(McMahon)	BSCC B195	----
00 000 0000	Samuel Wright	William	BPUT 469	----

00 000 0000	Washington Wright		HLOW	305	---
30 May 1802	William Wright	Jonathan	HLOW	616	---
00 000 0000	William Wright		BWMB	357	1807
00 00c 1791	William M. Wright		BGAS	431	---
00 000 0000	S.A. Wylie[Burns]		HLOW	305	---
00 000 1855	J.W. Yates		ASUL	168	1875
00 000 0000	Joshua Yeager		HCAR	352	1840
00 000 0000	Polly Yeates[Johnson]		BPUT	427	---
00 000 1798	Isom Yocum		CLOW	458	1832
00 000 0000	Elizabeth Young[Whittinghill]		HWSP	229	c1820
00 000 0000	Melton Young		HHHE	737	---
00 000 0000	William G. Young	John & Charlotte	BHCL	450	---
00 000 1800	William Youtser	In/Ger	BSCC	B196	---
00 000 1851	Amanthis A. Yowell[Christie]		HHHE	465	1855
00 000 0000	William Zike		HSHE	780	---
00 000 1828	William Zike	David & Catherine(Smith)Jessamine/Pa	CSHE	882	---

Abbett, Abraham 194
  Elizabeth 125
  James 125
  Nancy(Brent) 125
  O.H.P. 126
  Robert T.F. 114
  Sarah A. 194
Abbott, John M. 126
  Joseph C. 126
  Lenhart 161
  Mildred(Garriott) 126
Abel, Anna[Stewart] 114
Able, Robert 145
Ackman, Wiley F. 135
Adams, David 126
  E.N.H. 194
  Edward P. 176
  Eleanor 105
  Henry 194
  Hester[Hart] 81
  Hugh 126
  Isaac 176
  Jacob 194
  James 105
  John 194
  John C. 105
  Jennie[Stipe] 142
  Joseph 102
  Lamyan 52
  Mary(Long) 58
  Mary A(Batson) 33
  Nancy(Barton) 102
  Nancy(Rains) 238
  Nancy Ann 176
  Nancy(Polk) 176
  Peter 194
  Phoebe(Preston) 194
  Rachel[Wiggins] 39
  Robert S. 33
  Sarah E(Park) 105
  Seralda J(Youngman) 151
  Solomon 164
  T.S. 102
  Thomas 164
  Thomas S. 102
  William B. 33
Addington, Marinda L[Brown] 168
Adkins, Nancy(Drake) 209
Agan, John M. 152
Ahern, Catherine 169
  John 169
  Thomas C. 169
Aikman, James 85
  John 85
  Mary(Barr) 85
Akers, John H. 171
  Mary A[Stembridge] 161
Albin, George 161
  George T. 161
  Joseph 194
  Nancy(Foxworthy) 161
  Roxanna(Sheeks) 242
Alcone, Mary A[Burton] 194
Alcorne, Mary[Burton] 194
Aldridge, Elizabeth[Records] 84

Ales, Rachel E[Thompson] 119
  Rebecca[Pell] 140
Alexander, Archibald 146
  Augusta(Boetinger) 188
  Charlton 19
  Elizabeth(Lindsey)227
  Esther[Crowe] 180
  Fannie[Hollingsworth] 171
  George 19
  J.M[Ward] 194
  Kitty 19
  M.J. 119
  Melinda(Asher) 195
  Nancy[Shannon] 193
  Nancy[Spencer] 194
  Susan[Barton] 197
  William 109, 188, 194
Alfrey, Anna(Baunty) 152
  Henry 152
  Moses 152
Alkire, Sarah[Hurst] 195
Allan, James L. 162
Alle, Pleasant 79
  Susan 79
  William 79
  William M. 79
Allen, Abner W. 152
  Annie(Brinkley) 200
  E. 52
  Eli 152
  Elizabeth 79
  Elizabeth(McDonald) 152
  Elizabeth(Talbott) 246
  Elizabeth(Williams) 96
  Elizabeth[Williams] 189
  Elizabeth(Youel) 178
  George T. 158
  Hannah[Cleveland] 37
  Hannah(Levy) 85, 100, 179
  James 158
  James M. 178
  Jane[Logan] 178
  Jemima[Miller] 127
  Jeremiah 42, 52
  Joel R.M. 85
  Joseph 85, 178
  Josiah 178
  Martha(Braton) 197
  Mary[Gardner] 194
  Millie(Cooper) 205
  Nancy[Cain] 194
  Nancy[Hargis] 194
  Nancy(Young) 52
  Ormilda[Taylor] 160
  Robert 158, 178, 185, 195
  Sarah(Conley) 179
  Sarah(Gilkey) 100
  Sarah B[Corn] 179
  Sylvanus 42
  Thomas 100
  William 52, 79, 85, 178, 179
  William A. 100
  William L. 119
  Zeralda[Fyffe] 158

Allfrey, Joseph 164
Allison, Amos 175
  Asa 95
  Charles 195
  David 195
  Elijah 169
  Eliza[Leach] 81
  Ellen[Murray] 133
  George W. 152
  James 187
  John B. 85
  John F. 85
  Joseph H. 169
  Margaret(Frederick) 169
  Mary(Richardson) 175
  Mary T(Boswell) 199
  Matthew 175
  Rebecca(Mason) 96
Allnot, Mary Ann 171
  Ninian 171
  Thomas J. 171
Almon, Thomas 195
Alsman, H. 35
Alverson, Nancy(Overstreet) 116
  Pleasant 116
  Thomas 195
  Wesley 195
Alvis, Mary[Johnson] 223
Ambrose, H.L. 167
  Jacob 167
  Maria(James) 167
Ament, Catherine[Dodson] 120, 195
Amos, Christiana[Pruden] 195
  Elijah 85
  Rebecca(Neal) 85
  Sarah[Thomas] 89
  William 85
Amyx, Catherine[Branstetter] 79
Anderson, A.J. 37
  Andrew 152
  Ann(Monroe) 107
  B.T.W.S. 139
  Bathesda 37
  Charles 27, 35
  Charles B. 185
  Charles W. 185
  Elizabeth(Armstrong) 195
  Elizabeth(Fortner) 195
  George W. 17
  Hamilton 33
  Henry 82
  Isabella(Mosby) 203
  James 105/ 195
  Joel 195
  John 195
  Lucinda(Harlan) 216
  Margaret(Coy) 206
  Mary 152
  Mary(Logan) 105
  Mary A(Brown) 185
  Mary J(Lyon) 228
  Mason 82
  Mildred(Cornelius) 82
  Nathan 195
  Rebecca 52

Anderson(cont.)
Richard C. 27, 35
Ruth[Robbins] 127
Samuel L. 105
Sarah(Cannetsay) 202
Sarah C[Johnson] 195
Susan[McDaniel] 163
Steven 52
Thomas 37/52
Vincent 195
William 17/ 195
Wilson 105
Annis, Abraham 195
Armilda(Hopewell) 220
James 195
Ansley, Charles 52
Dilly(Johnson) 28
George 28
Johnson P. 28
Mary 52
William 52
Anthony, Jacob 85, 105
Applebay, Mary(Walker) 140
Philip 140
Sebith(Sears) 101
Applegate, Ann(Lemon) 42
Annie[Coons] 129
Benjamin 42
Benjamin F. 42
Cassandra(Newkirk) 129
Daniel W. 42
Ellen(Tenness) 146
J.D. 129
James D. 129
Mary A. 129
Nancy(Tolle) 195
Peter W. 146
Rebecca(Wall) 42
Samuel 129
Sarah A[McNary] 146
Vincent 42
Appleman, Saraphina[Renner]38
Arbuckle, Rachel[Peyton] 141
Archer, Catherine(McMullen) 230
Michael[Nutt] 60
Ardrey, Jane[Mathers] 88
Armstrong, Ambrose W. 109
Elizabeth[Anderson] 195
Elizabeth(Fisher) 109
Elizabeth[Kelly] 195
Frances(Brown) 151
Henry 109
J.D. 151
James F. 151
Jane(Trowsel) 248
John 195
Joseph D. 151
Margaret 195
Margaret[Wilson] 251
Mary[Taylor] 195
Robert A. 195
Arnold, Brent 19
C. 161
Elisha 97
J.U. 19
James T. 98
James W. 129
John 52, 97
Lucy J. 19
Mary 97
Mary[Williams] 251
Polly[Lantz] 83
Prudence(Moore) 129
Rachel 52
Rachel[Coats] 195
Rebecca 195

Richard 195
William Z. 129
Arpy, Jane[Bell] 143
Arrasmith, Alexander 195
Arrowsmith, Elizabeth(Kenton) 42
Ezekiel 42
Sarah[Haller] 43
Wesley 42
Arthur, Ambrose 138
Joseph 138
Mary(McFarland) 138
Arvin, Harry 190
James P. 190
Asbury, Elizabeth(Fisher) 109
S.W. 109, 145
W.D. 109
W.H.H. 109
Ash, Benjamin 195
Elizabeth[Cox] 195
Hannah(Fig) 195
Robert 195
Ashbrook, Benjamin 18
Claude 18
Elizabeth(Tucker) 18
Milanda[Cofer] 195
Ashby, F.W. 129
Fielding W. 129
Harrison 128
James 179
James S. 129
Julia[Dillon] 195
Nancy(Radford) 179
S.F. 179
Thompson V. 179
Ashcraft, Ann(Wilson) 117
B.K. 117
Benjamin K. 117
Jediah 117
Asher, Frances[Walters] 101
Melinda[Alexander] 195
Ashmore, Elizabeth(Roten) 127
Askren, John M. 126
Sarah(Davis) 207
Atchison, Nancy W[Edelman]122
Aten, Aaron M. 126
Adrian 52, 126
Atherton, David C. 140
John 140
Susan(Boatman) 140
Willis G. 105
Atkins, Alice(Atkinson) 37
Harvey 162
John 37
Priscilla 37
Atkinson, Alice[Atkins] 37
George Y. 116
Philip A. 195
Atley, Henry 52
Sarah 52
Aubrey, Jane[Parent] 120
Aust, Lucinda[McCoy] 196
Austin, John B. 81, 116, 122
John M. 122
Mary E[Hillman] 196
Nancy(Van Hook) 81, 116
Samuel W. 81/116
Avis, David 179
Awings, Minerva[Cassady] 196
Axton, Bayless E. 167
David J. 167
Elizabeth(Terry) 167
Robert J. 167
Babbitt, Martha M(Nichols) 119
Millard F. 119

Stephen B. 119
Bacon, Charles A. 99, 187
Charles P. 99
Hillary E. 187
Joseph 196
Margaret(Gibson) 187
Susan(Roulette) 97
Susan(Rowlette) 97
Badger, David 158
Dulcene 158
Elizabeth(Miller) 158
Oliver P. 158
Bagby, Mahala I(Bruce) 51
Walter J. 51
William 51
Bahn, Rosa[Falter] 21
Bailey, Elisha 85
Elizabeth[Faught]113
Fannie S(Shoemaker) 243
Harriet(Rial) 41
John 129
John A. 96
Luther 98
Mary[Grider] 78
Susan[Elkin] 193
Bain, Ann[McConnel] 27
Elizabeth(Baker) 187
Leroy 187
William C.A. 187
Baird, A.B. 109
Archibald 81
Ary A(Rose) 109
Dorothy(Camerer) 28
Elizabeth 81
James A. 105
John P. 185
John R. 81
L.M. 185
Martha(Burton) 126
Mary[Thompson] 196
Sarah(McDonald)185
Sarah M(Hodge) 57
Stephen 185
Thomas D. 179
William 28, 109, 176
William D. 28, 52
Baker, Andrew 105
Barbara 46
Delia(Manley) 230
Elisha 193
Elizabeth[Bain] 187
Emily B[Langworthy] 132
Frederick 118
I.C. 196
Jacob 46
James 193
James H. 196
Jesse 105
John 118, 126, 193, 196
John W. 196
Margaret[McCool] 104
Margaret R[White] 45
Martha(Griggs) 105
Mary[Burns] 196
Mary[Riddle] 196
Mary(Wynans) 19
Mary[Zaring] 126
Nancy(Kemper) 196
Nancy[Zaring] 171
Patsy(Sparks) 196
William 19, 52, 46, 196
William G. 19
Balay, Benjamin W. 118
Nancy(Hilburn) 118, 219
Obadiah 118
Baldon, Eliza[Pickens] 196

Baldwin, Elizabeth[Harrah]
110
James M. 196
Malissa(Green) 196
William 196
Bales, John L. 196
Balintine, George 27
Ball, Henry 187
Nancy(Wise) 187
William E. 187
Ballard, Beverly 196
Camdon 169
Curtis W. 179
James F. 179
John 196
Lavinia(Raley) 169
Mary(Moody) 179
Nancy(Fitzpatrick) 196
Polly A[Brown] 196
Ruth(Smock) 244
Taylor 196
W.J. 169, 179
Balleger, Priscilla(Thomas)
89
Ballenger, Milton 85
Ballu, Agnes(Repley) 191
Linzy 191
Banfield, Altha[Plumoner]133
Bannon, L.J. 168
Banta, Abram 196
Ann(Smock) 156
Anna 126
Catherine(List) 126
Cornelius 196
Daniel 126
Elizabeth[Hatfield] 52
Henry 196
Henry D. 126
J.D. 179
Jacob 126, 196
Jane(Fulton) 212
John P. 126
Mary[Bergen] 126
Mary(Demaree) 196
Mary A(Brewer) 153
Nancy[Carnine] 196
Peter 126
Peter J. 126
Rachel[Kerlin] 127, 196
Rebecca(Eckles) 210
Samuel 126
Sarah(Demaree) 208
Vooncha(Van Nuys) 126
Barbee, Lucy[Young] 196
Barber, Elizabeth K(Houts)220
Jahazy[Vice] 82
Barclay, James W. 146
Barker, Elizabeth(Willard)251
Nancy[Grigsby] 196
Nancy(Kemper) 224
Barklow, Benjamin 31
Stout 31
Barkwell, Harmon B. 196
Barlow, C. 190
Harvey R. 176
John 190, 196
Priscilla(Burris) 190
Ruth[Runkle] 196
Sarah E(Smith) 128
Sarah J(Smith) 244
Barnes, Alfred 35
Charles 35
Edward 152
Florence(Todd) 35
Harriet[Hodge] 142
John W. 144
Joseph 53

Julia[Moberly] 144
Martha A. 85
Mary[Law] 197
Mary(Wheeler) 144
Noah 144
Phebe[DeCoursey] 197
Stephen 33
William 152
Barnett, Ambrose D. 164
James F. 197
James M. 142
John 142
John P. 164
Sallie(McNeely) 142
Sarah(Jackson) 85, 87
Thomas 85
William H. 85
Barnhart, Catherine[Erdel]97
Barr, Hannah(Johnson) 87
James 53, 197
John 197
Julie(Burris) 201
Mary[Aikman] 85
Barrett, John 40
Nancy[Harris] 217
Barringer, G.H. 187
Barrow, Bennett 46
James 197
Bartholomew, Catherine
[McNaught] 197
Bartlett, Fanny(McQuaid)230
George 197
Lucinda[McKee] 197
Barton, James A. 85
Nancy[Adams] 102
Susan(Alexander) 197
Thomas 197
Winston 197
Basinger, Joseph S. 197
Bass, Elizabeth(Robinson)240
Jane(Dodd) 142
Jane(Todd) 142
John H. 142
Josiah 197
Nancy[Gray] 197
Nathan 197
Ruhama(Price) 197
Sion 142
Thomas W. 197
Bassett, Sarah[Thompson] 40
Bateman, Nancy[Monyham] 133
Bates, Ann F[Carpenter] 82
Batman, James 129
Maria(Malott) 132
Batson, Mary A[Adams] 33
Batterson, Polly[Wheeler]144
Batts, Alford 197
Baty, America[Swindler] 197
Baumgarden, Permelia 197
Baunty, Anna[Alfred] 152
Baxter, Mary 26
Reason R. 26
Sill 26
Bayless, Herman A. 53
Herman G. 53
Mary A(Strong) 53
Baysinger, Malinda[Chanley]
203
Beabout, Mary[Telmadege] 112
Beachem, Mary[Morris] 177
Bean, Fenton[Bigstaff] 17
Margaret(Whitmore) 251
Beard, Elizabeth(Wells) 186
Emily J(Morris) 114
J.H. 114
James H. 114
Joel 53

John 114
Margaret(Blue) 53
Stephen C. 185
William 53, 162
Beasley, Ellen[Herring] 197
Beatly, Anna M(Peniston) 236
Beatty, Eliza A[Patterson]
105
Ernest N. 27
James P. 27
John 85, 105
Mary E(Nutter) 27
Nancy 85
Sarah(Patterson) 85, 105
Beaucham, Martha[Maddox] 185
Beauchamp, Dorothy(Jubinal)
223
Isaac W. 185
T.J. 197
Beaver, David 122
Margaret(Coon) 122
Michael 122
Beazley, Augustine 126
Sally Ann 126
Sally Ann(Webb) 126
Bebout, Abner 109
Elijah 109
Peter 109
Beck, J. 109
James 109
Philip W. 197
Simeon 197
Beckes, Margaret(Jordan) 223
Beckett, Eleanor[Miller] 111
J.P. 139
James F. 85
Beckham, Elizabeth[Chisham]
135
Mary[Frost] 136
Becks, Elizabeth(Phillips)
237
Bedster, John 179
Polly(Southern) 179
Thomas 179
Bedwell, Clayborn 197
Elisha 197
Robert 197
Thomas 197
Beecher, W.H. 103
Beem, Daniel 197
Enoch 197
Levi 197
Beeson, Ellen N(Harvey) 217
Begley, Baxter 125
Frances(Hughes) 125
John 125
Behymer, William 197
Bell, Daniel 197
Elijah 85
Elizabeth[Duret] 197
Grizzy A[Dixon] 43
Henry 197
Keziah[Woods] 79
Jane(Arpy) 143
Mary A[Davis] 197
Osse[Ward] 197
Samuel 197
Sophia[Inlow] 110
William M. 146
Belt, Elizabeth[Sprague] 37
Benbow, Lydia(Atkins) 195
Bence, George W. 129
Benedict, Americus 97
Elizabeth(Herbert) 97
J.L. 97
Jeremiah 97
Benefiel, Esther[McLeland]100

-257-

Benfiel, Elizabeth 85
  Samuel 85
  William H. 85
Benham, M.A. 198
Bennett, Aurelia M[Goulding]
  47
  Elizabeth[Fulton] 43
  Elizabeth[Sullivan] 150
  George W. 42
  Isaac 85
  John 198
  Lovina[Lantz] 32
  Matilda(Nichols) 42
  Sarah 198
  William 198
  William A. 42
Bennington, Mary(Rains) 28
  Robert P. 28
  Thomas 28
  William 28
Benson, Ellen(Minor) 172
  John 172
  Polly[Hopkins] 87
  Walter M. 172
  William 129, 198
Bentley, Charles E. 198
  Henry 37
  Sophia[McCarty] 152
Bergen, Abraham 126
  Garrett C. 126
  Margaret[Covert] 198
  Mary(Banta) 126
Berger, George W. 47
Berkner, Elizabeth[Collins]
  109
Berkshire, Mary J[Hopping]
  198
Berry, E.B. 151
  J.L. 129
  Lucinda(Millison) 129
  Lucinda(Millon) 133
  Sarah(McDonald) 229
  William 141
  William A. 129
Bersman, Mary E. 129
  William 129
Best, Abner 42
  Benjamin D. 42
  Louisa(Reynolds) 42
Betts, Ruth[Campbell] 176
Betz, Elizabeth(Mehringer)
  198
  John 198
  Mary P[Schriver] 24
Biby, Nancy[Allen] 178
Bice, Lydia[Carnine] 202
Bickham, Robert 19
Bicknell, Jesse 198
Bicks, Reason 146
Biddle, Ann(Clark) 85
  Richard 85
Bigger, John 53
  Mary 53
  Mary[White] 64
  Thomas 53
Biggs, Alonzo C. 192
  Andrew 46
  Charlotte J(Hall) 192
  Edward 53
  Floyd J. 192
  Judith(Robertson) 46
  Nancy[Crist] 198
  William 31, 46
Bigstaff, Fenton(Bean) 17
  O.S. 17
  Samuel 17
Bilbo, Archibald 90

Mary 90
  William 90
Billingsley, John J.W. 189
Bird, Abram 179
  Henry 179
Bishong, Nancy[Lough]
Bishop, Asa J. 198
  Byron 179
  Eliza[Wilkinson] 104, 164
  Elizabeth(Turner) 179
  George 28
  George M. 152
  Harriet[Ewings] 109
  Henry 28
  John B. 179
  Lucy(Wells) 29
  Marine E(Horine) 152
  Richard M. 28
  Sarah[Roberts] 127
  Valentine 152
Black, Alexander 26, 53
  Cassandra[White] 198
  Elizabeth(Deem) 208
  F.G. 35
  George M. 158
  James 26, 53, 198
  James L. 26
  Jane(Crockett) 53
  Janet(Crocket) 26
  Janet(Crockett) 26
  John 198
  Lavina[Shuck] 126
  Margaret(Whittsitt) 158
  Martha(Coleman) 204
  Martha[Thompson] 198
  Sarah(List) 126
  Sarah[McIlvain] 53
  Miller 158
  Virginia(Campbell) 198
  William 126
  William F. 164
Blackburn, Katherine[Ellis]3?
  Sarah[Posey] 198
Blacklidge, Charlotte(Laville)
  226
  Harvey 173
Blades, Amanda(Gates) 42
  Betsy[Clark] 179
  William 42
  William F. 164
Blair, John T. 129
  Margaret(Cowen) 205
  Martha[Thompson] 198
  Robert 129
  Samuel 198
  Sarah E(Moore) 129
Blake, Elizabeth[Lamar] 149
Blakemore, George W. 198
Blakey, George T. 142
  Sarah E(McLean) 142
  William M. 142
Blanchard, Donald D. 129
  John L. 129
  Sallie H(McDonald) 129
Bland, Richard A. 162
Blankenbeker, Animy[Tyler]
  198
Blankenship, Amy 140
  John W. 141
  Noel 141
Blann, Allen S. 198
Blanton, Delilah(Ragland)238
  John 198
Bledsoe, Daniel 198
Blennerhassitt, Susan[Lark-
  ins] 38

Blevence, Rhoda 198
Blevins, Artemisia[Shake]
  170
Blincoe, Nancy[Mason] 119
Bliss, Maria S[Dickson] 103
Blockford, Jane[Kennedy]198
Bloom, Miranda(Roberts) 62
Blue, Margaret[Beard] 53
Blunk, Andrew 130
  Sarah[Brindley] 198
Blunt, Thompson 114
Blythe, James E. 105
Boardman, James R. 164
  Sally(Hazelrigg) 164
  William W. 164
Boatman, Melinda[Plummer]
  198
  Sarah[Willis] 135
  Susan[Atherton] 140
Bobbitt, Margaret(Mann) 59
Bodine, Margaret(Reynolds)
  239
Boetinger, Augusta[Alexan-
  der] 188
Bogan, Sarah[Scales] 198
Bogard, Elizabeth[Sills]199
  Levi 162
Boggs, Aaron 53
  Ezekiel 53
  William 114
Bohanan, Daniel A. 102
Bohannon, Abner 179
  Booten 199
  Daniel 199
  Elizabeth[Dooley] 209
  George 199
  Henry 199
  James 199
  John 179
  Mary(Sacrey) 179
  Nancy(Claten) 199
  Sarah(Rogers) 241
  Susan 199
Bohanon, Eliza(Todd) 248
Bohn, Christina[Franz] 125
Boldt, Charles 35
  Margaret(Schwenck) 35
Boles, Julia A(Franklin)154
Boling, F.M. 199
Bolinger, C.B. 199
  F.J. 146
  Henry 146
  J.S. 199
  James S. 146
  Susan 146
  Victoria(Close) 146
  W.H. 199
  W.T. 199
  William H. 146
Bollinger, C.B. 146
  Victory(Close) 146
  W.H. 146
Bolton, Ann[Smith] 49
  Malinda 199
Bond, Martha[Wilkinson] 199
Bondurant, E.G. 113
  Elizabeth(Woodfill) 113
  H.A. 199
  Thomas L. 113
Bone, John 199
Bonnell, Jonathan 152
  Rebecca(Dean) 152
  Thomas 152
Bonwell, Elizabeth[Pulse]53
Booker, Elizabeth[Ewing]211
  Jacob 113

Boon, George 199
  Mecca[Woods] 199
Boone, Benjamin 199
  Mary[Bryan] 172
  Moses 199
  Noah 174
  Squire 199
Booth, Abigail[McGinnis] 199
Borgman, William 130
Boring, Ailsey(Collett) 54
  Elsie(Collett) 54
Borude, George 199
Bosley, Catherine[Harris]188
Boston, J.W. 199
  James W. 185
Bostwick, Mary[Dickerson]130
Boswell, Mary T[Allison] 199
Bottom, James E. 90
Bottorff, Fletcher 199
  Sarah(Fry) 212
Bough, Frederick 81
  Rebecca(Sexson) 81
  William 81
Bourland, E.C.(Stice) 104
Bourn, Elijah 135
  Sarah[West] 172
  W.C. 199
Bourne, Ambrose 199
  Martha J[Vermillion] 199
Bowan, Mary A[Collins] 30
Bowen, Amanda(Vansant) 249
  Anthony 199
  Elijah 135
  Nancy 135
  Sampson 122
  Tavner 135
Bowers, Eliza[Hume] 199
Bowles, Elizabeth 122
  James 122
  Mary(Harris) 122
  Robert 122
  Sarah Ann(Smith) 124
  T. Jefferson 122
Bowling, Mary[Ritchie] 142
Bowman, Elizabeth[Asbury]
  109
  Samirah[Watson] 199
Boyce, Charles F. 35
  Edmond C. 35
Boyd, C.W. 40
  Charles C. 42
  Charles W. 40
  Elizabeth[Martindale] 144
  Henry 92
  Isabel(Higgins) 144
  James 40, 42
  Lucy[Williams] 22
  Margaret(Gibson) 40
  Mary[Dooley] 41
  Mary(Gibson) 40
  Nancy[Robbins] 85
  Phebe(Webster) 92
  Robert 199
  Robert F. 165
  S.G. 40
  Samuel 42, 144
  Samuel K. 144
  Susan A(Calvert) 42
  William 199
Boyers, Katie[Liter] 87
Boyle, John 199
Boyll, Arthur 185
  Catherine[Carr] 185
  Culbertson 185
  David 199
  Henry 185
  Ruth(Carr) 202

  Sarah(Park) 185
Bradbarn, J.W. 190
Braden, Jane(Newell) 33
  Robert 33, 53, 176
  Samuel 33
  William 176
Bradford, Anna(Wrightman) 18
  Hugh 47
  J.W.R. 18
  Margaret(Chalfant) 47
  William A. 47
  William R. 18
Bradley, Elisha 178
  Elizabeth(Ping) 174
  Emma S[Neal] 88
  Henry 113
  Hugh J. 199
  James L. 113
  Margaret[Williams] 105
  Mary(Jenkins) 113
  Reuben 174
Braiser, Gideon 200
Bramble, Sophia[Hollick]132
Bramkamp, Louis C. 35
Bramwell, William C. 140
Branch, John W. 200
  Lucy F[Branigin] 146
Brand, Abraham J. 200
  Fannie(Carter) 19
  John W. 200
  Joseph 85
  Joseph C. 19, 53
  Joseph F. 85
  Margaret(Hesson) 218
  Thomas 19, 53
Brandenburg, Jonathan 151
  Lydia(Charley) 151
  Philip 151
Brandon, Isaac P. 53
  Van S. 53
Branham, Alexander K. 176
Branigin, John 146
  Lucy F(Branch) 146
  N.S. 200
  Sarah J(Forsythe) 211
  Thomas 146, 200
Brannigin, Martha A[Feathern-
  gill] 200
Branson, Caroline(Mahen)230
Branstetter, Catherine
  (Amyx) 79
  John 79
Braselton, John 119
Brashear, Benjamin F. 18
  Sarah F[Temple] 189
Brasier, Sarah(Jones) 223
Braton, Martha[Allen] 197
Bratton, Maria[Washburn]178
Brazalton, John 152
Brazelton, Elizabeth
  (League) 90
  John 90
Bray, Nancy[Culver] 200
Brayfield, John 152
Breckinbridge, Rebecca
  [Carpenter] 200
Breeding, Alexander 78
  David 78
  Elza 78
  Mary(Hendrickson) 78
  Mary M(Hendrickson) 78
Bregle, Eliza J[Epperson]
  154
Brehmer, Catherine(Summers)
  23
  Fred W. 23
  Frederick 23

Bremer, Mary P(McPherson)130
  Simeon 130
  Susan 53
  William P. 130
Brener, Martha A[Michael]200
Brent, C.F. 37
  Elizabeth[Richardson] 200
  George 126
  Margaret C[MacKoy] 38
  Nancy[Abbett] 125
  Robert 44
  Samuel 114
  Sarah 114
Brentlinger, A.J. 130
  Andrew J. 130
  Christina[McCormick] 200
  Joseph 200
  Rosanna[Hoke] 130
Brenton, Henry 187
  Martha[Mack] 200
Breshears, A.F. 168
Bretz, Eliza J(Shively) 243
Brewer, Abraham 53, 153
  Abram 36
  Ann(Carrico) 147
  Ann(Comingore) 153
  Ann(Cummingoer) 153
  Daniel 153
  Ellen[Wade] 191
  Elizabeth[Farrow] 55
  Fannie(Webb) 128
  Garret 200
  George 147
  Hannah M[Johnson] 40
  Henry 153
  James T. 147
  John 40, 153
  John C. 153
  Mary[DeMott] 90
  Mary[Vanarsdall] 156
  Mary A[Banta] 153
  Rachel(Dunavon) 40
  Samuel 200
  Theodocia(Derland) 153
Bridewell, Benjamin 96
Bridges, Catherine[Dicks]109
  Charles C. 158
  Dillon 109
  George 109
  Matilda[Forsythe] 211
  Moses T. 109
  Rachel(Lockridge) 158
  William 158
Bridgewater, Elizabeth[Eaton]
  35
  Louisa[Wallace] 105
  William 105
Bridwell, Amanda(Shy) 119
  Hayden 162
  Henry L. 119
  Nancy(Cuppy) 162
  Noah 162
  Samuel L. 119
  William S. 141
Bright, Elizabeth(Pope) 140
  Harry 140
  Henry 140
  James H. 169
  Mary[Browning] 29
  Sarah[Quinn] 109
  Susannah(Truman) 169
  William H. 169
Brightwell, Catherine[Norris]
  92
Briley, Melinda(Newkirk)235

Brindley, George 200
  Sarah(Blunk) 198
Brinkley, Annie[Allen] 200
Briscoe, Elizabeth[Fisher]
  180
Brissey, James M. 171
  James W. 171
  Sarah(Osburn) 171
Bristow, Benjamin P. 103
  John 200
  Lucinda(Harding) 216
  Rachel[Roby] 103
  Sallie(Crawford) 103
Brite, J.M. 168
Brittingham, Nancy 53
Broadstreet, Melvina A. 95
Broadwell, Frances[Rice] 189
  Louisiana[Mannen] 44
Bronaugh, Charles T. 116
  Mary(Taylor)116
  Robert N. 116
Brookie, Amanda F(Rogers) 241
  John A. 169
  Mary(Dougherty) 169, 193
  Mary(McCullin) 149
  Robert A. 193
  William 169, 193
Brookover, Nancy A[Case] 42
Brooks, Ann(Comingore) 153
  Charles G. 37
  James L. 124
  John 27
  Laura(Tone) 37
  Lee 37
  Lucinda(Woodward) 124
  Mirian[Finley] 200
  Mosley 165
  Susanna(Geohegan) 165
  Thomas J. 124
  William 168
  William M. 165, 168
Broshears, A.F.[Houland] 168
  Ira 119, 200
  Jeremiah 119
  Manuel 168
  Margaret(Humphrey) 168
  Ruth(Sullivan) 119
Brothers, Amelia(VanPelt) 63
Brown, Agnes[Shannon] 183
  Alvis P. 168
  Anna 53
  Anna(Crow) 103
  Asa 53
  Azariah D. 162
  Barker 85
  Benjamin F. 53
  Betsey(Carter) 203
  C.V. 162
  Cadmus V. 162
  Christopher D. 103
  D.D. 103
  Daniel 200
  Elizabeth(Burroughs) 116
  Elizabeth[Smith] 200
  Etheelenda[Porter] 182
  Francis O. 200
  George W. 200
  Gustavus 103
  Harlin S. 53
  Hervey 122
  Isaac 179
  J.F. 168
  James 53, 98, 103, 179,
    200
  John 53, 85
  James F. 168
  James M. 200

John C. 200
John G. 85
  Katherine(Rogers) 62
  Lucy J(Pemberton) 201
  Malinda J[Ray] 82
  Marinda L(Addington) 168
  Martha(Summers) 53
  Mary[Walker] 53
  Mary A. 53, 201
  Mary A[Anderson] 185
  Mary A(Colvin) 54
  Mary E(Wright) 200
  Matilda[Ford] 120
  Nancy(Hughes) 162
  Nancy[Kelley] 173
  Oliver H. 201
  Perry 185
  Polly(Seabright) 85
  Polly A(Ballard) 196
  Rice E. 169
  Richard 169
  Robert 201
  Robert S. 201
  Ryland T. 139
  Samuel 179
  Sarah[Owens] 91
  Thomas 201
  Thomas L. 116
  Vincent 53
  William 169
  William A. 201
  William F. 116
  William H. 168
  William J. 147
Browne, Hannah(Mauzy) 88
Browning, Basil 29
  Edmund 147
  Elizabeth[Mann] 230
  Hannah 147
  Isaac 147
  Jemima[Mahan] 149
  Jennie[Ramsey] 101
  Mahala Q[Renner] 29
  Mary(Bright) 29
Brownlee, Kate[Montgomery]
  201
Broyles, Harriet 86
Bruce, Mahala I[Bagby] 51
  Nancy[Rose] 115
  Phoebe(McIntire) 229
Bruehl, W.A.R. 37
Brumfield, J.N. 90
  James B. 90
  Phoebe J[Grainger] 201
Brumleve, Leon J. 35
Bruner, Rachel[Demaree] 180
  Sarah[Key] 201
  W.L. 119
Brunner, Lydia[Rowan] 84
Brunson, Elizabeth(Ellis) 53
  John 53
  Jonathan 122
  Robert 201
  Thomas 122
  William 53
Brush, Blakely 179
  John 175
  Mary A[McCormick] 179
  Nancy 175
  William M. 175
Bryan, A.H. 191
  Alexander 86
  Alexander J. 86
  Anthony H. 191
  Edmund 191
  Elizabeth 86, 179
  Elizabeth[Ringo] 127

Eugene 103
  Gabriel 103
  George W. 172
  Hampton 172
  Isabella H. 179
  Lettice(Pierce) 191
  Luke 172
  Margaret(Gosney) 172
  Mary(Boone) 192
  Mary[Casey] 130
  Patience[Kemper] 116
  Samuel 172
  Susan M(Hayden) 103
  Thomas 179, 201
  William H. 86
Bryant, Eliza(Shoat) 18
  Frances(Russel) 34
  James H. 103, 201
  James M. 201
  Louis 103
  Mary T(Morris) 103
  Patience[Kemper] 116
  William B. 34
  William F. 34
Buchanan, Alexander 153
  Henry 53
  John H. 105
  Mary(Minton) 105
  Nancy 193
  Nancy[Gilkeson] 154
  Smith 105
Buchannan, Henry 53
Buchannon, Anna[Lawler] 201
  Levi 201
Buckner, Avery 201
  Etheline E(Conn) 18
  Henry 18
  James H. 18
  Margaret(Sturgeon) 201
  Mary Ann[Vandiver] 201
Buford, William H. 201
Bugg, E.T. 128
Bull, Sarah[Robinson] 201
  Susan[Tichenor] 164
Bullington, Isaac N. 201
Bullock, John R. 37
  Mary T(Clayton) 37
  William R. 37
Bunel, William 147
Bunnell, George 19
  Jonas 19
  Nancy[Reed] 201
  Sallie(Tomlin) 19
Bunten, Henry H. 153
  John 201
  Leanna(Wilson) 153
  William 153, 201
Buntin, Andrew 165
  Elijah 165
  Elizabeth(Lothridge) 165
  John L. 165
Bunton, Greenberry 165
Burcham, James 201
  Rachel(Evans) 211
Burford, W.D. 153
Burgess, Catherine(Holbert)
  219
  Dawson[Griggs] 201
  Edward 176
  Greenberry F. 176
  James W. 147
  John L. 147, 201
  Mordecai 147
  Sally(Ryan) 147
  Sarah(Fields) 176
Burk, Lucy[Kackley] 177

Burkhart, Benjamin F. 162
  J. 162
  Mary(Wilkinson) 162
Burnes, James H. 114
  Washington 122
Burnett, Isaac 201
  Jacob 201
Burns, Andrew 165
  Emeline 201
  John M. 201
  John T. 109
  Mary(Baker) 196
  O.P. 82
  S.A.(Wylie) 253
  Torrance 201
  Wiley 201
Burnside, James 201
  John 144
  Mary(Denton) 144
  Thomas 144
  William 144
Buris, Lucinda[McGinnis] 86
Burrer, Mary C[Dannettail]97
  James D. 165
Burris, Julie[Barr] 201
  Priscilla[Barlow] 190
  Rebecca(Miller) 165
  Robert 201
  Samuel 165
Burroughs, Elizabeth[Brown]116
Burrows, Hudson 130
Burton, Anna[Robertson] 82
  Elizabeth[Mobley] 101
  Henry 202
  Jesse 202
  Laban 126
  Martha[Baird] 126
  Mary(Alcone) 194
  Mary A(Alcone) 194
  Robert 116
  Sarah(Harris) 126
  Sarah(Williams) 116
  Stephen G. 90
Busby, Francis M. 81
Buselman, Henry 37
  Mary(McCarthy) 37
  William R. 37
Bush, Elizabeth(Defoe) 208
  Franey(Sears) 107
  Jane[Whaley] 82
  Lucinda[Christie] 202
Bushman, Henry 23
  Sophia(DeMoss) 23
  William H. 23
Buskirk, Alfred 185
  Letitia(Dayhoff) 185
  P.A. 185
Buster, Garrett 51
  Green B. 51
  Sophia(Hudson) 51
Butcher, Amanda(McIntyre)229
  Sandora(Hancock) 216
Butler, Edward 30
  Jane(Buzan) 202
  Jane(Hollywood) 30
  R.H. 30
  Sarah[Ernst] 37
Button, Elizabeth[White-sides] 171
  Lucy[Evans]
Buxbaum, Asher 35
  Morris C. 35
  Sarah 35
Buzan, Jane[Butler] 202
Byers, Elizabeth(Vandiver) 156
  Elizabeth(Wiley) 126

George 126, 153
Henry 126
L.S. 202
Philip 202
Byrd, William 202
Bynch, Francis E[Welty] 187
Byron, Addie[Cain] 130
Cabbage, James W. 175
  John 175
  Nancy 175
Cahall, Thomas 53
Cahill, Elizabeth[Tennant] 145, 150
  Margaret[Seggerson] 20
Cain, Addie(Byron) 130
  Barnabas 202
  Edward A. 130
  Edward B. 130
Cainbell, Sarah[Daniels] 53
Caldwell, Abigail(Nicholson) 235
  Elizabeth[McClain] 166
  Isabel D[Durham] 90
  James H. 117
  John 90
  Mary(Knox) 90
  Rebecca(Swineford) 117
  Thomas 117
  Wallace 202
Call, John 202
Callahan, Elizabeth(Phillips) 130
  James 130
  John 130
Callaway, Frankie(Hawkins)86
  John H. 86
  Micajah 86
  Noble 86
Callon, William 202
Calvert, Augusta[Kirk] 83
  John 190
  Mary[Jones] 38
  Mary A[Foxworthy] 110
  Mildred[Perkins] 84
  Preston 202
  Susan A[Boyd] 42
Calvin, Vincent 53
Camerer, Dorothy[Baird] 28
Camp, Sarilda(Myers) 111
Campbell, A. Morgan 37
  Alexander 17
  Andrew 192
  Braxton N. 37
  David 126
  Elizabeth(Davis) 17
  Elizabeth[Veasey] 32
  Harriet 81
  James 23, 126
  James H. 179
  James M. 17
  Jane 53
  John S. 179
  John V. 123
  Joseph 202
  Julia A(Miles) 179
  Leander M. 139, 147
  Lewis 139
  Lucy[King] 110
  Martha[Scrogin] 107
  Mary[Dean] 100
  Mary(Gilless) 192
  Matilda[Spaulding] 44
  May(Valentine) 23
  May[Wyatt] 99
  Michael D. 176
  Morgan 37
  Nancy(Choshow) 81

Nancy(Spears) 244
Polly 53
Rachel[Martin] 42
Sally 37
Sarah(Carter) 126
Susan 139
Susan(Love) 37
Thomas 142
William 192
Williamson 81
Canary, Barbara[Creager]202
  Christian 153
  Elizabeth(Terhune) 153
  Henry 153
  Margaret 153
Canby, Louisa[Noble] 83
  Samuel 82
Canfield, Newton 82
Canine, Abraham 179
  H. Rice 179
  Sarah(Lefler) 179
  W.B. 179
  William 179
Cannatsay, Sarah[Anderson] 202
Cannon, Euphemy[Wolfe] 178
  Greenbury C. 175
  John 175
  Laurena 175
Canon, Elizabeth[Sheeler] 31
Cantrill, David 54
Capp, Tracy[Harp] 202
Carbaugh, Isaac H. 122
Caress, Eva[Stafford] 134
  Simon 202
Carey, Mary A[Hayden] 155
Carico, George W. 130
Carl, Anna(Suffield) 246
Carle, Thomas 202
Carleton, Olive[Lombard] 24, 38
Carlisle, Cordelia[Collins] 31
  W. 104
Carlton, Fannie 79
Carman, Comfort(Clinton) 49
  Elias 49
  Isaac 179
  James 49
  Mary(Hughes) 179
  William N. 179
Carmony, Mary(Stansell) 44
Carnahan, Aaron 48
  Alvira(Mitchell) 48
  Elizabeth(Graham) 214
  Elvira 48
  Martha J(Jones) 223
  Robert 202
Carnes, Eliza(Decker) 117
  William 117
  Zachariah 117
Carnine, Andrew 202
  Lydia(Bice) 202
  Nancy(Banta) 196
Carothers, Clara(Cole) 23
  Ralph G. 23
  Robert 23
Carpenter, Ann F(Bates) 82
  Asahel 82
  Balden C. 29
  Baldwin C. 29
  Caleb 18
  Charles 82
  David 18, 54
  Julia A(Watson) 112
  Levi 118
  Margaret 54

Margaret[Goodpaster] 81
Mary[Thompson] 99
Michael 81
Peter O. 109
Rebecca(Breckinridge) 200
Sallie(Jones) 81
Sally(Fee) 29
Scythia[Goodpaster] 81
Simeon 29
T[Sweeney] 99
Zerelda[Holsclaw] 127
Carr, Catherine[Boyll] 185
Dorotha A(Foster) 120
Hiram 202
Letitia(McDole) 86
Louisa[Stodghill] 115
Moses 202
Rebecca(Kester) 224
Ruth[Boyll] 202
Carrico, Ann[Brewer] 147
Anne 202
Catherine[Trimble] 105
Elizabeth(Cissell) 204
George G. 203
Carrithers, Adam 130
E.S. 203
George 203
Carroll, William 54
Carruther, Elizabeth[Smock]
203
Jane B(Carson) 96
Carson, Mary(Wells) 250
Carter, Annie[Eskew] 189
Betsey[Brown] 203
Betsy[Westerfield] 190
Daniel T. 109
Elizabeth[Conder] 203
Elizabeth[McClure] 179
Fannie[Brand] 19
Henry 109
J.O. 102
Martha[Foley] 147
Mary(Green) 109
Sarah[Campbell] 126
Cartmill, Isabel(Ferguson)17
Patsy[Crockett] 26
Thomas 17
William 17
Carty, Augustus 203
Bertha[Walters] 203
Carver, J.W. 90
Jane(Durham) 90
Sterling 90
Case, James 203
John 203
Nancy[Brookover] 42
Reed 162
William 162
Case, James 203
John 203
Nancy[Brookover] 42
Reed 162
William 162
Casey, John J. 130
Mary(Bryan) 130
William 105, 130
Casper, Mary A(Sweat) 246
Cass, Daniel 190
Elizabeth(Plew) 190
James 190
Cassady, James J. 203
Minerva(Awings) 196
Cassatt, Jacob D. 153
Cassidy, Thomas 203
Cassity, Mary 203
Cast, Ezekiel 54
Mary 54

William 54
Casteel, Martha A(Dunlavy)
209
Castleman, Nancy[Richardson]
163
Cates, S.J. 161
Catherwood, Samuel 122
Catlin, William E. 190
Caughey, Sarah[Fleming] 203
Cave, Benjamin 46
Mary(Mounts) 46
Caven, Elizabeth(Scott) 44
Cavender, Susan[Dorsey] 203
Cavins, Samuel R. 118
Cawthorn, Martha[Johnson]
203
Chadwell, Nancy[Haines] 99
Chaffin, Tabitha[Spears] 29
Chafin, James 203
Sarah(Hall) 215
Chafins, Alexander G. 39
Kenas M. 39
Margaret(Goans) 39
Chalfant, America(Coburn) 21
James F. 21
Margaret[Bradford] 47
Thomas 21
Chamberlain, Esther(Moore)97
Martha J[Welman] 130
Matilda[Gally] 203
Chambers, George 203
Isaac 119, 203
Jesse 109
John 179
Margaret(Starkey) 109
Martha[Jackson] 87
Champ, Joseph 203
Chandler, Daniel 105
Lydia 171
Morgan 171
Uriah 105, 171
Chanley, George W. 203
Malinda(Baysinger) 203
William M. 203
Chappell, J.E. 130
Charley, Lydia[Brandenburg]
151
Chastain, Bartlett 203
Cynthia 203
Cheaney, & Bros. 203
Cheatham, Frances[Peters]127
Chenoweth, Elijah 43
Isaac 203
John F. 43, 54
Joseph 203
Maria(Risinger) 240
Rachel(Foster) 43
Cherry, John 203
Chesnut, Benjamin 203
Childers, Catherine(Lydic)
105
Lindsey 105
Chilton, Eelon(Stewart) 126
James S. 126
John 126
Chinn, Martha[Gates] 203
Chisham, Daniel 135
Elizabeth(Beckham) 135
William W. 135
Chism, Lucy W[Shoptaugh] 158
Samuel 158
Sarah 158
Choshow, Nancy[Campbell] 81
Chrisman, Elizabeth[Smith]
26
Christie, Amanthis A(Yowell)

Ella[Underwood] 203
John 203
Lucinda(Bush) 202
Christman, Mary J[Irwin]120
Church, Cynthia(Landford)
175
Elijah 175
Joel 175
Churchill, Lucinda[Crim]203
Cisco, Elizabeth(Hedges) 82
Francis 82
William F. 82
Cissell, Elizabeth[Carrico]
204
Clark, Alexander 165
Allen 204
Allen W. 179
Americal O(Hawkins) 142
Ann[Biddle] 85
Betsy(Blades) 179
Cornelius 162
Darmis[Sharp] 204
Elisha 145
Eliza J[Tapp] 135
Emily J(Durham) 145
Fielding 92
G.W. 179
James 204
John A. 142
John T. 145
Mahala(Young) 100
Martha 179
Martha(Webb) 250
Rhoda H[Long] 181
Robert 144
Tabitha A[Sanford] 150
Thomas 162
Thomas C. 142
Woodson 142
Clarke, Mary[Harmon] 204
Clarkston, Mary[Stuteville]
204
Claten, Nancy[Bohannon] 199
Claxon, Elizabeth[New] 172
Claxton, Jeremiah 204
Joshua 204
Clay, Arabella(McCoun) 86
Isabella[Dixon] 209
James H. 86
John H. 105
Littleberry 86
Susan(Fleece) 91, 211
Claypool, Elizabeth[Logan]
44
Jacob 54
Clayton, Louisa(Shawman) 62
Mary T[Bullock] 37
Clearwater, Matilda(Williams)
251
Cleaveland, Adin 130
Benjamin 130
Mary(Conyears) 130
Cleland, Ann[Wilson] 45
Clem, America[Peed] 204
Louisa E[Smith] 114
Nancy(Shepherd) 114
Nancy J[Vanarsdall] 126
Phebe(Miller) 126
Philip 126
Clemens, Elizabeth[Tomlin]
173
Martha[Jackson] 221
Mary[Nixon] 38
Clements, Elizabeth(Garr)
213
Gustavus A. 29

John N. 204
Mary(Gregg) 29
Mary E(Haskins) 217
Solomon G. 29
Cleveland, Elizabeth[Shuff]
20
Ezer 179
Francis L. 30
Hannah(Allen) 37
J.T. 122
James H. 30
John L. 37
Laura(Harlan) 30
Martha 179
Marvin 179
Washington 37
Click, John 204
Clifford, A.C. 104
A.W. 105
Allen W. 204
Elizabeth[Houchin] 204
Clifft, John J. 204
Melinda(Jones) 204
Thomas 204
Clifton, John W. 25
Lavina 25
William 25
Cline, Elizabeth[McClellan]
228
J.N. 204
Clinger, Mollie[Crowell] 43
Clinton, Comfort[Carman] 49
Elizabeth(Harcourt) 27
Isaac 27
John 27
Joseph 204
Clore, Frances(Deer) 83,
204
Howard 204
Israel 83, 204
James 170
John 170
Sarah(Keller) 170
Simeon 83, 204
Close, Mary E[Deer] 115
Victoria[Bolinger] 146
Victory[Bollinger] 146
Cloud, J.D. 23
Clough, Catherine(Thomas)
247
Clow, John 81
William 81
Cloyd, David 204
Clutter, Gilbert 86
John 86
Mary(Gilcher) 86
Clutts, Archibald A. 31
Mary(Gantz) 31
Robert 31
Coats, David 130
Rachel(Arnold) 195
Cobb, Mercy(Shelby) 242
Merise(Shelby) 152
Van B. 204
Wesley 144
Coburn, America[Chalfant]21
Sarah(Mallott) 132
Cochran, Elizabeth(Colvin)
205
Hugh 204
Sarah 86
Simon 46
Cockrell, Andrew 98
Cockrum, Sarah D(Thomas)247
Cofer, Milanda(Ashbrook)195
Stephen 204

Coffey, Delilah(Turpin) 248
Lewis 204
Sarah(Goodright) 214
Coffin, Leonora(Moore) 37
William M. 37
Coffman, Abraham 86
Albert H. 86
Mary[Payne] 79
Susan 86
Coghill, Catherine[Smith]
204
Mary(Slusher) 243
Cohen, Jeanette(Graumer)131
Cohn, Julia[Cruetz] 23
Cohorn, Elizabeth(Smith)112
Coldwell, Barton 165
Clarissa(Panly) 165
David 165
David A. 165
Elizabeth 165
John 165
Sarah 165
Thomas 165
William 165
Cole, Alexander 43
Cinderella(Shirley) 163
Clara[Carothers] 23
Martha(Ward) 158
Mary(Wallingford) 43
Robert 158
Thomas 43, 158
Coleman, Anna[Willes] 64
Elizabeth[Mitchell] 204
J.A. 79
James H. 54
Martha[Black] 204
Collett, Ailsey[Boring] 54
Elender[Hamilton] 191
Elsie[Boring] 54
Elizabeth[Cooper] 191
John 54
Colley, Sims A. 204
Collings, Abraham 179
Archibald 179
Nancy(Nutgrass) 179
Collins, Archibald 185
Cordelia(Carlisle) 31
E.J. 130
Edward J. 130
Elizabeth(Berkner) 109
J.O. 204
James A. 31
James O. 130
James W. 31
John 147
Joseph D. 30
Mary 109
Mary(Hoke) 130
Mary A(Bowan) 30
Susan(Ware) 185
Thomas 30
W.S. 204
William 109, 130
William O. 185
William S. 130
Zachariah 147
Colliver, Jefferson 54
John 54
Matilda(Robinson) 54
Samuel 158
Colt, Frances(Mills) 137
George B. 137
John D. 137
Colven, William 137
Colville, Susan A[Pattison]
204

Colvin, A.H. 119
Abraham J. 205
Boswell 205
Elisha 153, 205
Elizabeth[Cochran] 205
Elizabeth[Lightfoot] 173
Elizabeth(Hillman) 219
James 54
Margaret(Curry) 153
Martha 54
Mary A[Brown] 54
Matthew 153
Sarah 205
Thomas J. 205
Colwell, Lavina(Fitch) 55
Combs, Catherine(Lemons)162
Elizabeth[Smalley] 89
John 162
Mary[Dillard] 189
William H. 162
Cominger, John A. 205
Samuel 205
Comingore, Ann[Brewer] 153
Ann[Brooks] 153
Cynthia[Brewer] 205
Elizabeth(Smock) 153, 156
Henry 153
Henry R. 153
Compton, Abraham 54
Jacob 54
Conaway, James 205
John 109
Phebe(Plank) 109
Samuel 109
Conder, Elizabeth K(Carter)
203
John 205
Lucinda(Hack) 90
Martin 90
Peter 90
Condit, Byram 143
Conduitt, Alexander B.
187, 205.
Matilda(Moreland) 187
Melissa R. 205
Melissa R(Hardwick) 216
Willis G. 187
Conger, Hannah[Railsback] 61
Conlee, J.A. 157
Conley, John 205
Mary[Kellams] 205
Thomas 205
Conn, Etheline E[Buckner] 18
Connell, Joseph 83
Connelly, William A. 83
Conner, Daniel 205
Nancy 205
Rubin 205
Susan A(Reed) 33
William 153
Connolly, A.G. 205
Conrad, Joseph 205
Rachel 205
Thompson 205
Conroy, Catherine(O'Rourke)
37
Charles 37
James J. 37
Conry, Jonathan 54
Conway, Catherine(McShirley)
147
Elizabeth 205
Emily(Hoagland) 187
Emily(Hogland) 187
J. Randolph 187
J. Randolphus 187

John 147, 187
Miles 147
Richard 205
William 205
Conwell, Lorinda[Harlan]145
Conyers, Mary[Cleaveland]
130
Cook, Catherine[Tansell]178
Jane(Robb) 62
Louisa(Hild) 131
Simon A. 23
Sybia(Doerr) 23
William M. 185
Cooke, Mary 105
Coomes, F.M. 103
Coon, Margaret[Beaver] 122
Coons, Annie(Applegate)129
Elizabeth[McQuinn] 170
George 205
Mary A[Keyes] 106
Nancy[Willette] 20
Sarah[Guyton] 170
Cooper, Abraham 191
Alexander 168
Catherine[Myers] 159
Cornelius H. 168
Daniel W. 191
Elizabeth(Collett) 191
John 174, 205
John J. 205
Lucinda(Ward) 250
Mary A[McKinney] 174
Millie[Allen] 205
Nancy(DeCoursey) 52
Polly[Dolson] 205
Polly(Wilson) 205
Sallie(Miller) 168
Stanley 174
Cooprider, Belinda(Lankford)
226
Mary(White) 251
Melinda(Lankford) 226
Coots, Edwin M. 179
Elizabeth(Morton) 179
R.M. 179
Cope, Andrew J. 138
Jesse 138
Winnie(Lewis) 138
Copher, Sarah(Foley) 115
Coppin, Melissa[Davis] 24
Corbin, Amanda 136
Elizabeth[McConnell] 135
George 78
J.T. 79
Martin 136
Rebecca[Jackson] 136
Sarah F. 79
Cordrey, John 106
Malinda(Johnson)106
Corn, Elizabeth[Stewart] 205
George 126
Jemima[Robertes] 240
Jesse 140
John 205
Rhoda 126
Cornelius, W.H. 147
Cornett, Margaret(Bergen) 198
Cornwell, Anne[Grigsby] 131
B.H. 130
Benjamin 170
Edward 130
John 170
Mary F(Swan) 130
Minerva(Williams) 170
William 130
Coron, Helen[Willis] 32
Corum, Amanda K[Raison] 32

Corwin, Hannah[Phillips] 61
Joseph 54
Mathias 19, 54
Thomas
Cory, Dolly 205
Cotton, Elizabeth 205
Marion I. 126
Phebe[Dewit] 205
Robert G. 162
William 205
Coughlin, Margaret[Murray]
133
Coulter, Agnes[Steele] 28
Andrew 33
John 33
Counts, Elijah 19
Elizabeth(Frame)55
Isaiah D. 19
Jacob 54
Margaret(Wiley) 19
Courtney, James 205
Mary R[Parish] 155
Sanders 205
Cover, Eliza[Kelly] 205
Covert, Daniel 153
John 153
Joseph V. 153
Lemima[LaGrange] 155
Margaret(Bergen) 198
Rachel(Voorhies) 153
William V. 153
Covington, Anna[Kavanaugh]57
Cowan, Joseph 86
Nancy[Patton] 111
Joseph 86
Rachel L[Hill] 165
Coward, Charlotte(Ellings-
worth) 130
George W. 130
Harriet 205
Milton 130
Cowen, Margaret[Blair] 205
Cowes, E. 191
Cowgill, Ann S(Tarvin) 147
Elisha 147
Elisha P. 147
Hannah[Swann] 54
Cowher, Elmira[Lee] 179
Cox, Amy[Miller] 206
Anna[Epperson] 154
Arvis 126
Elizabeth(Ash) 195
James 206
Jesse 171
John 171
John P. 171
Joseph 147, 206
Levi 206
Lurana(Osborn) 171
Mary(Flack) 211
Mary A(Skaggs) 117, 243
Nancy(Dickens) 126
Nancy W(Harrah) 217
Polly[Flick] 206
Rebecca[Miller] 139
Samuel F. 206
Sussanah[Foreman] 185
William 126
Coy, Margaret[Anderson] 206
Crabb, Lione(Williams) 251
Cracraft, Elizabeth[Rinker]
206
Craig, Ann(Newell) 122
Barsheba[Huffman] 79
Esther[Hudelson] 166
Isaac 122

Jane[Van Hook] 122
John 122
Margaret(McIlvain) 122
Merit S. 206
Robert 122
Robert C. 122
Sarah J(Handley) 90
William H. 90
Crain, Elizabeth(Ketron) 46
Isaac N. 46
John G. 158
Lewis 54
Lewis F. 54
Richard M. 46
Cramer, John 54
Margaret(Hoover) 54
Thomas 54
Crandall, Susan[Hargan] 120
Crandell, Joshua T. 116
Mary(Marksberry) 116
Samuel M. 116
Crane, Isaac 122
William 122
Craven, J.J. 83
Cravens, William 145
Crawford, Charles W. 23
James R. 23
John 31
Martha(Ward) 23
Melinda(Graham) 214
Sallie[Bristow] 103
Thomas 54
William A. 206
William H. 31
Creager, Barbara(Canary) 202
Thomas J. 206
William 206
Creath, John 19
Margaret 19
William 19
Creech, Frank L. 193
Fred 193
Nancy(Riggs) 193
Creighton, Margaretta[Havlin]
37
Cretcher, Jabez 54
John 54
Sarah(Oldfield) 54
Creutz, Christopher 23
Julia(Cohn) 23
Otto 23
Crews, Elizabeth(McCowan)
225
Crim, Jesse 206
Jesse M. 180
Martin D. 206
Moses 180
Sarah(Jacobs) 180
Crisenbury, Anna 206
Crisler, Carleton G. 18
R.H. 18
Crist, Mary 206
Nicholas 206
Crocket, Jane[Black] 53
Crockett, Patsy(Cartmill)26
Robert 26, 54, 206
Shellin 206
Shellin 206
Crockrell, Sarah[Gulick]148
Cromeans, George 102
Jeremiah(Dobbs) 102
John 102
Cromwell, Huldah(Risby) 240
Lavina(MeekO 232
Oliver 190
Owen D. 206

Cronenger, Edward H. 54
Crook, Ann[Strange] 160
  Elizabeth[Hardwick] 159
  Sally[Owen] 144
Crooke, James M. 206
  Nancy(Cruse) 206
Crooks, William 206
Cropper, Allen S. 126
  Daniel 206
  Elizabeth(Frame) 40
  Frances[Demaree] 208
  James 40
  Wheatley 40
Crosby, Catherine 147
  Eleanor(Osborne) 235
  Elizabeth(Jackson) 43
  Jacob 147
  John R. 43
  Joseph 43
  William 147
Crose, Jonathan 165
  Nancy[Younger] 167
  Susan(Utterback) 249
Cross, Clarington G. 109
  John 109
  Joseph 161, 206
  Mary(Johnson) 109
Crouch, Elizabeth[Richard-
  son] 121
Crow, Ann[Evans] 141
  Anna[Brown] 103
  Benjamin 141
  Cassandra 180
  Edward H. 180
  Joseph 180
  Martin 153
  Susanna(Sullivan) 141
  William 141
Crowder, Nathaniel 206
Crowe, Elizabeth(Stephens)
  112
  Esther(Alexander) 180
  John F. 180
  Samuel 180
  Samuel S. 180
Crowell, John S. 35
  Mollie(Clinger) 43
  S.B. 35
  Simon 43
  W.C. 43
Crumbaugh, Samuel R. 41
Crume, Marks 206
Crumming, Benjamin 54
Cruse, Emilia[Nelson] 206
Crutchfield, Polly[Dufour]
  136
Culbertson, John H. 147
  Nancy[Crooke] 206
  Nancy(Hunter) 147
  Robert 147
Culkins, Elizabeth J(McStead)
  31
  John 31
  William C. 31
Cullen, Gilbert I. 23
  James 23
  Sarah E(Gallup) 23
Culver, Nancy(Bray) 200
Cumming, James 176
Cummingoer, Anna[Brewer] 153
Cummings, Eliza 24
  Frank 24
  Mary[Morris] 88
  Samuel 24
Cummins, Benjamin F. 86
  Eliza[Sowder] 175
Cunningham, Nancy[Peggs]188

Cuppy, Nancy[Bridwell] 162
Curlee, Abraham E. 130
  Samuel M. 130
  Susan S(Little) 130
Curry, Jane[McClure] 207
  Margaret[Colvin] 153
  William 207
Curtis, J.W. 137
  James J. 106
  Louise[Evans] 157
Curtner, James A. 207
Cushman, Catherine(Kennerly)
  224
Custer, Conrad 86
  Devora[Wilson] 90
  Joseph 86
  Leanna 86
Cutsinger, Elizabeth(Harris)
  217
  George 207
  John 207
  Rebecca 207
  Samuel 190
Cuzick, Rebecca[Kilgore] 123

Dailey, Elizabeth[Holder]207
  Mary A(Shirley) 243
  Nancy(Frazee) 212
Dale, Catherine[Kaler] 207
  George 193
  Jane[Mills] 29
  Joseph 193
Daley, Thomas 207
Dalton, C.P. 151
  Catherine[Hudnut] 148
  Lycurgus 171
  Patience[Griffith] 207
Danaldson, David S. 100, 207
  Ellen 100
  John 100
  Walter 100
  Walter C. 100
Daniel, Sarah 19
Daniels, Eliza(Hite) 180
  Ellen[Nolan] 38
  James W. 42
  Joseph 180
  Rhoda 43
  William 180
Dannells, John E[Scott] 207
Danner, Adam 130
  James 207
Dannettail, Mary C(Burrer)97
Darcas, Kilen[Hoback] 207
Darland, Jane[Eccles] 154
  John 36
Darnall, Agnes(Bridges) 136
  James 136
  Julia[Sharp] 89
  Zenas 136
Darnell, Daniel 158
  John F. 207
  Jonathan 158
  Nancy(Turpin) 158
  Salinda[Ferguson]
  Samuel 158
Darter, Jane A[Pendlay] 141
Daughtery, Henry C. 78
  J.M. 78
  James 207
  Jane(Smith) 78
  Mary A[Montgomery] 78
  Mary Ann(Mills) 233
  Stephen 78
Davidson, Charity[Bowen] 79
  David 49

James 207
John 43, 49
Judah 207
Margaret 49
Margaret[Wisehart] 147
Mary(Steele) 207
Robert 19
Robert P. 207
Sarah J(Schofield) 24
W.A. 24
William J. 24
Davis, Abner 207
  Achilles 153
  Bedial J[Harris] 153
  Benjamin 55
  Catherine(Putnam) 140
  Catherine[Tucker] 158
  Charlotte 207
  David J. 147
  Edward G. 120
  Eli 109
  Elijah T. 55
  Elizabeth[Campbell] 17
  Elizabeth(Henry) 109
  Elizabeth[Laney] 141
  Elizabeth(Vance) 55
  George 207
  Harriet[Meredith] 111
  I. 55
  Issachar 56
  J.T. 120
  J. Hazard 24
  James 158
  Jeptha 27
  Jesse 158
  John 158, 207
  John E. 153
  John H. 24
  Julia Ann[Gobbel] 207
  Justus 109
  Martha(Robinson) 153
  Martha(Smothers) 160
  Mary A(Bell) 197
  Mary E[Smith] 207
  Matthias 158
  Melinda(Moore) 153
  Melissa(Coppin) 24
  Nancy(Kidd) 158
  Nancy[Terhune] 156
  Nathan 158
  Rebecca[Miles] 207
  Richard 44
  Robert 109
  Rose(Knott) 103
  Samuel 109
  Samuel H. 109
  Sarah[Askren] 207
  Sarah[Reese] 177
  Susan[Frame] 212
  Thomas S. 153
  W.H.T. 168
  W.R. 153
  Waller 140
  Walter 158
  Warren 180
  William K. 140
  William M. 136
  William R. 153
Davison, Mahala J(Earlywine)
  210
Dawkins, Elizabeth A[Swift]
  171
Dawson, C.M. 151
  Daniel 170
  Keziah(Tanner) 170
  Lucy E[Tomlinson] 170
  Minerva B[Laycock] 97

Day, Ambrose 207
  Edmond 152
  Joanna 208
  John 153, 208
  John N. 208
  Nancy 153
Dayhoff, Elias 153
  Letitia[Buskirk] 185
Deadman, Elizabeth[Smyser]171
Dean, Daniel 46
  James 100, 208
  Jennie(Steele) 46
  Jeremiah 100
  Joseph 46
  Kirich[McCune] 136
  Mary(Campbell) 100
  Miranda(Tennell) 247
  Nancy[Wilson] 160
  Rebecca[Bonnell] 152
Dearing, G.T. 145
  James M. 190
  John 190
  John B.T. 208
  Polly 190
  William 208
Dearinger, Rebecca J[White] 104
Dearmond, William L. 208
Debaun, Abraham 154, 208
  Charity[Frakes] 208
  John 154
  Joseph 154
  Mary(Devine) 154
  Samuel 154
  Simon 208
DeBell, Anna[Turner] 112
DeBolt, Jane[Hatfield] 151
DeBon, Ann[Whitenack] 157
DeCamp, Margaret(Hutchison) 221
Deck, Sarah(Colvin) 54
Decker, Charlotte 55
  Elizabeth[Carnes] 117
  Elizabeth[Edwards] 117
DeCoursey, John 208
  Nancy[Cooper] 52
  Phebe(Barnes) 197
  William 24
Dedman, William 208
Deem, Elizabeth[Blank] 208
Deer, Benjamin F. 115
  Frances[Clore] 204
  Joel 83
  Mary E(Close) 115
  Simeon 115
Deere, Joel G. 180
Defoe, Elizabeth[Bush] 208
Delard, Etienne 154
  John 154
Demaree, Catherine[Vannuys] 184
  David 126, 180
  Frances(Cropper) 208
  George W. 154
  James T. 208
  Kate[Vannuys] 184, 249
  Mary[Banta] 196
  Mary(Johnson) 180
  Peter 180
  Rachel(Bruner) 180
  Samuel 208
  Sarah[Banta] 126, 208
  William U. 208
  William W. 180
Deming, C.S. 48
  U.C. 48
Demoss, Sarah[Pruett] 192
  Sophia[Bushman] 23

DeMott, Abram 126
  Ann[French] 208
  Daniel 90
  John B. 90
  Margaret[Aten] 126
  Mary(Brewer) 90
  Mary[Henderson] 208
Denis, Cecilia 24
  Harry 24
  William T. 24
Denney, John W.S. 208
  William 208
Denny, Catherine 208
  Elizabeth 208
  James 208
  James H. 154
  John 154
  William 208
Denton, Mary[Burnside] 144
DePauw, Charles 208
  James 208
  John 208
DePew, Elizabeth[Kirk] 208
DePrez, Anna M[Metzger] 133
DePriest, George W. 189
  Nancy 189
  William 189
Derland, Theodocia[Brewer] 153
Deupree, Abraham 145
  Thomas 208
  William 208
Devin, Joseph 189
Devore, Anna(Barnes) 196
  Henry 92
  Henry H. 124
  Jerry 92
  Nancy(Mann) 92
Dewey, Rhoda[McLain] 119
Dewit, Peter 208
  Phebe(Cotton) 205
Dewitt, Thomas 208
Dewitte, John 26
Dicers, J.F. 185
Dick, Margaret[Gray] 86
Dickens, Nancy[Cox] 126
Dickerson, Alexander W.C. 130
  Henry 157
  John R. 157
  John S. 130
  Mary(Bostwick) 130
  Mary(Grider) 157
Dickey, Maia R. 55
Dickin, Joel 208
Dicks, Catherine(Bridges)109
  Elizabeth[Reeves] 98
  Enoch 147
  John 147
  Mary 147
  Mary(Patterson) 147
  Rebecca[Wysong] 147
Dickson, Francis 103
  J.R. 115
  Maria S(Bliss) 103
  Mary 92
Dill, Wealtha[Langsdale] 115
Dillard, Elizabeth(Kearby) 223
  Henry 189
  John W. 189
  Mary(Combs) 189
Dilley, Adeline(Henry) 218
  Jonathan 208
  Jonathan R. 209
  Nancy(Johnson) 223
Dillman, Elizabeth[Powell]22

Dillon, Julia(Ashby) 195
  Luke 209
Dills, Agnes(Moreland) 233
  Jane[Hamilton] 122
  John 209
  Rachel(Stevenson) 63
  Samuel 55
Diltz, Cynthia(Kennard) 224
  Joseph 55
  Mary(Jarrard) 55
  Wesley 55
Dinsmore, J.J. 29
  Jacob 209
Dinwiddie, Martha[Ramsay] 209
Distrow, Rachel(Massey) 231
Dittoe, George M. 37
  Louis G. 37
Dix, Amy[Youngman] 151
Dixon, C.C. 209
  Grizzy A(Bell) 43
  H.T. 125, 209
  Henrietta[Ruggles] 34
  Isabella 209
  William 43
Doak, James W. 136
  Robert 136
Dobbins, Catherine(Graham) 118
  Charles G. 118
  Thaddeus 118
  William 83
Dobbs, Barthenia P[Parker] 209
Dodd, Cranston T. 106
  Elizabeth(Myers) 106
  Elizabeth(Osborne) 235
  John 209
  Thomas 106
Dodds, John Y. 209
  Margaret E(Ramsey) 116
  Samuel 116
  William F. 209
Dodson, Catherine(Ament) 120, 195
  David S. 120
  John B. 120, 209
Doerr, Sybia[Cook] 23
Doggett, Arthur D. 81
  Henry 81
  Nancy(Smith) 81
Dollman, Rosina[Klein] 137
Dolson, Polly(Cooper) 205
Donaldson, Christian[Shake] 134
  William H. 24
  William M. 24
Doniphan, Susan[Frazee] 147
Donley, John 55
Donnell, Sally[Hudelson] 87
Donnohue, Dillard C. 86,159
  Mahala(Tipton) 160
Donovan, Clemency[Johnson] 43
  Polly[Steele] 89
  Rebecca[Montgomery] 88
Dooley, Elizabeth(Bohannon) 209
  Martha J. 209
  Mary(Boyd) 41
  Moses 41, 209
  Silas 41
Dorothy, Harrison 209
Dorsey, Greenberry 209
  Greenberry W. 209
  John 109
  Nancy(Spiers) 109

Dorsey (cont.)
  Robert S. 109
  Susan(Cavender) 203
Doss, William W. 209
Doty, Thomas 55
Doubet, Joseph P. 130
  Peter 130
Dougherty, C.H. 120
  Mary[Brookie] 169
  Matilda(Brown) 120
  Samuel 120
Doup, John 131
  Kitura(Shadburn) 131
Douthitt, James H. 103
Downey, A.R. 209
  Archibald 165
  Jacob 165
  James 165
  Sarah(Cook) 165
Downing, Susan[Ferrine] 44
  Susan[Salle] 44
Downs, Caroline(Holden) 57
  Thomas J. 168
  William 168
Doyal, John W. 140
  Matilda 140
  Samuel H. 140
Doyle, John 83
Drake, Greenberry 80, 151
  Henry 162
  James 209
  Joel E. 151
  Levina[Morris] 60
  Nancy[Adkins] 209
  Nancy(Lane) 80
  Sarah[Seaton] 134
  Sarah J(Gish) 213
  Thomas 80
  William 162
Draper, Elizabeth(Wheeler)128
  Lydia J[Taylor] 32
Drennen, Catherine(Early) 109
Driskell, Robert 209
Drummond, Druzilla[Welch] 64
  Elizabeth[Helm] 218
Drury, Alexander G. 37
  Asa 37
  Elizabeth W(Getchell) 37
Dryden, Nancy[Hamilton] 122
Dubbs, Sabina[Smith] 134
Dubois, N.G. 168
  Nelson G. 168
  Rebecca 168
  Stephen 168
Duckings, Clarissa[Triplett]
  112
Duckworth, James J. 81, 203
  Pressley S. 209
Duddevar, Elizabeth[Scott]141
Dudley, Catherine(Monahan) 55
  Catherine(Sparrow) 55
Duff, Elizabeth[Pinckard] 44
Dufour, John F. 136
  Perret 136
  Polly(Crutchfield) 136
Dugan, Sarah[Tabor] 163
Duke, Betsey J[Todd] 106
  Jane 209
Duley, Louisa S[Whicker] 109
Dulweber, Anna(Lineman) 37
  Benjamin F. 37
  James 37
Dunavon, Rachel[Brewer] 40
Duncan, Mary(Henry) 109
  Mary[Piety] 95
  William 109, 209
  Zelphy[Saunders] 107

Dunee, George 138
Dungan, Margaret[Hornback]
  209
  Mary(Young) 55
  Polly(Hall) 33
Dunham, Elizabeth[Wilkes]209
  Gideon 55
Dunlap, Martha(Gamble) 131
Dunlavy, Daniel 159
  David 209
  Francis 159
  John Y. 159
  Martha(Yocom) 159
  Martha(Yocum) 159
  Martha A[Casteel] 209
Dunn, Frances(Piatt) 83, 86
  George G. 190, 209
  Isaac 83, 86
  James E. 144
  John 86, 142
  John P. 83, 86
  Joseph 209
  Margaret K(Karn) 142
  Nathan 144
  R.W. 120
  Samuel C. 91
  Samuel W. 142
  Sophia W(Irvine) 144
  Williamson 91
Dupaquier, John 131
  Louisa P. 131
  Mary(Shoppie) 131
Durbin, Amos 118
  Susan(White) 118
  Thomas 118
Duret, Elizabeth(Bell) 197
Durham, Harrison 154
  Isabel D(Caldwell) 90
  J.L. 209
  J.Y. 91
  Jacob 91
  Jane[Carver] 90
  Jane[Clark] 145
  Jesse 91
  Jesse B. 91, 154
  Jesse Y. 91, 154
  John L. 91
  Martha(Tarkington) 91
  Miranda[Tucker] 99, 154
Dutterow, May[Kelley] 55
Duzan, James 147
  William 191
Dye, Amanda(Manchester) 230
  Charity 147
  Frances(Moss) 154
  Hiram 230
Dyer, Azro 143, 161
  Dillis 143
  Julia[Woodward] 146
  Virginia P(Hawthorne) 24
  William H. 24
Dyke, James 191
  William 191
Dynes, George 29
Dyson, R. 122
Eads, Mary E[Rudisill] 116
  Phoebe[McClure] 123
Earle, Benjamin P. 35
  E.R. 35
  Mary(Roberts) 35
Earlewine, Sarah[McGinnis]210
Earley, Anthony 43
  Daniel 55
  William 43
Early, Catherine(Drennen)109
  D.W. 55
  Dorcas 165

Early(cont.)
  Elizabeth(Lynn) 55
  Jacob D. 109
  James 165
  Joseph 109
  Mary[Bell] 146
  Mary(Stockwell) 109
  Samuel S. 109
Earlywine, George W. 210
  Mahala J. 210
East, James 116
  Joseph 116
  Lucy(English) 116
Eastham, Eliza(Sweets) 162
  Isaac N. 162
  Thomas 162
Eastin, Mahala[English] 210
  Philip 210
  Sarah(Smith) 212
Easton, John 49
  Patience 50
  Polly(McMichael) 49
  Redwood 49
Eaton, Elizabeth(Bridgewater)
  35
  Greenup 86
  John H. 35
  Mahala(Turpin) 178
  William 109
  William G. 35
Eccles, G.D. 154
  Garrard D. 154
  Jane(Darland) 154
  Samuel 154
Eckert, Leonad 29
  Susan 29
  Thomas F. 29
Eckles, Delana R. 109
  Rebecca[Banta] 109
Eckstein, Martha[Lindenburg]
  18
Eddy, Jane(Gillespie) 126
  Julia F[McBride] 126
  Julia F[Prewett] 126
  William 126
Edleman, James H. 122
  Leonard 122
  Nancy W[Atchison] 122
Edmondson, Elizabeth(Fried-
  ley) 212
Edmondson-Chenoweth, Sarah
  [Edwards] 210
Edward, Dorcas 165
  James 165
Edwards, Catherine(Ellis)210
  Champion 117
  Elizabeth(Decker) 117
  Elizabeth[Jones] 46
  Jackson 117
  James 210
  John 131
  Sarah(Edmondson-Chenoweth)
  210
  William K. 131
Efner, C.V. 147
Egnew, Anthony 122
  Frances[Varner] 210
  James W. 210
  Mary(Richardson) 239
Ehrman, Christian 106
  E.D. 106
  Edward D. 106
  Sophia(Withers) 106
Elder, Alexander 144
  Ann[Jabboe] 210
  James M. 144
  Louisa[Headdy] 47

Elder(cont.)
  Sarah[Carter] 203
Eleyet, Eliza 55
Elkin, Benjamin 162
  Eliza(Williams) 162
  Merry 193
  Philip A. 162
  Susan A(Bailey) 193
  Walter 193
Ellers, James H. 191
  John 191
  Susan(Smith) 191
Ellert, B.J. 131
  C.H. 131
  E.M(Rogge) 131
Ellingsworth, Charlotte[Coward] 130
Elliott, Calvin A. 79
  Dorsey O. 165
  E.C. 92
  Elizabeth[Shaw] 180
  Jesse P. 82
  John 82
  Martha T[Moore] 193
  Mary[Calloway] 210
  Rachel(Pigman) 82
  Sarah(Turner) 165
  William 165
  Zulma 210
Ellis, Catherine[Edwards]210
  Charles R. 210
  Edward 210
  Elizabeth[Brunson] 53
  Elizabeth(Hopkins) 125
  Fannie 180
  Katherine(Blackburn) 37
  Martha(Holtzclaw) 220
  Nancy[Foulks] 137
  Nancy[Kendall] 210
  Parmelia(Roberts) 240
  S.A.C. 37
  Sarah(Turner) 165
  Wade H. 37
  William 165
Ellison, Mary(Polk) 237
Elliston, Elizabeth T[Sale] 172
  George 46
  Ida(Givens) 46
  Joseph L. 46
Ellsberry, Elizabeth(McClure) 58
  Michael 55
Elson, Jonas 210
  Nicholas 210
Ely, Elizabeth(Hatfield) 115
  Eugene A. 115
  John E. 115
Embry, Talton 41
Emerson, Jesse 210
  Reuben 210
Emmerson, Jesse 210
  Lemuel 210
Emmons, Mary[Hurst] 221
Engel, Mary[Winterhead] 36
Engelhart, Louise[Layer] 35
England, Sarah[Honaker] 18
English, Ann[Loyd] 118
  Eleanor(Taylor) 177
  Elisha G. 210
  Joenna(Kincaid) 81
  John 81
  John A. 81
  Lucy[East] 116
  Mahala(Eastin) 210
  Samuel 177
  William H. 177

Engle, Lydia[Riggs] 210
Enlow, Amanda(Gwathmy) 120
  John E. 120
  Thomas K. 120
Ennis, Edna[Skaggs] 210
Enochs, Garrard 170
  Samuel 131
  Sarah(Johnson) 170
  William P. 170
Ensminger, Mary A(Megee) 232
Epperson, Anna(Cox) 154
  Charles 189
  Daniel 180
  David 154
  Eliza J(Bregle) 154
  Elizabeth(Smith) 189
  Francis 180
  George W. 154
  J.S. 189
  James S. 189
  Rebecca(Sanders) 24
  Samuel 154
  Tabitha(Redding) 180
Erdel, Catherine(Barnhart)97
  George 97
Erlywine, Thomas 122
Ernst, Richard F. 37
  Sarah(Butler) 37
  Sarah A(Butler) 37
  William 37
Eskew, Annie(Carter) 189
  John 102
Eskridge, E.R. 210
  Fannie(Robinson) 210
  Joseph W. 210
Eurton, J.H. 131
Evans, Ann(Crow) 141
  Cassandra[McNab] 210
  David 25
  David T. 157
  Frances 25
  Hannah[Williams] 210
  Harmon 210
  Hugh 55
  John 25
  John B. 55
  John W. 25
  Keziah[Mavity] 211
  Lucy(Button) 157
  Mahala(Ward) 25
  Mary A[Harrison] 144
  Rachel[Burcham] 211
  Richard 211
  Robert 157
  Thomas 141
  Ursala[Snodgrass] 124
  William 55, 141
  William E. 25
Everman, Nancy[Gardner] 211
Everston, Julia[Sarels] 99
Evins, Anna(Martin) 81
  Samuel P. 81
  Thomas 81
Ewing, Elizabeth[Booker] 211
  John 24
  Margaret 24
  Robert 211
  Robert W. 211
  William 55
Ewings, Harriet(Bishop) 109
  James 109
  William W. 109
Fairchild, William 137
Falter, Joseph 21
  Katherine[Winter] 21
  Rosa[Bahn] 21
Far, Daniel C. 131

Farbery, Mary[Corkary] 21
Faris, Andrew 109
  Eli 109
  James C. 211
  John 109
  Sarah(Truitt) 109
Farley, J.I. 81
  Joseph F. 180
Farmer, Eli P. 113
  Mary[Harlan] 94
  Mary[Williams] 114
Farmster, Rachel[Morgan]101
Farnsley, James 211
  Joshua 211
Farr, Catherine(Kurry) 106
  James 106
  Jefferson 106
  Sarah(Miller) 233
Farrar, Caroline J(Jarvis) 131
  John J. 131
  John M. 131
Farris, Emily(Redmond) 193
  Eunice[Rainhart] 190
  J.H. 193
  John 193
  T.H. 98
Farrow, Alexander S. 159
  David P. 159
  Elizabeth(Brewer) 55
  Elizabeth(Nelson) 159
  Orson D. 55
  Rachel A. 55
Faught, Elizabeth[Bailey]113
Faulkner, Anna(Harned) 118
  James W. 52
  Joseph F. 118
  Martha 52
  William 118
Fear, Martha A[Gartin] 211
Fearman, Emily[Lashbrooke] 103
Featherngill, David F. 170
  John H. 170
  Joseph 170
  Martha A(Brannigin) 200
  Mary(Forsyth) 170
Featherston, Jeremiah 211
  William E. 136
Fee, Sallie[Carpenter] 29
Felkins, Jane(Williams) 116
  Thomas 116
  William 116
Fendley, Malinda(Ragsdale) 238
Fenton, Eliza(Setree) 18
  H.B. 18
  Jeremiah 55
  Jesse 55
  Thomas T. 18
Fergusin, Clemons 86
  Isabel[Cartmill] 17
  James C. 86
  John W. 211
  Ralston 139
  Salinda(Darnell) 158
  Sarah(Cochran) 86
  Sarah(Patton) 60
Ferree, Mary[Pirtle] 211
Ficklin, Philadelphia[Bradley] 113
Fidler, Fannie K[Mugg] 211
Field, George 86
  Harrison 86
  Jane(Rankin) 193
  Jemima(Wright) 86
  Joseph 86

Field(cont.)
  Nathaniel 131
  Sarah[Campbell] 211
Fields, Abraham 211
  Anna(West) 211
  Jane(Hansford) 216
  Keen 211
  Mary M[Durham] 91
  Sarah[Burgess] 176
  Susannah[Steele] 150
  William 211
Fife, Andrew 131
  Elizabeth(Wright) 131
  John 131
Fig, Hannah[Ash] 195
Figg, Asbury 180
  Francis 211
  Robert P. 211
  William H. 180
Finch, Ceci[Whipps] 44
  George W. 147
  Phillip 211
Finke, Christine[Storke]211
Finley, David 211
  Elizabeth 211
  Jefferson 211
  Miriam(Brooks) 200
Finnell, James R. 211
Fintress, Eliza[Howard] 161
Fischbach, Emma(Fischer) 24
  Frederick 24
  Victor W. 24
Fischer, Emma[Fischbach] 24
Fish, D.A. 98
  Elizabeth(Wilson) 98
  John B. 98
Fisher, B. 55
  Brandes 170
  D.S. 97
  Elizabeth 109
  Elizabeth(Briscoe) 180
  Elizabeth[Harrison] 180
  J.S. 211
  James 180, 211
  Lydia[Houk] 220
  Mahala(Webb) 194
  Marly(Mahoney) 230
  Rebecca[Hodge] 219
  Sally A[Lydick] 106
  Samuel 106
  Sophia[Galey] 106
  William J. 170
Fisk, Cynthia(Stevens) 137
  Harry 137
  William B. 137
Fislor, Susan H. 211
Fitch, George 21
  James W. 21
  Lavina[Colwell] 55
  Mary(Martin) 21
Fite, John W. 47
  Millie(Cotterill) 47
  O.P. 47
Fitzgerald, Joseph 126
Fitzpatrick, John M. 49
  John W. 49
  Mary S(Smallwood) 49
  Nancy[Ballard] 196
  Ruth(Webb) 171
  Samuel D. 180
  Sarah[Moore] 144
  Solomon 41
  Zerilda(Vanhook) 41
Fitzsimmons, Enos M. 180
  Martha(Miles) 180
  Richard 180
Fitzwalter, Elizabeth[Tal-
    bott] 183

Flack, Mary[Cox] 211
Fledderman, Kate[Langfermann]
    137
Fleece, Charles 91
  George 141
  Jacob H. 91
  John 91
  Mary(Harlan) 91
  Susan[Clay] 91, 211
  Susan[Clay] 91, 211
Fleming, Eleanor[Southgate]
    19
  Sarah(Caughay) 203
Fleshman, Mary[Redick] 133
Fletcher, Eliza[Matthewa] 81
  Eliza A[Matthews] 91
  John 55
Flick, Polly(Cox) 206
  Sarah(Hill) 219
Flinn, Agnes(Priest) 61
Floro, David 55
Flournoy, David J. 49
  Elizabeth(Cunningham) 49
  Elizabeth J[Stevenson] 49
Floyd, Erastus L. 211
  Jane[Penn] 133
Flusant, Alice[Foster] 43
Flynn, Ailsey[Ragland] 100
Fogle, George 55
Foley, James B. 147
  James P. 109, 211
  John J. 147
  Martha(Carter) 147
  Mary(Bradford) 147
  Sarah[Copher] 115
Forbis, B.F. 80
Ford, David 120
  Emily J(Thurman) 118
  James W. 120
  John L. 193
  Matilda(Jackson) 120
  Mordecai E.55
  Susan[Smith] 211
  Thomas J. 118
  Walter M. 118
Foreman, James G. 185
  Joseph 185
  Susannah(Cox) 185
Forman, Margaret[Lendrum] 168
Forrest, Harriet[Williams]18
Forsee, James 113
Forsyth, J. 211
  James 131, 211
  Jane[Sturgeon] 131, 211
  Mary(Ragsdale) 170
  Thomas 131
Forsythe, David 211
  Jane(Pierce) 145
  Joseph 145
  Margaret(Pritchard) 238
  Mary[Featherngill] 170
  Matilda[Bridges] 211
  Sarah J[Branigan] 211
  W.H. 211
  William H. 145
Forward, Elizabeth[Long] 228
Fosdick, Louise 35
  Phillip C. 35
  William 35
Foster, Alice(Flusant) 43
  Eliza(Frizell) 43
  Dorotha A[Carr] 120
  James A. 18
  John R. 43
  John V. 131
  Joshua 43
  Joshua F. 43

Nancy[Terrell] 164
  Otho D. 43
  Prudence(Knight) 18
  Rachel[Chenoweth] 43
Foulks, Nancy(Ellis) 137
  Peter 137
  Redland 137
Fowler, Elizabeth[Masters]
    212
  Jane(Riley) 106
  Maggie R[Johnson] 106
  Nancy(Wakeland) 249
  Susan(Marland) 216
  William A. 106
Fox, Abraham 191
  Elizabeth[Wilson]174, 176
Foxworthy, James H. 110
  Mary A(Calvert) 110
  Nancy[Albin] 161
  Samuel 110
Frakes, Charity(Debaun) 208
  Greyson 212
  Margaret(Priestland) 238
Fraley, Sarah A(Ketcham)224
Frame, Elizabeth 40
  Elizabeth[Counts] 55
  John 212
  Margaretta(Jerette) 86
  Susan(Davis) 212
  William 86, 212
Frames, John 212
France, Elizabeth(Whitestine)
    251
Francis, Catherine(Lowman)
    100
  Hannah[Hamilton] 212
  Jesse 100
  Lucinda[Rouse] 212
  Rhoda A[Hatfield] 185
  Sarah(Hardesty) 86
  Thomas 100
  William 86
  Willis 86
Frank, Catherine[Miller]212
  Henry 94
  John 24
  Phebe(Miller) 94
Franklin,Julia A[Boles] 154
  Sarah(Ritter) 240
Frary, Eleanor[Jones] 154
Frazee, Benjamin 92
  Catherine(King) 92
  Diadama[Keith] 148
  Ephrain 147
  Ephrain S. 147
  Nancy[Dailey] 212
  Susan(Doniphan) 147
  William 92
  William D. 147
Frazer, W.W. 137
Frazier, E.L. 212
  James 212
  Nancy(Hendrick) 218
  Rebecca[Jacquess] 222
  Sarah[Shuck] 128
Frederick, Margaret[Allison]
    169
Freeman, Reuben F. 18
Frelinger, J.W. 24
French, Alice 46
  Charles 46
  Clara 46
  Ann(Demott) 208
  Doris 212
  J.S. 154
  Simon 154
Fresh, Dovinda[Leisure]212

Freyhoff, Charles 23
　Eva 23
　James 23
Fridley, Louisa[Schweickart]
　21
Fried, Barbara[Miller] 140
Friedley, Elizabeth[Edmondson] 212
Friend, Nancy 212
Friesner, Fred 56
Fristo, R.C. 43
　Thompson 43
Fritts, Susan(Wooden) 252
Fritz, Phillip 100
Frizell, Eliza[Foster] 43
　Nancy[Hance] 56
Frost, James A. 136
　Mary(Beckham) 136
　Simeon 136
Fry, Elizabeth 56
　George 212
　Jacob 56
　James 19, 56
　John 212
　Sarah[Bottorff] 212
Fryman, Nancy[Hendrixson] 29
Fulenwider, Lucinda[Mount]
　180
Fulkerson, A.J. 103
　Anna M(Chenoworth) 103
　John V. 103
Fullenwider, Eleazar 180
　Fannie E(Shipman) 183
　Jacob 180
　Katie(Winters) 180
Fuller, Louisa[Keper] 118
　Lydia A[Hutchinson] 115
Fulton, Elizabeth(Bennett)43
　Jane[Banta] 212
　Joseph 43
　Margaret[Meikle] 133
　Titus B. 43
Funk, Anary(Gray) 32
　Eugene M. 32
　Margaret[Hornback] 202
　Mary[White] 135
　Michael 36
　Sarah[Morris] 38
　Thornton A. 32
Fuquay, John 95, 212
Furber, Charles S. 21
　John N. 21
　Martha M(Smith) 21
Furinash, Dorcas[Gosnell]122
Furlow, Elizabeth[Wishard]
　113
Fyffe, John T. 147
　Jonathan 147
　Thomas 147
　Zeralda(Allen) 158

Gabbert, Charles D. 212
　E.E. 103
　Eli E. 119
　William J. 119
Galbreath, David 212
　Margaret[Vickery] 212
Galey, Benjamin 154
　D.W. 154
　Eliza 212
　Elizabeth(Woods) 154
　Mary C(Bennett) 198
　Matilda(Chamberlain) 203
　Samuel 212
　Samuel S. 212
　Sophia(Fisher) 106
　William W. 180

Gallaway, Covey 92
Galliher, Sarah[Hughes] 212
Galloway, Elizabeth(Kirkpatrick) 19
　J.L. 19
　Mary(Elliott) 210
　Samuel 19
Gallup, Sarah E[Cullen] 23
Galway, Juliette[Richards]
　212
Gambill, Morgan 212
Gamble, Martha[Dunlap]131
Gammon, Harriet(Stewart) 32
　Joshua L. 32
　Joshua M. 32
Gannon, Hannah[Pennington]
　212
Ganoe, Martha(Meadley) 232
Gantz, Mary[Clutts] 81
Gard, Gershom 56
　Job 56
Garden, R.G. 120
Gardner, Mary(Allen) 194
　Mary E[Smith] 33
Garnell, H.W. 213
Garner, Catherine[Oliver]
　162
　Deborah 213
　Deborah(Lyons) 81
　Hannah 162
　Harrison B. 213
　Luke 162
　Maria(Glass) 120
　Royal G. 120
　Emily(Hensley) 159
　Eliza A[Smith] 101
　Nancy(Everman) 211
　Sallie[Osburn] 163
　Solomon 213
　Solomon P. 81
Garr, Elizabeth[Clements]
　213
　Permelia[Smith] 134
Garrard, Jeptha D. 56
Garrett, Malinda R(Hunt)110
　O.W. 213
Garriott, Mildred[Abbott]
　126
Garrison, Elijah 43
　James 43
　Mary(Sullivan) 43
　William 43
Garshwiler, Nancy[Hunt]213
　Sarah[Vandiver] 156
Garten, John 122
Gartin, Marta A(Fear) 211
Garwood, Sarah[Spain] 213
Gasaway, L. 94
　Samuel 213
Gash, Eliza(Wilson) 141
　Samuel G. 141
　Thomas 141
Gashwooller, Elizabeth
　[Canary] 153
Gaskins, S.A. 213
Gasteneau, Elizabeth 174
　Joab 174
　Sallie 174
Gastineau, Joab 174
　Rachel[Newman] 174
　Sarah(Hayes) 174
Gates, Amanda[Blades] 42
　Elizabeth M(Murdoch) 234
　Martha(Chinn) 203
Gault, William P. 43
Gaunce, Martin 47
　Melville M. 47

Gayle, Albert D. 171
　D. Howard 48
　James 47, 171
　Sally(Green) 171
　Sarah C(Green) 47
　Walter S. 213
Gear, Sarah(Watson) 250
Geary, Betsey(Stump) 246
　Josephus 213
Gegelbach, Christian 99
　Ernest E. 99
　Sophia(Martin) 99
Gentry, Barry 106
　David 144
　Elizabeth[Giles] 95
　Elizabeth(Hornback) 213
　Elizabeth J(Ludlow) 106
　Garland 213
　James 213
　Joseph 213
　Susan(Stringer) 247
Geohegan, Susanna[Brooks]
　165
George, Drusilia(Raborn) 18
　Mary[Prather] 111
　Mary[Shryock] 84
　Milton 188, 213
　Robert 18
　Thomas D. 188
　W.J. 213
　William E. 18
Gibbs, James 191
　John 191
　Mary 191
Gibson, Isaac 101
　Kate F[Harrison] 99
　Margaret[Bacon] 187
　Margaret[Boyd] 40
　Mary[Boyd] 40
　Mary(Scott) 84
　Nancy 101
　Nancy[Burnett] 93
　William 101, 162
　William M. 162
Gifford, Ann(Tennis) 148
　Elisha 148
　Lemira 148
　Nancy 148
　William H. 148
Gilaspie, Elizabeth[McCracken] 213
Gilbert, Alfred M. 131
　Charles H. 131
　Elizabeth(Reynolds) 116
　Frank R.M. 120
　Franklin R.M. 120
　Rosanne G(Endress) 131
Gilchner, Mary(Clutter) 86
Giles, Elizabeth(Gentry) 86
　Gentry 92, 120
　James 92
　John 92
Gilkeson, John C. 154
　Nancy(Buchanan) 154
　Thomas 154
Gilkey, Sarah[Allen] 100
Gilkinson, Annie(Hunt) 110
　John 110
　Robert A. 110, 213
Gill, Jonathan 81
　Seyth(Ingraham) 81
Gillaspy, Lydia(McGuire)100
　Lysander H. 100
　Martin 100
Gillen, Henry H. 213
Gillespie, Jane[Eddy] 126

Gilless, Mary[Campbell] 192
Gilliam, Martha(Hodge) 56
  Richard 56
  William 56
Gilliland, Diana[Summers]
  134
  Margaret[Jones] 80
Gillums, Sarah[Talbot] 178
Giltner, Abraham B. 106
  Daniel 213
  Elizabeth[Licklider] 56
  Enoch 213
  Nancy(Liter) 106
Ginn, Benjamin 43
  Lucy(Triplett) 43
  Richard(Neal) 60
  Rosann[McKnight] 213
Gish, Sarah J[Drake] 213
Givens, Ida[Elliston] 46
  Mary(Mitchell) 43
  William 43
Gladish, James 213
Glass, Duncan C. 129
  Elizabeth[Marshall] 111
  Kate H. 129
  M.C. 129
  Marie[Gardner] 120
Glasscock, Asa 29
  David B. 29
  Elizabeth[Dailey] 94
  Elizabeth(White) 56
  Gregory 56
  John R. 56
  Mary(Penquie) 29
Glazebrook, Lucinda(Smith)
  183
  Clifford 154
  Lloyd 154
Glenn, Henry 165
  Sarah[Clark] 165
  Thomas 193
Glidden, Charles C. 37
  Daniel A. 37
  Ellen(Robinson) 37
Glove, Nettie[Ward] 213
Glover, Azel 43
  Jane[Tichenor] 164
  Lovina E. 213
  Mary(McManus) 80
  Priscilla(Gaddis) 180
  Ruth[Reed] 213
  Thomas B. 180
  Thomas G. 180, 213
  Uriah 180
  Ware 213
Goans, Margaret[Chafins] 39
Gobbel, Julia A(Davis) 207
Gobin, William 213
Goble, Eunice(Pound) 237
Godfrey, Abraham 154
  Phoeba[Hart] 213
  Rosa(Ray) 154
  William 154
Godwin, Joseph 213
Goff, David 213
  Sarah 213
Gold, Bertha[Pink] 21
Golden, John M. 172
Golding, George 213
  Jane(Jackson) 222
Goodber, Henry H. 159
  John H. 159
  Mary 159
Gooding, Asa 110, 214
  David S. 110, 214
  Matilda 110, 214
  Sarah[Mauzy] 232
Goodman, Benjamin T. 80

  Elizabeth[Sheridan] 134
  M. 214
Goodnight, Rachel[Young] 184
Goodpaster, Anthony J. 81
  Margaret(Carpenter) 81
  Michael 81
  Scythia(Carpenter) 81
Goodpasture, David 214
  John 214
  Solomon 214
Goodright, Sarah[Coffey] 214
Goodwin, Rebecca[Heady] 217
Goodwine, Elizabeth(Snyder)
  214
  James 214
  Mehitabel 214
  Samuel 214
  Thomas 214
Gootee, Thomas 214
Gordon, David 180
  Granville C. 180
  James 214
  Mary S[LeGrange] 162
  Nancy(Tompkins) 28
  William 214
Gorham, Alexander 86
  Sarah(Tyler) 86
Gorman, Willis A. 110
Goslin, Sarah[Moore] 110
Gosnell, Alexander 122
  Benjamin 122
  Dorcas(Furinash) 122
  John 214
Gosney, Margaret[Bryan] 172
  Millie[Yelton] 173
Goss, Margaret M(Halbert)215
Gossar, Jestina[Wilson] 176
  Justina[Wilson] 176
Gossom, James M. 104
  Mary E(Jordan) 104
  W.G. 104
Gott, Robert 180
  William 180
Goulding, Aurelia M(Bennett)
  47
  C.C. 47
  Fred A. 47
Grady, Catherine[Talley] 108
Graham, Anci 51
  Catherine[Dobbins] 118
  Eliza[Carnahan] 214
  Henry D. 51
  James 56, 214
  James H. 180, 214
  Jane[Mitchell] 214
  John 56
  John W. 162
  Mary 56
  Mary[Campbell] 214
  Melinda[Crawford] 214
  Nancy J. Roswell 241
  Sarah(Urton) 51
  Thomas B. 214
  Tilghman 214
Grainger, Phoebe J(Brum-
  field) 201
Grant, Mary[Osburn] 214
Grate, Nancy[Wilson] 135
Graumer, Jeanette[Cohen] 131
Graves, Absalom 83
  Laura G[Wasson] 52
  Lucy(Mitchell) 52
  R.C. 52
  R.E. 83
  R.K. 83
  Sarah E(Mothershead) 83,
  172
  W.H. 168

Gray, Anary[Funk] 32
  Andrew 214
  Catherine(McKinley) 230
  Francis 37
  James S. 56
  Jane 37
  John 37, 86
  Joseph 113
  Margaret(Dick) 86
  Mathew 56
  Nancy 56
  Nancy(Bass) 197
  Nancy[Ristine] 240
  Robert 37
  Samuel 214
  Susan[Robb] 62
  Thomas 113
  Walter E. 37
  William 214
  William J. 86
  Zeralda[Wallace] 214
Grayham, Permelia A[Ryan]
  156
Greathouse, George 214
Green, Archibald 165
  Eli 144
  George 20
  George S. 148
  H.D. 188
  James 180
  Jemima[Scott] 145
  John 144
  Malissa[Baldwin] 196
  Margaret(Johnson) 180
  Margaret(Montgomery) 233
  Mary[Carter] 109
  Rachel 20
  Rachel[Johnson] 29
  Rebecca(Snider) 144
  S. 214
  Sally[Gayle] 171
  Sarah C[Gayle] 47
  Stephen 214
  Thomas 180
  William H. 215
Greene, J. 83
  Mary E(Smith) 26
  Matilda[Powell] 125
  Thomas M. 26
  W.H. 83
  William 26
Greenhow, Ann[Grierson] 27
Greenup, Christopher 177
  Henry H. 215
  John 177, 215
  John W. 177
  Louisa 215
  Mary A(Holland) 177
  Samuel 215
  Samuel G. 177, 215
Greenway, William 215
Greer, Aaron 20
  John E. 171
Gregg, George W. 177
  Martha[Whitaker] 215
  Mary[Clements] 29
  Mary(McMurtry) 177
  Samuel 177
Gregory, Artistica[Rawlins]
  91
  Elizabeth[Hatfield] 185
  Joel 215
  Margaret[Piers] 133
Gresham, Christian 177
  Margaret A[Wood] 113
  Nancy[Nichols] 190

Grider, Mary(Bailey) 78
  Mary[Dickerson] 157
  Rebecca[High] 215
  Simon 78
  William 78
Grierson, Ann(Greenhow) 27
  John 27
  W.D. 27
Griffin, G.W. 115
  Parmelia(Johnson) 223
Griffith, Abel 83
  Bartlett 215
  Hannah(Richeson) 177
  James 215
  Jane 215
  Jennie(Windsor) 83
  Nancy 81
  Owen 83
  Patience(Dalton) 207
  Thomas 177
  William 177
Griggs, Dawson(Burgess) 201
  Martha[Baker] 105
  Millicent[Thompson] 144
Grigsby, Anne(Cornwell) 131
  Bennett 131
  Nancy(Baker) 196
  Reuben 215
  W. 168
  William 131
Grimes, Mary[Stephenson] 127,
  215
  Nancy[Pruitt] 215
  William 119
Gritton, J.F. 190
Groom, Louisa(Stowers) 131
  Samuel J. 131
  William H. 131
Groover, Louvisa(Heflin) 218
Grover, Jeremiah
Groves, James A. 215
  Mary(Cart) 93
  Mary[McMains] 215
Grubbs, Eliza P(Prentiss)215
  James T. 215
  John W. 222
  Sarah[Johnson] 222
Gruber, Catherine[Hubig] 24
Grubs, Mildred A. 100
Grundy, E.S.(Kemper) 43
  R.C. 43
  William H. 43
Gudgel, Elvira(Wallace) 249
  Teressa[McClure] 228
Guffin, Henry C. 148
Gulick, John F. 148
  John H. 148
  Sarah(Cockrell) 148
Gullaway, Matilda(Hurst) 221
Gunkel, Frederick C. 24
  Henry C. 24
  Katherine(Weber) 24
Gunn, Naomi[White] 215
Gunynn, Jane[Wilson] 124
  Louisa J[Mason] 215
Gurton, Jane(Moore) 233
Guyton, Sarah(Coons) 170
Gwathmy, Amanda[Enlow] 120
Gwinn, John T. 102

Hack, Lucinda[Conder] 90
Hackley, Elizabeth[Lane]159
Haddan, Emily(Hobbs) 131
  James W. 171
  John 171
  Rebecca 171
Hagemeyer, C.C. 47

Hall 47
  Mary E(Hall) 47
Haines, Adaline 154
  David W. 154
  Garrett 99
  John G. 99
  Nancy(Chadwell) 99
  Wesley 154
  Willis 99
Hains, Edward B. 140
  Elizabeth(Wellingsford)
  140
  Joseph 140
Halbert, Elizabeth(Marks)
  162
  J.M. 162
  John 162
  Margaret(Woodsmall) 162
  Margaret M[Goss] 215
Hale, Bowen 148
  Catherine(Tucker) 103
  John 148
  Levi 103
  Nancy J[Wedding] 169
Halfhill, Andrew J. 48
  Elizabeth(Kellum) 48
  John 48
Hall, A. 122
  Bluford 215
  Catherine(Wasson) 184
  Charlotte J[Biggs] 192
  Christiana[Whitely] 31
  Daniel 86
  Elizabeth[Rutherford] 89
  Henry 86
  John 33, 56, 189
  Louise[Kerns] 175
  Mary[Thorpe] 44
  Mary A[Hensley] 159
  Polly[Dugan] 33
  Polly(Nichols) 180
  Polly(Thixton) 215
  Ransom A. 37
  Ransom C. 37
  Richard 33
  Samuel Q. 180
  Sarah[Chafin] 215
  W.J. 125
  William 215
  William L. 215
Hallenshade, Linda(Wright)
  45
Haller, John 43
  P. 215
  Paul 131
  Sarah(Arrowsmith) 43
  William 43
Ham, Elizabeth(Mathers) 86
  Lutitia[Rice] 22
  Michael 86
  Moses F. 86
Hamilton, Benjamin 122
  Betsey[Hartford] 181
  Charlotte J(Terrell) 164
  David 122
  David N. 122
  Dorothy[Hickman] 215
  Elender(Collett) 191
  Eliza(Rhodes) 56
  Elizabeth(Luyster) 155
  H.H. 215
  Hannah(Francis) 212
  Hannah(Ramsey) 86, 100
  Hulbert L. 100
  James 100, 191
  James E. 165
  James H. 86, 216

Jane(Keeney) 223
Jane(McCoy) 165
John 56, 191
Joseph 122
Justice 56
Nancy(Dryden) 122
Nathaniel 216
Orville S. 110
Philander 165
Robert 83
Robert A. 165
S.R. 86
Thomas M. 159
William 216
Hammer, Margaret[Knox] 87
Hammond, James H. 181
  John 216
Hammonds, Fannie(Pendlay)141
  Joseph 141
  William H. 141
Hamner, John 154
Hamrick, Ambrose D.
  Jack R.M. 159
  Thomas 159
Hanauer, Andrew 43
  Charles 43
  Mary A.M. 43
Hance, Benjamin 56
  John R. 30
  Joseph 56
  Margaret J(Knox) 30
  Nancy(Frizell) 56
  Richard 30
  William 56, 216
Hancock, Catherine(Jackson)
  221
  James T. 216
  Lewis T. 79
  Martha(Lacey) 79
  Orpha[Hankins] 216
  Sanders[Butcher] 216
  Stephen F. 79
  Virginia[Jett] 113
  William 216
Handy, Augustus C. 177
  William 177, 216
Handley, Sarah J[Craig] 90
Hanes, James W. 216
Hankins, Gilbert 181
  Mary 181
  Orpha(Hancock) 216
  William 181
Hanks, L.L.L. 129
  Thomas 216
Hanna, Hugh 177
  James 177
  Martha W[Glenn] 154
  Samuel 177
  William 181
Hansford, Jane[Fields] 216
Hanson, Elizabeth[Miller]59
Harber, Ida J(Poe) 21
  John J. 21
  Pearl C. 21
Harbison, James P. 216
Harbit, Isaac 216
Harcourt, Elizabeth[Clinton]
  27
Harden, Daniel 127
  Nancy[Province] 127
Hardesty, Amelia(Rudd) 115
  Richard 115
  Sarah[Francis] 86
  William H. 115
Hardin, Abner 170
  Catherine 165
  Elizabeth[Mackoy] 38, 59

Hardin(cont.)
Emma(Ritter) 120
Franklin 165
Henry 165, 170
James 94
Nettie[Blenn] 216
Susan[Dunham] 188
Harding, Ede 190
Israel 190
Lucinda[Bristow] 216
Margaret(VanWinkle) 164
Martha 190
Robert 190
Rush[Hopkins] 216
Samuel 162, 190
Hardins, Elizabeth(Miller)
181
John A. 181
Joseph 181
Hardwick, Charles 159
Dorcas[Mitchell] 127
Elizabeth(Crook) 159
Melissa R[Conduitt] 216
Silas 159
Hardy, Amy(Pedigo) 216
Benjamin 216
Jay 125
Kate(Semonin) 125
T.R. 125
J.J. 80, 216
J. 92
Hargan, Daniel 120
Susan(Crandall) 120
Thomas J. 120
Hargis, John 216
Nancy(Allen) 194
Hargrove, John 174, 216
Sallie(Jasper) 174
William 174, 216
Harlan, Austin 145
David M. 56
J.M. 216
John 94
John T. 94
Joshua 80
Laura[Cleveland] 30
Lorinda(Conway) 145
Lucinda[Anderson] 216
Lucy J(Huffman) 221
Mary(Farmer) 94
Mary[Fleece] 91
Nathan 92
Harland, Andrew J. 158
Joel W. 158, 216
Polly(Mulkey) 158
Mary(Mulkey) 158
Susan[Fowler] 216
Harlow, May 18
Michael 18
Thomas 18
Harman, James 174
Harmon, Elizabeth[Mitchell]
233
Mary(Clarke) 204
Susan[Pinnick] 216
Harned, Anna[Faulkner] 118
Harney, Charlotte(Kyle) 181
Gilbert T. 165, 181
James F. 181
Harp, Elizabeth[Talbot] 108,
217
Tracy(Capp) 202
Harper, Cynthia 56
James S. 171
Martha[Shepard] 217
Patsy[Shepard] 193
Perkins 56

Polly[Wasson] 87
Sanford 56
William 56
Harpole, John H. 189
Harrah, Daniel 106
Elizabeth(Baldwin) 110
Nancy W[Cox] 217
Robert 110
S.B. 110
Sarah B. 110
Harrell, Elizabeth(Watkins)
162
Isaac 162
Mary(Miley) 232
Waller 162
Harris, Addison J. 188
Bedial J(Davis) 153
Catherine(Bosley) 188
Charles B. 188
Cynthia(Rusher) 241
Dorcas[Mitchell] 127
Eleanor[Huls] 26
Eliatha[Miller] 217
Elizabeth[Cutsinger] 217
Frances[Patterson] 87
G.W. 162
Isabel(McKune) 163
James 217
James M. 217
John 217
Joseph 56
Kate(Hobbs) 115
Lucinda(Witham) 252
Mahala[Pugle] 217
Mahala[Woolfolk] 152
Mary[Bowles] 122
Mary(Murray) 133
Masterson 217
Nancy(Barrett) 217
Nicodemis 154
Polly(Emerson) 141
Robert 56
Sarah[Burton] 126
Sarah J. 56
Sophia[Rice] 217
William 217
Harrison, C.C. 100
Carter 217
Elizabeth[Fisher] 180
Elizabeth(Nix) 94
Gabriel 94
Henry W. 99
J.J. 100
James B. 100
James H. 181
Jemima[Nation] 117
John 100
Julia(St. Clair) 241
Kate F(Gibson) 99
Mary A(Evans) 144
Otho 144
R.F. 99
Reuben 181
Reuben C. 122
Reuben G. 217
Reuben T. 181
Rhoda(Paris) 181
Sarah(Paris) 181
Sarah A(White) 100
Thomas S. 100
Harrod, William 217
Hart, B.F. 81
Hester(Adams) 81
John 81
Nancy[Davis] 158
Phoeba(Godfrey) 213
Sarah[Herod] 173

William 154
Harter, Bennett J. 56
Elizabeth 56
Elizabeth(Smizer) 33
Emily[Shidaker] 56
Jacob 33, 56
M.G. 33
Martha L[Talbott] 217
Hartford, Betsey(Hamilton)
181
Philip T. 181
William 181
Hartley, Mary G[Sellards] 32
Hartman, Nancy[Siner] 217
Hartwell, Charlotte(Muldrumm)
131
Richard M. 131
Samuel A. 131
Harvey, Benjamin 217
Ellen N[Beeson] 217
Mary A(Thompson) 247
Nancy(Sellars) 217
Hash, John C. 217
Hasenour, George 217
Martin 217
Tharsila 217
Haskill, Susan E[Kinkead] 21
Haskins, Mary E[Clements]217
William 217
Hasty, Levi 174
Lydia 174
Hatfield, Elijah 103
Elizabeth(Banta) 52
Elizabeth[Ely] 115
Elizabeth(Gregory) 185
Emiline(Morgan) 103
James 103
Jane(DeBolt) 151
John 43, 217
S.B. 151
Sidney B. 151
Susan(Lockridge) 227
Thomas 217
William 151, 185
Havens, Hester(Jarvis) 110
James 110, 148
Sarah[Randall] 111
Havlin, John H. 37
Joseph 37
Margarette(Creighton) 37
Hawes, Mary[Malott] 132
Hawkins, Amerial O[Clark]142
Anthony C. 188
Anthony S. 188
Christian(Worthington) 20
Denisa[Hill] 217
Elizabeth J(Hopgood) 188
Frankie[Callaway] 86
Henry 217
Jameson 217
Jefferson 94
John J. 20, 87
Joseph 20
Joseph C. 87
Margaret[McCarty] 217
Mary[Mayhall] 217
Polly(Kephert) 94
Samuel 20
Silas 94
Hawthorne, Virginia P[Dyer]
24
Hayden, A.B. 217
Catherine[Stevens] 120
Daniel 120
Hannah(Shacklet) 120
Susan M[Bryan] 103
Haydon, Elizabeth[Piles]237

Hayes, Sarah[Gastineau] 174
Haymaker, Sarah(Poulter) 155
Hayman, Elizabeth(Tarvin) 24
  Isaiah T. 24
  Richard H. 24
Haynes, James H. 168
  John 217
  John H. 217
Hays, Elizabeth(Smith) 37
  Harmon H. 37
  Samuel K. 37
Hayward, James 131
  Napoleon B. 131
  V.A. 131
Hazelrigg, Elizabeth 217
  Elizabeth(Lloyd) 227
  Frances(Wright) 81
  H.G. 217
  Harvey G. 81
  James T.J. 81
  Joshua 81
  John W. 217
  Sally[Boardman] 164
  William 217
Hazlett, James 165
  Mary(Stephenson) 165
  Samuel 165
Heady, Almond 217
  Elizabeth(Slavens) 160
  Louisa 118
  Martha[Jackson] 217
  Rebecca(Goodwin) 217
  Thomas 217
Hearick, J.A. 115
Hearn, Isaac 97
  John P. 97
  Nancy A(Mason) 97
Hearne, Cannon 20
  Jonathan D. 20
  Sallie(Owen) 20
  Sarah[Wasson] 20
Heath, Betsey[Jarvis] 99
  Martha(Rodgers) 240
Heaton, David F.
  Joseph 110
Heavern, Martha[Williams]218
Hedelson, Esther(Craig) 166
  James 166
  John C. 166
Hedges, Elizabeth[Cisco] 82
  Nancy[Hinman] 168
  Nancy(Thurman) 186
  Peter 168
  Rebecca[McCray] 87
  Sarah A(Tanner) 168
  William J. 168
Heflin, Louisa[Groover] 218
Heiner, Frederick 81
  Rossalinda 81
  Samuel 81
Helm, Charlotte[Thomas] 218
  Elizabeth(Drummond) 218
  James 43
  Jefferson 148, 218
  Phoebe 43
  Samuel H. 43
  Sarah[Merrett] 149
  William 218
Heltsley, Ellen[Utley] 187
Hemingray, Anna J[Shinkle]39
Hemphill, Andrew 56
Henderson, D.H. 40, 56
  Elizabeth(Truesdale) 40
  Elizabeth(Vance) 175
  Emeline[Wolf] 218
  Hezekiah 218
  James 40, 107, 181

James C. 181
John P. 106
Joseph 175
Josiah 175
Martha(DeMott) 206
Mary(Demott) 208
Mary(Pierce) 182
Mary(Piercy) 182
Mary J[Myers] 218
Parth. M. 218
Paulina[Wray] 116
Hendrick, George F. 218
  Nancy[Frazier] 218
Hendricks, Ambrose 218
  Clarinda(Mayfield) 232
  John A. 173
  Lucinda[McFerran] 141, 229
  Sarah[Leman] 56
Hendrickson, Catherine[Shir-
  ley] 163
  Daniel 40
  Elizabeth(Rummans) 40
  Joel D. 40
  Mary[Breeding] 78
Hendrix, Anna R(Waler) 89
  Frances(Honey) 81
  George 218
  John 81
  Moses M. 81
Hendrixson, Allen 29
  Enoch 29
  Nancy(Fryman) 29
Henry, Adeline[Dilley] 218
  Elijah 218
  Elizabeth[Davis] 109
  Hamilton 218
  John C. 56
  Sarah[Woollen] 252
  Thomas C. 123
Hensley, Emily[Gardner] 159
  J.W. 218
  John W. 159
  Mahala[McNutt] 218
  Mary A(Hall) 159
  Nancy[Shepherd] 218, 242
  Sarah(Icenangoe) 218
  Sarah(Peterson) 218
  William 218
Herbert, Charles 97
  Elizabeth 97
  William J. 97
Herman, Magdalene[Sulzer]134
Herod, E.D. 218
  Edmund D. 83
  John H. 173
  Lucinda(Kendall) 224
  Luther 173
  William 87
Herrell, Austin 127
  Elizabeth[Kephart] 127
  Rachel(Wiley) 127
  William 127
Herrin, Jesse 174
Herring, Azariah 218
  Ellen(Beasley) 174
  Isabella(Worrell) 124
  Jackson 123
Herron, Elizabeth[Howard] 94
  John 141
Hert, William 80, 141
Heslar, Catherine(Waits) 56
  George L. 56
  William 56
Hesler, Elizabeth[Trester]89
Hess, Jacob 29
  Thurza[Sheppard] 218
Hesse, Anthony 37

Raphael 37
Hessemer, P. 131
Hesson, Elizabeth(Tuley)248
  Margaret[Brand] 218
Hester, Adam 110
  Ann M(Van Zandt) 112
Hethington, Elizabeth[Wil-
  liams] 135
Hetzler, David 56
  Mary A(Thornell) 56
  Thomas 56
Hiatt, Frances[Overturf]218
Hibbs, Jeremiah 218
Hickman, Dorothy(Hamilton)
  215
Hicks, Ann(Reed) 218
  C. 218
  Eleanor 80
  James 218
  James B. 80
  Jefferson 218
  John 80
  Lucinda(Ragsdale) 238
  Melinda I. 22
  Samuel J. 22
  Sarah[Linthicum] 143
  William T. 22
Higby, Polly A[Nave] 219
Higgins, Elizabeth(Plasters)
  237
  Henry 219
  Isabel[Boyd] 144
Higgs, Permelia[Palmer] 127
High, Rebecca(Grider) 215
  Tilman 219
Highland, Sarah[Shrout] 87,
  167
Hight, Letice[Manner] 155
  Mary[Legge] 219
Hikes, George G. 219
Hilburn, Nancy[Balay] 118
Hild, Louisa[Cook] 131
Hiles, Catherine[Sullivan]
  150
Hill, Alice(Newland) 131
  Allen 174
  Amanda 34
  Denisa(Hawkins) 137
  Edmund 38
  Edward N. 131
  Elizabeth(Jones) 175
  Frank 131
  James 166, 174, 175, 219
  John W. 38
  Jordan 37
  Mary K. 151
  Nancy[Henderson] 219
  Rachel L(Cowan) 165
  Sarah 148
  Sarah[Fletcher] 219
  W.W. 137
  William 166, 175, 219
  William W. 137
Hillis, Abram 110
  Elizabeth(Peck) 111
  Elizabeth(Scobee) 160
  James 219
Hillman, Daniel 219
  Mary E(Austin) 196
Hilton, Sarah A(Jones) 223
Hinkle, J.S. 219
  Jackson 219
  James S. 219
  James W. 131
  Margaret[Rankin] 219
  Margaret A. 219
  Martha(Reed) 131

Hinkle(cont.)
  Philip 131, 219
Hinkson, Benjamin 33
  Margaret[Smart] 166
  Thomas 33
Hinman, James 168
  Nancy(Hedges) 168
  Rhodia[Perigo] 168
  Samuel 168
Hinton, J.C. 110
  Mary[Riley] 219
Hitch, Mary(McMullen) 230
Hite, Eliza[Daniels] 180
  Mary(Meyers) 59
  May A(Lowery) 228
  Sarah[Russell] 150
  William 91
Hitt, D.C. 20
  John 57
  Samuel 57
Hixon, William
Hoagland, Isaac 185
  John 27
  Levi 27
  Lucy(Mallory) 27
Hoback, John 219
  Kilen(Darcas) 207
Hobbs, Elizabeth 131
  Emily[Haddan] 131
  Emory 115
  J.P. 117
  James 131
  Kate[Harris] 115
Hobgood, L.P. 192
Hobson, Elizabeth 24
  George 24
  James 24
Hockaday, Nancy[McWilliams]
  144
Hocker, Joseph E. 219
Hodge, Andrew 46
  Fidelo T. 142
  Harriet(Barnes) 142
  Isabell(McTeer) 46
  James H. 46
  Jesse 219
  Martha[Gilliam] 56
  Perlina[Rhodes] 219
  Rebecca(Fisher) 219
  Samuel E. 46
  Sarah M[Baird] 57
  Thomas 142
Hodges, John 219
Hodkins, Henry E. 131
  Joseph 131
  Margaret 131
Hoey, Barnaby 57
Hoffer, Jane[Pollitt] 111
Hoffman, John 57
  L.F. 80
  Nancy[House] 83
  Susan 57
Hogan, Sallie[Parker] 19
Hoggegg, Mary M[Naugle] 219
Hoggett, S. 219
Hogland, Emily[Conway] 187
Hoke, Andrew J. 131
  Catherine[Howard] 132
  Jacob 131
  Jacob F. 131
  Mary[Brentlinger] 132
Holcomb, Dosha[Kelley] 184
Holden, Caroline[Downs] 57
Holder, Elizabeth(Dailey)
  207
Holdson, James 219
Holeman, Elizab(Street)246

J.M. 219
Holland, Mary[Jones] 24
  Mary A[Greenup] 177
Hollcraft, Eliza[Stratford]
  219
Hollick, Martin 132
  Sophia(Bramble) 132
  William 132
Holliday, Elizabeth(Martin)
  123
  Mary(Isgregg) 221
  Rebecca[McClintock] 123
  Samuel 123
  William A. 123
Hollingsworth, Bros. 181
  Fannie(Alexander) 171
  Nancy A(McKee) 229
Hollis, Anna[Weaver] 219
  C.L. 125
Hollon, G. 91
Holly, Mary[Pearcy] 182
Hollywood, Jane[Butler] 30
Holman, Daniel 144
  George 219
  Jesse L. 91
  Joseph 219
  Rebecca 144
  Sarah[Radcliff] 144
Holmes, Alexander 87
  Frances(Stogsdale) 245
  Jacob 219
  James 123
  James M. 87
  Margaret(McClure) 228
  Prudence(Klampet) 123
  Sarah 87
Holsclaw, Joshua 127
  Wickliffe B. 127
  Zerelda(Carpenter) 127
Holt, Vine 219
Holton, Nancy[Robinson] 148
Holtzclaw, Martha[Ellis] 220
Hon, M.M. 87
Honaker, Charles W. 18
  Cornelius 18
  Sarah(England) 18
Honey, Frances[Hendrix] 81
  Sarah[Reeves] 150
Hood, Bonaparte 78
  J.W. 78
Hooton, Thomas 220
Hoover, James 220
  Margaret[Cramer] 54
Hope, Abigail 220
  Isaac 181
  James 220
  James A. 181
  Mildred[VanPelt] 63
  Susan(Ellis) 181
Hopewell, Armilda[Annis] 220
  John 220
  Katherine(Lisman) 227
Hopkins, A.V. 57
  Eldridge 131
  Elizabeth(Ellis) 125
  Ezekiel 87
  Hiram A. 87
  J.N. 162
  James 97
  Milton B. 166
  Polly(Benson) 87
  Richard 125
  Richard H. 125
  Rush(Harding) 216
  Sarah(Smathers) 81
  Tabitha M[Warring] 99
  William 81

Hopper, James A. 220
Hopping, Mary J(Berkshire)
  198
Hord, Elias 148
  Elizabeth S(Moss) 148
  Francis T. 148
  Kendall M. 148
  Oscar B. 148
Horine, Mary E[Bishop] 152
Hornaday, Elizabeth(Meadows)
  232
Hornback, Adam 220
  Elizabeth[Gentry] 213
  Isaac 220
  Margaret(Dungan) 209
  Margaret(Funk) 220
Horton, George W. 83
  Lettie[Manning] 149
Hoskins, Joseph 220
  Nancy(Thompson) 247
Houchin, Elizabeth(Clifford)
  204
  Jesse 220
Houck, J.J. 220
Houghland, A.E. 162
  A.F(Broshears)168
  Cyntha 175
  Susan(Ward) 250
Houghton, Aaron 148
  Celia A(McKay) 148
  William 148
  William H. 148
Houk, John 220
  Lydia(Fisher) 220
  William 220
House, Jemima[Means] 220
  Masten 83
  Nancy(Hoffman) 83
Houseman, Walter 181
Houston, David 57
  John M. 57
  Mary[McGinnis] 88
  Mary[Talbott] 246
  Sarah[Tucker] 220
Houts, Eliza K[Barber] 220
  George 220
  Jennie(Graham) 220
Howard, Aaron 220
  Aletha(March) 231
  C. 220
  Catherine(Hoke) 132
  Cornelius 170
  D.S. 185
  Eliza(Fintress) 161
  Elizabeth(Herron) 94
  George 132
  Huston 94
  James 132
  John 148, 185
  Joseph 170
  Lucius S. 42
  Mahala[Chesnut] 220
  Nathaniel 161
  Oscar F. 161
  Phila(Summers) 185
  Rual 132, 220
  Sallie[Woolley] 28
  Samuel B. 94
  Sarah 170
  Sarah(Thornton) 247
  Thomas M. 161
Howe, Lucinda[Stewart] 220
  Robert 220
Howell, Mason J. 129, 193
Howes, Esther[Smith] 132
  Mitchell P. 132

Howlet, Elizabeth 220
  Robert 220
Howlett, Elizabeth(Thompkins)
  160
Howser, Jacob 43, 57
  Sarah(Loveless) 43, 57
Hubanks, Clarissa[Zink] 148
Hubbard, Mary[McHenry] 220
  Melinda M(White) 157
  R.N. 96
  Sarah(Vest) 249
  William 116, 220
Huber, Manasas 57
  Nancy(Makeinson) 59
Hubig, Catherine(Gruber) 24
  Simon 24
Huddleston, Fielding 220
  Susan(Philips) 220
  William 220
Hudelson, Alexander 106
  Catherine(Irvin) 87
  David 87
  Esther(Craig) 166
  James 166
  John C. 166
  John M. 87
  Robert J. 123
  Sally(Donnell) 87
  William 166
  William H. 87
Hudnut, Catherine(Dalton)148
  Joseph 148
  Theodore 148
Hudson, Sophia[Buster] 51
  Thirza(LeMasters) 227
Hudspeth, Thomas 189
  Thomas J. 189
Huff, Henry 94
  Margaret[Powell] 221
  William 221
  Wilson 94
Huffman, Adam S. 151
  Barsheba(Craig) 79
  Delilah I(Stapleton) 119
  Henry 79
  George 119
  John H. 119
  John S. 151
  Lucy J[Harlan] 221
  Rebecca(Stptaugh) 151
  Stephen F. 79
Hufford, Christopher 57
  Cornelius 57
  Joel 166
Huffstetter, Catherine(Sears)
  87
  David S. 87
  George 87
Huffstutter, Mary[Sears] 89
Hughes, C.K. 22
  David 57
  Elizabeth[Parks] 88
  Frances[Begley] 125
  George N. 221
  Hethinger[Woten] 221
  Jacob 221
  James B. 221
  Jane[Wilson] 113
  Jesse 57
  Margaret[Marshall] 120
  Mary[Carman] 179
  Nancy[Brown] 162
  Rachel[Rannells] 44
  Sarah(Galliher) 212
  Stephen T. 132
Hughbanks, Mary[Lee] 221
Hulet, John 221
Hull, Benjamin 57

John 168
Huls, Eleanor[Harris] 26
Hume, Eliza(Bowers) 199
  Joel 137
  Madison 221
Humphrey, Margaret[Broshears]
  168
Humston, Charles M. 127
  Milton L. 127
  Susan M(Tiplett) 127
Hungate, Jesse J. 155
Hunt, Basil 110
  Bazell 110
  Elizabeth(Rivers) 240
  John R. 221
  Johnson 159
  Joseph 221
  Joshua 221
  Lemuel 166
  Malinda R[Garrett] 110
  Martha J(Vanlandigham)112
  Mary 110
  Matilda 166
  Meshack 221
  Miles 110
  Nancy(Garshwhiler) 213
  Simeon 221
  William R. 221
Hunter, Anderson B. 170
  Eliza C[Barrows] 221
  Eliza M[Read] 97
  Elizabeth 181
  Henry 181
  Lewis S. 110
  Margaret[White] 251
  Margaret M[Peggs] 188
  Nancy(Culbertson) 147
  Ralsamon 170
  Samuel 181
  Sarah[Ragsdale] 182
Hurd, Dorcus(Morrison) 57
  John 57
  Thomas 57
Hurst, Mary(Emmons) 221
  Mary[McMurrays] 24
  Matilda[Gullaway] 221
  St. Clair 221
  Sarah(Alkire) 195
  William 221
Huser, John 221
Husk, Mary J(Kellams) 155
  V.W. 103
  W.J. 103
Huston, David 163
  Jonathan 163
  Margaret(Herron) 163
  Samuel M. 163
Hutchins, William D. 106
Hutchinson, Alexander 115
  John 115
  Lydia A(Fuller) 115
  Margaret[DeCamp] 221
  William 221
Hutford, Louisa J(Miller)233
Hutson, Frankie(Lewis) 227
  Sarah 20
  William 221
Hutton, Albert G. 221
Hyatt, Elisha 221, 149
  John 149
  Margaret(McPharson) 149
  Margaret(McTerren) 149
  Thomas 149
Hydron, Edwin W. 127
  Mary F(Schermerhorn) 127
  William 127

Icenangoe, Sally[Hensley]218
Iglehart, Ann(Taylor) 168,
  221
  Asa 168, 221
  Janet[Miller] 169
  Levi 168, 221
Iles, Elizabeth[McCann] 173
  Thomas 221
Inderrieden, Elizabeth(Weh-
  moff) 24
  Henry 24
  John D. 24
Ingraham, Seyth[Gill] 81
Ingram, James 170
  Jefferson 170
Inlow, Abraham 110, 221
  John J. 110
  Sophia(Bell) 110
  Susan(Sparks)244
Inman, Mary[Milburn] 232
Iredell, Charles J. 18
  James W. 18
  Virginia(Rust) 18
Ireland, Andrew 87
  Elizabeth 87
  James B. 115
  Mary[Purviance] 20
  Rachel[Works] 172
  S.I.H. 87
  Sallie(Lancaster) 115
  Sarah[Wilson] 49
  William W. 115
Irons, W.C. 119
Irvin, Ann[McDowell] 45
  Catherine[Hudelson] 87
  Martha 221
  Polly 221
  William 221
Irving, Mary[Page] 78
Irwin, Benjamin 95
  Christopher C. 120
  Ellen C(King) 120
  Isaac 120
  Jane[Wright] 57
  Mary[Doak] 136
  Mary(Thomson) 63
  Obed A. 120
  Smiley D. 120
  Thomas 57, 100
Irwine, Susan[Jenkins] 120
Isbell, Abel H. 163
  Livingston 80
Isgregg, John 221
  Mary 221
  Mary[Holiday] 221

Jabboe, Ann(Elder) 210
  Peter 221
Jack, Samuel 193
  Wade H. 115
Jackson, Armilda A(Stephen-
  son) 245
  Carter T. 87
  Catherine[Hancock] 221
  Elizabeth[Crosby] 43
  Elizabeth[Mason] 169
  Evan 29
  George W. 172
  J.H. 221
  J.W. 145
  James 87
  James H. 221
  James W. 145
  Jane[Golding] 222
  John 145, 222
  John H. 221
  John T. 145, 190, 222
  Martha(Chambers) 87

Jackson(cont.)
  Martha(Heady) 218
  Mary L(Pirtle) 145, 190
  Matilda[Ford] 120
  Nancy 29
  Nancy[Long] 181
  Newton J. 87
  Salathiel 177
  Sarah[Barnett] 85, 87
  Sarah(Richart) 82
  Thomas 29
  William 87, 221
  William A. 190
  Yula[Satterwhite] 172
Jacobs, Elizabeth(Turner) 63
  James 222
  Leander 149
  Mary 149
  Samuel 149
  Sarah[Crim] 180
Jacquess, Asbury C. 222
  Christian[Smith] 124
  Jonathan 222
  Jonathan G. 123
  Rebecca(Fraizer) 222
James, Enoch R. 163
  Harriet 149
  Marie[Ambrose] 167
  Mary A[Smith] 167
  Ruth[Lenn] 125
  Stanfield P. 149
  Thomas 149
Jameson, John M. 87
Jamison, John 222
  John W. 222
Janes, Elizabeth(McCollum)97
  Samuel 97
  William M. 97
January, James 27
  Robert 27
Jarrard, Mary[Diltz] 55
Jarvis, Betsey(Heath) 99
  Caroline J[Farrer] 131
  Hester[Havens] 110
  Reason 99
  William 99
Jeems, Elizabeth[Smith] 186
Jeffres, James 222
Jeffries, Fielden 181
  Francis 222
  Harvey 222
  Margaret 222
  Melinda(King) 225
Jenkins, James 120
  James A. 120
  Jane[Pruett] 222
  John E. 151
  L. 222
  Mahala 94
  Martha(Webster) 96
  Mary[Bradley] 113
  Richard 222
  Robert A. 96
  Susan(Irwine) 120
  Thomas 96
Jennings, Ceclia[Wedekind]
  123
  George B. 24
  Mary 155
  William 155
  William H. 155
Jerette, Margaretta[Frame]
  86
Jett, Elizabeth[Smoot] 222
  John W. 113
  M.L. 113
  Virginia(Hancock) 113

Jewell, Nancey[Roberts] 177
  Sally A[Napier] 163
  V. 185
Johns, Israel 57
  Jacob 120
  Robison 177
  Abram 177
  Elizabeth 177
Johnson, Alfred 222
  Andrew 83
  Arthur 110
  Catherine[Roe] 222
  Clemency(Donovan) 43
  Cornelius 222
  Daniel 222
  Dolly[Ansley] 28
  Edward H. 222
  Elias 163
  Elijah 222
  Eliza 120
  Elizabeth 120
  Elizabeth[Salle] 169
  Ellen[Kamp] 120
  Emily[Dunlap] 55
  Grafton 155
  Hannah[Jones] 222
  Harriett[Sparks] 222
  Henry G. 57, 29
  Hiram 222
  J.N. 163
  Jacob 29, 141
  James 43, 57, 155, 222
  James L. 222
  Jeremiah 222
  Jesse 57
  John 29, 132, 222
  Joseph R. 43
  Lawson W. 100
  Lewis 222
  Luke 141
  Maggie R(Fowler) 106
  Malinda[Cordrey] 106
  Malinda[Threlkeld] 222
  Margaret[Green] 180
  Maria(Martin) 231
  Martha(Rafferty) 61
  Mary(Alvis) 223
  Mary[Cross] 109
  Mary[Demaree] 180
  Mary(McClure) 83
  Mary(Taylor) 155
  Mary A[Stalling] 222
  Mary A.W(Stubblefield)100
  Martha(Cawthorn) 203
  Mary J[Prenat] 36
  Mary J[Waldren] 155
  Nancy[Dilley] 223
  Nancy(Murphy) 234
  Nancy[Tate] 135
  Nancy[Williams] 164
  Parmelia[Griffin] 223
  Perry C. 110
  Peter 29
  Polly(Yeates) 253
  Rachel(Green) 20, 29
  Rebecca[Michael] 57
  Robert 83
  Rosamond[Noble] 27
  Sarah[Enochs] 170
  Sarah(Grubbs) 222
  Sarah(Mitchell) 223
  Sarah(Whitehead) 163
  Sarah C(Anderson) 195
  Sophia(Linn) 25
  Susan(Stines) 141
  Susan[White] 80
  Susannah[Peak] 188

Thomas 20, 223
  Thomas B. 223
  Thomas F. 223
  Thornton A. 100
  Tom L. 49
  William 223
  William D. 43
Johnston, Arthur 50
  Charles 41
  Frances 50
  Francis 50
  Lydia 27
  Martha(Karney) 223
  Waller 27
Jones, Ann[Amos] 85
  Ann(Lewis) 181
  Berryman 223
  C.J. 24
  Calvin 103
  Charles 24
  Craig 223
  David E. 46
  Elizabeth(Edwards) 46
  Elizabeth[Hill] 175
  Elza 127
  Hannah(Johnson) 222
  Hannah[Page] 33
  Harrison 149
  Isabella(Peggs) 188
  James 103
  Jane(Kirk) 110
  John 46, 223
  John F. 110
  Joseph 223
  Joseph B. 120
  Lucinda(Myers) 110
  Lucy(Thompson) 149
  Margaret(Gilliland) 80
  Maria S(Tucker) 248
  Martha J[Carnahan] 223
  Martin 110
  Mary 57
  Mary(Calvert) 38
  Mary(Holland) 24
  Mary(King) 225
  Mary A(Poe) 237
  Melinda[Clifft] 204
  Nancy(Pritchett) 238
  Nancy C[Servies] 223
  Rebecca(Kirk) 103
  Richard B. 38
  Ruth[Thornhill] 57
  Sallie[Carpenter] 81
  Sarah[Braiser] 223
  Sarah[Ryker] 83
  Sarah[Whitmore] 57
  Sarah A[Hilton] 223
  Thomas A. 110
  Thomas D. 110
  Thomas M. 110
  Thompson 80
  William 38, 149
  William H. 57, 80
  William S. 163
Jordan, Elizabeth[Bandy] 93
  Lucy[Wheat] 79
  Margaret[Beekes] 223
  Mary E[Gossom] 104
Joseph, Humphrey S. 163
  Lydia(Sapp) 163
  Simeon S. 163
Jubinal, Dorothy[Beauchamp]
  223
Judd, F.M. 78
Judy, Benjamin 223
  Jesse 57
  John 29

Junken, Betsey 80
Edward A. 80
Harvey 80
Justus, Fannie(Shryock) 243
Juvinall, Jacob 57
Kackley, Elias 177
James E. 177
Lucy(Burke) 177
Kaiper, Charles H. 24
Nellie C(Wilson) 24
Samuel E. 24
Kaler, Catherine(Dale) 207
Kallams, Mary J[Husk] 155
Kamp, Ellen(Johnson) 120
Peter G. 120
Susannah[Lasswell] 175
William H. 120
Kandle, William A. 120
Karn, Margaret K[Dunn] 142
Karney, Martha[Johnston] 223
Kasson, Frances 38
Henry 38
Henry C. 39
Kavanaugh, Anna[Covington]57
Keach, Hannah(Meade) 223
John R. 223
Louisa[Swaim] 223
Kearby, Eliza[Dillard] 223
Kearns, G.M. 57
George E. 30
Josephine(Salendar) 30
Martin J. 30
William 223
Keeling, James 190
John 190
Mary 190
Keen, Archibald 38
George A. 38
Rebecca(Kirkpatrick) 38
Keeney, Jane[Hamilton] 223
Kehoe, Edwin J. 38
Elizabeth(McHenry) 38
Timothy 38
Keightley, Elijah T. 170
John W. 170
Keith, Diadema(Frazee) 149
George H. 223
I. 149
Isham 149
John A. 149
Rachel[Chambers] 223
W. 223
Keithler, Mary[Thatcher] 93
Kellams, Mary(Conley) 205
Keller, Mary[Krausgill] 123
Sarah[Clore] 170
Kelley, Charlotte(Walton) 223
David 125
David B. 169
David M. 184
Dosha(Holcomb) 184
Francis H. 223
Gideon 120
Isaac 223
Isham 79, 125
James 120
Joseph 184
May(Dutterrow) 55
Nancy 125
Nancy(Brown) 173
Perry 223
William 173
Kellum, Elizabeth[Halfhill] 48
Kelly, Eliza(Cover) 205
Eliza(Patterson) 107

Elizabeth(Armstrong) 195
Greenup 105
Isaac 141
Isham 223
J.W. 94
John 132
John H. 83
John J. 110
Mary J[Wells] 224
Matthew 223
Kelsey, Mary[Hays] 224
Marinda[McCoy] 189
Kemp, James 224
Kemper, Arthur S. 116
Caleb 27
E.S[Grundy] 43
Harriet 27
Nancy[Baker] 196, 224
Kendall, James R. 172
John R. 224
Lucinda[Herod] 224
Mary[Melton] 224
Nancy(Ellis) 210
Kendrick, Susan[Phillips] 61
Kennard, Cynthia[Diltz] 224
Kennedy, Aria[Talbot] 89
Benjamin F. 87
Elizabeth[Scott] 191
Elizabeth(Sharrer) 87
Florence G. 38
Jane(Blockford) 198
John M. 38
Joseph 87
L.C. 120
Luke C. 224
Mary(Kimbro) 87
Peter 120
Peter S. 87
Rachel 120
Robert 116
Thomas 87
Thomas G. 38
Kennett, Joseph H. 185
N.B. 185
Rhoda(St. Clair) 185
Kenney, David 20
Elam 20
Martha 20
Kenning, Patsy[English] 122
Kenton, Elizabeth[Arrowsmith] 42
Elizabeth[Neff] 91
Mark 57
Matilda[Parkison] 224
Susan(Markley) 57
William 57
William M. 155
Keper, J.D. 118
Louisa(Fuller) 118
Roscoe 118
Kephart, Elizabeth(Herrell) 127
Hannah[Mitchell] 224
James 127
Jemima(Swift) 127
John S. 127
Polly[Adams] 126
Polly[Hawkins] 94
William 127
Kercheval, Maria A. 97
Robert T. 97, 137
Samuel E. 97
Kerlin, George 127, 224
James 127, 224
Lou J(Tyler) 135
Margaret(Smith) 224
Rachel(Banta) 127, 196

Kern, Abraham 166
Anne[Sears] 167
Kerns, Christopher C.H. 175
Isham 175
Louise(Hall) 175
William 224
Kerr, Agnes[McMichael] 44
Kersey, Thomas 166
Kesler, Elizabeth[Beauchamp] 224
Isaac N. 185
Rebecca[Carr] 224
Kester, Ephraim 185
Nancy[Weeks] 186
William 185
Ketcham, Daniel 181
John 224
John L. 224
Mary A[Mitchell] 182
Sarah A[Fraley] 224
Ketherwood, Charles 33
Ruth 33
Ketron, Elizabeth[Crain] 46
Key, Hannah(Level) 224
Sarah(Bruner) 201
William 224
Keyes, John L. 106
Mary A(Coons) 106
Nelson R. 106
Kidd, Nancy[Davis] 158
Kidwell, J[Mattingly] 224
John H. 190
Kilgore, David 123
James 20
John 20
Lydia 20
Obed 123
Rebecca(Cuzick) 123
W.W. 224
Kimberlain, Fountain 224
Henry 224
Jacob 224
John 224
John C. 224
Kimbrell, Vina[Spry] 105
Kimbro, Mary[Kennedy] 87
Kime, R.R. 117
Kincaid, John 224
John J. 224
Kincheloe, Allen L. 151
Jesse W. 151
Susan(Marlay) 151
King, Benjamin 224
Catherine[Frazee] 92
Cynthia 225
Ellen C[Irwine] 120
Elizabeth J[Williams] 110
Enoch W. 110
Isaac 224
James 175, 224, 225
James W.D. 225
Jesse 225
John 225
Joseph 225
Judith(Roundtree) 225
Lucinda[Pinnick] 225
Lucy(Campbell) 110
Mary[Jones] 225
Melinda[Jeffries] 225
Rachel[Kirts] 225
Rebecca[Culbertson] 225
Robert 225
Sarah[Rector] 225
William 175, 225
Kinkead, E.G. 225
Edna A(Manser) 38
Joseph D. 38

Kinkead(cont.)
  Oscar E. 21
  Susan E(Haskill) 21
  William 21
Kinneman, Charlotte[Weaver]
  151
Kinnett, Thomas I. 185
Kinsey, Gertrude[Weaver] 135
Kinsley, Jane[Kilgore] 225
Kiplinger, Mahala(Shockey)62
Kirk, Augusta(Calvert) 83
  Clarence L. 83
  David 225
  Edmond 225
  Elizabeth(DePew) 208
  Jane[Jones] 110
  John W. 83
  Martha 225
  Rebecca[Jones] 103
  Thomas 188
  William J. 225
Kirkendall, Sarah[Williams]
  184
Kirkham, Robert 163
Kirkman, James 225
  Jane S. 190
  Joseph 225
Kirkpatrick, Anna(Mays) 123
  David 225
  Elizabeth[Galloway] 19
  Emma[Denton] 192
  John S. 225
  Moses 225
  Rebecca[Keen] 38
  William 123
Kirtley, Elizabeth 225
  Eusebius 83
Kirtsinger, Harrison 225
  John W. 225
  Sarah 225
Kise, William C. 106
Kiser, James 87
  Joseph 87
  Rebecca 87
Kitch, Elizabeth[Leak] 92
Kitchen, Dennis B. 95
  Mary[Risk] 225
Kitcher, Mary[Tucker] 128
Kite, R.H. 225
Klampet, Prudence[Holmes]123
Klein, Charles E. 38
  Elmer A. 38
  George J. 137
  George L. 137
  Katherine(Peters) 38
  Rosina(Dollman) 137
Kline, Sarah 57
Klotter, George F. 35
  Magdalene 35
Knaper, Mary E[Martins] 32
Knecht, Joseph 24
Knetzer, Catherine 149
  Charles 149
  Francis M. 149
Knight, Amanda(Winans) 83
  John 83
  Margaret[Mahan] 111
  Prudence[Foster] 18
  William P. 83
Knott, Roser[Davis] 103
Knowland, William 225
Knowles, Comfort S[Marvel]
  142
  Margaret[West] 36
  William 149
Knox, John 87

Margaret(Hammer) 87
Margaret J[Hance] 30
Mary[Caldwell] 90
  William 87
Koebler, Mary[Wilhite] 171
Koleapple, Julia A. 225
Korbly, Charles A. 225
Korby, Charles 132
  Charles A. 132
Krausgrill, David 123
  Mary(Keller) 123
  Philip 123
Krutz, Josephine[Moore] 115
Kurry, Catherine[Farr] 106
Kurtz, Henry 163
  Henry F. 225
Kyle, Charlotte[Harney] 181

Labold, Fannie(Rosenfeld)38
  Henry 38
  Simon 38
Lacefield, Catherine[McClain]
  181
Lacey, Martha[Hancock] 79
Ladd, Charles W. 132
  Mary E(Steele) 132
  W.W. 132
Laffoon, Hattie(Parker) 35
  Polk 35
LaGrange, Aaron 225
  Daniel C. 155
  Lemima(Covert) 155
  Peter 155
  Peter D. 155
  Patsy M(Ramsdell) 156
Lair, Alice[Smith] 34
Lake, Asa 57
  Asa M. 57
  Cloe 57
  Eliza[Sharpe] 107
  Lydia[Wolford] 57
  Martha[Rose] 57
Lamar, Elizabeth(Blake) 149
  John H. 149
  William W. 149
Lamaster, Isaac 225
Lamb, Elizabeth[Walters]119
  Evarilla[Walters] 136
  Mary P[Wilson] 225
Lamberson, Samuel 92
  Thoughgood 92
Lambert, Sarah[Walden] 125
Lamme, David 30, 57
  Elizabeth(Martin) 59
  Nancy(Ralston) 30
  Nathan 30
  Samuel 58
Lancaster, Edith E. 18
  Martha A(Tanner) 18
  Sallie[Ireland] 115
Land, James 136
Landford, Cynthia[Church]175
Lane, Amos 83, 226
  Charles 226
  Elizabeth(Hackley) 159
  George W. 83
  Henry 226
  Henry S. 159
  Higgins 159
  John F. 226
  Mary 83, 226
  Nancy[Drake] 80, 151
  R.H. 159
  Robert G. 159
Laney, Elizabeth(Davis) 141
  James 141

  Levi D. 141
Lang, James 226
  Thomas 103
Langfermann, Kate(Fiedder-
  man) 137
Langsdale, J.M.W. 115
  John 115
  R.G. 226
  Wealtha(Dill) 115
Langworthy, Emily B(Baker)
  132
  George W. 132
  James N. 132
Lanier, Lucretia[Williams]
  226
Lankford, Belinda[Cooprider]
  226
  Larkin 226
  Melinda[Cooprider] 226
Lansdowne, Zachariah M. 58
Lantz, Henry 32
  John B. 83
  Lovina(Bennett) 32
  Mary 83
  Polly(Arnold) 83
  Thomas C. 32
Larkins, Charles W. 38
  George W. 38
  Susan(Blennerhassitt) 38
Larsh, Charles 58
Lashbrooke, Emily(Fearman)
  103
  Grayson 103
  P.S. 103
Lasher, Abraham 95
Lasswell, John J. 175
  Susannah(Kamp) 175
  William 175
Latimore, John 58
Latta, Lida[Rigsby] 133
Laughlin, John O.M. 226
Lauman, Anna J(Shanklin)29
  George M. 29
  Gordon F. 29
Laville, Charlotte[Black-
  ledge] 29
Law, John 170
  Mary(Barnes) 197
  Mary(Tracy) 170
  William 170
Lawler, Anna(Buchannon) 201
Lawrence, Elizabeth[Riley]
  226
  Sarah[Reeves] 98
Lawson, Elizabeth(Rauling)
  32
  Jacob 32
  John M. 32
Lay, Harriet[McNeil] 22
Laycock, Minerva B(Dawson)
  97
  Thomas B. 97
  William H. 97
Layer, Gottlieb 35
  Louise(Engelhart) 35
  W.G. 35
Layman, Alfred 226
  J.H. 226
  John 226
Laymon, Alfred 226
  Jennie(Steele) 226
  John 226
Layne, Elisha 226
  P.M. 226
Leach, Eliza(Allison) 81

Leach(cont.)
  Enos 226
  Jane[Powell] 189
  John A. 226
  Mary[Stafford] 178
  Meredith 81
  Sarah[Leak] 226
  William W. 81, 169
Leachman, James 149
  Mary(Reeves) 149
  William 149
League, Elizabeth[Brazelton]
  90
Leak, Elizabeth 92
  Elizabeth(Kitch) 92
  George W. 92
  Landrum 226
  Louis 92
  William 92
Leathers, James M. 113, 226
Leavell, Benjamin 106
  Robert 106
Leavitt, George B. 111
Ledbetter, Dorothy(Linkart)
  17
  Thomas 17
  Warren 17
Ledgerman, William 226
Ledgerwood, Colonel 184
Lee, Anna(McCoy) 149
  Catherine[Shepherd] 177
  Cecilia J(Runey) 113
  Charles 174
  David 226
  Elizabeth(Mitchell) 181
  Elizabeth[Sommervill] 112
  Elmira(Cowher) 179
  Eunice(Atherton) 105
  G.G. 173
  Gashum 143
  Henry 181, 226
  James N. 226
  John 149, 181
  Joseph 80
  Maurice 113
  Morris 113
  Nancy[Mille] 182
  Nice 174
  Noah 174
  Rebecca[Taylor] 104
  Spencer 226
  William 181
Leffew, Arah 141
  Samuel 141
  William S. 141
Leffler, Sarah[Canine] 179
Lefler, Catherine 227
  Peter 227
Legge, William A. 227
LeGrange, Mary E(Gordon)162
  Richard 163, 227
Lehmeyer, J.H. 132
Leisure, George W. 116
  John P. 227
  Nathan 116
  Sarah(Irvin) 116
Lemaster, Zachariah 227
Lemasters, Sarah 174
  Thirza[Hudson] 227
Lemen, Sarah(Hendricks) 56
Lemmon, James H. 113
  John 181, 185, 227
  John M. 177
Lemon, Ann[Applegate] 42
  Sarah[McNight] 22
Lemons, Catherine[Combs]
  162

Lendrum, Charles K. 144
  Margaret(Forman) 168
Lenmell, David F. 132
  John 132
  Margaret 132
Lenn, James 125
  Lewis 125
  Ruth(James) 125
Letherman, Barbara 227
Lett, Fieldea 172
  John A. 227
  Randall 227
  Sarah(Tyndall) 227
Levy, Hannah[Allen] 85
Lewellen, Philip 23
Lewis, Alexander H. 38
  Anna[Jones] 181
  David S. 227
  Eugene 38
  Frankie[Hutson] 227
  G. 177
  Gideon 227
  Martha(Montgomery) 24
  Mary[Rutledge] 58
  Mary[Shallcross] 134
  Nancy[Phillips] 36
  Sarah(Marion) 38
  Winnie[Cope] 138
Licklider, Elizabeth(Gilt-
  ner) 56
Lidikay, Catherine(Yenawine)
  132
  George E. 227
  Jacob 132
  Jacob E. 132
Lightfoot, Alfred C. 173
  Elizabeth(Collin) 173
  William B. 173
Limpus, Isaac 227
  John 227
Lincoln, Leonard 227
  Mary[Mitchell] 24
Lindeman, Benjamin J. 58
  Joseph 58
  Mary 58
Lindenburn, Jacob 18
  Martha(Eckstein) 18
  Philip 18
Lindley, Rebecca(McKittrick)
  107
Lindsay, Charles 115
  D.F. 177
  Eleanor(Montgomery) 177
  Enoch M. 127
  Joseph 177
  Leander 115
  Lucinda(Powers) 84
  Minerva(Williams) 115
  Thomas 227
Lindsey, Elizabeth[Alexan-
  der] 227
  Leander 115
Line, Elizabeth(McClellan)
  58
Lineman, Anna[Dulweber] 37
Lingenfelter, Valentine 100
Linkhart, Dorothea[Ledbet-
  ter] 17
Linn, Angelina[Blair] 25
  Joseph 25
  Sophia(Johnson) 25
  T.T. 227
Linthicum, Edward 143
  Porter 143
  Rufus 143
  Sarah(Hicks) 143
Lisman, Katherine[Hopewell]

  227
  Margaret(Lovelace) 228
List, Albert 127
  Anna 227
  Catherine[Banta] 126
  Sarah[Black] 126
  Susan(Vannuys) 156
  Theodore 227
Liter, Henry 87
  Katie(Boyers) 87
  Nancy[Giltner] 106
Little, George 145
  I.W. 161
  Jane[Prewett] 91
  Mary[Thompson] 145
  Polly[Wheeler] 227
  Reynold 145
  Sarah(Prather) 145
  Susan S[Curlee] 130
Littlejohn, Unia E[NcDan-
  iel] 174
Livingston, Hannah[King] 227
Lizenby, Huldah[Cunningham]
  227
Lloyd, Anna 227
  Elizabeth[Hazelrigg] 227
  James M. 227
  John G. 227
  Philip 227
Lockerbie, Janette[McOust]
  107
Lockhart, Jorman 227
  Judith[Warren] 227
  Susan[Hatfield] 227
Lockridge, Andrew M. 159
  Dulcenia 159
  Elizabeth(Malone) 159
  Rachel[Bridges] 158
  Robert 159, 227
Lockwood, Benjamin 87
  Narcie[Ritter] 87
  Rebecca(Smith) 87
Logan, Amzi 181
  Benjamin 58
  David R. 58
  Elijah 58
  Elijah R. 58
  Elizabeth[Emerson] 141
  Ezekiel D. 228
  Jane(Allen) 178
  Mary[Anderson] 105
  Nancy[Zaring] 171
  Phoebe(Richards) 58
  Roxoline(Powell) 61
  Samuel 58
Logsdon, Samuel 124
Lombard, David R. 58
  H.D. 24
  Harry D. 38
  Jesse 24, 38, 58
  Olive 58
  Olive(Carlton) 24, 38
Long, Benjamin 106
  David 193
  Elizabeth[Forward] 228
  Elizabeth(Martin) 193
  Isabella(Thompson) 58
  John 58, 193
  Marcus D.L. 181
  Margaret A. 106
  Mary[Adams] 58
  Nancy(Jackson) 181
  Nancy[Pool] 113
  Rhoda H(Clark) 181
  Robert 58
  Sarah(Reeves) 111
  Stephen 58

Long(cont.)
T.A. 106
Thomas 181
Thomas A. 166
W.D. 181
William 58
William D. 181
Longfellow, Joseph 58
Longley, Anber H. 149
Looney, Martha K[Wiley] 140
Lorenz, John H. 132
Loring, Richard 228
Lory, Barbara[Procaskey] 119
Losley, Joseph D. 228
Lothridge, Elizabeth[Buntin]
165
Loudon, Charles 58
Lough, Jacob B. 102
Nancy(Bishong) 102
Thomas 102
Love, Susan[Campbell] 37
Lovelace, Margaret[Lisman]
228
Loveland, Mary[Sweeringen]40
Loveless, Sarah[Howser]43,
57
Lovitt, C.G. 192
Lowe, Catherine[Shanklin] 81
Elijah 228
George 123
Jonathan 228
Kate(Voris) 228
Lawrence 228
Littleton 228
Simon P. 228
Susan(Endicott) 122
Lowery, Mary A[Hite] 228
Lowman, Catherine[Francis]
100
Loyd, Greth J. 118
Joseph H. 118, 228
Phoebe A(English) 118
William 118, 228
Lucas, Sarah[Wilson] 184
Ludiker, Gerhard 137
Ludlow, Elizabeth J[Gentry]
106
Lurton, Charles F. 132
Lutes, F.C. 151
Wilson B. 151
Luyster, Elizabeth[Hamilton]
155
Lydic, Catherine[Childers]
105
Lydick, Andrew 87
Harriet(Wilson) 108
Sally A(Fisher) 106
Lyle, Benjamin F. 49
John 49
Mary(Phillips) 49
Lynam, J.S. 228
Lynch, Delilah[Turner] 228
Lynn, Dann 100
Elizabeth[Early] 55
Lyon, Mary J[Anderson] 228
Lyons, Deborah[Garner] 81
Harvey S. 155
Jane(Vanarsdall) 155, 156
John M. 155
Robert 155
Lytle, Nancy 149

McAtee, Daniel 228
McAuley, Jane[McIntosh] 106
McBride, Julia F[Eddy] 126
McCallie, Annie[Selby] 123

M'Callister, Jesse 91
McCammon, Eliza J[Stillwell]
228
Hugh 128
McCane, Mary[Richardson] 58
McCart, Benjamin 228
McCarthy, Mary[Buselman] 37
McCartney, Margaret 228
McCarty, George M. 152
Sophia(Bentley) 152
William T. 152
McCaslin, Alexander 155
Allen 181
David 155, 181
Mary(Marrs) 181
Polly(Sellers) 183
McClain, Alexander 166
Catherine(Lacefield) 181
Elizabeth(Caldwell) 166
Francis P. 166
Jacob 181
James 181
Thomas 228
McClary, James 111
John 58, 111
Margaret 111
McClaskey, James 228
McClellan, Elizabeth(Cline)
228
Elizabeth[Line] 58
James H. 188
Jane 58
Joel C. 228
Joseph 58
Robert 58
William 188, 228
McClelland, Sarah[Cunningham]
29
McClennahan, Mary A[Morris]
92
McClery, Elizabeth[Watts] 228
McClintock, Elizabeth[McKee]
20
Joseph 228
Louise(Stipp) 20
Rebecca(Holliday) 123
Thomas 166, 228
William H. 228
McCluer, Samuel 33
McClure, C.W.H. 83
David F. 81
Elenor[Sharp] 124
Elizabeth(Carter) 179
Elizabeth[Ellsberry] 58
Elizabeth[McKee] 59
Jane 27
Jane(Curry) 207
John 27
Louisa[Steele] 228
Margaret[Holmes] 228
Martha 228
Martha J. 27
Mary[Johnson] 83
Phoebe(Eads) 123
Samuel 33, 189, 228
Sarah(Curry) 188
Teressa(Gudgell) 228
William 123
McCollins, Narcissus[Rice]228
McCollum, Elizabeth[Jones]97
John 228
McCone, Irene(Nelson)24
James 24
William P. 24
McConkey, Archibald 58
Daniel 58
McConnel, Ann(Bain) 27

McConnell, Elizabeth(Corbin)
135
James H. 100, 228
McCook, Nancy[Strange] 181
McCool, Joseph 104
Margaret(Baker) 104
William 104
McCord, J.A. 229
John 149
Samuel H. 229
William R. 144
McCorkill, Bryson 106
William F. 106
McCorkle, Abraham 111
Mathew S. 229
McCormick, Andrew 181
Christina(Brentlinger)200
John 181
Maria J(Perry) 143
Martha J(Todd) 181
Mary A(Brush) 179
Phillip 229
Preston 181
McCoun, Arabella[Clay] 86
McCowan, Elizabeth[Crews]229
McCoy, A.H. 229
Anna[Lee] 149
Anna[Piatt] 19
Charlotte 58
Isaiah 115
James B. 58
Jane[Hamilton] 165
Jesse C. 166
John 116, 229
Joseph 58
Lucinda(Aust) 196
Marinda(Kelsey) 189
Mary 116
Nancy 58
Nancy(Waple) 115
Stark 189
William 115
William W. 83
Willis 116
Willis F. 189
McCracken, Elizabeth(Gillas-
pie) 213
James 229
John 229
S.W. 58
Sally(Meek) 229
McCray, Fleming 87
Rebecca(Hedges) 87
Samuel 87
William 89
McCrosky, James 58
McCullin, David 149
Elizabeth 149
Mary[Brookie] 149
McCulloch, Druzilla(Morgan)
229
William 229
William M. 229
McCullough, Eleanor[Tilford]
178
Eliza[Sorrell] 18
F.B. 159
Margaret 229
McCune, Isaac 136
James 136, 229
Keziah 229
Kirich(Dean) 136
McCutchen, Joseph 33
McDaniel, Catherine[Mann]47
Elizabeth[Allen] 152
Harvey 174
John 174, 229

McDaniel(cont.)
  John T. 163
  John W. 163
  Martha 174
  Spencer 174
  Susan(Anderson) 163
  Unia E(Littlejohn) 174
  William 149
McDermitt, Katherine[Walden]
  125
McDonald, Anne[Yeager] 98
  Catherine(Vannest) 155
  Daniel 155
  David 88
  Eleanor[May] 141
  James 155
  James A. 166
  Jennie[Turpin] 192
  Preston 163
  Robert 229
  Sallie H[Blanchard] 129
  Sarah[Baird] 185
  Sarah[Berry] 229
  William 33
McDougal, Stephen 59
McDowel, Elizabeth[Utterback]
  128
McDowell, John A. 45
  Margaret[McIndoo] 181
  Mary[Starling] 45
McDuffie, Polly M[Taylor] 59
  Robert 123
  Robert G. 123
  Sarah(Taylor) 123
McElfresh, Abigail 229
  Samuel 229
McEntee, James A. 38
  Maria(McKean) 38
  Patrick 38
McFadin, Fannie T[Montgomery]
  132
McFarland, Benjamin 97, 229
  Green 104
  Jane[McCullom] 229
  John A. 192
  Mary[McCullom] 229
  Nancy(Winkler) 192
  Presley 192
McFerran, Lucinda(Hendricks)
  141, 229
  Marion W. 141, 229
  Thomas 141, 229
McGary, Harrison 229
McGaughey, Michael 229
McGee, William 59
McGhee, Annie[Story] 112
McGill, Isabella[Perigo]169
McGillicuddy, Tim D. 35
McGinnis, Abigail(Booth)199
  Dulcina[Moore] 92
  Elisha 229
  John 88
  Joseph T. 229
  Lucinda(Buris) 86
  Margaret 59
  Mary(Houston) 88
  Reuben 88
  Samuel 166, 229
  Sarah(Earlewine) 210
  William 166
  William F. 229
McGowan, Christina[Kemp]229
  D.J.(Ramsey) 191
  David 174
  Delila J(Ramsay) 191
  J.W. 191
  Mary(Haynes) 191
  Samuel 174

William J. 191
McGown, John 163
McGravin, H. 132
McGregory, Alexander 38
  Rachel(Willoughby) 38
McGrew, Rebecca[Miller] 185,
  229
McGuire, Edward 193
  Elizabeth(Stagg) 124
  Lydia[Gillaspy] 100
  Sarah[Thompson] 229
McHaley, William 229
McHargue, Andrew 139
  James 139
  Phebe 139
McHatteon, Betsey[Junken] 80
McHenry, Elizabeth[Kehoe] 38
  George A. 229
  Mary[Moore] 133
McIlvain, James 106
  Margaret[Craig] 122
  Moses 59
  Samuel 59
  Sarah(Black) 53
McIndoo, Jacob 181
  John 181
  Margaret(McDowell) 181
McIntire, Phoebe[Bruce] 229
McIntosh, A.B. 19
  Ann C. 19
  David 106
  Jane(McAuley) 106
  William J. 19
  William R. 19
McIntyre, Amanda[Butcher]229
  Sarah[Netherland] 99
Mack, Martha(Brenton) 200
McKay, Alexander 80
  Celia A[Houghton] 148
  George 80
  John 132
  William H. 95
Macke, Bernard 38
  Margaret(Weber) 38
  William 38
McKean, Maria[McEntee] 38
McKee, Agnes[Scott] 20
  Agnes[Wilson] 116
  Elizabeth(McClintock) 20,
  59
  John 20, 59
  Joseph 229
  Louise(Stipps) 63
  Lucinda[Bartlett] 197
  Nancy A[Hollingsworth] 229
  Samuel 107
  William 20, 59
McKeen, Benjamin 230
McKenney, Sarah[Thrailkell]
  230
McKenzie, Charles 166
McKeown, Leah[Malott] 133
  Leah P[Malott] 133
McKewen, Eliza A[Pottorff]
  133
McKim, Florence 19
  Gordon F. 19
  William F.19
McKinley, Catherine[Gray]
  230
  Mary[Russell] 186
  Mary A[Ringo] 230
McKinney, D.J. 176
  Esther 107
  James 107
  James W. 107
  M.J. 185
  Thomas R. 107, 230

William 174
MacKinnon, Sarah[Taylor]44
McKittrick, Rebecca[Lindley]
  107
McKnight, James 230
  Mary[Washburn] 47
McKown, Leah[Malott] 133
  Leah P[Malott] 132
McKoy, Elizabeth(Hardia)
  38, 59
  Harry B. 38
  John 38, 59
  Margaret C(Brent) 38
  W.H. 38, 59
  William H. 38
McKune, Isabel[Harris] 163
McLain, Archibald 119
  James 119
  John 230
  Rhoda(Dewey) 119
McLane, Elizabeth(VanZant)
  177
  Robert 177
  William 177
McLary, Hugh A. 230
McLaughlin, Samuel F. 143
  Susan(Reaves) 143
  Thomas 143
McLean, Sarah E[Blakey] 142
McLeland, Esther(Benefiel)
  100
  Robert 100
  William E. 100
McLoed, George 88
  Katie(Miller) 88
  Oliver 230
McLeod, Ingels 59
  Susannah[Wasson] 90
McMahan, Jesse L. 92
McMains, Robert 230
McMaken, John 59
McManis, George 59
McManus, Mary[Glover] 80
McMichael, Agnes(Kerr) 44
  James M. 44
  Polly[Easton] 49
  William 44
McMillen, George O. 22
  Martha 22
McMullen, Catherine[Archer]
  230
McMurrays, Mary(Hurst) 24
  Robert 24
  William J. 24
McMurtry, Alexander 117
  John S. 117
  Joseph A. 80
  Louisa(Perkins) 80
  Mary[Gregg] 177
  Polly(Smith) 117
  Samuel B. 80
McNab, Cassandra(Evans) 210
  Henry 230
  Jane[Stackhouse] 95
McNary, John 149
  John W. 149
  Sarah 149
  Sarah A(Applegate) 146
McNaught, Catherine(Bar-
  tholomew) 197
McNeely, Sallie[Barnett]
  142
McNeill, David G. 22
  Harriet(Lay) 22
  James 22
McNelly, William 59
McNight, Alexander 22
  Augustus M. 22

McOuat, Janette(Lockerbie)
107
Robert L. 107
Thomas 107
McOust, Robert L. 107
McPharson, Margaret[Hyatt]
149
McPherson, Jame W[Cowan] 59
Mary K[Bremer] 130
McQueen, Mary[Thomas] 140
McQuaid, Fannie[Bartlett]
230
McQuinn, Elizabeth(Coons)
170
Jeptha 170
Ezekiel 170
Martin 230
McRae, Louisa A[Poulter] 155
McRoberts, Artemus 141, 230
William 59
McShirley, Catherine[Conway]
147
McStead, Elizabeth[Gulkins]
31
McTaggart, Catherine 230
McTeer, Isabel[Hodge] 46
McTerren, Margaret[Hyatt]149
McWilliams, John C. 144
Nancy(Hockaday) 144
R.C. 144
Madchen, Lydia[Williamson]
84
Madden, Lydia[Williamson] 84
Maddox, Delilah[Todd] 182
Elijah 182
Emily(Todd) 182
John W. 230
Martha(Beaucham) 185
Martha[Long] 185
Nelson 185
Maddux, Alexander 152
Thomas 152
Magee, R.S. 38
Magill, John 230
Mathew 230
Magruder, John 96
Levi 96
Mary(Straney) 96
Maguire, Douglas 107
Mahan, Caroline[Branson] 230
Isaac 111
James 149
Jemima(Browning) 149, 230
Jeremiah 230
Jerry 149
John 59
John R. 111
Margaret(Knight) 111
Nary[Read] 230
Mahin, John 149
Mahoney, Fielding 127
Marly[Fisher] 230
Mahorney, Morgan D. 230
Makemson, John 33
Margaret(Lindsey) 58
Nancy(Huber) 59
Thomas 59
Mallory, Edie[Raff] 95
Lucy[Hoagland] 27
Mallott, Hiram 132
Leah P(McKeown) 132
Leah P(McKown) 132
Volney T. 132
William 132
William H. 132
Malone, Elizabeth[Lockridge]
159

Malott, Benjamin 132
Elijah 132
Hiram 132
James H. 132
Leah(McKeown) 133
Leah(McKown) 133
Maria[Batman] 132
Mary(Hawes) 132
Michael A. 132
Sarah[Coburn] 132
Manchester, Amanda[Dye] 230
Hiram 230
Manley, Delia[Baker] 230
Mann, Catherine(McDaniel)47
Elizabeth(Schooling) 155,
230
George 47
Jacob 47
James B. 137, 155, 230
Josiah 155, 230
Josiah T. 155
Margaret[Bobbitt] 59
Nancy[Devore] 92
Nancy[Waddle] 49
Rachel[Stone] 23
Mannen, Louisiana[Broadwell]
44
Nancy[Newcomb] 44
Manners, George 155
James 155
Letice(Hight) 155
Manning, B.P. 149
Frank R. 149
Lettie(Horton) 149
Manser, Edna A[Kinkead] 38
Mansfield, William 230
Maple, John 88
Mappin, Rebecca[Powell] 230
March, Aletha[Howard] 231
Mark, James 27
Nancy(Vankirk) 20
Markley, Susan[Kenton] 57
Marks, Elizabeth[Halbert]
162
James 163
Marksberry, Mary[Crandell]
116
Marlay, Susan[Kincheloe]151
Marlow, Alphonso B. 177
George 177
Mary(Reid) 177
William 231
Marmaduke, Milton 149
Marrs, Mary[McCaslin] 181
Urban 143
Urbin 143
Marsh, Abi(North) 115
George W. 115
Sophia[Wood] 88
William 115
Marshall, Ambrose 231
Elizabeth(Glass) 111
Hannah[Preble] 231
Hugh 59
Isom 231
Jane 59
Jesse 59
John G. 107
John W. 120
Joseph G. 111
Margaret(Hughes) 120
Martin, A.C. 182
Abner 182
Absalom 38
Anna[Evins] 81
Cliff E. 38
Edmund W. 182

Elizabeth[Holliday] 123
Elizabeth[Lamme] 59
Elizabeth[Long] 193
Elizabeth(Randall) 127
Enoch 231
Henry 59
J.M. 141
Jane[Lane] 231
John 231
Jonathan J. 182
Joseph C. 127
Joseph W. 231
Lewis 182
Lucy[Scroggan] 231
Manoah 182
Maria[Johnson] 231
Mary[Fitch] 21
Mary(White) 182
Mary A(Wayman) 182
Moses H. 136
Patsy[Martin] 231
Philip 137
Rachel(Campbell) 42
Robert 111
Sarah(Singleton) 136
Sophia[Gegelbach] 99
Thomas 231
William 182
William C. 127
William D. 231
William E. 136
Martindale, Elizabeth(Boyd)
144
Margaret[Long] 231
Marting, Henry 32
Henry A. 32
Mary E(Knaper) 32
Marvin, Jesse 149
Marymee, L.W. 96
Mason, Anthony S. 190
Christopher J. 169
Edwin 144
Elizabeth(Jackson) 169
James 190
John 231
John H. 169
Lincoln 231
Mary[Wheat] 231
Nancy J. 144
Rankin 231
Rebecca[Allison] 96
Rebecca(Sandusky) 190
William F. 231
William M. 144, 231
Massey, Elizabeth[Ranard]
174, 231
Rachel[Disbrow] 231
Massie, A.W. 101
Charles E. 101
Elizabeth[McCulla] 231
Henry 59
James B. 123
Kate 102
Nathaniel 59
Salestine(Ford) 101
Susan B(Thompson) 63
Masters, Elizabeth(Fowler)
212
Masterson, Dorcas[Louden]34
Julia[Sudwell] 231
Matchet, Polly[Wilson] 113
Mateer, Isabel[Hodge] 46
Matheny, Francis A. 231
Matherly, Frances M. 138
Henry B. 138
Melvina P(Miller) 138
Mathers, Elizabeth[Ham] 86

Mathers(cont.)
  James 88
  Jane(Ardrey) 88
  Thomas N. 88
Mathes, J.M. 231
  John 182
Mathews, Richard 231
Mathis, Frederick W. 120
  John 188
  Mary(Warden) 188
  William 188
Matthews, Claude 81
  Eliza A(Fletcher) 81
  Polly[Young] 231
  Thomas A. 81
Mattingly, Henry 231
  James 149
  Thomas 231
Maurer, Wilhelmina[Morehead]
  125
Mauzy, Hannah[Browne] 88
  William 88
Mavity,Keziah(Evans) 211
Mawzy, Lucinda[Pattison] 88
Maxwell, Mary E[Pattie] 169
  John 88
May, Anna[Parris] 101
  David 141
  Eleanor(McDanald) 141
  George 232
  George A. 232
  Jacob 141
  James G. 141
  Maria 104
  Matilda[Miller] 99
  William 104
  William T. 104
Mayfield, Amelia 182
  Catesby J. 182
  Clarinda[Hendricks] 232
  Francis 188
  Francis F. 188
  Jane(Buchanan) 174
  Jeptha 232
  John C. 174
  Joshua 188, 232
  Lucinda(Ouseley) 188
  Pleasant W. 174
  Southerland 182
  W.C. 232
Mayhall, John B. 232
  Mahala[Turpin] 232
  William 232
Mays, Anna[Kirkpatrick] 123
Maze, Maragaret[Titus] 107
  Thomas 88
Meadley, Martha[Ganoe] 232
Meadows, Elizabeth[Hornaday]
  232
Means, Edward 133
  Elizabeth[Myers] 133
  J.H. 159
  Sarah 133
Medcalf, Elizabeth[Myers]
  133
  J.H. 159
  Sarah 133
Meder, Mary A[Widerin] 135
Meek, Edwin 232
  John 123, 232
  Joseph 232
  Lavina[Cromwell] 232
  Rachel 232
  Samuel 123
Mefford, Thomas 44
Megee, Mary A[Ensminger]232
Megenity, James L. 127

Meharry, Sarah(Wood) 64
Mehne, Barbara(Price) 232
  John 232
Mehringer, Elizabeth[Betz]
  198
Meike, Hugh F. 133
  Margaret(Fulton) 133
  Thomas 133
Mellin, Fredericka 133
Melton, Martha[Wilson] 232
Meldrumm, Charlotte[Hartwell]
  131
Menaugh, John L. 185
Menefee, Elizabeth A[Walker]
  232
Menzies, Gustavus 83
  Sally(Winslow) 83
  Samuel G. 83
Mercer, Rebecca[Payne] 186
Meredith, Harriet(Davis) 111
  James W. 111
  William R. 111
Meriwether, Caroline[Reay]
  133
Merrett, Reuben 149
  Sarah(Helm) 149
  William 149
Merritt, Judith[Polloch] 133
Metcalf, A.F. 104
  Thomas S. 107
Metcalfe, J.J. 166
  Lucy C[Ogden] 22
Metesser, Lewis 188
Metzger, Anna M(DePrez) 133
  Peter 133
  Silas 133
Meyers, Louisa[Stucky] 134
  Mary[Hite] 59
  Nancy[Power] 22
Michael, Rebecca(Johnson) 57
Middleton, Susan[Thompson]59
Miers, Sarah[Risinger] 133
Milam, Ambrose 232
  Henry R. 232
Milburn, Francis 232
  Jonathan 155
  Mary(Inman) 232
  Richard F. 232
Mile, Sarah[Weddle] 232
Miles, Elhanan 182
  Franklin 232
  Isaac 193
  James 182
  John L. 188
  Martha[Fitzsimmons] 180
  Nathan 107
  Rebecca(Davis) 207
  Samuel 232
  Susan(Simmons) 182
Miley, Mary[Harrell] 232
Miller, Aaron 123
  Abigail[Leach] 232
  Amy(Cox) 206
  B.W. 233
  Barbara(Fried) 140
  C.I. 233
  Catherine(Frank) 212
  D.L. 169
  David 186, 233
  Elizabeth 233
  Elizabeth(Hanson) 59
  Elizabeth[Hardins] 181
  Elizabeth(Miller) 158
  Ephraim 127
  Francis 127
  Francis M. 233
  George 233

H.W. 140
Hamilton 149
Harvey 182
Henry 177
J. 133
Jacob 140, 233
James 107, 149, 182
James F. 233
Jemima(Allen) 127
John 111, 177
John W. 233
Katie[McLoed] 88
Louisa J[Hufford] 233
Lucy[Ramsey] 101
Margaret 177
Mary 101
Mary[Morris] 177
Matilda[Potter] 233
Melvina P[Matherly] 138
Michael 101
Milton M. 59
Nancy 158
Nancy(Lee) 182
Nancy(Robinson) 149
Nicholas 234
Phebe[Clem] 126
Phebe[Frank] 94
Rebecca[Burris] 165
Rebecca(Cox) 139
Polly (Ravencroft) 123
Rebecca(McGrew) 185
Robert 59, 177
Sallie[Cooper] 168
Samuel 59
Sarah[Farr[233
Sarah[Weakley] 178
Sarah[Wolfe] 178
Thomas 20, 123
William 59. 111
Millison, Lucinda[Berry] 129
Millon, Lucinda[Berry] 133
Mills, Abner C. 59
  Benjamin 233
  Ellen(Spencer) 95
  Frances[Colt] 137
  Harriet[Sweet] 112
  James 29
  Jane(Dale) 29
  John A. 233
  Lewis D. 111
  Mary A[Daugherty] 233
  Thomas 29
Milner, Isaac L. 94
  Mary A(Wilkerson) 94
  Patrick D. 94
Milton, Abigail[Throop] 167
Milus, Chris 24
  Jacob 24
  Louisa 24
Miner, Rhoda[Moore] 97
Minery, Jane[Standley] 89
Minor, John 91
  John W. 91
  Mary E[Benson] 172
  Polly(Owens) 91
Minter, Lucy 59
  Melinda(Pinkston) 107
  William 182, 234
Minton, Mary[Buchanan] 105
Miranda, Isaac 92
  Jonathan 92
Mitchell, Aaron 233
  Alfred 83
  Alvira[Carnahan] 48
  Andrew 127
  B.H. 127
  Benjamin 83

Mitchell(cont.)
  C. Garnett 83
  Cassandra(Biddle) 93
  Dorcas(Hardwick) 127
  Elijah 59
  Elizabeth(Coleman) 204
  Elizabeth(Harmon) 233
  Enfield(Ralls) 159
  Harriet[Williams] 184
  Hugh 59
  James L. 182
  Jane[Graham] 214
  John F. 159
  Lewis 59
  Lucy[Graves] 52
  Mary[Givens] 43
  Mary(Lincoln) 24
  Mary A(Ketcham) 182
  P.L.D. 182
  P. Lincoln 24
  Paul 233
  Pleasant L.D. 182
  Richard 78
  Richard H. 24
  Robert 233
  Robert H. 24
  Solomon 94
  Thomas 233
  Thomas V. 78
  Vincit 59
  William 159
Moberly, Julia(Barnes) 144
  Martha(Robertson) 144
  Thomas 144
  William 144
Mobley, C.W. 101
  Elizabeth(Burton) 101
  Walter E. 101
Moenkhaus, Charles 133
  Frederica(Ramsbrok) 133
  William 133
Moffatt, Mary[Scott] 36
Moffet, J.W. 104
Moffett, George 52
  James D. 52
Mogan, Michael 152
Mollenkamp, M. 133
Monahan, Catherine(Dudley)55
Monk, Simon S. 80
Monroe, Ann[Anderson] 107
  David P. 170
  Dora V. 138
  William 173
  William Y. 170
Montgomery, Eleanor[Lindsay]
  177
  Elizabeth[Steers] 178
  Fannie T(McFadin) 132
  James 233
  John 111
  John R. 233
  Joseph 177
  Kate(Brownlee) 201
  Margaret[Green] 233
  Martha[Lewis] 24
  Mary A(Daugherty) 78
  Polly(Donovan) 111
  Rebecca(Donovan) 88
  William 177
  William A. 88
  William R. 111
  Zachariah 88
Monyhan, Henry 133
  Nancy(Bateman) 133
  Turn 133
Mooar, Cornelia(Moore) 24
  Luke M. 24

  W. Emerson 24
Moody, Mary[Ballard] 179
Moore, Alexander 97
  Amanda(Sellers) 139
  Betsey(Todd) 107
  Christiana[Coon] 60
  Cornelia[Mooar] 24
  Daniel 127
  Dulcina(McGinnis) 92
  Eleven 133
  Elizabeth 20
  Elizabeth(Roberts) 127
  Elizabeth(Tyler) 133
  Esther[Chamberlain] 97
  Eveline[Pierce] 176
  Ida N[Wheatcraft] 115
  Jackson L. 139
  James 107
  John 92, 107, 115
  John H. 133
  John W. 133
  Joseph 133
  Josephine(Krutz) 115
  Joshua 233
  Lee 233
  Leonora[Coffin] 37
  M. 60
  Martha T(Elliott) 193
  Mary(Law) 233
  Mary(McHenry) 133
  Melinda[Davis] 153
  Nathaniel 107
  Prudence[Arnold] 129
  Rhoda(Miner) 97
  Sarah(Fitzpatrick) 144
  Sarah(Goslin) 110
  Sarah[Wilkerson] 64
  Sarah E[Blair] 129
  T.S. 144
  Uriah 139
  Walker 139
  Wilford W. 92
  William 20, 111, 127
Moorhead, George A. 125
  James 125
  Wilhelmina(Maurer) 125
Moreland, Agnes[Dills] 233
  Matilda[Conduitt] 187
Morgan, Emiline[Hatfield]
  103
  Jesse 149
  John D. 166
  John S. 190
  John T. 82, 127
  Lorilda(Turman) 82
  Preston 127
  Rhoda 127
  William C. 82
  William H. 233
Morris, Austin W. 88
  Benjamin W. 38
  David 38
  Emily J[Beard] 144
  John B. 38
  John D. 166
  John P. 92
  Joseph 60, 136
  Joseph R. 136
  Levina(Drake) 60
  Mary(Beacham) 177
  Mary(Cummings) 88
  Mary(Miller) 177
  Mary A(McClennahan) 92
  Mary H. 177
  Mary T[Bryant] 103
  Morris 166, 88
  Rachel 166

  Sarah(Funk) 38
  Sarah(Rodman) 136
  Theodore 177
  Thomas A. 166
  Thomas B. 92
  William 88, 177
Morrison, Andrew 88
  Dorcas[Hurd] 57
  I.N. 111
  James 111
  James H. 57
  John 166
  Joseph 111
  Leander 88
  Sally 166
  Sally A[McClary] 111
  William 166
Morrow, Thomas 25
  Thomas V. 25
  William 88
Morton, Elizabeth[Coots] 179
  Elizabeth[Dearing] 208
  Jane 60
  Joab 60
  John 60
  N. 91
Mosby, Frances[Wilhoit] 194
  Isabella[Anderson] 233
Mosley, B.C. 143
Moss, Charles W. 186
  Elizabeth S[Hord] 148
  George 182, 186
  Jacob B. 182
  Lydia(Vuilderback) 182,
  186
  William H. 234
Mothershead, Alvin 172
  John L. 177
  Nathaniel 177
  Sarah E[Graves] 83, 172
Mount, Elizabeth P(Woodward)
  182
  Letitia[Schwindler] 183
  Lucinda(Fulenwider) 180
  Matthias 182
  P.J. 182
  William 234
Mounts, D.A. 152
  Garrarad 234
  Isabella(Smith) 62
  Mary[Cave] 46
  Providence 60
  William 60
Moxley, Joseph 50
Mugg, Fannie K(Fidler) 211
  John 234
  William 234
Mulkey, Polly[Harland] 158
Mull, Annie(Stites) 141
  David 141
Mullen, Catherine[Stafford]
  234
Mundell, James 234
Murdock, Archie C. 115
  Christopher C. 115
  Elizabeth M[Gates] 234
  Mary J(Winters) 115
Murgrave, Benjamin 143
Murlin, Ann[Upton] 33
  Daniel 32
  John A. 32
  Sally 32
  Susanna 32
Murphey, Kanlum 234
  Mary A.C[Sims] 234
  Nancy(Sicklesworth) 234
  Thomas 234

Murphy, Aaron 234
  Winnie[Rowland] 102
  Nancy[Johnson] 234
Murray, Carrie R[Willan]124
  Charles D. 118
  Dennis 133
  Ellen(Allison) 133
  Jeremiah 149
  Malinda(Steele) 149
  Margaret(Coughlin) 133
  Mary[Harris] 133
  T.C. 133
  W.T. 149
Musgrave, Benjamin 161, 234
  Rebecca(Davis) 161
  Samuel 161
Musselman, Henry 234
  Rebecca(Smyser) 171
Myers, Abram 60
  Catherine(Cooper) 159
  Elizabeth 60
  Elizabeth[Dodd] 106
  Elizabeth(Means) 133
  Hannah(Salisbury) 140
  Henry 140
  Hiram 159
  Isabella(White) 32
  John 234
  John A. 32
  John S. 140
  John T. 60
  John W. 32
  Lewis 159
  Lucinda[Jones] 110
  Sarilda[Camp] 111
  Thomas 234

Napier, Henry C. 163
  James B. 163
  Sally A(Jewell) 163
Nash, Marvel W. 234
Nation, Jemima(Harrison)117
  Wesley 117
  William K. 117
Nave, Elizabeth[Woodard]234
  Solomon 234
Nay, Asa B. 170
  Eusebia N. 170
  Lucinda(Whitesider) 170
Nayles, Elizabeth[Hendrick-
    son] 155
Naylor, Charles B. 234
  James 44
  Samuel 44
Neal, Annie(Turpin) 89
  Asa 234
  Benjamin 30
  Charles W. 88
  Emma S(Bradley) 88
  George W. 234
  J. 30
  Lucy A(Wells) 234
  Mary(Sellers) 30
  Matilda[Wilson] 234
  Moses H. 136
  Nathaniel 88
  Rebecca[Amos] 85
  Richard 60
  Robert H. 234
  Sallie(Sandusky) 88
  Tavner 88
  William M. 136
Neff, Elizabeth(Kenton) 91
  Frank 91
  John 91
  Leonard 60
  Michael 60

Willis G. 91
Neil, Robert 26
Neiles, James 111
  Sarah 111
Nelson, Charles 234
  Elias 234
  Elizabeth[Farrow] 159
  Emilia(Cruse) 206
  Frances(Doniphan) 149
  Franklin P. 159
  Irene[McCone] 24
  James 234
  James I. 159
  James L. 159
  John J. 234
  Joseph A. 234
  Lucy[Sallee] 62
  Margaret H[Ridge] 146
  Nelly(Crouch) 234
  Pauline(Yeates) 159
  Thomas H. 149
  Thomas W. 149
  William N. 44
Nesbit, John 88, 234
  John J. 234
  Joseph A. 234
  Mary 234
  William O. 234
Netherland, Christian P. 99
  Joseph H. 99
  Sarah(McIntyre) 99
New, Elizabeth(Claxon) 172
  John C. 172
  William J. 172
Newby, Edmund 174
  Granville 174
  Mary(Tumbleson) 174
Newcomb, Charlotte(Nolan) 60
  J.C. 44
  James 44
  Nancy(Mannen) 44
  Rachel[Spurgeon] 176
Newell, Ann[Craig] 122
  Jane(Braden) 33
  Margaret 33
Newkirk, Cassandra[Applegate]
    129
  Melinda[Briley] 235
Newland, John H.B. 113
Newlon, Nancy 235
  Richard 235
  William 235
Newton, J.A. 161
Nicholas, John 235
Nichols, Elizabeth[Rice]
    96, 192
  Martha M[Babbitt] 119
  Matilda[Bennett] 42
  Nancy(Gresham) 190
  Nathan 190
  Noah 96
  Polly[Hall] 180
  Thomas 163
Nicholson, Abigail[Caldwell]
    235
  Benjamin 136
  D.D. 136
  David D. 136
  Edward W. 235
  Isaac J. 88
  James 235
  Jemima(Stars) 136
  Jesse C. 235
  Samuel 60
  William 235
Nickell, Joseph B. 235
Nix, Elizabeth[Harrison]
    94

Nixon, John S. 38
  Mary(Clemens) 38
  William D. 38
Noble, George 138
  George T. 83, 84
  Louisa(Canby) 83, 84
  Noah E. 83
  Rosamond(Johnson) 27
  Samuel C. 84
  Thomas 138
  Thomas B. 84
  Thomas H. 27
  Thomas S. 27
Noel, William T. 234
Nolan, Charlotte[Newcomb] 60
  Edward J. 38
  Ellen(Daniels) 38
  James 38
Noland, William 144
Norman, James G. 186
  Thomas 92
Norris, Catherine(Brightwell)
    92
  Edward 92
  Norris J. 92
  Phebe[Garrison] 235
  William R. 92
Noland, William 144
Norman, James G. 186
  Thomas 92
North, Abi[Marsh] 115
  Martha 60
Northcott, John 235
Northcutt, George 60
  Runyan 60
  Ruth(Taylor) 60
  Shadrick 60
Nourse, Charles 163
  Joseph W. 163
  Rosanna(Logan) 163
Nowels, John 235
Nowland, Matthia T. 113
Nowlin, Martha E(Pride) 235
  Silas 235
  Zachariah 235
Nutgrass, James 182
  Mary(Page) 182
  Nancy[Collings] 179
  William 182
Nutt, Aaron 60
  Abigail 60
  Ann 60
  Bethesda 60
  Levi 60
  Mary 60
  Michael(Archer) 60
  Moriah 60
  Sarah 60
Nutter, Clement H. 107
  Hewitt 107
  John 107
  Mary E[Beatty] 27
  Susan(Talbot) 107
Nye, Catherine(Oyler) 36

Oakerson, Elizabeth(Todd)235
  John 235
  William 235
Oard, Diana[Teegardin] 60
O'Bannon, Presley N. 235
  John 235
  William 235
O'Bryan, Sylvester 234
Offutt, Charles G. 177
  Elizabeth 177
  Lloyd 177

Ogden, Frances(Threlkeld)92
  Henry 22
  Henry T. 22
  James W. 92
  John 92
  Lucy C(Metcalfe) 22
Oglesby, Samuel D. 133
O'Hair, James E.M. 157
  Michael 159
Oldfield, Sarah[Cretcher]54
Oldham, Joses 235
  O.D. 80
Oliver, Agnes H[Wishard]
  107, 167
  Catherine J(Gardner) 162
  Dandridge H. 127
  Nancy[Stone] 101
Olleman, Ezra A. 155
  James 155
  Mary(Tsinger) 155
Ollis, Ellen[Marshall] 235
O'Neal, George 19
  Sarah(Sleet) 19
  Wenden 19
O'Neall, Martha A(Salle) 52
Ooley, John H. 235
Orewiler, Adam 60
Orme, Moses 140
  Nicholas 140
Ormes, Charles 140
  Moses 140
O'Rourke, Catherine[Conroy]
  32
Orr, John 166
  Nancy[Saxon] 166
  Susan 166
Ortblieb, Catherine 24
  Constance 24
  William L. 24
Osborn, David 60
  Eleanor[Crosby] 235
  John 235
  Lurana[Cox] 171
  M. 235
  Sarah[Brissey] 171
  Sarah[Cooper] 235
  Silas 235
  Thomas 235
Osborne, Elizabeth[Dodd] 235
  Isaiah 235
  M[Strode] 96
Osburn, John 163
  Sallie(Gardner) 163
  Thomas 163
Osmon, Philip W. 235
Ouseley, Lucinda[Mayfield]
  188, 235
Overstreet, Aaron 99
  Gabriel M. 170
  James 99
  Laurena M[Shirley] 171
  Nancy[Alverson] 116
  Nancy[Yager] 171
  Susan 99
Overture, James 235
Owen, Abraham B. 129
  Abraham M. 129
  Frances(Driskel) 99
  H.C. 144
  Henry C. 144
  Horatio 101
  John E. 129
  Jonathan 174
  Margaret(Sears) 101
  Rebecca[Short] 174
  Sallie[Hearne] 20
  William 99, 144, 174

  William L. 99
Owens, Andrew 191
  John 159
  Kate(Tyree) 175
  Mary(Ewen) 159
  Mary[Preston] 61
  Nancy[Williams] 175
  Owen W. 191
  Polly[Minor] 91
  Robert N. 175
  Sarah(Brown) 191
  Virginia[White] 45
  William 175, 235
  William B. 159
  William W. 149
Oyler, Catherine[Nye] 36

Pace, B.T. 159
  Beverly T. 80
  Harriet L(Whitlow) 80
  J.W. 102
  Joseph W. 80
Paddock, Ebenezer 236
Padgett, Permelia A[Scifres]
  121
Page, Elizabeth[Cunningham]
  143
  Hannah(Jones) 33
  James C. 33
  Jonathan 33
  Lafayette F. 78
  Mary(Irving) 78
  Mary[Nutgrass] 182
  Robert 78
Painter, Isaac 236
  Mary A. 236
Palsey, Ann[Plough] 145
Palmer, Permelia(Higgs) 127
  Truman H. 127
  William 127
Parent, David 120
  Jane(Aubrey) 120
Parido, Charles W. 26
  Mary H. 26
  William 26
Paris, James H. 88
  Rhoda[Harrison] 181
  Sarah[Harrison] 181
  Sarah(Peoples) 88
  Stephen 88
Parish, Charles J. 155
  Eliza A(Seths) 155
  Mary R[Courtney] 155
Park, Sarah[Boyll] 185
  Sarah E[Adams] 105
Parker, Hattie[Laffoon] 35
  Barthenia F(Dodds) 209
  James D. 19
  Jane Z[Smith] 111
  L.P. 129
  Nancy[Pratt] 236
  Nancy(Stanton) 129
  Nancy[Toner] 236
  Orene 28
  P.C. 32
  Richard 19
  Robert 236
  Sallie(Hogan) 19
  Thomas 129
  William 20
Parkhurst, Daniel 236
  John 182
Parkison, John 236
Parks, Charity 60
  Charity(Runyan) 80
  Curtis 80

  Elizabeth(Hughes) 88
  George 60
  J.O. 236
  James 88
  James O. 88, 236
  L.F. 35
  Samuel 60, 80
Parmer, Isaac 236
  James 236
  Sarah(Wishard) 236
Parris, Anna(May) 101
  Berry 101
  James 101
Parrish, Edmond 145
Parvin, Ann[McDoughty] 37
Paten, Susan[Ross] 127
Patrick, Elizabeth L[Powell] 82
Pattan, James 50
Patten, Margaret[McCorkle]
  236
Patterson, A.F. 92
  Alexander L. 98
  Anderson 92
  Catherine 28
  Eliza[Kelly] 107
  Eliza A(Beatty) 105
  Evan L. 92, 150
  Frances(Harris) 87
  J. 84
  Jefferson 28
  Mary[Dicks] 147
  Rebecca[Ward] 22
  Robert 107, 123
  Robert L. 28
  Sarah[Beatty] 37, 105
Pattie, John 169
  Marie E(Maxwell) 169
  R.B. 169
  Robert B. 169
Pattison, Lucinda(Mawzy) 88
  Susan A(Colville) 204
  William B. 236
Patton, Andrew D. 111
  D.H. 111
  Isabell 102
  Mary 20
  Nancy(Cowan) 111
  Sarah[Ferguson] 60
Pauley, William 236
Pauly, Benjamin 236
  Clarissa[Coldwell] 165
Paxton, Martha 61
  Samuel 61
  Thomas 61
Payne, Allen F. 186
  Bennet 182
  Caroline 30
  J.C. 186
  J.H.P. 28
  Jacob 28
  John W. 182
  Rebecca(Mercer) 186
  Robert H. 182, 186
  Sarah(Whitecotten) 182
  William 186
Payton, A.M. 236
  Jacob 236
  James 236
  John H. 88
Peach, Fannie(Taylor) 32
  George 32
  John 32
Peak, Grafton 188
  Susannah(Johnson) 188
  William A.J. 188
Peake, John 236

Pearce, Charles 44
  Charles D. 44
  John 29
  John W. 145
  Mary(Taylor) 29
  Samuel 29
Pearcy, Henry 236
  Mary(Holly) 182
  Nancy[Radford] 182
  Robert 236
  S.H. 182
  William 182
Pearman, John 121
  Sebert 121
Pebworth, James H. 182
Peck, Delia[Howard] 38
  Elizabeth[Hillis] 111
  Hiram D. 33
  Jane(Veach) 33
  John W. 33
  Joseph 123
Peckinpaugh, Eleanor(Sheck-
  ell) 121
  John 94
  Nicholas 94, 121
  Peter 94
Pedigo, E. 169
  Ezekiel 169
  Dudley L. 124
  Isabell(McGill) 169
  James W. 124
  Jane(Richardson) 124
  Jesse S. 124
  Jonathan 169
  Robert 169
Peed, Elizabeth 150
  James 236
  John R. 150
  William 150
Peer, Jane(Dawson) 207
Peggs, Evan O. 188
  Isabella[Jones] 188
  Joseph 188
  Margaret M(Hunter) 188
  Nancy(Cunningham) 188
Pell, John 140
  Rebecca(Ales) 140
  Richard D. 140
  William F. 140
Pendlay, Fannie[Hammonds]
  141
  Jane A(Darter) 141
  John 141
  Joshua 141
Pemberton, Lucy J[Brown]201
Peniston, Anna M[Beatly] 231
Penn, Charlotte[McLoed] 236
  Ephraim 182
  George F. 133
  Huldah 236
  James C. 133
  Jane(Floyd) 133
  John W. 182, 236
  Mary 182
Pennington, Hannah(Gannon)
  212
  Isaac 236
Penny, Dennis 61
  Lewis 61
  Peter 61
Penquie, Mary[Glasscock] 29
Peoples, Sarah[Paris] 88
Percy, Hannah[Ross] 237
Perfect, Middleton 61
  William 61
Perigo, Samuel H. 236
Perkins, Aaron 61
  Abbariller[Keith] 237

Abbie[Keith] 237
Frank H. 38
George 19
James 84
James N. 84
John H. 38, 19, 182
Louisa[McMurtry] 80
Maria(Stinsifer) 38
Mildred(Calvert) 84
William 22
William W. 22
Perrill, Margaret(Sparks)63
Perrine, Daniel 44
  Joseph 44
  Susan(Downing) 44
  William C. 44
Perry, E. 172
  Elizabeth 28
  Elizabeth(Stewart) 133
  Elizabeth[White] 113
  John S. 133
  Maria J[McCormick] 143
  Lewis 172
  Norval W. 138
  Orphy E(Said) 172
  Sylvester 133
Peters, Frances(Cheatham)
  127
  John A. 127
  John R. 236
  Jonathan 236
  Joseph 127
  Joseph T. 127
  Katheryn[Klein] 38
  Mary(Tatum) 236
Pettit, H.M. 173
Peyton, Anthony 150
  James F. 150
  John J. 113
  Margaret(Wllington) 150
  Martin 141
  Rachel(Arbuckle) 141
  William 141
Pfingstag, Richard J. 98
Phillips, Abraham 36
  Anna(Ross) 61
  Brannock 159
  Columbus 61
  Elijah 61
  Elizabeth[Becks] 237
  Elizabeth[Callahan] 130
  Hannah(Corwin) 61
  Jesse C. 61
  John 61
  Lloyd 36
  M. 237
  Marion 61
  Mary[Lytle] 49
  Nancy(Lewis) 36
  Nancy[Pottorf] 114
  P.T. 61
  Susan(Kendrick) 61
Piatt, A. Sanders 19
  Anna(McCoy) 19
  Benjamin M. 19
  Frances[Dunn] 83, 86
  Hannah A. 19
  Jacob 19
  John H. 19
  Kentucky B. 19
  R.J. 19
Pickens, Eliza(Baldon) 196
  Samuel 237
Pickerill, Lovell 44
  Mary 61
  Samuel 44, 61
  William F. 61
Pierce, Eveline(Moore) 176

J.S. 176
J.T. 176
Jane[Forsythe] 145
John 237
Lettice[Bryan] 191
Mahala(Shively) 186
Mary[Henderson] 182
Piercy, George 88
Piers, Joseph 133
  Margaret(Gregory) 133
  Thomas J. 133
Pierson, Malinda[Smith] 88
  Moses 237
Piety, James D. 121
  Mary(Duncan) 95
  Thomas 95, 121
  William D. 95
Pigman, Caroline A. 92
  George W. 92
  Rachel[Elliott] 92
  William A. 92
Piles, Elizabeth(Haydon)237
  John J. 237
  William 237
Pilchard, Hester A[Tull] 93
Ping, Christina 237
  Elizabeth[Bradley] 174
  Job 237
Pinckard, Elizabeth(Duff) 44
  G. 44
  Grandison 44
  J.W. 44
  William 44
Pink, Abraham J. 21
  Benjamin P. 21
  Bertha(Gold) 21
Pinkston, Elizabeth 116
  John 116
  John A. 237
  Melinda[Minter] 107
  William O. 116
Pipe, Catherine[Survant]237
Piper, Alexander 61
  George 19
  Harry M. 19
  W.D. 61
Pirtle, Alford 237
  Mary(Ferree) 211
  Mary[Jackson] 190
  Mary[Nosler] 237
  Mary L[Jackson] 145
Plake, John 237
Plank, Phebe[Conaway] 109
Plasters, Elizabeth[Higgins]
  237
Pleak, Narcas 159
Plew, Elizabeth[Cass] 190
  W.M. 190
Plough, Ann(Patsey) 145
  Henry 145
  Joseph 145
Plow, J. 84
Plummer, Jeremiah 61
  Melinda(Boatman) 198
Plumoner, Altha(Banfield)
  133
  John 133
  Thomas J. 133
Plunkett, Jonathan 237
Poague, Nancy[McClaskey]237
Poe, Andrew 22
  David 22
  Elizabeth(Richey) 22
  Ida J[Harber] 21
  Mary A[Jones] 237
Polk, A.H. 163
  Clayborn 237
  Elizabeth[Spencer] 163

Polk(cont.)
George W. 163
James 163
James M. 186
John A. 163
Lizzie F[Wilson] 96
Mary[Ellison] 237
Nancy 163
Nancy(Adams) 176
Richard 163
Sarah(Shoptaugh) 96, 186
Thomas 237
W. 237
William 96, 186
Pollard, Allison 182
Mary 182
Pollitt, Alexander 40
Alexander D. 111
Eleanor 40
James S. 40
Jane(Hoffer) 111
Nehemiah 111
Polloch, Henry 133
Judith(Merritt) 133
William 133
Pool, Nancy(Long) 113
Pope, Elizabeth[Bright] 140
Popham, Mary[Selser] 152
Porter, A.M. 111
Albert G. 111
Andrew 111
Cynthia(Davis) 111
Elizabeth[Steele] 237
Etheelenda(Brown) 182
Jeptha 182
L.G[Prentiss] 107
Samuel 182
Seth W. 111
William W. 237
Portland, John L. 105
Leonard 105
Martha(Portwood) 105
Portwood, Martha[Portland] 105
Posey, Sarah(Blackburn) 198
Postlewaite, Mary(Neal) 133
Thomas N. 133
William 133
Pottenger, 61
Pottorf, Eliza A(McKewen) 133
George 114
Nancy(Phillips) 114
Simeon 133
Wesley 114
William A. 133
Poulter, Louisa A(McRae) 155
Sarah[Haymaker] 155
William R. 155
Pound, David 186
Eunice[Goble 237
Harvey M. 186
Massie(Sparks) 186
Powell, Abraham 61
Adam 22
Elizabeth(Dillman) 22
Elizabeth L(Patrick) 82
Jackson 155
James(Leach) 189
James M. 125
James W. 189
John 82, 237
John W. 125
Joseph 22
Mary(Dunlap) 55
Mary(Thompson) 155

Matilda(Greene) 125
Roxaline[Logan] 61
Samuel 61
Thomas E. 189
Thomas M. 82
Timothy 61
Power, Benjamin F. 22
Nancy(Meyers) 22
Robert 22
Powers, Isaac 237
Lucinda[Lindsay] 84
Poynts, James 177
Rebecca(Ross) 177
William R. 177
Prather, Basil 111
James 111
Mary(George) 111
Sarah[Little] 145
Pratt, Artemas 237
Preble, Benjamin B. 237
Lucretia(Marshall) 237
M.M. 237
Prenat, Francis H. 36
Francis X. 36
Mary J(Johnson) 36
Prentiss, Eliza P[Grubbs] 215
L.G(Porter) 107
Laura G[VanTrees] 107
Thomas G. 107
Pressel, David 237
John 237
Motley(Larndy) 237
Preston, Mary(Owens) 61
Phoebe[Adams] 237
Thomas 61
Prewett, Albert G. 91
Jane(Little) 91
Joseph 91
Price, G.C. 174
Nancy 174
Ruhama[Bass] 197
Shadrach 174
William 61
William F. 61
Prichard, C.G. 238
D.S. 238
Isabella(Spears) 238
Priest, Agnes[Flinn] 61
David 159
George W. 159
Powell 159
Priestland, Margaret[Frakes] 238
Prince, William 61
Prine, Henry 29
Mary[Rhoten] 61
Robert T. 29
Pringlem Sarah(Vance) 63
Prior, John 61
Pritchard, David P. 238
Henry R. 88
Margaret[Forsythe] 238
Walker 238
Pritchett, Elisha 238
Nancy[Jones] 238
Procaskey, Barbara(Lory)119
George 119
George J. 119
Protsaman, William 91
Province, Nancy(Harden) 127
Samuel 127
W.M. 127
Pruden, Christina(Amos) 195
Pruett, Calvin 192
Mary[Wilkinson] 91
Sarah(DeMoss) 192

William 192
Pruitt, Catherine H[Shake] 170
Hannah[Wilson] 238
Daniel 170
Eli 170
John 238
Moses 78
Nancy(Grimes) 215
Nancy(Williams) 170
Phoebe(Williams) 78
William 78
Pullan, Ann 177
Gonel B. 177
Sidney S. 177
Pulse, Eliza(Bonwell) 53
Purcell, Alfred 44
Augustus 238
Purdum, Elizabeth[Rees] 61
Pursell, Melinda 238
Thomas 238
William 238
Pryatt, Nathan 189
Purviance, David 20
John 20
Lewis W. 89
Mary(Ireland) 20
Putnam, Hannah 40
Henry 44
Robert H. 40, 44
Thomas D. 40
Zecharia 44
Putoff, Eli 238
John 238
Mark(Hoke) 238
Pyeatt, Nathan 189
Pyle, Emery C. 24
Lemuel T. 24
Liza(Willison) 24

Quinn, James 111
John 111
Sarah(Bright) 109

Rabourn, Drusilla[George] 18
Fried 238
Radcliff, Sarah(Holman) 144
Rademacher, Catherine 133
Charles 133
Frances 133
Radford, Elizabeth(Tabor) 163
Nancy(Pearcy) 182
William 182
Raff, Charles 95
Edie(Mallory) 95
Horace E. 95
Rafferty, Martha[Johnson] 61
Ragan, Abner 238
James M. 238
Mary(MacCoun) 238
Reuben S. 155
Ragland, Benjamin F. 26
Delilah[Blanton] 238
Dudley 101
Elizabeth[Stevenson] 238
Henry 26
Ragsdale, Frederick 182
Lucinda[Hicks] 238
Malinda[Fendley] 238
Mary[Forsyth] 170
J.T. 182

Ragsdale(cont.)
Sarah(Hunter) 182
Railey, G.R. 146
Railsback, Delthia J(Rey-
nolds) 163
E.D. 238
Hannah(Conger) 61
Isaac C. 61
John 20, 61
John S. 163
Lewis D. 163
Raines, Cornelius 160
Tabitha 160
Walter 160
Rains, George W. 117
John 117
Mahala 117
Mary[Bennington] 28
Nancy[Adams] 238
Rairden, Jane[Walker] 238
Rairdon, Henry 238
Raison, Amanda K(Corum) 32
Charles L. 32
Raley, Lavinia[Ballard] 169
Ralls, Enfield[Mitchell]159
Ralston, Nancy[Lamme] 30
Ramsay, Martha(Dinwiddie)
209
Ramsbrok, Frederica[Moen-
khaus] 133
Ramsey, Alexander 101
Andrew 101
Hannah[Hamilton] 86, 100
Jennie(Browning) 101
Margaret E[Dodds] 116
Mary 238
Robert M. 238
Samuel 192, 238
W[McGowan] 191
William 238
Ranard, Benjamin 174
Elias 174
Elizabeth(Massey) 174
Randall, Richard S. 111
Sarah(Havens) 111
William C. 111
Randolph, J.A. 174
Samuel C. 238
Raney, James 238
Rankin, George I. 238
Jane[Field] 193
Lovisa[Wood] 238
Rannells, Rachel(Hughes) 44
Samuel 44
William J. 44
Ranner, Mahala Q(Browning)
29
Ransdell, Patsy M[Legrange]
156
Wheron 156
Ransom, R.H. 38
Rariden, James 123
Ratcliff, J.T. 84
Rau, Frederick G. 133
John 133
Rebecca(Schneider) 133
Ravencroft, Polly[Miller]
123
Rawling, Aaron 127
Elizabeth[Lawson] 32
James 29
Mary(Tibbe) 29
Thomas 29
Rawlings, James 61
Rawlins, Aristica(Gregory)
91
Charles 91

F.J.C. 177
John 177
Joseph 91
Patsey 177
Ray, Edwin 160
James B. 133
James H. 82
Joel 82, 102
John 191
John F. 191
Malinda J(Brown) 82
Martin M. 239
Polly 191
Rea, James A. 101
Leanna(Rice) 101
William 101
Read, De Granton 97
Eliza M(Hunter) 97
H.E. 97
Hiram E. 97
James G. 239
Reading, Alexander D. 239
Reape, H. 138
Reaves, Susan[McLaughlin]143
Reay, Caroline(Meriwether)
133
John O. 133
William 133
Records, Alexander 84
Alfred 84
Elizabeth(Aldridge) 84
Rector, John 239
Redding, John 170
Tabitha[Epperson] 180
Redick, John 133
Mary(Fleshman) 133
Philip 133
Redman, Minerva[Mounts] 239
Redmond, Emily[Faris] 193
Reed, A. 239
Absalom 20, 61
Armer 239
Cyrus 61
Elizabeth(Wilson) 90
Green B. 190
Isaac 62
James 150
Margaret[Arthur] 62
Martha[Hinkle] 131
Nancy(Bunnell) 20
Nancy[Lamme] 30
Ruth(Glover) 213
Samuel 20
Rees, Abel 62
Reese, Benjamin 177
Mary[Rose] 156
Sarah(Davis) 177
Reeve, Benjamin F. 150
George W. 150
Reeves, Andrew W. 111
Elizabeth(Dicks) 98
Ila 239
James 150, 239
John 98, 150
Mary 239
Mary[Leachman] 149
Sarah(Holton) 150
Sarah[Long] 111
Stacy 98
Stacy L. 98
Reid, Mary[Marlow] 177
Reiley, Barney 150
James 150
John 150
William F. 98
Reinhart, Caleb 190
Eunice(Farris) 190

John J. 190
Maria[Ackerman] 93
Renbarger, Abraham 239
Renner, George J. 38
Saraphina(Appleman) 38
Retherford, David 89
Elizabeth(Hall) 89
Levi R. 89
Reynolds, Delthia J[Rails-
back] 163
Elizabeth[Gilbert] 116
J. 239
Louisa[Best] 42
Margaret[Bodine] 239
Mary 239
Sarah J(Tower) 121
William 239
William R. 121
William V. 121
Rhea, John 62
Rheuby, John 91
Rhodes, Benjamin 239
Eliza[Hamilton] 56
Isaac H. 239
Samuel 239
Susan(Wishard) 239
Rhoten, Josiah 44
Mary(Prine) 61
Rial, Harriet[Bailey] 41
Rice, Elizabeth(Nichols)
96, 192
Ida[Sickles] 36
James R. 192
Jesse 183
John 239
Joseph 189
Laban M. 192
Leanna[Rea] 101
Lewis N. 183
Lucinda[McHaley] 239
Lutitia(Ham) 22
Martha(Wilcoxson) 183
Frances(Broadwell) 189
Michael 22
Miles 189
Philena[Powers] 239
Robert D. 22
William A. 239
Richards, Juliette(Galway)212
Phebe[Beem] 239
Rebecca[Metsker] 239
Samuel 239
Richardson, Amy(Thompson)
239
Anna[Tucker] 239
Basil 239
Dudley 239
Ebenezer 121
Elizabeth[Brent] 200
Elizabeth(Crouch) 121
Jacob 121
John 111, 163, 239
Joseph C. 163
Mary 239
Mary[Allison] 175
Mary[Egnew] 239
Nancy(Castleman) 163
Phoebe[Logan] 58
Rhoda[Portland] 239
Thomas 121
William B. 121
Richart, Sarah[Jackson] 82
Richeson, Hannah[Griffith]
177
Richey, Elizabeth[Poe] 22
Richie, Unis[Shewmaker]
138

Ricketts, Dillard 101
  Edward 111
  John 111
  Jonathan 239
  Sarah(Storey) 111
  Sarah(Story) 111
  William 111
Riddle, Isaac 146
  Joseph C. 146
  Margaret H(Nelson) 146
Ridge, Mary(Baker) 196
Riely, L.A. 95
Rigdon, Martha[White] 113
Riggs, Dora V. 138
  Lydia(Engle) 210
  Nancy[Creech] 193
Right, Samuel 239
Rigsby, Charles R. 133
  Lida(Latta) 133
  Thomas D. 133
Riker, Mary E[Warner] 90
Riley, Edward 240
  Ezekiel 96
  Jacob 121
  Jane[Fowler] 106
  Mary E[Shaw] 98
  Noble S. 240
  Zachariah T. 123
Ringo, Elizabeth(Bryan) 127
  George 127
  Major 127
  Morgan B. 127
  Walter B. 240
Rinker, Elizabeth(Cracraft)
  206
Risinger, Charles W. 133
  Daniel 133
  M.L. 133
  Mariah[Chenoweth] 240
  Sarah(Miers) 133
Risk, Elswie 240
Risley, Huldah[Cromwell]
  240
Ristine, Benjamin T. 240
  Henry 240
  Nancy(Gray) 240
Ritchie, Mary(Bowling) 142
  Simpson 142
  William 142
Ritter, Agnes(Butler) 142
  Emma[Hardin] 170
  Henry 62
  John 136
  John A. 136
  Narcie(Lockwood) 87
  Sarah[Franklin] 240
Rivarde, Mary C[Hall] 37
Rivers, Elizabeth[Hunt] 240
Roach, Frances 161
Robards, Nancy P[Thompson]
  45
Robb, Jane[Cook] 62
  Robert 62
  Susan(Gray) 62
Robbins, John 127
  Nancy(Boyd) 85
  Ruth(Anderson) 127
  Sarah 240
  William A. 127
Robertes, Andrew W. 240
  Jemima(Corn) 240
  Minor 240
Roberts, Billingsley 177
  C.L. 89
  Elizabeth[Zuck] 240
  Israel 240

James 127
John 177
John H. 240
Mary[Earle] 35
Miranda[Bloom] 62
Moses 127
Nancy(Jewell)
Parmelia[Ellis] 240
Reden 240
Robert 240
Sarah(Bishop) 127
William R. 240
Robertson, Addison 240
  Anna(Burton) 82
  Cassandra 183
  Elias 145
  Eliza 240
  Elizabeth[McKnight] 240
  George W. 240
  Henry 82
  Jemima(Green) 145
  John H. 82
  Margaret[Mogan] 240
  Martha[Moberly] 144
  Martin 145
  T.B. 240
  William 240
Robins, William 240
Robinson, Abner 123, 240
  Albert 38
  Alfred 49
  Allen 49
  Annie(Stevenson) 38
  Burton E. 38
  Ellen[Glidden] 37
  Fannie[Eskridge] 210
  George W. 240
  Lucretia(Sanford) 241
  Martha[Davis] 153
  Martha J. 240
  Matilda[Colliver] 54
  Nancy(Holton) 148
  Nancy[Miller] 149
  Osman 150
  Osmyn 240
  Ozias 240
  Sarah(Bull) 201
  Sarah(Lyon) 240
  William 240
  William C. 123
Robison, Thomas 111
Robuck, Aaron 62
Roby, John 104
  Robert 104
Rochner, J.H. 134
Rodgers, Martha[Heath] 240
Rodman, Sarah[Morris] 136
Roe, E.F. 78
Rogers, Alexander 241
  Amanda F[Brookie] 241
  Asa L. 241
  Elias 84
  Elizabeth(Pearson) 241
  Elizabeth(Smith) 121
  George 241
  Jacob 48
  John 121
  Katherine[Brown] 62
  Lewis T. 136
  Martha[Stark] 100
  Mary 240
  Mary A(Truston) 48
  Sally(Stricker) 84
  Sarah[Bohannon] 241
  Shacklet 121
  William 54

William M. 48
Rogge, E.M. 131
Rollison, Rebecca[Vann] 125
Rooks, Joseph 241
Rooksberry, W.A. 134
Rose, Archibald 115
  Ary A[Baird] 109
  Charles 156
  Elizabeth(Pearson) 241
  J.B. 241
  Jacob 115
  Jonathan H. 111
  Lewis A. 156, 189
  Martha(Lake) 57
  Mary(Reese) 156
  Mary R[Warner] 241
  Nancy(Bryce) 115
  Walker 241
Roseberry, William N. 89
Rosenfeld, Fannie[Labold]
  35
Ross, Anna[Phillips] 61
  Elizabeth(Wilson) 84
  Jenetta[Summers] 84
  John 241
  John H. 112
  Joseph B. 89
  Judson 150
  Margaret B(Walton) 89
  Nathan 84
  Nathan O. 84
  Nepthfalum R. 127
  Samuel 89
  Susan(Paten) 127
  W.T. 193
  William 84
  William T. 193
Roswell, Nancy J[Graham] 241
Roten, Elizabeth[Ashmore]
  127
Roulette, Susan[Bacon] 99
Roundtree, Judith[King] 241
Rouse, Lucinda(Francis) 212
  Nathaniel 241
Rousk, Annie(Roberts) 107
Rousseau, Lovell H. 141
Rout, John 121
  Levisa 121
  Richard 121
Rowe, Ellen[Winspear] 21
Rowen, Francis 84
  Lydia(Brunner) 84
  William 84
Rowland, Thomas J. 102
  Wade 102
  Winnie(Murphy) 102
Rowlette, Susan[Bacon] 99
  Royal, Richard 241
Royse, Martin 241
Royster, Pheba 241
Ruby, Ambrose S. 123
  James 241
Rucker, Edward P. 134
  Wilson H. 62
Rudd, Amelia[Hardesty] 115
Rudder, James 241
Rudisill, Mary[Allison] 175
Rudulph, Joab 49
Ruggles, Cynthia[White] 241
Rulon, Morrison 241
Rumbarger, Elizabeth(Miller)
  59
  Mary E(Eads) 180
Rummans, Elizabeth[Hendrick-
  son] 40
Rumsey, John E. 150

Runey, Cecilia J[Lee] 113
Runkle, Ruth(Barlow) 196
Runyan, Catherine[Springer]
  30
  Charity[Parks] 80
Runyon, Daniel 150
  David L. 150
  Robert 62
Rush, Greenberry 173
  Nancy[Brooner] 93
  William P. 241
Russel, Frances[Bryant] 34
Russell, Alexander W. 114
  Andrew 163
  Cynthia 163
  E.C. 163
  J.W. 241
  J.P. 89
  James 114, 186
  John W. 150
  Jonathan 150
  Mary(McKinley) 186
  Sarah(Hite) 150
  Spencer 186
Rust, Virginia[Iredell] 18
Rutledge, Mary(Lewis) 58
Ryan, James G. 156
  Patrick D. 156
  Permelia A(Grayham) 156
  Sally[Burgess] 147
  Thomas 95
  Wilson 241
Ryker, Gerardus 183
  John G. 183
  Sarah(Jones) 183
Ryman, Elizabeth[Parson]
  241
Rynerson, Isaac 156
  Isaac N. 156
  John 156

Sacrey, Mary[Bohannon] 179
Sadler, W.D. 241
Said, Orphy E[Perry] 172
  Presley 18
St. Clair, John 241
  Julia[Harrison] 241
Sale, Clayton 241
  F.H. 172
  Elizabeth T(Elliston) 172
  James H. 172
  Samuel 241
Salendar, Josephine[Kearns]
  30
Sales, Richard 62
Salisbury, Hannah[Myers]
  24, 140
Salle, Abraham 62
  Benjamin K. 169
  Elizabeth(Johnson) 169
  James 62
  Joseph 52
  Lucy(Nelson) 62
  Martha A[O'Neall] 52
  Oliver P. 169
  Susan(Downing) 52
Sallerfield, Eliza 241
Salt, Elizabeth(Davis) 38
  Enoch 38
Salter, Lucinda[White] 157
Sample, Nancy[Wellever] 241
  Robert 241
Sandefur, Elizabeth(Shipp)
  156
  Samuel D. 156
Sanders, Jane 112
  John 112

Margaret 20
Mary[Turner] 62
Rebecca[Epperson] 241
Samuel(Morton) 241
Thomas 241
Wesley 112
Sands, Isaac 163
  Martha[Sloan] 241
  Samuel 163
Sandusky, James 89
  Rebecca[Mason] 190
  Sallie[Neal] 88
Sandy, Lucinda(Thompson)247
Sanford, Elizabeth[Vermilion]
  157
  Elizabeth[Vermillion] 157
  Hamilton 150
  Tabitha[Small] 150
  Tabitha A(Clark) 150
Sapp, Edward 62
  Lydia[Joseph] 163
Sarels, Julia(Everston)99
  Richard 99
Satterwhite, Harvey 188
  Yula[Jackson] 172
Saunders, Charles 107
  Jennie J. 134
  Louis 107
  Zelphy(Duncan) 107
Sawyer, Ella M. 51
  Louis B. 51
  Nathan L. 51
Saxon, Nancy(Orr) 166
Scales, Sarah(Bogan) 198
Scanland, J.T. 146
Scantlin, Elizabeth(Young)
  107
  James 107
  Thomas 107
Scearce, Ezra W. 183
  George W. 183
  Jeff B. 52
  Martha(Shepherd) 183
Schackelford, James M. 91
Scherer, Michael 32
Schermerhorn, Mary F[Hydron]
  127
Schneider, Rebecca[Rau] 133
Schnurrenberger, Elizabeth
  62
Schofield, Sarah J[Davidson]
  24
Schonling, Joseph 242
Schooling, Elizabeth[Mann]
  155, 230
Schriver, Louis H. 24
  Mary P(Betz) 24
  Walter A. 24
Schumann, J. 134
Schweickart, Frederick 21
  Louisa(Fridley) 21
  William L. 21
Schwench, Margaret[Boldt]
  35
Schwindler, Jonathan 183
  Letitia(Mount) 183
  William 183
Scifres, David 121
  Permelia A(Padgett) 121
  William C. 121
Scott, Agnes(McKee) 20
  David 183
  Elizabeth[Caven] 44
  Francis L. 36
  James C. 89
  Jane 62, 89
  Jane E(Dannells) 207
  John 62, 89

John T. 80
Martha 177
Martin 145
Mary[Gipson] 84
Nancy[Brent] 126
Nancy[Underwood] 242
Obedience[Straughan] 183
Rebecca(Welch) 108
Robert 62
Thomas P. 36
Scrogen, John H. 242
Scroggen, Lucy(Martin) 231
Scroggin, Joseph 107
  Martha(Campbell) 107
  Robert H. 107
Seabright, Polly[Brown] 85
Sears, Catherine 87
  Daniel 89
  Franey[Bush] 107
  Jaob 89
  Margaret[Owen] 101
  Mary[Huffstutter] 89
  Sebith[Appleby] 101
Seaton, Allen R. 134
  George 134
  Mary[Tyler] 135
  Sarah(Drake) 134
Sebree, Elizabeth[Fenton]
  18
  Fannie[Watts] 108
Secrest, Henry 112
  James 112
  Lydia A[Welch] 113
Seggerson, John 20
  Margaret(Cahill) 20
  Patrick 20
Selby, Annie(McCallie) 123
  James H. 123
  John 123
Self, George 124
Sellards, Abraham G. 32
  Andrew J. 32
  Mary G(Hartly) 32
Seller, James 123
  Mary D. 123
  William A. 123
Sellers, Abigail[Parkhurst]
  183
  Amanda[Moore] 139
  Amelia(Staton) 139
  Edward 139
  J.M. 139
  Mary[Neal] 30
  Nancy 89
  Polly[McCaslin] 183, 242
Selser, Harvey G. 152
  Henry H. 152
  Mary(Popham) 152
Semonin, Kate[Hardy] 125
Sentemary, Jane[Short] 242
Seright, Sarah J[Riffe] 242
Service, William T. 242
Seths, Elizabeth A[Parish]
  155
Servier, James 101
  Samuel E. 101
  Susanna(Warren) 101
Servies, Eliza(Pilcher) 183
  William A. 183
  William T. 183
Seward, Emma J. 125
Sexon, Rebecca[Bough] 81
Sexton, Enoch 242
  Lucy[Cox] 94
  Phebe(Stansbery) 245
Seybold, James 112
Seymour, Polly[Smith] 92

Shackleford, J.M. 142
James M. 142
Shacklet, Hannah[Hayden]
120
Shadburn, Kitura[Doup] 131
Shafer, Henry 62
Shaffer, E.C. 242
Shake, Adam R. 134
Artemisie(Blevins) 170
Christian(Donaldson) 134
David 170
George 134
George W. 134
J.B. 170
Jacob 170
John 170
Lemuel H. 170
Nancy(Donelson) 170
Sarah A(Sturgeon) 170
Venalia 170
Shallcross, John 134
Mary(Lewis) 134
William L. 134
Shambs, Clara C. 36
Shannon, Agnes(Brown) 183
Alexander 183
David 193
Ignatius F. 193
John 134
Mary A. 134
Nancy(Alexander) 193
Samuel 134
Thomas B. 183
Sharp, Darmis(Clark) 204
George 89
James M. 89
Julia(Darnall) 89
Stephens 123
Sharpe, Ebenezer 107
Eliza(Lake) 107
Thomas H. 107
Shanklin, Anna J[Lauman] 29
Catherine(Lowe) 81
Elizabeth 242
John 242
Johnson 242
Shaptaw, A.H. 96
Sharp, Archibald 124
Elenor(McClure) 124
Hubbard 242
Mary(Reeves) 239
Stephen 242
William 124
Sharrer, Elizabeth[Kennedy]
87
Shaw, Benjamin 242
Coleman 98
David 62
Elizabeth(Elliott) 180
James H. 186
John C. 92
John N. 98
John T. 62
George W. 98
Margaret[Vermillion] 78
Martha[Vermillion] 157
Mary E(Riley) 98
Shawman, Louisa[Clayton] 62
Sheckell, Eleanor[Peckin-
paugh] 121
Sheeks, Rosanna[Albin] 242
Sheeler, Elizabeth(Canon)31
Jacob 31
Jerry 31
Shelburn, John 242
Shelburne, Benjamin 183

James S. 183
Johanne(Webb) 183
Shelby, Mercy[Cobb] 242
Merise[Cobb] 152
Shelton, John 150
John F. 150
Shepard, George 242
Horace B. 193
Mary[McQuigg] 242
Otis 242
P.W. 176
Patsy(Harper) 193
Shepherd, Abraham 62
Catherine(Lee) 177
Daniel 242
David 242
Francis B. 177
Horace B. 242
James 242
James T. 40
John 40, 62
Joseph 62
Martha[Scearce] 183
Mary 62
Mary(Ship) 243
Mary A(Smith) 46
Nancy[Clem] 114, 126, 183
Phillip B. 177
Stephen 242
Thomas 242
Sheridan, Elizabeth(Goodman)
134
Jesse 134
Sherley, William S. 171
Sherman, Susan[Barger] 93
Shewmaker, Samuel M. 243
Shidaker, Emily(Harter) 56
Shields, Clement N. 80
Mary(Stewart) 80
Patrick 80
William 62, 243
Shinkle, A. Clifford 39
Amos C. 39
Ann J(Hemingray) 39
Bradford 39
Ship, Mary[Shephard] 243
Shipman, Fannie E[Fullenwid-
er] 183
Shipp, Elizabeth[Sandefur]
156
John 62
Nancy[Hogeland] 187
Shircliff, Catherine(Cissell)
204
Shirk, Elizabeth(Stout) 246
Shirley, Catherine(Hendrick-
son) 163
Cinderella[Cole] 163
D.J. 178
Isaac 163
James W. 243
Laurenda M(Overstreet) 171
Lawrence 62
Mary A[Dailey] 243
William S. 171
Shively, Fannie S[Bailey]
243
Mahala[Pierce] 186
Shoat, Augusta 18
Eliza J[Bryant] 18
Sarah 18
Shockey, Mahala[Kiplinger]62
Shockley, Samuel 112
Shoemaker, Fannie S[Bailey]
243
Shofstall, Robert C. 150

Shoppie, Mary[Dupaquier] 131
Shoptaugh, Jacob 243
Sarah[Polk] 96
Short, Ezekiel 243
Jane(Sentemay) 242
John 243
John C. 28
Mary(Symmes) 28
Milton 174
Peyton 28
Rebecca(Owen) 174
Wesley 174
Shortridge, Morgan 243
Shoulders, Thomas 189
Shouse, Alice[Mason] 243
Shrout, A.W. 89
Sarah(Highland) 87
Shryock, Fannie 243
Hillary 243
John G. 84
Mary(George) 84
Mary(Lewis) 243
Valentine J. 84
Shuck, Elizabeth[Vories]128
Levina(Black) 126
Samuel 128
Sarah(Frazier) 128
William A. 128
Shuff, Elizabeth(Cleveland)
20
Isaac 20
John L. 20
Shy, Amanda[Bridwell] 119
W.W. 102
Sickles, H. George 36
Ida(Rice) 36
Simon 36
Sicklesworth, Nancy[Murphey]
234
Sicks, Philip 82
Siddens, Hugh 243
James 243
Sarah 243
Sidewell, Joseph 243
Sill, Elizabeth[Smyth] 243
Sills, Elizabeth(Bogard)199
John W. 243
Silvers, Nancy 243
Simmons, Elizabeth[Lemmon]
243
Susan[Miles] 182
Simms, Amanda(Smith) 89
Craven 89
Michael M. 89
Simons, Hiram W. 243
Simpson, John T. 187
Margaret[Warmouth] 116
Mary T. 44
Sims, Asbury 139
Mary[Wiley] 158
Mary A.C(Murphey) 234
Starlin 139
Sinclaire, Samuel 243
Siner, Benjamin 95
Nelson 95
Singleton, Hunley 243
Nancy(Tolbert) 243
Sarah[Martin] 136
William 243
Sisson, Benjamin 243
Benjamin W. 136
John S. 115
Skaggs, Edna(Ennis) 210
John 243
Mary A[Cox] 117, 243
Skellon, James A. 243

Slade, John 62
Slaughter, Delilah(Spencer)
 183
 James B. 163
Sleet, Sarah[O'Neal] 19
Slegar, David 96
 Ellison 96
 Margaret(Stafford) 96
Slout, J.C. 186
Slusher, Mary[Goghill] 243
Small, Tabitha(Sanford)150
Smalley, Alfred 89
 Elizabeth(Combs) 89
 Jackson 89
Smallwood, Mary S[Fitzger-
 ald] 49
Smathers, Sarah[Hopkins]81
Smelser, Margaret[Smith]89
Smiley, John 243
Smith, A. 116
 Adam 98
 Albertus 33
 Allen 243
 Amanda[Simms] 89
 Andrew 169
 Ann(Bolton) 49
 Anna M(Tull) 193
 Aquila 92
 Barbara 175
 Benjamin 169
 Berryman 178
 Bolton 49
 Caroline(Wagner) 25
 Catherine(Coghill) 204
 Catherine[Nation] 124
 Catherine[Orthblieb] 24
 Catherine[Rice] 243
 Charles S. 62
 Christian(Jacquess) 124
 Daniel 25, 101
 Daniel R. 150
 Eliza(Settles) 163
 Eliza A(Gardner) 101
 Elizabeth(Brown) 200
 Elizabeth(Chrisman) 26
 Elizabeth(Cohorn) 112
 Elizabeth[Epperson] 189
 Elizabeth[Hays] 37
 Elizabeth[Jeems] 186
 Elizabeth[Rogers] 121
 Elizabeth[Thompson] 243
 Forrest W. 62
 Fountain P. 112
 Francis P. 128
 George D. 134
 George W. 134
 Hannah[Butler] 243
 Harriet[Albro] 46
 Henry G. 163
 Henry W. 134
 Hezekiah 150
 Hubbard M. 101
 Ina(Wardill) 62
 Isaac 244
 Isabella[Mounts] 62
 J.C. 26, 145
 Jacob G. 33
 James 243
 James H. 193
 Jane[Daugherty] 78
 Jane Z(Parker) 111
 Jemima 161
 Joel F. 124
 John 49, 243
 John M. 78
 John P. 89, 244
 John W. 101

 Jonathan 175
 Katherine W. 169
 Levi 175
 Louisa[Sullivan] 244
 Lucinda[Glazebrook] 183
 Lucinda[Talbott] 122
 Lucy A[Ragan] 244
 M.L. 244
 Malinda(Pierson) 88
 Manoah 244
 Margaret(Smelser) 89
 Margaret[Stone] 80
 Martha M[Furber] 21
 Mary 243
 Mary A[Shepherd] 40
 Mary A[Smith] 150
 Mary E(Davis) 207
 Mary E(Gardner) 33
 Mary E[Greene] 26
 Morgan 186
 Nancy[Doggett] 81
 Oliver 49
 Paul 124
 Permelia(Garr) 134
 Peter 89, 134, 244
 Polly[McMurtry] 117
 Polly(Seymour) 92
 Rebecca(Lockwood) 87
 Reuben 186
 Rhoda 178
 Richard 244
 Robert 112
 Sallie D[Todd] 136
 Samuel 152
 Samuel H. 62
 Sarah[Eastin] 210
 Sarah A[Bowles] 124
 Sarah J[Barlow] 244
 Sarah E[Barlow] 128
 Susan[Ellers] 191
 Temple 244
 Thomas D. 247
 Thomas M. 176
 William 161, 193
 William A. 244
 William B. 244
 William D. 25
 William E. 134
 William H. 116
 William W. 26, 134, 39
Smitha, Emma(Robinson) 240
 Granville T. 193
 John 193
 W.B. 244
Smither, John 244
Smizer, Elizabeth[Harter]33
Smock, Abraham 244
 Ann(Banta) 156
 Cornelius 244
 David 96
 Dorcas 96
 Elizabeth(Carruther)203
 Elizabeth[Comingore]
 153, 156
 Isaac 156
 Jacob 96, 156
 John B. 156
 Ruth[Ballard] 244
 Simon 156
 Thomas C. 156
Smoot, William P. 244
Smyser, Elizabeth(Deadman)
 171
 Joseph 171
 Rebecca[Musselman] 171
Smyth, Ebenezer 244
 Elizabeth(Sill) 243

Smythe, Edward 244
Snapp, R.H. 134
Snider, Caroline 136
 Elizabeth(Cravens) 136
 John 136
 Rebecca[Green] 144
 William 244
 William H. 244
Snoddy, George W. 89
Snodgrass, Benjamin 124
 Napoleon B. 124
 Ursala(Evans) 124
Snyder, Catherine[Hutchin-
 son] 27
 Elizabeth[Goodwine] 214
 Mary(Snyder) 131
 S.W. 186
Sommervill, Elizabeth(Lee)
 112
 Joseph 112
 William A. 112
Soper, Charles 89
Sorrell, Elisha 18
 Eliza(McCullough) 18
 J.D. 18
Southard, Matthew R. 150
Southern, Polly[Bedslar]
 179
Southgate, Bernard 19
 Eleanor(Fleming) 19
Sowder, Charles R. 175
 Daniel R. 175
 Eliza(Cummins) 175
Spalding, Mary(Strange) 191
Sparks, G.W.G. 134
 James B. 244
 Margaret[Perrill] 63
 Massa[Pound] 244
 Massie[Pound] 186
 Norval 138
 Patsy[Baker] 196
 Susan[Inlow] 244
Sparrow, Catherine[Dudley]
 55
Spaulding, Daniel 44
 Hillary 190
 Matilda(Campbell) 44
 William D. 44
Spear, A.B. 244
 Ann(Voris) 244
 Moses 244
Spears, Isabella[Pritchard]
 238
 John 91
 Martha 91
 Nancy[Campbell] 244
 Robert 91
 Sophia[Pritchard] 244
 Spencer 29
 Tabitha(Chaffin) 29
Spees, George 22
 Mary(Wright) 22
 Samuel J. 22
Spencer, Delilah[Slaughter]
 183
 Ellen[Mills] 95
 James W. 244
 Nancy(Alexander) 194
 Spear 163
 Spier 183
 Thomas 28
Speyer, H.M. 245
 Henry 245
 Margaret(Pickens) 245
Spiers, Nancy[Dorsey] 109
Spilman, Narcissus[Tyner]
 245

Spilman(cont.)
  Sarah[White] 98
Spink, Francis X. 245
Sprague, Elizabeth(Belt) 37
Springer, A.W. 245
  Catherine(Runyan) 30
  Charles 30
  Elizabeth[Welch] 136
  Priscilla[Stewart] 245
  Reuben R. 30
Spry, Catherine(White) 101
  John 105, 245
  Malvina(Kimbrell) 245
  Vina(Kimbrell) 105
Spurgeon, Eli 176
  Ezekiel 63
  George M. 176
  Martha J. 63
  Milton A. 128
  Rachel(Newcomb) 176
  William 128
Spurger, Nancy[Weedman] 118
Spurlen, Elizabeth(Goodpast-
  er) 214
Spurlock, Martha M[Burgess]
  21
Spyker, Elizabeth(Todd) 63
Stackhouse, Hugh 95
  Jane(McNab) 95
  Sanford 95
  William 95
Stafford, Benjamin 134
  Catherine(Mullen) 234
  James 178
  Margaret[Seegar] 96
  Malinda[Toon] 172
  Mary(Leach) 178
  Shelby 178
Staggs, Athel 245
  Elizabeth[McGuire] 124
Stalling, Samuel 96
  Sarah 96
  William 96
Stamper, Elizabeth[Davidson]
  93
Standley, Jane(Minery) 89
  Moses 89
Stansberry, Phoebe[Sexton] 245
Stansell, Henry 44
  Mary[Carmony] 44
Stansifer, John 138
  Sarah(Herod) 138
  Simeon 138
Stapleton, Delilah I[Huffman]
  119
Stapp, Joseph 178
  Milton 178
Stark, C. 186
  David W. 150
  Malinda[Phillips] 245
  Martha(Rogers) 150
Starkey, Margaret[Chambers]
  109
Starling, Lyne 45
  Mary(McDowell) 45
  Sarah[Sullivant] 63
  William 45
Stars, Jemima[Nicholdson]136
Staton, William 128
Staube, James T. 245
Steele, Agnes(Coulter) 28
  Asbery 150
  Bluford 96
  Catherine(McClure) 245
  Harvey 89
  James 245
  Jemima[Layman] 245

Jenny[Dean] 46
John 28, 245
Joseph 150
Lacy[Walts] 79
Malinda[Murray] 149
Mary[Davidson] 207
Mary E[Ladd] 132
Polly(Donovan) 89
Robert 28
Samuel 89
Susannah(Fields) 150
Thomas 245
William S. 245
Steeley, Basil 245
Steers, Elizabeth[Montgomery]
  178
  William 178
Stembridge, Mary 161
  Mary A(Akers) 161
Stephens, Ausburn T. 138
  Elizabeth[Crowe] 112
  James 138
  James F. 245
  Josiah 176
  Sarah(Trail) 138
Stephenson, Armilda A[Jackson]
  245
  Benjamin 128, 245
  Elizabeth(Ragland) 238
  Frankie[Reeves] 245
  John 121, 245
  Madison 245
  Mary(Grimes) 127
  Thomas 245
Stevens, Catherine(Hayden)
  120, 121
  Cynthia[Fisk] 137
  Henderson 121
  R.J. 44
  Samuel 44
  Stephen C. 245
  Warder W. 121
  Wardner W. 121
  William 190
Stevenson, Alexander C. 193
  Annie[Robinson] 38
  Charles W. 63
  David E. 84
  Eeleon[Chilton] 126
  Elizabeth(Ragland) 238
  James D. 245
  Mary(Grimes) 127, 215
  Mary[Hazlett] 165
  Mary[McBerry] 145
  Morgan 245
  Patton 245
  Payton 245
  Rachel M[Dills] 63
  Sarah 245
Steward, Elizabeth[Watson]
  245
Stewart, Andrew 92
  Anna(Abel) 114
  Asa 245
  David B. 124
  Eliza J[Walker] 25
  Elizabeth(Corn) 205
  Frances(Sanders) 134
  Harriet[Gammon] 32
  Isaac 134
  J.H. 134
  James 134, 150
  James A. 114
  James W. 124
  Joseph 245
  Margaret 124
  Mary[Shields] 80

Thomas P. 134
William 150, 245
Stice, E.C[Bourland] 104
  Hiram H. 97
Still, George 183
  Murph D. 183
Stillwell, Charles W. 128
  James 245
  Jeremiah 183, 245
Stines, Susan[Johnson] 141
Stipe, Henry 142
  Jennie(Adams) 142
  William H.H. 142
Stipp, Louise[McClintock]20
Stipps, Louise[McKee] 63
Stites, Annie[Mull] 141
Stockslager, S.M. 124
Stockwell, John M. 112
  Mary[Early] 109
Stogsdale, Frances[Holmes]
  245
Stone, Dudley 245
  George P. 80
  John L. 142
  Joseph H. 102
  Joseph P. 246
  L.D. 101
  Margaret(Smith) 80
  Nancy(Oliver) 101
  Rachel(Mann) 23
  Stanford 80
  W.H. 125
  W.O. 183
  William 101
Stoptaugh, Rebecca[Huffman]
  151
  Sarah[Polk] 186
Storey, Sarah[Ricketts] 111
Storm, Elizabeth[Keith] 246
Story, Annie(McGhee) 112
  G.W. 112
  James 112, 246
  Lewis 112
  Sarah[Ricketts] 111
Stott, John 114
  William T. 114
Stout, Arsula(Taylor) 186
  Elijah M. 186
  Elizabeth 186
  Elizabeth[Shirk] 246
  George W. 186
  James 186
  Jane C[Lanning] 246
  Mary(Van Dyke) 186
  Peter 246
  Robert 186, 246
  Sarah[Boston] 185
  William 186
Stowers, Louisa[Groom] 131
Strain, William 246
Straney, Mary[Magruder] 96
Strange, Harriet(Eubanks)101
  John 101
  Mary 101
  Mary[Spalding] 191
Stratford, Joshua 246
Stratton, Lot 63
Straughan, John 183
  Nathaniel 183
  Obedience(Scott) 183
Street, Elizabeth[Holeman]
  246
Strickler, Sally[Rogers] 84
Stringer, Susan[Gentry] 247
Strode, Joshua 96
  M(Osborne) 96
  William 96

Strom, John 63
Strong, Mary A[Bayless] 53
Stroud, Edward 31
  Henrietta[West] 31
Stubblefield, Mary A.W[John-
  son] 100
Stubbs, William C. 98
Stucker, David W. 114
Stucky, Frederick 95, 134
  John M. 134
  Louisa H(Myers) 134
Stump, Betsey[Geary] 217
  George 84
  John 84
  Martha(Talbot) 84
Sturgeon, Jane[Forsyth]
  131, 211
  Sarah A[Shake] 176
Sturgus, Robert 247
Stuteville, John A. 247
  Mary[Clarkston] 204
Suffield, Anna[Carl] 242
  Austin 150
  Catherine(Hiles) 150
Sullivan, Dennis 247
  Elizabeth(Bennett) 150
  George R.C. 134
  Jonah 150, 247
  Joseph 247
  Lewis 150
  Mary[Garrison] 43
  Ruth[Brosheers] 119
  Susanna[Crow] 141
  W.H. 150
  William C. 247
Sullivant, Sarah(Starling)
  63
Sulzer, Joseph F. 134
  Magdalene(Herman) 134
  Samuel 134
Summers, Catherine[Brehmer]
  23
  Diana(Gilliland) 134
  George G. 134
  George L. 84
  George T. 134
  J.R. 191
  James S. 134
  Jenetta(Ross) 84
  Martha[Brown] 53
  Moses 84
  Phila[Howard] 185
Summerville, Moriah 247
Sumption, George 108
Survant, Catherine J(Pine)
  237
  James 247
  Jane 247
  William 247
Sutton, Jonathan 63
  W.W. 63
Swallow, John 247
Swan, D.B. 121
  Mary[Cornwell] 130
  Mary F[Cornwell] 130
  William S. 63
Swann, Hannah(Cowgill) 54
Swank, Jacob 63
Swearingen, Francis A. 40
  John 40
  Mary(Loveland) 40
Sweat, Moey A[Casper] 247
Sweeney, Dennis J. 39
  G.T. 99
  John 39
  Julia 39
  T(Campbell) 99
  Z.T. 99

Sweet, Austin 112
  Benjamin 112
  Harriet(Mills) 112
Sweets, Eliza[Eastham] 162
Swift, Elizabeth A(Dawkins)
  171
  Jemima[Kephart] 127
  John 171
  William T. 171
Swindler, America(Baty) 197
  Rhoda A. 183
Swineford, Rebecca[Caldwell]
  117
Switzer, James 247
  John 247
Swope, James H. 145
Symmes, Mary[Short] 28

Taber, Enoch S. 152
Tabor, Elizabeth[Radford]
  163
  Enoch S. 163
  Sarah(Dugan) 163
Tadlock, Elisha 246
Taggat, James 101
  Samuel G. 101
Tague, V.T. 246
Talbot, Aria(Kennedy) 89
  Courtney 89, 108
  Elizabeth(Harp) 108
  Gassaway 178
  Harrison 178
  Henry H. 108
  Martha[Stump] 84
  Nicholas 89
  Sarah(Gillums) 178
  Susan[Nutter] 107
Talbott, E.P. 183
  Elizabeth[Allen] 246
  Elizabeth(Fitzwalter) 183
  Hester(Scott) 183
  J.E. 183
  Josiah 63
  Lorenzo 183
  Lucinda(Smith) 112
  Mary(Houston) 246
  Othoniel 183
  Washington H. 246
  William 246
Talge, John B. 135
  John H. 135
Talley, Catherine(Grady)108
  James 108
  John 108
Talmadege, Jesse 112
  Jonathan 112
  Mary(Beabout) 112
Talmage, Jonathan 112
Tanner, Andrew 84
  J.L. 84
  Jeremiah S. 156
  Keziah[Dawson] 170
  Martha A[Lancaster] 18
  Sarah A[Hedges] 168
Tansel, Eliza J(Clark) 135
  James P. 135
  Peyton 246
Tansell, Catherine(Cook)178
  Francis 178
  Leland 178
Tapp, William 246
  William H. 135
Tarkington, Martha[Durham]
  91
Tarleton, Robert H. 150
Tarlton, Caleb B. 108

Tarvin, Ann S[Cowgill] 147
Tate, David 135
  Nancy(Johnson) 135
  Samuel 135
Tateman, Lucinda[Wills] 160
Tatman, James 63
  Mary 63
  Samuel 63
  Stephen 112
Taylor, Annie[Iglehart] 168
  Augusta 160
  Arsula[Stout] 186
  Eliza(Thornton) 29
  Elizabeth W[Smith] 101
  Fannie[Peach] 32
  George H. 29
  Griffin 44
  Henry F. 29
  J.F. 114
  James 135
  James F. 160
  James J. 104
  John 44
  Louisa[Owen] 174
  Lydia J(Draper) 32
  Manuel 104
  Martha[Turpin] 178
  Martyn 32
  Mary(Armstrong) 195
  Mary[Bronaugh] 116
  Mary[Johnson] 155
  Mary[Pearce] 29
  Mary(Vyze) 98
  Napoleon B. 98
  Ormilda(Allen) 160
  Rachel[Town] 246
  Robert 98
  Robert A. 98
  Sarah 63
  Sarah(MacKinnon) 44
  William H.H. 164
Tatum, Mary[Peters] 236
Tegarden, Annie(Todd) 183
  Basil 183
  Bazil 108
  Columbus 183
  Elizabeth[Lee] 246
  John 183
  Nancy(Todd) 108
  Robert 108
Temple, Jonathan C. 189
  Sarah F(Brashear) 189
  Walter R. 189
Templin, James 63
  John 63
Tencher, Mary[Knowland] 246
Tennant, John G. 150
  Elizabeth(Cahill) 145,
  150
  Richard S. 145, 150
  William E. 145
Tennell, J.B. 28
  Joseph 28
  Miranda[Dean] 247
Tenness, Ellen[Applegate]
  146
Tennis, Ann[Gifford] 148
Terhune, Ann[Smock] 247
  David 112
  Elizabeth[Canary] 153
  Garret 156
  James 156
  Nancy(Davis) 156
Terrell, Charlotte J[Hamil-
  ton] 164
  Henry H. 164
  Nancy(Foster) 164
Terry, Eliza[Axton] 167

Tevis, Fletcher 93
Thomas 93
Tharp, Bernice(Rowlins)
Callen 146, 247
Clinton K. 146
Isaac 29
Jacob 29
Perry 247
Thatcher, George W. 93
Jesse 93
Joseph 93
Mary(Keithler) 93
Thickstan, Mary G. 142
Thixton, Polly[Hall] 215
Thomas, Alfred G. 121
Alvin 247
Catherine[Clough] 247
Daniel 89, 140
Elizabeth[Whisler] 247
Fountain 247
Frances[Smith] 247
George 140
Hezekiah 183
Hiram 138
Huldah[Boothe] 183
Isaac 121
James 191, 247
Joel 247
John F. 191, 247
Malinda[McGowen] 247
Mary(McQueen) 140
Mary(Sayfres) 183
Mary(Trotter) 191
Mary(Watts) 121
Philemon 247
Priscilla[Balleger] 89
Sarah(Amos) 89
Sarah F[Cockrum] 247
William 89, 183
William S. 167
Thomasson, William P. 128
Thompkins, Elizabeth[Howlett] 160
Thompson, A. 95
Andrew H. 40
Arthur 247
Frances[Wheeler] 247
George N. 93, 150
George W. 40
Hamilton 247
Isabella[Long] 58
J.B. 121
James 247
James A. 167
James H. 45
James L. 247
James W. 247
Jesse 145
John 108
John B. 45, 63
John D. 247
John F. 99
John W. 191
Joseph 247
Lewis G. 108
Louisa[Hamilton] 247
Lucinda[Sandy] 247
Lucretia(Webster) 21
Lucy[Jones] 149
Marion 189
Martha(Blair) 198
Mary(English) 247
Mary(Baird) 196
Mary(Little) 145
Mary[Powell] 155
Mary A[Harvey] 247
Mary C(Carpenter) 99
Mathew 40

Millicent(Griggs) 144
Nancy[Hoskins] 247
Nancy P(Robard) 45
Rachel E(Ales) 119
Richard 247
Robert 247
Sam 247
Samuel 247
Samuel(Hill) 43
Sarah(Bassett) 40
Squire 145
Susan(Middleton) 59
Susan(Wilson) 247
Susan B[Massie] 63
Thomas 247
Thomas F. 99
W.E. 247
William 21, 191
William J. 21
Wilson 194, 25
Thornell, Mary A[Hetzler] 56
Thomson, Mary[Irwin] 63
Thornhill, Ruth(Jones) 57
Thornley, Mary[Beckett] 85
Thornsburg, Benjamin 156
James 108
Thornton, Eliza[Taylor] 29
Sarah[Howard] 247
Thorpe, Andrew J. 44
John 44
Mary(Hall) 44
Thrailkill, Sarah(McKenney) 230
Thrasher, Woodson W. 173
Threilkield, Dennis 248
George 248
Threlkeld, Elizabeth[Sanford] 183
Frances[Ogden] 92
Throop, Abigail(Milton) 167
George A. 167
James H. 167
Thurman, Angeline[Low] 248
Elijah 248
Emily J[Ford] 118
Nancy[Hedges] 186
Tichenor, Daniel 164
Daniel N. 164
Ebenezer 164
H.T. 164
Hannah[LeGrange] 248
Jane(Glover) 164
Susan(Bull) 164
William N. 164
Tilford, Alexander 178
Eleanor(McCullough) 178
Joseph M. 178
Tilley, Eleanor[McCoy] 248
Joe 183
Tilman, J.R. 103
James H. 78
Mary(Brown) 78
Morris A. 78
Tinchenor, William L. 248
Tindall, Isaac 248
Job D. 178
Tiplett, Susan M[Humston]127
Tipton, Andrew 248
Mahala[Donnohue] 160
Nancy(Vance) 39
Wiley C. 39
William 39
Titus, Catherine[Wingate]172
Margaret[Maze] 107
Tivis, Susamma[Wheeler] 145
Todd, Annie[Tegarden] 183
Betsey[Moore] 107
Catherine 25

Charles W. 25
David 136
Delilah(Maddox) 182
Eliza[Bohanon] 248
Eliza[Spyker] 63
Elizabeth[Oakerson] 235
Emily[Maddox] 182
Florence[Barnes] 35
Henry G. 135
Jane[McCormick] 181
Jane[Wilson] 248
John 89
John M. 248
Johnson 183
Levi L. 108
Nancy[Tegarden] 108
Robert N. 108, 136, 248
Sallie D(Smith) 136
Thomas J. 25
Walter J. 25
William S. 136
Tolbert, Nancy[Singleton] 243
Tolin, Alexander B. 82
Tolle, Denton 40
Harrison 63
Joseph 63
Nancy[Applegate] 195
Stephen 40
Tomlin, B.F. 173
Sallie 19
Simeon 173
Tomlinson, Lucy E(Dawson) 170
Tompkins, Nancy[Gordon] 28
Tone, Laura[Brooks] 37
Toner, Nancy(Parker) 236
Toon, John 172
Malinda(Stafford) 172
Martin S. 172
Tower, Sarah J[Reynolds]121
Town, Rachel(Taylor) 246
Uriah 248
Townsend, Anne[Weir] 89
James 248
Joseph 248
Mary H.D[Layman] 248
Tracy, Brazzie 150
John 150
Mary[Law] 170
Nancy 150
Sarah F[McClain] 248
Trail, Sarah[Stephens] 138
Traylor, J.G.W. 160
Mary(Trimble) 160
Nicholas 160
Sarah J. 89
Trester, B.F. 89
Edward H. 248
Elizabeth(Hesler) 89
Martin 89
Samuel 248
William 89
Tribbe, Mary[Rawling] 29
Tribby, Leander M. 248
Mahala(Myers) 248
William 248
Trimble, Catherine(Carrico) 105
James 248
Joseph 108, 208
Mary[Traylor] 160
Triplett, Charles 112
Charles E. 112
Clarissa(Ducklings) 112
Lucy[Ginn] 43
Trosper, William 248
Trout, Hannibal 188

Troutman, A.D. 104
Trowsel, Jane[Armstrong]
248
True, Lucy[Wells] 136
Truesdale, Elizabeth[Hen-
derson] 40
Truitt, Sarah[Faris] 109
Truman, Susannah[Bright]
169
Truston, Mary A[Rogers] 48
Tucker, Anna(Richardson)
239
Catherine[Hale] 103
Dandridge 99
Elizabeth[Ashbrook] 18
Franklin 248
James 128
Lee 99
Maria S[Jones] 248
Mary(Kitcher) 128
Miranda(Durham) 99
Samuel 128
Tulay, Preston F. 135
Tuley, Elizabeth[Hesson]
248
John 248
Tull, Anna M[Smith] 193
Hester A(Pilchard) 93
Isaac D. 93
Joseph 93
Tullis, Aaron 49
John T. 49
Tumbleson, Mary[Newby] 174
Turman, Lorilda[Morgan] 82
Turnam, D. 248
Turner, Anna(DeBell)112
Elizabeth[Bishop] 179
Elizabeth[Jacobs] 63
Esther[Evans] 21
James H. 112
Joel 112
John 248
Mary(Sanders) 62
Sarah[Elliott] 165
William S. 145
Turnham, D. 248
Turpin, Alfred 248
Anderson 89
Annie[Neal] 89
Delilah[Coffin] 248
Eveline(Reupert) 89
George 192
Jacob 178
James 192
Jennie(McDonald) 192
Mahala[Eaton] 178
Mahala(Mayhall) 232
Martha(Taylor) 178
Rachel(Powell) 89
Robinson 89
Turrin, Nancy[Darnell] 158
Turvey, America(Cupp) 93
William M. 93
William S. 93
Tyler, Elizabeth[Moore]133
George 249
Lou J[Kerlin] 135
Mary(Seaton) 135
Milton W. 135
Sarah[Gorham] 86
Tyner, Narcissus(Spilman)
245
Tyree, Kate[Owens] 175

Ulrey, Hannah(West) 63
Jacob 63
Uncel, Rachel[Young] 121

Underwood, Ella(Christie)
203
Franklin 183
George 249
John 183
Mary[Wildman] 249
Nancy(Scott) 242
Rebecca(Radford) 183
William 183
Upton, Ann(Murlin) 33
Edward 33
John 33
Thomas 33
Urton, Sarah[Graham] 51
Utley, David H. 187
Ellen(Heltsley) 187
James P. 187
Utterback, Elizabeth(Mc-
Dowel) 128
Lucy[Vandiver] 249
Martin 128
Susan[Grose] 249
William H. 128

Vager, E.H. 91
Vail, Lydia A(Voriss) 150
Valentine, May[Campbell] 23
Vanarsdall, Catherine 156
Cornelius A.B. 156
Jane[Lyons] 155
Jane[Voris] 157
John 156
John W. 156
Nancy J(Clem) 136
Simon 156
Vance, Elizabeth[Davis] 55
Elizabeth[Henderson] 175
Elizabeth[Lowe] 249
Joseph C. 44
Nancy[Tipton] 39
Sarah[Pringle] 63
Sarah(Wilson) 44
Wilson 44
Van Cleave, James 249
Ruth A[Todd] 249
Stephen B. 89
Vandament, Henry 63
Vandaveer, Elizabeth[Murphy]
249
Vandervoot, Elizabeth(Wil-
kerson) 64
Vandiver, Elizabeth[Byers]
156
Henry 249
James H. 156
Mary[Luyster] 249
Mary A(Buckner) 201
Peter 156
Sarah(Garshwiler) 156
VanDyke, Martha[Stout] 186
Mary[Stout] 186
VanHook, Martin 89
Nancy[Austin] 116, 181
Zerilda[Fitzpatrick] 41
VanHorn, Elizabeth[Wheeler]
128
VanKirk, Nancy[Mark] 20
Vanlandigham, Martha J[Hunt]
112
Vanlaningham, Jeremiah 112
VanLiew, Blanche(Weaver)
135
Dennis 135
John R. 135
Vanlue, John 249
Vann, Absalom 125
John A. 125

Rebecca(Rollison) 125
VanNada, Martin 249
Solomon 249
Vannest, Catherine[McDonald]
155
VanNice, Margaret[Kurtz] 249
Vannuys, Catherine 183
Catherine(Demaree) 184
Cornelius D. 183
H.L. 249
Hervey L. 184
John H. 184
Kate(Demaree) 184, 249
Samuel 184
Susan[List] 156
Tunis 183, 184, 249
Vooncha[Banta] 126
Vonosdol, Jacob 156
Thomas J. 156
VanPelt, Amelia[Brothers]63
Cyrus N. 63
Mildred(Hope) 63
Vansant, Amanda[Bowen] 249
VanScholack, L.T. 249
VanTrees, Laura G(Prentiss)
107
Vantress, William 249
VanWinkle, Margaret[Harding]
164
VanZandt, Ann M[Hester] 112
Elizabeth[McLane] 177
Varner, Frances(Egnew) 210
Vaughan, Elizabeth 116, 142
Joseph L. 116
Thompson 116, 142
Vaughn, William 63
Vaught, H.C. 249
Vawter, Elizabeth[Scott] 249
Sarah B(Watts) 84
Smith 178
William 249
Veach, A.C. 124
Adam C. 124
Jane[Peck] 33
Veasey, Armour K. 32
Elizabeth(Campbell) 32
Joseph W. 32
Veazey, A. King 32
Elizabeth(Campbell) 32
Joseph W. 32
Verbrike, Samuel A. 156
Vermillion, Cornelius 157
Elizabeth(Sanford) 157
George 157
Joel 157
Martha(Shaw) 157
Martha J(Bourne) 199
Thomas S. 157
Vessels, Cornelius 121
Elijah 121
Elizabeth 121
Vest, Sarah[Hubbard] 249
Vice, Drury B. 82
Jahazy(Barber) 82
Vinson, Irwin 249
Virt, Rebecca 249
Vodrey, William H. 36
Vontrece, Rebecca[McKnight]
184
Voohres, Stephen 157
Voorhees, Peter 157, 249
Stephen 157, 249
Voorhies, Andrew C. 157
Rachel[Covert] 153
Vorhies, Isaac B. 157
Jacob 157
Margaret 157

Vories, Elizabeth(Shuck)
128
Hervey 249
John 128, 249
Rachel B(Whitenack) 157
William T. 128
Voris, Abraham B. 108
Ann[Spear] 244
Elizabeth[List] 127
Harrison R. 157
Isaac 157
Jane(Vanarsdale) 157
Sarah(Lyons) 106
Voriss, Lydia A[Vail] 150
Voshell, A.R. 84
Vuilderback, Lydia[Moss]
186
Vyze, Mary[Taylor] 98

Wade, Ellen(Brewer) 191
Evan 191
James 191
Wadkins, Martha[Cleveland]
179
Waggoner, John 124
Wagner, Caroline[Smith] 25
Wagoner, Milton L. 124
Sarah[Weatherholt] 95
Waits, Catherine[Heslar] 56
Wakeland, Nancy[Fowler] 249
Walden, James 125
James W. 125
Katherine(McDermitt) 125
N.B. 125
Nathan B. 125
Sarah(Lambert) 125
Waldren, Mary J(Johnson)155
Waler, Anna R[Hendrix] 89
Walker, August R. 39
Charles A.J. 39
Charles H. 249
Eliza L(Stewart) 25
Elizabeth A(Menefee) 232
Jacob P. 128
James 84
Jane[Cromer] 139
Jane(Rairden) 238
Kiziah[Watson] 164
Kizzia[Watson] 186
Margaret(Nieman) 39
Mary[Applebay] 140
Mary(Brown) 53
Nancy 63
Nancy(Young) 128
Rhoda(Blevence) 198
Robert 60, 249
Rudolph 39
Samuel 128
Thomas 121
William 63
William M. 63
William O. 112
William P. 112
Wall, Rebecca(Applegate) 42
William 63
Wallace, Catherine 44
Edwin S. 46
Elvira[Gudgel] 249
Joseph 46
Louise(Bridgewater) 105
Mary 44
John M. 99
John T. 169
Thomas 44, 249
Zeralda G. 249
Zeralda(Gray) 214
Waller, John W. 249

Wallingford, Amanda[Cofield]
Mary[Cole] 43
Mary[Warder] 112
Walls, John 95
Walter, David 136
Sarah[Woodruff] 36
Walters, Bertha(Carty) 203
Elizabeth(Lamb) 119
Evarilla(Lamb) 136
Frank 108
Luke 136
Joel O. 136
Richard 101
Sampson 108
Samuel 119
William P. 119
Walterfield, Jacob 28
Walton, Margaret B[Ross] 89
Waple, Nancy[McCoy] 115
Ward, Beverly R. 250
Durbin 22
Greenberry 194
J.M(Alexander) 194
James 108
Lucinda[Cooper] 250
Martha[Crawford] 23
Martha[Cole] 158
Nettie(Glove) 213
Rebecca(Patterson) 22
Susan[Houghland] 250
Warden, Mary[Mathis] 188
Warder, Hiram K. 112
Luther F. 112
Mary(Wallingford) 112
Wardill, Ina[Smith] 62
Ware, Susan[Collins] 185
Warfield, Anna R[Gordon]
250
Warner, Andrew J. 250
J.W. 250
Josiah 90
Mary E(Riker) 90
William I. 90
Warren, James 192
Reuben 192
Susanna[Sevier] 101
Warring, John M. 99
Tabitha M(Hopkins) 99
Thomas E. 99
Warrum, Harmon 250
Washburn, Isaac 178
Maria(Bratton) 178
R.R. 178
Washbun, James W. 250
Matilda(Dean) 250
Robert D. 250
Washburn, Ira D. 47
John B. 47
Mary(McKnight) 47
Wasson, Alexander 184
Barton W. 20
Catherine[Hall] 184
Fleming 90
Jane 184
Jane A[Ashby] 135
John J. 90
Joseph 20, 90
Polly(Harper) 87
Samuel 90
Sarah(Hearne) 20
Susanah(McLeod) 90
Waters, Isaac 63
James 63
Watkins, Elizabeth[Harrell]
162
Watson, Abraham 44
Cooper K. 63
Elizabeth(Steward) 245

James M. 164
Jonathan 250
Julia A[Carpenter] 112
Kiziah(Walker) 164
Kizzie(Walker) 186
Michael 44
Richard 186
Samirah(Bowman) 199
Sarah[Gears] 250
Scarlet 164, 186
Watt, Samuel 64
Watts, Fannie(Sebree) 108
Howard 108, 112
John 108
John S. 84
Johnson 108
Mary[Thomas] 121
Sarah B[Vawter] 84
Wayman, James V. 98
Moses 90
Weakley, Conrad 178
Jerry 178
Sarah(Miller) 178
Wealthy, P.H. 95
Weatherholt, Jacob 95
Sarah(Wagoner) 95
William 95
Weaver, Blanche[Van Liew]
135
Charles A. 135
Gertrude(Kinsey) 135
Joseph 135
Magdalene[Motz] 34
Webb, Fannie[Brewer] 128
James 28
Johanne[Shelburne] 183
John 44
Mahala[Fisher] 194
Martha[Clark] 250
Richard 44
Ruth[Fitzpatrick] 171
Sallie A[Beazley] 126
Zachariah 108, 250
Weber, August J. 135
Katherine[Gunkel] 24
Margaret[Macke] 38
Webster, Lucretia[Thompson]
21
Martha[Jenkins] 96
Wedding, Charles L. 169
Columbus V. 169
Mark 169
Milliard F. 169
Nancy J(Hale) 169
Weddle, Sarah(Mile) 232
Thompson 250
Wedekind, Cecilia(Jennings)
123
Weeks, Louis L. 186
Nancy(Kester) 186
William L. 186
Wehmoff, Elizabeth[Inder-
rieden] 24
Weir, Ann E(Townsend) 89
David T. 184
William M. 184
Welborn, Sarah[Stephenson]
250
Welch, Benjamin F. 64
Druzilla(Drummond) 64
Elizabeth[Mitchell] 250
Elizabeth(Springer) 136
James E. 113
John A. 136
Lydia A(Secrest) 113
Noble 113
Rebecca[Scott] 108
Thomas B. 64

Wellingsford, Elizabeth
  [Hains] 140
Wellington, Margaret[Peyton]
  150
Welliver, Isaac 250
  Nancy(Sample) 241
Wells, Elizabeth[Beard] 186
  Frank 250
  Jacob 137
  Lemuel 250
  Lucy[Bishop] 29
  Lucy(True) 136
  Lucy A[Neal] 234
  Mary[Carson] 250
  Sarah 137
  William 128
Welman, Andrew N. 171
  Elizabeth(Williams) 171
  Jeremiah L. 171
Welsh, Mary 250
Welty, Frances E(Bynch) 187
  George B. 187
  John 187
West, Alexander 192
  Anna[Fields] 211
  Hannah[Ulrey] 63
  Henrietta(Stroud) 31
  Isaac 192
  John 172
  John A. 36
  Margaret(Knowles) 36
  Robert H. 36
  Samuel 250
  Sarah 192
  Sarah(Bourn) 172
  Van 172
  William 250
Westerfield, Betsey(Carter)
  190
  David 157
  James 157
Weyman, Frances[Wooden] 184
Whalen, Mary A[Bond] 93
Whaley, Benjamin 82
  Benjamin F. 82
  Jane(Bush) 82
Wharton, Mary C[Sadler]250
Wheat, Mary(Mason) 231
Wheatcraft, Ida N(Moore)115
Wheeler, Elizabeth[Draper]
  128
  Elizabeth(VanHorn) 128
  Frances(Thompson) 247
  James 95
  Jesse 250
  John 145
  Jonathan 124
  Juda[Williams] 78
  Mary[Barrus] 144
  Nancy[Robertson] 145
  Reason 145
  Susanna(Tivis) 145
  Thomas 250
  Tilson 145
  William 128
Whetstine, Elizabeth[France]
  251
Whicker, Louisa D(Duley)109
Whipps, A.J. 44
  Arah[Worthington] 45
  Cecil(Finch) 44
  William 44
Whitaker, Bland B. 118,
  184
  Grafton 251
  Levi 118, 184
  Margaret(Seaton)118, 184

Martha(Gregg) 215
White, Alfred P. 113
  Asa 251
  Burr 157
  Carr D. 45
  Cassandra(Black) 198
  Catherine[Spry] 101
  Charles 28
  Charles W. 28
  Convard 98
  Cynthia(Ruggles) 241
  David 32
  E.A. 135
  Elias 25
  Elizabeth[Glasscock] 56
  Elizabeth(Perry) 113
  Elmer S. 104
  Emiline[Wood] 32
  Enoch 251
  Frank S. 98
  George B. 184
  Hazel 113
  Isabella[Myers] 32
  J.M. 135
  James 164
  John D. 45
  Joseph 164
  Lucinda(Salter) 157
  Margaret(Hunter) 251
  Margaret R(Baker) 45
  Martha(Rignon) 113
  Mary(Bigger) 64
  Mary[Cooprider] 251
  Mary(Funk) 135
  Mary[Martin] 182
  Melinda M[Hubbard] 157
  Naomi(Gunn) 215
  Nelson 113
  Peyton 45
  Rebecca J(Dearinger) 104
  Simon 135
  Stephen 64
  Susan A[Harrison] 100
  Susan[Durbin] 118
  Thomas 64
  Thomas T. 113
  Vincent 251
  Virginia(Owens) 45
  Willis G. 104
Whiteaker, Thomas 251
Whitecotton, Margaret[Losley]
  251
  Sarah[Payne] 182
Whitehead, Sarah[Johnson]
  163
Whitenack, Abram 157
  Ann(Debon) 157
  Catherine[Vanarsdall] 156
  John 157
  Peter 157
  Rachel B[Voorhies] 157
Whitesides, Elizabeth(But-
  ton) 171
  John 251
  Joseph 171
  Lucinda 171
  Lucinda[Nay] 170
Whitlock, J.W. 251
Whitlow, Harriet L[Pace] 80
Whitmer, Barbara A(Shaver)
  161
  Ephraim 161
  Michael 161
Whitmire, David M. 137
  John 137
Whitmore, Margaret[Bean]251
  Sarah(Jones) 57

Whittinghill, David 251
Whittington, Frances 184
  Littleton 184
  S.T. 184
  William 184
Wible, Samuel 164
Widerin, Christian 135
  G.L. 135
  George L.T. 135
  Mary A(Meder) 135
Wiggens, Galton 178
Wiggins, David 251
  Joseph F. 251
  O.B. 39
  Orville J. 39
  Rachel(Adams) 39
Wiggs, H.R. 251
Wikoff, Elizabeth[Bur-
  gess] 251
Wilbern, Andrew 251
  Jerry W. 251
  Sarah(Walker) 251
Wilcoxson, Martha[Rice]
  183
Wiley, Elizabeth[Byers]
  126
  James 140
  James F. 140
  John 158
  John H. 251
  Lytle 114
  Margaret 64
  Margaret[Counts] 19
  Mary(Sims) 158
  Martha K(Looney) 140
  Rachel[Herrell] 127
  Thomas H. 158
  William 114, 251
Wilhite, Aaron L. 171
  Lamech 171
  Mary(Koebler) 171
  Noah 171
  Polly(Williams) 171
  Thomas 171
Wilhoit, Abram 194
  Francis(Mosby) 194
  Jacob 194
Wilkerson, Elizabeth 64
  Elizabeth[Vandervoot]
  64
  James 64
  John 64
  Mary A[Milner] 94
  Sarah(Moore) 64
Wilkes, Elizabeth(Dunham)
  209
Wilkinson, Charles 64
  Eliza(Bishop) 104, 164
  Isaac T. 104
  James W. 164
  John G. 104, 164
  Martha(Bond) 199
  Mary[Burkhart] 162
  William 28
Willan, Carrie R(Murray)
  124
  Elzy B. 124
  Ira C. 124
Willard, Elizabeth[Bar-
  ker] 251
Willes, Anna(Coleman)64
  Benjamin C. 64
  Samuel W. 64
Willette, Carlton 20
  Nancy(Coons) 20
  William H. 20
Williams, Allen 175

Williams(cont.)
Anderson 22
Asa C. 164
Baylis 251
C.T. 101
Catherine[Colvin] 54
Charles H. 251
Eliza[Elkin] 162
Elizabeth(Allen) 189
Elizabeth(Hethington) 135
Elizabeth[Welman] 171
Elizabeth J(King) 110
Garland 184
Hannah(Evans) 210
Harriet(Forrest) 18
Harriet(Mitchell) 184
Henry 184
Hezekiah 175
Hugh T. 95
James C. 175
Jane[Felkins] 116
Jefferson 251
Jesse 174
John 184, 251
John D. 105
John R. 135
Joseph 64
Juda(Wheeler) 78
Keziah[Patrick] 82
Liona[Crabb] 251
Lucy(Boyd) 92
Margaret(Bradley) 105
Martha[Carleton] 202
Mary(Arnold) 251
Mary(Farmer) 114
Matilda[Clearwater] 251
Melatiah 64
Micaiah 64
Minerva[Lindsay] 115
Nancy(Johnson) 164
Nancy(Owens) 175
Otho 95
Parker 114
Phoebe[Pruitt] 78
Rememberance 251
Robert 251
Samuel A. 18
Sarah[Burton] 116
Sarah(Kirkendall) 184
Thomas 174, 251
Urbane 164
Vincent E. 114
William 18, 105, 135, 251
William A. 22
Z.G. 251
Williamson, Delano E. 84
James H. 49
Lydia(Madchen) 84
Robert 84
Willis, A.J. 251
Edward 32, 142
Helen(Coron?) 32
J.W. 251
James D. 84
Richard 142
William M. 32
Willison, Liza[Pyle] 24
Willoughby, Rachel[McGregor] 38
Wills, Lucinda[Tateman]160
Wilson, Abel 184, 251
Alexander 184
Andrew 45
Andrew P. 64
Aaron 176
Ann[Ashcraft] 117
Anna(Cleland) 45
Benjamin 251

Daniel 64
David 124, 252
Devora(Custer) 90
Eliza[Gash] 141
Elizabeth[Brown] 169
Elizabeth[Fish] 98
Elizabeth(Fox) 174
Elizabeth[Oldham] 252
Elizabeth[Reed] 90
Elizabeth[Ross] 84
Elizabeth J[McClelland]251
George P.R. 164
Hannah(Pruitt) 238
Harriet[Lydick] 108
Helen[Self] 160
Henry 176
Isaac 64
J.W. 176
Jacob 64
James 90, 45, 113, 252
James W. 176
Jane(Guynn) 124
Jane(Hughes) 113
Jestina(Gossar) 176
John 108, 135, 176, 252
John F. 252
John H. 113
John W. 252
Leanna[Buntem] 153
Letitia[Cornelius] 252
Lizzie F(Polk) 96
Loretta 252
Margaret 252
Margaret(Armstrong) 251
N.B. 138
Mary P(Lamb) 225
Nancy(Grate) 135
Nelly[Kaiper] 24
Nelly 49
Polly[Cooper] 205
Polly(Matchet) 113
Rice 176
Robert M. 64
Sarah(Lucas) 184
Sarah[Vance] 44
Susan[Smith] 252
Thomas 113, 174, 188, 252
Thomas C. 45
Thomas W. 174
Urias 252
Valentine 31
W.L. 184
W.P. 252
Walter 157
William 90
William D. 31
William R. 176
Wilton, James 104
Winans, Amanda[Knight] 83
John 124
Mary D[Baker] 19
Winchester, Serrill 121
Windsor, Jennie[Griffith] 83
Winfrey, Jordan G. 103
Wingate, Catherine(Titus) 172
Smith 172, 252
Winkler, Elizabeth[Medcalf] 104
Frances[Medcalf] 119
Nancy[McFarland] 192
Winspear, Ellen(Rowe) 21
John B. 21
Wheelock 21
Winston, Elizabeth 25
Harry C. 25
L.C. 25

Sally[Menzies] 83
Winter, Katherine(Faller)21
Winterhead, Pacific
Winters, John 28
Mary J[Murdock] 115
William B. 64
Wise, Albena[Stevenson]252
Nancy[Ball] 187
Wiseheart, Jacob 164
John D. 164
Margaret(Davidson) 147
Mary E. 164
Wishard, Agnes H(Oliver)167
Elizabeth(Furlow) 113
James L. 252
John 167
John O. 252
Robert C. 113, 167
William 113
William H. 167
Witham, Lucinda[Harris] 252
Withers, Sophia[Ehrman] 106
Witting, Mary E[Frecks] 21
Woerner, Conrad 135
Frank 135
Mary(Zwirman) 135
Wolcott, Mary E[Sparrow]39
Wolf, David 252
George 252
Wolfe, Conrad 178
Euphemy(Cannon) 178
G.W. 157
Jacob 178
Joel 178
Sarah(Miller) 178
William 178
Wolford, Lydia(Lake) 67
Woner, Malinda W(Hayden)155
Wood, Caleb 167
Emeline[White] 32
George 90
John 167
Lewis 252
Lovisa(Rankin) 238
Margaret A(Gresham) 113
Nicholas 64
Phebe 64
Robert 104
Sarah[Meharry] 64
Sophia(Marsh) 88
Susan 167
William G. 252
Willis 252
Woodard, Franklin 171
Wooden, Frances(Weyman) 184
Jefferson 135
John L. 184
Levi 184
Malinda 135
Robert M. 135, 184
Susan[Fritts] 252
Woodfill, Andrew 184
Elizabeth[Bondurant] 113
Gabriel 172, 184
William S. 172
Woodruff, Sarah(Walter) 36
Woods, Benjamin 252
Elizabeth 114
Elizabeth(Cunningham) 207
Ezekial S. 51
Jeremiah 93
John 114
Margaret 93
Mecca(Boon) 199
Robert 93, 114
Woodsmall, Margaret[Halbert] 162

Woodward, Elizabeth P[Mount]
  182
  George 64
  James 146, 252
  Lucinda[Brooks] 124
  William 146
Woollen, Leonard 252
  Milton 252
  Sarah(Henry) 252
Woolley, A.H. 28
  Charles W. 28
  Sallie(Howard) 28
Woolfolk, John F. 152
  Mahala(Harris) 152
  Thomas H. 152
Woolsey, T. 189
Works, Andrew 172
  J.A. 172
  James A. 172
  Rachel(Ireland) 172
Worland, Rachel 108
Worley, Robert E. 121
Worrell, David 252
  Isabella[Herring] 124
  Robert 252
Worthington, Christian[Hawkins] 20
  William 252
Wright, Alvin T. 91
  Frances[Hazelrigg] 81
  Elizabeth[Fife] 131
  Jemima[Field] 86
  Jane(Irwin) 57
  Joel 252
  Jonathan 252, 253
  Linda[Helenshade] 45
  Mary[Spees] 22
  Mary E[Brown] 200
  Rachel(McMahon) 252
  Samuel 252, 253
  Washington 253
  West L. 192
  William 192, 252, 253
  William M. 253
Wrightman, Anna[Bradford] 18
Wyatt, George C. 99
  James S. 99
  Mary(Campbell) 99
Wylie, J.L. 17
  S.A. 253
  Sarah(Cook) 17
  Thomas 17
Wynans, Mary[Baker] 19
Wysong, Rebecca(Dicks) 147

Yager, John T. 171
  Nancy(Overstreet) 171
  William 171
Yancey, Simeon T. 114
Yater, Abram 117
  J.L. 117
Yates, John F. 102
  Martha[Padgett] 135
  J.W. 253
  William 135
Yeager, Absalom 98
  Anne(McDonald) 98
  Joel 98
  Joshua 253
Yeates, Paulina[Nelson] 159
  Polly[Johnson] 253
Yelton, Charles 173
  Hayden 173
  Millie(Gosney) 173
  Milly[Hall] 86
Yenawine, Catherine[Lidikey]
  132

Yocom, John W. 64
  Martha[Dunlavy] 159
  Solomon 64
Yoke, John B. 124
Youel, Elizabeth[Allen]
  178
Young, Adam 121
  Alexander 64
  Caleb 100
  Charlotte 253
  Elizabeth[Scantlin] 107
  Elizabeth[Whittinghill]
    253
  Jacob 121, 184
  James 22
  John 64, 253
  L.R. 82
  Lucy(Barbee) 196
  Mahala[Clark] 100
  Mary(Dugan) 55
  Melton 253
  Nancy[Allen] 52
  Nancy[Dodd] 141
  Nancy[Morris] 95
  Nancy[Walker] 128
  Rachel(Goodnight) 184
  Rachel(Uncel) 121
  Robert L. 64
  Thomas 64
  William 22, 98
  William B. 253
  William H. 184
Younger, John 167
  Lewis 167
  Michael 167
  Nancy(Crose) 167
  William P. 167
Yount, Jonathan 184
Youtser, William 253
Yowell, Amanthis A[Christie] 253

Zaring, Benjamin 171
  Lewis 171
  Mary(Baker) 126
  Nancy(Baker) 171
Zerner, Adam 90
Zike, Catherine(Smith)253
  David 253
  William 253
Zimmerman, Sarah A[Tweedy]
  103
Zink, Clarissa(Hubanks)
  148
Zuber, Charles H. 25
Zuck, Elizabeth(Roberts)
  240
Zwirman, Mary[Woerner]
  135